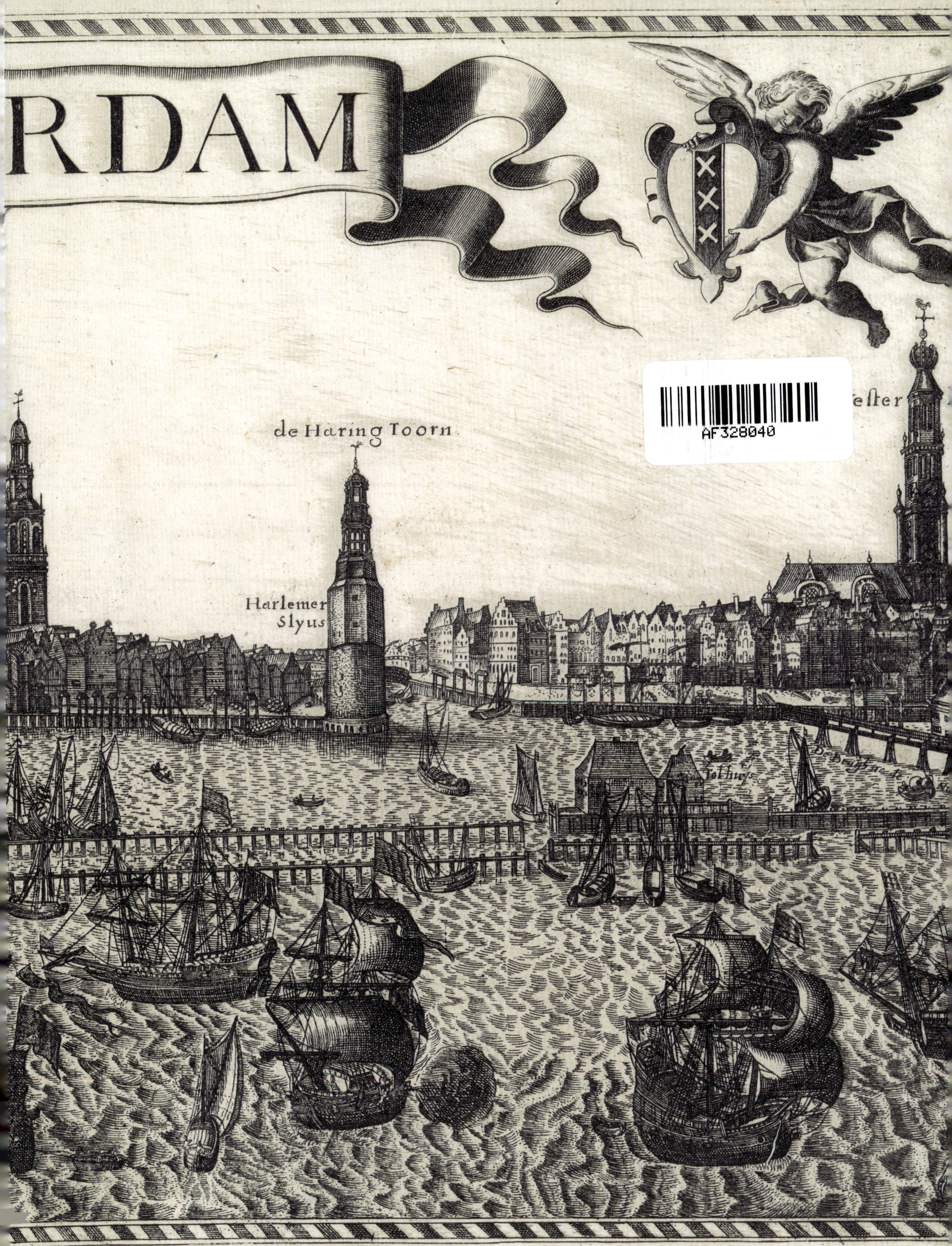
RDAM
de Haring Toorn
Harlemer
Slyus
Tolhuys

Rembrandt
in Amsterdam

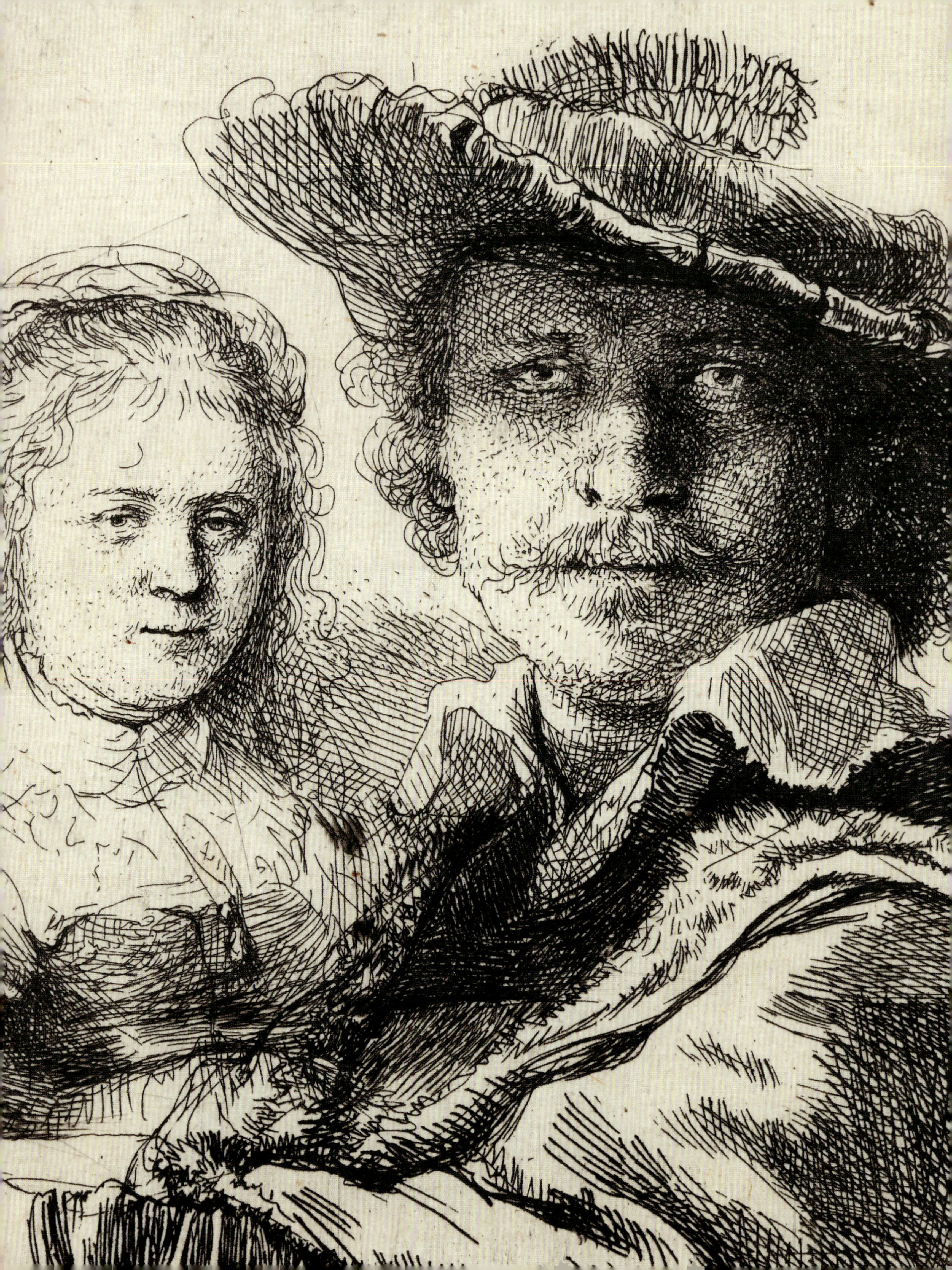

Rembrandt
in Amsterdam

Creativity and Competition

Edited by

Stephanie S. Dickey and Jochen Sander

With contributions by:

Jonathan Bikker

Jan Blanc

Sonia Del Re

Stephanie S. Dickey

Rudi Ekkart and Claire van den Donk

Robert Fucci

Jasper Hillegers

Maarten Prak

Jochen Sander

Friederike Schütt

Martin Sonnabend

National Gallery of Canada, Ottawa
Städel Museum, Frankfurt am Main
Distributed by Yale University Press,
New Haven and London

The exhibition at the Städel Museum was made possible by

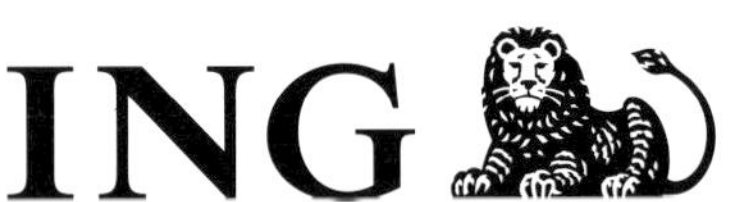 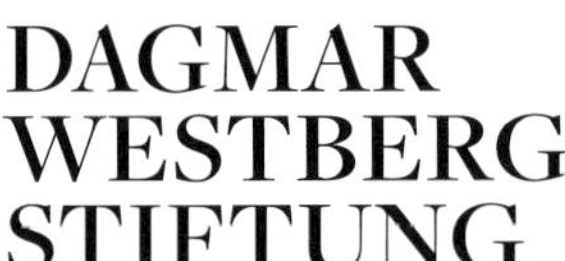

When he moved to the international business and trade capital Amsterdam, Rembrandt was hoping for an environment that would both challenge and inspire him in his artistic activities. Following a number of recent presentations revolving around Rembrandt's early and late work, the exhibition at the National Gallery of Canada and the Städel Museum is the first to devote itself to the dynamic and extremely successful course the artist's career took between 1630 and 1655. It was in this phase that – spurred on by his friends, patrons and rivals in a process of constant competition and exchange – he managed to establish the unmistakable "Rembrandt" brand and, with the aid of his pupils and assistants, expand its reach in the world.

Rembrandt went his way – with inspiration, commitment to innovation, a feel for fertile networks, a strong sense of self, and a high degree of willpower and determination. These qualities, which undoubtedly contributed to shaping Rembrandt's artistic personality and work, but also his entrepreneurial activities, still play an important role today when it comes to realizing one's projects. The ING believes in art's power to stimulate innovation and change.

We at ING Germany, an institution with a head office in Frankfurt am Main and strong ties to Amsterdam, are delighted to have this opportunity to support the Städel Museum in the realization of a unique exhibition, and together explore the world of Rembrandt.

Nick Jue
CEO of ING in Germany

Table of Contents

Foreword

Rembrandt van Rijn (1606–1669) was already a successful painter and printmaker in his native Leiden when he made the audacious decision in 1631 to try his luck with a portrait commission from Amsterdam – the Dutch Republic's centre of global trade and home to the largest, most competitive art market in northern Europe. By 1634 he was established there as an independent master. This exhibition traces the central decades of Rembrandt's career, from his arrival in Amsterdam to the emergence of his late style in the mid-1650s, in the transformative context of the dynamic city that became his home. While building his own career, Rembrandt mentored dozens of younger artists in a studio whose products ranged from penetrating portraits and emotionally charged history paintings to homely genre scenes and placid landscapes. As his own style and interests evolved, acolytes became rivals while competitors offered tempting alternatives to catch the attention of an increasingly sophisticated clientele. By bringing Rembrandt's work into dialogue with stellar paintings, drawings and prints by talented contemporaries active in Amsterdam, this exhibition reveals the synergy between a gifted master and the stimulating artistic environment that challenged and inspired him.

Conceived by Stephanie Dickey, Bader Chair in Northern Baroque Art at Queen's University (Kingston, Ontario) and guest curator for the National Gallery of Canada, this exhibition is co-organized by the National Gallery of Canada, Ottawa, and the Städel Museum, Frankfurt am Main. We are grateful to the curators, Stephanie Dickey and Jochen Sander, Vice Director of the Städel Museum and Professor of Art History at Goethe-Universität, Frankfurt am Main, for their vision, dedication and thorough research. We also thank Sonia Del Re, Erika Dolphin, Kirsten Appleyard and Friederike Schütt for their valuable work as members of the curatorial team, and Martin Sonnabend for his support with numerous loans from the Städel Museum's Prints and Drawings collection. Among the international community of colleagues providing welcome insights and advice, we especially thank the other scholars who contributed essays to the catalogue – Jonathan Bikker, Jan Blanc, Rudi Ekkart and Claire van den Donk, Robert Fucci, Jasper Hillegers and Maarten Prak – and members of our advisory committee, including Melanie Gifford, Volker Manuth, William W. Robinson, Eric Jan Sluijter, Gregor J.M. Weber, Arthur K. Wheelock, Jr., and Marieke de Winkel. We sincerely thank the many staff members at both of our institutions whose diligence and creativity brought this project to fruition.

In Ottawa, we are grateful to the National Gallery of Canada Foundation for encouragement and assistance.

In Frankfurt, we are indebted to ING Germany, which has generously supported us in this ambitious project. In this context, we would like to express our deep gratitude to Nick Jue, Chairman of the Board, and Joachim von Schorlemer, member of the Board, for their commitment and confidence in our work. We would also like to thank the Dagmar-Westberg-Stiftung, which once again provided us with essential support for an internationally oriented project. Its founder, Dagmar Westberg, has followed the scientific work especially in the field of Old Masters at the Städel Museum with great interest over many years and has shown far-sighted pioneering commitment. Our gratitude goes to the Foundation's Board of Directors; their great loyalty and support of this exhibition is exceptional and ties in with the patronage of the founder.

Finally, we extend our immense gratitude to the lenders, both public and private, without whom this exhibition, and the new insights it offers, would not have been possible. The National Gallery of Canada is delighted to present Rembrandt's incomparable *Blinding of Samson* from the Städel Museum, and other masterpieces never before shown in Canada.

From the 1650s onward, the Dutch Republic concluded a period of tremendous growth with a series of naval wars and other challenges. An epidemic that began in 1663 brought death to over 24,000 Amsterdam citizens. It may have claimed the life of Rembrandt's partner, Hendrickje Stoffels. Then as now, the global circulation of goods and people meant that illness knew no political boundaries. By 1665 the Great Plague had spread to London. Yet, Rembrandt and his contemporaries continued to produce extraordinary works to serve a vibrant market at home and abroad.

Since planning for this exhibition began, the world has weathered an unfathomable crisis. The generosity of artists and institutions everywhere in providing solace through online resources has shown that the power of art, too, surpasses boundaries, those of time and space as well as geography. As the world slowly recovers, we celebrate the return of visitors to our galleries. With this exhibition, we invite you to rediscover the art of one of the European tradition's great masters and the lively milieu that pushed him to reach his full potential – a confluence of creativity, innovation and resilience that continues to inspire today.

Sasha Suda
Director and CEO
National Gallery of Canada

Philipp Demandt
Director
Städel Museum

Acknowledgements

This exhibition and catalogue could not have been accomplished without the help of numerous colleagues and friends. When we began work on this project years ago, no one could have predicted how the museum landscape would be transformed by COVID-19. Throughout the process, colleagues at our home institutions and elsewhere have sustained us with kindness and generosity. We are delighted that this catalogue pictures the exhibition as we envisioned it. The installations in Ottawa and Frankfurt am Main present the very best interpretations we are able to offer in these challenging circumstances.

We extend warm thanks to our catalogue authors and to our advisory committee for their inspiring contributions and wise counsel. In addition, we are grateful to colleagues at participating institutions and among the international network of scholars of Dutch art who have shared their time, support and expertise. These include Clifford Ackley, Sébastien Allard, Dita Amory, Thomas Andratschke, Christopher Atkins, Ronni Baer, Ellinoor Bergvelt, Holm Bevers, Marten Jan Bok, David Bomford, Maria del Mar Borobia, Alicia Boutilier, Peter van den Brink, Christopher Brown, Stephanie Buck, Cynthia Burlingham, Connie Butler, Quentin Buvelot, An Van Camp, Caroline Campbell, H. Perry Chapman, Keith Christiansen, James Clifton, Peter van der Coelen, Bart Cornelis, Jacquelyn Coutré, Pierre Curie, Dolores Delgado, David de Witt, Sandra Diefenthaler, Thomas Döring, Blaise Ducos, Adam Eaker, Bernd Ebert, Ildikó Ember, Wayne Franits, Michiel Franken, Carina Fryklund, Silke Gatenbröcker, Jeroen Giltaij, Amy Golahny, Hilliard Goldfarb, Liesbeth Helmus, Helen Hillyard, Erik Hinterding, Olenka Horbatsch, Holger Jacob-Friesen, Laurence Kanter, Katja Kleinert, Jan de Klerk, Christi Klinkert, Stefanie Knöll, George Kremer, Friso Lammertse, Justus Lange, Leah Lembeck, Alexandra Libby, Krista van Loon, Austėja Mackelaitė, John Marciari, Norbert Middelkoop, Tom van der Molen, Otto Naumann, Uta Neidhardt, Larry Nichols, Kirk Nickel, Petria Noble, Liesbeth van Noortwijk, Maggie North, Nadine Orenstein, Cynthia Osiecki, Sander Paarlberg, Eva de la Fuente Pedersen, Sabine Pénot, Sandra Pisot, Michiel Plomp, Teresa Posada Kubissa, Thomas Rassieur, Marrigje Rikken, Laura Ritter, Pieter Roelofs, Manja Rottink, Martin Royalton-Kisch, Epco Runia, Peter Schatborn, Stephanie Schrader, Gary Schwartz, Jennifer Scott, Christian Tico Seifert, Anja Ševčík, Leonore van Sloten, Nicolette Sluijter-Seijffert, Irina Sokolova, Ron Spronk, Júlia Tátrai, Laura Thiel-Convery, Oliver Tostmann, Kevin W. Tucker, Ilona van Tuinen, Jane Shoaf Turner, Alejandro Vergara, Annette de Vries, Adriaan Waiboer, Andrew Weislogel, Dennis Weller, Ernst van de Wetering, Betsy Wieseman, Anne Woollett, Lara Yeager-Crasselt, and students at Queen's University, Kingston, who shared in our research.

This project builds on many years of research on Rembrandt and his contemporaries made possible by generous support from Alfred and Isabel Bader, the Social Sciences and Humanities Research Council of Canada, and Queen's University.

At the National Gallery of Canada, we extend our gratitude to Sasha Suda, Director and Chief Executive Officer; Kitty Scott, Deputy Director and Chief Curator; and Isabelle Corriveau, Director of Exhibitions and Outreach. We would also like to thank Sonia Del Re, Erika Dolphin and Kirsten Appleyard in Curatorial; Whitney Gattesco, Virginie Denis, Florence Pinard-Lefebvre, Ceridwen Maycock and Caroline Côté in Exhibitions and Loans; Junia Jorgji and Ellen Treciokas in Design; Gary Goodacre, Andrea Gumpert and Katja Canini in Education and Public Programs; and all our colleagues in the following departments: Collections; Conservation; Facilities Planning and Management; Finance; Marketing, New Media and Communications; Membership and Annual Giving; Multimedia; Partnerships and Community Engagement; Publications and Copyright; Sponsorship and Corporate Giving; and Technical Services. We are also grateful to staff at the National Gallery of Canada Library and Archives and the National Gallery of Canada Foundation. Finally, we thank Karen Colby-Stothart, Anne Eschapasse, Paul Lang, Christine La Salle, Marc Mayer, Marie-Claude Rousseau and Christine Sadler, who provided key support in the early phase of development.

At the Städel Museum, we are particularly grateful to Philipp Demandt, Director; Heinz-Jürgen Bokler, Deputy Director and Head of Finances; and Katja Hilbig, Head of Exhibitions. We would also like to thank Martin Sonnabend, Jan Bielau and Katharina Frohneberg in Prints and Drawings; Hannah Vietoris in Exhibition Organization; Johanna Schick, Assistant of the Director and International Relations; Eva Mongi-Vollmer in Catalogue Management; Martin Kaufmann in Graphics; Chantal Eschenfelder, Anne Sulzbach, Janine Burnicki, Anne Dribbisch, Anna Huber, Antje Lindner and Natalie Marie Meyer in Education; and all colleagues in these teams and the following departments: Conservation; Technical/Installation Crew; Engagement; Marketing; Press and Public Relations; Events; Administration; and Library. Special thanks go to Friederike Schütt as Assistant Curator in the Department of German, Dutch and Flemish Painting before 1800, assisted by Samuel Fickinger and Leslie P. Zimmermann, Student Assistants.

Stephanie S. Dickey
Guest Curator
National Gallery of Canada

Jochen Sander
Vice-Director and Curator of German, Dutch and Flemish Painting before 1800
Städel Museum

Lenders to the Exhibition

Hungary
Museum of Fine Arts, Budapest

Netherlands
Amsterdam City Archives
Amsterdam Museum
Centraal Museum, Utrecht
Dordrechts Museum, Dordrecht
Frans Hals Museum, Haarlem
The Kremer Collection, Amsterdam
Mauritshuis, The Hague
Rembrandt House Museum, Amsterdam
Rijksmuseum, Amsterdam
The Royal Collections of the Netherlands, The Hague
Stedelijk Museum Alkmaar

Russia
The State Hermitage Museum, St. Petersburg

Spain
Museo Nacional del Prado, Madrid
Museo Nacional Thyssen-Bornemisza, Madrid

Sweden
Nationalmuseum, Stockholm

United Kingdom
Ashmolean Museum, University of Oxford
The British Museum, London
Dulwich Picture Gallery, London
National Galleries of Scotland, Edinburgh
The National Gallery, London

United States
Allentown Art Museum
Fine Arts Museums of San Francisco
Hammer Museum, UCLA, Los Angeles
Herbert F. Johnson Museum of Art, Cornell University, Ithaca
High Museum of Art, Atlanta
The J. Paul Getty Museum, Los Angeles
The Leiden Collection, New York
Los Angeles County Museum of Art
The Metropolitan Museum of Art, New York
Michele and Donald D'Amour Museum of Fine Arts, Springfield
The Morgan Library & Museum, New York
The Museum of Fine Arts, Houston
National Gallery of Art, Washington
North Carolina Museum of Art, Raleigh
Philadelphia Museum of Art
Wadsworth Atheneum Museum of Art, Hartford
Yale University Art Gallery, New Haven

And lenders who wish to remain anonymous.

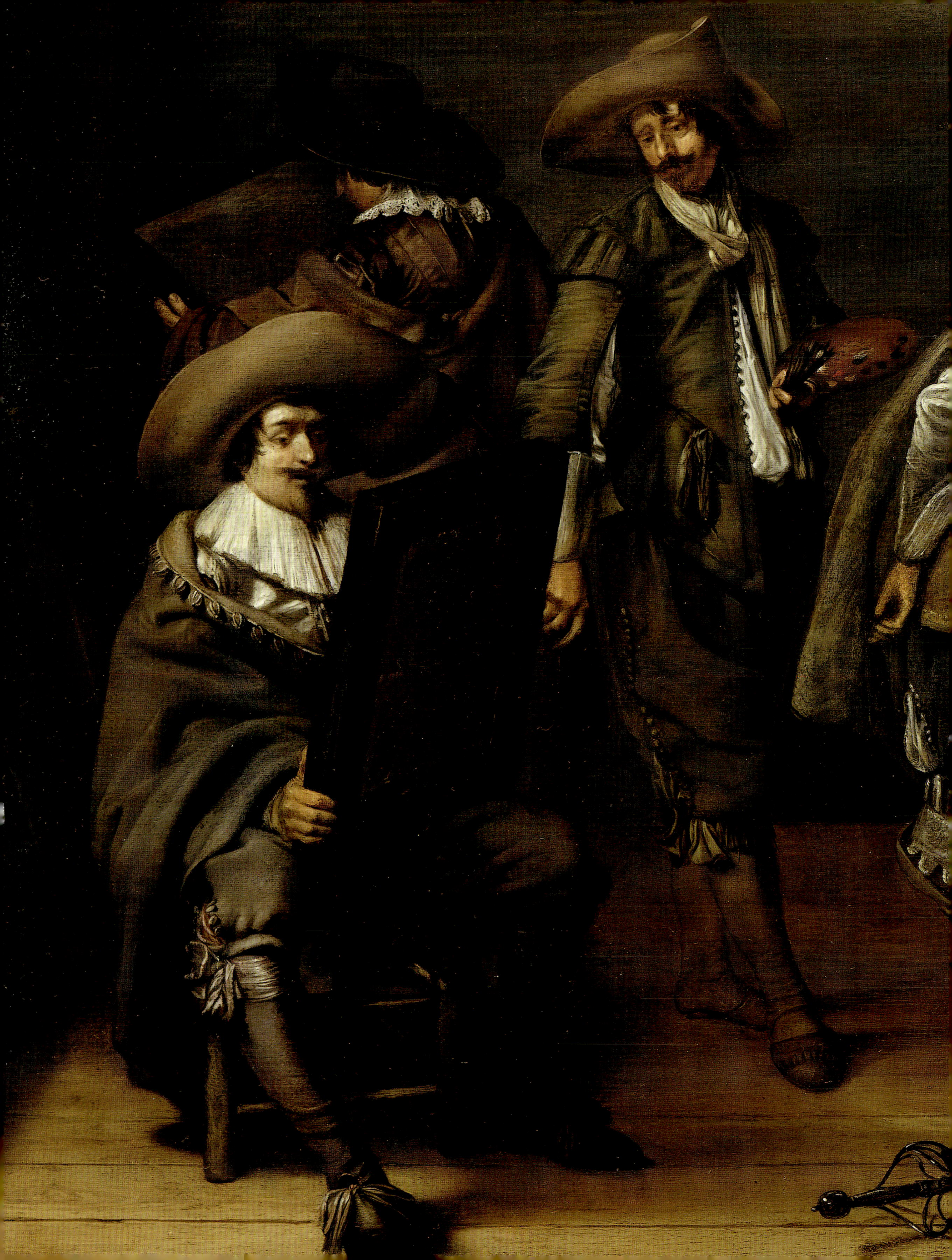

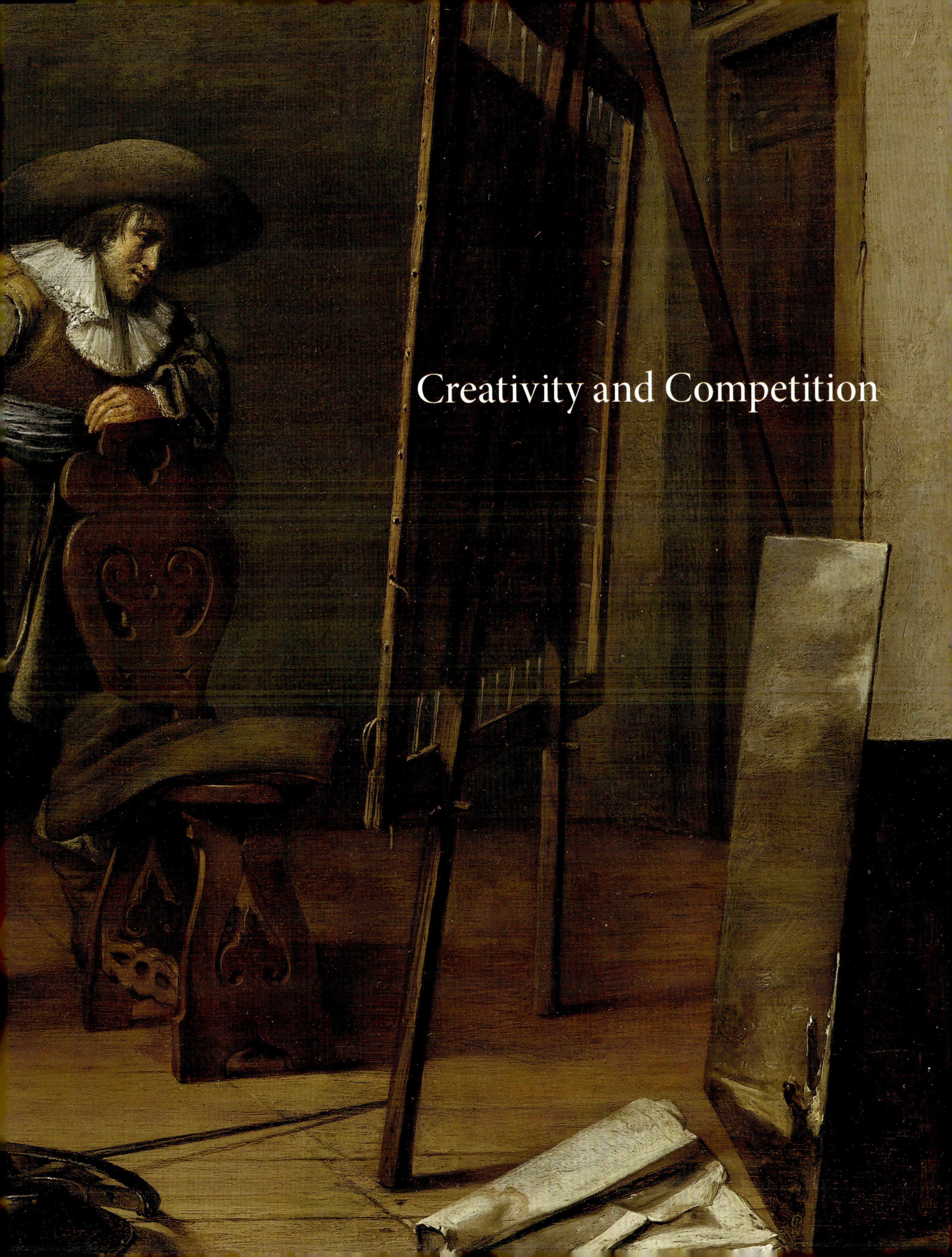

Creativity and Competition

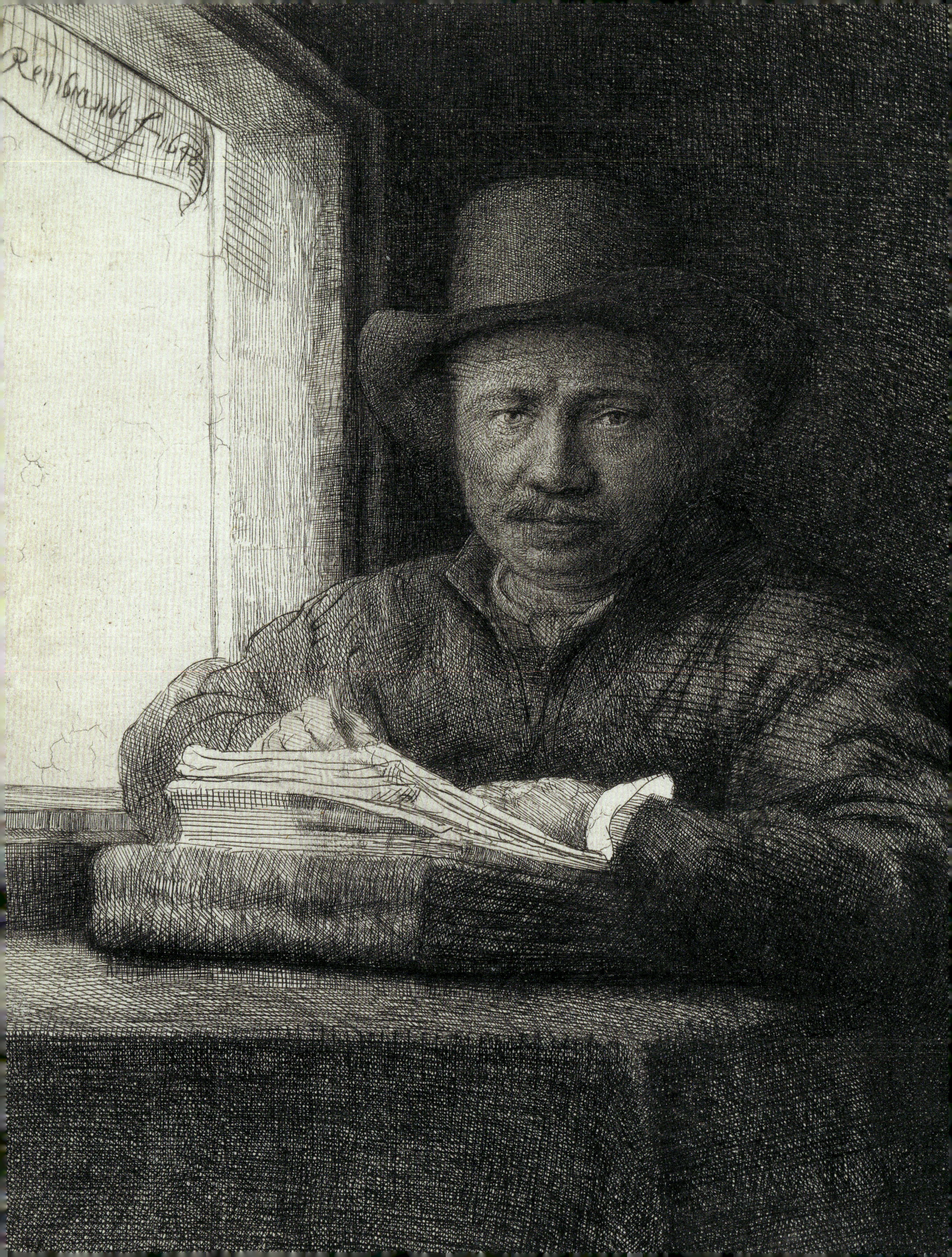
Rembrandt f 1648

STEPHANIE S. DICKEY

Becoming Rembrandt

Rembrandt van Rijn was not supposed to be an artist. Born in Leiden in 1606, he was the ninth of ten children of Neeltgen van Zuytbrouck and Harmen Gerritsz van Rijn, the prosperous owners of a malt mill that had been in the family for generations. Rembrandt must have been a gifted child. While his siblings joined the family business or pursued artisanal careers, his parents sent him to the Latin School and enrolled him at Leiden University. Typically, this type of education would lead to a career in law, theology or medicine. He registered at the university on 20 May 1620 as "Rembrandús Hermanni Leydensis," age fourteen, and did not, as was once thought, drop out quickly. A recently discovered document shows that he remained enrolled until at least 1622 before leaving to apprentice with the local history painter Jacob van Swanenburg.[1]

Seventeenth-century artists usually began their training around the age of ten. From the start, Rembrandt must have felt a sense of urgency to make up for lost time. His years in Leiden were characterized by hard work, creative experimentation and bold ambition.[2] In the winter of 1624–25, he augmented his training with six months in the Amsterdam workshop of Pieter Lastman, a renowned master of small-scale narrative scenes packed with lively figures and classical details (pl. 19).[3] In early history paintings such as *David Playing the Harp for Saul* (pl. 34), Rembrandt adopted Lastman's vocabulary of turbans, rich fabrics and antique accessories while enhancing drama through strong contrasts of light and shadow.[4] He even depicted himself in the garb of a Turkish potentate (fig. 1.1).[5]

Although Leiden was then the second-largest city in the Dutch Republic, Amsterdam was three times the size, and Rembrandt would have found himself in a bustling environment quite different from his home.[6] Leiden was a conservative community dominated by industrial textile production, beer brewing and the university. Competition from other talented artists was limited, and the coterie of art lovers was small, consisting mainly of scholars such as Theodorus Schrevelius, Rector of the Latin School, and the historian and poet Petrus Scriverius. In 1641 the Leiden historian Jan Jansz Orlers wrote that Rembrandt's talent quickly attracted the admiration of connoisseurs.[7] Returning home to set up his first studio, Rembrandt signed early works with the monogram RHL, for Rembrandt, son of Harmen, from Leiden, a loyal patronymic echoing his university registration. He joined forces with Jan Lievens, also an alumnus of Lastman's shop, who was a year younger and already established. They shared models, props, subject matter and experimental techniques.[8] One elderly male model features in several works by both artists, posing as the drunken Lot in a drawing by Rembrandt, later dated 1633 (pl. 152), as Saint Jerome in an etching by Lievens (pl. 21), and as the biblical patriarch Job in Lievens' monumental painting of 1631 (pl. 22). These works capture the pensive dejection of old age, a theme the artists explored repeatedly.[9] In addition to history paintings, they helped to popularize the rising genre of character studies, called *tronies* (faces) in Dutch inventories (pl. 20).[10]

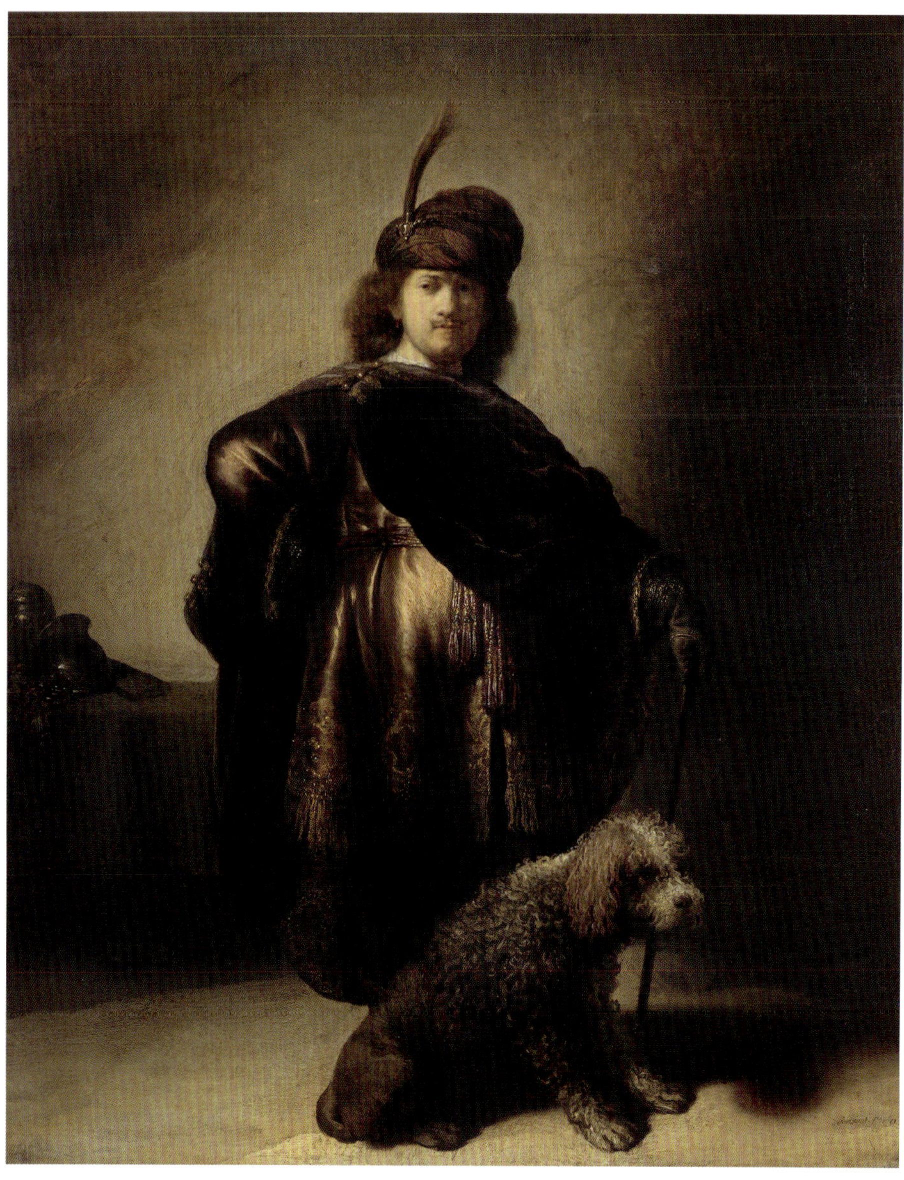

fig. 1.1 Rembrandt van Rijn, *Self-portrait in Oriental Costume*, 1631, oil on panel; 66.5 × 52 cm. Petit Palais, Musée des Beaux-Arts de la Ville de Paris. Dutuit Bequest 1902 (PDUT925)

Leaving Leiden

A year or so after Rembrandt returned to Leiden, Lievens talked his way into painting the portrait of Constantijn Huygens, secretary to Stadtholder Frederik Hendrik (see fig. 6.1). Court commissions for both artists soon followed (pl. 47, see figs. 13.2, 13.3).[11] Huygens declared the pair "a young and noble painterly duo," with potential to surpass even the great masters of the Renaissance.[12] In the winter of 1631, he may have introduced them to Anthony van Dyck when the Flemish master visited the stadtholder's court in The Hague.[13] Although Van Dyck was just a few years older than Rembrandt and Lievens, the combination of power and grace that flowed through his portraits and history paintings had already captured elite patronage across Europe (pl. 104, fig. 1.11). Within a year, Lievens had left Leiden to join Van Dyck's entourage

at the court of King Charles I in London. Rembrandt, too, was getting restless. An etched self portrait of 1630, in the role of a beggar with his hand out, satirically suggests his irritation with the demeaning process of soliciting attention from potential buyers.[14]

In Leiden, Rembrandt trained his first two pupils, Isaac de Jouderville and Gerrit Dou, and collaborated with the printmaker Jan van Vliet (pl. 165).[15] It is clear that he was not – then nor ever – the isolated genius nineteenth-century Romantics imagined him to be.[16] From the beginning of his career to the end, Rembrandt surrounded himself with talented students and peers.[17] In Amsterdam, at least forty younger artists would pass through his workshop. Some, such as Gerbrand van den Eeckhout and Philips Koninck, came as friends rather than pupils.[18] Only a few, such as Govert Flinck, produced work that rose to the level of serious competition, but all of them played a role in expanding the reach of his brand. Sources such as Rembrandt's etched portraits of the Italianate landscape painter Jan Asselijn (pl. 1), the goldsmith Jan Lutma (pl. 23), the printseller Clement de Jonghe (pls. 170, 171), and the apothecary and avid art collector Abraham Francen (pl. 24) document further contacts outside his immediate circle.[19]

Accounts of Rembrandt's network have usually emphasized his impact on others, but inspiration in creative communities flows in all directions. In 1678 Samuel van Hoogstraten, who studied with Rembrandt in the mid-1640s, counselled young artists that competition could ignite creativity. "It is no Herezy to outlymn Apelles," he wrote.[20] This invitation to rival the legendary painter of ancient Greece had contemporary relevance, since Apelles was an established role model. Rembrandt was compared with Apelles in several contemporary texts, but so were Lievens and Flinck.[21] No less than that of his peers, Rembrandt's art was shaped by creative exchange with talented colleagues and discerning patrons.

The Wise Merchant

On 9 January 1632, the humanist Caspar Barlaeus stood before an assembly of businessmen and magistrates to deliver his inaugural address at the opening of the Athenaeum Illustre, an educational institution founded to prepare the sons of Amsterdam's mercantile elite for study at Leiden University. Speaking in Latin, Barlaeus described the ideal Amsterdam citizen as a *mercator sapiens* (wise merchant), whose devotion

Rembrandt van Rijn, *Portrait of Jan Asselijn*, 1647. Städel Museum, Frankfurt am Main

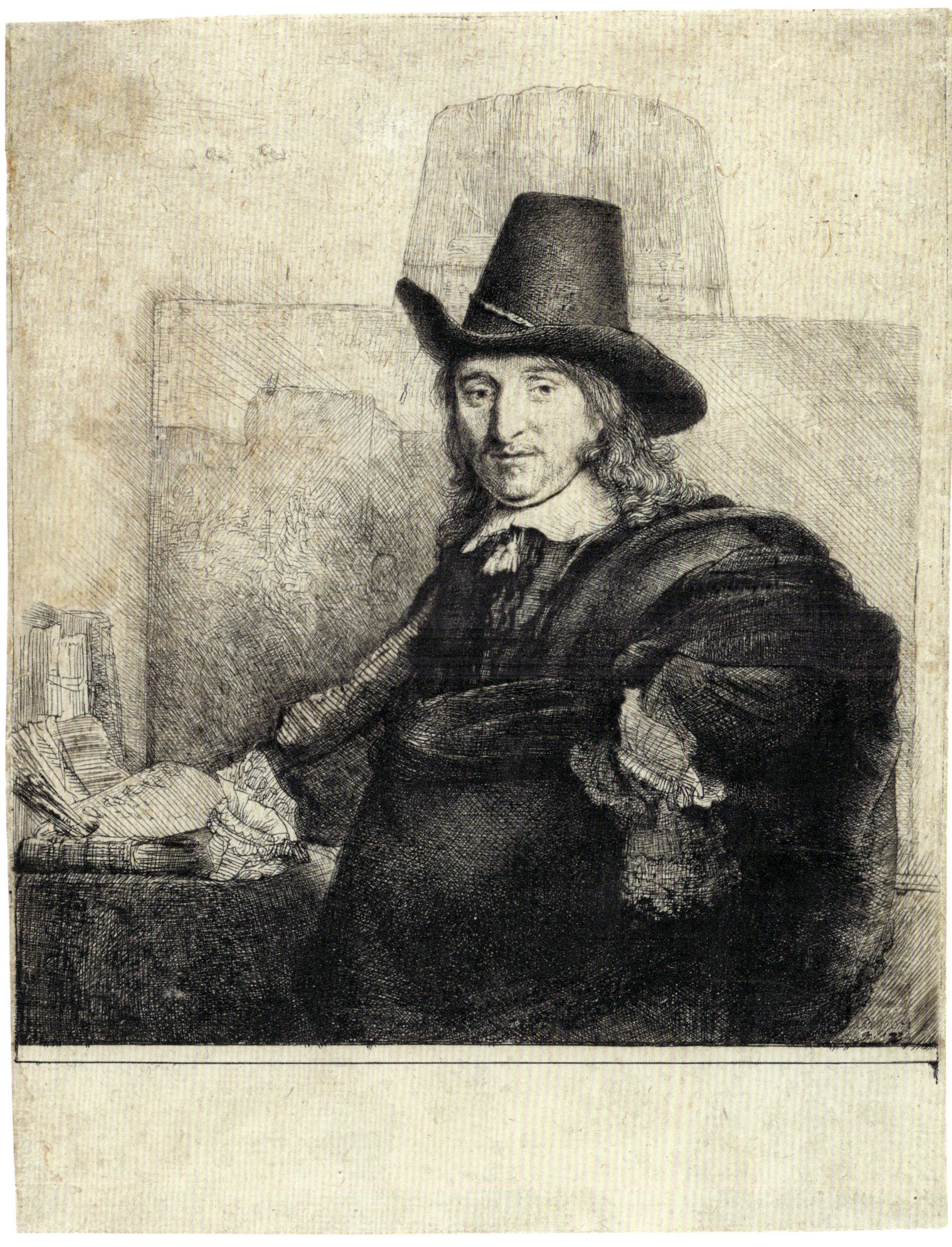

2   Rembrandt van Rijn, *View of the Montelbaans Tower in Amsterdam*, c. 1644–45. Rembrandt House Museum, Amsterdam

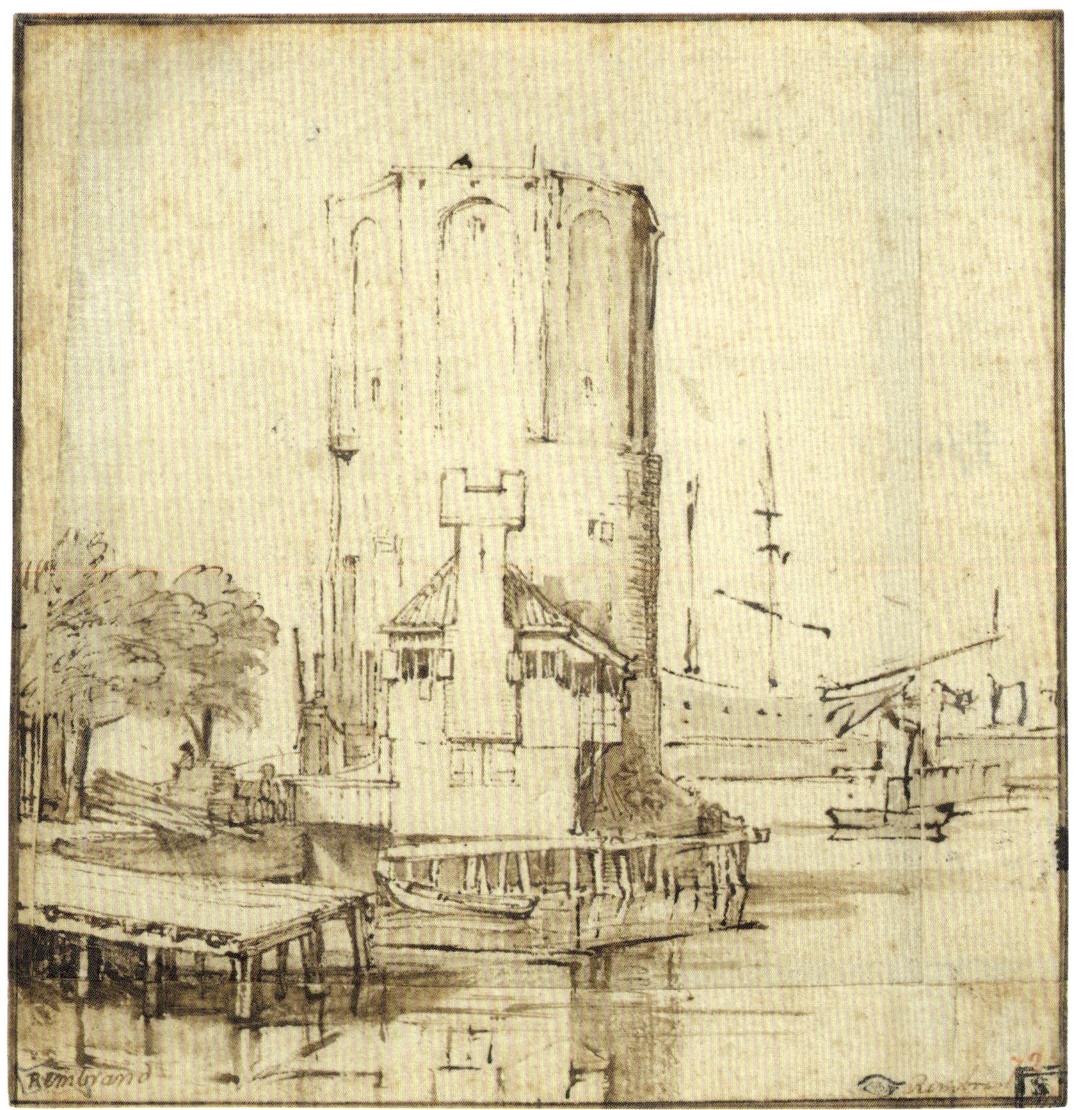

to profitable trade was tempered by a philosophical understanding that some things in life are more important than money.[22] Barlaeus and Rembrandt moved to Amsterdam from Leiden around the same time and may well have crossed paths.[23] In his oration, Barlaeus described making his way through teeming but orderly crowds, stopping to admire "churches sacred to God ... many lofty homes for the afflicted poor, towers, lighthouses rising up to the sky; ... elsewhere the lofty porticoes of the traders; everywhere so many bridges' arches and ceilings. ... I can look in astonishment at the tremendous amount of goods shipped in from abroad, the multitude and strength of the ships, the capacious ports, the landing stages for fleets that surround the city. ... I am distracted by the splendour of its buildings."[24]

It is easy to imagine that Rembrandt felt a similar excitement. Sketches preserve his observations of the city's architecture and street life (pl. 2, fig. 1.2).[25] Most important for him was the chance to compete

in the largest and most diverse art market in the Dutch Republic. Two days after Barlaeus' speech, Rembrandt signed and dated his portrait of Marten Looten, a wealthy textile merchant (fig. 1.3).[26] Looten's Mennonite faith would have sustained him in practising Barlaeus' ideal of moderation, and it probably brought him into contact with Rembrandt by way of Hendrick Uylenburgh, the Mennonite art dealer and entrepreneur whose workshop offered Rembrandt the launching pad for his luminary career in Amsterdam.[27]

Rembrandt's partnership with Uylenburgh began with an investment: sometime before 20 June 1631, he lent the dealer the substantial sum of 1,000 guilders.[28] This makes it clear that he had done well in Leiden and that he entered into this phase of his career with further financial success in mind. In two paintings from 1632 (pl. 35 and Burrell Collection, Glasgow) and in an etching completed between 1631 and 1633 (pl. 3), he portrayed himself for the first time

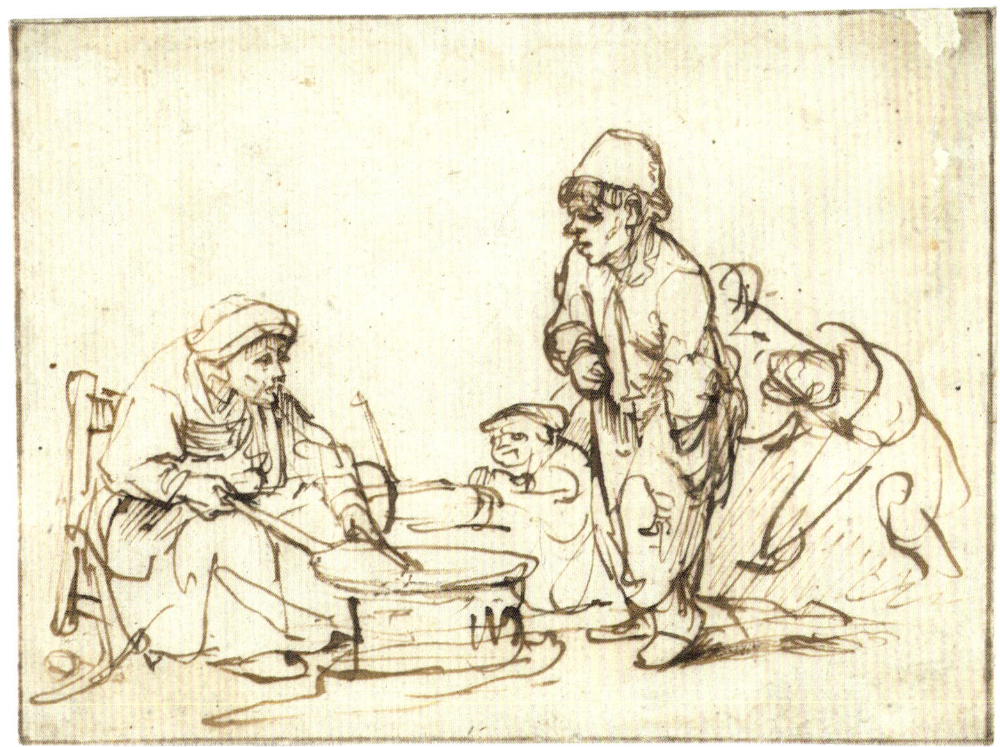

fig. 1.2 **Rembrandt van Rijn,** *The Pancake Woman*, **c. 1635, pen and ink on laid paper; 10.8 × 14.4 cm. Rijksmuseum, Amsterdam. Purchased with the support of the Rembrandt Association (RP-T-1891-A2424)**

dressed as a prosperous burgher.[29] The monogram "RHL" on early states of the print gives way to his mature signature, "Rembrandt."[30]

To hire an untested portraitist from another city, Uylenburgh must have been desperate for talent to fill the growing demand.[31] For Rembrandt, the shift from history painting was a strategic move: portrait commissions opened the door to other sales.[32] His early experiments with character studies and self-portraits laid a foundation for formal likenesses that combine close attention to detail with expressive effects of light and colour, evoking both personality and physical presence. While some clients continued to prefer the sober and dignified portraits of established masters such as Nicolaes Eliasz Pickenoy and Thomas de Keyser, Rembrandt's refreshing approach soon caught on. Over the next two years, he lodged with Uylenburgh while keeping his Leiden studio open

and travelling to The Hague and Rotterdam. His portrait clients included not only Amsterdam merchants but also the stadtholder's wife, Princess Amalia von Solms (pl. 47), and Reverend Johannes Wtenbogaert, former court chaplain and distinguished leader of the Remonstrant movement (see fig. 6.2).[33]

Three weeks after Barlaeus' speech, a thief known as Aris the Kid was hanged for assaulting a man while attempting to steal his cloak. His body was dissected in a public demonstration that served as both a medical lesson and a moral warning to onlookers. This event provided the basis for Rembrandt's first group portrait, *The Anatomy Lesson of Dr. Nicolaes Tulp* (fig. 1.4). Although he had not yet attempted a history painting with life-size figures, Rembrandt transformed the portrait into a unified, dramatically lit action scene. Tulp's colleagues watch with rapt attention as he lectures on the anatomy of the arm. Glowing light endows

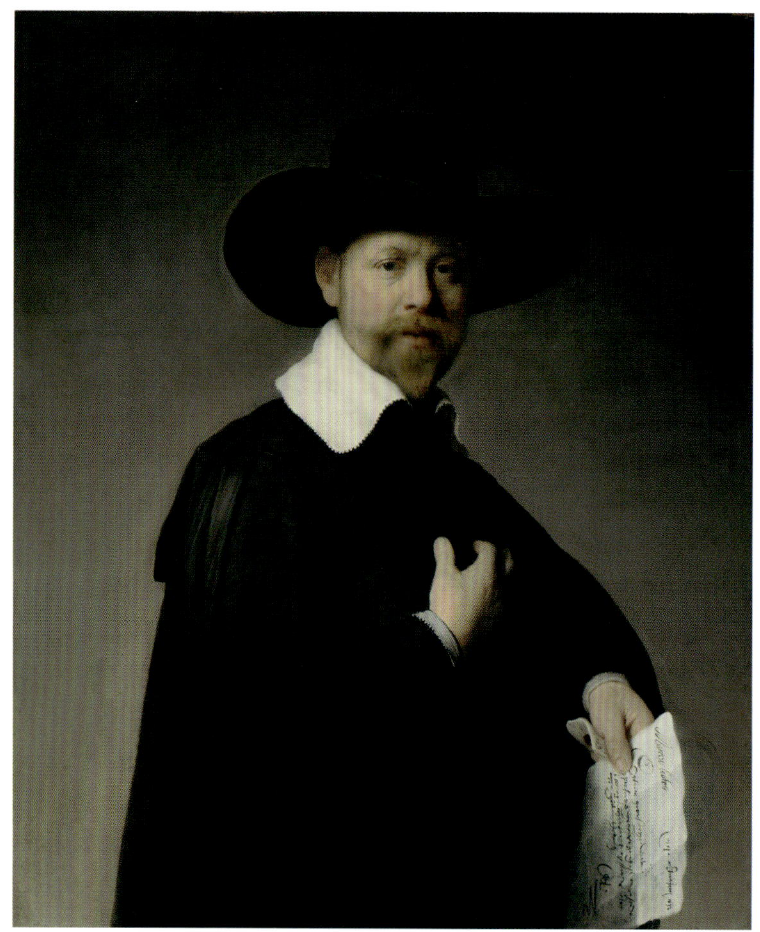

fig. 1.3 **Rembrandt van Rijn,** *Portrait of Marten Looten,* **1632, oil on panel; 92.7 × 76.2 cm. Los Angeles County Museum of Art. Gift of J. Paul Getty (53.50.3)**

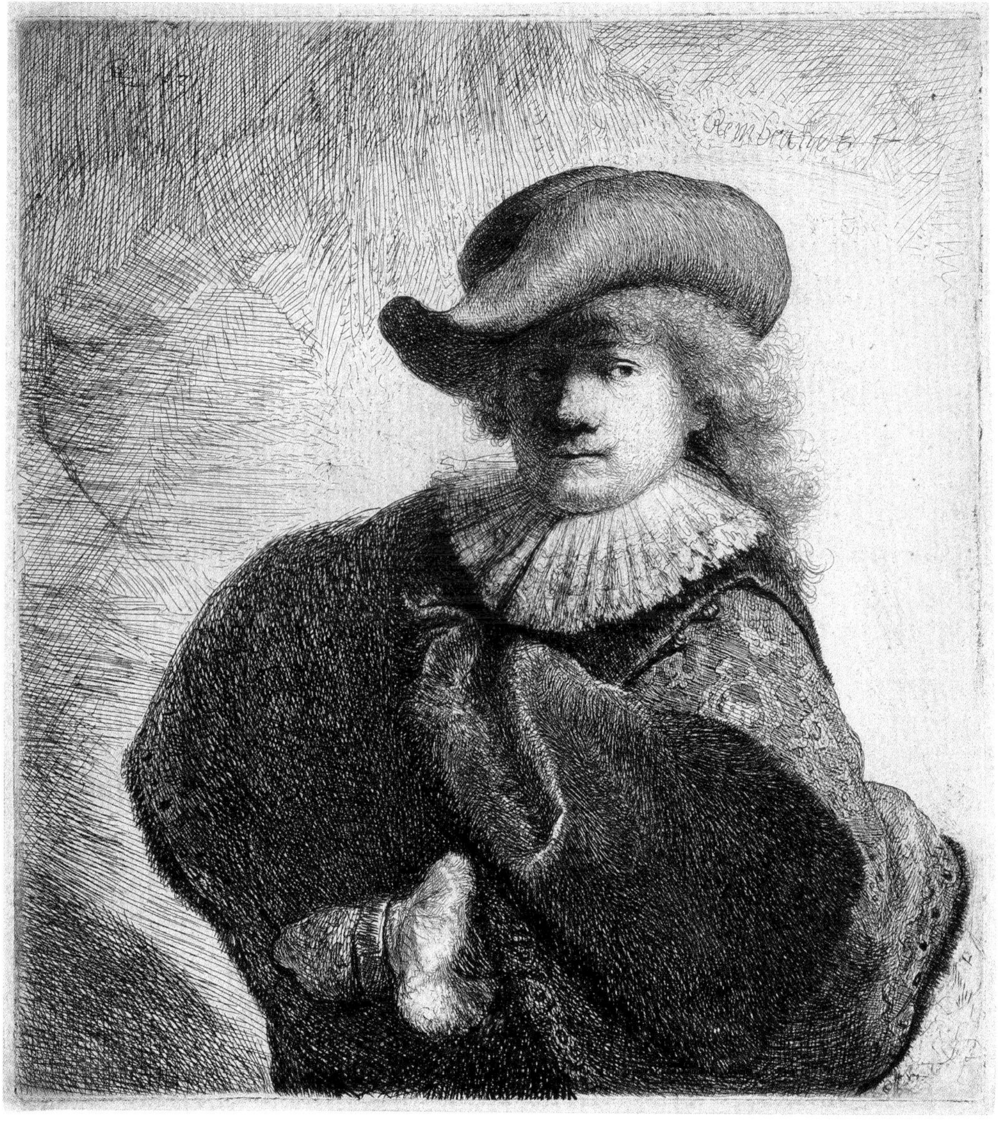

the prostrate corpse with sacral pathos, an effect that would come to fruition in *The Blinding of Samson* of 1636 (pl. 106).[34] Displayed in the headquarters of the Amsterdam Guild of Surgeons, the group portrait was a bold advertisement of Rembrandt's skill and ambition.[35] By 1633 he had moved to Amsterdam and joined Uylenburgh's shop full time.

At the peak of demand, Rembrandt (or Uylenburgh) must have engaged in some of the production methods common to masters of large portrait workshops, such as Gerard van Honthorst in Utrecht or Michiel van Mierevelt in Delft. This included allowing assistants to complete parts of his compositions, and even signing works that were largely painted by others. Technical analyses suggest that many of the portraits and *tronies* produced in Uylenburgh's workshop were collaborative efforts or copies. Who the assistants might have been demands further research. One may have been Dirck van Santvoort, a successful portraitist in his own right (pl. 53).[36]

fig. 1.4 **Rembrandt van Rijn,** *The Anatomy Lesson of Dr. Nicolaes Tulp,* **1632, oil on canvas; 169.5 × 216.5 cm. Mauritshuis, The Hague (146)**

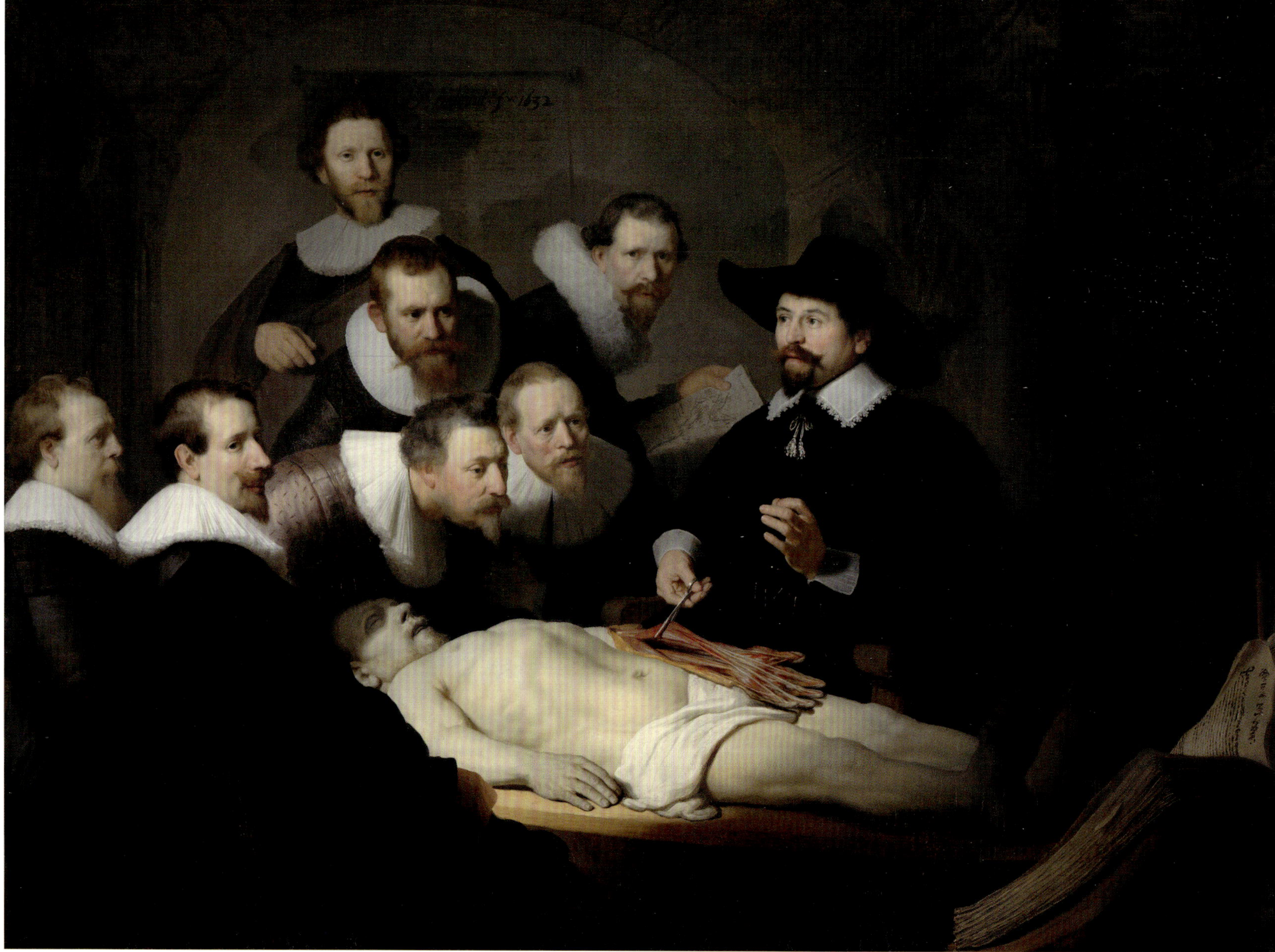

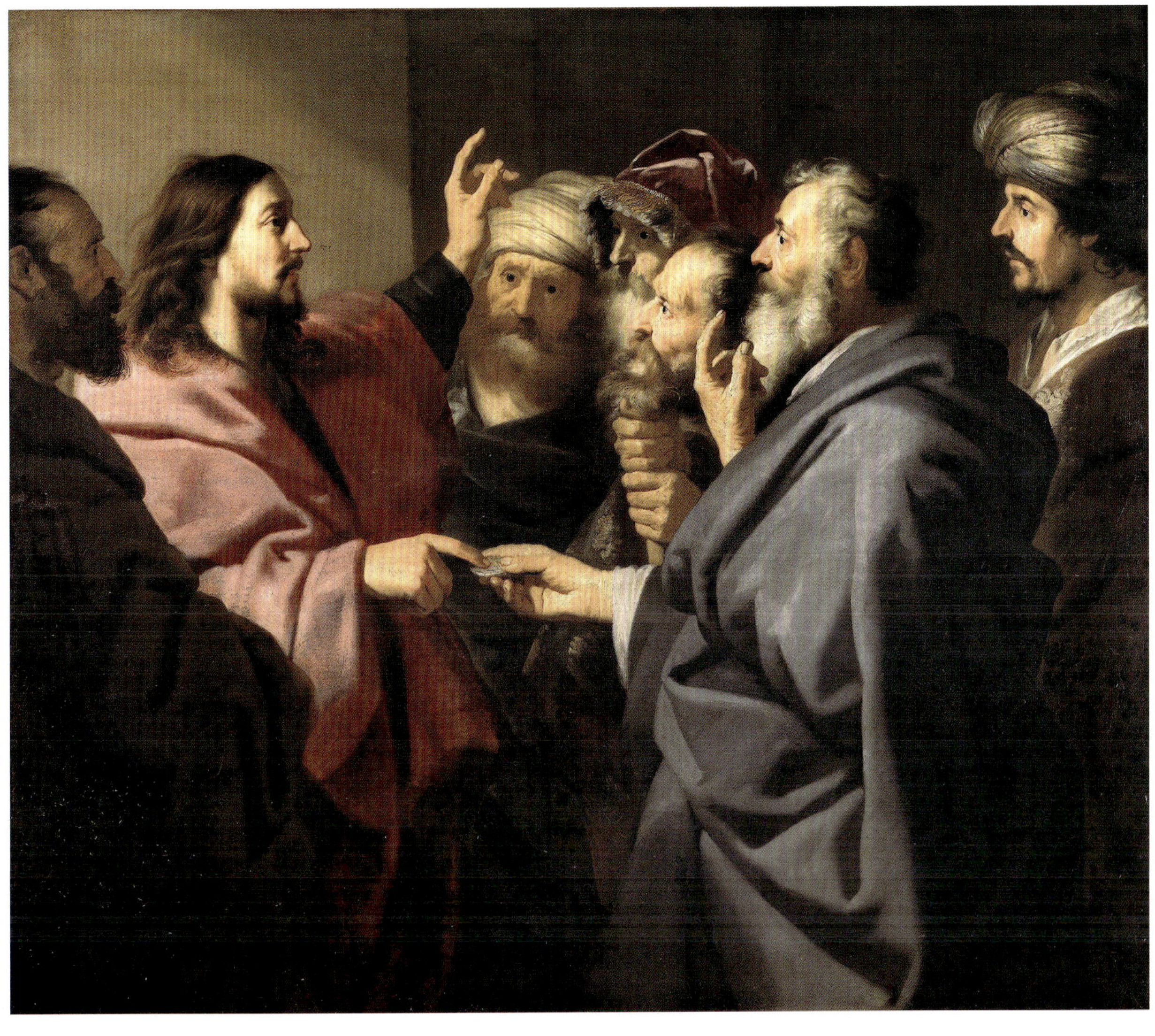

fig. 1.5 Jacob Backer, *The Tribute Money*, c. 1631, oil on canvas; 139 × 159 cm. Nationalmuseum, Stockholm (NM 631)

Rembrandt, Backer and Flinck

Rembrandt was not the only artist whose career was launched by Hendrick Uylenburgh. Jacob Backer learned the basics of painting in Amsterdam, possibly from Lastman's associate Jan Pynas, but in 1626 he travelled north to Leeuwarden to work for the Mennonite preacher and painter Lambert Jacobsz. There, Backer was joined by Govert Flinck, whose Mennonite parents had sent him from Cleves. Jacobsz maintained close ties with Uylenburgh, exchanging consignments of paintings by Backer, Flinck and Rembrandt. By February 1633 Backer had returned to Amsterdam. He was not, as once thought, a follower of Rembrandt, but a talented competitor on several fronts. The German artist and biographer Joachim von Sandrart, who lived in Amsterdam from 1637 to 1645, commented on the speed and fluency of his painterly style, telling the story of a woman from Haarlem who sat for a portrait and took

it home the same day.[37] Van Hoogstraten admired the warmth of Backer's flesh tones, a quality evident in paintings such as *Portrait of a Man (Jan Pietersz van den Eeckhout?)* (pl. 51).[38] Backer's first group portrait, *Regentesses of the Burgerweeshuis* (1634, Amsterdam Museum), brought him into contact with patrons from four powerful regent families.[39]

In addition to portraits and figure studies, Backer introduced to the Amsterdam market a Jacobsz specialty: history paintings with a few life-size figures interacting through gesture and conversation. These works posed a challenge for Rembrandt, who produced his first large-scale history painting around 1634 (see fig. 13.5). The combination of speaking and intense listening that activates *The Anatomy Lesson of Dr. Nicolaes Tulp* is anticipated in Backer's *Tribute Money* (fig. 1.5), painted in Leeuwarden and offered for sale by Uylenburgh in Amsterdam.[40]

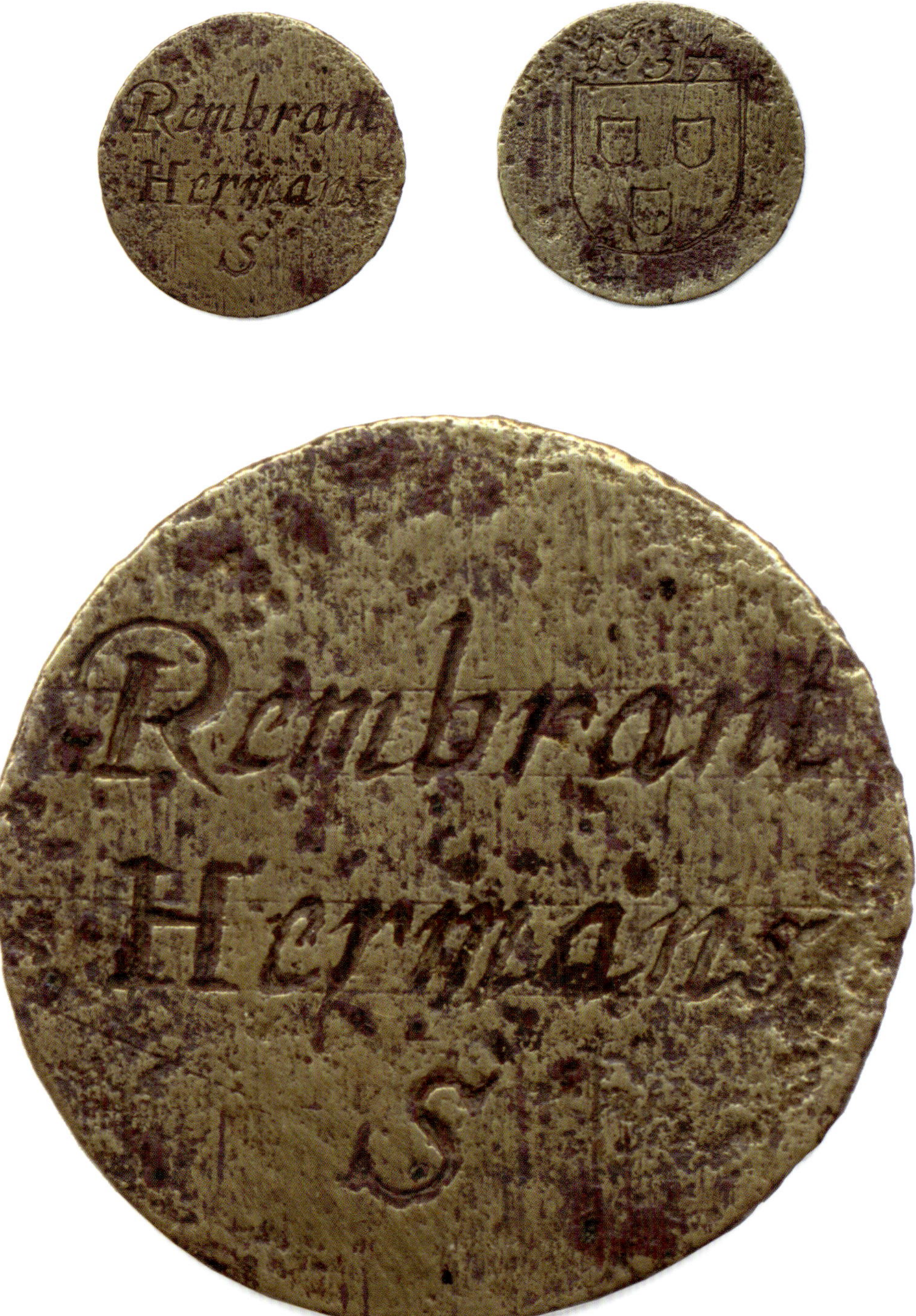

4 *Rembrandt's Funeral Medallion* (recto, verso and enlargement of recto), 1634. Rembrandt House Museum, Amsterdam

Backer's composition reflects the Flemish master Peter Paul Rubens' treatment of the theme, publicized in reproductive prints by Lucas Vorsterman and Claes Jansz Visscher.[41] Rembrandt probably studied the same prints,[42] but he must also have encountered Backer's painting.

Backer became an active participant in the city's creative network. Thomas de Keyser painted his portrait, and Backer portrayed the Italianate history and landscape painter Bartholomeus Breenbergh and his wife.[43] The sitter in *Portrait of a Man*, mentioned above, has been identified as the father of Rembrandt's friend Gerbrand van den Eeckhout.[44] Backer also kept in contact with Flinck, who arrived in Amsterdam in 1634 to work in Uylenburgh's shop under Rembrandt's direction. In the 1640s they met together with other artists to draw from the nude female body, producing sketches in black chalk on toned paper that are difficult to tell apart.[45]

In 1634 Rembrandt joined the Amsterdam Guild of Saint Luke and received the brass medallion all members were required to present when they attended the funerals of their colleagues.[46] Remarkably, this small object has survived, a material trace of Rembrandt's living presence in the city's artistic community (pl. 4). The same year, he married Hendrick Uylenburgh's cousin, Saskia. In 1635 they moved out of Uylenburgh's home to rented quarters, and in 1639 purchased the house on St. Anthonisbreestraat that is now the Rembrandt House Museum. Rembrandt filled the house with art and curiosities, for his own pleasure and for sale, while dozens of younger artists came to work and study there.[47] Saskia's likeness is a radiant presence in her husband's work until 1642, when she died at age twenty-nine, leaving him with an infant son, Titus (pls. 5–7, 155–157).[48] There followed a troubled affair with Titus' nursemaid, Geertje Dircks. After 1650 a number of paintings and drawings reflect Rembrandt's affection for Hendrickje Stoffels (pl. 91), who entered his household as a servant and became his late-life partner and mother of their daughter, Cornelia.[49]

When Rembrandt became an independent master, Flinck took over as head of Uylenburgh's workshop. Early patronage came from wealthy members of Flinck's extended family.[50] By 1644 Flinck, too, was on his own, purchasing two adjacent houses on the Lauriergracht.[51] Arnold Houbraken (biographer and former student of Van Hoogstraten) described an impressive studio filled with classical busts, weapons, fabrics and exotic costume elements – a workspace designed in emulation of Rembrandt's cabinet of curiosities.[52] Like Rembrandt, Flinck built his reputation through portraiture but also excelled in history painting, *tronies* and landscape. Portraiture was a strategic choice rather than a true calling; as a mature artist, according to Houbraken, he preferred to pass portrait commissions along to Bartholomeus van der Helst.[53]

Disciples from Dordrecht

Ferdinand Bol arrived in Amsterdam in 1636 after basic training in Dordrecht and worked with Rembrandt until about 1640, producing variations on Rembrandt's history paintings (pl. 119) as well as competent portraits. His style was deeply imprinted by Rembrandt's approach to storytelling, colour and composition, but with smoother brushwork and more restrained emotion; he became an expert at rendering material detail.[54] Bol took up the art of etching more seriously than any other Rembrandt pupil (pl. 115).[55] He witnessed several of Rembrandt's iconic works in the making, including the 1639 etching *Self-portrait Leaning on a Stone Sill* (pl. 45) and the 1640 painting *Self-portrait at the Age of 34* (see fig. 5.6). These closely related self-portraits, based on Renaissance examples, combine dignity, fantasy and illusionism in a consummate statement of artistic authority. Bol and Flinck were the first of many artists to emulate this influential formula in both self-portraits and commissioned works (pls. 39, 40, 64, 66, 67).[56] As an independent artist after 1640, Bol flourished as a painter of histories and portraits, winning major public and private commissions. His marriage to Elisabeth Dell in 1653 brought useful connections in civic government and the admiralty.[57]

Samuel van Hoogstraten arrived from Dordrecht in 1642. He returned there by 1648, but later travelled widely, developing a polished style that had little to do with Rembrandt apart from a continuing fascination with illusionism. From 1649 he was also a published author; his treatise of 1678, *Introduction to the High School of Painting*, is larded with advice and anecdotes picked up in Rembrandt's shop.[58] Nicolaes Maes studied history painting with Rembrandt around 1646–52 but began to produce innovative genre paintings when he returned to Dordrecht (see fig. 15.3); later, he became a fashionable portraitist.[59]

5   Rembrandt van Rijn, *Studies of the Head of Saskia and Others*, 1636. Städel Museum, Frankfurt am Main

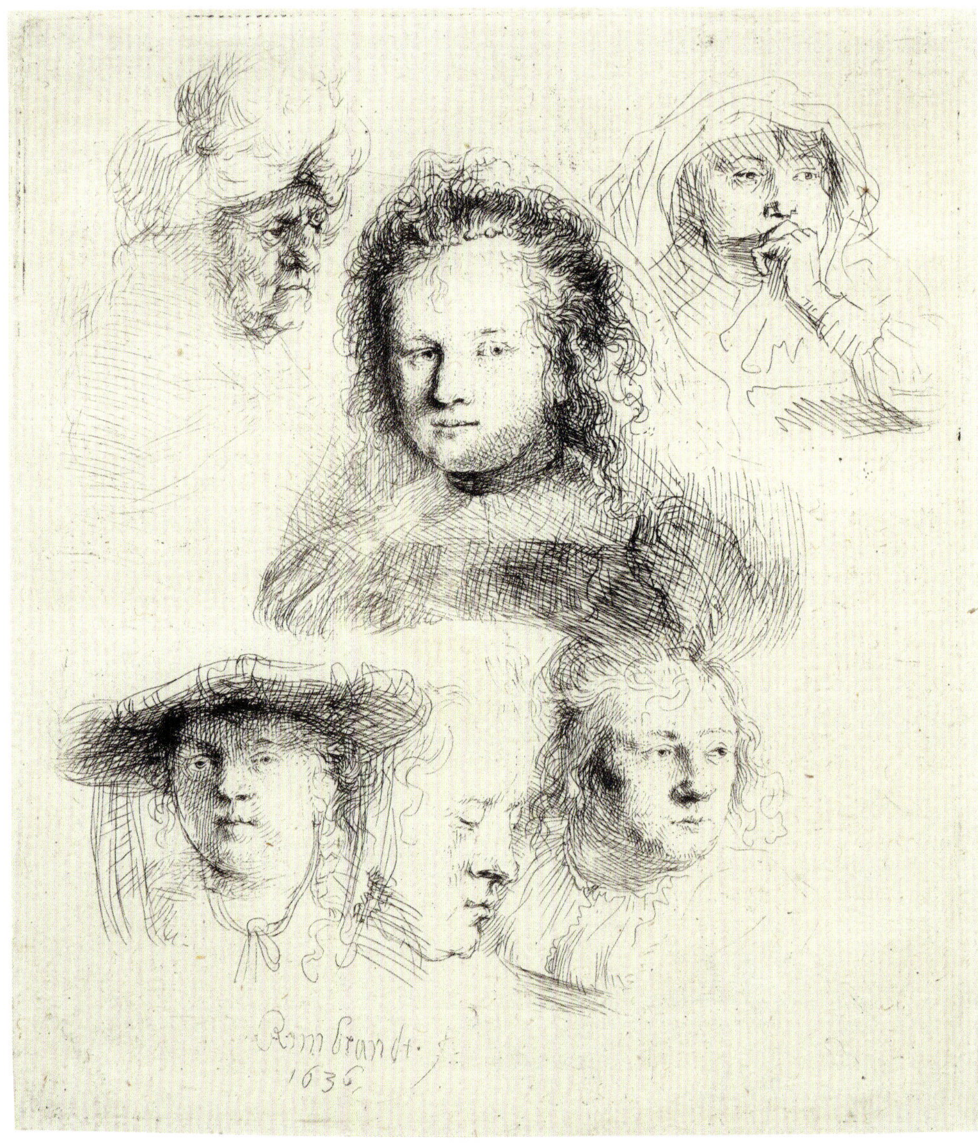

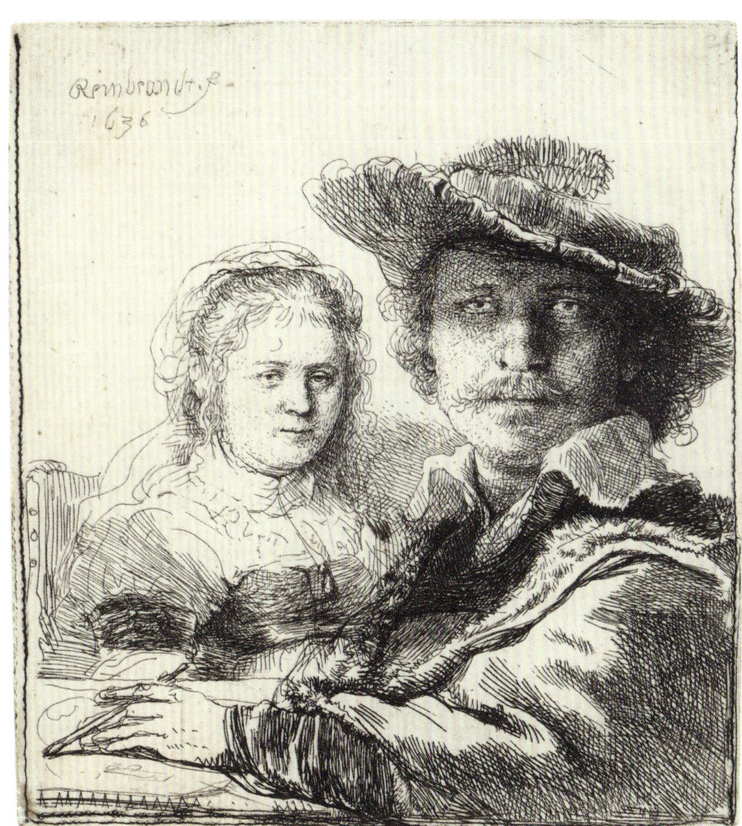

7   Rembrandt van Rijn, *Saskia van Uylenburgh, the Wife of the Artist*, c. 1634/35–1638/40. National Gallery of Art, Washington

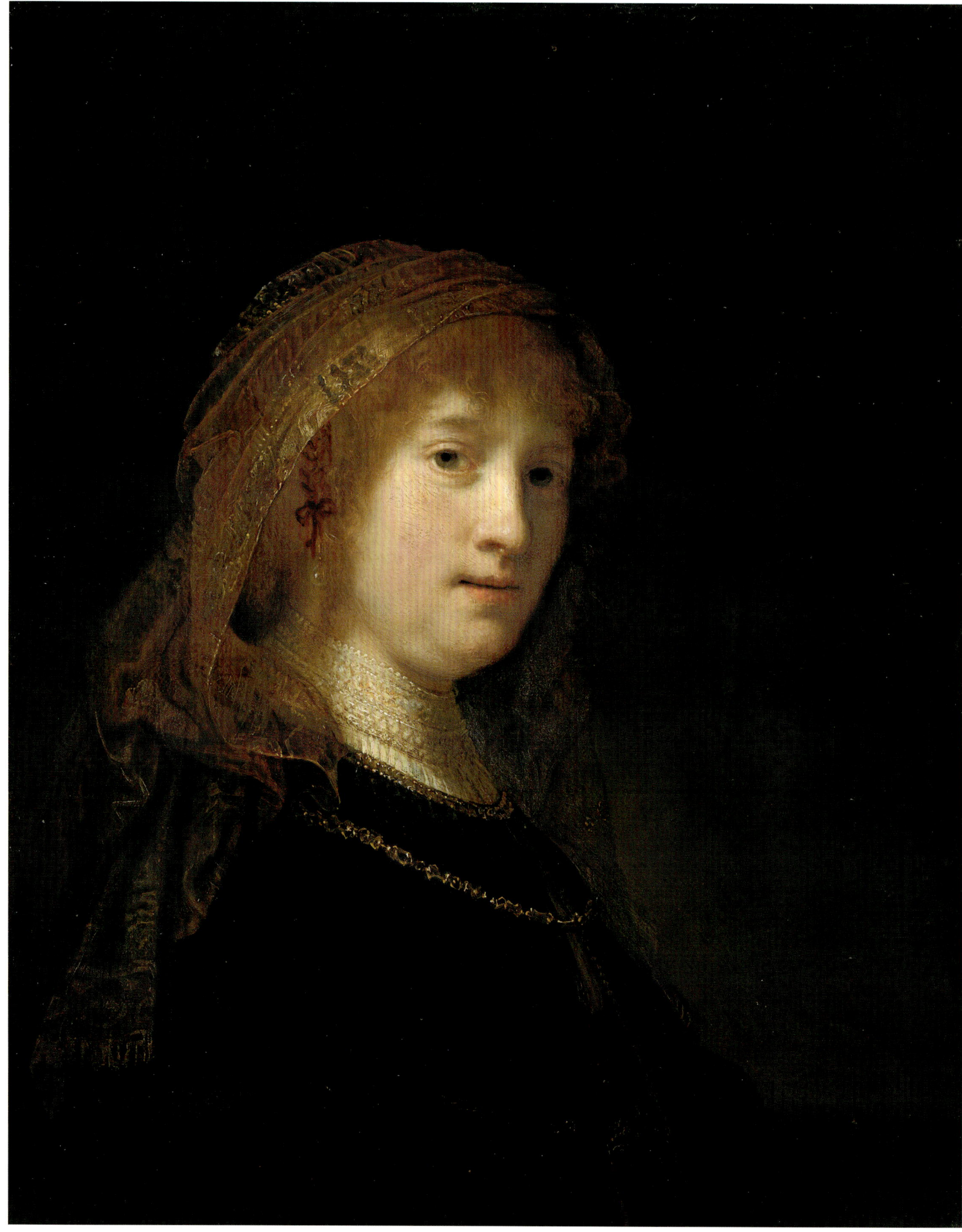

Building a Brand

It is not possible to discuss all of Rembrandt's pupils here, but a few key points can be made. Most importantly, Rembrandt took teaching seriously. In the 1640s his own productivity declined, perhaps in part because much of his time was taken up with mentoring younger masters. Sandrart observed that Rembrandt profited handsomely from tuition fees and sales of student work.[60] Rembrandt's most innovative strategy was to encourage them not only to copy his works but also to develop their own creative variations. This prepared them for independent careers while also expanding the product line. Like any good teacher, Rembrandt was surely energized by the creative enthusiasm of ambitious disciples. Sometimes the student's version might improve on the original.

Artists who were not strictly pupils, such as Gerbrand van den Eeckhout, Salomon Koninck and Jan Victors, also borrowed motifs and ideas.[61] It has been suggested that the proliferation of derivative products cut into Rembrandt's market share.[62] However, only a few other painters in Amsterdam commanded his prices or served the same elevated segment of the market. It is more productive to understand the reach of his brand as a collective enterprise in which talented associates expanded the market with more affordable works. Some also took his ideas and pushed them in new directions. For instance, while Rembrandt painted few genre scenes, a surprising number of followers became innovators in this increasingly popular category.[63] Dou founded a dynasty of genre painters in Leiden who developed Rembrandt's meticulous early style. The genre imagery of Maes, Van Hoogstraten and others built upon the commitment to naturalism evident in Rembrandt's homely treatments of biblical subjects.[64] Van den Eeckhout, while painting mostly histories, played a key role in reviving the guardroom scenes and elegant merry companies pioneered in Amsterdam by Pieter Codde and Willem Duyster. He did this in tandem with Jacob van Loo, an artist working in a very different style (see figs. 15.4–15.6). Van Loo lived in Amsterdam from 1642 to 1660, painting mostly mythologies (pl. 100) and portraits. His cool elegance contrasts markedly with Van den Eeckhout's ruddy palette and expressive touch.[65] Side by side, they set the stage for the high-life genre scenes of Gabriel Metsu and Johannes Vermeer.

Versatility in a Specialized Market

Theorists considered history painting the pinnacle of artistic achievement, but elite urban consumers increasingly collected more contemporary subjects as well. Between 1630 and 1660, the open market for landscapes, genre scenes and still lifes grew exponentially. History paintings remained popular in Amsterdam at all price levels, but claimed a smaller share of the market.[66] Many talented artists, especially in Amsterdam, diversified their skills. Pickenoy and De Keyser painted mostly portraits but also produced a few history paintings.[67] Codde worked in both these genres, but is best known today for scenes of elegant leisure.[68] Yet, by mid-century, it had become increasingly possible to secure a market niche by specializing in specific pictorial categories. For instance, after returning from Italy in 1647, Jan Asselijn painted only lucid landscapes, such as *The Tiber River with the Ponte Molle at Sunset* (pl. 134), that interpret his experience of the sunny south for Amsterdam collectors.[69]

Rembrandt embraced the ideal of the universal master, proficient in all aspects of his craft.[70] Despite his training as a history painter, already in Leiden he was exploring figure painting of all kinds, from allegories to genre scenes and *tronies*. He took up portraiture in 1631 and landscape a few years later (pl. 131). There is evidence that he also painted still lifes, although few surviving works fit this description (pl. 150).[71] Significantly, his approach was disruptively fluid: group portraits became action scenes, lofty historical figures were brought down to earth, and the flat Dutch landscape gained a numinous mystery through nuanced effects of light.

Christ in the Storm on the Sea of Galilee (fig. 1.6), painted in 1633, is a dramatic biblical scene and also Rembrandt's only seascape, a specialty aligned with the broad impact of seafaring in Dutch life (pl. 33). The painting's original owner was Jacques Specx, former governor general of Batavia in the Dutch East Indies.[72] In 1633 Rembrandt produced a single illustration for Elias Herckmans' treatise in praise of seafaring, an allegory in which Fortuna sets sail from imperial Rome, perhaps steering a course toward a future when the Dutch rule the seas (pl. 8).[73] Book illustrations were mundane work for printmakers, and when Rembrandt accepted such a task again it was for a close friend and patron, the wealthy textile merchant Jan Six (see figs. 17.9, 17.10).[74]

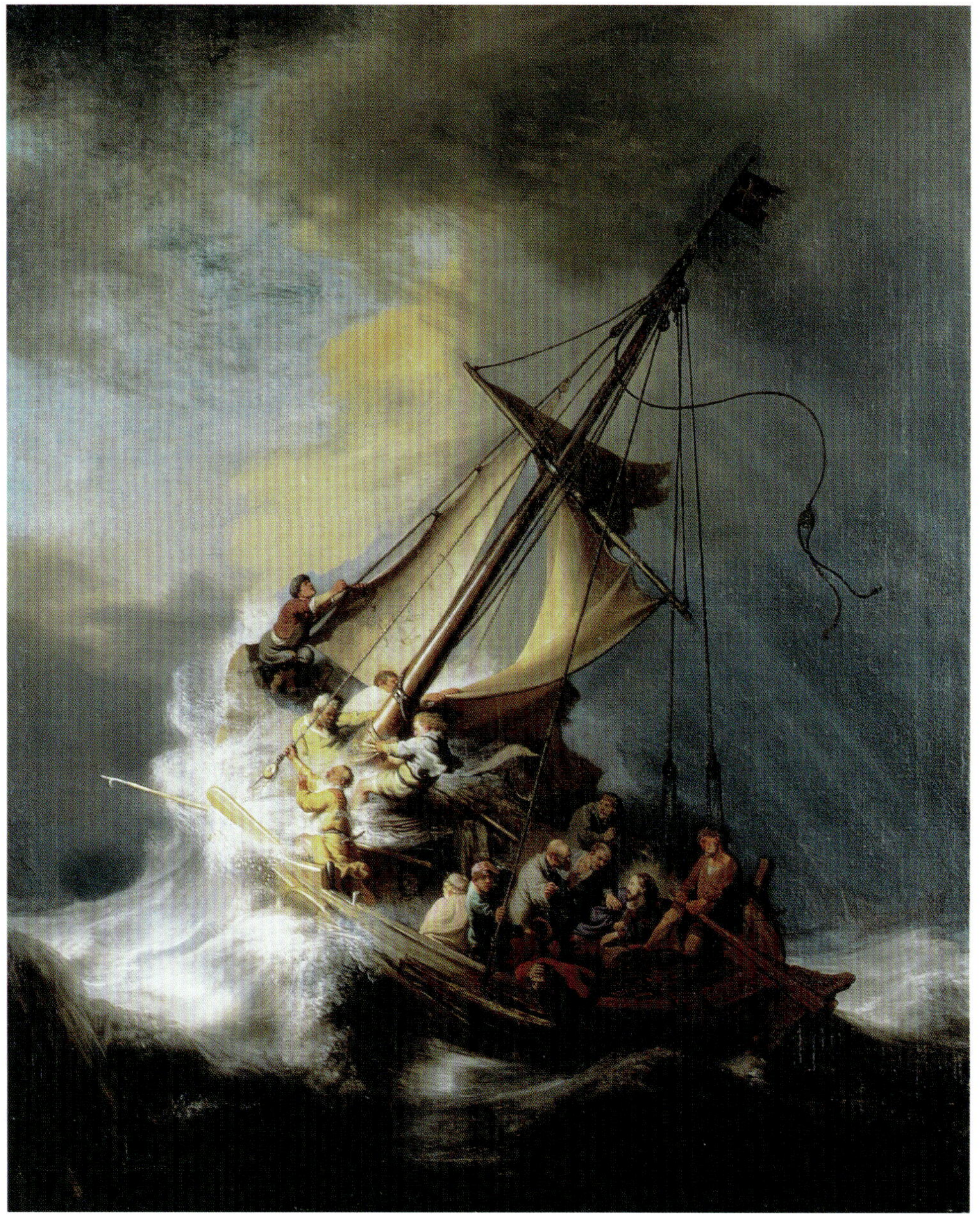

fig. 1.6 **Rembrandt van Rijn,** *Christ in the Storm on the Sea of Galilee*, 1633, oil on canvas; 160 × 128 cm. (Formerly) Isabella Stewart Gardner Museum, Boston (P21S24)

Rembrandt's versatility is especially evident in his prints, which treat a remarkable range of subjects and demonstrate a fearlessly inventive approach to technique. Recent studies of watermarks on the papers he used have revealed patterns in his production. Impressions were printed in small batches, and he would pull out and reprint a plate years later to meet demand, or perhaps when he needed extra income.[75] His rare proof impressions, characterized by subtle effects of inking and printing, appealed to the nascent market for fine print collecting, leaving the commercial market to printmakers such as Salomon Savery and Theodor Matham.[76] In a self-portrait etching of 1648, Rembrandt presents himself as a printmaker at work (pl. 9). Soberly dressed and seated like a scholar at his desk, he fixes the viewer with an appraising stare.[77] In the mid-1650s, financial exigency forced him to sell his stock of copperplates. Many of them came into the hands of the Amsterdam printseller Clement de Jonghe, whose portrait he had etched in 1651 (pls. 170, 171).

97

DER
ZEE-VAERT LOF,
Derde Boeck.

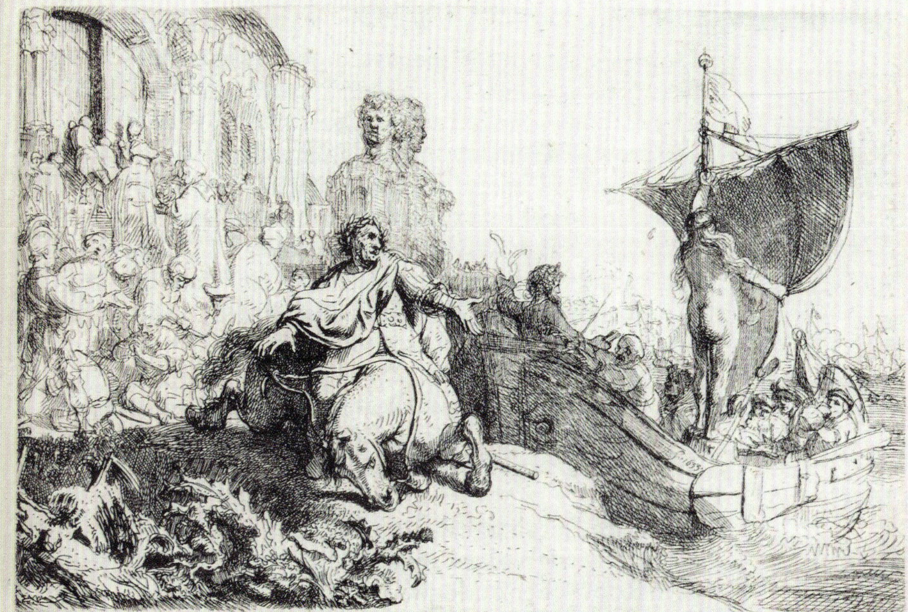

Ellone [a] (die te gaer met Mars te velde torsten
'tGehamerd yser, tot bescherm, van buyck en borsten:
Wen sabels blixems-flagh en dond'rend' veld-geschrey
Iav'lijn en flitsen stroyd op Mavors oorloghs rey)
Verbied (om weynigh rusts en adem locht te scheppen)
'T allarm trompets geluyt en 't nare brand-klocks kleppen
Te water en te land, beyd' krijger en matroos;
So langh, tot nieuwe twist heur stael ten [b] rechter koos.
Weshalven dat den vorst [c] August' de heyl'ge tempel
Des achtersienden [d] Gods doet sluyten, aen den drempel

Anno Mvndi 3935.
Ætat. Romę 723.
[a] *Bellone*, de suster van *Mars*, beyde God ende Goddinne des oorloghs.
[b] Wanneer tusschen twee partyen twisten opstaen, ende sich onder malkander door bereden niet vergelijckē konnen, kiesen gemeenelijck den degen van Mars en Bellone, om hun scheydsman te wesen, diens degen dan langhst is, diens recht alder-grootst is, so de wijse Seneca seyd: *Ius est in armis, opprimit leges pudor.* [c] *Octavius Cæsar Augustus, Monarcha ende Roomsch Keyser.* [d] Den achtersienden God was *Janus*, die eertijds by den Heydenen eenen koninck gheweest is, den eersten Politicus, ofte Burgerlijcken, die het grove woeste ende rouwe leven der menschen veranderde tot een eerlijcke sachte en reckelijcke burgherlijckheyd van leven, daeromme hem eerst de Romeynen als eenen half God ghe-eerd, ende namaels Numa Pompilius hem eenen tempel ter eeren ghebouwd heeft, hem met twee aensichten uytbeeldende, te weten, met het achterste siende op de voorgaende rowe manier van leven, en met het voorste aengesicht siende op 't gene dat alreede door hem verniewt, ofte verbeterd was, door welcke manier van leven de luyden vredelijck malkanderen beminden; daerom hem de Romeynen in tijd des oorloghs gheduyrigh offerden; want als de

N   De

9   Rembrandt van Rijn, *Self-portrait Etching at a Window*, 1648. Städel Museum, Frankfurt am Main

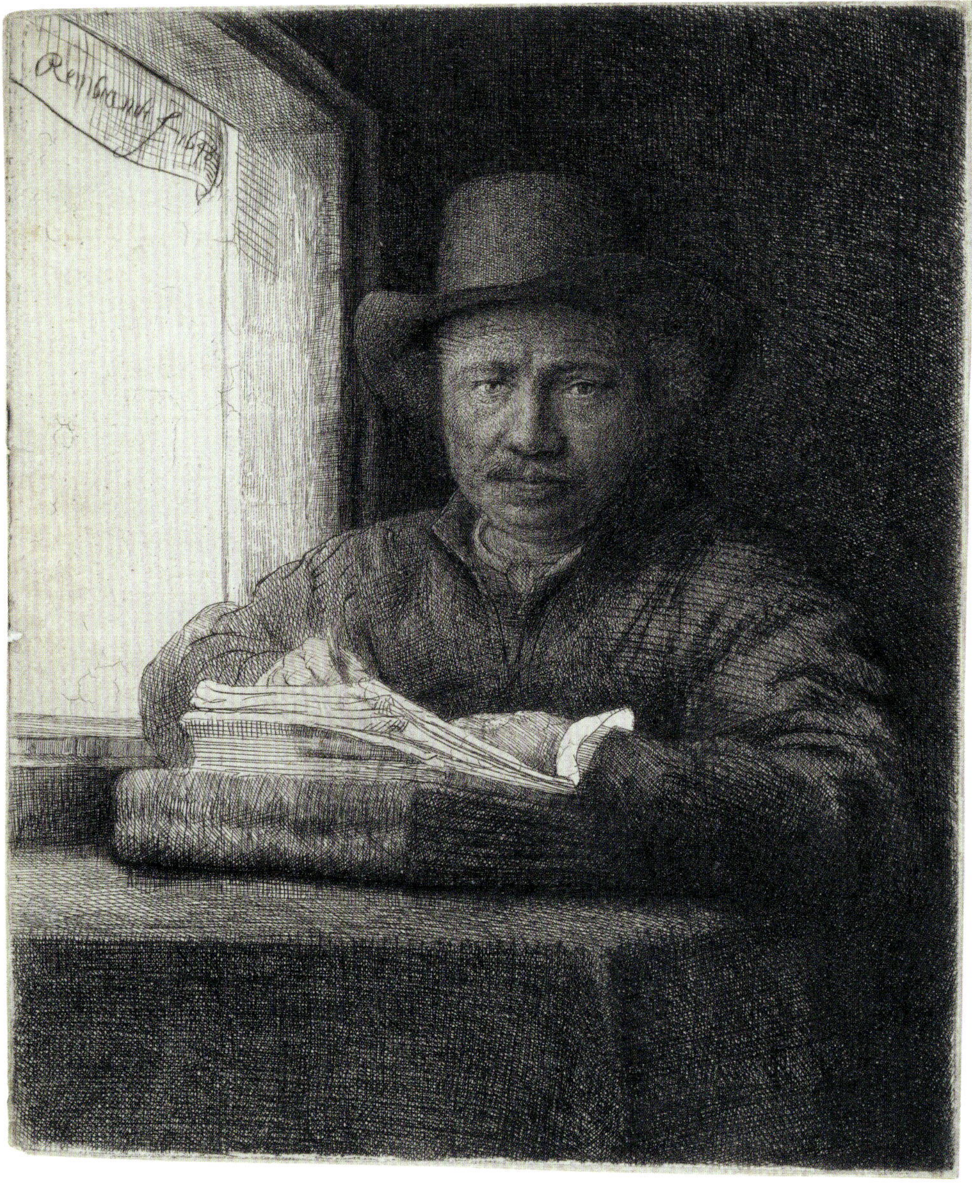

The Artist as Dealer

Like many of his contemporaries, Rembrandt profited from trading in the work of others. At public auctions, dealers and collectors competed for treasures both local and imported.[78] At the estate sale of the painter Jan Bassé in March 1637, Rembrandt purchased seashells, drawings and prints, including several sets of Albrecht Dürer's renowned woodcut series *The Life of the Virgin*. Among other buyers were Pickenoy, Flinck, Rembrandt's student Leendert van Beijeren, and Sandrart's cousin Michel LeBlon.[79] LeBlon, a printmaker, silversmith, art dealer and diplomatic agent born in Frankfurt am Main, lived in Amsterdam from 1628 to 1647. He supported Sandrart in cultivating a network of elite patrons quite different from Rembrandt's.[80] In October 1637, Rembrandt attended a sale of works by the still-life painter Jan Jansz den Uyl (see fig. 2.3), possibly for the dubious purpose of bidding up prices, for which he received a small commission.[81] On 9 April 1639, Rembrandt sketched Raphael's *Portrait of Baldassare Castiglione* at the estate sale of the wealthy merchant Lucas van Uffelen (see figs. 5.4, 5.5). Sandrart nearly bought the painting for himself.[82] At some point, Rembrandt acquired a copperplate by the innovative landscapist Hercules Segers. Around 1653 he deftly reworked it, transforming *Tobias and the Angel* into *The Flight into Egypt* (figs. 1.7, 1.8).[83]

The journey of one painting by Rubens is illuminating. Painted in Italy around 1604, *Hero and Leander* (pl. 46) depicts a tragic love story told by Ovid. By 1637 it was in Amsterdam, where Den Uyl gave it to his accountant, Trojanus de Magistris, as security for a debt. On 8 October 1637, Rembrandt purchased it from Magistris for the substantial price of 424 guilders.[84] The investment paid off in 1644, when he sold it to the merchant Lodewijk van Ludick for 530 guilders.[85] The city's two most prominent poets, Joost van den Vondel and Jan Vos, dedicated poems to Rubens' painting, the latter locating it in 1662 in the collection of Jan Six's brother, Pieter.[86] Owning such a prestigious work would have raised Rembrandt's cultural capital, but it appears he was more interested in profiting financially.

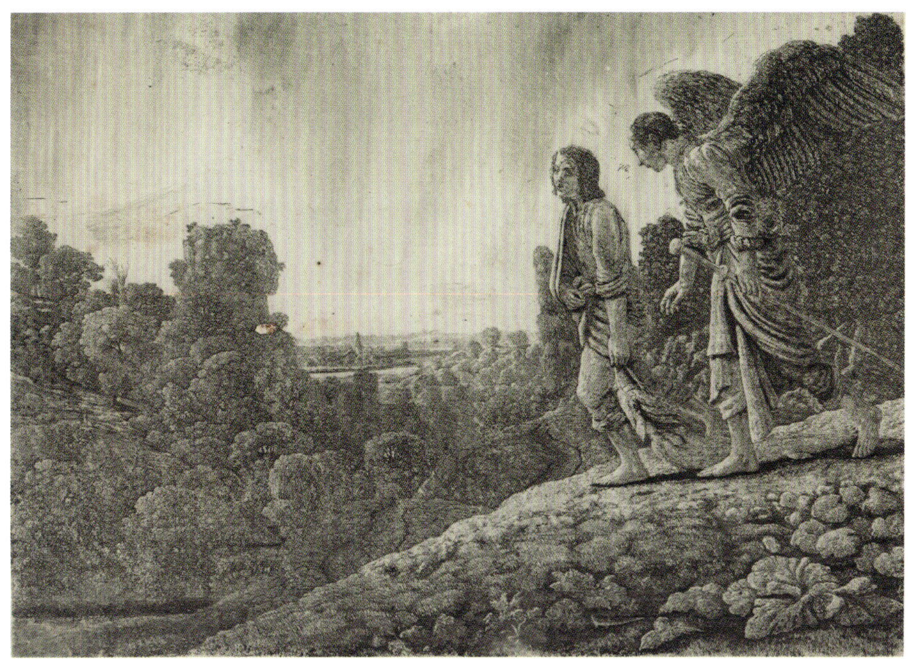

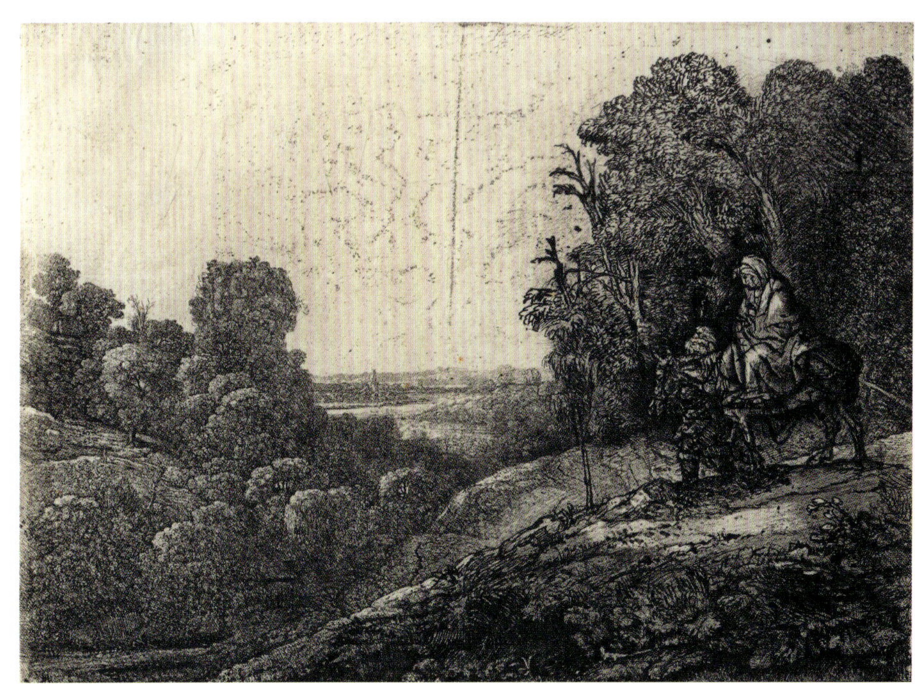

fig. 1.7 Hercules Segers, *Tobias and the Angel*, c. 1630–33, etching on laid paper; 20.2 × 27.6 cm. Rijksmuseum, Amsterdam. Transferred from the Koninklijke Bibliotheek (Den Haag), 1816 (RP-P-oB-796)

fig. 1.8 Rembrandt van Rijn, *The Flight into Egypt, altered from Hercules Segers*, c. 1653, etching, engraving and drypoint on laid paper; 21.2 × 28.4 cm. Collection of Dr. Jonathan Meakins and Dr. Jacqueline McClaran, Montreal

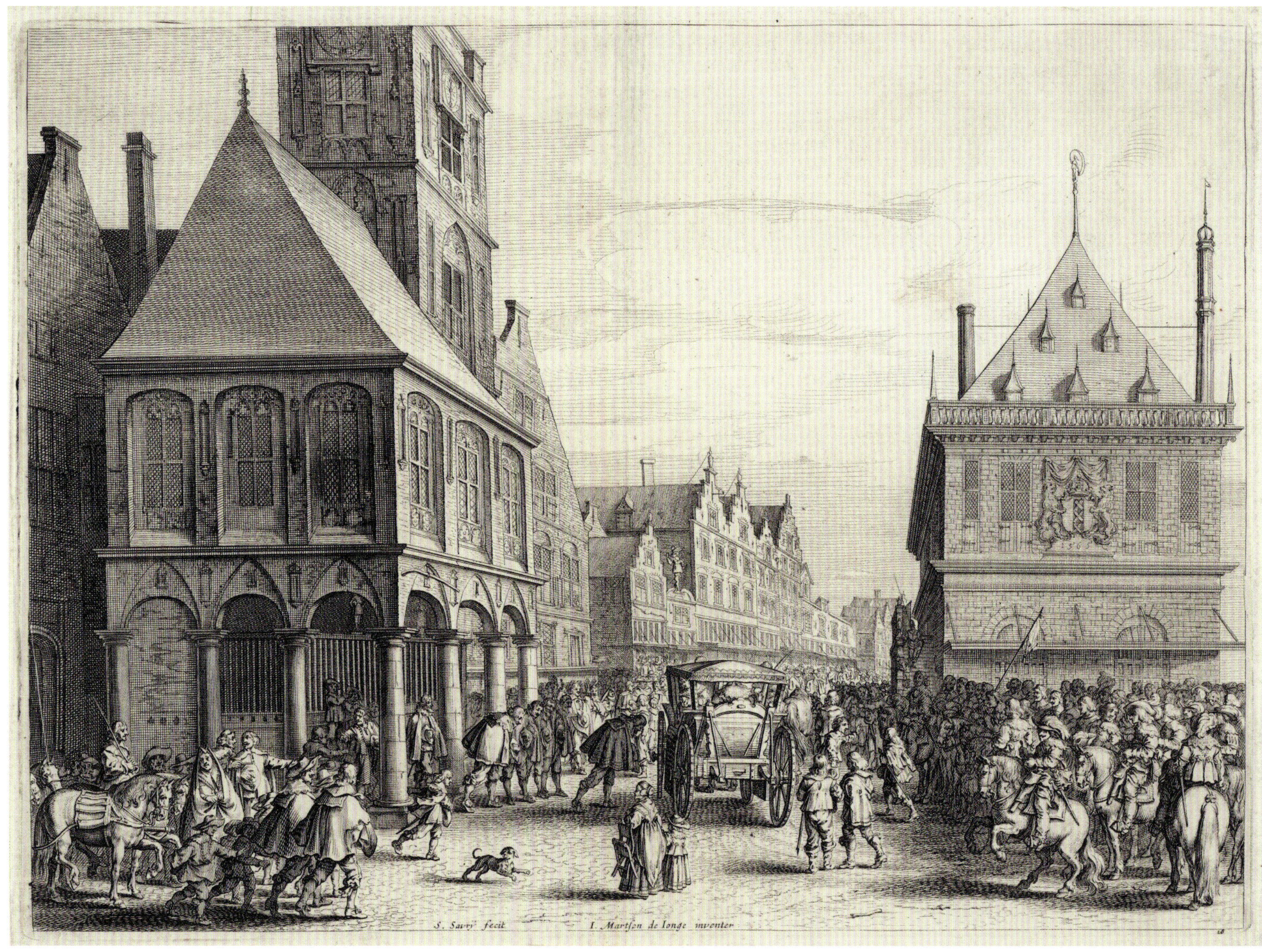

10   Salomon Savery (after Jan Martszen de Jonge), *Mayors of Amsterdam Bidding Farewell to Marie de' Medici in Front of the Amsterdam Town Hall on Dam Square*, 1638. Amsterdam City Archives

Public Occasions, Prestigious Commissions

In 1638 Marie de' Medici visited Amsterdam. Her retinue included the stadtholder's wife, Amalia von Solms. The city fathers welcomed the exiled French queen with all the pageantry of a triumphal entry. Claes Moeyaert, one of Lastman's associates, was hired as principal designer, and Barlaeus wrote an account of the festivities. One of Salomon Savery's illustrations shows Marie's carriage making its way past city officials lined up to salute her on the Dam Square (pl. 10).[87] The state visit brought portrait commissions for Rembrandt and others, commemorating Amsterdammers who took part in this prestigious event.[88]

In 1642 Rembrandt contributed to one of the city's most impressive public projects: a sequence of life-size group portraits for the Kloveniersdoelen, the meeting hall of the Kloveniers (musketeers) civic guard (fig. 1.9). The dark tonality of Rembrandt's painting prompted its nickname, *The Night Watch*, but in fact it depicts a daytime rally. The presence of children underfoot suggests that the company of citizen volunteers is mustering for a parade, or another festive occasion, rather than military action. Commissions from other districts went to Pickenoy, Backer, Sandrart, Flinck and Van der Helst – a who's who of Amsterdam portraitists.[89]

Van der Helst devoted his life to the art of portraiture. Ninety-five per cent of his extant oeuvre belongs to this genre.[90] As Sandrart noted, Van der Helst was well paid for his efforts.[91] In 1650 he earned 330 guilders for a pair of half-length portraits, plus room and board for six weeks.[92] For a large family portrait in 1656 he was paid 1,400 guilders, just under what Rembrandt earned for *The Night Watch*.[93] When Van Hoogstraten later recalled that *The Night Watch* made the other paintings look as flat as playing cards,[94] he was speaking in part of Van der Helst's contribution to the hall, depicting Captain Roelof Bicker's company gathered outside the De Haan brewery, across the street from

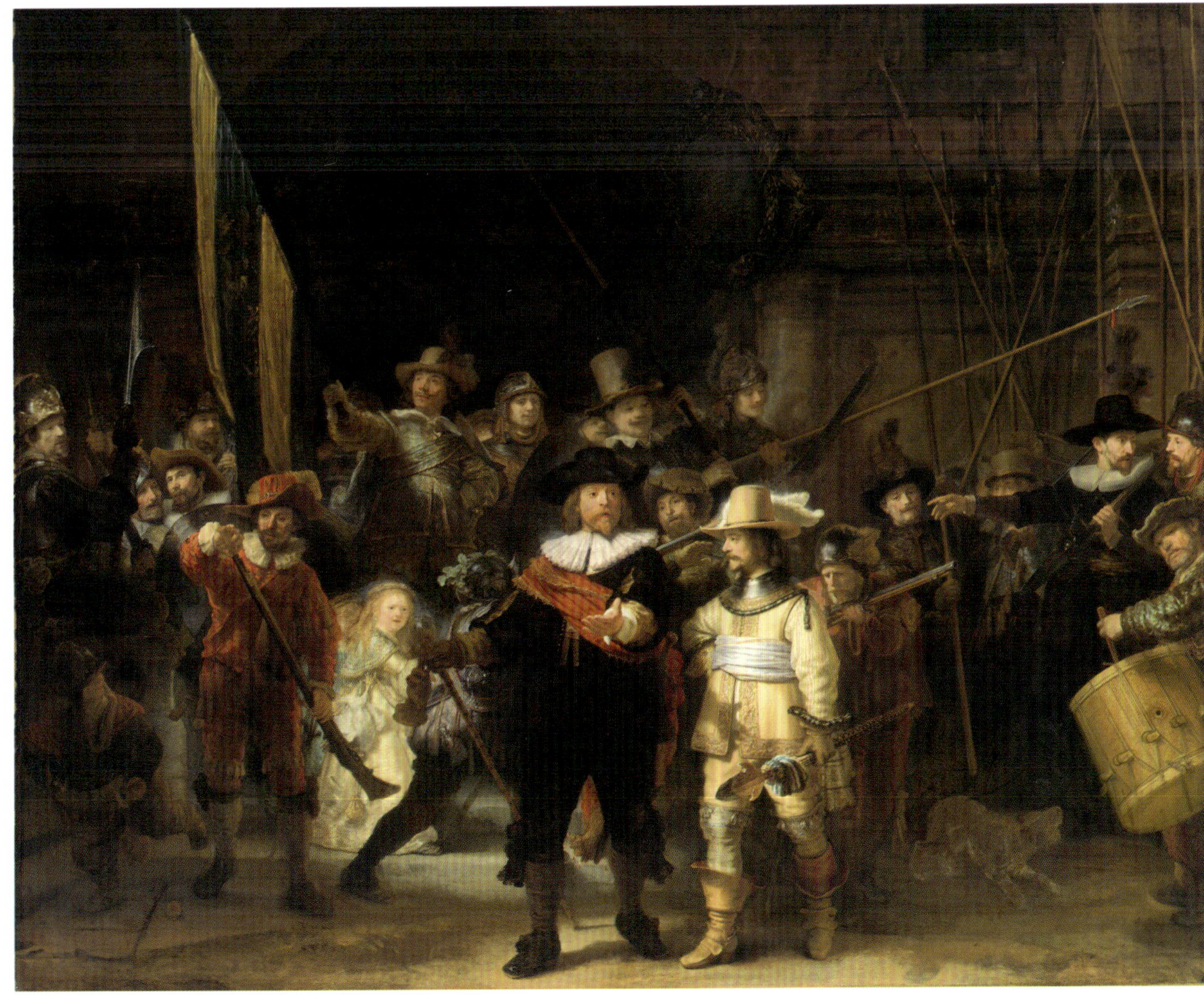

fig. 1.9 **Rembrandt van Rijn,** *Militia Company of District II under the Command of Captain Frans Banninck Cocq* (*The Night Watch*), **1642, oil on canvas; 379.5 × 453.5 cm. Rijksmuseum, Amsterdam. On loan from the City of Amsterdam (SK-C-5)**

the artist's house (fig. 1.10).[95] In fact, Van der Helst deserves admiration for his artful balancing of the tension between group dynamics and individual likeness. Like Rembrandt's *Night Watch,* the scene is enlivened with displays of musketry, including shots being fired in the background. The two compositions were developed simultaneously, probably over several years, making it unclear who first decided to include these dramatic features.[96] Van der Helst received further portrait commissions from the Bicker family. Another member of the company, Joan Hulft, may be the fashionably dressed man portrayed in the life-size painting now in the Montreal Museum of Fine Arts (pl. 74). His canine companion appears in both works.[97]

In the 1640s Rembrandt lost his place as the preeminent portraitist in the city. The unconventionality of *The Night Watch* was once believed to be the cause for this, but in fact, the painting was widely admired. More to blame was a generational shift: competition increased as younger talents perfected their skills and younger patrons opted for a more polished approach to technique and characterization. Van der Helst's civic-guard portrait is a prime example. Flinck adapted quickly to what Houbraken termed the "bright style," replacing the sober dignity of Pickenoy and the ruddy chiaroscuro of Rembrandt with casual elegance and clear daylight (pls. 66, 67).[98] This shift was stimulated by developments in Baroque painting in France and Flanders, introduced to Amsterdam by Sandrart, who had travelled widely before settling there in a house purchased for him by LeBlon. In 1639 Sandrart portrayed the Amsterdam patrician Jacob Bicker (pl. 62) in a genteel pose derived from Anthony van Dyck's elegant portrait of LeBlon (fig. 1.11), painted between 1630 and 1635, and recorded in a reproductive print engraved around 1645 by Theodor Matham in Amsterdam.[99]

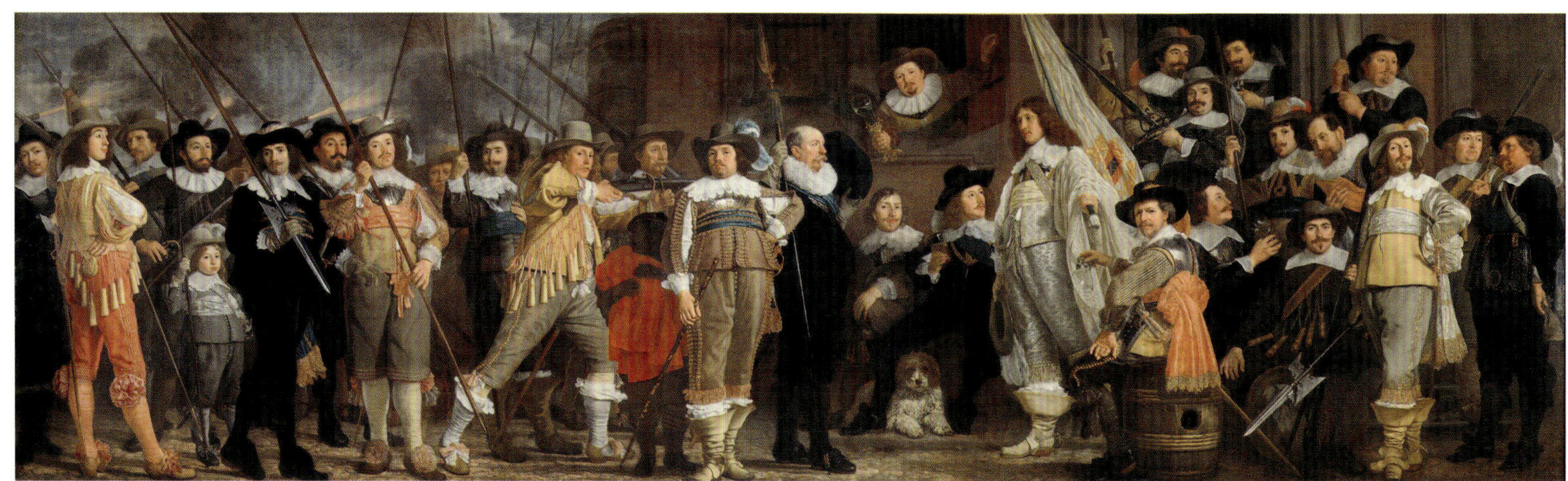

fig. 1.10   **Bartholomeus van der Helst, *Militia Company of District VIII under the Command of Captain Roelof Bicker,* c. 1640–43, oil on canvas; 235 × 750 cm. Rijksmuseum, Amsterdam. On loan from the city of Amsterdam (SK-C-375)**

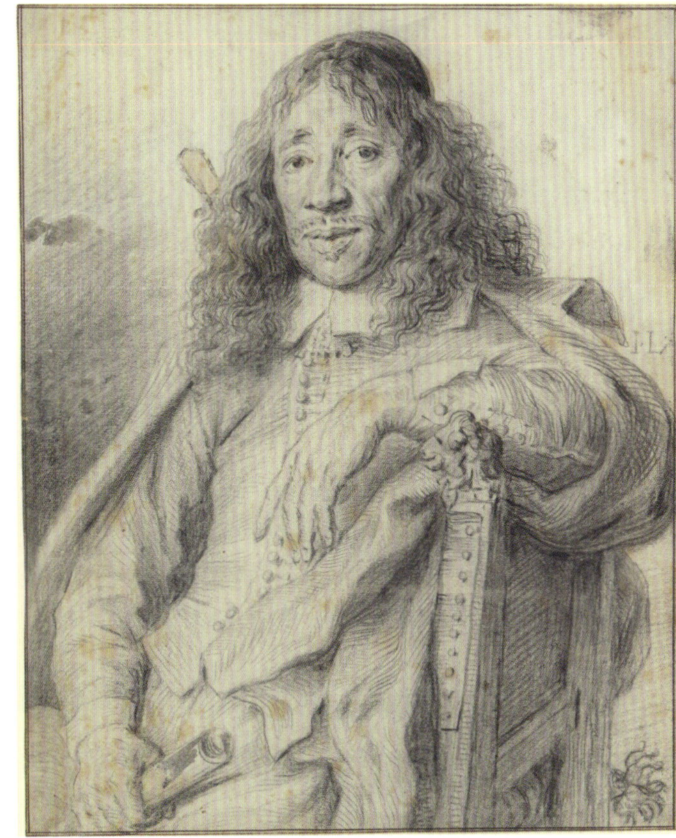

fig. 1.11 **Anthony van Dyck,** *Portrait of Michel LeBlon*, c. 1630–35, oil on canvas; 78.1 × 61 cm. Art Gallery of Ontario, Toronto. Bequest of J.J. Vaughan, 1965 (64/45)

fig. 1.12 **Jan Lievens,** *Portrait of Jan Vos*, c. 1660, black chalk on laid paper; 32.5 × 25.6 cm. Städel Museum, Frankfurt am Main (836)

The Return of Lievens

A satirical drawing dated 1644 seems to capture Rembrandt's response to the shifting terrain (pl. 12). A connoisseur's visit to an artist's studio was a social occasion, as depicted in a painting by Pieter Codde (pl. 11). In Rembrandt's drawing, two men on the right seem to pantomime judicious appraisal of a large canvas held up for their inspection. To the left, a critic seated on a barrel gestures with his pipe (suggesting that his words are worthless smoke) toward two paintings of half-length figures, a staple product of the Rembrandt workshop. Donkey ears poke through his hat and an evil asp slithers up his arm. At lower right, the artist demonstrates his response to this critique by squatting to defecate.[100]

In 1644 Rembrandt faced renewed rivalry with an old friend. After years in London and Antwerp, where he absorbed the Flemish elegance of Rubens and Van Dyck, Jan Lievens settled in Amsterdam. His international resumé must have impressed local patrons, who commissioned history paintings and portraits (pl. 76).[101] His accomplished portrait drawings record prominent Amsterdam residents such as Andries de Graeff (painted by Rembrandt in 1639, pl. 73), the poet Jan Vos (fig. 1.12), and the philosopher René Descartes.[102] Like Rembrandt, Lievens took up landscape painting in mid-career. His beautifully finished landscape drawings differ dramatically in style from Rembrandt's atmospheric sketches, but the two artists recorded similar motifs, such as rustic farmsteads (pls. 163, 164).

11   Pieter Codde, *Connoisseurs Visiting an Artist's Studio*, c. 1630. Staatsgalerie Stuttgart

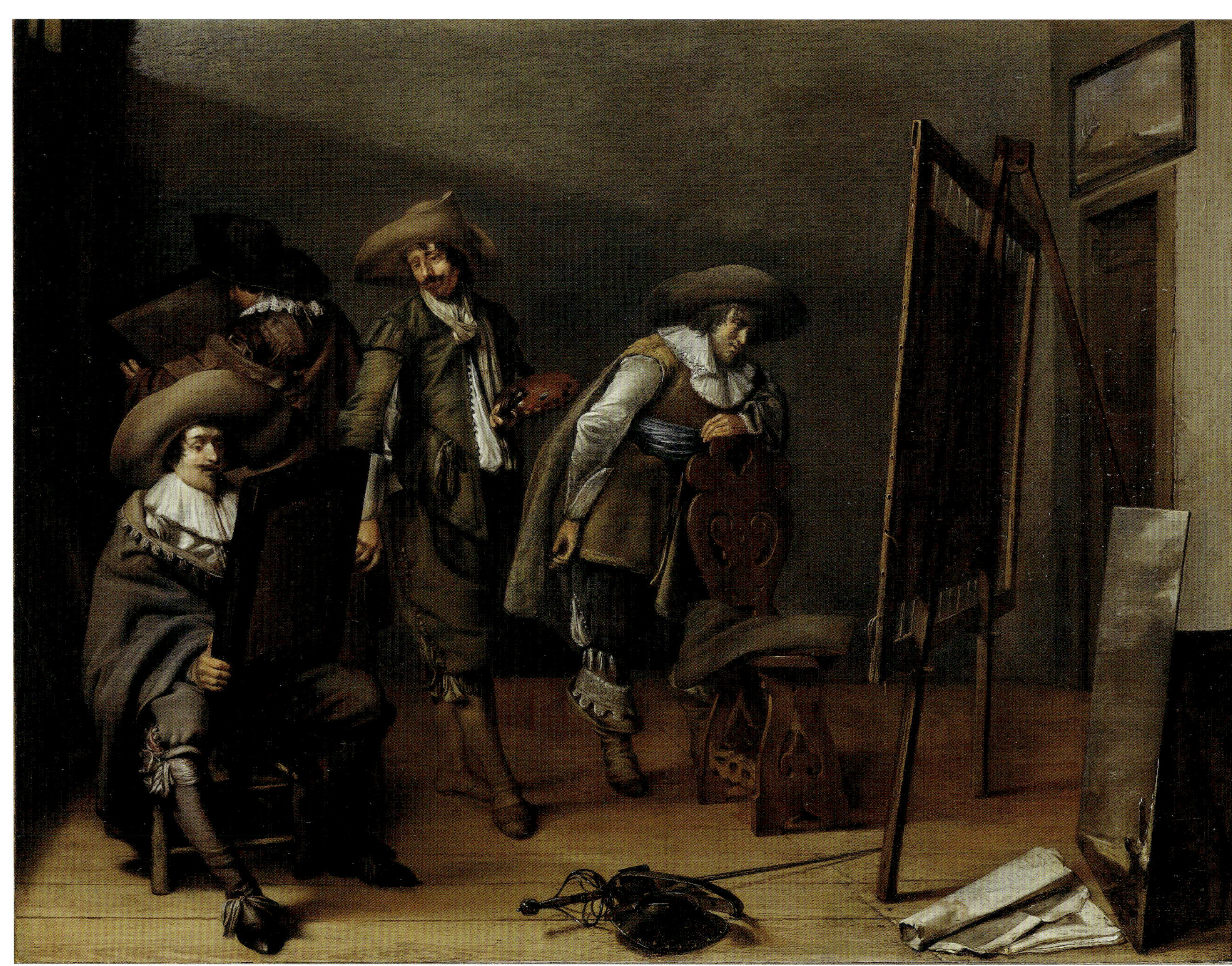

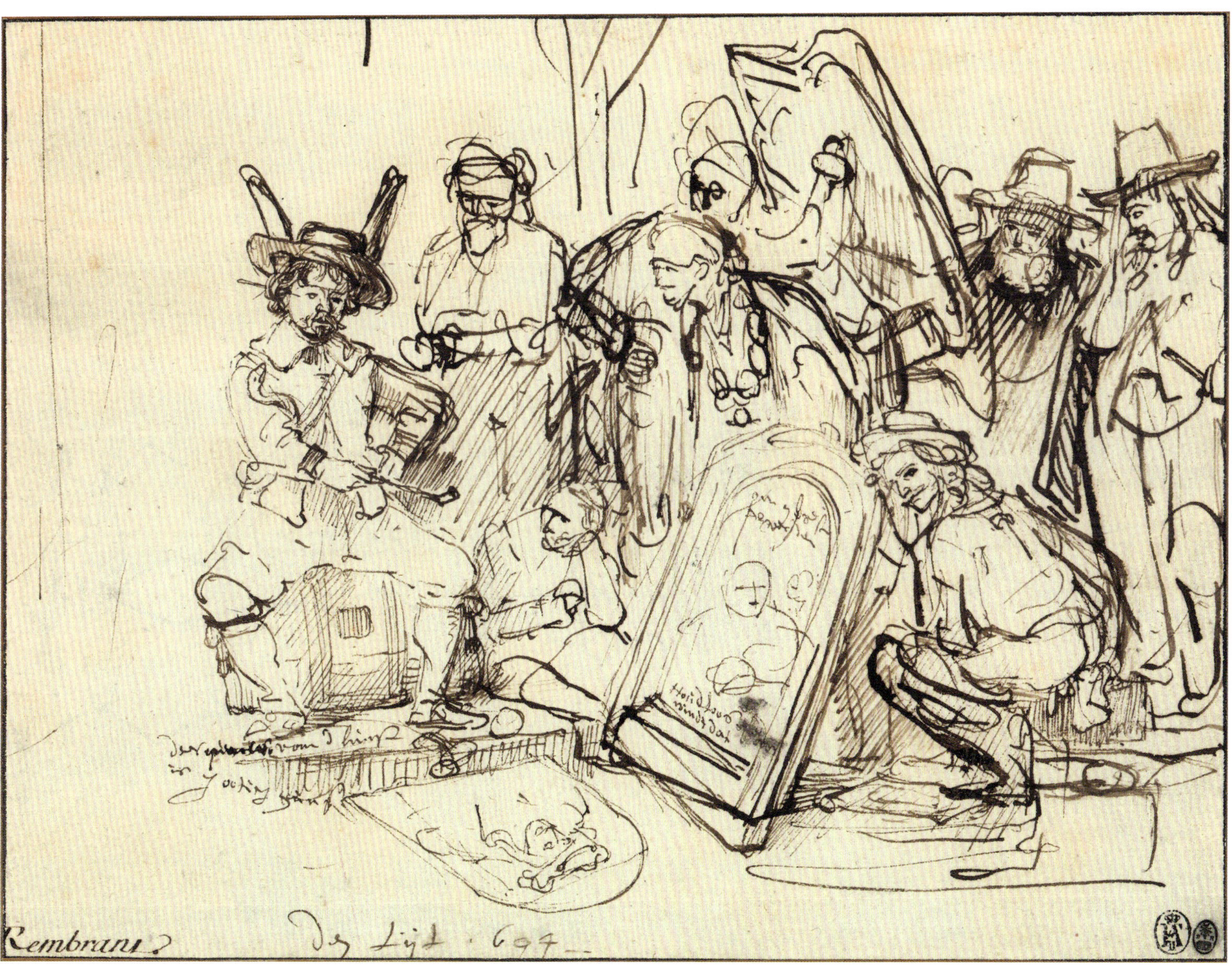

13 Rembrandt van Rijn, *Portrait of Jan Six*, 1647. Städel Museum, Frankfurt am Main

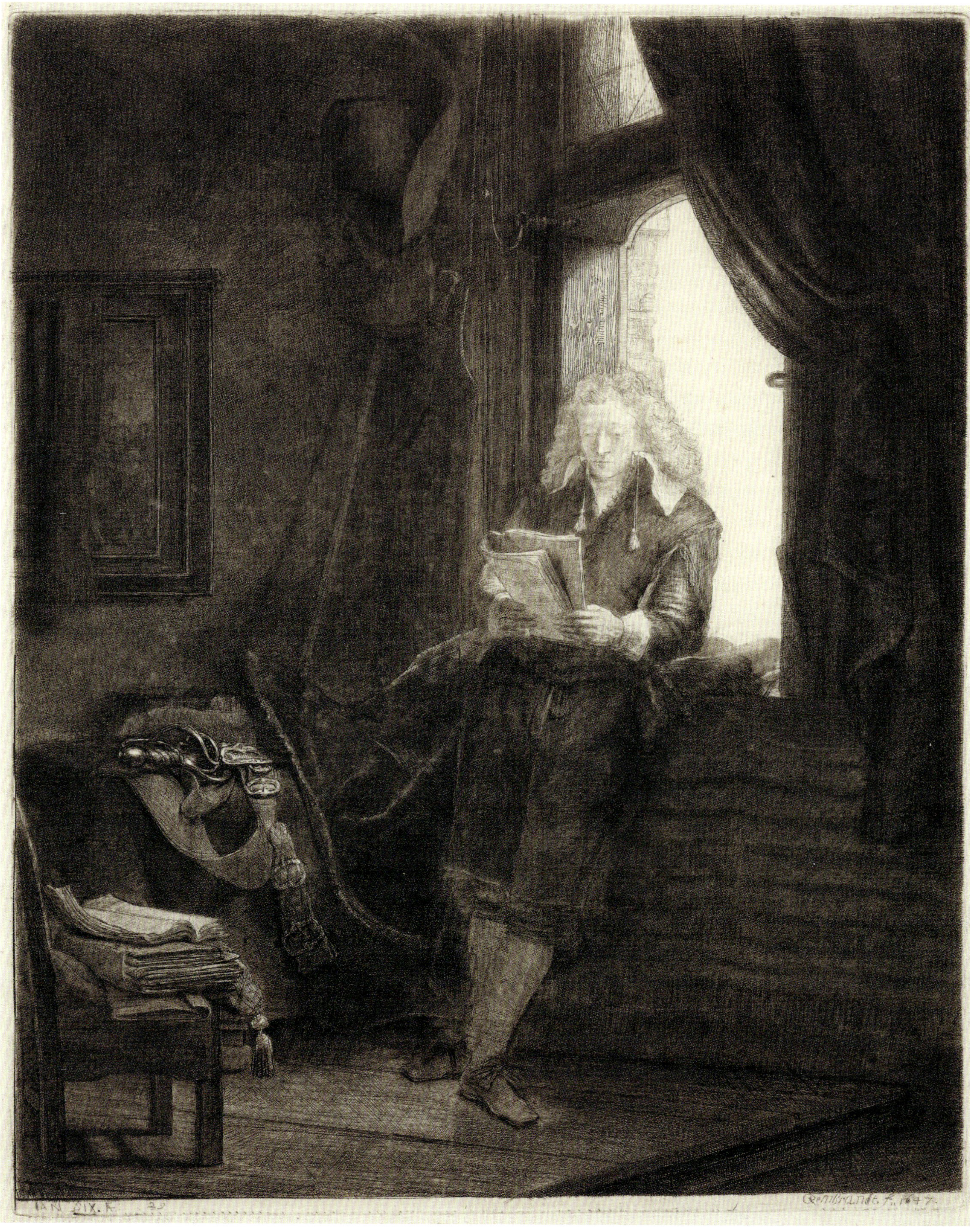

They may even have gone sketching together.[103] In 1656 Rembrandt had several Lievens landscape paintings on display in his reception room, perhaps for sale to support his old friend, or to hedge his bets on the competition.[104]

Both Jan Six and the prominent art dealer Johannes de Renialme owned paintings by Lievens as well as Rembrandt.[105] In De Renialme's estate inventory of 1657, by far the highest valuation was 1,500 guilders for Rembrandt's *Christ and the Woman Taken in Adultery* of 1644 (see fig. 9.2), one of the masterpieces of his middle years.[106] In 1646 Rembrandt completed a series of paintings on the life of Christ begun in Leiden for Stadtholder Frederik Hendrik, receiving 1,200 guilders each for *The Nativity* (*The Adoration of the Shepherds*, Alte Pinakothek, Munich) and a lost *Circumcision of* *Christ*.[107] Lievens' 1644 *Adoration of the Magi* (Agnes Etherington Art Centre, Kingston), painted in the same size and format, suggests an effort to share in this prestigious and lucrative commission.[108]

Between 1647 and 1654, Jan Six was Rembrandt's most important patron, lending him money, making numerous purchases and welcoming the artist to his home. Rembrandt's etched portrait of Six from 1647 (pl. 13) and painted portrait of 1654 (fig. 1.13) are among his most brilliant performances in either medium. While the painting captures a moment in the life of a busy man, the etching portrays Six, an amateur poet and playwright, absorbed in reading.[109] In 1655 Six married Dr. Nicolaes Tulp's daughter Margaretha. For her own portraits, she preferred the Van Dyckian elegance adopted by Flinck (fig. 1.14).[110]

fig. 1.13 **Rembrandt van Rijn,** *Portrait of Jan Six*, 1654, **oil on canvas; 112 × 102 cm. Six Collection, Amsterdam (CS 00070)**

fig. 1.14 **Govert Flinck,** *Portrait of Margaretha Tulp*, c. 1658, **oil on canvas; 96 × 78 cm. Six Collection, Amsterdam (CS 00037)**

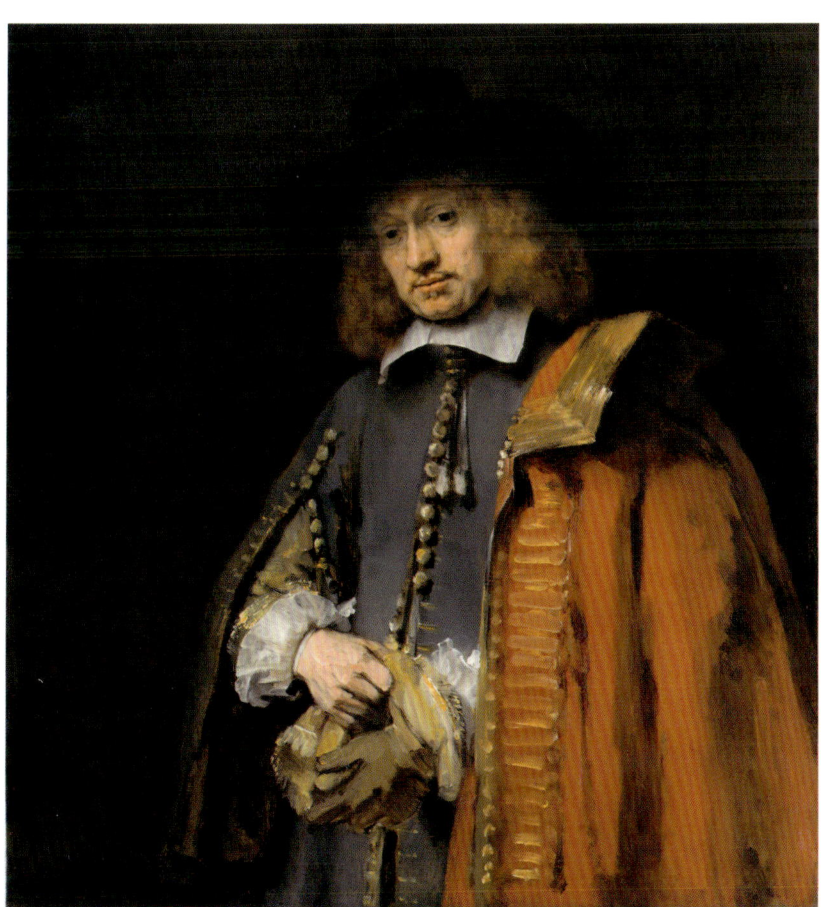

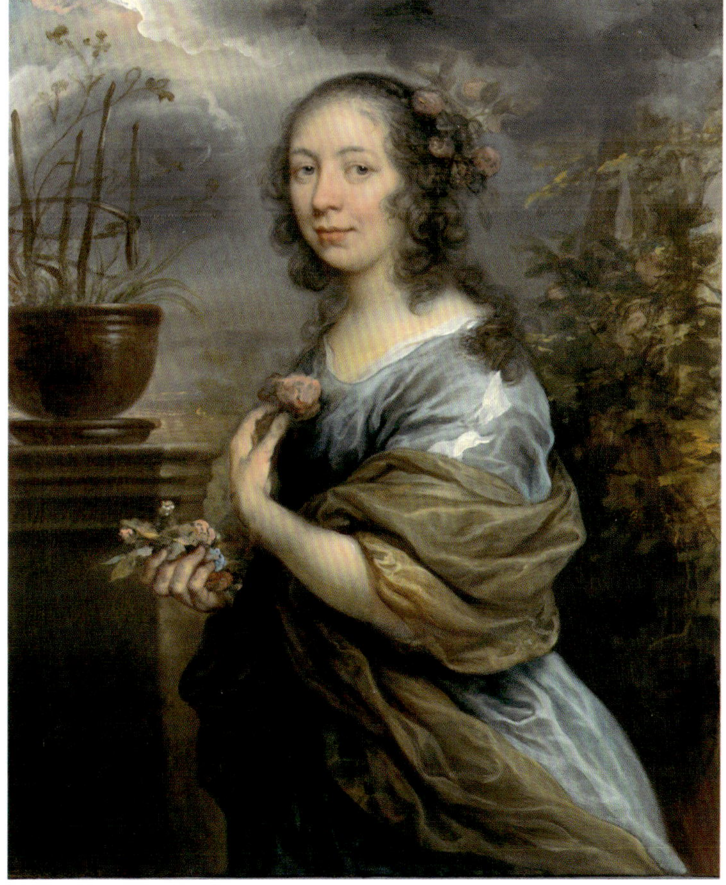

City on Fire

On 7 July 1652, the medieval town hall on the Dam Square, already being demolished, was destroyed by fire. The spectacle prompted numerous paintings, prints and drawings.[111] We can imagine Rembrandt, his student Pieter de With, and other artists standing together to sketch the smoldering ruins (pl. 14, fig. 1.15).[112] The grand building that rose in its place was the most important public art project of the century, asserting the city's economic and political might (pl. 30). Bol and Flinck painted several large canvases for the meeting rooms (pl. 95), and in 1659, Flinck won the plum commission for a cycle of monumental canvases recounting the ancient Batavians' revolt from Rome, a legendary antecedent of the Dutch Republic's struggle for independence from Spain. Flinck died a few months later, leaving the work to be parcelled out among other history painters, including Lievens and the Flemish artist Jacob Jordaens. Rembrandt's contribution, *The Conspiracy of the Batavians under Claudius Civilis*

(see fig. 9.3), was rejected and removed in 1662, shortly after it was installed. While the circumstances are unclear, it is likely that his late style, powerful as it seems today, did not meet the commissioners' standards of decorum for such a politically charged installation.[113]

On 20 October 1653, Amsterdam's artistic community gathered for a banquet honouring Saint Luke and celebrating the city's success as a centre of cultural production. Van der Helst was one of the organizers, and Rembrandt, Flinck and Bol attended, along with Jacob van Loo, Salomon and Philips Koninck, and many others. Jan Asselijn's brother Thomas delivered a poetic oration honouring "the union of Apelles and Apollo," that is, art and poetry.[114] Joost van den Vondel was the guest of honour. Vondel held a central position in the city's cultural community. His plays, based on classical drama, were performed at the Schouwburg, and his occasional verses are a goldmine of evidence for personal connections and patronage.[115]

fig. 1.15 **Rembrandt van Rijn,** *Ruins of the Old Town Hall after the Fire of 1652*, 1652, pen and ink with wash, touches of red chalk, on laid paper; 10.5 × 21 cm. Rembrandt House Museum, Amsterdam (245)

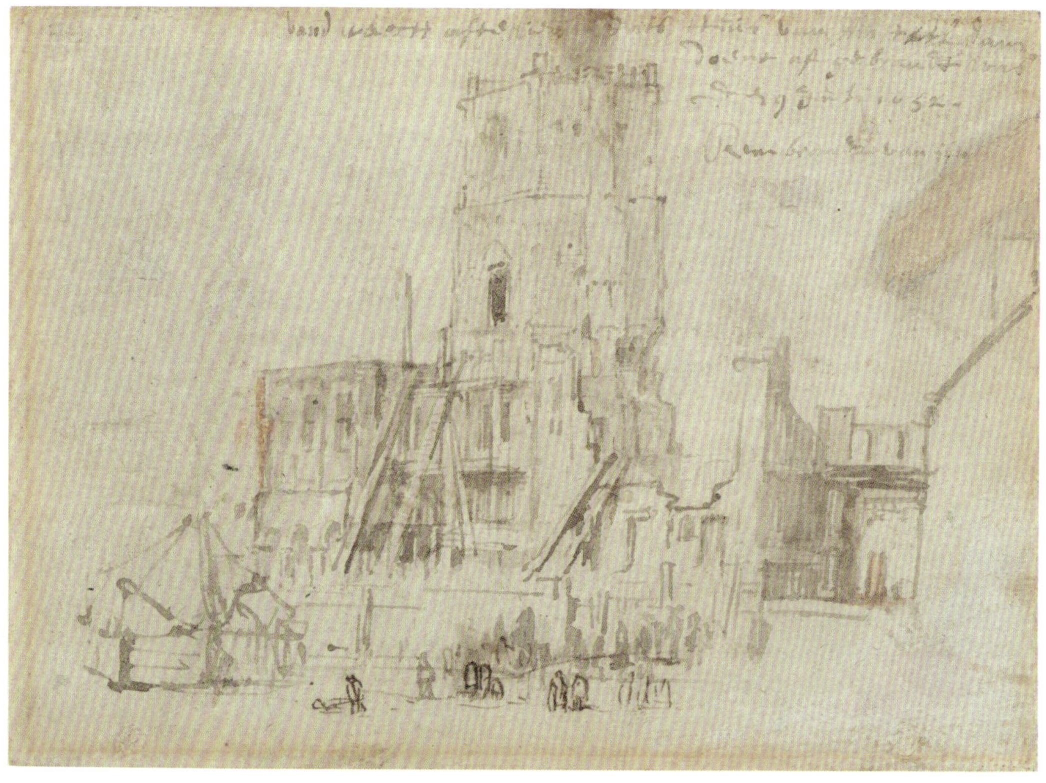

14   Rembrandt Workshop, attributed to Pieter de With, *Amsterdam Town Hall after the Fire of 7 July 1652*, c. 1652. Herzog Anton Ulrich-Museum, Kunstmuseum des Landes Niedersachsen, Braunschweig

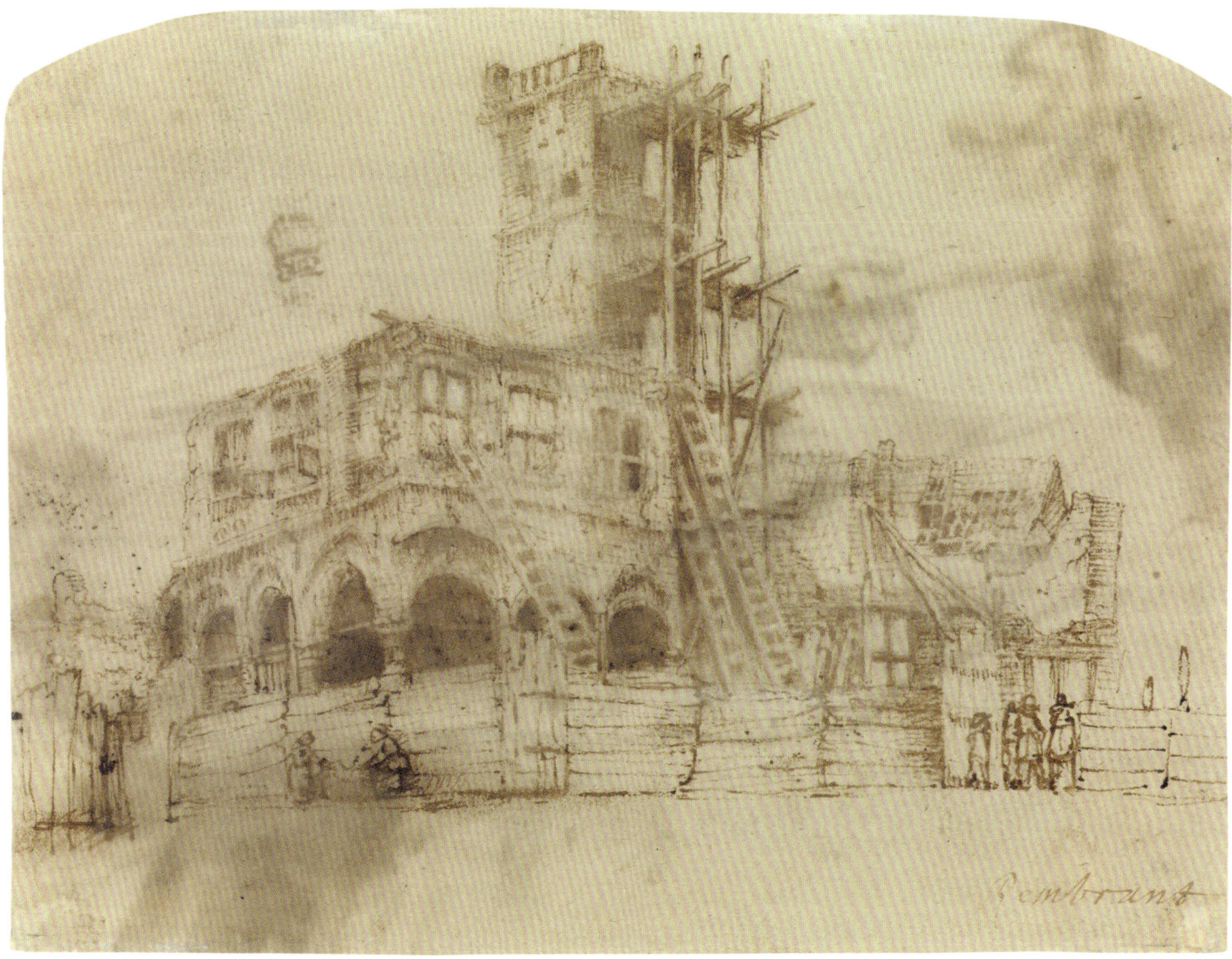

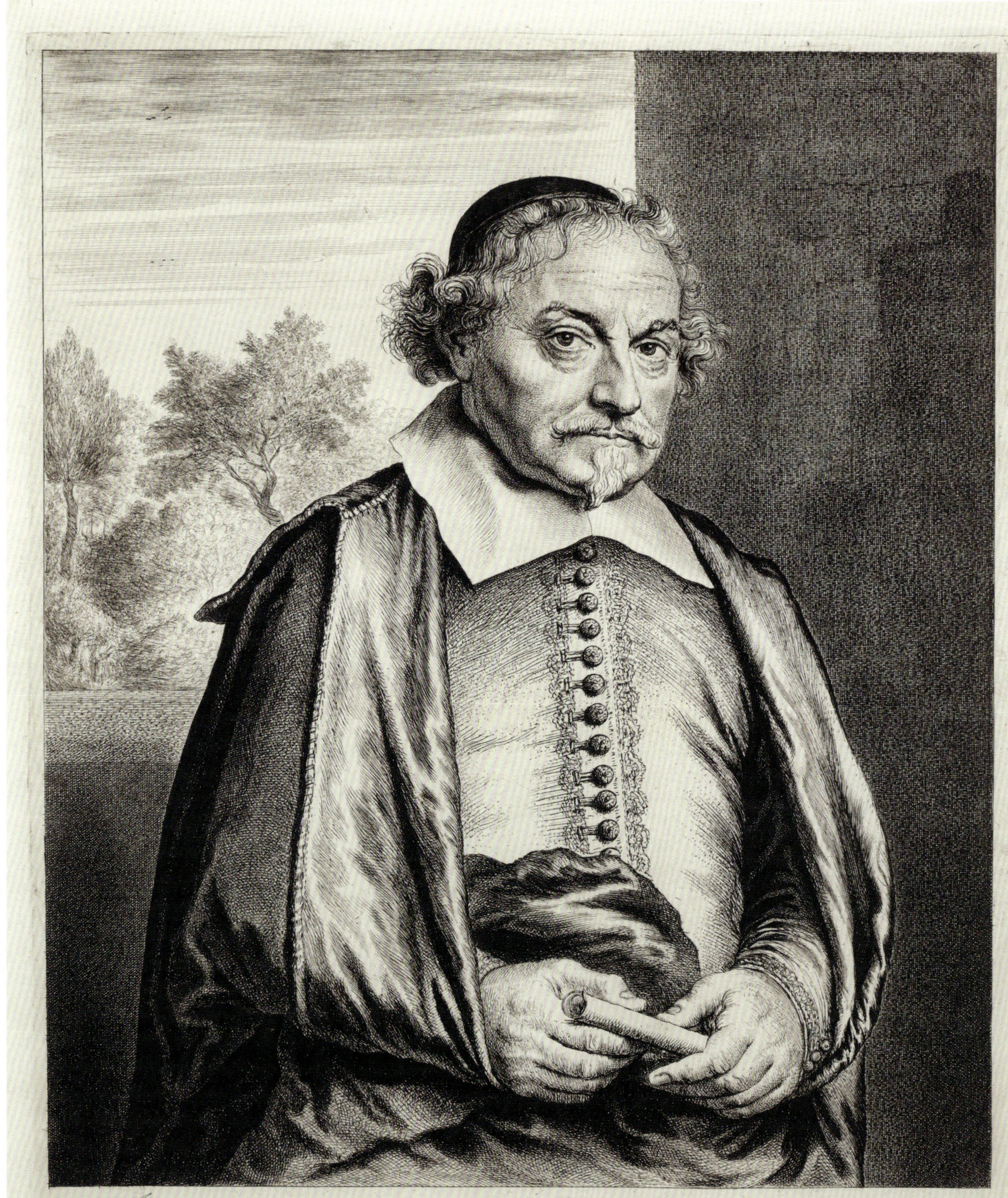

IOOST VANDE VONDEL.
I. Sandrart
Delineavit.
Sandrart heeft VONDEL dus naer 'taenzicht uitgedruckt,
Niet zijn gedachten; want die waren wech-geruckt,
Verslingert op d'aeloude en bloende treurtooneelen,
Om ernstigh af te zien, wat zol d'uitheemschen spelen.
Vint niemants brein in bloet noch gal noch tranen smaeck,
Hy leeft in treurdicht. ay, vergun hem dat vermaeck.
Theod: Matham Sculp.
C. Dankertz exc.

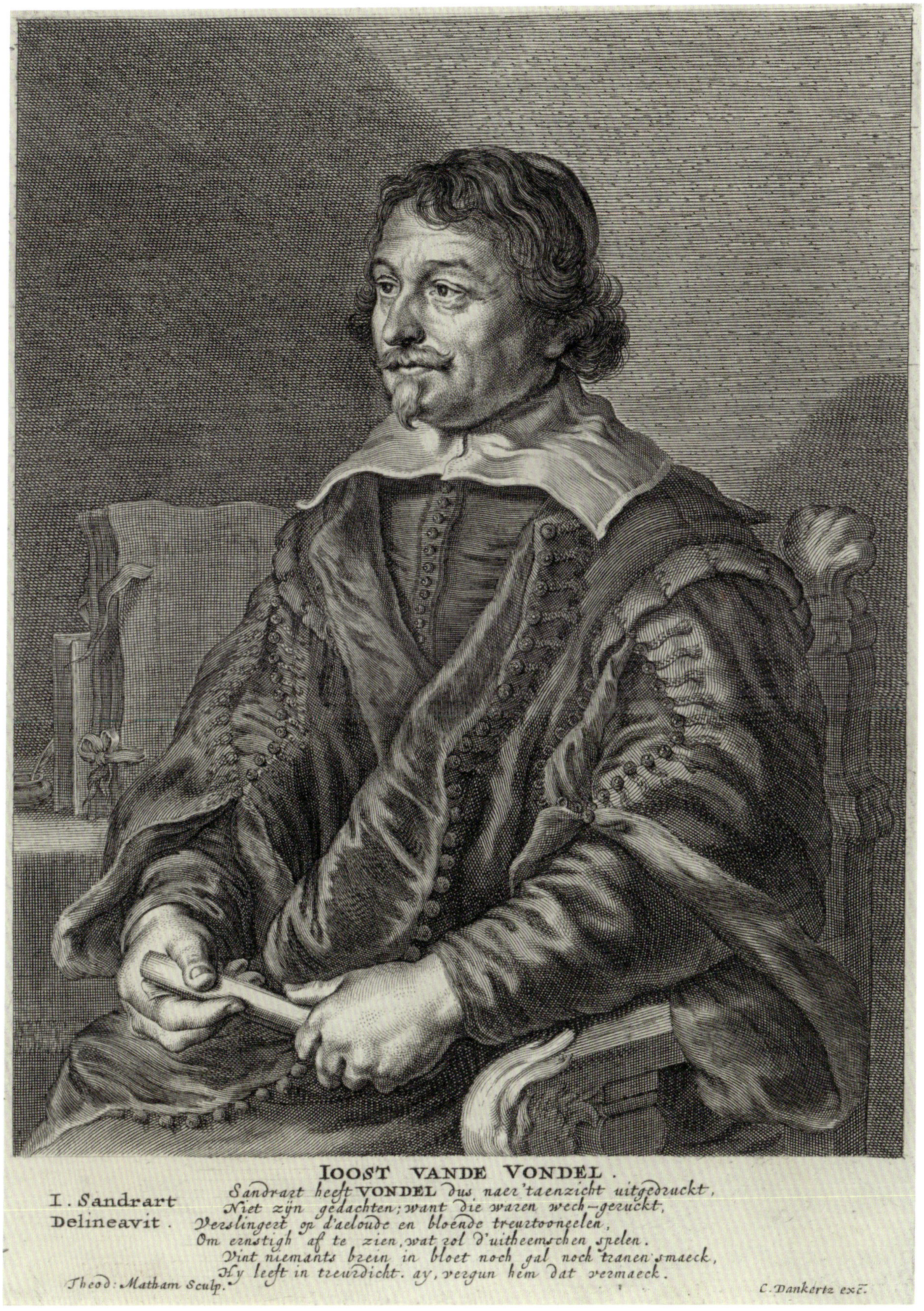

17 Cornelis Visscher, *Portrait of Joost van den Vondel*, c. 1657. Städel Museum, Frankfurt am Main

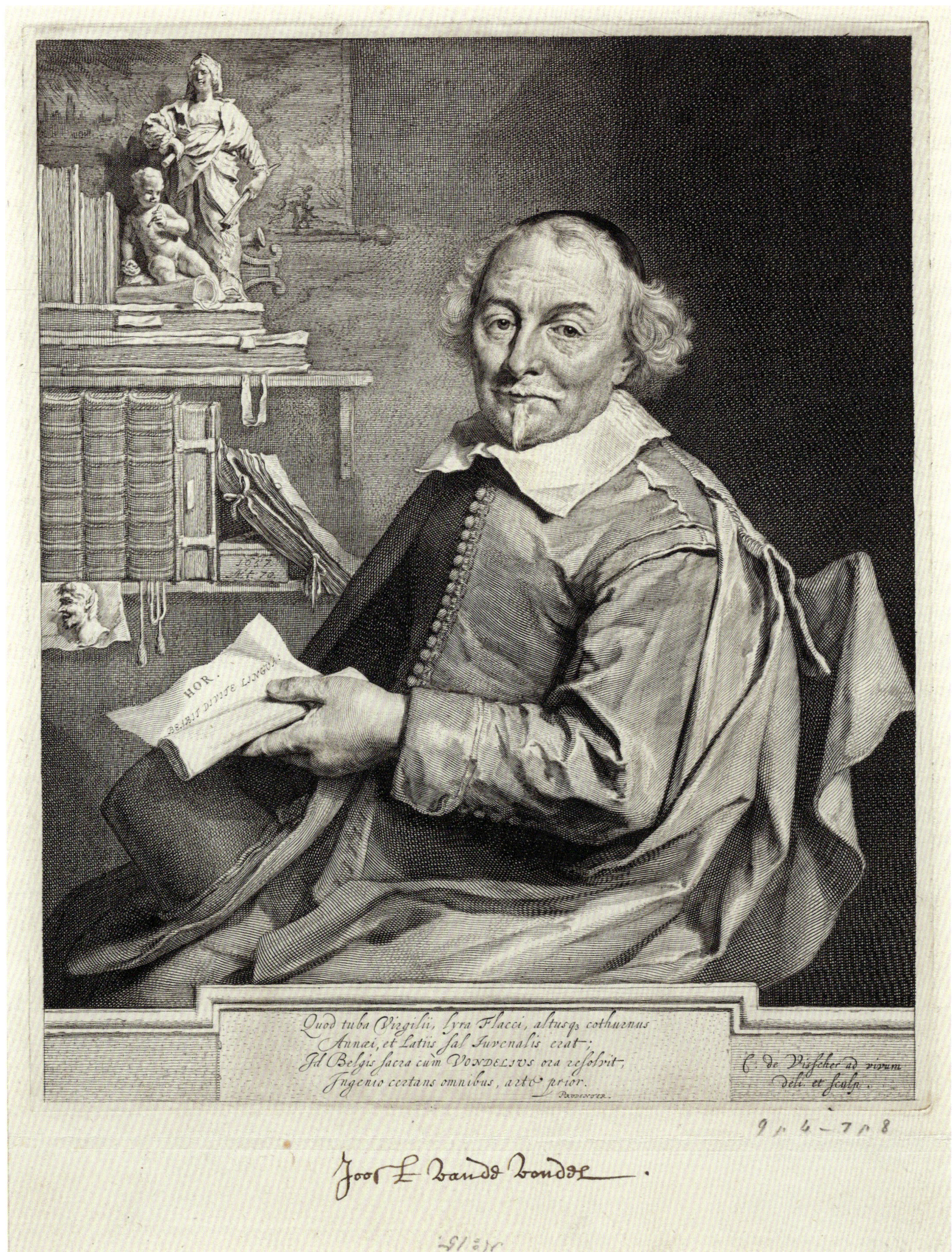

Among numerous portraits of Vondel are accomplished prints by Lievens, Sandrart (working with Theodor Matham) and Cornelis Visscher (pls. 15–17).[116] Why did Vondel not sit to Rembrandt? Multiple poems indicate that his favourite artists were Sandrart, Lievens and Flinck, placing him among advocates of the bright style. He devoted only one poem to a portrait by Rembrandt, depicting the Mennonite preacher Cornelis Claesz Anslo (fig. 1.16), to whose congregation Vondel belonged before converting to Catholicism around 1640. The quatrain challenges Rembrandt to "paint Cornelis' voice" because "the visible self is the least of him." While this has been seen as a pejorative comment on Rembrandt's abilities, it is a fitting metaphor for a preacher. Still, the challenge may have echoed in Rembrandt's mind when he etched an even more vivid "speaking likeness," the posthumous portrait of Saskia's guardian, the Calvinist minister Jan Cornelisz Sylvius, in 1646 (fig. 1.17). Barlaeus provided a Latin eulogy, inscribed by a professional calligrapher, praising Sylvius' inspirational ministry.[117]

A second banquet took place in October 1654, this time with the prominent art patron Joan Huydecoper as the guest of honour, and his favourite poet, Jan Vos, as master of ceremonies. In 1628 Huydecoper was the first known Amsterdammer to purchase a painting by Rembrandt.[118] By the 1650s his taste had shifted to the polished elegance of Van der Helst.[119] Vos' poetic oration lists the city's fifteen leading painters, including Rembrandt as well as several whose style could not be more different from his, such as Nicolaes van Helt Stockade and Jacob van Loo.

Changing Times

Rembrandt's participation in the cultural life of Amsterdam was multifaceted. He was active as a painter, draughtsman, printmaker, teacher, dealer, investor and collector, husband and father, and mentor and friend. Yet, no one has ever described him as a wise merchant. At the height of his career in the early 1640s, his assets were valued at more than 40,000 guilders, but by 1654 he was facing financial ruin. The Dutch Republic was fighting the first of three naval wars against the British, and, as often happens in times of crisis, the market for luxury goods stagnated. In 1649 Rembrandt had stopped making mortgage payments on his house, and he was mired in debt. A document notes that he suffered "losses at sea," suggesting that,

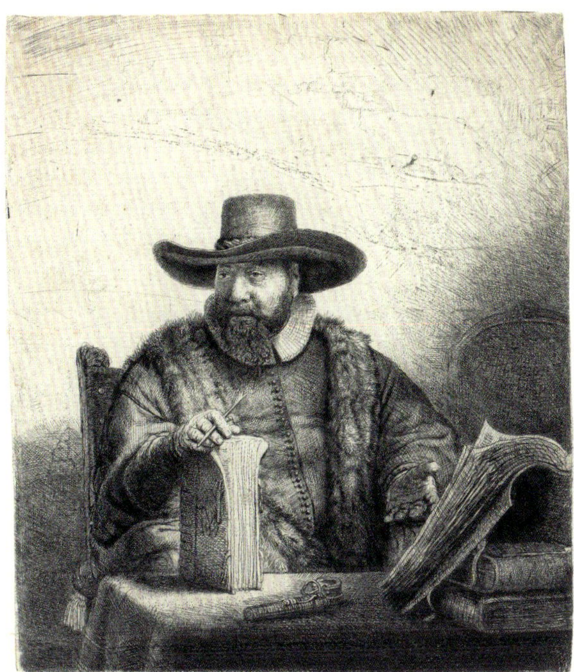

fig. 1.16 **Rembrandt van Rijn,** *Portrait of Cornelis Claesz Anslo, Preacher,* 1641, etching and drypoint on laid paper; 18.5 × 15.6 cm. National Gallery of Canada, Ottawa. Purchased 1923 (2938)

fig. 1.17 **Rembrandt van Rijn,** *Posthumous Portrait of Reverend Jan Cornelisz Sylvius,* 1646, etching on laid paper; 27.8 × 18.8 cm. Städel Museum, Frankfurt am Main (53672)

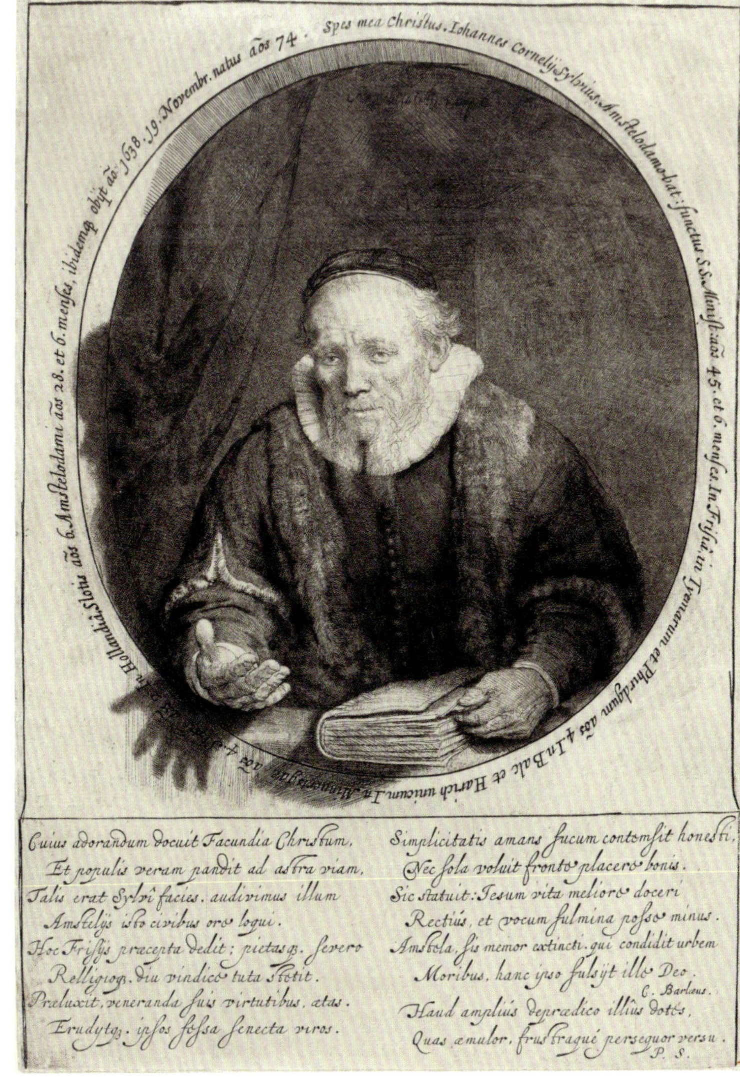

like many of his contemporaries, he had invested in global trade, but the bulk of his assets were tied up in material objects. In 1655 he auctioned off much of his collection, and in 1656 he declared insolvency.[120] Forced to forfeit his house on the Breestraat, he moved to more affordable quarters in the Jordaan district, working as an employee for a company Hendrickje and Titus set up to shield his remaining assets from creditors. There, he found a new creative community and continued to mentor younger artists. His last pupil, Aert de Gelder, another recruit from Dordrecht, would carry the Rembrandt brand into the eighteenth century.[121]

The scumbled canvases of Rembrandt's final years engage in a sculptural encounter with pigment that classicist critics found impossible to explain or admire.[122] Yet, his late paintings found favour with a select circle of connoisseurs who appreciated their layered brushwork, glowing colour and introspective emotion (pls. 78, 79, 93). From the mid-1650s to his death in 1669, Rembrandt was still the only Amsterdam artist with a truly international reputation, renowned for his prints even more than his paintings. He received commissions from Italy, and foreign visitors such as Cosimo III de' Medici called at his studio.[123] One such visitor may have been the dark-haired man recorded in a portrait of 1658 (pl. 78). His stance and expression project arrogant self-confidence. His costume is inconsistent with Dutch formal attire and not quite as fanciful as the historicizing attributes typical of Rembrandt's *tronies*. His identity remains a mystery.

A glimpse of Rembrandt in his painter's smock, probably recorded around 1652 by his talented pupil Willem Drost, conveys an irrepressible force of personality (pl. 18). We will leave him there to sort out his bankruptcy and settle into the Jordaan, still an innovator but no longer a trendsetter. Today, Rembrandt's stubborn commitment to following his own vision contributes to his enduring fame, but for consumers in Amsterdam's evolving marketplace, his earthy style was superseded by other appealing options. We invite you here to discover the diversity of artistic styles available to art lovers in seventeenth-century Amsterdam, a thriving creative community unique for its time. In doing so, we acknowledge the rich context that inspired a young artist from Leiden to become the master we know today as Rembrandt. ■

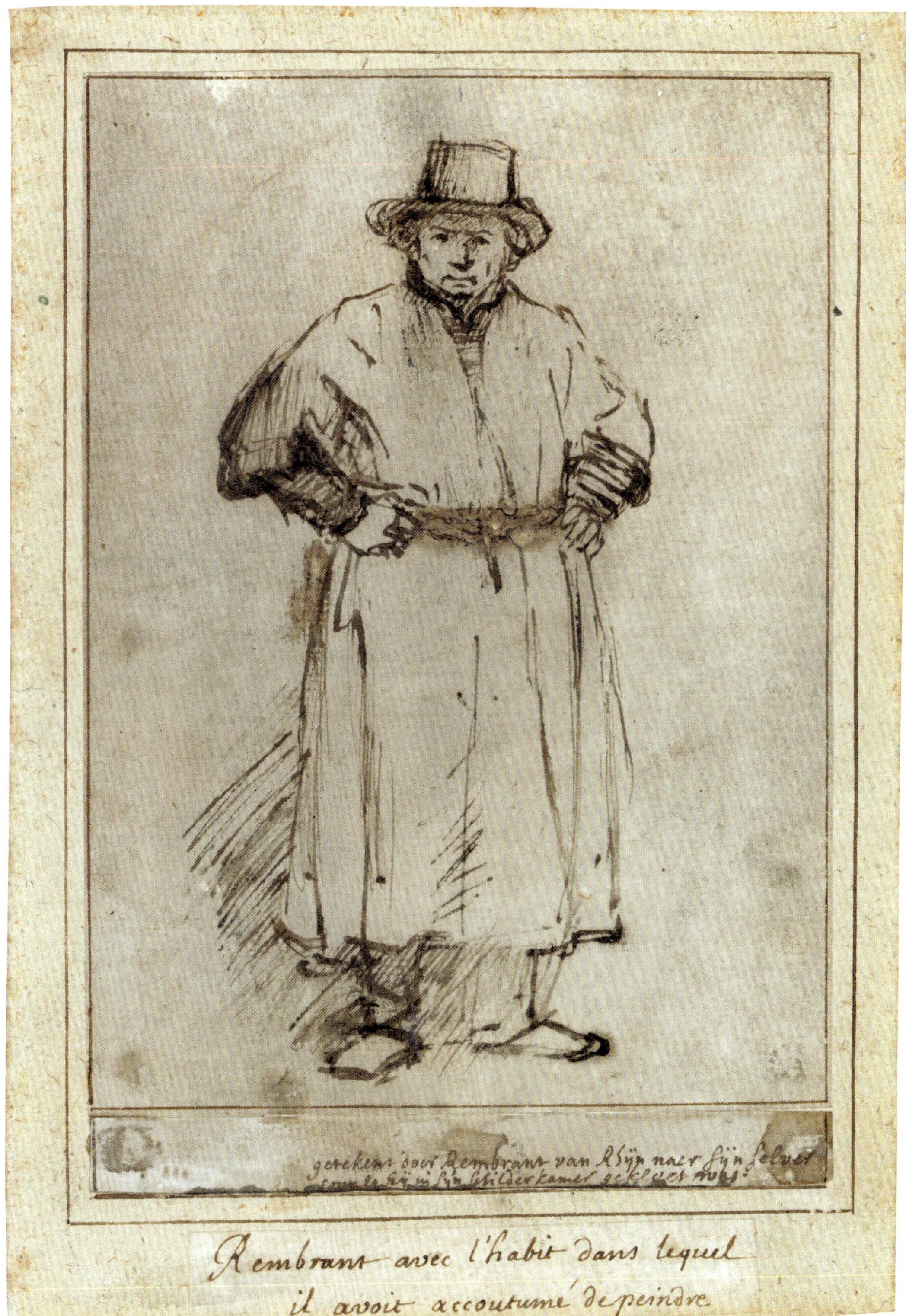
getekent door Rembrant van Rhijn naer sijn selver
soo als hij in sijn schilderkamer gekleet was
Rembrant avec l'habit dans lequel
il avoit accoutumé de peindre

NOTES

1 Schaeps and Van Duin 2019, 28–31. On Rembrandt's education, see also Golahny 2003. For Rembrandt's biography, see, among others, Schwartz 1985; Schwartz 2006; Westermann 2000; Büttner 2014; Bikker 2019. Endnotes in this volume cannot encompass the vast literature on Rembrandt and his milieu. Please see the Bibliography for a full list of sources consulted.

2 See recently Schnackenburg 2016; Leiden and Oxford 2019–20; Kingston, Edmonton, Regina and Hamilton 2019–21.

3 On Lastman, see Seifert 2011, with further references, esp. no. A14.

4 On *David Playing the Harp for Saul*, see Neumeister 2005, 363–379; *Corpus*, vol. 6, no. 38, and the essay by Jochen Sander in this volume.

5 De Winkel 2006, 260–261; *Corpus*, vol. 6, no. 53; Paris 2016–17, no. 12.

6 Around 1630, the population of Leiden was about 45,000, and that of Amsterdam was about 120,000; Lourens and Lucassen 1997, 112; Marten Jan Bok, "Rembrandt's Fame and Rembrandt's Failure: The Market for History Paintings in the Dutch Republic," in Kofuku 2004, 159–178, esp. 163.

7 Orlers 1641, 375. See, among others, Mariët Westermann, "Making a Mark in Rembrandt's Leiden," in Boston 2000–01, 25–49; Sluijter 2015, 25–26, Christiaan Vogelaar, "Ten Years of Struggle: Rembrandt in Leiden and Amsterdam, 1624–34," in Leiden and Oxford 2019–20, 15–35, esp. 15–20.

8 See esp. Van Straten 2005; Washington, Milwaukee and Amsterdam 2008–09; Schnackenburg 2016.

9 On Rembrandt's drawing, see recently Dresden 2019, no. 29.2, with further references, and the essay by Sonia Del Re in this volume. On Lievens' etching and painting, see Washington, Milwaukee and Amsterdam 2008–09, nos. 72, 25.

10 *Corpus*, vol. 6, no. 21; on *tronies*, see esp. Hirschfelder 2008, Gottwald 2011.

11 See Leerintveld 1989; Washington, Milwaukee and Amsterdam 2008–09, no. 16. On Rembrandt's series for Frederik Hendrik, see the essay "The Life of Christ" by Stephanie S. Dickey in this volume.

12 Noted in his unpublished autobiography; for a recent English translation, see Leiden and Oxford 2019–20, 297–299.

13 NHD Van Dyck 72; Stephanie S. Dickey, "Van Dyck in Holland: The Iconography and its Impact on Rembrandt and Lievens," in Vlieghe 2001.

14 Blanc 2006, 12; Dickey 2013.

15 NHD 50. De Jouderville apprenticed with Rembrandt in 1629–31; Strauss and Van der Meulen 1979, doc. 1631/7, 1631/8. On Dou, see, among others, Washington, London and The Hague 2000–01.

16 See McQueen 2003 and the essay by Jan Blanc in this volume.

17 On Rembrandt as a teacher, see, among others, Berlin, Amsterdam and London 1991–92b; Blanc 2006; Los Angeles 2009–10; Amsterdam 2015; Sluijter 2015; Amsterdam 2017–18; Amsterdam 2019. On his role in the art market, see the essay by Jasper Hillegers in this volume.

18 On Van den Eeckhout and Rembrandt, see Sluijter 2015, 346–361; Eric Jan Sluijter and Nicolette Sluijter-Seijffert, "Rembrandt's Pupils? The Attribution of Early Drawings to Gerbrand van den Eeckhout and Jan Victors," in Dumas, Ekkart and Van de Puttelaar 2020. Koninck's portraits, history paintings and landscapes (pl. 132)

reflect Rembrandt's impact; in 1641, he married the sister of Rembrandt's pupil Abraham Furnerius. For connections to Rembrandt, see Strauss and Van der Meulen 1979, doc. 1639/9, 1659/11 and [p.] 615.

19 For a survey of Rembrandt's portrait prints, see Dickey 2004; for Rembrandt's social network, see Amsterdam 2019.

20 Van Hoogstraten 1678, 215; see also Sluijter 2006, 262.

21 Houbraken 1718–21, vol. 2, 25; Slive 1988, 15, 47–48, 205; Tom van der Molen, "How Nature Fears the Painter Who Gave Life to His Canvases: Poems on the Life and Work of Govert Flinck," in Cleves 2015–16, 32–43, esp. 37; Amsterdam 2017–18, 82–84. On Apelles and Amsterdam, see also Sluijter 2015, 13–14.

22 See Barlaeus 2019, with further references.

23 Schwartz 1985, 33, 72, 123, 144–146, 185–186, 235–236.

24 Barlaeus 2019, 73.

25 For more examples, see Kassel and Leiden 2006–07, nos. 22–32; Schwartz 2006, 244–253.

26 Strauss and Van der Meulen 1979, doc. 1632/1; *Corpus*, vol. 2, no. A52; Schwartz 1985, 147. His first known Amsterdam portrait commission is *Portrait of Nicolaes Ruts* (see fig. 4.2); *Corpus*, vol. 6, no. 59.

27 On Uylenburgh and Rembrandt, see London and Amsterdam 2006; Büttner 2014, 51–66; and the essay by Jasper Hillegers in this volume.

28 Strauss and Van der Meulen 1979, doc. 1631/4; see also Amsterdam 2017–18.

29 *Corpus*, vol. 6, nos. 69, 66; Marieke de Winkel, "Costume in Rembrandt's Self-Portraits," in London and The Hague 1999–2000, 62–64 and nos. 32, 33.

30 The plate was begun in 1631, the "Rembrandt" signature added in 1633; see esp. NHD 90; Amsterdam and London 2000–01, no. 13; Dickey, "Van Dyck in Holland," in Vlieghe 2001, 289–303. On Rembrandt's signatures, see the essay by Jochen Sander in this volume.

31 Sebastien A.C. Dudok van Heel, "Rembrandt and Frans Hals Painting in the Workshop of Hendrick Uylenburgh," in Dickey 2017b, 17–43, esp. 19–21.

32 For example, *The Holy Family* (see fig. 13.5) was purchased by his portrait client Marten Soolmans. See the essay by Jasper Hillegers in this volume.

33 *Corpus*, vol. 6, nos. 65b, 90. See Dickey 2004, 34–47, and the essay by Rudi Ekkart and Claire van den Donk in this volume.

34 For *The Blinding of Samson*, see the essay "Desire and Enchantment" by Friederike Schütt in this volume.

35 *Corpus*, vol. 6, no. 76; see, among others, Heckscher 1958, esp. 115; Schwartz 1985, 144–146.

36 Michiel Franken, "Learning by Imitation: Copying Paintings in Rembrandt's Workshop," in Amsterdam and Berlin 2006, 153–177, esp. 153; Dudok van Heel, "Rembrandt and Frans Hals," in Dickey 2017b, 36. One connection is Santvoort's faithful drawing after Rembrandt's 1632 *Self-portrait* (Teylers Museum, Haarlem).

37 Sandrart 1675–80, vol. 2, book 3, 307. See Peter van den Brink, "Uitmuntend schilder in het groot. De schilder en tekenaar Jacob Adriaensz. Backer," in Amsterdam and Aachen 2008–09, 27–84, esp. 27. On Backer and Rembrandt, see Sluijter 2015, 110–127.

38   Van Hoogstraten 1678, 227–228; Van den Brink, "Uitmuntend schilder," in Amsterdam and Aachen 2008–09, 28.

39   Amsterdam and Aachen 2008–09, no. 8, oeuvre catalogue, no. A21; Sluijter 2015, 112, 114.

40   Jaap van der Veen, "Hendrick Uylenburgh's Art Business: Production and Trade between 1625 and 1655," in London and Amsterdam 2006, 178, 182; Amsterdam and Aachen 2008–09, no. A3; Sluijter 2015, 110–127, esp. 112–113. Rembrandt's etching *The Tribute Money* (NHD 138) may also be a product of this exchange. Watermark evidence dates it to 1629–34; Hinterding 2008, 143–144. The 1629 painting *The Tribute Money* in the National Gallery of Canada, Ottawa, presents a very different composition; a possible attribution to Rembrandt requires further research.

41   Peter Paul Rubens, *The Tribute Money* (1610–15, Fine Arts Museums of San Francisco); Sluijter 2015, 112–113, reproductive print by Vorsterman, fig. IIB–24.

42   As noted by Reznicek 1977, 104; Schwartz 1985, 143.

43   Jaap van der Veen, "Jacob Backer, een schets van zijn leven," in Amsterdam and Aachen 2008–09, 15, 20–21; Jacob Backer, *Portrait of Bartholomeus Breenbergh* and *Portrait of Rebecca Schellingwou* (1644, Amsterdam Museum), ibid., 140–141, no. 25a-b. On Breenbergh and Rembrandt, see Sluijter 2015, 127–148; Sluijter 2017.

44   Van den Brink 2016; Volker Manuth, "Rembrandt's Artist Friends," in Amsterdam 2019, 84–87.

45   See, among others, Edinburgh and London 2001, 29–54; Amsterdam and Aachen 2008–09, no. 54a-b; Amsterdam 2016.

46   Strauss and Van der Meulen 1979, doc. 1634/10.

47   On the house, heavily mortgaged, and Rembrandt's finances, see Strauss and Van der Meulen 1979, doc. 1639/1; Schwartz 2006, 120–141; Crenshaw 2006. On Rembrandt's collection, see, among others, Strauss and Van der Meulen 1979, doc. 1656/12; Amsterdam 1999–2000; H. Perry Chapman, "Curiosity and Desire: Rembrandt's Collection as Historiographic Barometer," in Dickey 2017b, 99–121.

48   On Rembrandt and Saskia, see, among others, Broos 2012; Leeuwarden and Kassel 2018–19; Dresden 2019, 127–149; and the essay "Powerful Women" by Stephanie S. Dickey in this volume. Titus was baptized on 22 September 1641, and Saskia was buried on 19 June 1642; Strauss and Van der Meulen 1979, doc. 1641/4, 1642/4.

49   On Rembrandt's personal relationships, see, among others, Sebastien A.C. Dudok van Heel, "Rembrandt: His Life, His Wife, the Nursemaid and the Servant," in Edinburgh and London 2001, 19–27; Büttner 2014, 89–108.

50   See recently Tom van der Molen, "The Life of Govert Flinck," in Cleves 2015–16, 10–21; Erna Kok, "Prosperous Friends and Distinguished Gentlemen: The Patrons of Govert Flinck," in ibid., 22–31; Erna Kok, "Govert Flinck, Ferdinand Bol and Their Networks of Influential Clients," in Amsterdam 2017–18, 58–79, esp. 59–70.

51   Cleves 2015–16, 15–16. The purchase price was 10,000 guilders. Rembrandt paid 13,000 guilders for his house on St. Anthonisbreestraat; Strauss and Van der Meulen 1979, doc. 1639/1.

52   Houbraken 1718–21, vol. 2, 22; Cleves 2015–16, 16.

53   Houbraken 1718–21, vol. 2, 19.

54   See David de Witt and Leonore van Sloten, "Ferdinand Bol: Rembrandt's Disciple," in Amsterdam 2017–18, 40–53.

55   See Leonore van Sloten, "Ferdinand Bol, the Etcher," in Amsterdam 2017–18, 206–221.

56   See Dickey 2004, 89–104; Amsterdam 2017–18, 50–53, 72–73, and the essay by Jonathan Bikker in this volume.

57   See Kok 2013, 63–65.

58   See Brusati 2003, with further references.

59   See London and The Hague 2019–20.

60   Sandrart 1675–80, vol. 2, book 3, 326.

61   See Sluijter 2015, 199–214 (Koninck), 346–361 (Van den Eeckhout), 352–375 (Victors).

62   Bok, "Rembrandt's Fame and Rembrandt's Failure," in Kofuku 2004, 168.

63   See also the essay "Art and Life" by Stephanie S. Dickey in this volume.

64   Compare, for instance, Rembrandt's *Holy Family with a Curtain* (1646, Gemäldegalerie Alte Meister, Kassel) and Maes' *Young Woman at a Cradle* (1652–62, Rijksmuseum, Amsterdam); London and The Hague 2019–20, no. 7.

65   Franits 2004, 177–180; Mandrella 2011, 47. See also Sluijter 2015, 375–379.

66   John Michael Montias, "Works of Art in Seventeenth-century Amsterdam: An Analysis of Subjects and Attributions," in Freedberg and De Vries 1991, 331–372; Bok, "Rembrandt's Fame and Rembrandt's Failure," in Kofuku 2004, 165–166; Jager 2015.

67   Sluijter 2015, 272–292.

68   Franits 2004, 57–64; Sluijter 2015, 272–311.

69   For Asselijn's painting, see www.nga.gov/collection/art-object-page.159836.html (accessed 26 Feb. 2020). On process and product innovation in landscape, see Montias 1987.

70   See esp. Boudewijn Bakker, "Rembrandt and the Humanist Ideal of the Universal Painter," in Dickey 2017b, 67–98.

71   See, for instance, *The Slaughtered Ox* (see fig. 18.4), *Corpus*, vol. 6, no. 240. Still lifes by Rembrandt are listed in his inventory of 1656; Strauss and Van der Meulen 1979, doc. 1656/12.

72   See, among others, Schwartz 2006, 230–233, and the essay "Portraits of Prosperity" by Stephanie S. Dickey in this volume.

73   NHD 123. For interpretations, see Golahny 2003, 38–39; Schwartz 2006, 233; Van de Grind 2016.

74   For *Medea, or The Marriage of Jason and Creusa*, see figs. 17.9, 17.10 and the essay by Robert Fucci in this volume.

75   See esp. Amsterdam and London 2000–01; Hinterding 2006.

76   On print production in Amsterdam, see Amsterdam 2011.

77   NHD 240. For interpretation, see Dickey 2004, 125–130.

78   For an overview, see Montias 2002.

79   Bredius 1915–22, vol. 5, 7–12; Strauss and Van der Meulen 1979, doc. 1637/ 2. On Rembrandt's print purchases, see also the essay by Robert Fucci in this volume.

80   Dickey 2004, 75, 98–100, 187, 191; Sluijter 2015, 71–74, 80–81; Badeloch Noldus, "A Spider in its Web: Agent and Artist Michel LeBlon and His Northern European Network," in Keblusek and Noldus 2011, 161–191.

81   Strauss and Van der Meulen 1979, doc. 1637/5.

82 Sandrart 1675–80, vol. 1, book 3, 55. On Rembrandt and Sandrart, see Dickey 2004, 89–104; Dickey 2007; Kok 2013, 115–130; Sluijter 2015, 71–95. On Rembrandt and the art market, see esp. Bok, "Rembrandt's Fame and Rembrandt's Failure," in Kofuku 2004, 159–178; Schwartz 2006, 117–129; and the essays by Jasper Hillegers and Jonathan Bikker in this volume.

83 NHD 271; see recently Dresden 2019, nos. 48.1–48.2, with further references. In 1656 Rembrandt owned six paintings by Segers; Strauss and Van der Meulen 1979, doc. 1656/12.

84 Strauss and Van der Meulen 1979, doc. 1637/5, noting that Rubens owned three paintings by Den Uyl. In 1640 Den Uyl's brother-in-law, still-life painter Jan Jansz Treck, invested in Uylenburgh's business; London and Amsterdam 2006, 171. Provenance history rules out the version of Rubens' painting in the Gemäldegalerie, Dresden, as the one discussed here.

85 Strauss and Van der Meulen 1979, doc. 1659/20.

86 Vos' poem was inscribed in Jan Six's *album amicorum*, to which Rembrandt had contributed two drawings in 1652. See Golahny 1990; Dickey 2004, 113–114; Sluijter 2015, 81–83. See also Toronto 2019, 238–243.

87 Barlaeus 1638; Blocksom 2018. On Savery, see esp. Jasper Hillegers and Lotte Jaeger, "Salomon Saverij, een plaatsnijder en zijn vrienden," in Amsterdam 2011, 120–163.

88 Rembrandt's portraits of Maria Trip (c. 1641, Rijksmuseum, Amsterdam) and her mother Aletta Adriaensdr (1639, Museum Boijmans Van Beuningen, Rotterdam), who hosted Amalia von Solms during the visit, have been linked with this occasion; *Corpus*, vol. 6, nos. 169, 184b; Schwartz 1985, 206–207.

89 *Corpus*, vol. 6, no. 190. See esp. Haverkamp-Begemann 1982; Sluijter 2015, 90–95 (noting connections to the Medici entry); Müller 2015.

90 Van Gent 2011, 418.

91 Sandrart 1675–80, vol. 2, book 3, 317; Van Gent 2011, 417.

92 Van Gent 2011, 128–130, 417.

93 Ibid., 417. One participant testified that sixteen sitters in *The Night Watch* paid about 100 guilders each; Strauss and Van der Meulen 1979, doc. 1659/16.

94 Van Hoogstraten 1678, 176; Thijs Weststeijn, "The Rules of Art and Rembrandt, 1630–1730," in Franits 2016, 202–233, esp. 210–213.

95 Van Gent 2011, no. 3, 152–155, 418.

96 Van Gent 2011, 153, suggests Van der Helst worked on this enormous canvas from 1639 to 1643. Rembrandt received the commission for *The Night Watch* before December 1640 and completed it in 1642; *Corpus*, vol. 3, no. A146, 450.

97 Van Gent 2011, 168–170, no. 15; pendant (current whereabouts unknown), no. 16; related drawing, Kunsthalle, Hamburg, 129, 374, no. T1.

98 The term "bright style" (*helder schilderen*) in contrast to Rembrandt's manner is established in Houbraken's biography of Flinck; Houbraken 1718–21, vol. 2, 21; Kok, "Govert Flinck, Ferdinand Bol," in Amsterdam 2017–18, 64, 243n17. See also Lootsma 2007–08.

99 NHD Van Dyck 467. Barnes et al. 2004, no. III.93, dates Van Dyck's painting stylistically to his second Antwerp period, c. 1627–34, which includes Van Dyck's visit to The Hague in winter 1631–32. Sellin 1998, 112, suggests 1635, when both Van Dyck and LeBlon were in London.

100 For interpretations, see esp. Blanc 2006, 22; Crenshaw 2013.

101 See Washington, Milwaukee and Amsterdam 2008–09, 18–25 and nos. 43–55; Sluijter 2015, 379–384.

102 *Portrait of Andries de Graeff* (1657, Teylers Museum, Haarlem), *Portrait of Jan Vos* (fig. 1.12) and *Portrait of René Descartes* (c. 1644–49, Museum voor Stad en Lande, Groningen); Dickey 2004, 133–135; Washington, Milwaukee and Amsterdam 2008–09, nos. 117, 118, 112.

103 See Amsterdam and Paris 1998–99; Washington, Milwaukee and Amsterdam 2008–09, nos. 121–139, esp. 131.

104 Dickey 2008.

105 On Six and Lievens, see Dickey 2004, 134–135.

106 Strauss and Van der Meulen 1979, doc. 1657/2; *Corpus*, vol. 6, no. 196; Sluijter 2015, 58–59, 346; Friso Lammertse and Jaap van der Veen, "Der Amsterdamer Kaufmann und Kunsthändler Johannes de Renialme und sein Gemäldebestand in den Jahren 1640, 1650 und 1657," in Hamburg 2017–18, 170–191.

107 Strauss and Van der Meulen 1979, doc. 1646/6; Sluijter 2015, 54. A studio copy of *The Circumcision of Christ* is in the Herzog Anton Ulrich-Museum, Braunschweig; *Corpus*, vol. 6, no. 211; *The Adoration of the Shepherds*, no. 211b. For more on the series, see the essays "A Letter from Rembrandt" and "The Life of Christ" by Stephanie S. Dickey in this volume. A 1662 business transaction with the dealer Lodewijk van Ludick suggests that Rembrandt later profited from studio versions of these compositions; Strauss and Van der Meulen 1979, doc. 1662/6.

108 Jan Lievens, *Adoration of the Magi* (1644, Agnes Etherington Art Centre, Kingston) may be the work listed in 1654 in the collection of Amalia von Solms, but there is no evidence it was exhibited with Rembrandt's series; De Witt 2008, 199–200, no. 118.

109 On Rembrandt and Six, see, among others, Dickey 2004, 115–119; Amsterdam 2017; Amsterdam 2019, 100.

110 For Flinck's *Portrait of Margaretha Tulp*, see Amsterdam 2017–18, 84–85, 157. On Flinck and Van Dyck, see Lootsma 2007–08.

111 Jan Beerstraten made a specialty of cityscapes recalling the event. See, for instance, *The Ruins of the Old Town Hall of Amsterdam after the Fire of 7 July 1652* (1652–66, Rijksmuseum, Amsterdam), and a 1652 drawing (Amsterdam Museum).

112 See also, for instance, drawings by Abraham Furnerius (1652, Teylers Museum, Haarlem) and Roelant Roghman (1652, Rijksmuseum, Amsterdam).

113 The remaining fragment is now in the Nationalmuseum, Stockholm; *Corpus*, vol. 6, no. 298. See also the essays by Maarten Prak and Friederike Schütt ("Illustrious Histories") in this volume.

114 See, among others, Dickey 2004, 109–111; Mandrella 2011, 32; Tom van der Molen, "Flinck and Bol's Companions in Art," in Amsterdam 2017–18, 82.

115 For an overview, see Bloemendal and Korsten 2012.

116 On Lievens' print, see Washington, Milwaukee and Amsterdam 2008–09, no. 85. Sandrart produced a series of five portraits of leading literary figures, also including Barlaeus; see Norbert Middelkoop, "New Light on Sandrart's Scholar Portraits," in Ebert-Schifferer and Mazzetti di Pietralata 2009, 97–107; Sluijter 2015, 74–75.

117 On Rembrandt, Vondel, Anslo and Sylvius, see Dickey 2004, 30–65.

118 Schwartz 2006, 131. See pl. 20 and the essays by Jasper Hillegers and Jonathan Bikker in this volume.

119 See, for instance, Bartholomeus van der Helst, *The Governors of the Voetboogdoelen* (1656, Amsterdam Museum); Van Gent 2011, no. 87.

120 Strauss and Van der Meulen 1979, doc. 1656/10. On Rembrandt's financial affairs, see Montias 2002, 180–187; Bok, "Rembrandt's Fame and Rembrandt's Failure," in Kofuku 2004; Crenshaw 2006.

121 See esp. Von Moltke 1994; Cologne and Dordrecht 1998–99.

122 On the classicist critique, see, among others, Slive 1988; Emmens 1968; Sluijter 2006. On the late work, see London and Amsterdam 2016.

123 Strauss and Van der Meulen 1979, doc. 1667/6. On Rembrandt's dealings with Antonio Ruffo of Messina, see Giltaij 2017, with further references. On an unresolved commission from Genoa in 1666, see Magnani 2007.

19   Pieter Lastman, *The Triumph of Sesostris*, 1631. Fine Arts Museums of San Francisco

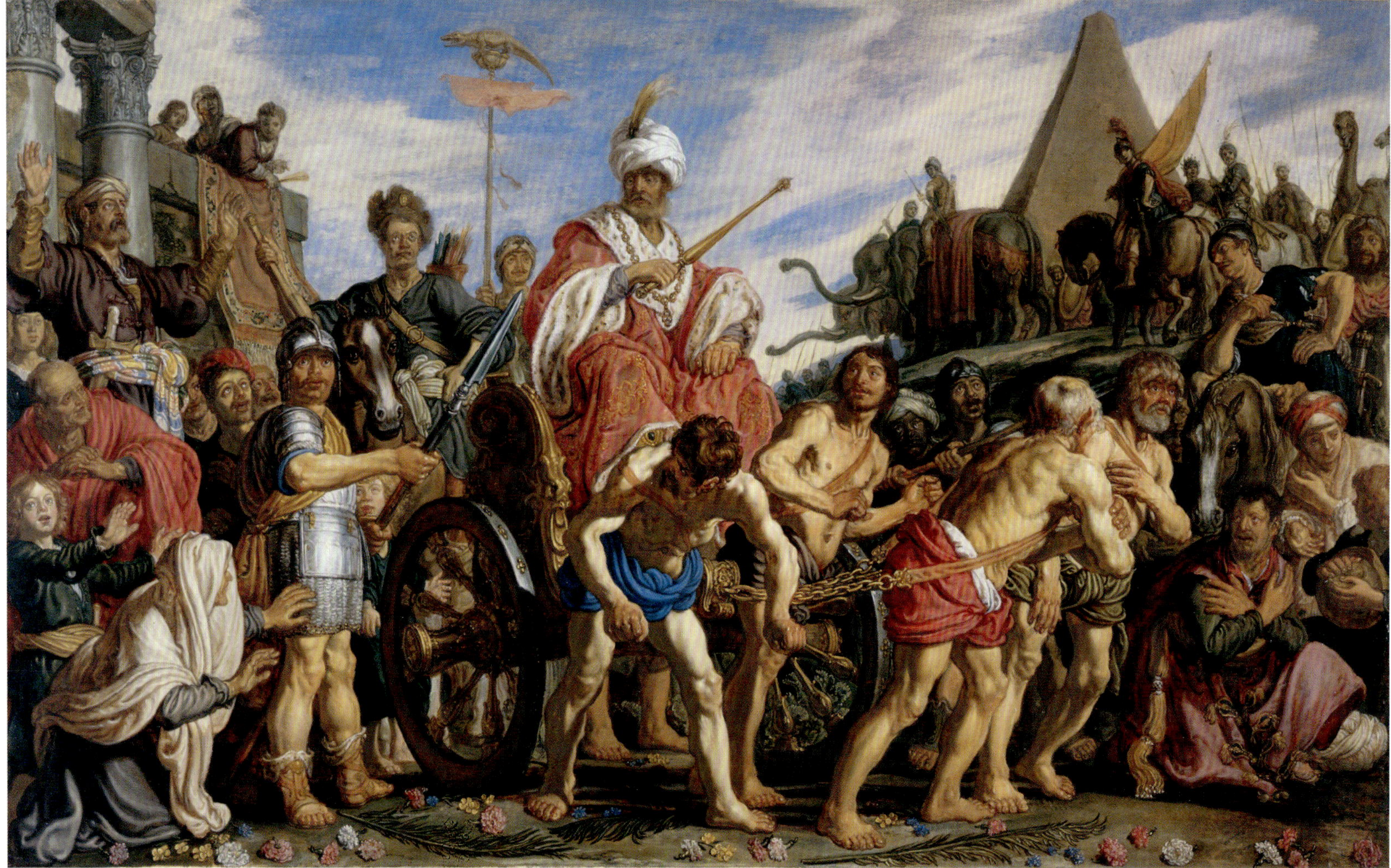

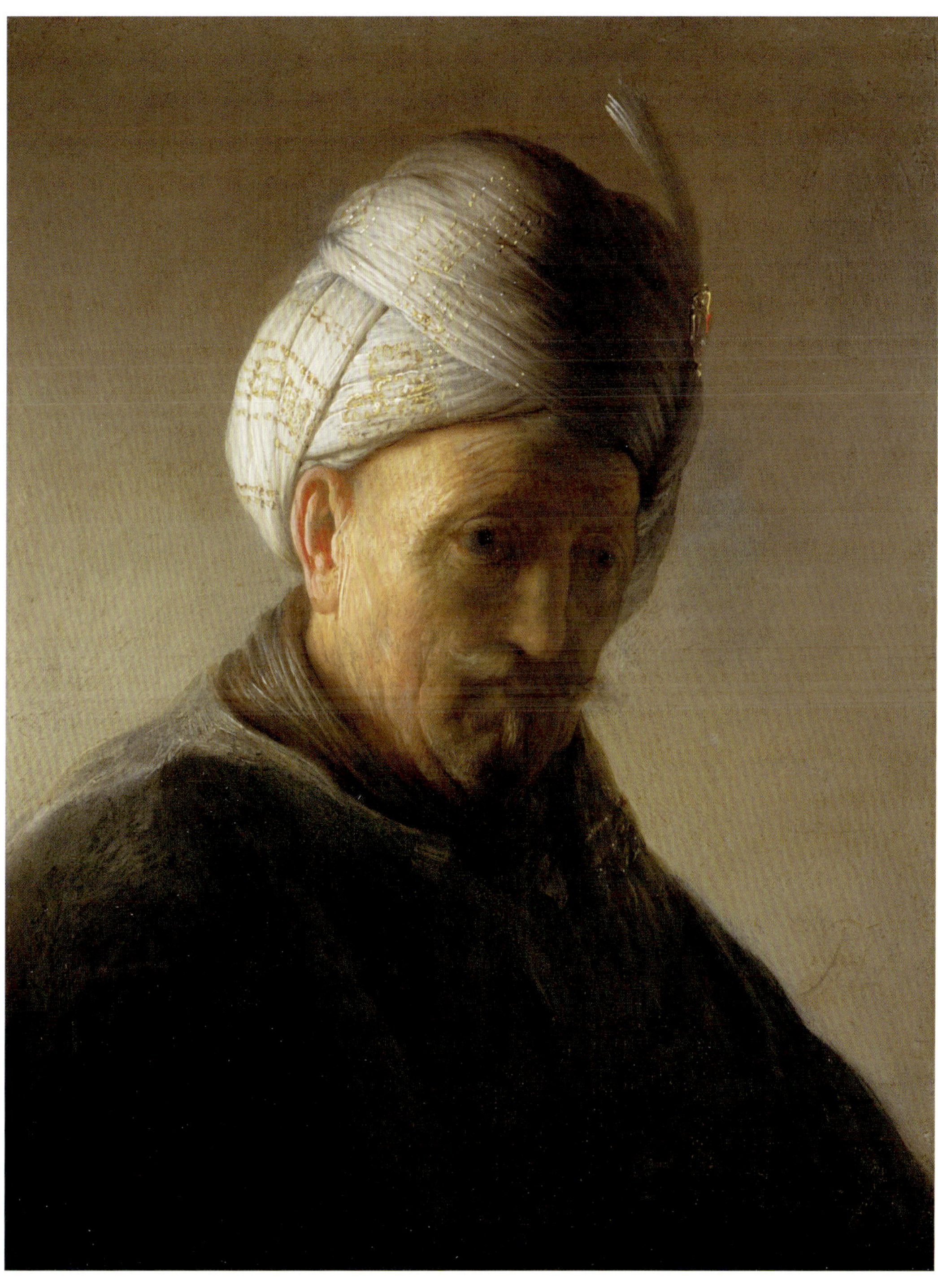

21 Jan Lievens, *Saint Jerome Meditating in a Grotto*, c. 1630. Städel Museum, Frankfurt am Main

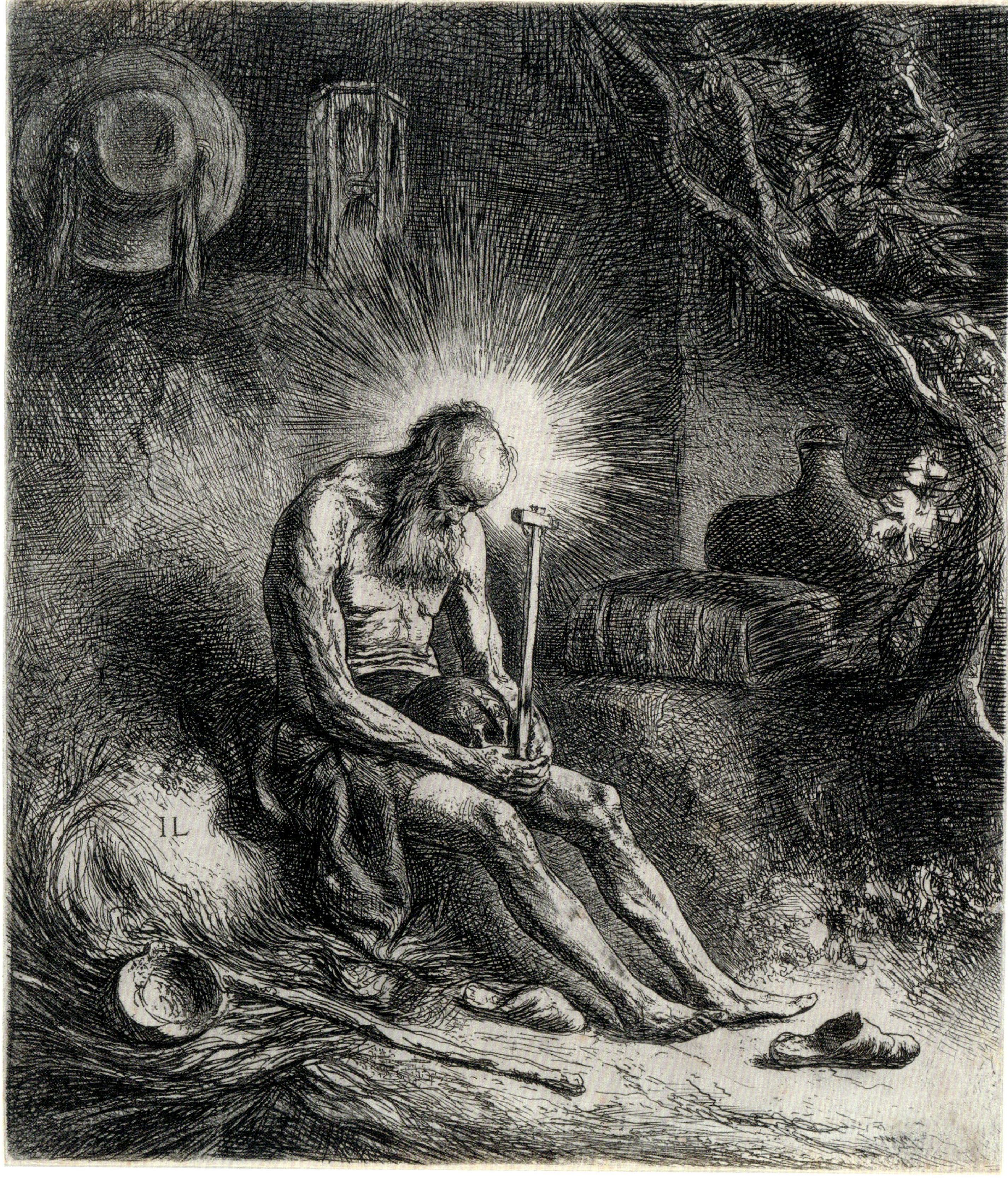

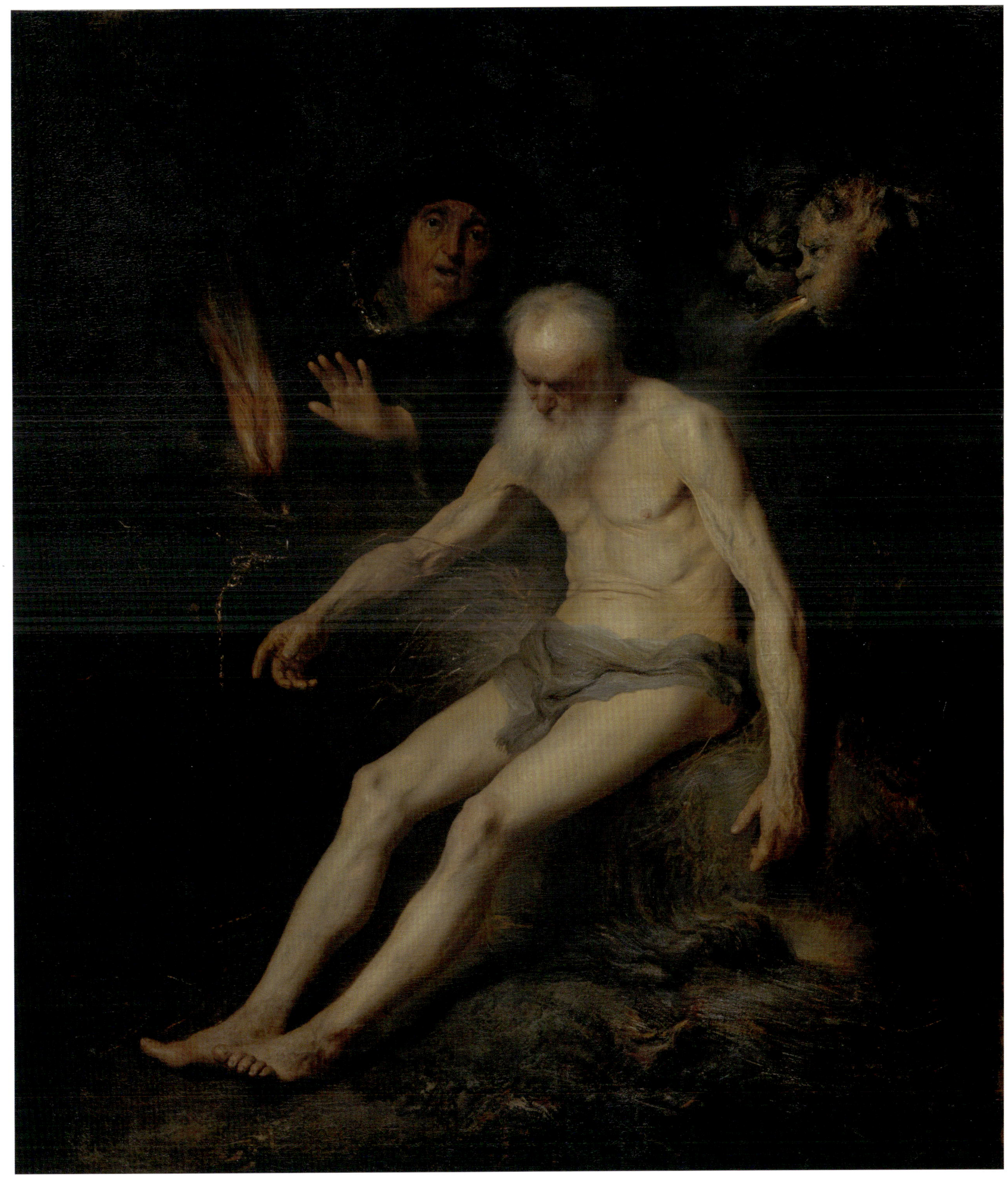

23 Rembrandt van Rijn, *Portrait of Jan Lutma, Goldsmith*, 1656. National Gallery of Canada, Ottawa

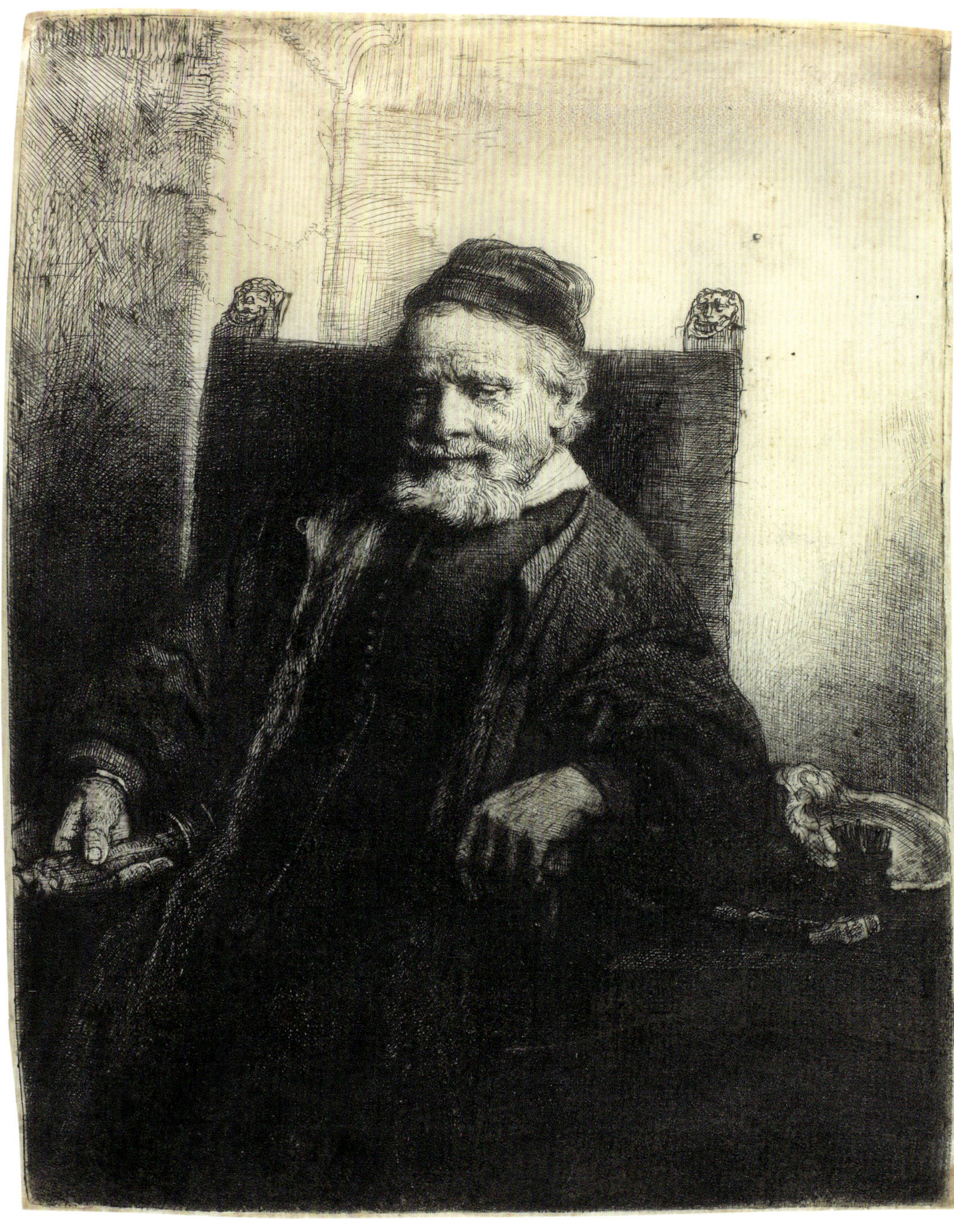

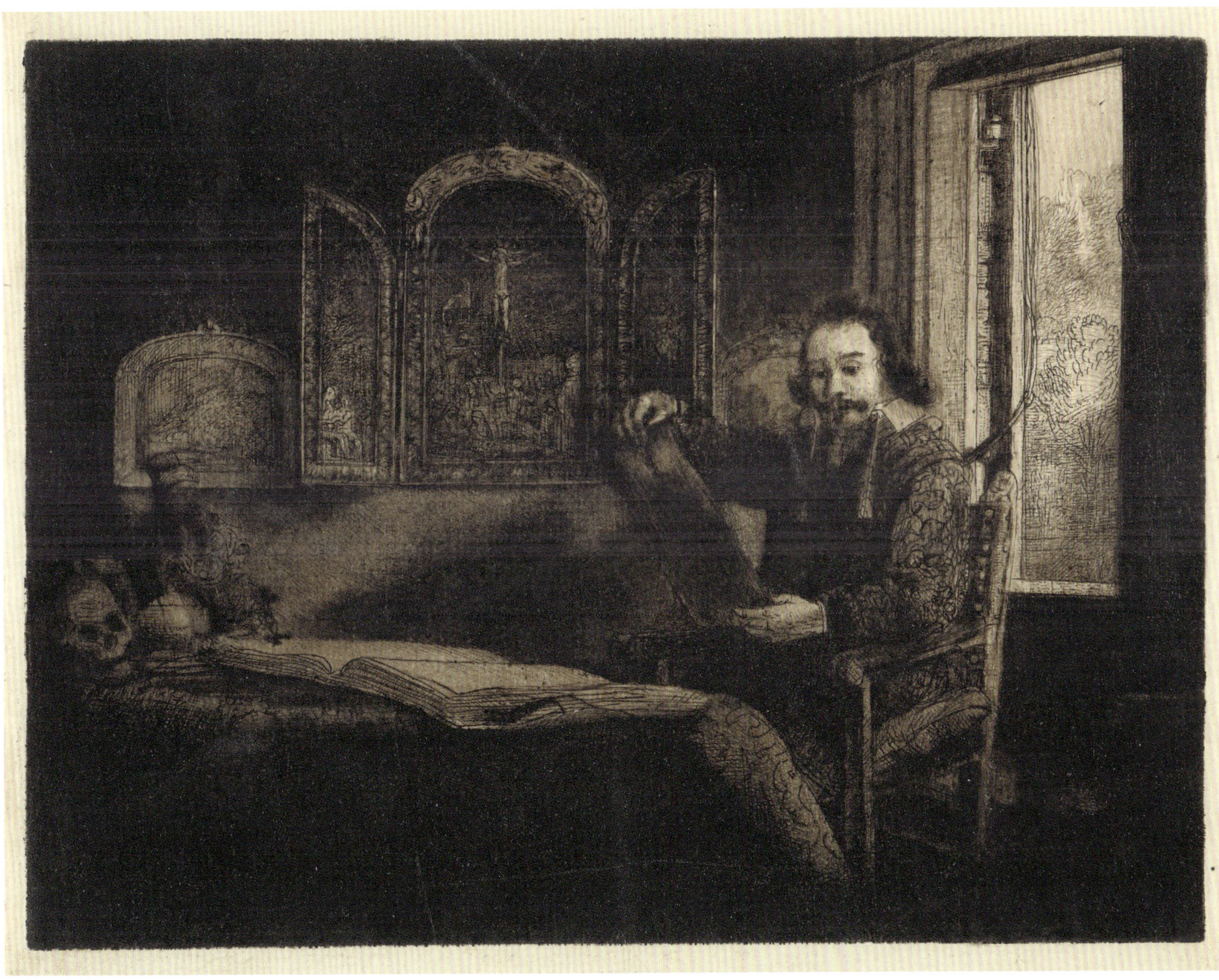

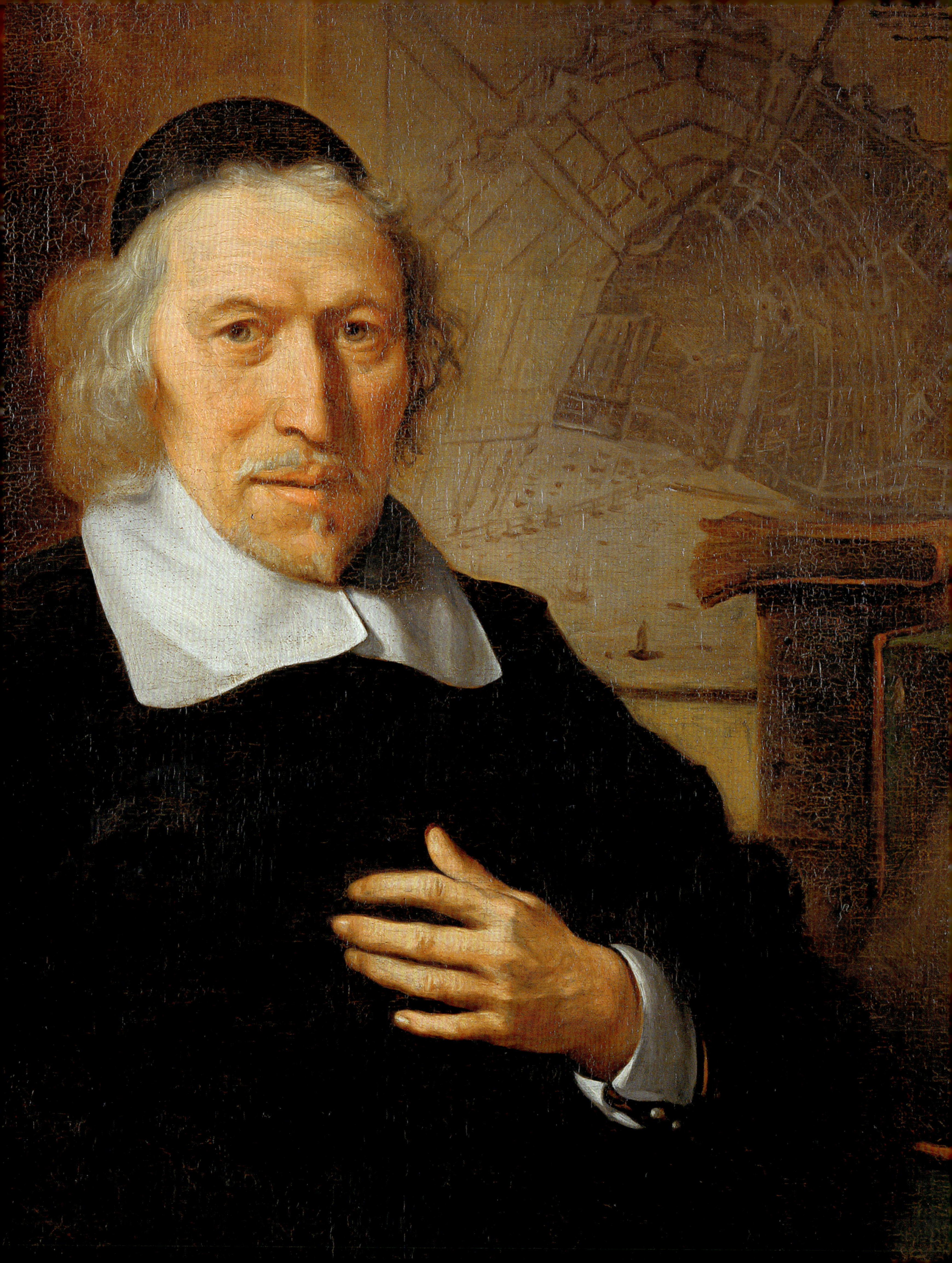

MAARTEN PRAK

Rembrandt's Amsterdam

When Rembrandt van Rijn moved to Amsterdam from his native Leiden in the early 1630s, he settled in a burgeoning city with ample opportunities for a young artist (pls. 25, 32). From around 30,000 inhabitants some fifty years earlier, Amsterdam's population had quadrupled. It was already in the league of Europe's ten largest cities, and by the end of the century, with a population of more than 200,000, it would rank third, behind London and Paris. Amsterdam's spectacular growth helped make Holland – the largest and most affluent province of the newly formed Dutch Republic – the wealthiest region on Earth.[1] That prosperous era, traditionally known as the Dutch Golden Age, witnessed at one and the same time an economic boom, a social transformation, a political revolution and a creative explosion. This essay outlines these four aspects of Amsterdam life during the middle decades of the seventeenth century, when Rembrandt was one of its prominent inhabitants.

Economic Boom

For much of the previous century Amsterdam had been a commercial outpost of Antwerp, northwestern Europe's most important trade hub. Antwerp had managed to combine three distinct trade flows. The first was the wool trade between England and the Continent, established centuries before, that supplied an important wool industry in Flanders, and in the region that is now northern France, but was then also part of the Low Countries. The second was trade with a large German hinterland that suffered from poor access to the sea. The third, and most recent, was trade between Europe and Asia, conducted initially by Italians, but from around 1500 also by Portuguese and Spanish merchants. This global trade increasingly also encompassed Africa and the Americas.[2]

Amsterdam itself had a much more limited trade portfolio in the sixteenth century. Its mainstay was the grain trade with the Baltic, Holland's "mother trade."[3] Holland had been dependant on grain imports for more than a century, to an extent that was very unusual at a time when high transport costs were making imported basic foodstuffs too expensive. The Dutch had responded to this challenge by designing ships that were increasingly efficient. By the end of the century, this series of innovations consolidated in the "flute" type of vessel that would make the Dutch into Europe's transporters.

After 1585 traditional commercial networks, combined with new shipbuilding technology and an injection of foreign capital, transformed Amsterdam from a secondary harbour into the world's centre of trade (pl. 33). In 1629, shortly before Rembrandt moved there, Amsterdam's merchants boasted "that we, through our frugality and cunning, have managed, during the Twelve Years' Truce [1609–21] to out-compete all our rivals, pulled other countries' commerce over here, and serviced all of Europe with our ships."[4] This was a remarkably accurate observation. During the seventeenth century, the Dutch merchant navy was larger than those of England and France combined, even though the populations of those two countries together were around 12.5 times larger. Dutch shipping was in many ways the foundation for its economic success.[5]

That success was, however, also due to the aggressive commercial policies that the Dutch state, and the town of Amsterdam in particular, were willing to pursue under the cloak of war.[6] The first, and perhaps single most important blow that the Dutch managed to strike was the blockade of Antwerp harbour after the city fell to the Spaniards in August 1585. The blockade made it much more difficult, and therefore more expensive, to transport goods in and out of Antwerp.

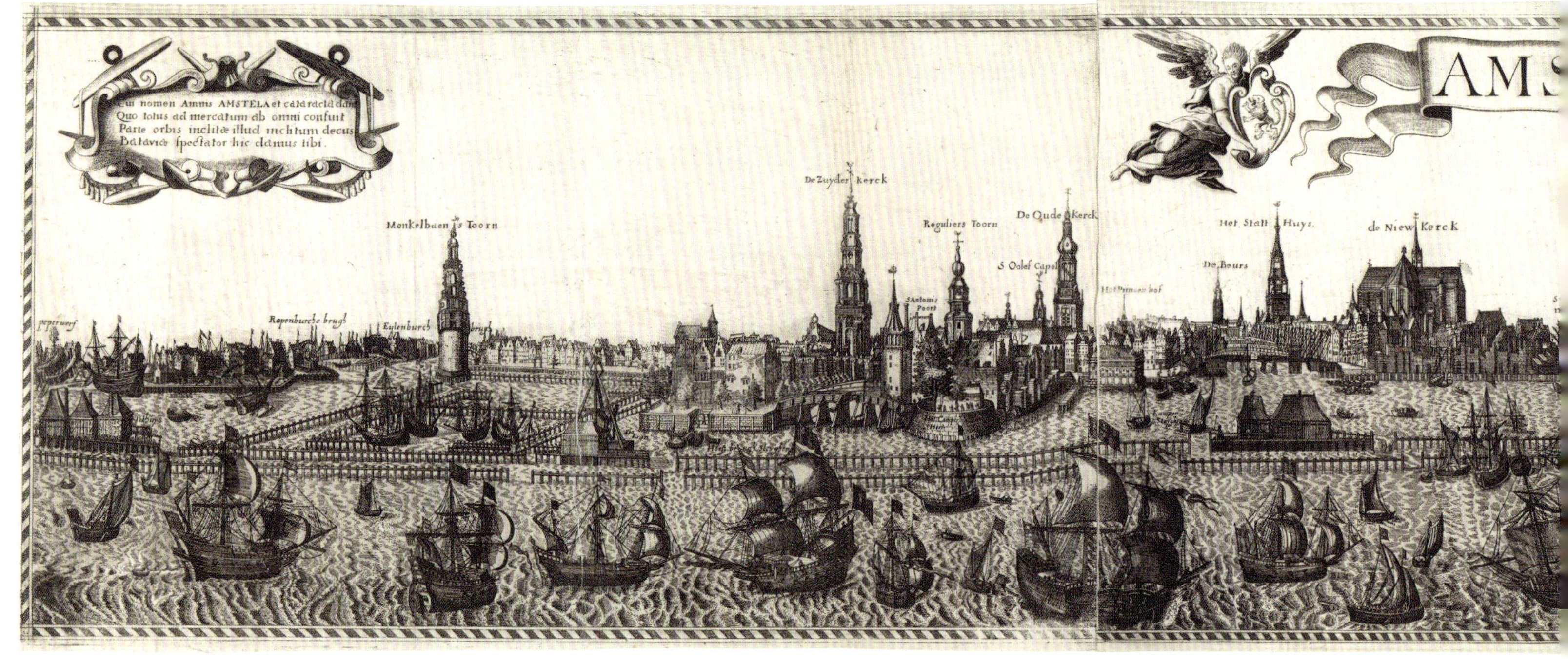
Cui nomen Amnis AMSTELA et cataracta dant
Quo totus ad mercatum ab omni confluit
Parte orbis inclitæ illud inclitum decus
Batavicæ spectator hic damus tibi.
AMS
peper werf
Rapenburchs brugh
Eulenburch brugh
Monkelbaen is Toorn
De Zuyder kerck
S Antonis Poort
Reguliers Toorn
De Oude Kerck
S Oolef Capel
Het Prinsen hof
De Beurs
Het Statt Huys.
de Niew Kerck

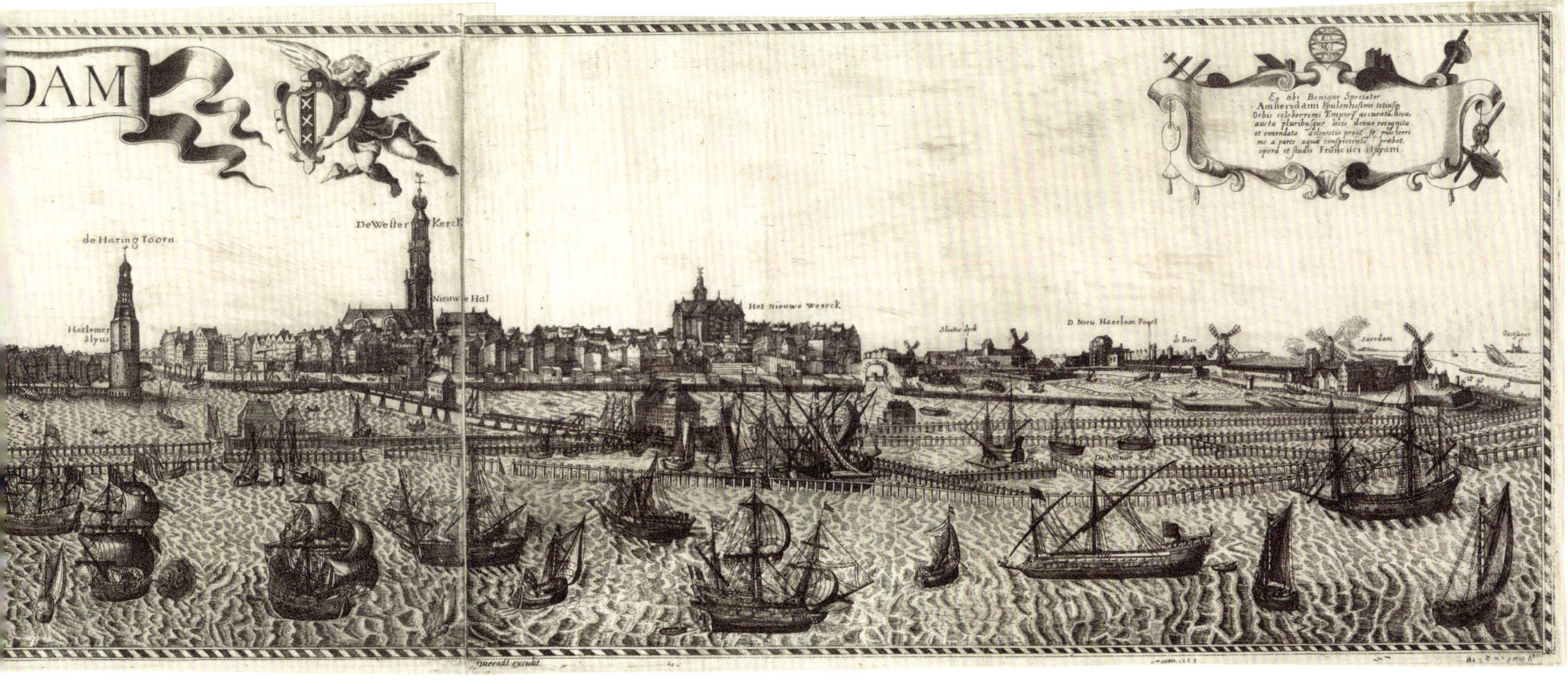
DAM
de Haring Toorn
De Welter Kerck
Nieuwe Hal
Haerlemer Sluys
Het Nieuwe Werck
Sluter Syck
D Nieu Haerlam Poort
de Boer
Saerdam

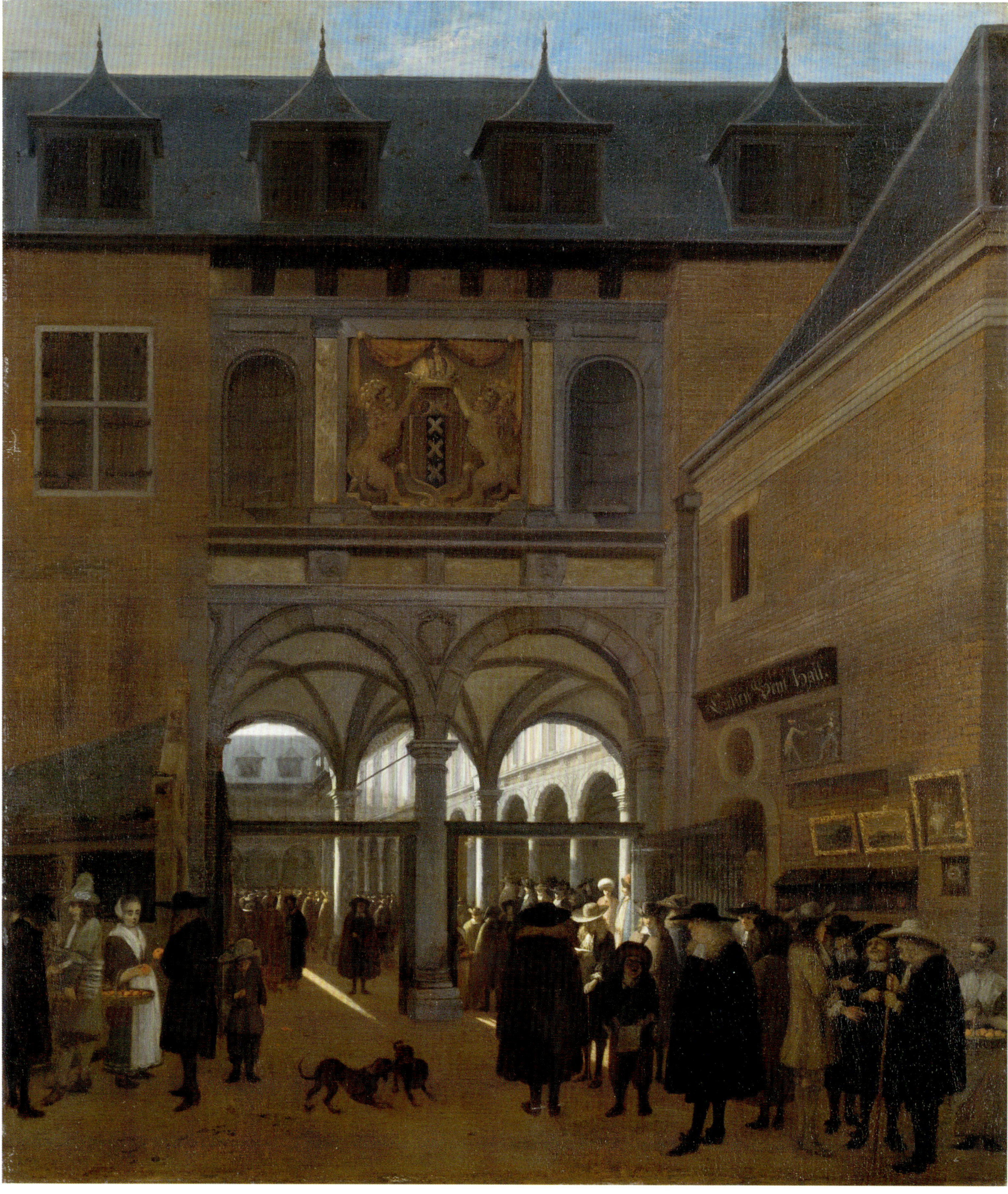

26 Job Adriaensz Berckheyde, *The Stock Exchange in Amsterdam*, c. 1675–80. Städel Museum, Frankfurt am Main

For this and other reasons, the Spanish conquest triggered an exodus of refugees. Antwerp itself lost half its population. Around 100,000 migrants from the south settled in the north, many of them in Amsterdam.

During the 1590s, ships from Amsterdam started to explore the sea routes to Asia. These had been laid open by Portuguese and Spanish merchants, and now the Dutch were trying to get a piece of this potentially very profitable trade as well. Their attempts were consolidated with the establishment in 1602 of the VOC (Dutch East India Company), which saw its mission as a combination of trade and warfare, especially in its early years. Around half of the activities of the VOC were funded by Amsterdam capital. From 1621 trade with the Americas was consolidated in the WIC (Dutch West India Company), again with substantial participation from Amsterdam. The two companies would contribute significantly to the Dutch Republic's economic success, and at the same time represented the period's darkest side, which was slavery. The WIC was a major force in the Atlantic slave trade, while the VOC was likewise involved in human trafficking in Asia.[7]

All these developments had made Amsterdam, by the time Rembrandt settled there, into the hub of world trade (pl. 26). To be sure, world trade at the time was still a very modest enterprise compared to that of the twenty-first century. But of what there was, Amsterdam and the rest of Holland had managed to grab a remarkably large slice. Of all the European shipping enterprises that ventured past the southern tip of Africa, going to Asia or returning from one or another Asian port, a staggering two-thirds were Dutch. With Amsterdam sending out more than half of the VOC fleet, the implication is that around a third of the overseas trade between Europe and Asia at the time was controlled by Amsterdam alone.[8] The city's position in trade between Holland and northern Europe was equally impressive, and in fact even more important for the local economy.[9]

The expansion of the commercial, and most dynamic, sector of the economy in turn had a major effect on other sectors. Some benefitted from the importation of new raw materials. The first sugar refinery was established in Amsterdam in the 1570s; by 1600 there were fifteen, and by 1630 around thirty.[10] Others benefitted from the increased demand for goods. The building sector, for example, had to construct homes for the rapidly expanding population.[11] Those same people also had to be fed and clothed. The home and studio that

Rembrandt acquired in 1639, now the Rembrandt House Museum, had been built only thirty years before.

Around 1650, however, the economic current started to shift. The change was imperceptible at first, because business was still booming,[12] but clouds were gathering. In 1652 England launched the first of three naval wars against the Dutch Republic that were designed to curtail Dutch commercial dominance. As a country with little in the way of raw materials, and a small population to boot, the Dutch Republic was vulnerable to such pressure. From 1672 the French also threw in their weight during the Franco-Dutch War, during which the Dutch were forced to spend increasingly large sums of public money on defence. But it is easy to overstate the problems. Even by the end of the eighteenth century, when the "Golden Age" was well and truly over, the Dutch Republic, Holland in particular, was probably still the richest region in the world. But it so happened that Rembrandt lived in Amsterdam precisely during the years when it reached its economic pinnacle.

Social Transformation

The economic boom that Amsterdam experienced during the first half of the seventeenth century was both cause and consequence of an upsurge in immigration. During this period, Amsterdam became a "city of migrants."[13] The marriage registers, which note spouses' places of origin, are not entirely reliable for mapping patterns of migration (not every migrant married in Amsterdam, and some people never married at all), but they do give a reasonably accurate picture, and that picture speaks volumes. Whereas immigration had been dominated in the final decades of the sixteenth century by refugees from Antwerp and other locations in the Spanish Netherlands, it was now the turn of Germans and Scandinavians to flock to Amsterdam. For Germans, the devastating Thirty Years' War (1618–48) provided a strong incentive to move, but the influx of Scandinavians demonstrates that the pull of the Amsterdam labour market was an equally important factor in attracting people to the city.

In the first half of the seventeenth century, almost half (45 per cent) of all those who married in Amsterdam were foreigners, while only a quarter were local. The others came, as Rembrandt did, from elsewhere within the Dutch Republic. First-generation foreign immigrants, in other words, constituted the largest group within Amsterdam's population. Among

27 Gerbrand van den Eeckhout, *Portrait of Isaac Commelin*, 1669. Städel Museum, Frankfurt am Main

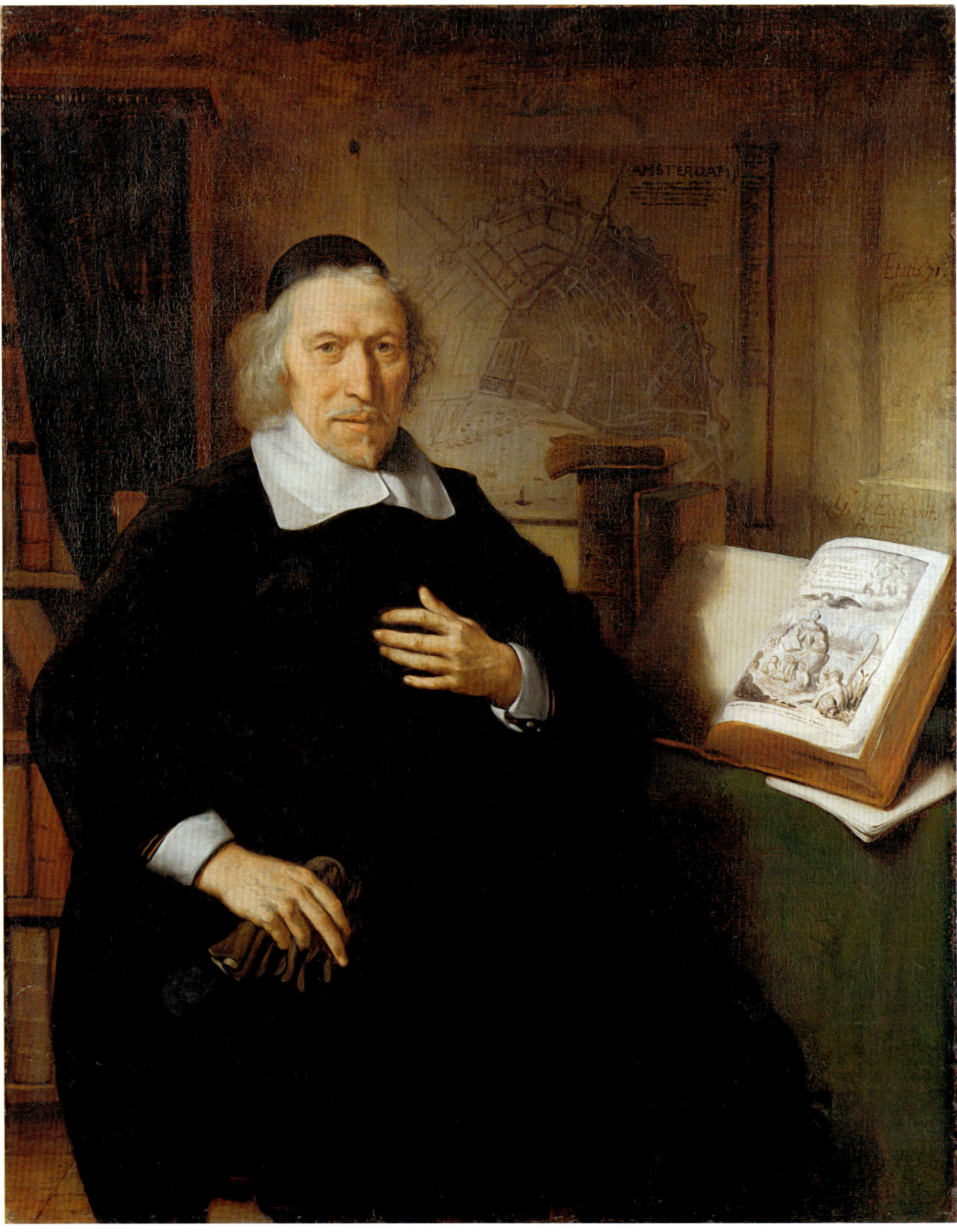

the foreigners, more than half (about 55 per cent) came from Germany, one in ten from Scandinavia, and a similar percentage from the Spanish Netherlands.[14] On top of that, smaller groups arrived from many other European regions.

Among the most noteworthy of the smaller immigrant communities were Jews from Spain and Portugal, a group that was to produce the philosopher Baruch Spinoza as their most famous descendant. Although Spinoza's family were merchants and relatively well off, after a series of setbacks much of the family fortune evaporated, and Spinoza had to make a living grinding lenses.[15] Most immigrants, however, including the majority of Jewish migrants from east-central Europe, had to settle for worse jobs from the very start. Amsterdam's economic boom transformed it from a town of mostly self-employed artisans, shopkeepers and merchants into one of wage-labourers and paupers.[16] Because, just as today, "capital" benefitted more from the economic boom than "labour," inequality increased in the city during the seventeenth century.[17]

This observation sits uncomfortably with the concept of a "Golden Age." How good was life in seventeenth-century Amsterdam for the majority of its inhabitants? There is no doubt that wages rose, and possibly doubled between 1585 and 1660. However, the cost of living went up as well. The average rent in Amsterdam around 1660 was on the order of six times higher than it had been in 1585. Luckily, the cost of food did not increase as much, so wages divided by the cost of living (the so-called real wage) still rose over these same decades, but only by about 10 per cent. As a result, and because Amsterdam had a relatively generous system of poor relief and offered numerous job opportunities, it remained an attractive destination for migrant workers.[18]

There is strong evidence that the top tier of urban society, comprising the wealthiest Amsterdammers, was growing and becoming wealthier still.[19] These were Rembrandt's customers, so they deserve our attention.[20] Traditionally, Amsterdam's elite consisted primarily of merchants, specialized in overseas trade. As we saw, the opportunities in that area had expanded rapidly in the decades around 1600. At the same time, the ranks of the Amsterdam merchant class were swollen by the arrival of immigrants, most notably from the Spanish Netherlands and Iberia. We have no proper way of counting the number of these families, but there must have been hundreds of them. They also

became more visible. During the 1610s, Amsterdam had expanded its enclosed territory on the western side to accommodate the many new arrivals. Specific areas had been created for the rich, notably what would turn out to be the first phase of the now famous canal zone. The canals themselves allowed merchants, who usually conducted business from their homes, to receive goods delivered to their doors by boat.[21] The zoning regulations required owners of plots along the canals to build substantial houses, while at the same time industrial activities were banned.[22] Amsterdam's canal zone became part of an urban landscape that was celebrated in several local histories, as well as in presentation maps that people used to adorn their homes (pls. 27–29). Rembrandt did not buy a property on one of the canals, but rather settled in a large house in a neighbourhood that was already home to many other artists.[23]

Political Revolution

Traditionally, merchant families dominated Amsterdam's local government, which consisted of a council of thirty-six, representing the community as a whole but recruited through co-optation and with membership for life. Seven aldermen, who were usually selected from the councillors, and four burgomasters, who usually were not, took care of day-to-day business. The aldermen and burgomasters sat for one or at most two years and then had to step down, but could return to office after a year, and often would.[24] The independence of the Dutch Republic cast local politics into a completely new role. Amsterdam was represented, together with seventeen other towns and the hereditary nobility, in the States of Holland. The States of Holland, in turn, represented one of the provinces that made up the States-General – in effect, the government of the Dutch Republic. On paper, Amsterdam was one of more than fifty towns that participated in the governing of this new state, but since Holland was more populous and wealthier than all the other provinces combined, and since Amsterdam was by far the largest and richest town in Holland, it carried greater responsibilities than any of the other towns. It arguably had more influence than any of them. However, the Dutch Republic had no official capital city, and as Amsterdam had joined the Dutch Revolt at a relatively late point in time, there was no way the other towns would allow Amsterdam a formal position

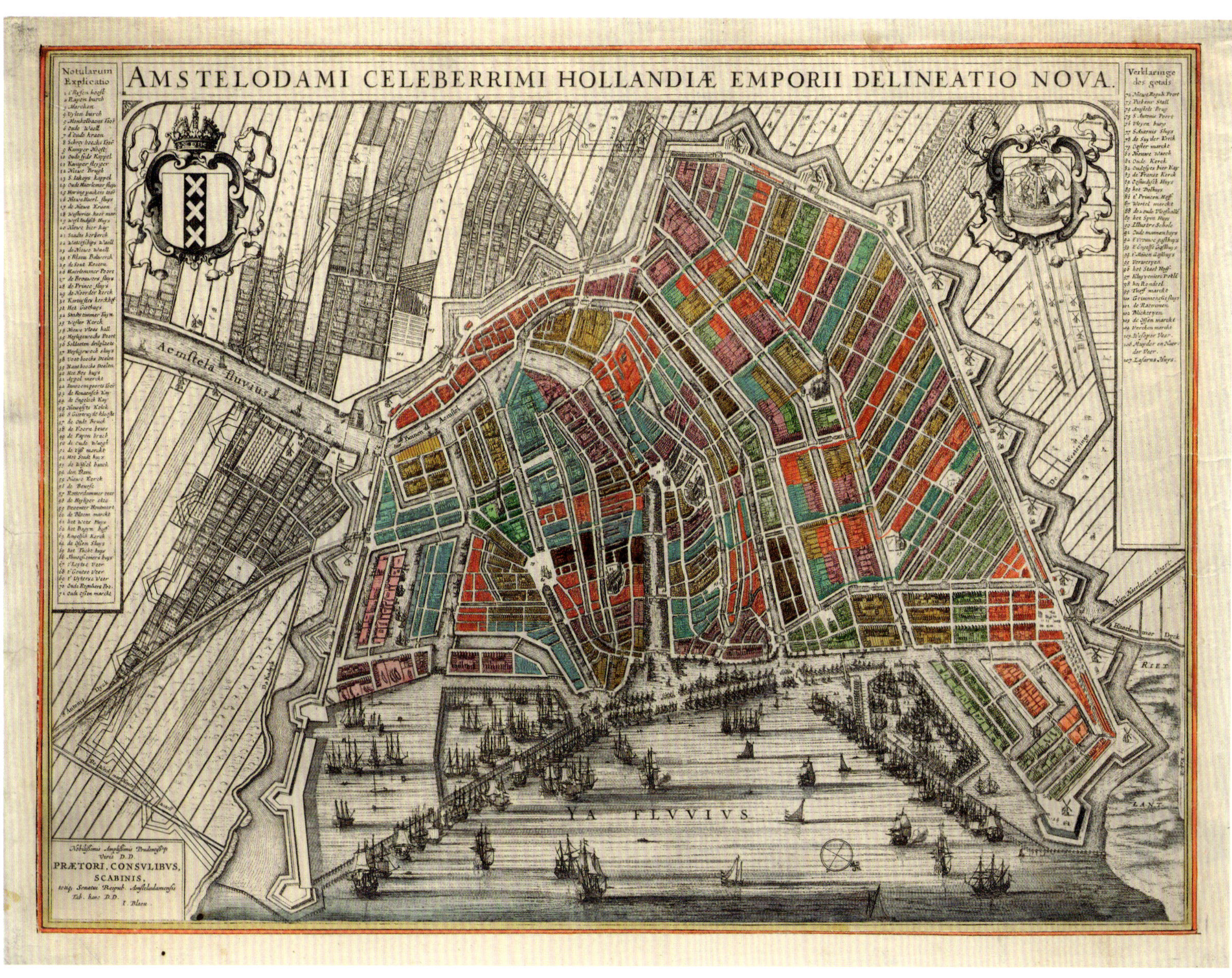
AMSTELODAMI CELEBERRIMI HOLLANDIÆ EMPORII DELINEATIO NOVA.
Aemstela Fluvius
YA FLUVIUS

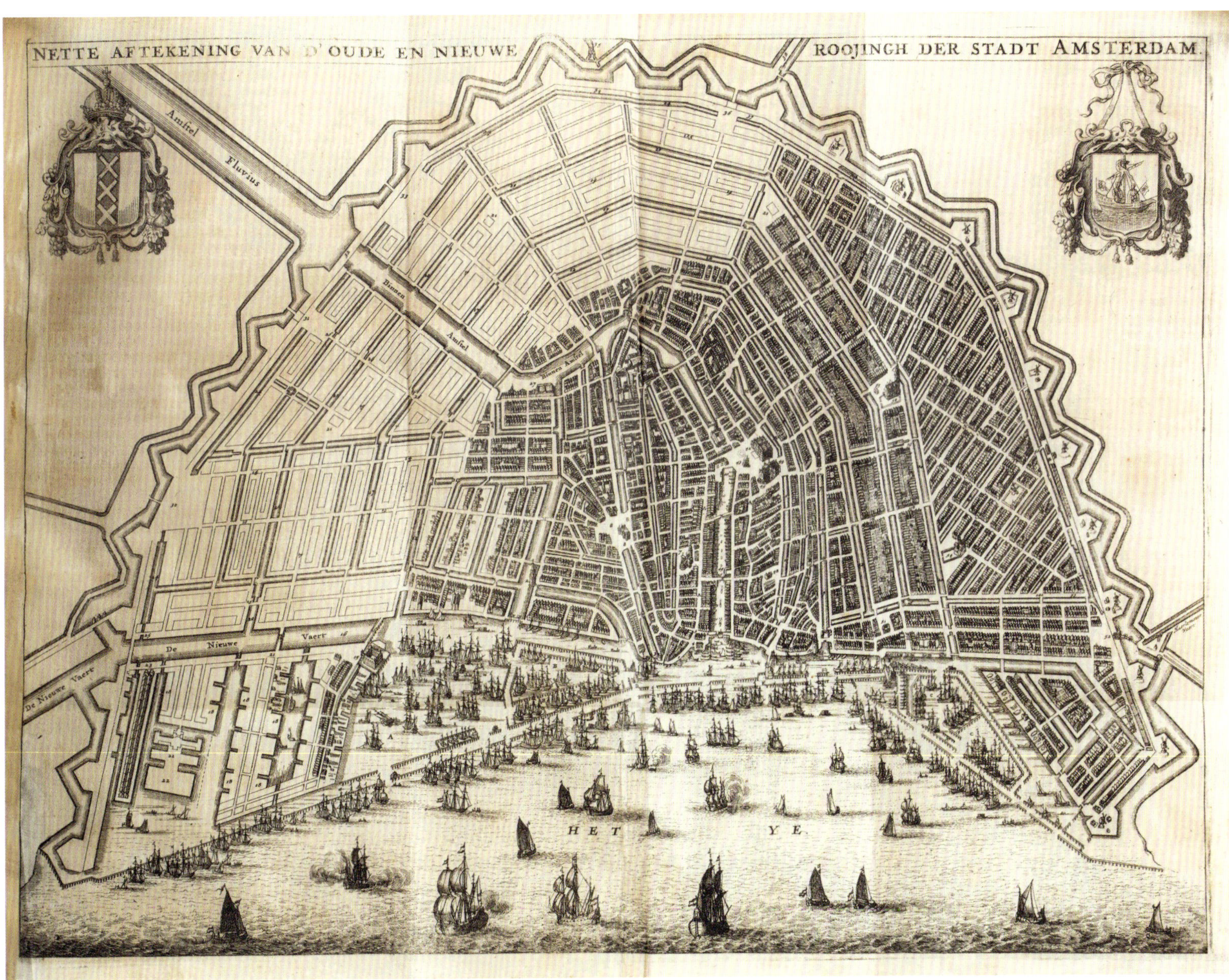
NETTE AFTEKENING VAN D'OUDE EN NIEUWE   ROOJINGH DER STADT AMSTERDAM.
Amstel
Fluvius
Binnen
Amstel
De Nieuwe Vaert
De Nieuwe Vaert
HET   Y E.

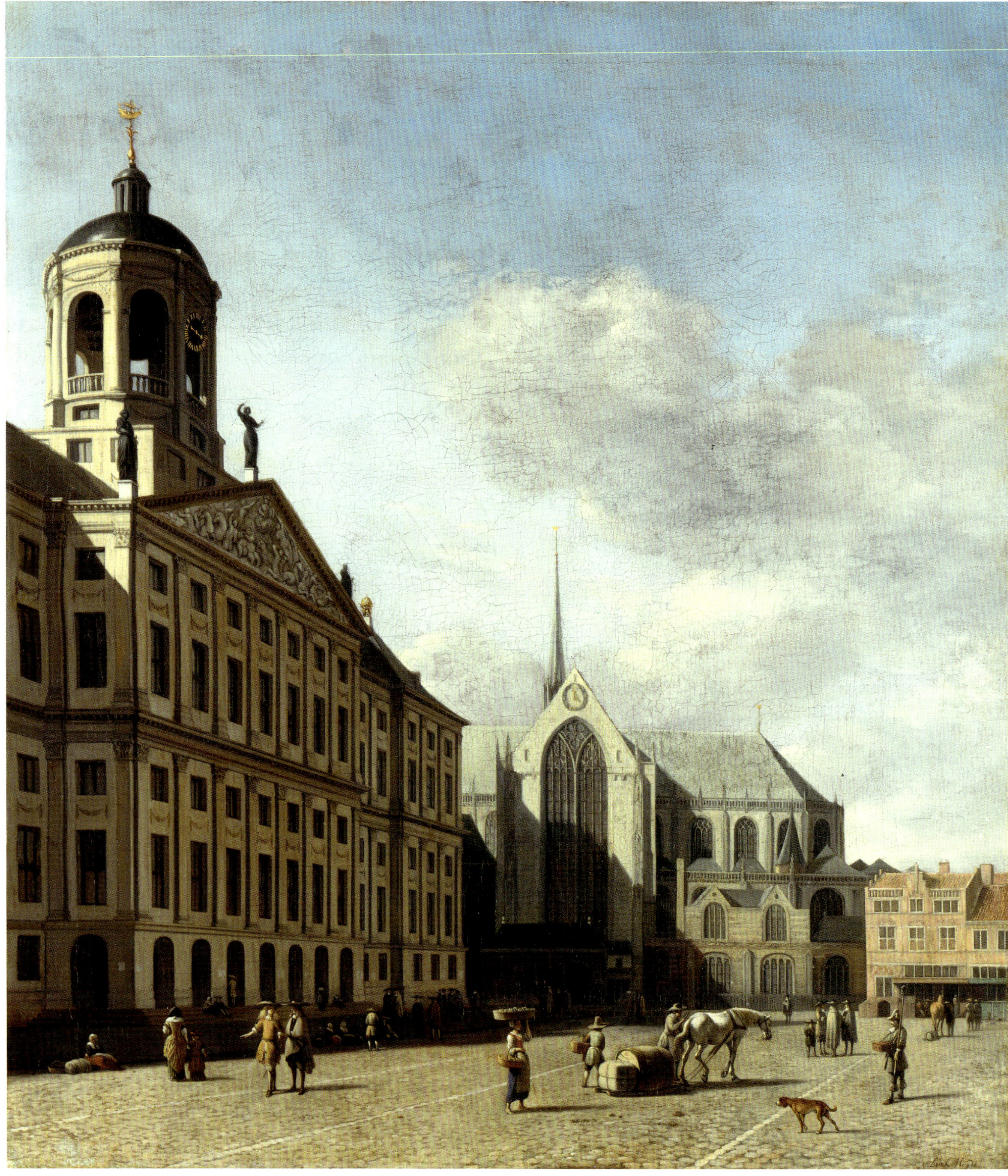

30 Gerrit Adriaensz Berckheyde, *The Town Hall in Amsterdam*, c. 1674. Städel Museum, Frankfurt am Main

to match its influence. Instead, the institutions of government would remain where they always had been, in The Hague, home of the stadtholder's court, which technically was not even a town and hence not represented in the States assembly.[25]

Behind the scenes, and at times also in the forefront, Amsterdam's power was significant, but the way the Dutch Republic was organized ensured that it could be balanced by coalitions of other towns, just as Holland was faced in the States-General by coalitions of the other provinces. During the 1630s and 1640s, Dutch politics was torn apart by the question of whether to continue with war or negotiate peace with Spain. Three provinces were in favour of peace; three others favoured war. Holland was divided: Amsterdam preferred peace, but enough other towns wanted to continue fighting, which they reckoned to be beneficial to their economies, to create a stalemate.[26]

The fact that Amsterdam's formal position did not match its real punch, or indeed its self-image, may go a long way toward explaining the building of the grand town hall (now the Royal Palace) on Dam Square, replacing the antiquated structure that burned down in 1652 (pls. 14, 30, see fig. 1.15). The actual construction of what was to become the largest public building erected in seventeenth-century Europe was launched in 1648. The lavishly decorated interior of the town hall celebrated at once Amsterdam's global economic reach and the wisdom of its governors.[27] Rembrandt was commissioned to contribute to the interior decoration, but the painting he made, *The Conspiracy of the Batavians under Claudius Civilis* (see fig. 9.3), was removed in 1662, only months after its completion, for reasons that remain shrouded in mystery. His former students Ferdinand Bol and Govert Flinck fared better (pls. 94, 95).

The town hall was first and foremost a celebration of Amsterdam's success in previous decades, but it could also be taken as the symbol of a new type of society. None of Amsterdam's politicians were portrayed individually inside the building. Rather, the virtues of collective civic identity were on display there – and on a monumental scale. Whereas in other European societies of the time the aristocracy was in charge, the Dutch Republic had become a society dominated by its bourgeoisie.[28] For Rembrandt's studio, the patronage of the political class had always been an issue, and this may have been a factor in the removal of his work from the town hall.[29]

Creative Explosion

The Dutch Republic was itself the product of a revolution, but its economic and social transformations in turn engendered another revolution, this time in consumption and taste. This revolution also deeply affected the creative industries, including the visual arts.[30] Historians have been discussing the idea of a "consumer revolution" for some time now. The concept was initially developed in relation to the Industrial Revolution in eighteenth-century England, with Josiah Wedgwood's ceramics as a prime example. More recently, however, sixteenth-century Antwerp and seventeenth-century Holland have been pinpointed as the cradles of modern consumerism.[31] In both locations, new products fuelled a new demand for "populuxe goods."[32] In Amsterdam, sugar refineries were established around 1600, supplied by cane sugar imported from the New World. As soon as the VOC started trading in 1602, it imported not only pepper and other spices, but also silk and porcelain, two products from Asia that became hugely popular in seventeenth-century Holland.[33] Later in the century, tea and coffee started to make an appearance in Amsterdam homes.[34] Rembrandt is known to have made more than twenty drawings after Indian Mughal miniatures that may have been in his private collection (fig. 2.1).[35] In addition, a number of his works depict figures that were possibly inspired by Black people he observed in his own surroundings (fig. 2.2).[36]

These developments took place throughout Holland, and to a lesser extent in the rest of the Dutch Republic. Amsterdam, however, was in many ways the eye of this cultural storm. This was all the more remarkable because statistics suggest that the city had been little more than a cultural wasteland until the late sixteenth century. Among its already substantial population, Amsterdam counted merely two booksellers in 1570, five in 1585. Of the 136 painters in the city whose activities were recorded between 1580 and 1609, only eighteen were locals, whereas ninety-nine were identified as immigrants.[37] The number of painters rapidly increased, as did booksellers, who were usually also publishers. By 1610 Amsterdam had thirty-four booksellers; by the middle of the seventeenth century there were well over one hundred. By this time, Holland, and Amsterdam in particular, had become the "bookshop of the world."[38]

A dramatic expansion happened in the painting industry. The word "industry" is used deliberately here, because painting developed on a truly industrial scale in Holland during the seventeenth century. The American economist-turned-art-historian John Michael Montias estimated that by the middle of the century some 650 to 750 painters were active in the Dutch Republic, which at the time had a population of about 1.5 million people. Of these painters, Montias estimated that 175 worked in Amsterdam. New data suggest that, in fact, Amsterdam painters numbered on the order of 250 around 1650, and this would grow to well over 300 by the late 1660s.[39] These statistics imply that during the middle decades of the seventeenth century there was one painter active in Amsterdam for every 650 to 700 inhabitants. Rembrandt was, in other words, surrounded by a small army of colleagues and competitors.[40]

Mass markets emerged in several cultural areas simultaneously, but most spectacularly in publishing and the visual arts. To some extent these two overlapped, most obviously in book illustrations and prints. In these trades, significant innovations can be directly related to the new possibilities offered by

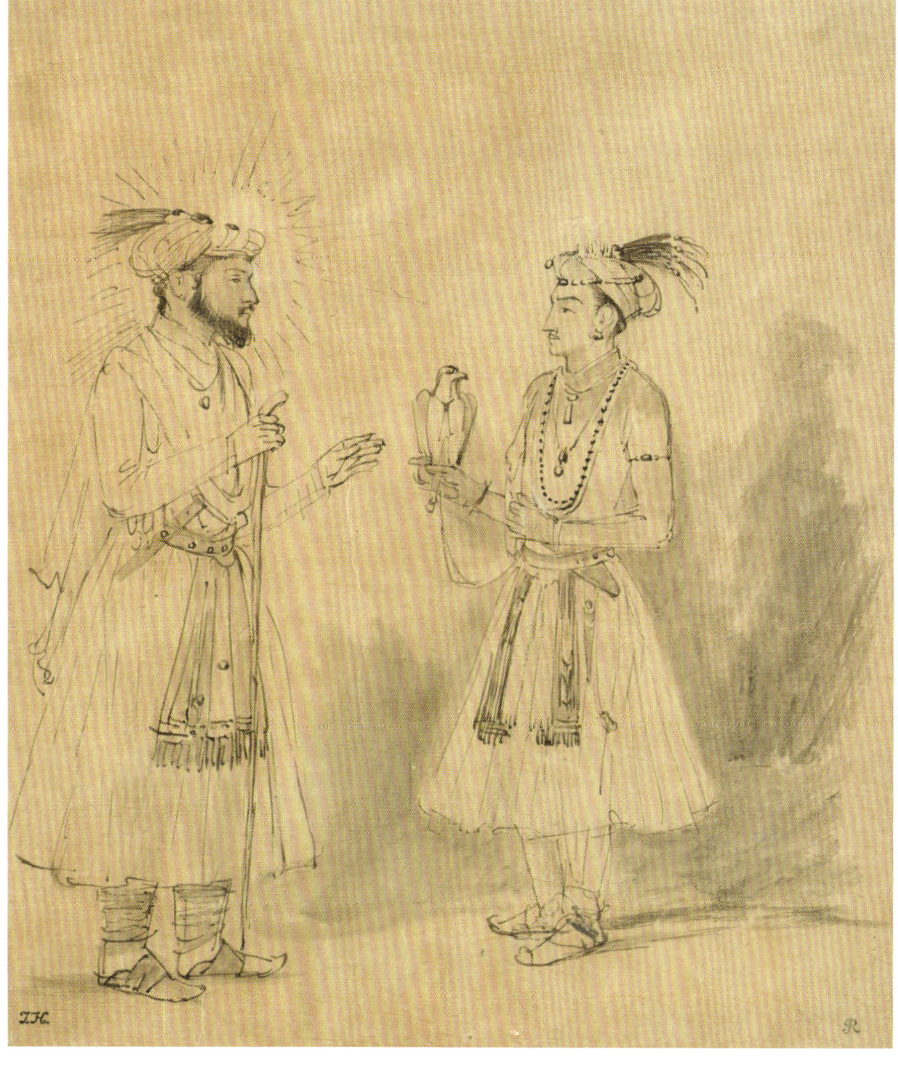

fig. 2.1 **Rembrandt van Rijn,** *Shah Jahan and Dara Shikoh*, **c. 1656–61, pen and brown ink with wash and white bodycolour on Asian paper; 21.3 × 17.8 cm. The J. Paul Getty Museum, Los Angeles (85.GA.44)**

the rapidly expanding customer base, but also to the specific requirements set by a mass market.

In publishing, those innovations covered a spectrum extending from book design to content to entirely new forms of communication. A spectacular example of the latter was the rise of the newspaper in Amsterdam during the 1620s. The regular publication of news items had originated in Germany shortly after 1600. The earliest news bulletins were published as pamphlets, which were relatively expensive and short-lived. Two publishers in Amsterdam developed the modern newspaper, consisting of large sheets of paper – initially just a single sheet – densely printed in columns. As a centre of trade, Amsterdam was bustling with news. Because these newspapers were cheaper than pamphlets they reached a larger audience than earlier news outlets and managed to stay in business. Amsterdam became the capital of news. Other publishers in the city developed small-format books that could be carried in one's pocket, and commissioned new fonts that would be easier to read in small print.[41]

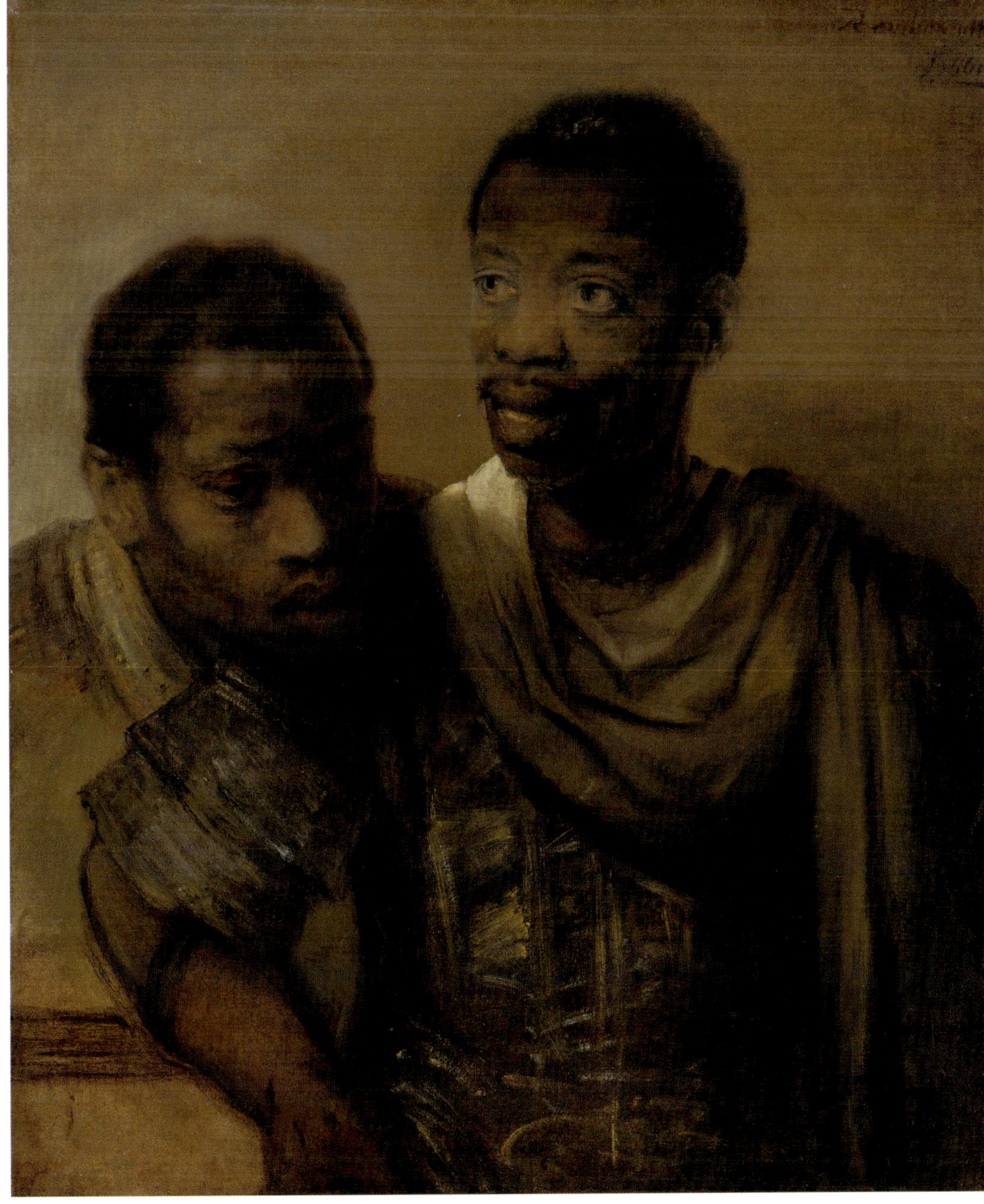

fig. 2.2 **Rembrandt van Rijn,** *Two African Men*, **1661, oil on canvas; 77.8 × 64.4 cm. Mauritshuis, The Hague (685)**

Similar innovations took place in the visual arts. Publishers and printmakers developed novel ways of capturing the world on paper. One notable area of innovation was related to overseas trade. Map-making was still in its infancy around 1600, but Amsterdam booksellers such as Cornelis Claesz and Johannes Janssonius acquired copper plates from Antwerp's famous map pioneer Gerardus Mercator that allowed them to launch a profitable business in increasingly accurate maps and globes.[42] Rembrandt himself developed a newly refined etching technique, which produced more subtle shades between light and dark. He also increased his market by selling multiple states of his designs.[43]

In painting, artists began developing techniques to reduce the time required to produce a saleable work. Famously, François van Knibbergen, Jan Porcellis and Jan van Goyen competed to see who could produce the best painting in a single day.[44] As a result, the range of prices became so broad that paintings were affordable to several social classes. Foreign travellers remarked on the wide distribution of paintings. Meanwhile, different topics were introduced, while others that had been pioneered in Antwerp were developed in new directions. An example of the latter was the "breakfast piece" that Pieter Claesz and Willem Claesz Heda developed as a sub-genre of still-life painting, adopted by Amsterdam artists such as Jan Jansz den Uyl (fig. 2.3). Porcellis created more realistic seascapes, while Van Goyen, Salomon van Ruysdael and Pieter de Molijn, all working in Haarlem (Van Goyen only briefly) did the same for landscape. Again, these developments found their way to Amsterdam. Jacob van Ruisdael moved there from Haarlem around 1656 and painted several views of the city (pl. 31).[45] During the 1620s, Dutch painters experimented with a narrower range of colours, requiring less work to prepare them as well as smaller investments in pigments. Landscape was the single most popular subject for paintings, and several painters who had visited Italy developed an Italianate style of landscape painting that was uniquely Dutch (pl. 134). At the same time, a group of Utrecht painters who had also worked in Italy introduced Caravaggesque compositions to a Dutch audience.[46] Elements of these developments could be found all over Holland, but especially in Amsterdam, which had the largest concentration of painters and the most affluent customers. All of this coincided with the early stages of Rembrandt's career, and much of it influenced him, one way or another.

Rembrandt's work was truly original, but also part of an explosion of creativity and innovation in the Dutch Republic during the first half of the seventeenth century. There is no single explanation for this remarkable phenomenon. An economic historian might point to the confluence of an established tradition of overseas trade, mainly with northern Europe, and the arrival of migrant merchants, especially from Antwerp, with contacts in Mediterranean Europe and beyond. He or she would also mention how

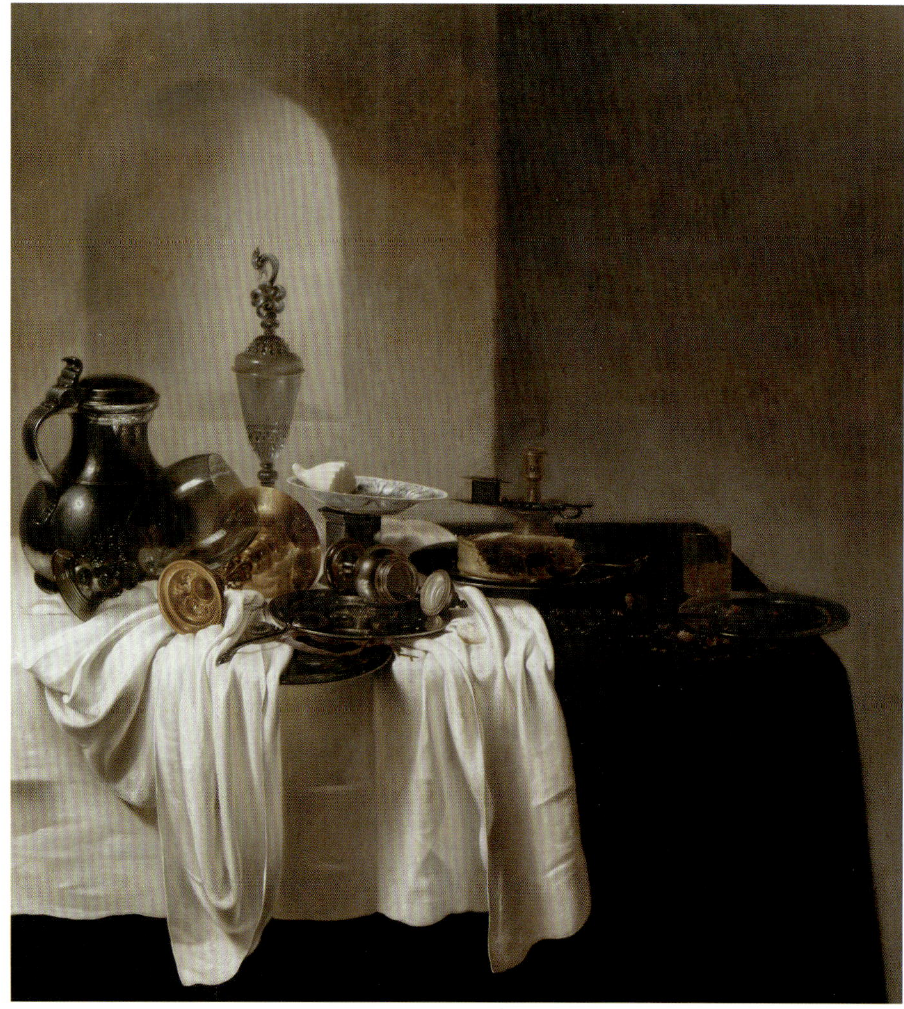

fig. 2.3 **Jan Jansz den Uyl,**
Breakfast Still Life with Glass
***and Metalwork*, c. 1637–39,**
oil on panel; 130.5 × 115.5 cm.
Museum of Fine Arts, Boston.
Anonymous gift (54.1606)

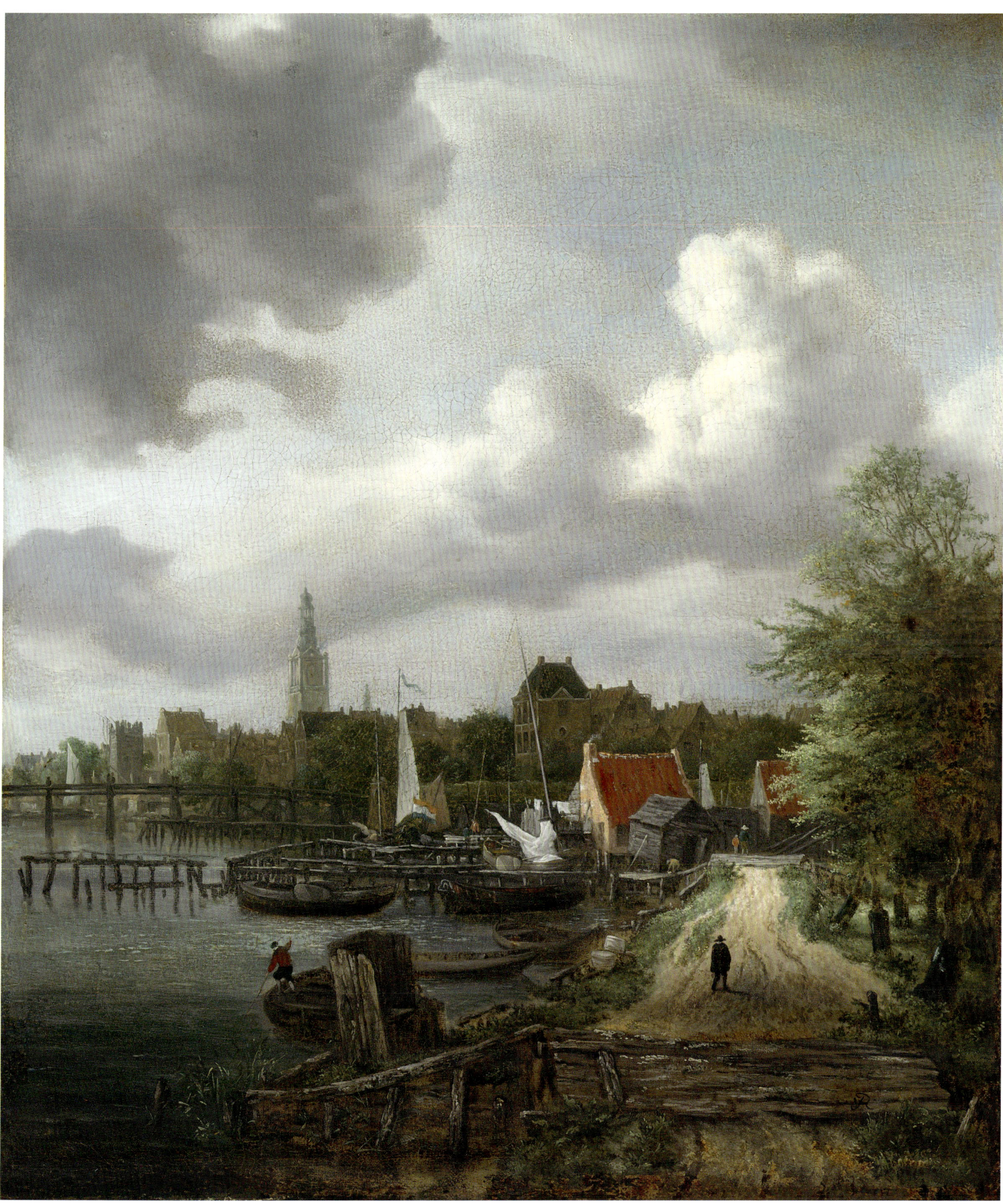

Amsterdam had benefited from the war and the closure of the Scheldt River, which contributed to Antwerp's decline. A social historian would, no doubt, highlight the role of immigrants, who brought new ideas and techniques to Amsterdam and who were so important to the blossoming of the creative industries, and would probably also mention increased purchasing power among the population as a whole. A political historian could point out that this was happening in a newly established country, eager to make its mark. Cultural historians, finally, have highlighted the newly emerging markets for paintings and other material goods. John Michael Montias thought that this helped create a "critical mass" of artists, and hence the likelihood of a genius emerging.[47] Claartje Rasterhoff has added that Holland was blessed with a geography that stimulated creativity through the proximity of rival towns. Competition increased quality, while proximity ensured that new ideas were circulating rapidly.[48]

Taken together, these various explanations suggest that during the first half of the seventeenth century Holland was a place in flux, with many innovations occurring everywhere. At the same time, until its official independence in 1648, the Dutch Republic was still fighting for its survival against the Spanish Habsburgs. In combination, these factors created a fertile environment for experimentation. By the time Rembrandt died in 1669, the mood was becoming, slowly but surely, more conservative. Rembrandt's experiments were going out of fashion. However, for most of his working life, he was able to ride a wave of change and creativity of which he was both an instigator and a beneficiary. ∎

NOTES

1　For a general history of the Netherlands at the time, see Prak 2005.

2　De Zwart and Van Zanden 2018; see also Brook 2008; Parker 2010.

3　Van Tielhof 2002. For a broader discussion of the Dutch economy of the period, see De Vries and Van der Woude 1997.

4　Cited by Clé Lesger, "De wereld als horizon: De economie tussen 1578 en 1650," in Frijhoff and Prak 2004, 103; see also Lesger 2006.

5　Davids 2008, vol. 1, 92–107; see also Jan de Vries, "Connecting Europe and Asia: A Quantitative Analysis of the Cape-route Trade, 1497–1795," in Flynn, Giráldez and Von Glahn 2003, 35–106.

6　't Hart 2014; see also Onnekink and Rommelse 2019.

7　Fatah-Black and Van Rossum 2015, 63–83; Van Rossum 2015, 29–57.

8　De Vries, "Connecting Europe and Asia," in Flynn, Giráldez and Von Glahn 2003, 46, table 2.2.

9　Lesger 2006, chap. 2.

10　Poelwijk 2003, 56.

11　Ad Knotter, "Bouwgolven in Amsterdam in de 17e eeuw," in Klep et al. 1987, 25–37.

12　Israel 1989, chap. 6.

13　Kuijpers 2005; see also Van Lottum 2007; Janssen 2017, 233–252.

14　Kuijpers 2005, 359–360.

15　Nadler 2011.

16　Kuijpers 2005.

17　Soltow and Van Zanden 1998, chaps. 3, 5.

18　De Vries and Van der Woude 1997, chap. 12; Lesger 1986.

19　Zandvliet 2018.

20　For Rembrandt's customers, see Schwartz 2006, chap. 6.

21　It was still common for merchants to have large storage facilities in their homes.

22　Abrahamse 2010, 58–71.

23　Marten Jan Bok, "The Rise of Amsterdam as a Cultural Centre: The Market for Paintings, 1580–1680," in O'Brien et al. 2001, 192.

24　Maarten Hell, "De Oude Geuzen en de Opstand: Politiek en lokaal bestuur in tijd van oorlog en expansie 1578–1650," in Frijhoff and Prak 2004, 242–251.

25　Marjolein 't Hart, "Intercity Rivalries and the Making of the Dutch State," in Tilly and Blockmans 1994, 196–217; see also Price 1994.

26　Israel 1979, 41–69.

27　Fremantle 1959; Goossens 1996.

28　Maarten Prak, "The Dutch Republic as a Bourgeois Society," in Van Berkel and De Goei 2010, 107–138.

29　Bikker 2019, 176.

30　For the concept of "creative industries," see Caves 2000.

31　A recent survey of this revolution in consumption is provided in Trentmann 2016.

32　The term was used by Cissie Fairchilds in "The Production and Marketing of Populuxe Goods in Eighteenth-century Paris," in Brewer and Porter 1993, 228–248.

33　Van Campen and Eliëns 2014; Salem and Amsterdam 2015–16.

34　McCants 2008, 175–176.

35　Salem and Amsterdam 2015–16, 283; Los Angeles 2018.

36　Kolfin 2013, 40–41, 43; Amsterdam 2020.

37　Rasterhoff 2017, 40, 174.

38　Pettegree and Der Weduwen 2019.

39　Montias 1990, 59–74; recent data from the ECARTICO database: www.vondel.humanities.uva.nl/ecartico/analysis/?task=numberssvg (accessed 20 Aug. 2019).

40　On his competitors, see Sluijter 2015.

41　Pettegree and Der Weduwen 2019, chap. 3; Rasterhoff 2017, 69–72, 75–78.

42　Pettegree and Der Weduwen 2019, chap. 4; Zandvliet 2002.

43　Erik Hinterding, "'The Incomparable *Reinbrand*:' Rembrandt als onafhankelijk prentmaker in 17de-eeuws Amsterdam," in Amsterdam 2011, 165–199.

44　Montias 1987, 460.

45　Norbert E. Middelkoop in Budapest 2014–15, no. 144.

46　Rasterhoff 2017, 196–202.

47　Montias 1987, 455–456.

48　Rasterhoff 2017, 292–294.

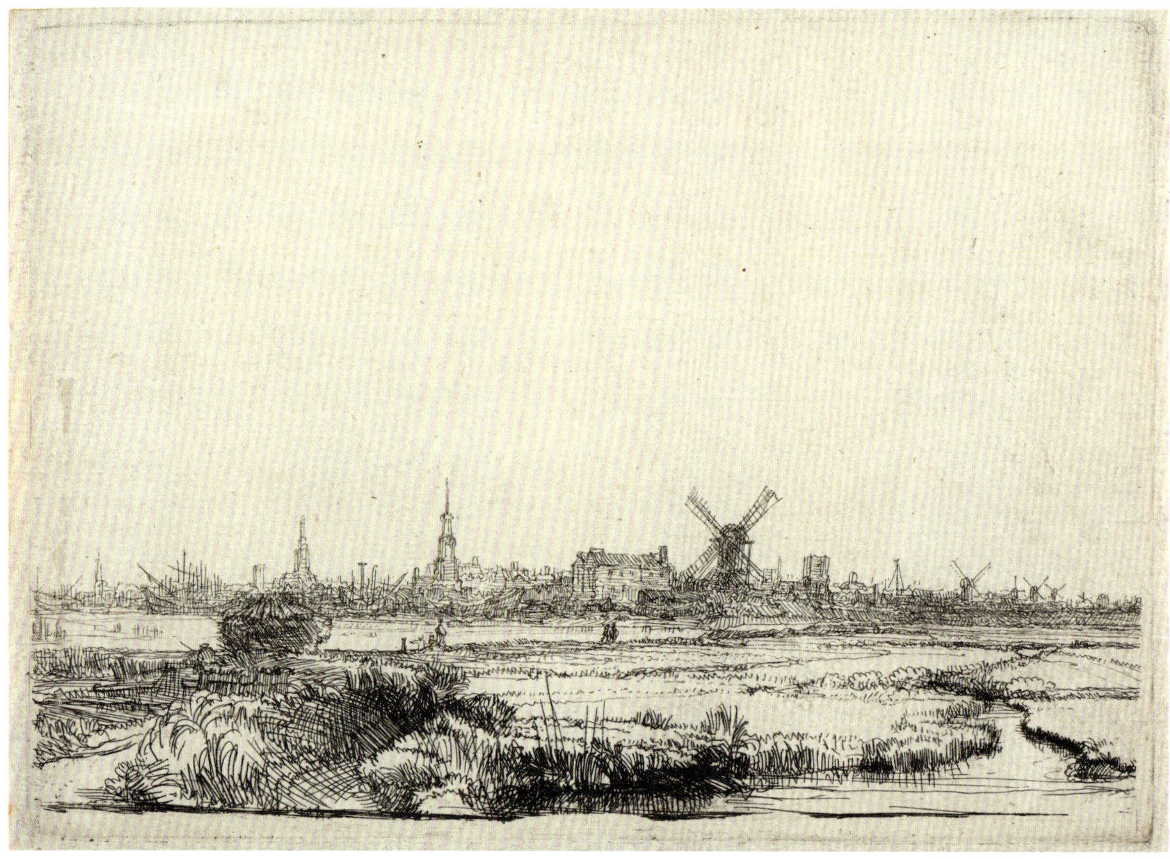

32 Rembrandt van Rijn, *View of Amsterdam Seen from the Kadijk, from the Northeast*, c. 1641. Städel Museum, Frankfurt am Main

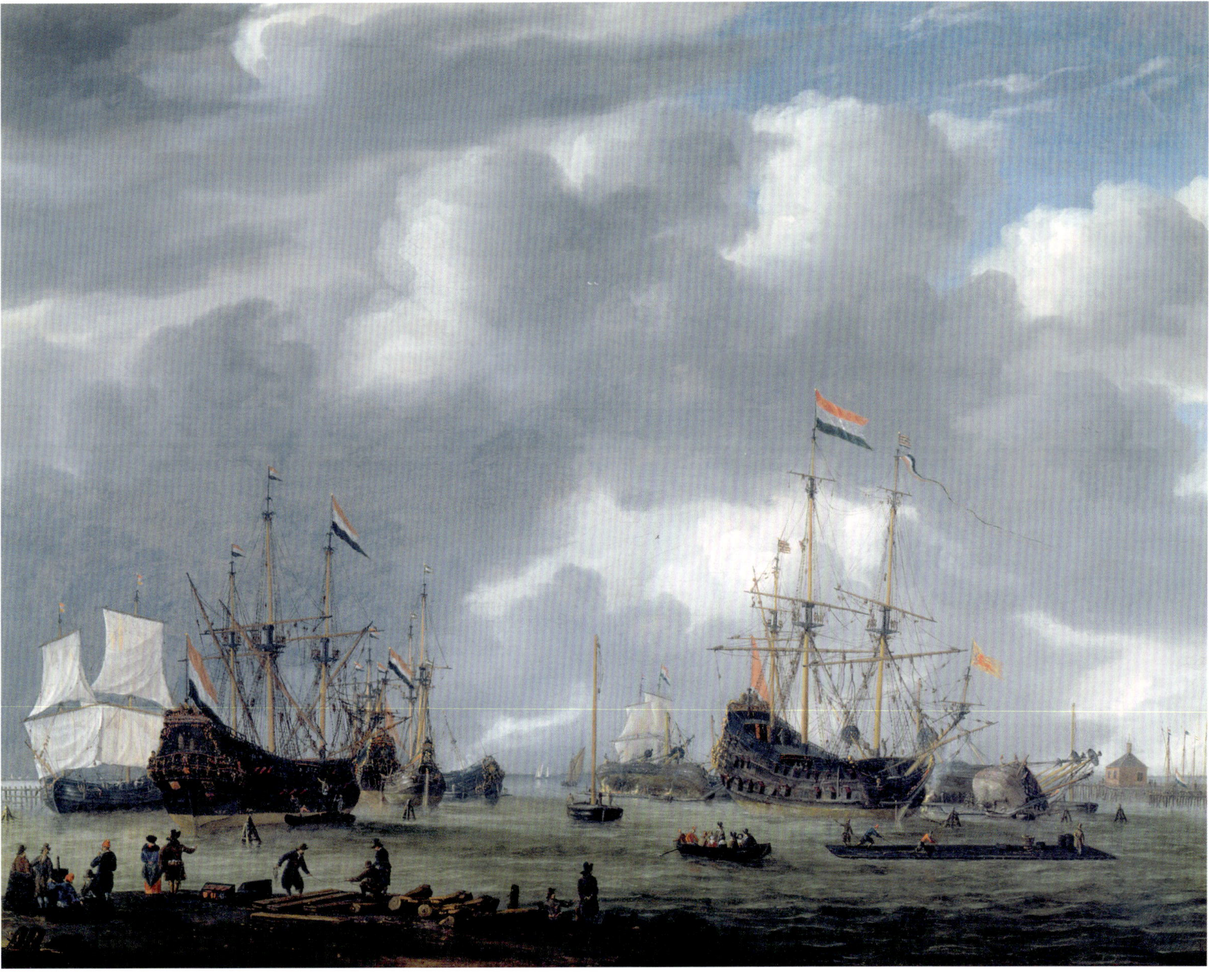

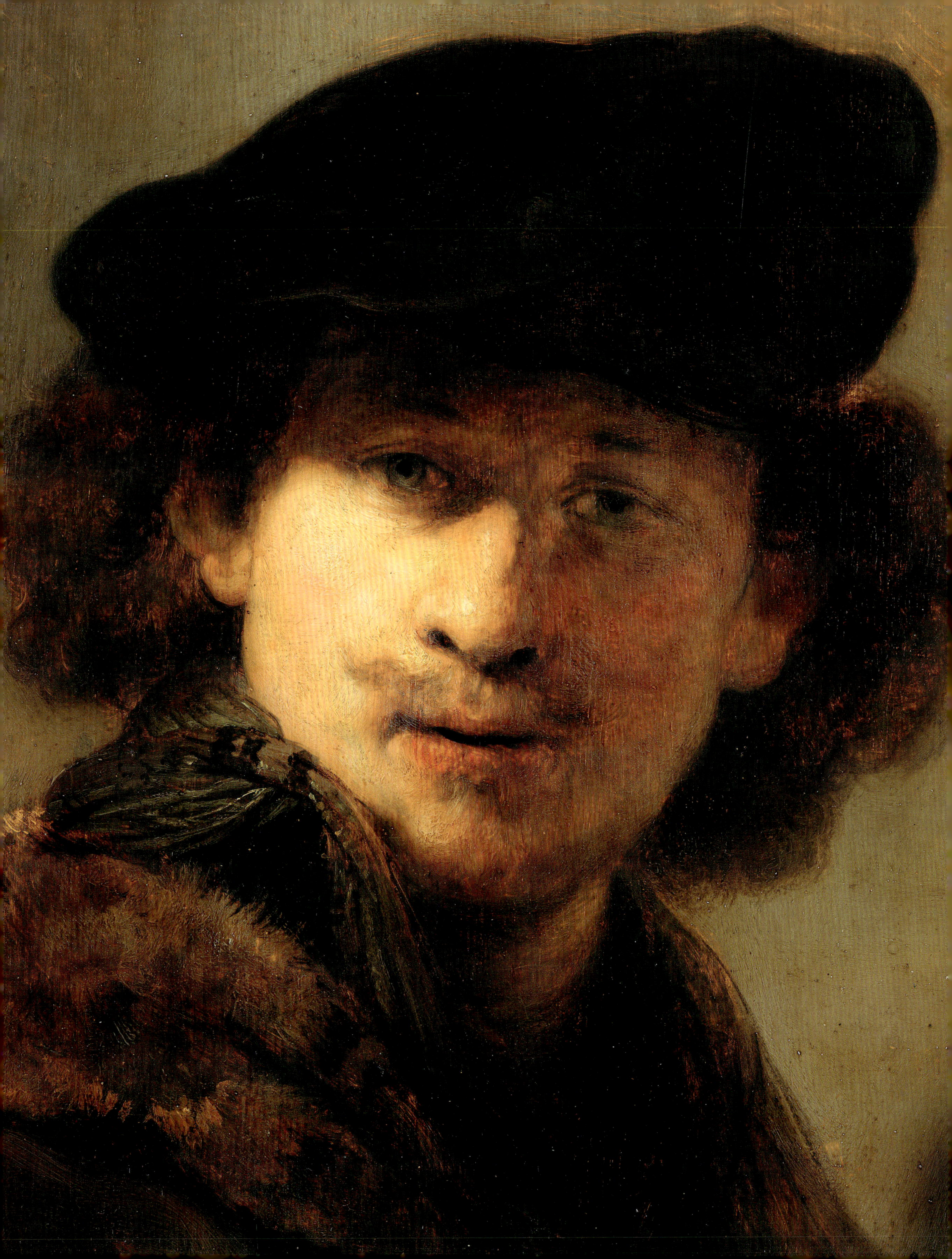

JOCHEN SANDER

Rembrandt as a Brand

"Rembrandt": the name is an internationally renowned trademark, and the works of this artist are among the "blue chips" of the art market. Recently, the Netherlands and France jointly purchased from the Rothschild collection the pendant portraits of Marten Soolmans and Oopjen Coppit painted by Rembrandt in 1634 (figs. 3.1, 3.2).[1] It remains uncertain whether this joint acquisition was driven by the record price for the two paintings or the prestige of the two national collections – the Rijksmuseum, Amsterdam, and the Musée du Louvre, Paris – each of which would probably have liked to be the sole owner of both works.

Of course, the name "Rembrandt" as a trademark is no recent phenomenon. It was the artist himself who took the decisive step, soon after his arrival in Amsterdam, to establish his brand by abandoning traditional forms of the signature he had used earlier.[2] Around 1624/25 he signed his works with the monogram "RHF" – "Rembrant, son of Harmen, made this" (*Rembrant Harmenszoon fecit*).[3] He briefly experimented with just the first letter of his forename in 1625[4] and the monogram "RH" (Rembrant Harmenszoon) a year later.[5] From 1628 onward he used "RHL" or "RL,"[6] with the "L" for Leiden indicating that his art was now creating a stir well beyond the borders of his native city. In 1632, presumably as he began to spend more time in Amsterdam, the artist briefly signed with "RHL van Rijn" and "Rembrant van Ryn,"[7] but from the end of 1632 he used just his first name, spelling it "Rembrant" (pl. 35),[8] then "Rembrandt" – the form that became his trademark. This was unprecedented for artists in the northern Netherlands.

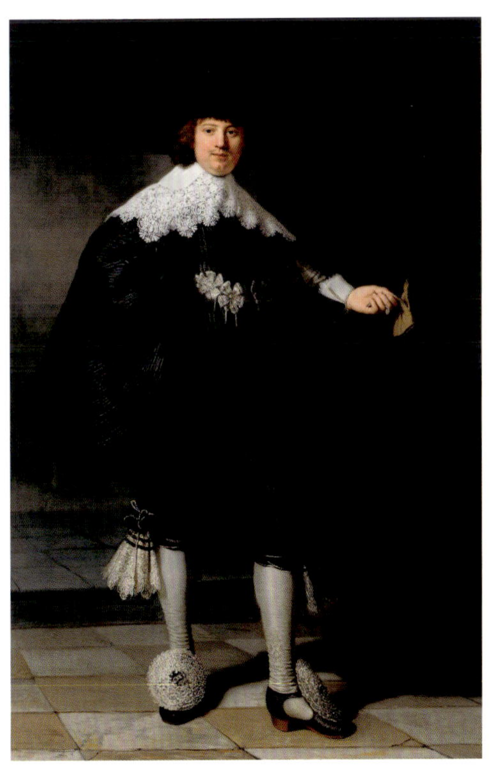

fig. 3.1 **Rembrandt van Rijn,** *Portrait of Marten Soolmans,* 1634, oil on canvas; 207.5 × 132 cm. Rijksmuseum, Amsterdam / Musée du Louvre, Paris. Joint acquisition by the Dutch State and the French Republic (SK-A-5033)

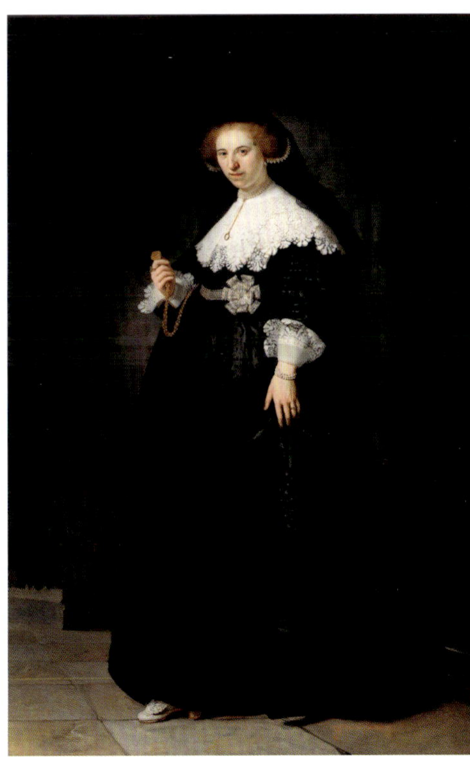

fig. 3.2 **Rembrandt van Rijn,** *Portrait of Oopjen Coppit*, 1634, oil on canvas; 207.5 × 132 cm. Rijksmuseum, Amsterdam / Musée du Louvre, Paris. Joint acquisition by the Dutch State and the French Republic (SK-C-1768)

With this decision to sign his works with his first name, Rembrandt seems to have deliberately adopted a custom that was already being followed by his early patrons and admirers. In 1628 the Amsterdam collector Joan Huydecoper, describing one of the painter's works in his collection, referred to him simply as "Rembrant,"[9] while Constantijn Huygens, the influential secretary of Stadtholder Frederik Hendrik, elevated him to "Rembrantio" in the laudation he wrote in Latin around 1630.[10] This was only possible because the artist's first name was relatively rare – painters called Jan or Pieter would have found their names less easy to market. Rembrandt may have emulated Italian artists, such as "Tiziano" or "Tintoretto," highly esteemed in the Amsterdam art market at the time, who had signed their paintings with their first names, or even more frequently, with their nicknames.[11]

The young Rembrandt had already caught the attention of Frederik Hendrik and his court in The Hague in the late 1620s. By 1632 the stadtholder had acquired several small-format paintings for his collection. In his inventory, some were attributed to Rembrandt, others to Jan Lievens, Rembrandt's friend and colleague in Leiden,[12] but today they are identified as Rembrandt's 1628 *Samson and Delilah* (Gemäldegalerie, Berlin) and his 1631 paintings of Minerva and Proserpina (both Gemäldegalerie, Berlin) and *Simeon's Song of Praise* (Mauritshuis, The Hague).[13] Huygens described the qualities of the pictorial narratives Rembrandt created in Leiden that were admired by connoisseurs at the stadtholder's court. In diary entries written between 1628 and 1630, he records a visit to Rembrandt's workshop. On this occasion he must have seen the artist's painting of the repentant Judas returning the thirty pieces of silver, completed in 1629 (fig. 3.3), which he praised profusely.[14] According to Huygens, whose judgment was undoubtedly coloured by local patriotism, Rembrandt's ability to depict different emotions surpassed not only the Italian masters but also the art of classical antiquity.[15]

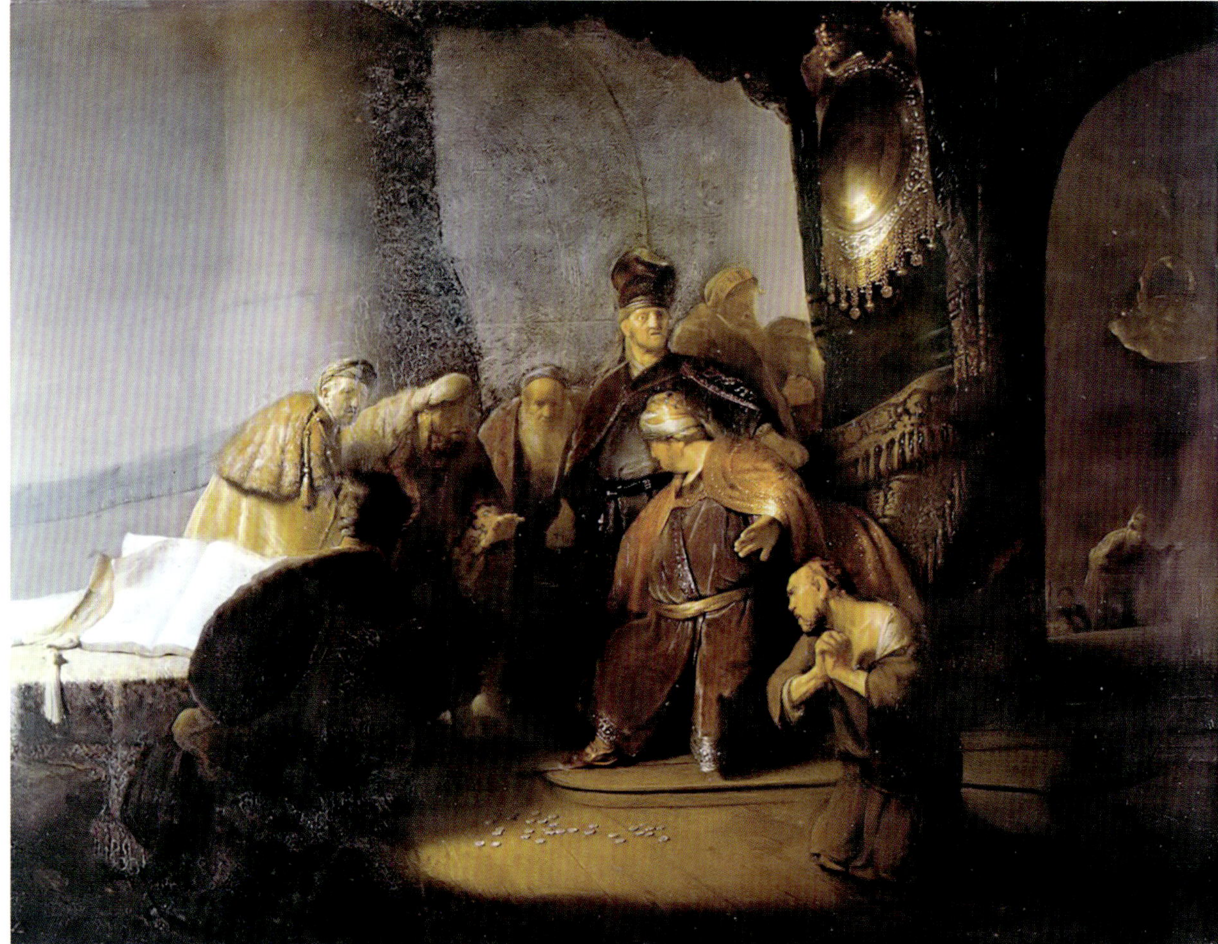

fig. 3.3 **Rembrandt van Rijn,** *Judas Repentant, Returning the Thirty Pieces of Silver,* 1629, oil on panel; 79 × 102.3 cm. **Private collection**

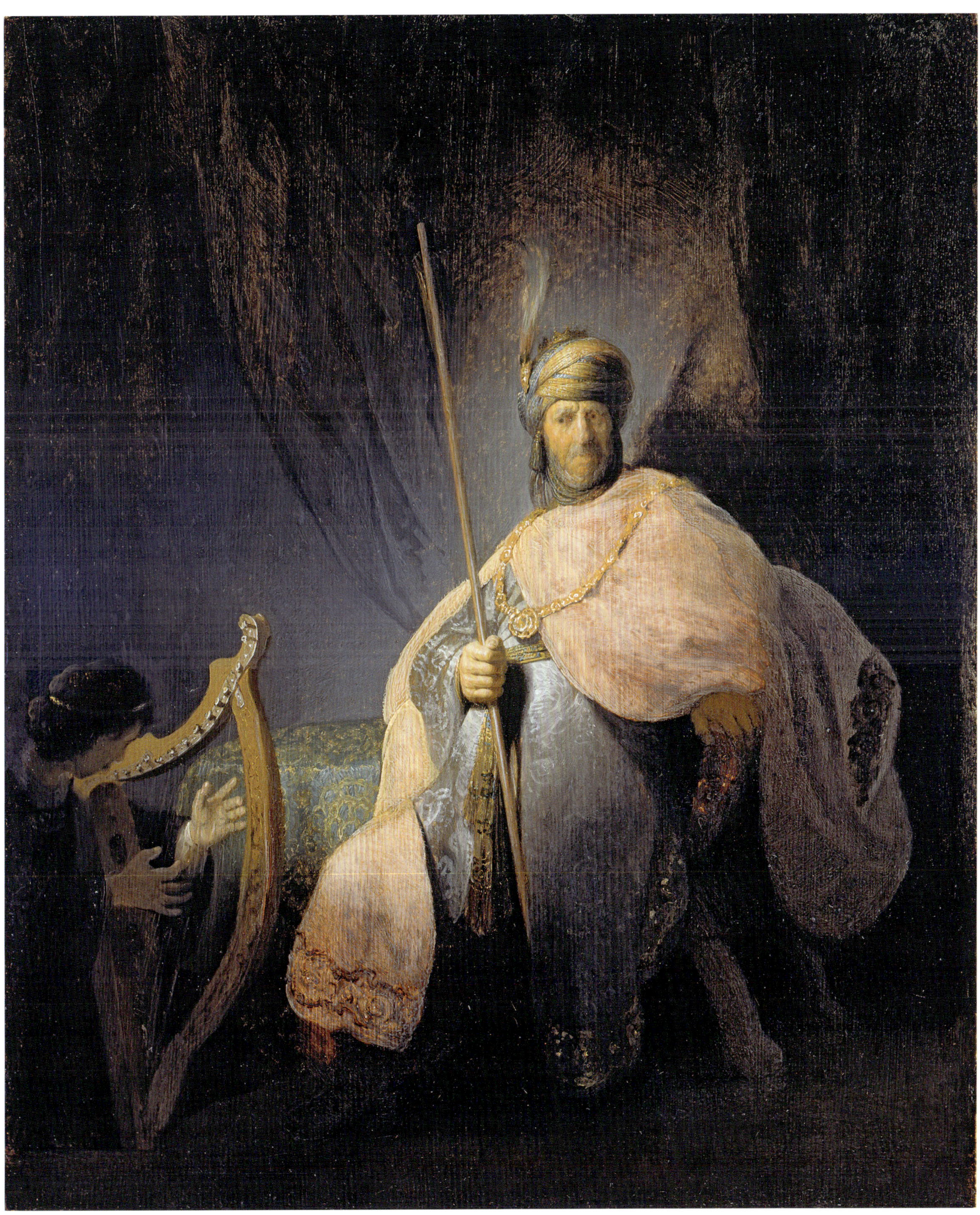

Rembrandt's extraordinary ability to capture the psychology of his figures in all their depth, which the artist is known for to this day, is evident not only in his early work from Leiden but also in the paintings and prints he created in Amsterdam. A comparison of two of Rembrandt's major works, created before and after his relocation, shows how he sharpened his brand profile after moving to the metropolis. *David Playing the Harp for Saul* (pl. 34) was created around 1630–31, while *The Blinding of Samson* (pl. 106) is dated to 1636; thanks to some happy coincidences in the history of collecting, both paintings are today held by the Städel Museum, Frankfurt am Main. If the former is a brooding chamber piece, the latter presents both the viewer and protagonist with agonizing drama on a grand, boldly illuminated stage. In *David Playing the Harp before Saul*, Rembrandt masterfully captures a scene of acute psychological tension, a moment of uncanny calm just before violence erupts, while *The Blinding of Samson* confronts the viewer with the piercing of Samson's eyes, allowing no escape from the story's brutal climax. The faces of the protagonists, especially Delilah, display an astounding variety of emotional reactions to what they see.

With these qualities of directness, dramatic storytelling, realistically rendered details and deft handling of light effects, Rembrandt claimed his place in the Amsterdam art market as a painter of historical subjects: the category held in highest esteem in academic circles. Yet, immediacy and nonchalance, paired with psychological depth, would also become the hallmarks of the many portraits he executed in Amsterdam. The life-size painting of Andries de Graeff in the Gemäldegalerie Alte Meister in Kassel is a good example (pl. 73). When compared with a more traditional work such as Nicolaes Eliasz Pickenoy's *Portrait of a Man* in the Staatliche Kunsthalle Karlsruhe (pl. 72), it makes the latter seem old-fashioned. With these innovations in portraiture, Rembrandt struck a chord with the up-and-coming bourgeois elite of Amsterdam, as shown by the large number of portrait commissions he received in the 1630s and early 1640s.

In the field of portraiture, the success of Rembrandt's branding remained solidly bourgeois. His one attempt to gain a foothold with the stadtholder was unsuccessful. In 1632 he was commissioned to paint a portrait of Frederik Hendrik's wife, Amalia von Solms (pl. 47), to serve as a pendant to an existing portrait of the stadtholder by Gerard van Honthorst (see fig. 6.3).[16] However, it seems that Rembrandt's painting did not meet the court's expectations since it was soon replaced with a new portrait, again by Honthorst, which shows the princess consort in a more idealized, courtly pose (see fig. 6.4). Yet, this setback did no harm to Rembrandt's court patronage as a history painter. In 1633 the stadtholder purchased *The Raising of the Cross* and *The Descent from the Cross* (see figs. 13.3, 13.2), the first works in the Passion series. Between 1636 and 1639, further paintings in the series, depicting the Ascension, Entombment and Resurrection, would follow (see figs. 10.1, 10.2).[17] Rembrandt's self-confident asking price of no less than 1,000 guilders per painting, which he noted in a letter to Huygens,[18] shows how successfully he had promoted his brand, even in court circles, by the end of the 1630s. By then, he was established as the most important artist in the bourgeois society of Amsterdam, a status strengthened by the fact that he was active in all genres (pls. 73, 150).

Throughout his life, Rembrandt seems to have regarded depictions of himself as an effective marketing tool (pls. 35, 41, 42).[19] Already in his Leiden years he showed a keen interest in his own physiognomy. The study of his face – whether in paintings, drawings or prints – allowed him to explore the expression of every possible emotion or mood. To call these representations self-portraits in the conventional sense would be to overlook their iconographic ambiguity, a characteristic they share with the artist's numerous *tronies*,[20] to which he often lent his own features. In many cases – as for example in *Tronie of a Man with a Feathered Beret* (pl. 36) – it is not easy to draw a clear line between study heads or *portraits historiés* and Rembrandt's self-portraits in the proper sense.[21] This play with the viewer's expectations seems to have made a deep impression on Rembrandt's younger collaborators and competitors, some of whom, such as Govert Flinck, portrayed Rembrandt himself in various guises,[22] while others, such as Jacob Backer, Ferdinand Bol and Wallerant Vaillant (pls. 37, 40, 38) delivered their own versions of self-portraits in diverse roles, thus demonstrating the power of the Rembrandt brand. ■

NOTES

1   *Corpus*, vol. 6, no. 120a-b; Manuth, De Winkel and Van Leeuwen 2019, nos. 241–242.

2   See Joshua Bruyn, "A Descriptive Survey of the Signatures," in *Corpus*, vol. 1, 53–59; *Corpus*, vol. 6, 66; Van 't Zelfde 2012; Manuth, De Winkel and Van Leeuwen 2019, 89; Christopher Brown, "The Evolution of Rembrandt's Early Style," in Leiden and Oxford 2019–20, 37–55. Bruyn, "A Descriptive Survey," in *Corpus*, vol. 1, 53, also reproduces four autograph signatures by Rembrandt from archival sources of the early 1630s showing that the artist signed as "Rembrant Harmensz van Rijn" in civil life.

3   See *Corpus*, vol. 6, no. 4; as well as Rembrandt van Rijn, *The Unconscious Patient (Allegory of Smell)* (c. 1624–25, The Leiden Collection, New York); Manuth, De Winkel and Van Leeuwen 2019, no. 120a.

4   See *Corpus*, vol. 6, no. 5.

5   Ibid., nos. 6–14.

6   Ibid., nos. 17–19, 21, 29–31, 37, 39–40, 42–44, 47, 50–52, 55–60, 63a-b, 72 (RHL); nos. 23, 27, 32 (RL).

7   Ibid., nos. 61, 64a-b, 65b, 66–68, 70–71, 73–75, 78–84, 86–87.

8   Ibid., no. 69. See also nos. 53, 76, 77a-b, 85, 88b, 100, 102, 105.

9   See "Joan Huydecoper buys a tronie by Rembrandt," 10/15 June 1628, Remdoc, no. e4385. The same form of name appears in the estate inventory of the Amsterdam painter Barent Teunisz, dated 19 Oct. 1629; see Strauss and Van der Meulen 1979, doc. 1629/1; "A Rembrandt painting in the inventory of Barent Teunisz," 19 Oct. 1629, Remdoc, no. e4387.

10 Huygens 1987, 74–94.

11 Van 't Zelfde 2012; Thijs Weststeijn, "Rembrandt and the Germanic Style," in Dickey 2017b, 44–66, esp. 44–45.

12 "Paintings in the collection of Prince Frederik Hendrik of Orange," 16 Aug. 1632, Remdoc, no. e4400; Strauss and Van der Meulen 1979, doc. 1632/3.

13 *Samson and Delilah* (1628, Gemäldegalerie, Berlin), see *Corpus*, vol. 6, no. 37, and Manuth, De Winkel and Van Leeuwen 2019, no. 5; *Minerva in Her Study* (c. 1631, Gemäldegalerie, Berlin), see *Corpus*, vol. 6, no. 54, and Manuth, De Winkel and Van Leeuwen 2019, no. 95; *The Abduction of Proserpina* (c. 1631, Gemäldegalerie, Berlin), see *Corpus*, vol. 6, no. 49, and Manuth, De Winkel and Van Leeuwen 2019, no. 96; *Simeon's Song of Praise* (1631, Mauritshuis, The Hague), see *Corpus*, vol. 6, no. 47, and Manuth, De Winkel and Van Leeuwen 2019, no. 44.

14 See Manuth, De Winkel and Van Leeuwen 2019, no. 38.

15 Quoted recently in Leiden and Oxford 2019–20, 298, after Huygens 1987, 74–94; see also Sluijter 2014, 66–68.

16 *Corpus*, vol. 6, no. 65a.

17 See *Corpus*, vol. 6, nos. 106–107, 145, 162–163.

18 "The fourth letter to Constantijn Huygens," Jan. 1639, Remdoc, no. e4459, referencing the recently completed *Entombment* and *Resurrection*; Strauss and Van der Meulen 1979, doc. 1639/3.

19 See, for example, Chapman 1990; London and The Hague 1999–2000; *Corpus*, vol. 4.

20 See Hirschfelder 2008; Gottwald 2011.

21 *Corpus*, vol. 6, no. 157.

22 See, for example, Franziska Gottwald, "Tronies in Govert Flinck's Oeuvre: Fantasy Portrayal versus Mimetic Representation," in Cleves 2015–16, 54–61; David de Witt, "Govert Flinck Learns to Paint Like Rembrandt," in Amsterdam 2017–18, 28, fig. 17, 226, no. 5.

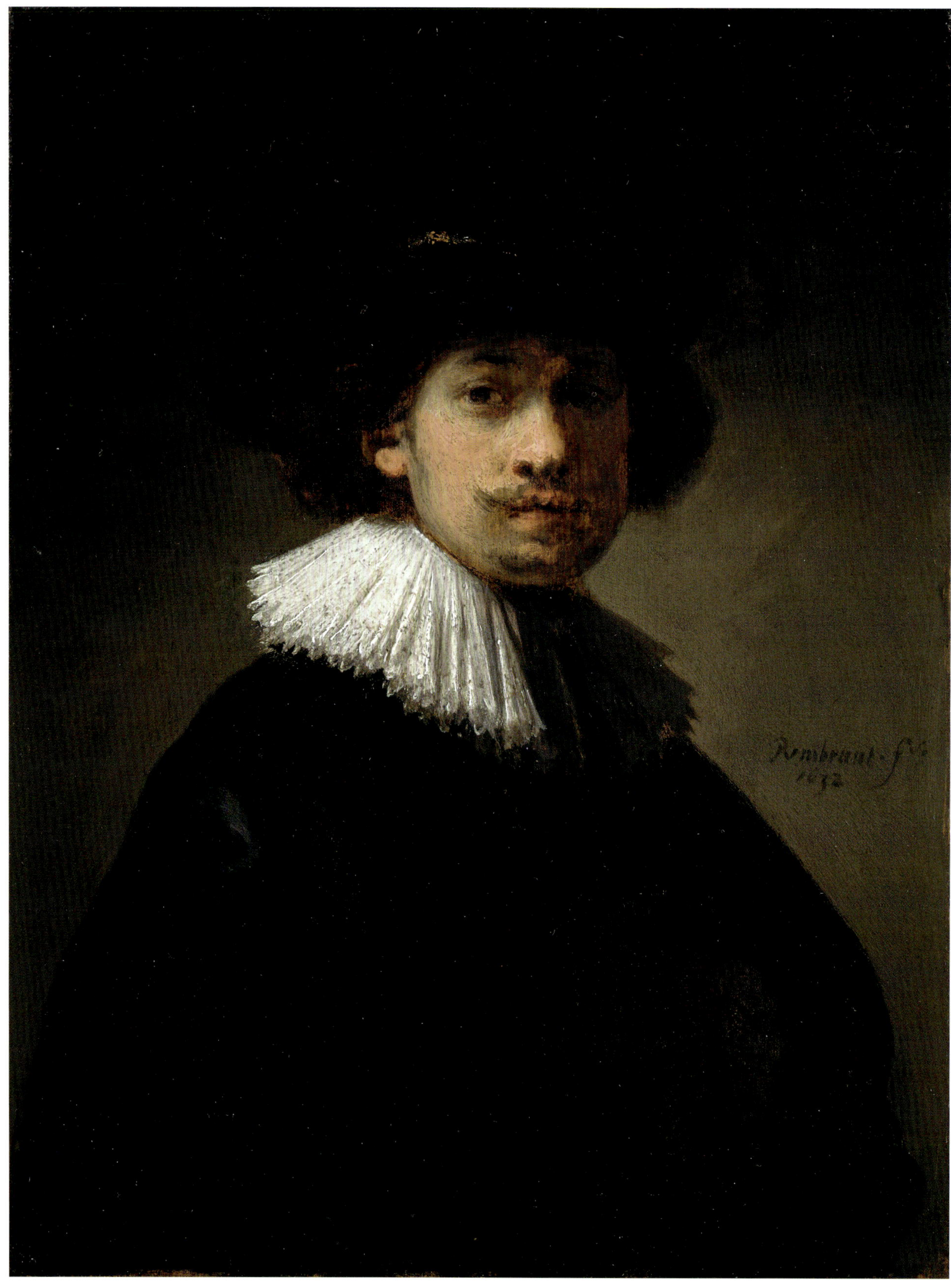

35   Rembrandt van Rijn, *Self-portrait in a Wide-brimmed Hat*, 1632. Private collection

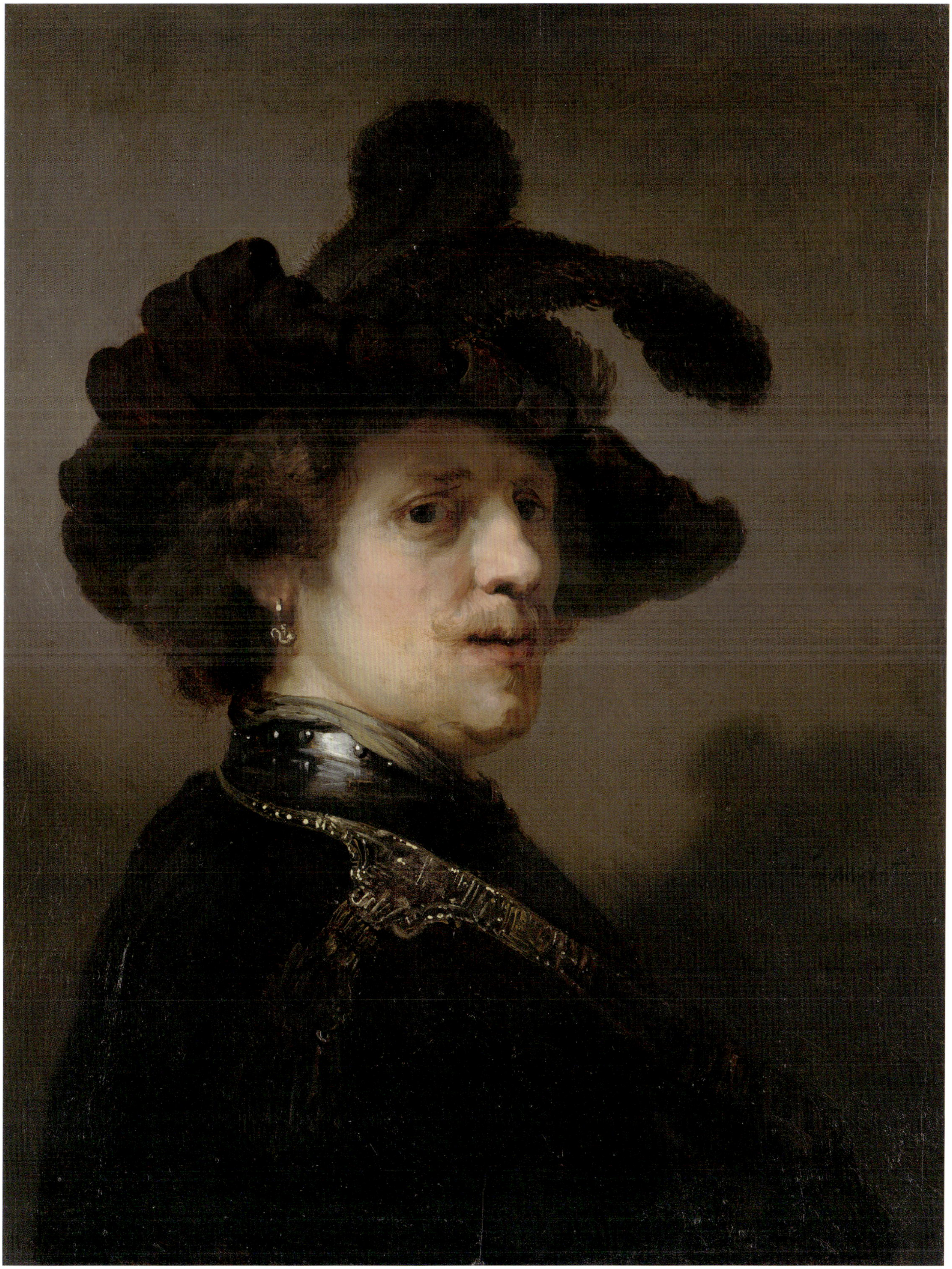

37 Jacob Backer, *The Drinker (Allegory of Taste)*, c. 1634. Staatliche Museen zu Berlin, Gemäldegalerie

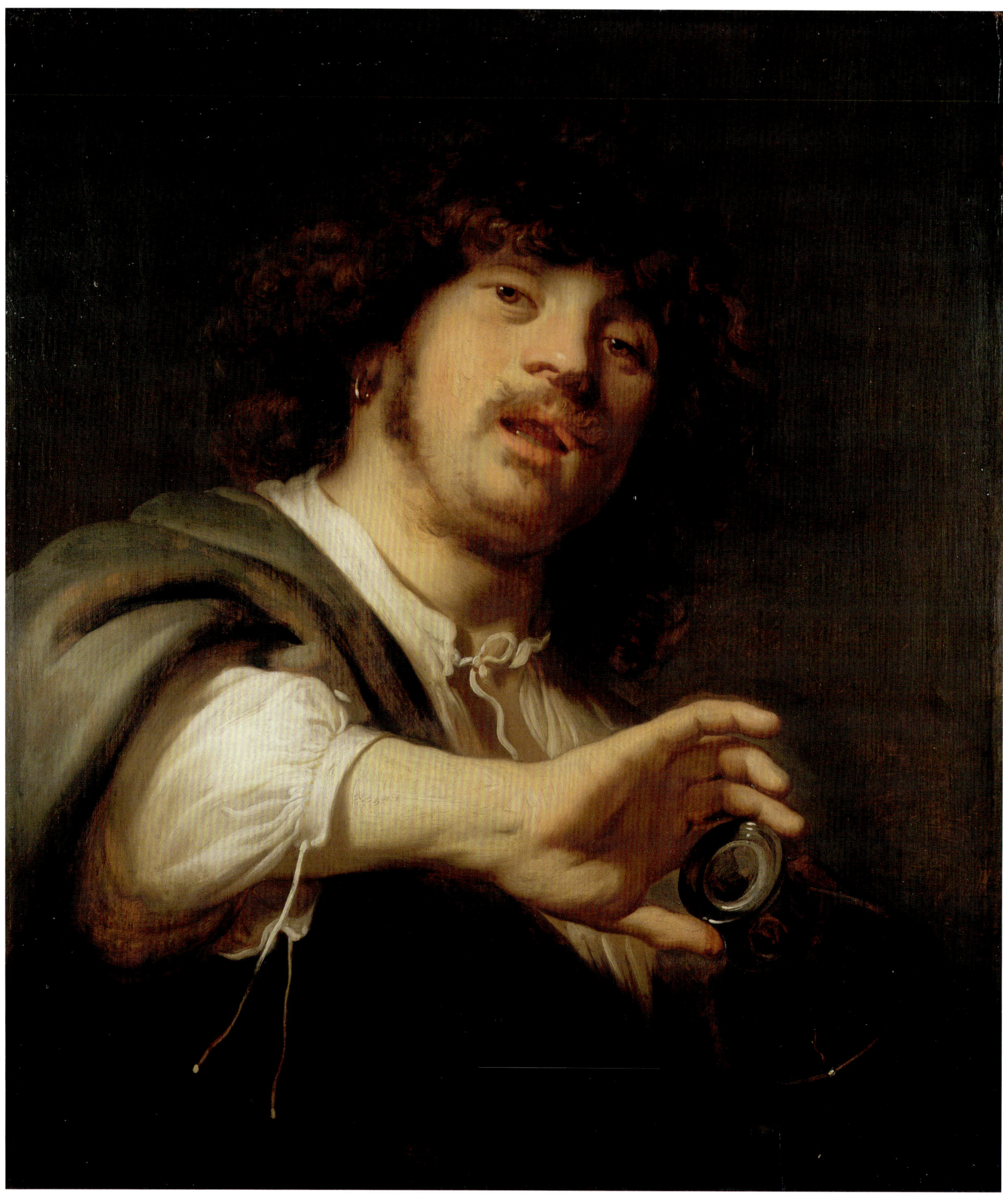

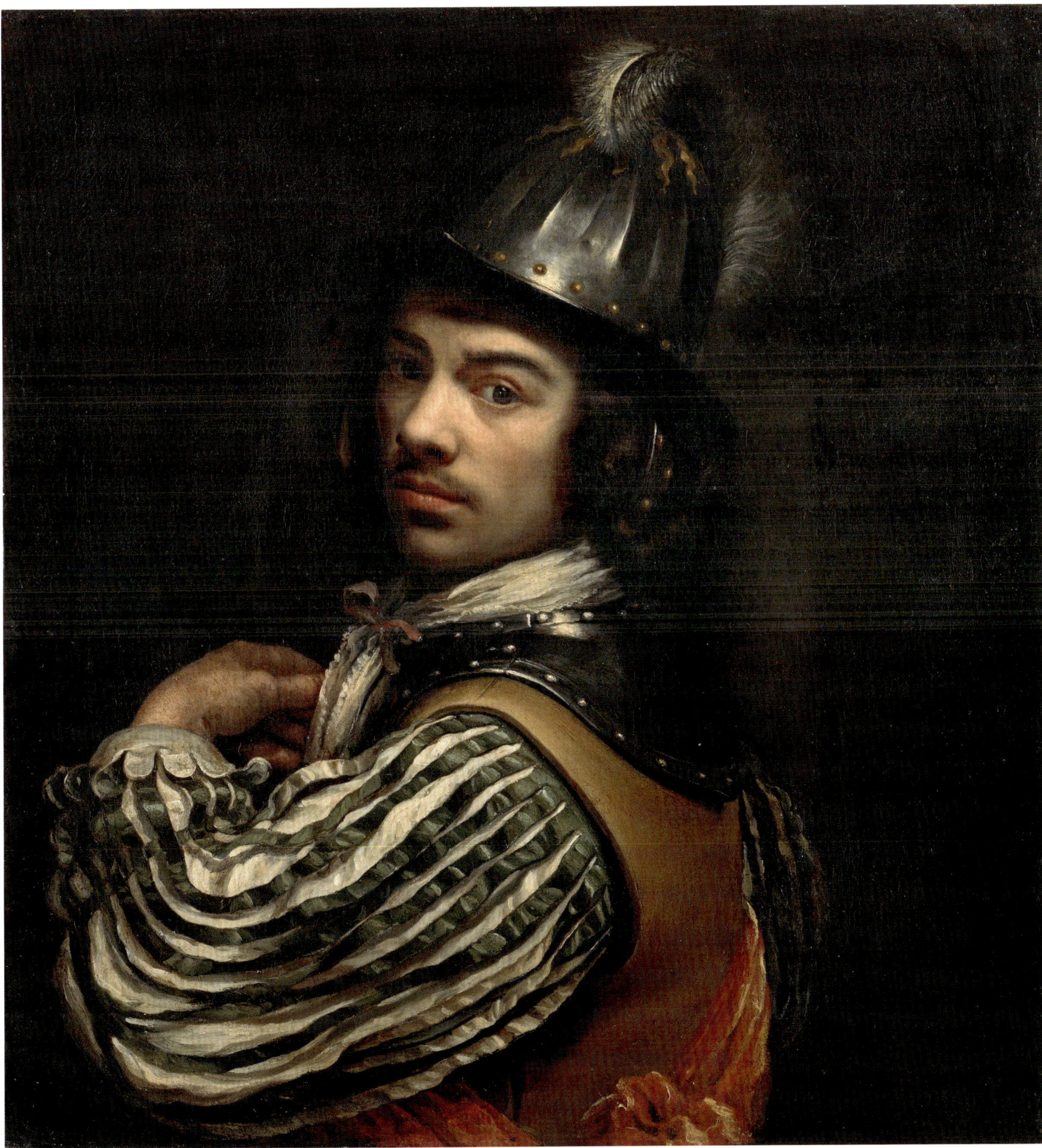

39 Ferdinand Bol, *Self-portrait*, 1642. Städel Museum, Frankfurt am Main

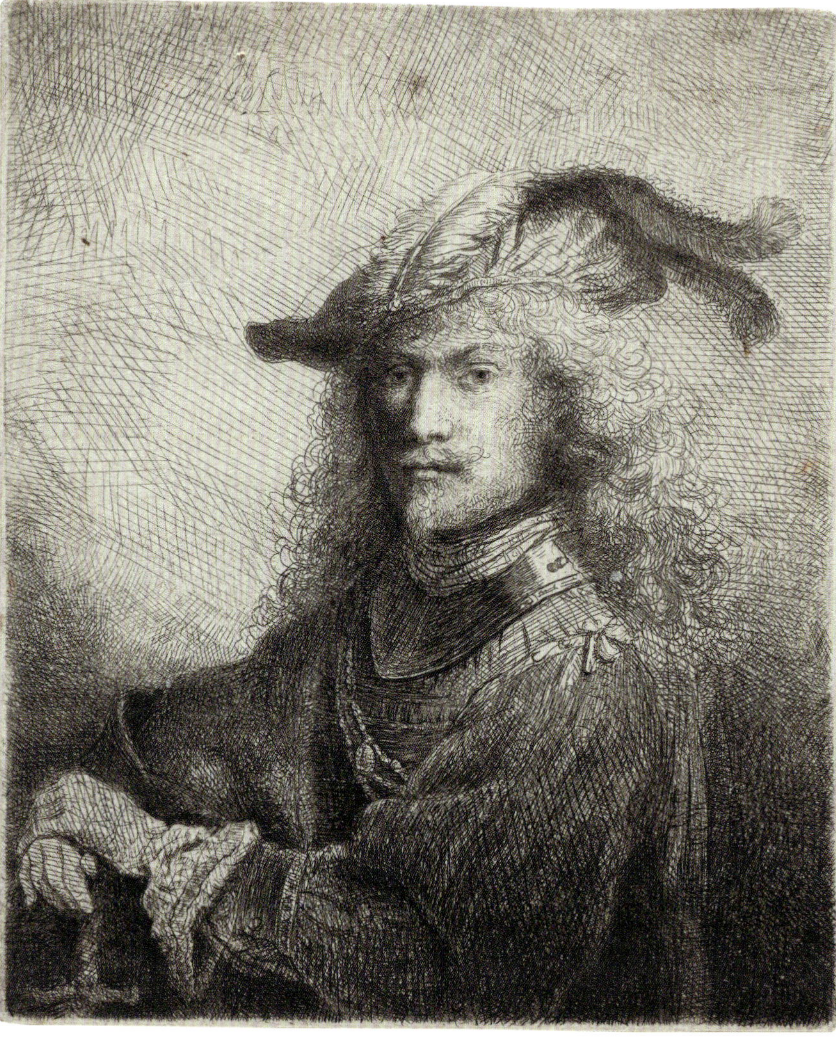

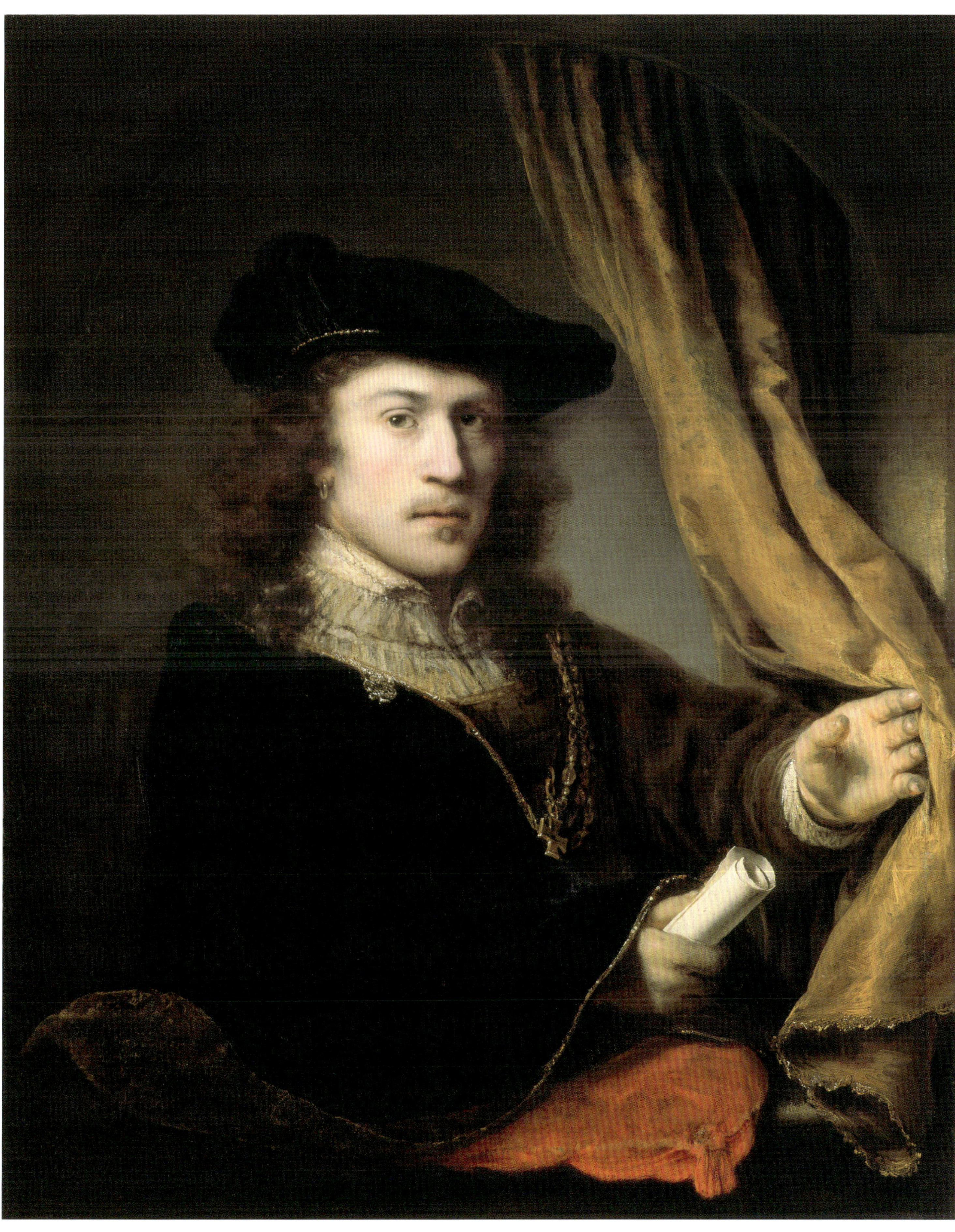

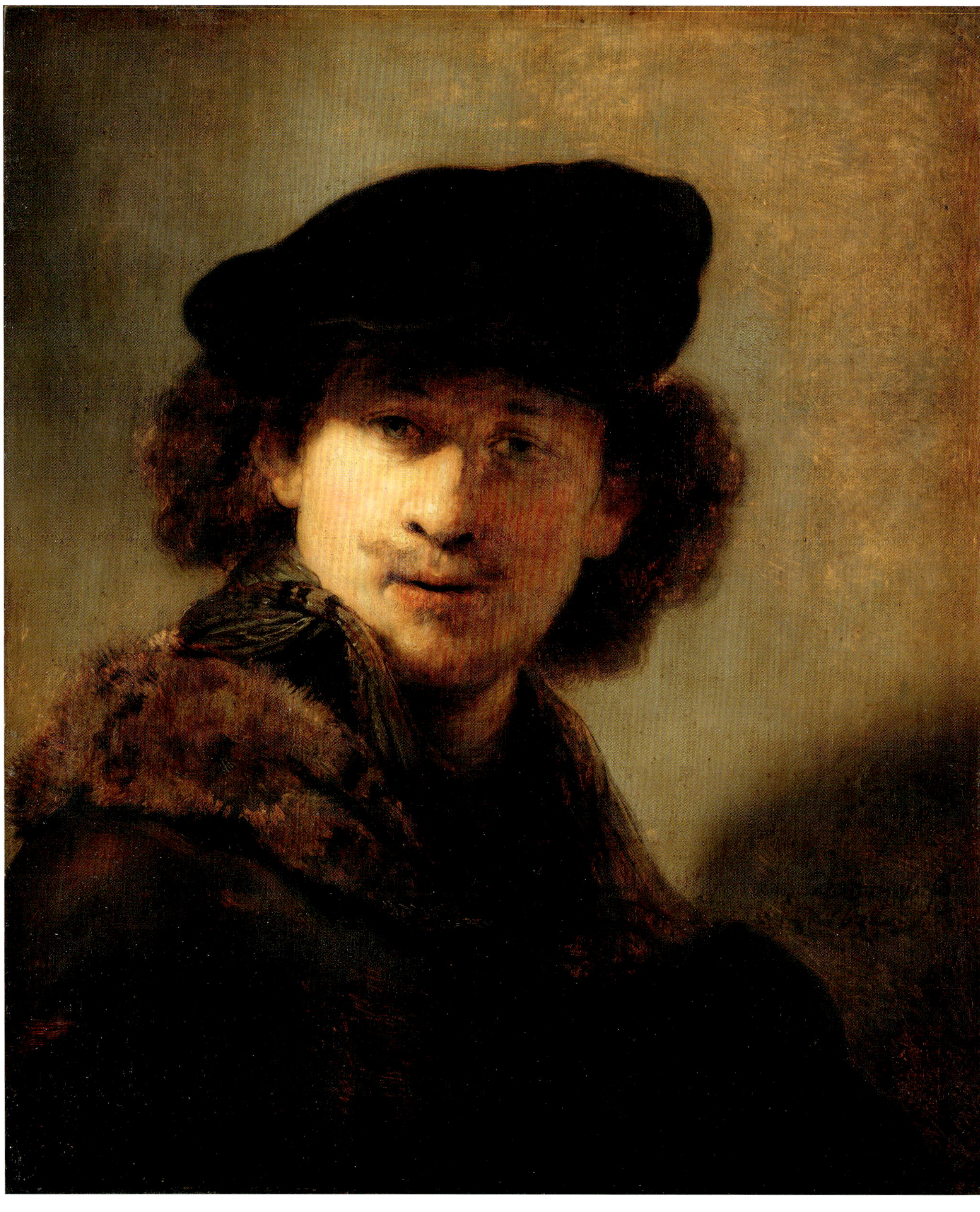

41 Rembrandt van Rijn, *Self-portrait in a Cap and a Fur-trimmed Cloak*, 1634. Staatliche Museen zu Berlin, Gemäldegalerie

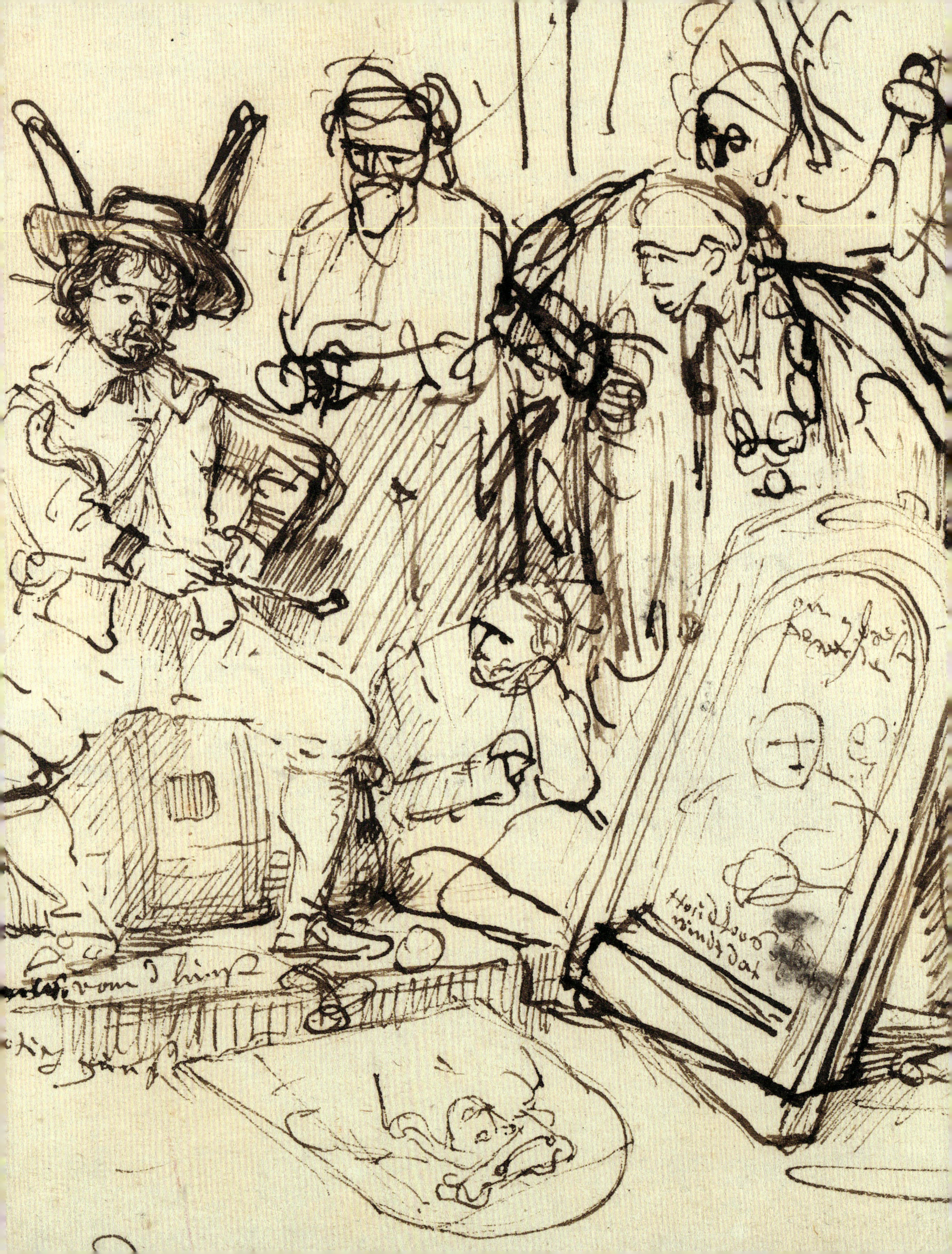

...af: von d hing
...kig hang
en pen har
Hosi boog
nimby dat

J A S P E R   H I L L E G E R S

Rembrandt and the Amsterdam Art Market

"Today, 16 July 1632, I, Jacob van Zwieten, notary public … visited the house of Mr. Heijndrick Ulenburch, painter living on Breestraet near St. Anthonissluijs in this city [Amsterdam], and asked a certain young girl who came to the door whether Mr. Rembrant Harmensz van Rijn, painter (who had taken lodgings at the house), was at home and available. This girl replied 'yes,' and on request the aforementioned Mr. Rembrant Harmensz van Rijn, painter, was called to the entrance hall, where … I asked him if he was Mr. Rembrant Harmensz van Rijn, the painter. And he replied 'yes.' And I then said to him that that was all, and that it appeared to me that he was still fresh and vigorous, and in good health. To which he replied: 'That is true, I am – thank God – in good health and feeling great.'"[1]

This brief summertime visit to the Amsterdam home and studio of the painter and international art dealer Hendrick Uylenburgh documents a major step in Rembrandt's life. What prompted it? In March 1631 Rembrandt, still living in Leiden, had subscribed to a tontine – a peculiar investment scheme, popular at the time, in which the participant who outlived the others would claim the prize. Each year, the depositors' status had to be verified. In 1632, however, Rembrandt was absent from Leiden and so, after waiting four months, the organizers hired the notary Jacob van Zwieten to look for him in Amsterdam. The document testifying that on 16 July of that year he found Rembrandt alive and "feeling great" is the earliest dated confirmation that the artist was residing in his new hometown, under the roof of Uylenburgh, his business associate.[2]

Rembrandt was no stranger to the St. Anthonisbreestraat area of Amsterdam. In the winter of 1624–25 he had studied with the renowned history painter Pieter Lastman on the other side of the lock, and possibly with Jacob Pynas at the nearby St. Anthonismarkt.[3] Having soaked up everything he had learned in Amsterdam, Rembrandt returned home to Leiden and within a few years morphed into the most sensationally promising artist of his time: a history painter with his own well-paying pupils, gifted with an incomparable talent for capturing emotions and rendering light in all its dramatic power. For this and more he had already earned abundant praise, most recently from no less than Constantijn Huygens, Stadtholder Frederik Hendrik's brilliant secretary, who was responsible for the presence of four of Rembrandt's history paintings and a portrait of Frederik Hendrik's spouse, Amalia von Solms (pl. 47), in the stadtholder's collection as early as 1632.[4] Rembrandt's portrait of Amalia complemented the one of her husband by Gerard van Honthorst (see fig. 6.3), who in recent years had become an international court painter – an honourable and lucrative position, arguably the pinnacle of what a painter could achieve.[5] In 1632 Rembrandt again received a courtly commission for an ambitious cycle of paintings depicting the Passion of Christ. The promise of being a court artist in The Hague may have been tempting, especially as Rembrandt's undisputed idol, the internationally renowned painter Peter Paul Rubens, served many royal patrons. However, the pull of Amsterdam was stronger, specifically through the person of Hendrick Uylenburgh.

The Uylenburgh Years

When Rembrandt appeared before Van Zwieten on Uylenburgh's doorstep, he and the art dealer must have been in business for some time. In fact, Uylenburgh, twenty years Rembrandt's elder, may be linked with the earliest references to the young painter's works in Amsterdam. The first documented purchase of Rembrandt's artwork by an Amsterdam patron is a "*tronitgen* [a small head or character study] *van rembrant* 29 [guilders]," mentioned in June 1628 in the cashbook of the Amsterdam regent Joan Huydecoper.[6] The second, another small head ("*tronijtge*"), is found in the October 1629 death inventory of the painter Barent Teunisz.[7] An earlier – only partially overlapping – inventory of Teunisz's paintings had been drawn up in January 1629, in which Rembrandt's "*tronijtge*" is not yet mentioned.[8] One of these citations may refer to *Bust of an Old Man in a Turban*, painted around 1627–28 (pl. 20).

Given the turnover in his holdings, Teunisz probably dealt in art. In fact, the new paintings in the second inventory form a specific group: in addition to Rembrandt's "*tronijtge*" they include a landscape by the Leiden painter Pieter de Neyn (for a typical example of his work, see fig. 4.1), a "*stuckie*" (small piece) by De Neyn's teacher Esaias van de Velde, and four landscapes by Jan van Goyen, who was also from Leiden and was De Neyn's fellow apprentice (tellingly, these are also the earliest works by De Neyn and Van Goyen in Amsterdam). De Neyn was a business associate of Uylenburgh in Leiden; his dealership might even be called a branch of the Uylenburgh firm.[9] Might one infer that these works arrived in Amsterdam through the agency of De Neyn and Uylenburgh? Uylenburgh is documented in Leiden in March 1628 (three months before Huydecoper's purchase), where he might have met Rembrandt, possibly through De Neyn.[10] Clearly, business was done during his visit, for on 7 April someone (possibly De Neyn) stated before a Leiden notary that he had ordered several "skilful" paintings from Uylenburgh.[11]

Twenty months after Teunisz's October inventory, the Uylenburgh-Rembrandt partnership was up and running. On 20 June 1631, a notary confirmed that Rembrandt had lent the dealer the considerable amount of 1,000 guilders, apparently to buy himself into his business.[12] Moreover, Rembrandt's portraits of Uylenburgh's coreligionists – the Amsterdam Mennonite merchants Nicolaes Ruts, dated 1631 (fig. 4.2), and Marten Looten, dated 11 January 1632 (see fig. 1.3) – make clear that in 1631 Rembrandt, travelling from Leiden, received commissions in Amsterdam via Uylenburgh.[13] The dealer, it seems, had "talent-scouted" Rembrandt. What the artist contributed (besides 1,000 guilders) is clear. But what could Uylenburgh offer? Firstly, there was the promise of a fully equipped studio – with some assistance by apprentices and journeymen – in the epicentre of the fastest growing art market in Europe.[14] Secondly, Uylenburgh provided access to a network of wealthy customers, both in Amsterdam and regionally: while De Neyn acted as an agent in Leiden, in Leeuwarden Uylenburgh relied on the Mennonite painter and art dealer Lambert Jacobsz. Similar contacts in cities such as Haarlem, Utrecht and even Antwerp, although undocumented, seem no less logical. Thirdly, by working for Uylenburgh, Rembrandt might well have bypassed guild stipulations that would have prevented him, as an outsider to the city, from joining the painters' guild.[15] Lastly, and importantly, Uylenburgh was a master salesman and marketer; he brokered the sales, so Rembrandt could focus on producing art.

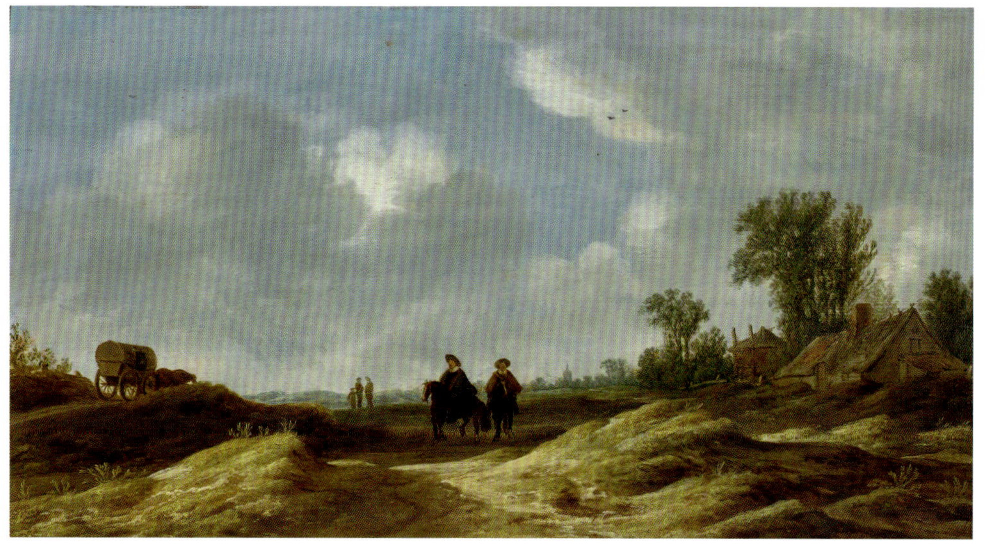

fig. 4.1 **Pieter de Neyn,**
Dune Landscape with Figures on Horseback, **1628, oil on panel;
30.5 × 56 cm. Private collection**

Rembrandt did exactly that. Taking Ernst van de Wetering's *Rembrandt's Paintings Revisited: A Complete Survey* of 2014 as a basic list of Rembrandt's output, the artist painted an astonishing ninety-seven pictures between 1632 and 1635 (80 per cent are dated, and the rest are assigned to this period on stylistic grounds).[16] In reality, this number must have been significantly higher: it does not include lost works, paintings whose attribution is unclear,[17] workshop copies,[18] or independent workshop products in Rembrandt's style.[19] A statistical analysis based on the *Complete Survey*, spanning the period from Rembrandt's arrival in Amsterdam (1632) until the year prior to his bankruptcy (1655), indicates that he painted almost as many paintings in these four years as in the remaining twenty altogether: 97 versus 105. Additionally, Rembrandt's production of prints, which peaked in Leiden, declined in 1632 but soon rose again, totalling twenty-nine etchings in the period from 1632 to 1635.[20] Among these we find *Christ before Pilate* (see fig. 17.3) and *The Descent from the Cross* (pl. 166). It appears these were part of an exceptionally ambitious series that Uylenburgh planned to publish, targeted at his own Mennonite community and capitalizing on the Passion Series commissioned for Frederik Hendrik in The Hague.[21] This productivity was noted by Rembrandt's contemporary biographers, such as the German painter Joachim von Sandrart, who knew Rembrandt from his own time in Amsterdam (1637–45). Sandrart wrote that, in addition to "innate predilection," Rembrandt achieved high esteem through "immense hard work."[22]

Portraiture

In Amsterdam, Rembrandt's production took a whole new direction. Whereas he painted virtually no portraits in Leiden, forty-four of the ninety-seven paintings (45 per cent) produced in Amsterdam between 1632 and 1635 were commissioned portraits. Five of these feature multiple sitters, starting with the paradigm-shifting *Anatomy Lesson of Dr. Nicolaes Tulp* of early 1632 (see fig. 1.4), which Rembrandt brilliantly conceived as a history piece, with reference to Rubens' *Tribute Money* (1612, Fine Arts Museums of San Francisco).[23] In this magisterial business card, he switched from the signature he had used in Leiden, "RHL" (Rembrandt Harmensz Leidensis), to his first name "Rembrant," an inspired marketing trick alluding to the greats of the Italian Renaissance: Leonardo, Michelangelo, Raphael and Titian who, unlike most Dutch artists, were known by their first names. Did Uylenburgh, with his international outlook, suggest the idea? As a statement of personal ambition and self-regard, it echoes Rembrandt's likewise exceptional production of self-portraits from around 1629 onward.[24] He painted at least seven of them (excluding studio copies and many prints) between 1632 and 1635, which made him exceptionally visible for an artist still in his twenties.

The portrait market was lucrative. After Cornelis van der Voort's passing in 1624, Amsterdam counted few serious competitors – Nicolaes Eliasz Pickenoy and Thomas de Keyser being the only high-end specialists.[25] Against Pickenoy's sophisticated but restrained conservative approach (pls. 56, 57) and

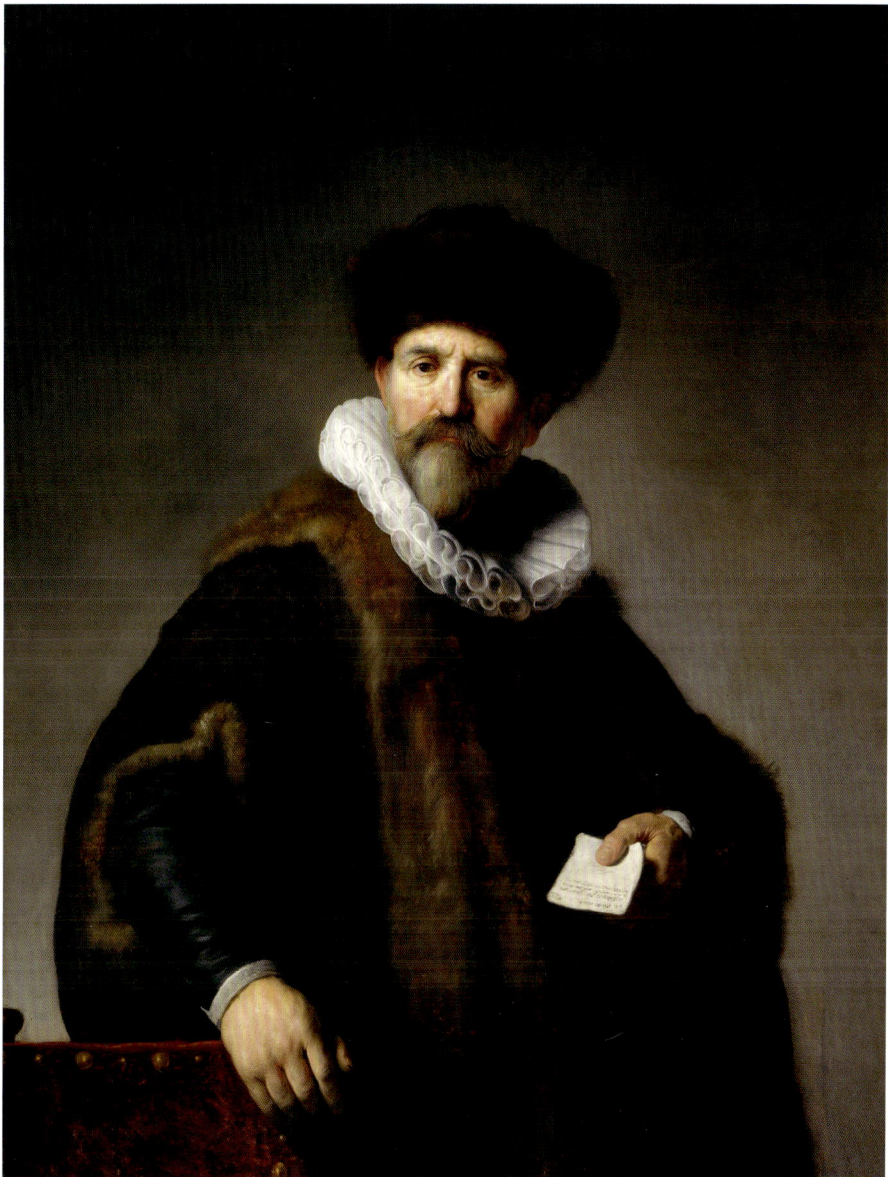

fig. 4.2 **Rembrandt van Rijn,** *Portrait of Nicolaes Ruts*, 1631, oil on panel; 116.8 × 87.3 cm. The Frick Collection, New York. Purchased 1943 (1943.1.150)

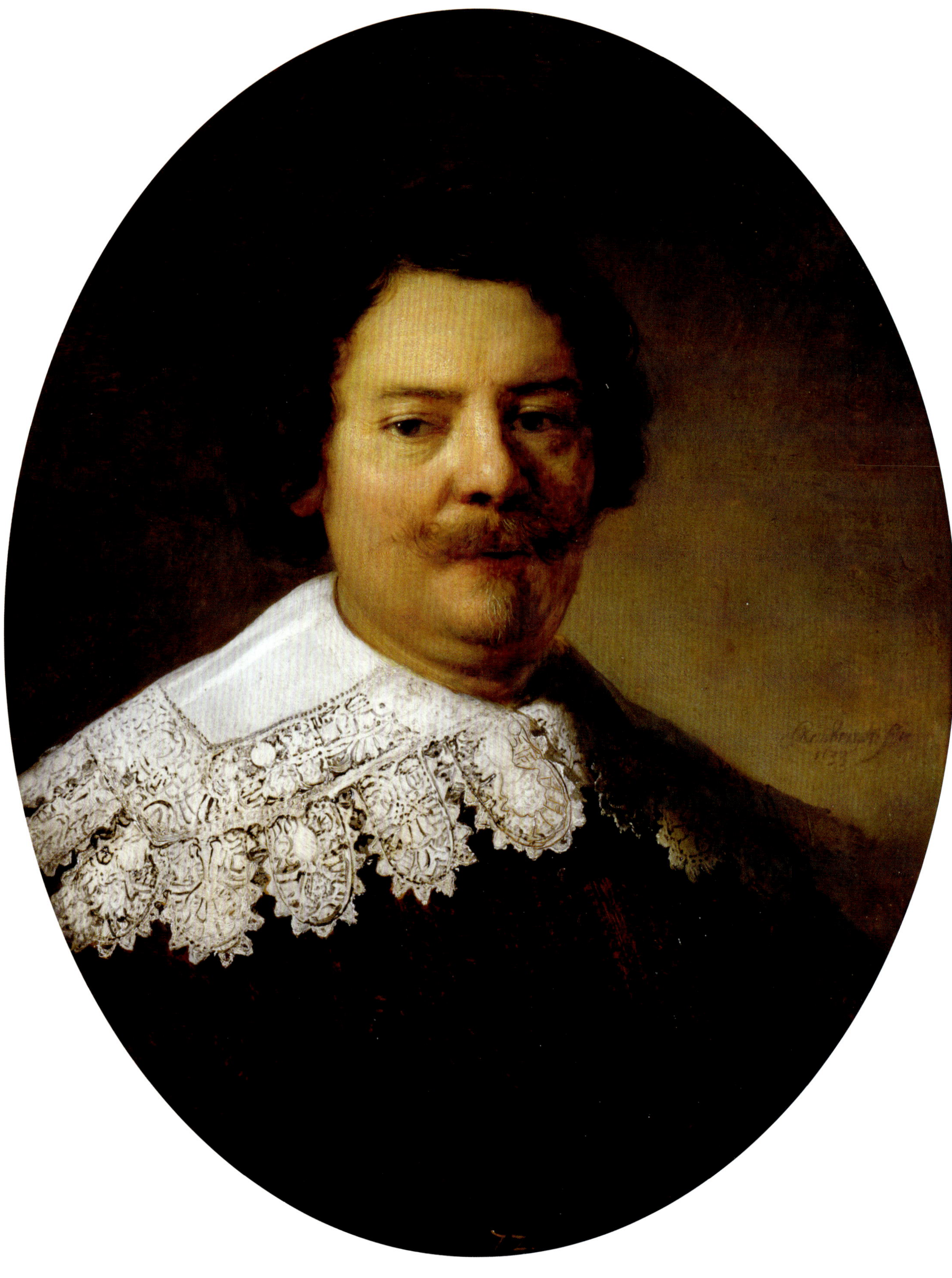

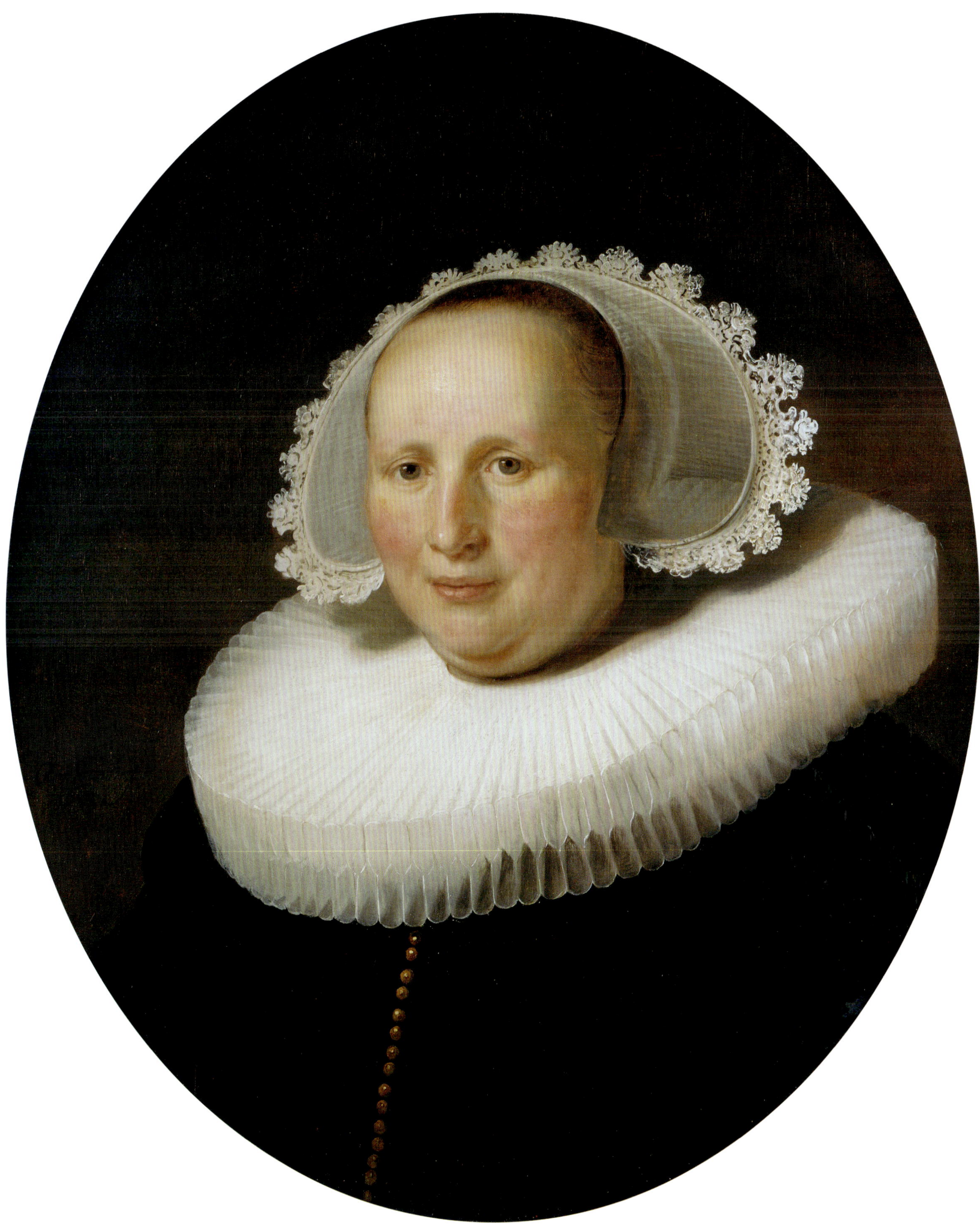

De Keyser's neatly executed, small portraits (pls. 58, 59) Rembrandt offered a novel, dynamic alternative (pl. 68). Perhaps more serious competition came from the talented Mennonite painter Jacob Backer, who had worked in Leeuwarden with Uylenburgh's associate Lambert Jacobsz. Once Backer arrived in Amsterdam, he also started producing portraits, yet not as many as Rembrandt (eleven, or 31 per cent of a total production of thirty-five known works from 1632/33 to 1635), and although elegantly painted (pl. 69), these were not as novel as those of Rembrandt.[26]

Portraiture offered networking opportunities, the chance to come face to face with wealthy buyers who could also become potential clients for Rembrandt's expensive history paintings and other products of the Uylenburgh studio. These included copies or variations after Rembrandt's historical compositions and *tronies*, painted by Rembrandt himself (nine in the first two years) and by others in the workshop (twelve assignable works between 1632 and 1635).[27] Tellingly, among Rembrandt's early Amsterdam sitters we find that more than half owned other works by him as well.[28] Jacques Specx – former governor general of Batavia in the Dutch East Indies and commissioner of the portraits of his sister-in-law Petronella Buys and her husband Philips Lucasz (pls. 61, 60) – also owned Rembrandt's *Abduction of Europa* (see fig. 11.1), his "Saint Peter's Ship" (probably *Christ in the Storm on the Sea of Galilee*, see fig. 1.6) and a *Saint Paul*. In addition to their own double portrait,[29] the cloth merchant Jan Pietersz Bruyningh and his wife Hildegond Pietersdr Moutmaker owned a landscape by Rembrandt and had him paint a portrait of Hildegond's father.[30] Marten Soolmans and Oopjen Coppit – portrayed by Rembrandt in 1634 (see figs. 3.1, 3.2) – also owned his *Holy Family* (see fig. 13.5), while Soolmans' cousin Martin van den Broeck possessed four paintings by Rembrandt in 1647.[31] Such cases testify to Uylenburgh's, and Rembrandt's, successful customer-relations strategy.

Contacts, thus, were key, both inside and outside Amsterdam. In 1632 Rembrandt portrayed at least four sitters from The Hague (where Rembrandt had pre-Uylenburgh contacts),[32] possibly two from Delft,[33] and in 1633/34 a group of prominent Rotterdam Remonstrants belonging to the Pesser-Couwenhoven clan.[34] That such commissions relied on word-of-mouth shows from the portrait of Jacob Jacobsz van Couwenhoven, dated 1633 (see fig. 6.11).

That year Van Couwenhoven must have attended the Dutch Remonstrants' general assembly in Amsterdam, a festive moment after years of religious-political hardship. On 13 April, the Remonstrant preacher Johannes Wtenbogaert noted in his diary that he sat for Rembrandt at the request of Amsterdam's Remonstrant leader Abraham Anthonisz Recht, the portrait's commissioner (see fig. 6.2).[35] Van Couwenhoven, close with both Wtenbogaert and Recht, would have followed suit. One thing led to another: the next year Rembrandt is documented in Rotterdam, where he portrayed four more family members, including Van Couwenhoven's wife, Maritje Jansdr Pesser.[36] Moreover, in 1659 Reynier van der Wolf, a son-in-law of the Pessers, owned a *Paracelsus* by Rembrandt.[37]

In 1633 Rembrandt may have returned to Leiden to portray Maertgen van Bilderbeecq (pl. 44). The daughter of Leiden's city mason, Maertgen was sister-in-law to both the Leiden professor Johannes Meursius and Uylenburgh's associate Pieter de Neyn.[38] Did De Neyn mediate the commission? Possibly, yet one must also consider that on 16 November 1625 Maertgen had married the Leiden baker and grain merchant Willem Burchgraeff.[39] Headman of the Leiden baker's guild in 1638, Burchgraeff belonged to the same Leiden milieu of bakers and millers as Rembrandt's family.[40] Rembrandt, thus, could have gained this commission on his own. In fact, it consisted of two portraits: one of Maertgen and one of Willem. For a long time it was thought that a 1635-dated male portrait by Daniel Mijtens was the pendant depicting Maertgen's husband.[41] However, that identification cannot be accepted.[42] A more likely candidate is Rembrandt's 1633 portrait in the Gemäldegalerie Alte Meister, Dresden (pl. 43).[43]

History Painting

Although we know little about Rembrandt's business arrangement with Uylenburgh, the seventeenth-century Florentine author Filippo Baldinucci lifted a tip of the veil in writing about Rembrandt's pupil and soon-to-be successor Govert Flinck, who had come to Amsterdam around 1633 from the Leeuwarden workshop of Lambert Jacobsz. Flinck worked under Rembrandt's supervision in Uylenburgh's workshop for about a year (presumably between 1634 and 1635). According to Baldinucci, Flinck "in his younger day handed out his services to a certain merchant [Uylenburgh]," who, by giving him plenty of money, employed him "almost constantly, as his [Flinck's] fantasy prompted him."[44]

Rembrandt, we presume, was likewise well-remunerated and granted considerable artistic freedom. In 1632, 63 per cent of his production consisted of portraits, but this dropped to 37 per cent between 1633 and 1635, with renewed attention to history subjects (44 per cent). Around 1630 the Amsterdam market for history paintings had been dominated by Rembrandt's teachers: Pieter Lastman led the field, and in his slipstream the brothers Jan and Jacob Pynas, Claes Moeyaert, Jan Tengnagel, Pieter Isaacsz and François Venant. All mainly produced small-figure histories, often set in a landscape, characterized by clear narrative and bright colours. As with his portraits, Rembrandt's history pieces were game-changers, available in an idiosyncratic variety, and catering to different preferences. The enigmatic, gem-like *Heroine from the Old Testament* from 1632/33 (pl. 85), which deliberately withholds from the viewer the essential *clavis interpretandi* (a known Rembrandt method[45]) was a conversation piece custom-made for intellectual connoisseurs. The mysterious 1634 *Judith at the Banquet of Holofernes* (pl. 82, also identified as Sophonisba, Esther or Artemisia) starts from the same premise – a calculated shortage of identifying details – but its sheer monumentality and size put it in a different category. And for other reasons, the magnificent *Abduction of Ganymede* from 1635 (pl. 97) was a conversation piece as well. The gods' wine-pourer, Ganymede, depicted not as a handsome youth but as a life-size, peeing and screaming toddler, was Rembrandt's "in-your-face" statement that art should follow nature and nature alone. Whoever bought it (perhaps the connoisseur Lucas van Uffelen, as Eric Jan Sluijter temptingly suggests[46]) must have been the talk of the town: its shock value would have caused a stir among Amsterdam art lovers, some of whom would have appreciated such witty, risqué realism, while others surely would not. Rembrandt probably enjoyed being the centre of such gossip, which would have cemented his reputation, an invaluable asset on the art market.

These large figural works were new to Rembrandt. Having previously preferred a smaller scale, he now faced competition from top-tier painters, even under his "own" roof. Halfway through the 1630s, Uylenburgh had in his dealer's stock a "life-size *Adam and Eve*" and a "Satyr seducing a beautiful lady," by Honthorst, a "slightly less than life-size" *Ruth and Naomi* by Pieter de Grebber from Haarlem, and a "large painting with life-size figures" depicting *The Tribute Money* by Jacob Backer (see fig. 1.5), the other "new kid in town" and a serious competitor.[47] Paintings such as *Judith at the Banquet of Holofernes*, *The Abduction of Ganymede* and *Belshazzar's Feast* (see fig. 5.13) were Rembrandt's phenomenal (but also labour-intensive) answers to such works, in which he pulled out all the stops: a strong chiaroscuro, motion, emotion, drama and tension were his irresistible trademarks. In these qualities he equally excelled on a small scale, as demonstrated in refined works such as *Diana and Her Nymphs Bathing, with the Stories of Actaeon and Callisto* of 1634 (pl. 99).

The previous year, Rembrandt had received the exceptionally high price of 600 guilders each for his *Raising of the Cross* and *Descent from the Cross* (see figs. 13.3, 13.2), painted for Frederik Hendrik.[48] One wonders if Uylenburgh collected a percentage for the Passion Series, as Rembrandt had surely gained this major commission without Uylenburgh's assistance. Looking back at this period, Arnold Houbraken wrote: "in those days Rembrandt's manner was praised by everyone, so that everything had to be in that style if it were to please the world" and "his art was so regarded and sought after in his time, that people had to beg him and give tithing."[49] Such success, his ability to land commissions himself, and the huge demand for his work must have fostered Rembrandt's confidence that he should start a business for himself. In 1634 he joined the Amsterdam Guild of Saint Luke and married Uylenburgh's cousin Saskia. It was time to spread his wings.

On His Own

Artists in Amsterdam produced paintings to suit a wide range of budgets and tastes. As recent research has shown, a large but nearly vanished part of the market consisted of mass-production by little known "galley-painters" working for art dealers who hired them to produce inexpensive paintings on familiar themes.[50] At the pinnacle of the market, Rembrandt's working arrangement with Uylenburgh shows a peculiar parallel. No other high-end dealer employed a first-class painter to work for him exclusively.[51] Rather, successful masters had their own workshops, in which students and assistants contributed to the production. Rembrandt aspired to do the same. The first document showing true independence is a February 1636 letter to Huygens. It reveals that Rembrandt was no longer lodging with Uylenburgh and gives his new address as "*niuwe doelstraet*" (Nieuwe Doelenstraat), likely both his home and studio.[52] He did not stay there long: in 1637 he and Saskia moved to the Binnen-Amstel, and in 1639, he bought the imposing house at Breestraat 3 that is now the Rembrandt House Museum. As an independent master, Rembrandt could have pupils and assistants of his own, and this became an increasingly important part of his business. Among the first to stay with Rembrandt for several years were Ferdinand Bol from Dordrecht (c. 1636–1640/42), Leendert van Beijeren from Amsterdam (c. 1636–38) and, possibly, Jan Victors (c. 1637–39) and Gerbrand van den Eeckhout (1637–40?), both natives of the city.[53] With this team, Rembrandt built his brand in the increasingly competitive art market of Amsterdam.

The dynamic growth of the market for paintings and other luxury goods was the result of many inter-related factors. An influx of immigrants from the southern Netherlands, beginning earlier in the century, brought talented craftsmen and a taste for decorating homes with paintings.[54] In the booming international trade market, merchants made incredible fortunes and invested in material goods ("Here [in Amsterdam] is the stock exchange, and the money, and the love of art," wrote the poet Thomas Asselijn).[55] Building projects, both private and municipal, ensured endless walls to fill. In a society constructed on credit and eager for risky profit, paintings were viewed as commodities with trade value and the potential for financial gain. The creative industry catered to the craze for novel subjects and themes, forming a complex socio-economic maze of producers (overseen by their guild), dealers (some of whom were producers themselves), appraisers, agents, auctioneers, experts, connoisseurs, collectors and commissioners.[56]

When Rembrandt moved back to the Breestraat in 1639 it was the epicentre of the market, home to many painters, studios, shops and guild offices (at St. Anthonismarkt).[57] A drawing from 1818 still shows the street much as it looked in Rembrandt's time (fig. 4.3). Rembrandt was an active player in this network. He attended auctions, such as the 1638 estate sale of the merchant Gommer Spranger, where he bought prints and drawings by Albrecht Dürer and Hendrick Goltzius, and the record-breaking sale of the Lucas van Uffelen collection in 1639 (see fig. 5.4).[58] Baldinucci stated that Rembrandt would outbid others "in order to emphasize the prestige of his profession,"[59] a suggestion seemingly confirmed by Sandrart's statement that Rembrandt spent an incredible 1,400 guilders on fourteen prints by Lucas van Leyden.[60] He also traded in other artists' work, for instance selling *Hero and Leander* by Rubens (pl. 46) around 1644 for a fair profit to the connoisseur and dealer Lodewijk van Ludick,[61] and a *Simeon* by his old friend Jan Lievens in 1652 to Jan Six.[62] Rembrandt's 1656 estate inventory shows that he and another painter, Pieter de la Tombe, held 50-per-cent shares in a *Rich Man* by Palma Vecchio and a *Samaritan Woman* by Giorgione.[63] Like many prominent artists, Rembrandt was also consulted for his expert opinion; in 1653, he validated the attribution of a painting to the landscape painter Paul Bril.[64]

Still, Rembrandt was primarily a painter and printmaker. Once independent of Uylenburgh and no longer focusing on portraiture, his production slowed.[65] In the period from 1636 to 1639, he produced at least six to seven paintings per year, down from twenty-four between 1632 and 1635. Clearly, running his own workshop demanded precious time

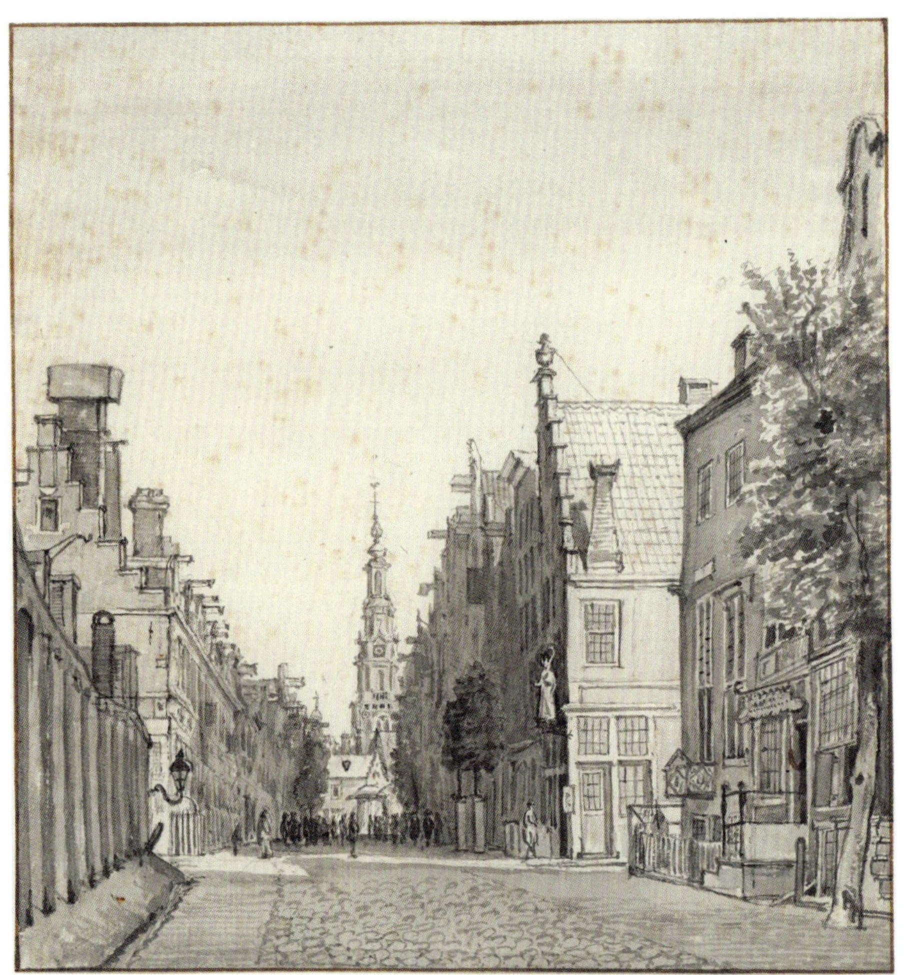

fig. 4.3 **Gerrit Lamberts**, *View of the Jodenbreestraat (formerly St. Anthonisbreestraat)*, 1818, pencil and grey wash on paper; 18.4 × 17 cm. Amsterdam City Archives. Collection Koninklijk Oudheidkundig Genootschap (KOG-AA-2-16-298)

previously spent on painting. Creatively, however, Rembrandt was at his peak, delivering explosive history pieces such as *The Blinding of Samson* (pl. 106), renewing his interest in genre and still life (e.g., *Still Life with Peacocks*, pl. 150), and brilliantly venturing into new subject types, including landscape (pl. 131) and political allegory (*The Concord of the State*, 1642, Museum Boijmans Van Beuningen, Rotterdam). Thirty-one known paintings were made between 1640 and 1644, including *The Night Watch* (see fig. 1.9), showing a continued rate of production of about six paintings per year, with portraiture picking up again at 39 per cent.

Not a single dated painting is known from 1649, but Rembrandt's production otherwise remained relatively steady at twenty-one works from 1645 to 1648 (five per year), and twenty-seven from 1650 to 1655 (four and a half per year). Remarkably, fifty-five of the eighty-two works painted over the period of 1640 to 1655 (67 per cent) depict single figures – whether portrait, *tronie*, genre or historical character – rather than narrative compositions, a statistic that reflects a profound shift in Rembrandt's art, away from spectacle and toward the depiction of introspection. Of twenty-two historical compositions, only five (23 per cent) measure more than one metre (either height or width), as opposed to 41 per cent in the 1630s. These smaller works were probably easier to sell.

The Rembrandt Brand

To understand why Rembrandt's personal production may have declined, one has to bear in mind Joachim von Sandrart's remark that the painter's studio was filled with "almost innumerable youths of good family, who came to him for instruction and tuition. Each paid him 100 guilders per year."[66] Teaching offered a guaranteed source of income, and talented pupils' efforts were perfectly salable, forming a lower-cost product line of the "Rembrandt brand." Sandrart observed that the "profit which [Rembrandt] made out of the pictures and engravings of these pupils [amounted] to some 2,000 to 2,500 guilders."[67] On the reverse of a drawing from around 1637, Rembrandt noted the sale of an unnamed pupil's *Standard Bearer* for 15 guilders, a *Flora* for 4.6 guilders, and "a work of Ferdinand [Bol] and another of his / The *Abraham* and *Flora* / Sold Leendert [van Beijeren's] *Flora* [for] 5 [guilders]."[68] The low prices suggest these were copies after Rembrandt's originals.[69]

More unusually, the workshop produced numerous high-quality variants of autograph work. These were both crucial training exercises and profitable merchandise. An early example is *Abraham's Sacrifice of Isaac* of 1635 and its variant of 1636 (see figs. 12.1, 12.2), thought to be painted by Flinck, in which the angel approaches from a different angle.[70] Similarly, *The Angel Departing from the Family of Tobias* (see fig. 12.7), painted in 1637, inspired several variations. Two depict the angel flying toward the family instead of away and add a planter in the lower right.[71] The better of the two has been attributed to Bol, while the other is possibly a later copy by an anonymous Bol student.[72] Intriguingly, a third version of this variation recently surfaced (pl. 119),[73] which more accurately follows Rembrandt's example,[74] and is painted more competently than the other two.[75] The wood panel has been shown to come from the same tree as Rembrandt's 1638 *Landscape with the Good Samaritan* (Czartoryski Museum, Cracow), locating it firmly within Rembrandt's studio at just the right time.[76] Who painted this high-quality, creative variation? Was it Bol, or was it Flinck, who was still working for Uylenburgh?[77] Rembrandt's ties with Uylenburgh and Flinck were still strong, as may be inferred from the latter's artistic adherence to Rembrandt until at least 1640/42. A document of 20 January 1640 shows that Rembrandt remained invested in Uylenburgh's firm as part of a consortium of intimates that included the heirs of Lambert Jacobsz and Pieter de Neyn's widow.[78]

These works testify to the workshop's *modus operandi* while also highlighting a theme they helped to popularize: the supernatural – specifically the angelic – encounter. Rembrandt's interest in this theme is not surprising considering his fascination with evocative light effects. From 1634 on, a string of heavenly messengers appeared in his art, becoming a distinguishing feature of the Rembrandt brand. For decades, angelic subjects such as the Angel Appearing to the Shepherds (see fig. 12.3),[79] Abraham's Sacrifice, Manoah's Sacrifice, the Angel Appearing at the Sepulchre, the Angel Appearing at Gideon's Sacrifice, the Angels Appearing to Jacob in His Dream and Saint Peter Released from Prison – often directly quoting from Rembrandt's work – were favoured among his former pupils' repertoires (pls. 114, 117).

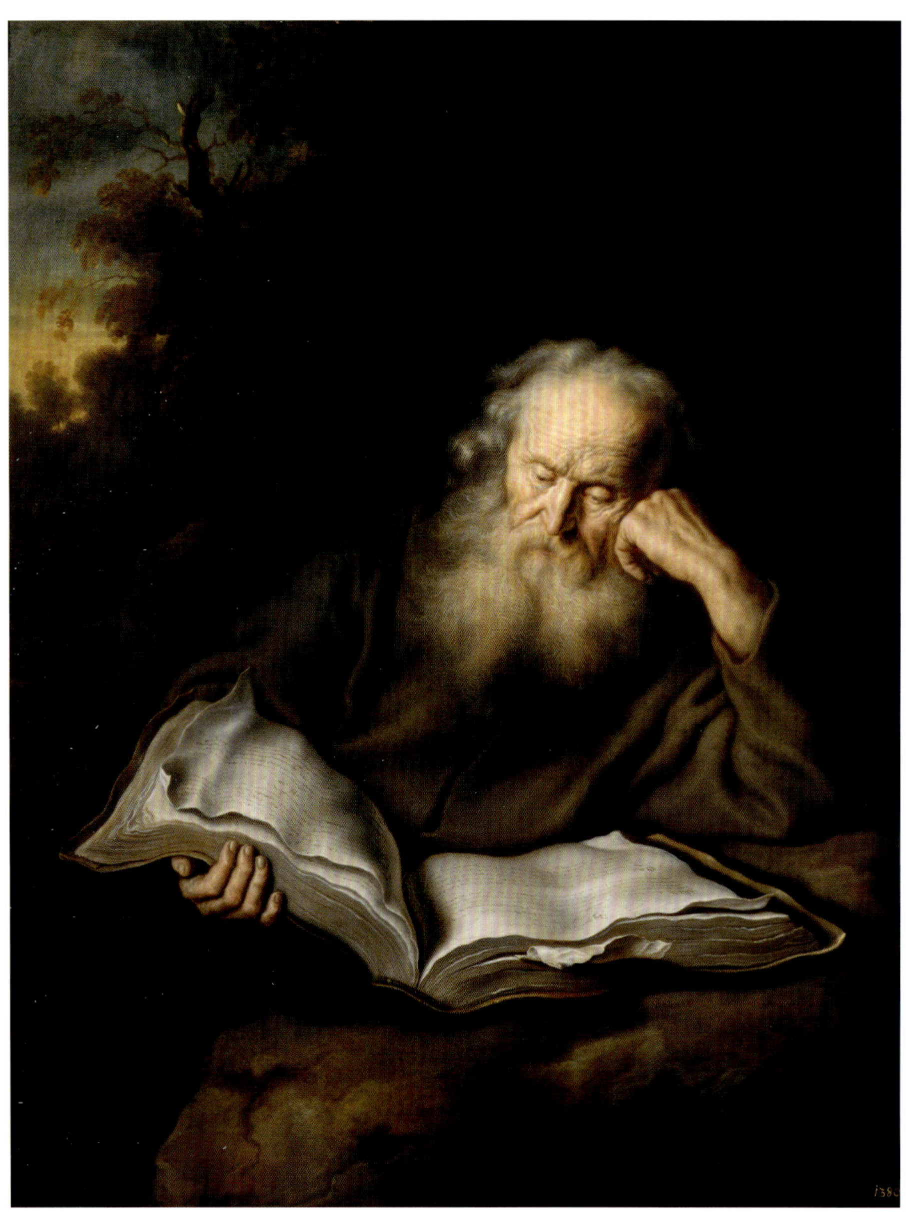

fig. 4.4 **Salomon Koninck,**
***The Hermit*, 1643, oil on canvas;**
121 × 93.5 cm. Staatliche
Kunstsammlungen Dresden,
Gemäldegalerie Alte Meister
(1589)

Rembrandt's Rivals

Houbraken claimed that "Rembrandt's art, as something new, enjoyed such general appreciation in its time that artists, if they wanted their work to be marketable, were compelled to adopt his style."[80] This is a clear indication of Rembrandt's extraordinary impact, but is also an exaggeration. Throughout Rembrandt's career, Amsterdam art buyers could choose from a multitude of artists, styles, subjects, media and levels of price and quality. In his important book *Rembrandt's Rivals*, Eric Jan Sluijter analyzes thirty Amsterdam history painters of diverse backgrounds, strategies and output.[81] While few came close to Rembrandt's talent, they did perform in the same arena. Less thoroughly studied is the market for other genres in which Rembrandt and his workshop also excelled – portrait, landscape, still life, genre and *tronies*. What follows is a glance into this complex market and its functioning.

The Expulsion of Hagar

Fraught with family dysfunction and moral ambiguity, the Old Testament story of Abraham's dismissal of the serving maid Hagar and her son Ishmael became the most popular subject among Amsterdam history painters.[82] Pieter Lastman's masterful painting of 1612 (pl. 107) set the stage, followed by Jan Pynas in 1614 (Rembrandt House Museum, Amsterdam) and others. Lastman's painting must have remained in an Amsterdam collection, for around 1637 Rembrandt made a drawing after it (pl. 108). His subsequent etching emphasizing Abraham's conflicting emotions (pl. 112) prompted a cascade of variants among his (former) pupils and followers: Flinck (pl. 113), Barent Fabritius (pl. 111), Jan Victors, Van den Eeckhout, Bol and Nicolaes Maes all took up the subject.[83] Fabritius looked back to Lastman's work, while Flinck developed Lastman's "*houding*" (accomplishing spatial unity through differentiating colour and tone) and Rembrandt's emphasis on "*naetuereelste beweechgelickheijt*" (the natural, most convincing expression of motion and emotion) into a fresh, personal interpretation.[84] Thus, Rembrandt and his entourage catalyzed supply and demand for an engaging pictorial theme. Minor Amsterdam masters outside his orbit, such as Pieter Potter, Rombout van Troyen, Johannes Urselincx, Jan Dammeroen and Jan Micker, followed suit with works for the lower end of the market.[85]

Salomon Koninck

The history painter Salomon Koninck was a native of Amsterdam and a Breestraat regular, but never a pupil of Rembrandt. He studied with David Colijns (on the St. Anthonismarkt) and Lastman's brother-in-law, the painter François Venant, and in 1638 married the daughter of the painter Adriaen van Nieulandt. He no doubt knew Rembrandt and his

oeuvre, and might also have worked for Uylenburgh.[86] His *Esther Reading the Decree of the Extermination of the Jews* (pl. 84) strongly relies on Rembrandt's *Heroine from the Old Testament* (pl. 85), implying first-hand knowledge and dating the work to the 1630s.[87] While adhering to Rembrandt's figure types, manner of spatial arrangement and narrative emphasis through strong chiaroscuro, light and tone,

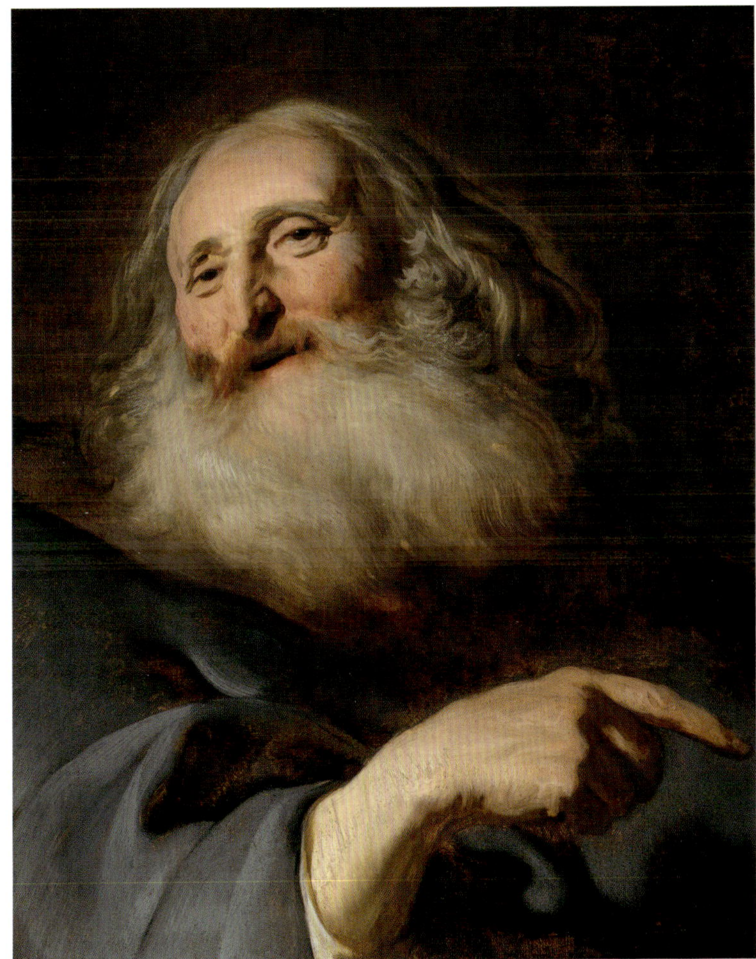

fig. 4.5 Jacob Backer,
Laughing Old Man (Democritus),
c. 1635, oil on panel;
60 × 46.5 cm. Salomon Lilian,
Amsterdam/Geneva

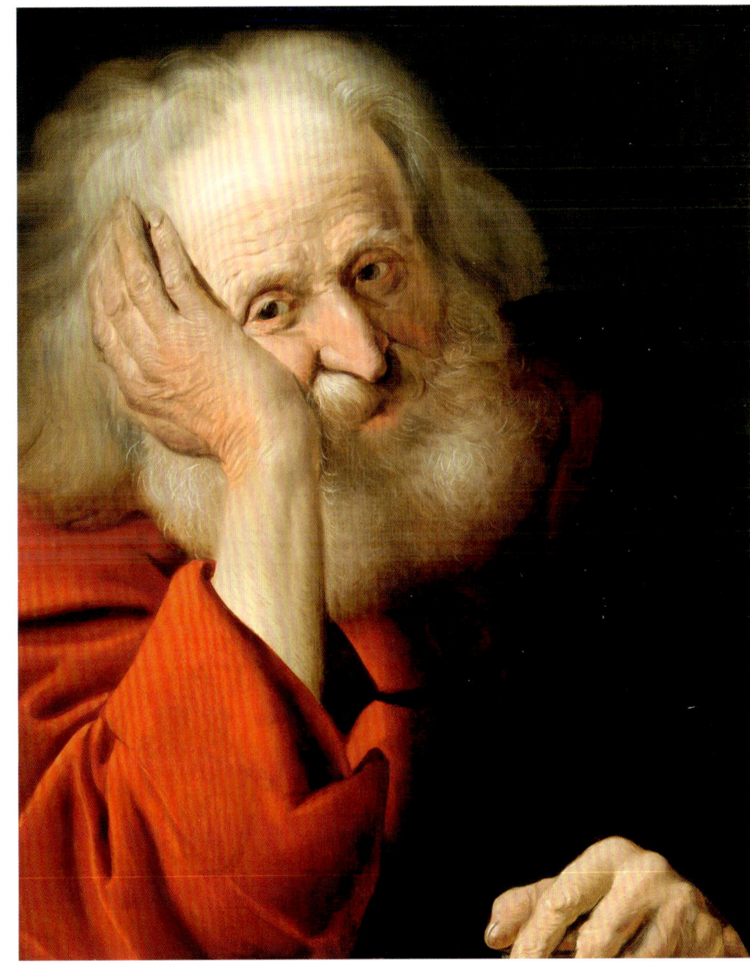

fig. 4.6 Simon Kick, *Tronie of
an Old Man*, c. 1640, oil on panel;
48 × 38 cm. Private collection

Koninck's refined way of rendering shiny draperies and glimmering gold thread seems unique to him. His subject matter, too, reflects his admiration for Rembrandt, whose predilection for greybeards he shared. Cornelis de Bie informs us that the painter Jan Tengnagel owned a *St. Jerome in the Wilderness* by Koninck, probably the painting now in the Gemäldegalerie Alte Meister, Dresden (fig. 4.4), for which he employed a popular Amsterdam model, also used by Backer, De Keyser and Simon Kick (figs. 4.5, 4.6).[88] Rembrandt's work continued to challenge him, as demonstrated in a monumental, recently surfaced *Susanna and the Elders* (fig. 4.7), clearly inspired by Rembrandt's 1647 *Susanna* now at the Gemäldegalerie, Berlin (sold by Rembrandt for an impressive 500 guilders).[89] Two smaller

variations, dated 1649, were already known,[90] and one wonders who encouraged Koninck to paint this subject three times in a row. An intriguing prospect is the art dealer Johannes de Renialme, documented as owning twelve paintings by Koninck in 1650, and later thirteen works by Rembrandt (including a *Susanna*).[91] Another is the connoisseur/dealer Marten Kretzer, who owned a *Ceres at Night Searching for Proserpina* by Koninck and a work by Rembrandt, probably sold in 1650.[92] Lodewijk van Ludick possessed several works by Koninck, including a *David and Bathsheba*, and was a friend, patron and financial supporter of Rembrandt.[93] The key point is that Rembrandt and Koninck mixed with the same dealers, who, as "taste leaders," might have steered them in developing marketable subjects.

Portraiture Again

Returning to portraiture from 1639 to 1644, Rembrandt faced stronger competition. Not only were Pickenoy, De Keyser and Backer still around, but Rembrandt's former pupils Flinck and Bol had become extremely capable portraitists, Bol working in a Rembrandtesque style (pls. 64, 65), with Flinck adopting a more fashionable, Flemish-oriented manner (pls. 66, 67). The most important of several newcomers was Pickenoy's former pupil Bartholomeus van der Helst, whose portraits paired unprecedented realism with idealized characterization (pls. 71, 74, 77). In his wake, London-born Isaack Luttichuys, arriving in 1638, claimed his corner of the market with exquisite, cool and distinguished portraits for a specific group of merchants. Many were of German ancestry like himself, such as the Hamburg-born merchant Martijn Gaertz, who died in Amsterdam in 1664 (fig. 4.8); his brother Johannes lived on the Keizersgracht.[94] Joachim von Sandrart's portraits exuded – as he did himself – restrained grandeur (pls. 62, 63), while Lievens, back in 1644 from a thirteen-year stay in London and Antwerp, brought a Van Dyckian *noblesse* that landed well with Amsterdam's elite. For instance, Lievens' fashionable portrait of Adriaen Trip (pl. 76), one of his earliest Amsterdam portraits, must have made an impression.[95] Gradually, Rembrandt lost his market share, probably from a combination of increasing competition and a personal loss of interest: between 1645 and 1655 only six portraits are known (13 per cent of his total production).

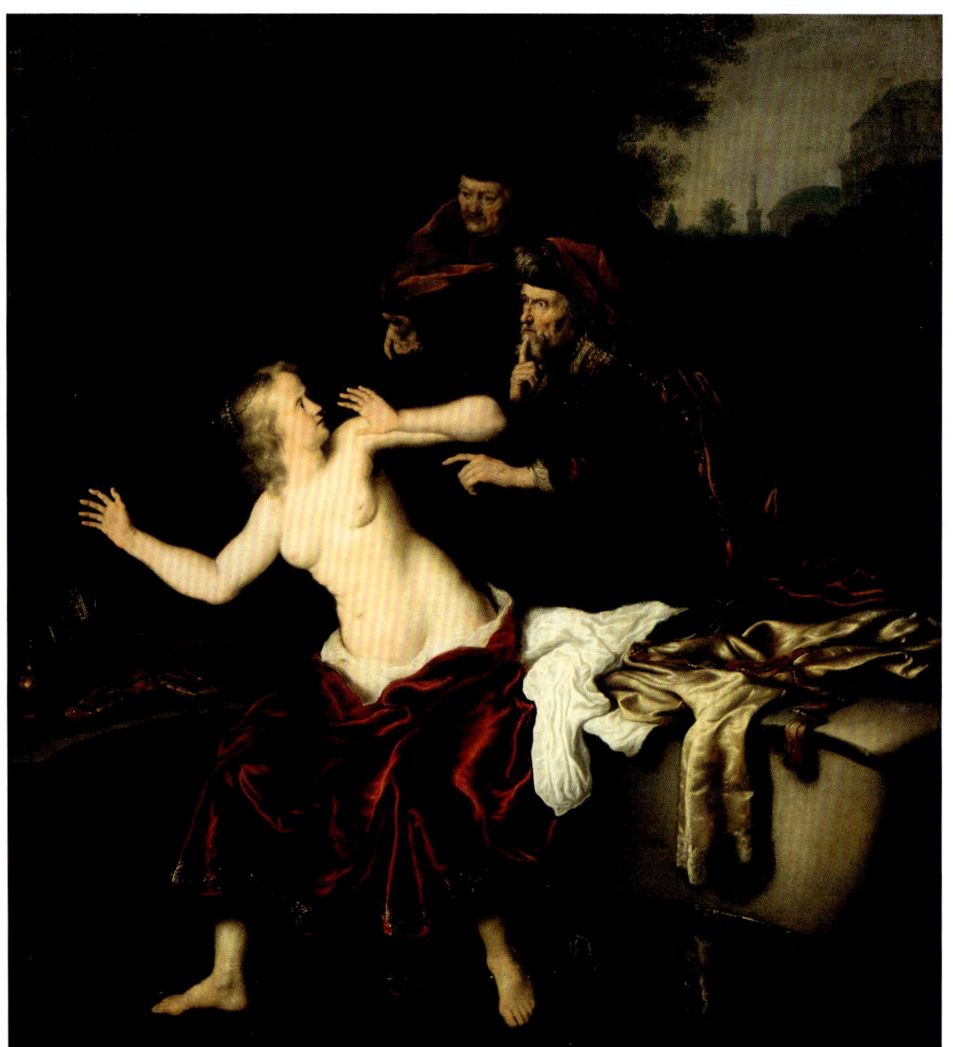

fig. 4.7 **Salomon Koninck,** *Susanna and the Elders*, **c. 1649, oil on canvas; 152.5 × 138 cm. Private collection**

Landscape

Rembrandt's venture into landscape – a genre that steadily gained in popularity[96] – lasted roughly a decade.[97] His production, although consisting primarily of (topographical) drawings and prints, also yielded several spectacular paintings, in which brooding local light causes magnificent suspense (pl. 131). Highly original, they feed on examples by Hercules Segers (pl. 130), whose work Rembrandt owned, while likewise alluding to Rubens' metaphysical landscapes of the 1630s. Rembrandt was well paid for his landscapes, but kept most for himself,[98] while his workshop produced others that must have been for sale.[99]

For consumers, the Amsterdam art market provided many options. Flinck, still in Uylenburgh's service, offered landscapes that were extremely close to those of Rembrandt.[100] Philips Koninck (Salomon's cousin), who associated with Rembrandt during the early 1640s, created a distinctive pictorial world, adopting the latter's warm tones, but surveying the local landscape with a wide panoramic gaze (pl. 132). Lievens, too, produced landscapes, prominently featuring robust, dark trees, recalling those of his deceased Antwerp friend Adriaen Brouwer.[101] Many are found in Amsterdam inventories, including that of Rembrandt himself.[102] Gorinchem-born Aert van der Neer settled in Amsterdam around the same time as Rembrandt. His spectacular moonlit nightscapes, highlighting his talent for rendering reflections in the dark water, were popular with local buyers (pl. 133).

There were also Italianate artists. Bartholomeus Breenbergh from Deventer started his career in Amsterdam in 1619, but moved to Rome the same year where he stayed for over a decade.[103] Upon his return around 1630, he settled in or near the Breestraat, where he produced neat landscapes with Roman ruins, often with biblical or mythological *staffage* (pl. 121), or with subjects from pastoral plays, betraying his intimate knowledge of the work of colleagues active in Rome, such as Adam Elsheimer, Paul Bril, Filippo Napoletano and, most of all, Cornelis van Poelenburch.[104] Jan "Crabbetje" Asselijn, whose portrait Rembrandt etched (pl. 1), returned in 1647 after ten years in Rome to reposition himself on the market with highly fashionable Italianate landscapes that brought warm southern light into the dark and cold houses of wealthy Amsterdammers (pl. 134).

Competition was not restricted to Amsterdam painters. Through the art trade, buyers could choose from a variety of out-of-town landscapists such as Salomon van Ruysdael, Jan van Goyen or Pieter de Molijn. Not everybody could stand (or was attracted to) this competitive atmosphere. The young Paulus Potter (son of the successful painter Pieter Potter), for instance, who grew up in the Breestraat and probably studied with Moeyaert, mastered the specialty of animal-filled landscapes developed by earlier Amsterdam artists such as Roelant Savery and Gillis de Hondecoeter, but successfully opted to try his luck in Delft and The Hague.

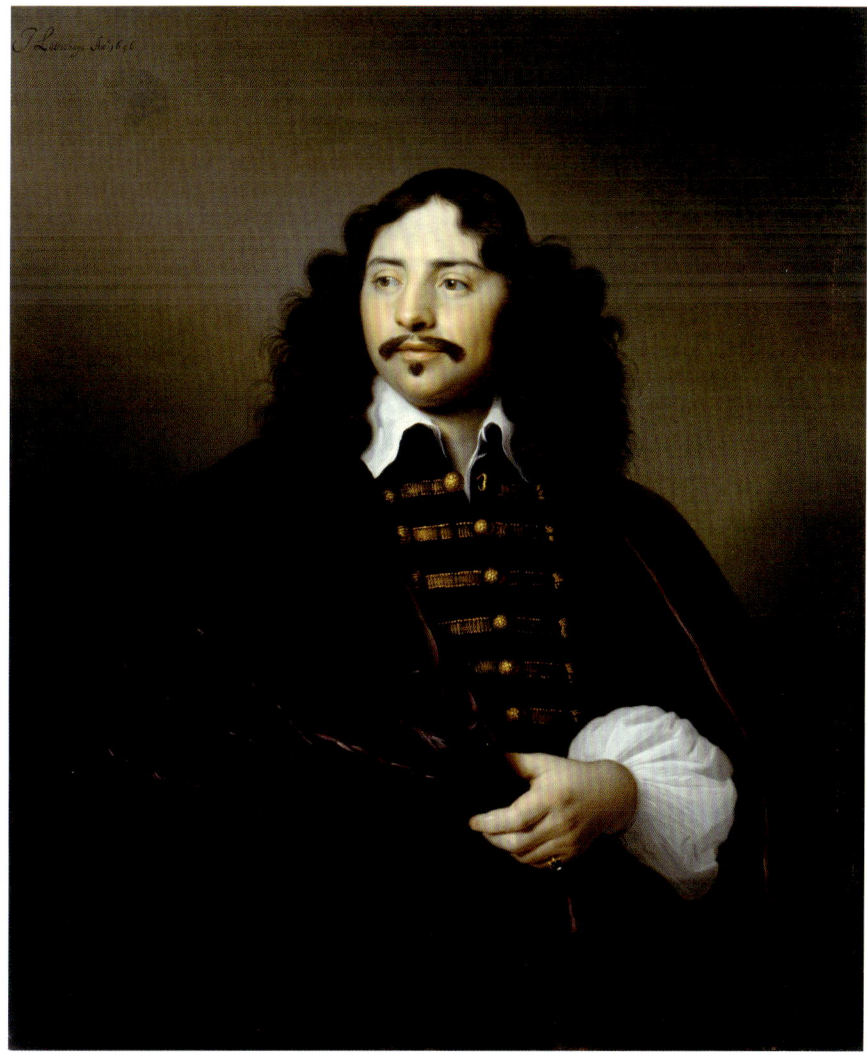

fig. 4.8 **Isaack Luttichuys,** *Portrait of Martijn Gaertz*, 1656, oil on canvas; 98.4 × 81.6 cm. The Museum of Fine Arts, Houston. Gift of Mr. and Mrs. Jimmy J. Younger in memory of Douglas F. Younger (2001.84)

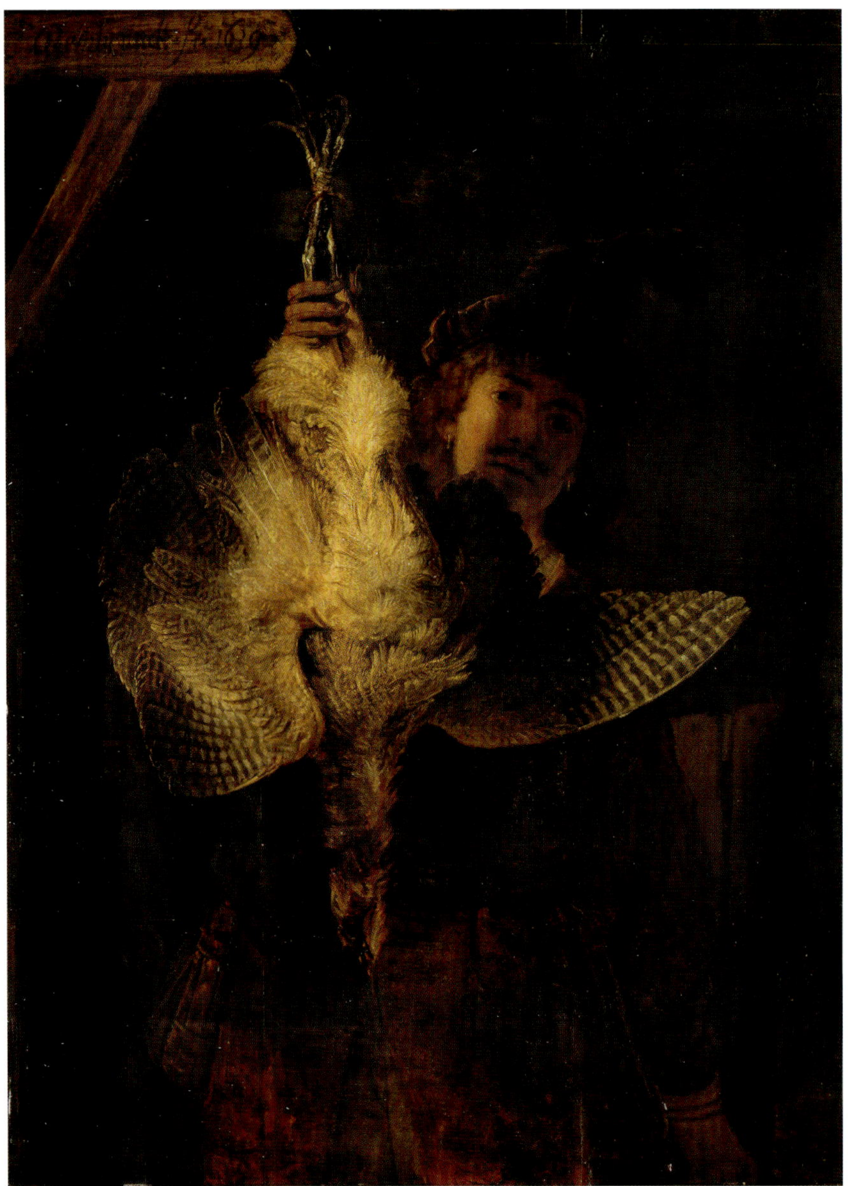

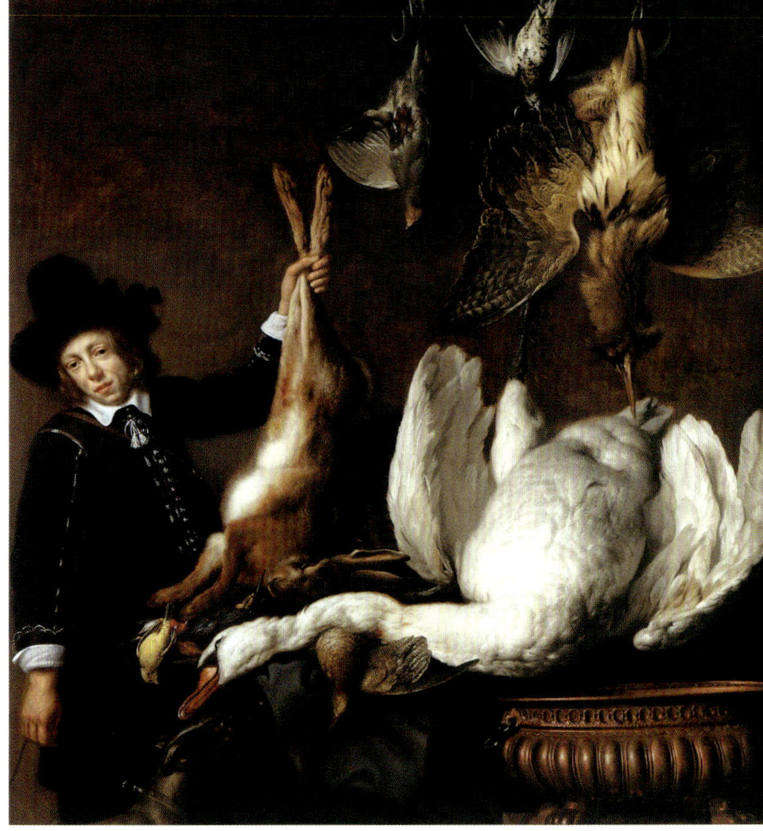

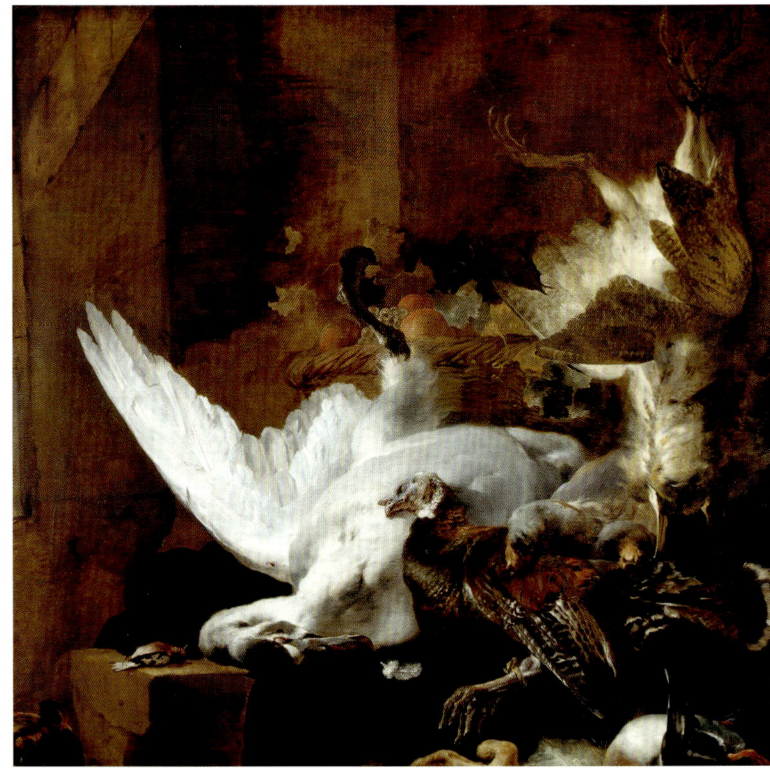

fig. 4.9 Rembrandt van Rijn,
The Bittern Hunter, 1639,
oil on panel; 120.7 × 88.3 cm.
Staatliche Kunstsammlungen
Dresden, Gemäldegalerie
Alte Meister (1561)

fig. 4.10 Elias Vonck, *Boy Holding
a Hare near a Hunting Still Life
with Dead Birds*, c. 1645–50,
oil on canvas; 162.5 × 146 cm.
Private collection

fig. 4.11 Jan Baptist Weenix,
Still Life with a Dead Swan, c. 1651,
oil on canvas; 152.4 × 153.7 cm.
Detroit Institute of Arts. Gift of
Ralph Harman Booth (26.22)

Still Life

Still life held a market share of only around 8 per cent during the period from 1630 to 1659.[105] Several still lifes by Rembrandt are mentioned in his inventory,[106] but only the large *Still Life with Peacocks* (pl. 150) remains. Although this work was recently interpreted – together with *The Bittern Hunter* (fig. 4.9) – as primarily a study in the shape, form and light of feathers in preparation for history painting,[107] the theme of hanging dead fowl had a long pictorial tradition in Amsterdam, introduced in the sixteenth century by Pieter Aertsen.[108] Rembrandt's contemporary, Elias Vonck, travelled to Poland but was back in Amsterdam in or before 1639.[109] His *Boy Holding a Hare near a Hunting Still Life with Dead Birds* (fig. 4.10) postdates Rembrandt's painting by several years, but Vonck is known to have already painted dead fowl in the 1630s.[110] Against Rembrandt's warm palette, Vonck offered a more realistic alternative, paralleled in the work of Jan Baptist Weenix, another Amsterdam native and a talented pupil of Moeyaert.[111] Paintings such as Weenix's equally imposing *Still Life with a Dead Swan* (fig. 4.11) must have catered to an increasingly opulent taste.

Genre

Until the 1630s, the Amsterdam market for "genre" figures from modern life, sometimes referred to by contemporaries as "*moderne beelden*" (modern images), had primarily been dominated by the merry companies and guardroom scenes of Pieter Codde (see fig. 15.4) and Willem Duyster, both Amsterdam natives. Rembrandt, in his Amsterdam years, mostly reserved "genre" for drawings and prints (pls. 144, 145, 148, 153).[112] What he and his workshop did produce in abundance were *tronies*, character busts of men and women in often fanciful costume; these ranged from sketchy studies to elaborate portrait-like figures, some transcending the genre's narrower definition (pls. 36, 81).[113] A specific sub-group featuring girls leaning out of windows quickly became a recognizable product of the Rembrandt brand. Although the theme developed from the painter's exploration of the illusionistic impact of portrait sitters leaning over balustrades, as in his *Self-portrait at the Age of 34* (see fig. 5.6), followed by self-portraits and commissioned portraits,[114] the first to single it out was not Rembrandt but Jan Victors in 1640, in

his earliest signed painting (pl. 88). From 1641 on, Rembrandt and his pupils developed this innovative and appealing motif in paintings of women leaning out of frames, beds and windows (pl. 151).[115]

Rembrandt and his (former) pupils held a firm grip on the Amsterdam *tronie* market, but others participated as well.[116] Lievens' *tronies* are often found in inventories.[117] Jacob Backer and the genre painter Simon Kick, who grew up around the Breestraat and married the sister of Willem Duyster, also produced *tronies*; as noted above, they even employed the same model.[118] Relatively easy to produce, *tronies* were among the less expensive products available from Rembrandt's workshop. During his lifetime, eight by the master himself were inventoried at a modest average value of 45 guilders, while three copies of *tronies* after Rembrandt averaged no more than 13 guilders apiece.[119]

Meanwhile, Amsterdam attracted several capable genre painters. In 1637 Jan Miense Molenaer, who had studied with Frans Hals in Haarlem, settled in Amsterdam with his wife Judith Leyster. With his peasant scenes (pl. 142), Molenaer was able to fill an empty niche in the market. Backer cultivated a market for pastoral images featuring shepherds and shepherdesses that was taken up by Flinck and Jacob van Loo, who arrived in the city around 1642.[120] Primarily a history painter (pl. 100), Van Loo also practised portraiture and genre. Around 1650, both he and Van den Eeckhout turned their attention to the growing market for elegant genre imagery, introducing increased refinement of gesture, rendering of materials and descriptive realism (see figs. 15.5, 15.6). Using a bright palette, they achieved a vibrant clarity far removed from Rembrandt's saturated "*houding.*" As Wayne Franits aptly states, their work "testifies to the changing expectations and tastes among increasingly wealthy and civilized buyers who desired more sophisticated renderings of established imagery."[121]

In genre as in portraiture, a classicizing tendency toward brighter colours and a greater sophistication and elegance was initiated by the painters themselves, but nourished by changing consumer taste from the 1640s onwards. After immersing themselves in Rembrandt's manner, Flinck, Bol and other pupils gradually developed a brighter, more legible style. Expressing eloquence and referencing Flemish examples (Rubens, Anthony van Dyck), this new manner was especially suitable for public spaces, for which in time they received numerous commissions. Artistically, Rembrandt did not compete with his Amsterdam colleagues in following this fashion. *Hors catégorie*, he operated in a different artistic league, more concerned with his great predecessors. Still, he too had bills to pay, which would have been a major incentive for commercial success.

Selling His Art

In 1675 Joachim von Sandrart suggested that, if Rembrandt "had been able to please people and to look after his affairs properly, he would have increased his wealth considerably."[122] Documents concerning Rembrandt's dealings reveal a self-assured, commercial attitude. In a much-discussed series of letters to Huygens between 1636 and 1639 (pl. 96), Rembrandt writes of trying to get the full price of 1,000 guilders each for five paintings in the Passion Series commissioned for Frederik Hendrik.[123] Eventually, he received 600 guilders apiece for the *Entombment, Ascension* and *Resurrection*, still an incredible price; moreover, in 1646, for the final two works, he earned an astonishing 2,400 guilders.[124] In a 1641 letter, the French painter Claude Vignon asked the art dealer François Langlois to greet Rembrandt, to "bring back something by him," and to inform him that he had just appraised Rembrandt's *Bileam*, "which Mr. Lopez bought from him."[125] Besides underlining Rembrandt's international stature, Vignon's letter informs us that Rembrandt deftly sold a 1626 "*winkeldochter*" (a product that has remained unsold) to a major collector: the aforementioned Alphonso Lopez, who resided in Amsterdam from 1636 to 1640.[126]

Two cases concerning portraits show how Rembrandt did not refrain from seeking arbitration when it could benefit him. In 1654 he brought a dispute with the merchant Diego d'Andrade over the likeness of a "young daughter's portrait" to the guild officers.[127] And in 1659 Uylenburgh testified that in 1642 Rembrandt had called upon a group of "good men" (including Uylenburgh) to mediate in a matter concerning a "painting or *conterfeitsel*" created for the regent and future burgomaster Andries de Graeff, probably the latter's portrait now in the Gemäldegalerie Alte Meister, Kassel (pl. 73).[128] The good men judged that De Graeff should pay Rembrandt 500 guilders, the same price he received that year for a now lost double portrait of the director of the West India Company, Abraham van Wilmerdonx, and his wife

Anna van Beaumont.[129] In 1652 Rembrandt sold Jan Six three paintings, including the very personal *Portrait of Saskia in a Red Hat* (c. 1633–42, Gemäldegalerie Alte Meister, Kassel).[130] In 1662 he sold a *Nativity* and a *Circumcision* to his friend Lodewijk van Ludick for the substantial amount of 600 guilders.[131] Later on, Rembrandt made lucrative deals with the Italian noblemen Antonio Ruffo from Sicily (1,300 guilders for three paintings) and Francesco Maria Sauli from Genoa (1023.15 guilders for two *modelli*).[132] In fact, throughout his career, Rembrandt received numerous important commissions, public and private.[133] A recent insight reconfirms this: Rembrandt's 1655 *Joseph Accused by Potiphar's Wife* (Gemäldegalerie, Berlin) belonged to a prestigious commissioned six-part cycle on Joseph's life, closely related to the theatre, to which Flinck, Breenbergh and Salomon Koninck also contributed.[134] Moreover, Baldinucci mentioned that "in the house of a merchant who was a magistrate of Amsterdam, [Rembrandt] painted in oils on the wall many pictures of stories of Ovid."[135] Nothing else is known about this important cycle, but we can be sure that its commissioner – possibly the merchant and burgomaster Cornelis Witsen[136] – paid Rembrandt well for it.

Rembrandt continued to work with art dealers as well. His relationship with Uylenburgh remained cordial.[137] Johannes de Renialme, dubbed "Rembrandt's preferred dealer" by John Michael Montias, catered to a clientele of select connoisseurs.[138] Among the "commercial wares" in his estate inventory one finds an amazing thirteen paintings by Rembrandt, varying from a *Moor* (African) for 12 guilders to a *Christ and the Woman Taken in Adultery* for no less than 1,500 guilders – averaging a substantial 291 guilders.[139] From a variety of sources (inventories, cash books, divisions of estates, sales records, deeds of purchase, correspondence, etc.) fifty-nine priced paintings by Rembrandt recorded during his lifetime can be gathered. Their average price of 303.16 guilders (or 324.77 guilders including *The Night Watch*) is astonishingly high.[140]

Despite this list of impressive deals and prices, it is sometimes stated that Rembrandt was a commercial failure. This point of view is fostered by remarks such as those of Sandrart, and by Rembrandt's dramatic bankruptcy in 1656. In contrast, Flinck is sometimes held up as Rembrandt's opposite: a suave, successful painter who built a network that brought him commissions, prestige and wealth. Erna Kok has shown the basic underlying principle of such networks to be "service and service in return."[141] By cultivating relations with close-knit networks of elite families, intertwined through religion, politics and social status, and by following the societal conventions of favours, gifts, reciprocity, honour and reputation instead of commercial "supply and demand," painters at the upper end of the market were able to establish favourable positions. Rembrandt, it is stated, did not possess the attributes – either by nature or by will – necessary for this career path. His insistent correspondence with Huygens over the remuneration for the Passion Series is frequently cited.[142] For instance, the phrasing "if His Highness with reasonable persuasion [*met goede vougen*] cannot be moved to pay a higher price, even if [the paintings] are clearly worth it, I shall be content with 600 k. guilders each," has been interpreted as overreaching.[143] However, in the same 1639 letter Rembrandt addresses Huygens as a friend: "I have full faith in you … If things had gone according to your wishes and to propriety, no objection would have been raised to the asking price."[144] Moreover, the fabulous 2,400-guilder remuneration in 1646 for the two remaining paintings marks the court's eventual realization that Rembrandt offered *hors concours* quality.[145]

This is, of course, not to argue that Rembrandt was in fact a gallant networker. He was clearly difficult, but also someone who stood his ground – a confident entrepreneur who firmly believed in his exceptional product, and got unparalleled prices, confirming his

beliefs. Daring to ask and then settling for less was neither a *faux pas* nor a sign of defeat, but rather a negotiating strategy. Similarly, in 1659 Lievens was commissioned to portray Joan Huydecoper's family. While initially asking a steep 2,500 guilders, he settled for 1,600, still an enormous figure (64 per cent of the original asking price, close to Rembrandt's 60 per cent). Interestingly, Huydecoper's diary reveals that Lievens and the Huydecoper family were extremely friendly during the project: dinners (with and without Lievens' wife), drinks and joint visits to the tavern are mentioned.[146] Thus, asking full price was not a social mistake per se. As a thank you, Lievens painted an *Entombment* for Huydecoper, but the latter disposed of it quickly, so as not to "have any obligation."[147] Hcrc we see another parallel with Rembrandt, whose generous gift to Huygens (a large painting, thought to be *The Blinding of Samson*, pl. 106) was possibly refused or regifted.[148]

Rembrandt strongly believed he should be remunerated not for the amount of time or work invested – the normal custom among Dutch painters and craftsmen – but for the quality of the work and his distinguished reputation.[149] The idea that the rigidity with which he practised this belief caused him social and economic problems,[150] ultimately leading to his bankruptcy in 1656,[151] is contradicted by the number of impressive commissions and prices he attracted throughout his career, not from one family network, but from an international clientele of serious lovers of art. ■

NOTES

1   "Rembrandt's certification of well-being," 26 July 1632, Remdoc, no. e4399 (trans. modified).

2   On Uylenburgh, see esp. Jaap van der Veen's essays in London and Amsterdam 2006, chaps. 1, 3.

3   Houbraken 1718–21, vol. 1, 254–255, is the only source to name Pynas.

4   "Paintings in the collection of Prince Frederick Hendrick [Frederik Hendrik] of Orange," 16 Aug. 1632, Remdoc, no. e4400; cf. Sluijter 2015, 26.

5   On Honthorst, see Judson and Ekkart 1999.

6   "Joan Huydecoper buys a tronie by Rembrandt," 10/15 June 1628, Remdoc, no. e4385; Roscam Abbing 2006, 11, NRD3, notes that it could also read 20 guilders.

7   "Een kleijn tronitge van Remlandt"; "A Rembrandt painting in the inventory of Barent Teunisz," 19 Oct. 1629, Remdoc, no. e4387.

8   Bredius 1915–22, vol. 1, 287–290.

9   Jaap van der Veen, "Hendrick Uylenburgh's Art Business: Production and Trade between 1625 and 1655," in London and Amsterdam 2006, 171–173, 184–186. Uylenburgh co-signed De Neyn's testament in 1638, and De Neyn's widow invested money in Uylenburgh's firm in 1640. Moreover, we conspicuously find De Neyn's paintings in Amsterdam collections that contain works by other painters associated with Uylenburgh (e.g., Reijncke Gerrits, death inventory, Montias Database, 1647, no. 234, with works by De Neyn, Rembrandt, Govert Flinck, Claes Moeyaert, Simon de Vlieger and Dirck van Santvoort; "Paintings in the estate of Jacques Specx," 13 Jan. 1653, Remdoc. no. e4626, with works by De Neyn, Rembrandt, Flinck, De Vlieger, Jacob Backer and Jan Adriaensz van Staveren).

10 "The earliest record of Hendrick Gerritsz Uylenburch [Uylenburgh] residence at Amsterdam," 8 Mar. 1628, Remdoc, no. e4384. See also Van Straten 2005, 74; Jaap van der Veen, "Hendrick Uylenburgh, Agent of the King of Poland and Art Dealer in Amsterdam," in London and Amsterdam 2006, 24, 51.

11 Bredius 1915–22, vol. 5, 1686; cf. Montias 2002, 122.

12 "Acknowledgement of a debt owed to Rembrandt by Hendrick Uylenburch [Uylenburgh]," 20 June 1631, Remdoc, no. e4393.

13 A signed receipt for the tuition fee of Rembrandt's pupil Isaac de Jouderville indicates that Rembrandt was still active in Leiden in November 1631; "Receipt for the apprenticeship fee paid by Rembrandt's student Isaack [Isaac] de Jouderville," 19 Nov. 1631, Remdoc, no. e1686.

14 On the question of studio assistance in the Uylenburgh years, impossible to address extensively here, see, among others, Amsterdam and Groningen 1983; Josua Bruyn, "Studio Practice and Studio Production," in Corpus, vol. 3, 12–50; Liedtke 2004; Michiel Franken, "Learning by Imitation: Copying Paintings in Rembrandt's Workshop," in Amsterdam and Berlin 2006, 153–177; "Salomon Koninck (1609–1656): His Amsterdam Career until c. 1650," in Sluijter 2015, 199–213 (Salomon Koninck, Jacob de Wet, Willem de Poorter).

15 See Ernst van de Wetering, "Problems of Apprenticeship and Studio Collaboration," in Corpus, vol. 2, 59–60; Chapman 1990, 57.

16 Corpus, vol. 6, "Notes to the Plates," 480–687, nos. 1–324. Hereafter, all numbers preceded by "CS" refer to this list.

17 Corpus, vol. 6, lists 349 paintings by Rembrandt (not included here is CS184a, Portrait of a Man [Balthasar Coymans?] [1641?, private collection], listed as "mainly executed by a member of Rembrandt's workshop"). Over the period of 1632 to 1655, one can count 202 works (CS50, CS61–242). From the initial eighty-three rejected in earlier volumes of the Rembrandt Research Project's Corpus of Rembrandt Paintings over this period (B8–11, C45–122), Corpus, vol. 6, reaccepts thirty-six works (43 per cent!). However, A82 and A83 have been excluded without further explanation, whereas A97 was rejected in Corpus, vol. 4, 602.

18 To estimate the number of copies is extremely treacherous. Taking Corpus, vol. 6, as a basis, for CS50, CS61–143 (Rembrandt paintings, 1632–35), one can count at most forty-three possible period copies (copies listed in Corpus, vols. 1–3, categories A, B and C, excluding drawings and works evidently produced after 1635 and/or outside the Uylenburgh studio). For works from 1632 to 1635 not included in Corpus, vol. 6 (Corpus, vols. 1–3, A82–83, A97, B11, C45, C50, C54–55, C57–59, C62–64, C75–77, C81–82), one can count another ten possible period copies. However, these numbers remain inadequate, as many paintings listed in Bredius and Gerson 1969 lack separate entries in the Corpus.

19 Many such paintings have been lost over time. Attribution issues, recent discoveries, etc., rule out true "completeness."

20 Schwartz 1977, 8–11, charts etchings per year; for a full chronology, see also NHD. After Rembrandt's move to Amsterdam, biblical subjects replaced beggars and old men, possibly because Uylenburgh felt there was a good market for them.

21 The caption reads "cum pryvlo: Amstelodami Hendrickus Ulenburgensis," asserting copyright privilege for Uylenburgh. Ernst van de Wetering describes this project as "exceptionally ambitious, not to say megalomanic," theorizing that "Rembrandt and Uylenburgh together had great plans for this print [that was] the launch of a major project for more prints whose copyright had to be safeguarded," and argues that the chosen subjects had specific meaning for Mennonites; Corpus, vol. 5, 176–185.

22 Joachim von Sandrart in Ford 2007, 29. Huygens addressed Rembrandt's (and Lievens') "tireless perseverance and hard work"; quoted in Van Straten 2005, 345–346. Filippo Baldinucci said he "toiled restlessly and completed very few pictures"; Ford 2007, 43.

23 Reznicek 1977, 75–107, esp. 84. See also Corpus, vol. 2, A51, A184.

24 Van de Wetering in Corpus, vol. 4, xxv, suggests that Rembrandt made self-portraits mostly to supply a demand, rather than as a marketing tool. In 1632 Rembrandt sometimes spelled his name without the "d."

25 Sebastien A.C. Dudok van Heel argues that Uylenburgh took over Van der Voort's portrait workshop, subcontracting outside painters to produce portraits; Dudok van Heel 2006, 330–337; cf. Van der Veen in London and Amsterdam 2006, 47–49, 119–121.

26 Peter van den Brink, "Oeuvrecatalogus," in Amsterdam and Aachen 2008–09, 204–249, lists thirty-two paintings produced by Backer in Amsterdam between 1632/33 and 1635 (A6–9, A12–39). Van den Brink 2016 (NB: A10–11 as painted in Leeuwarden) adds three works (figs. 8, 10, 11) bringing the total to thirty-five, including eleven portraits (31 per cent).

27 In addition to the nine accepted tronies in Corpus, vol. 6, twelve tronies from 1632 to 1635 not accepted as by Rembrandt are listed in Corpus, vols. 1–3, C50, C52, C54–60, C62–64.

28 Eleven (combined) Amsterdam sitters can be identified, six documented as owning/having commissioned more work by Rembrandt: Looten; Uylenburgh/Sylvius; Bruyningh/Moutmaker; Rijcksen/Jans; Soolmans/Coppit; Lucasz/Buys (commissioned by Specx). For five this cannot be established: Ruts; Krul (identification doubtful); Wtenbogaert (commissioned by Recht); Pellicorne/Van Collen; Elison/Bockenolle (commissioned by their son).

29   This double portrait (CS61, identification of sitters is not confirmed) and *Christ in the Storm on the Sea of Galilee* (CS105)
were stolen in 1990 from the Isabella Stewart Gardner Museum,
Boston.

30   The portrait of Pieter Jansz Moutmaker is listed in the 1647
inventory of his son-in-law Jan Pietersz Bruyningh; "Paintings
in the inventory of Jan Pietersz Bruyningh," 30 Jan. 1647, Remdoc,
no. e4552; Van Eeghen 1977, esp. 67–71. Moutmaker was probably
born around 1570–75. In 1623 he lived in Amsterdam, but probably
moved away before 1630. He signed his last will in January 1632
in Amsterdam, and died before October 1635. The portrait might
be the *Portrait of a Man* in the Metropolitan Museum of Art,
New York (CS73), from 1632, the year Moutmaker was in
Amsterdam to sign his will and the same year as the double
portrait of his daughter and her husband (CS61), who likely commissioned the father's portrait for their house. The given age of
the sitter, forty, is a later addition applied to make it fit with
Rembrandt's female portrait in the Nivaagaards Malerisamling,
Nivå (CS74), where a similar inscription was added. See Liedtke
2007, vol. 2, no. 141, esp. 550–552n2.

31   "Paintings in possession of Martin van den Broeck bartered for
marine supplies," 28 Mar. 1647, Remdoc no. e4551.

32   In addition to Amalia von Solms, Rembrandt portrayed Maurits
Huygens, Jacques de Gheyn III, Joris de Caullery and – possibly
at this time as well – the latter's son Johan (presumably lost, but
listed in the fathers' will in 1661); CS65b, CS67, CS68, CS70. That
the identification of Johan de Caullery with the sitter of
Rembrandt's 1632-dated *Portrait of a Man* (CS71, pl. 50) cannot
be correct was convincingly demonstrated by Ben Broos, who
pointed out that Johan was only five years old in 1632; Broos in
The Hague and San Francisco 1990–91, 373. See also the essay
by Rudi Ekkart and Claire van den Donk in this volume.

33   Whether the so-called Van Beresteyn pendant portraits
(CS63a-b, see figs. 6.8, 6.9) depict members from the Van Beresteyn
family (tentatively Cornelis van Beresteyn and his second wife
Corvina van Hofdyck, who lived in Delft; see Liedtke 2007, vol. 2,
no. 143), or Frederik Hendrik's treasurer Thomas Brouaert and his
wife Johanna van Clootwijk (resident in The Hague), they were
most likely painted in The Hague. See also the essay by Ekkart and
Van den Donk in this volume.

34   CS116, 117a-b, 119a-b. Sebastien A.C. Dudok van Heel identifies
Rembrandt's pendants in Pasadena and Louisville as Jacob van
Couwenhoven and Maritje Pesser; Sebastien A.C. Dudok van
Heel, "Rembrandt's Surprising Start as a Portrait Painter: Hendrick
Uylenburgh's Role in the Production of Portraits in Amsterdam,"
in Madrid 2020, 137–138; see also Dudok van Heel 2020. The
couple were again portrayed by Bartholomeus van der Helst in
1647; Van Gent 2011, nos. 38, 39. See also Van der Veen 2003, in
which the pendants are tentatively identified as Pieter Seijen and
his wife Marritje Cornelisdr van Grotewal. For two further additions to this group by Van der Helst in 1647, see Jasper Hillegers,
"Bartholomeus van der Helst," in Hillegers et al. 2014, 36–43.

35   "The portrait of Rev. Johannes Wtenbogaert," 13 Apr. 1633, Remdoc,
no. e4404.

36   "Rembrandt gives power of attorney to his brother-in-law Gerrit
van Loo to negotiate on his behalf with debtors in Frisia," 22 July
1634, Remdoc, no. e4415.

37   Van der Wolf was married to Maria Dircksdr Pesser, the daughter
of Dirck Pesser and Haesje Cleyburg, who were among the family
members painted by Rembrandt in 1634 (CS117a-b). In 1659 the
Paracelsus was offered for sale to Leopoldo de' Medici, who

apparently did not buy it. See Rutgers 2003, 10, 18n68; see also
Roscam Abbing 2006, vol. 2, 76, NRD53. The painting was again
for sale in 1676 for 200 guilders (a minor price compared to many
other works in this sale). See Hoet 1752–70, vol. 2, 340.

38   In the 1620s Maertgen was witness to the baptism of four children
of her sister Neeltgen and Pieter de Neyn, the latter two along
with her husband; Leiden archive, DTB, archive 1004, inv. 232,
8 Mar. 1622 (Maertien); 14 Nov. 1623 (Adriaen); inv. 221, 23 Jan. 1626
(Adrianus); inv. 233, 7 Aug. 1633 (Cornelia).

39   Sigal 1961. At their intended marriage, Burchgraeff is described
as "*jongman van Renegens*" (young man from Renegens), no doubt
Reningelst in West Flanders; Leiden archive, DTB archive 1004,
inv. 9, fol. 30v, 25 Oct. 1625. He died in 1647 at the age of forty-
three; Maertgen died in 1653 at the age of forty-seven.

40   Leiden archive, 0506, inv. 471, fol. 9 (notary Jacob Jansz de Haes),
Mar. 1638.

41   Mijtens resided in London until 1634. It is extremely unlikely
that the female portrait (dated 1633) was painted before the male
portrait.

42   See *Corpus*, vol. 2, A82. The identification of Maertgen relies on
an eighteenth or nineteenth-century inscription on the reverse
of the panel: "*Margareta Hendrikse van Bilderdijk* [sic] *Huisvrouw
van Willem Burggraaf* [sic]." The reverse of the Mijtens portrait
carries an inscription in the same handwriting: "*Willem
Burggraaf.*" This implies that the works once belonged to the
same family collection. The Mitjens portrait is inscribed "*Aetatus
[Age] 50 Ao 1635.*" Thus, Mijtens' sitter cannot be Maertgen's
husband (d. 1647), who would have been thirty-one in 1635. Rather,
he shows a striking resemblance to the sixty-two-year-old sitter
in Bartholomeus van der Helst's *Portrait of a Man* (1647,
The Metropolitan Museum of Art, New York), as noted in Liedtke
2007, vol. 1, 326–327, no. 76. Perhaps there was another Willem
in the Burchgraeff clan.

43   The authors of *Corpus*, vol. 2, considered the painting (C77) to
be executed by the same hand responsible for C56 (*Bust of
Rembrandt*, Gemäldegalerie, Berlin), probably Flinck. In 2014
C56 was reassigned to Rembrandt, c. 1633–36 (CS146). The *Corpus*
authors rejected the Burchgraeff/pendant to Bilderbeecq identification due to lack of resemblance with the Mijtens portrait
and dissimilar panel construction, compositions and "artistic
approach." None of these reasons seems valid. Moreover – and
not considered in the *Corpus* – when the female portrait was
bought by the Städel Museum, Frankfurt am Main, in a Rotterdam
auction in 1844, it was accompanied by a copy after the Dresden
portrait, first mentioned in Dresden as early as 1722. Apparently,
when the pendants were separated (by inheritance?) around
1722, a copy of the male portrait was painted to remain with the
female portrait. This copy is listed in the Städel Museum's 1844
inventory, but not in the 1846 and subsequent inventories. See
Neumeister 2005, 380–394, esp. 382–383. Walter Liedtke and
Sebastien A.C. Dudok van Heel consider A82 and C77 to be autograph pendants; Liedtke 2004, 66; Dudok van Heel in Madrid
2020, 140, fig. 79.

44   Baldinucci 1974, vol. 5, 321–322.

45   E.g., *Kneeling Saint Peter* (1631, Israel Museum, Jerusalem,
CS40), bridging the distinctive pictorial traditions of Saint
Peter repentant and Saint Peter in prison. The *Leiden History
Piece* (1626, CS7, see fig. 5.2) still lacks a satisfying interpret-
ation, although it is doubtful whether this was Rembrandt's
intention.

46   Sluijter 2015, 40–41.

47   Straat 1928, 76. The paintings belonged to Lambert Jacobsz in Leeuwarden, whose possessions were inventoried in 1637, after his passing in 1636. Uylenburgh no doubt had the works on consignment from Jacobsz and would have received a commission if he sold them. Clearly, they were produced for the open market. Honthorst's *Satyr* is no doubt the work in the Rijksmuseum (inv. SK-C-1759), on loan from the Broere Charitable Foundation (see Judson and Ekkart 1999, no. 122); De Grebber's *Ruth and Naomi* is probably the 1628-dated work in the sale at Christie's, New York, 23 Jan. 2004, lot 21; Backer's *Tribute Money* exists in several versions; the principal version is in the Nationalmuseum, Stockholm (see fig. 1.5); see Van den Brink 2016, nos. A3, A3a-c. Backer, originally from Harlingen, spent the latter part of his youth in Amsterdam, but left for Leeuwarden around 1626–28.

48   See "The sixth letter to Constantijn Huygens," 13 Feb. 1639, Remdoc no. e4461.

49   Houbraken 1718–21, vol. 1, 269.

50   Jager 2016.

51   In 1645 the art dealer Marten Kretzer hired Pieter van den Bosch to paint whatever Kretzer demanded – winter dawn to dusk and summer 7 am to 7 pm – for 1,200 guilders yearly; Bredius 1934. Although Kretzer was a prestigious dealer, Van den Bosch was not in the same league as Rembrandt, or as Govert Flinck, his successor with Uylenburgh.

52   "The first letter to Constantijn Huygens," Feb. 1636, Remdoc, no. e4428.

53   For an overview of Rembrandt's pupils, see Ben Broos, "Fame Shared is Fame Doubled," in Amsterdam and Groningen 1983, 35–58, esp. 46–47; Liedtke 2004, esp. 68, Appendix B. Arnold Houbraken, who seems to have been well informed on Van den Eeckhout, states that he was Rembrandt's pupil and friend; Houbraken 1718–21, vol. 2, 20–21, vol. 3, 206. Eric Jan Sluijter is convinced – with strong arguments – that neither Van den Eeckhout nor Victors were Rembrandt's pupils; Sluijter 2015, 346–348, 363–364.

54   Sluijter 2009.

55   Thomas Asselijn, quoted in Sluijter 2015, 7.

56   Of the vast literature on the Dutch and Amsterdam art markets, see esp. Boers 2012; Bok 1994; Marten Jan Bok, "Rembrandt's Fame and Rembrandt's Failure: The Market for History Paintings in the Dutch Republic," in Kofuku 2004, 159–178; Bok and Schwartz 1991; Li 2018; Li 2019; John Michael Montias, "Works of Art in Seventeenth-century Amsterdam: An Analysis of Subjects and Attributions," in Freedberg and De Vries 1991, 331–372; Montias 1999; Montias 2002; Montias 2004–05; Rasterhoff 2017, chaps. 7–8; Eric Jan Sluijter, "Determining Value on the Art Market in the Golden Age: An Introduction," in Tummers and Jonckheere 2008, 7–28; Sluijter 2009.

57   Dudok van Heel reproduces part of Balthasar Florisz van Berckenrode's 1625 city map showing the Breestraat neighbourhood, with the locations of many artists' and other residents' homes and studios; "Rembrandt van Rijn [1606–1669]: A Changing Portrait of the Artist," in Berlin, Amsterdam and London 1991–92b, 58–59, and Dudok van Heel 2006, 74–75. On the Breestraat's history, see Ten Cate 1988.

58   Rembrandt is documented at seven sales. See "Rembrandt's purchases at the sale of the Van Someren collection," 22–29 Feb. 1635, Remdoc, no. e4420; "The sale of the Jan Bassé collection by Pieter Jacobsz Indische Raven," 9–30 Mar. 1637, Remdoc, no. e4438; "Rembrandt's presence at an art sale," 7 Oct. 1637,

Remdoc, no. e4442; "Rembrandt's purchase at the Nicolaes Bas sale," 10 Sept. 1637, Remdoc, no. e4440; "Rembrandt's purchases at the sale of Gommer Spranger's collection," 9 Feb. 1638, Remdoc, no. e4447; "The sale of a painting by Raphael, the so-called 'Portrait of Baldassare Castiglione,' at the Van Uffelen auction...," 9 Apr. 1639, Remdoc, no. e4464; "Rembrandt's purchase of marble statues," 13 Sept. 1646, Remdoc, no. e4544 (he purchased several marble statues from the Antwerp dealer Matthijs Musson for 186.10 guilders). Rembrandt might also have attended the sales of Cornelis Boissens in Leiden in 1636 and of his own pupil Leendert van Beijeren in 1648/49. For Rembrandt as an art buyer, see Roelof van Gelder and Jaap van der Veen, "A Collector's Cabinet in the Breestraat: Rembrandt as a Lover of Art and Curiosities," in Amsterdam 1999–2000, 33–89, esp. 37–43.

59   Baldinucci in Ford 2007, 45.

60   Sandrart 1675–80, vol. 2, book 3, 240. Dudok van Heel 1978, esp. 152–153n4, suggests Sandrart refers to an estate auction of Rembrandt's late pupil Van Beijeren, c. 1650–52. See also "Rembrandt's purchase of Lucas van Leyden's print 'Ulenspiegelken,'" 1642, Remdoc, no. e4515, in which Harderwijk burgomaster Ernst Brinck declares that Rembrandt "recently" paid 179 guilders for an impression of Van Leyden's print *The Beggar's Family*, nicknamed "*Uylenspiegel*" (NHD 159, see fig. 17.6).

61   "Deposition by Lodewijck [Lodewijk] van Ludick concerning Rembrandt's purchase of a painting 'Hero and Leander' by Rubens," after 7 Oct. 1659, Remdoc, no. e12836. Rembrandt had bought Rubens' painting in 1637 from the accountant Trojanus de Magistris for nearly 425 guilders and thus made a profit.

62   An agreement with Jan Six dated 5 Oct. 1652 is no longer extant but is referred to in "Cancellation of agreements between Rembrandt and Six," 13 Sept. 1658, Remdoc, no. e12788.

63   Inventory of Rembrandt's insolvent estate (Cessio Bonorum), 25–26 July 1656, fol. 30r and 31v, Remdoc, nos. e12713, e12716. For a transcription of the inventory, see Jaap van der Veen in Amsterdam 1999–2000, 147–152, Appendix 2.

64   "Rembrandt's appraisal of a painting by Paulus [Paul] Bril," 16 Sept. 1653, Remdoc, no. e4641.

65   For 1636–39 only three portraits are known, but more once existed; see Jaap van der Veen, "Faces from Life: *Tronies* and Portraits in Rembrandt's Painted Oeuvre," in Melbourne and Canberra 1997–98, 78; Montias 2002, 164–170.

66   Sandrart 1675–80, vol. 2, book 3, 326.

67   Ibid.

68   Inscription on the reverse of *Susanna and the Elders* (Kupferstichkabinett, Berlin); "Rembrandt's notation on the verso of the drawing 'Susanna at the Bath' (Benesch 448)," c. 1634–37, Remdoc, no. e13493.

69   Grey/brown brush drawings after Rembrandt's *Standard Bearer* (1636, Rothschild Collection, Paris) and *Saskia as Flora* (1635, The National Gallery, London) are in the British Museum, London, while a sketch signed by Bol after Rembrandt's *Minerva* (1635, The Leiden Collection, New York) is in the Rijksmuseum, Amsterdam (inv. RP-T-1975-85). See Peter Schatborn, "Govert Flinck and Ferdinand Bol: Drawings," in Amsterdam 2017–18, 185, figs. 241–243. Could these be the works referred to in Rembrandt's inscription (above)?

70   On didactic imitation and reproduction in Rembrandt's workshop, see Franken, "Learning by Imitation," in Amsterdam and Berlin

2006. On *Abraham's Sacrifice of Isaac*, see, among others, *Corpus*, vol. 3, A108; Pieter J.J. van Thiel in Berlin, Amsterdam and London 1991–92b, 181–183, no. 21 (copy by Bol); Liedtke 2004, 54–55; *Corpus*, vol. 6, CS136; David de Witt, "Govert Flinck Learns to Paint Like Rembrandt," in Amsterdam 2017–18, 24–25.

71   On this group, see Ernst van de Wetering, "Two Nearly Identical Variations on Rembrandt's 1637 *The Angel Raphael Leaving Tobit and His Family* in the Louvre," in *Corpus*, vol. 5, 276–282, Appendix 3; David de Witt and Leonore van Sloten, "Ferdinand Bol: Rembrandt's Disciple," in Amsterdam 2017–18, 46–48.

72   Ernst van de Wetering in *Corpus*, vol. 5, 276–282 ("possible … no more than a conjecture … a constellation of external evidence"); De Witt and Van Sloten, "Ferdinand Bol," in Amsterdam 2017–18, 47 ("common features that are clear and sufficient enough to attribute the work to him with a high degree of certainty"). One supporting argument is that two of the figures in Rembrandt's original appear, slightly modified (one with a different hand gesture, the other transformed from a man into a woman), in Bol's 1644 *The Three Women at the Sepulchre* (National Gallery of Denmark, Copenhagen), implying Bol's familiarity with these figures and the availability of the composition in his studio. Bol's 1669 inventory lists a "Tobias"; Bredius 1910, 234, no. 22. These arguments speak just as much, if not more, for the recently surfaced third variation, which is superior in execution.

73   Sale, Christie's, London, 4 July 2019, lot 6, as School of Rembrandt. The painting was known from an eighteenth-century reproductive engraving, and subsequently mentioned in the literature, but overlooked for more than one hundred years (mentioned last by Hofstede de Groot, 1908–27, vol. 6 [1916], under no. 70, as "a later replica"), and never illustrated.

74   E.g., in details such as the curve of Tobias' coat (next to Tobit's head), the shape of the balustrade behind Tobias' left hand, Anna's closed eyes (opened in the variation given to Bol), or her headgear, which is flatter in Rembrandt's original and the newly surfaced variation, but higher in the variation given to Bol. In fact, elements such as the shape and expression of Tobias' head and face seem to indicate that the variation given to Bol was based on the newly surfaced variation.

75   Elements rendered more capably include the angel Raphael's face, the folds of his garment, Anna's hands, the faces of Tobit and Tobias, the detailed complexity of their garments, and Tobit's heel.

76   Dendrochronological information: sale catalogue, Christie's, London, 4 July 2019, lot 6.

77   Flinck's departure from Uylenburgh's studio is not documented, but Sandrart stated he was there for many years. On the basis of the presumed sale of Flinck's *Angel Appearing to the Shepherds* (Musée du Louvre, Paris) in 1639 to Uylenburgh (as noted by Baldinucci), Erna Kok assumes that Flinck was then no longer in Uylenburgh's service; Kok 2013, 49, 171–172n222. For a suggested date of 1644 (when Flinck bought a house at Lauriergracht), see Tom van der Molen, "The Life of Govert Flinck," in Cleves 2015–16, 15, and Sophia Thomassen, "Timeline," in Amsterdam 2017–18, 11.

78   Strauss and Van der Meulen 1979, doc. 1640/2; "Hendrick van Uylenburgh's hypothecation to creditors [afschrift]," 20 Jan. 1640, Remdoc, no. e12929. See Van der Veen, "Hendrick Uylenburgh's Art Business," in London and Amsterdam 2006, 188–196.

79   Baldinucci wrote that Flinck sold this painting, based on Rembrandt's etching of the same theme, to an Amsterdam merchant, most likely Hendrick Uylenburgh himself; Baldinucci 1974, vol. 5, 308; see, among others, Dickey 2017a, 10–11.

80   Houbraken 1718–21, vol. 2, 20–21 (biography of Govert Flinck) and vol. 3, 206 (biography of Aert de Gelder).

81   Sluijter 2015.

82   Weixuan Li, "5. Tipping Point: Case Study of the 'Epidemic' of The Dismissal of Hagar," in Li 2018, 89–93.

83   Sluijter 2015, 367–369, figs. VII-48–VII-53.

84   De Witt in Amsterdam 2017–18, 37.

85   Sluijter 2015, 261–263, fig. IV-83 (Johannes Urselincx, *Expulsion of Hagar*, 1630s, Museum of Religious Art, Uden).

86   Ibid., 100. Koninck was a master of the Amsterdam guild by 1630 according to Cornelis de Bie, whose unusually detailed biography suggests that he was informed of this by Koninck himself. Koninck's intimate knowledge of Rembrandt's work suggests a close acquaintance with Uylenburgh's studio.

87   A version of the Copenhagen *Esther* with a more extensive background is in the North Carolina Museum of Art, Raleigh; Sumowski 1983–94, vol. 3, no. 1079. For other variants, see ibid., nos. 1086, 1087 (both whereabouts unknown).

88   On this model, see Jasper Hillegers, "Jacob Backer," in Hillegers et al. 2019, 6–13.

89   "Deposition by Adriaen Banck concerning a painting of 'Susanna,'" 1659, Remdoc, no. e12833. Attestation by Adriaen Banck, widower of Helena Swalmius, daughter of Eleazer Swalmius and Eva Ruardus (all portrayed by Rembrandt) on the 1647 purchase of a *Susanna* from Rembrandt for 500 guilders.

90   Sumowski 1983–94, vol. 3, no. 1095 (1649, formerly Nystad Oude Kunst, The Hague), citing references to two other versions.

91   On De Renialme, see John Michael Montias, "Art Dealers II; Johannes de Renialme," in Montias 2002, 130–143.

92   "Lambert van den Bos' praise of Rembrandt in 'Konst kabinet van Marten Kretzer,'" 1650, Remdoc, no. e4590, mentions Rembrandt's name but not the subject of the painting. Two versions of *The Mocking of Ceres* by Koninck are known, one formerly in the Buchenau Collection, Niendorf, the other in the Ackland Art Museum, University of North Carolina, Chapel Hill; Sumowski 1983, vol. 3, nos. 1088, 1089.

93   From Van Ludick's March 1659 attestation on the value of Rembrandt's art collection, it appears that the two were well acquainted from at least 1640; "Deposition by Lodewijck [Lodewijk] van Ludick and Adriaen Hendricksz De Wees regarding the value of Rembrandt's art collection," 19 Mar. 1659, Remdoc, no. e12829. In 1659 Rembrandt agreed to paint and deliver a *Jonathan and David* within a year to Van Ludick; "Agreement between Rembrandt and Lodewijck [Lodewijk] van Ludick," Mar. 1659, Remdoc, no. e12830. In 1662 Rembrandt sold a *Nativity* and a *Circumcision* to Van Ludick for 600 guilders; "A new agreement between Rembrandt and Lodewijck [Lodewijk] van Ludick," 28 Aug. 1662, Remdoc, no. e12924.

94   Ebert 2009, no. Is. A62, identifies the sitter in a portrait by Isaack Luttichuys in the Museum of Fine Arts, Houston, as Martijn's brother Johannes (see also no. Is. A67).

95   On the Amsterdam patronage of Lievens' portraits, see Jaap van der Veen, "Patronage for Lievens' Portraits and History Pieces, 1644–1674," in Washington, Milwaukee and Amsterdam 2008–09, 28–39. Although few identified portraits remain, Van der Veen demonstrates that Lievens was a significant player on the Amsterdam portrait market.

96   Montias, "Works of Art," in Freedberg and De Vries 1991, 336, 350–355, tables 2–5.

97   For Rembrandt's landscapes in all three media, see Kassel and Leiden 2006–07. Six autograph paintings dated c. 1637/38–46 are accepted, not including *Landscape with the Good Samaritan* (1638, National Museum, Cracow, CS159) and *Landscape with the Rest on the Flight into Egypt* (1647, National Gallery of Ireland, Dublin, CS214). See also the essay by Martin Sonnabend in this volume.

98   Rembrandt's 1656 inventory lists twelve landscapes by himself. One priced landscape by Rembrandt is recorded during his lifetime, in the 1644 sale catalogue of Boudewijn de Man from Delft, for 166 guilders. See "A landscape by Rembrandt in the estate of Boudewijn de Man," 15 Mar. 1644, Remdoc, no. e4527; "Further information about the three half-figures Antonio Ruffo ordered from Rembrandt," 1 Jan. 1668, Remdoc, no. e1644. Other owners of Rembrandt's landscapes were Jan Pietersz Bruyningh, portrayed by Rembrandt together with his wife in 1632 (probably the painting formerly in the Isabella Stewart Gardner Museum, Boston, CS61), and Martin van den Broeck, a first cousin of Marten Soolmans, who also owned portraits of Rembrandt's wife, Rembrandt himself, and Rembrandt's "*minnemoer*" (nurse). See "Paintings in the inventory of Jan Pietersz Bruyning," 30 Jan. 1647, Remdoc, no. e4552; "Paintings in possession of Martin van den Broeck bartered for marine supplies," 28 Mar. 1647, Remdoc, no. e4551; Montias 2002, 180–187; Jacquelyn N. Coutré, "Painted Landscapes by Lievens and Rembrandt: The View from Seventeenth-century Amsterdam Collections," in Dickey 2017b, 122–150.

99   Melanie Gifford in Kassel and Leiden 2006–07, 137, identifies the canvas of *Landscape with the Baptism of the Eunuch*, attributed to Bol (c. 1640, Niedersächsisches Landesmuseum, Hannover), and that of Rembrandt's *Still Life with Peacocks* (CS165, pl. 150) as being from the same bolt.

100 Kassel and Leiden 2006–07, 30, fig. 16; 62, fig. 46.

101 Sumowski 1983–94, vol. 3 (1983), nos. 1301–1311; Lloyd DeWitt and Arthur K. Wheelock, Jr., in Washington, Milwaukee and Amsterdam 2008–09, nos. 37, 42, 43.

102 In 1656 Rembrandt owned three landscapes by Lievens ("The inventory of Rembrandt's insolvent estate [Cessio Bonorum] [Fol. 29v.]," 25–26 July 1656, nos. 18, 19, 22, Remdoc, no. e4707); Johannes de Renialme owned five (Montias Database, 1657, no. 180); Herman Becker, who lent money to Lievens, Rembrandt and other artists and dealers, owned six (Montias Database, 1678, no. 254); J. Meurs had one (Montias Database, 1678, no. 1377). In March 1644, just after his arrival in Amsterdam, Lievens filed a lawsuit against the painter Jan Miense Molenaer (with whom he lodged) over an unfinished landscape. See Arthur K. Wheelock, Jr., "Jan Lievens: Bringing New Light to an Old Master," in Washington, Milwaukee and Amsterdam 2008–09, 18–19; Coutré, "Painted Landscapes," in Dickey 2017b, 122.

103 On Breenbergh in Amsterdam, see Sluijter 2015, 127–148.

104 According to their 1634 testament, Breenbergh and his wife lived in the Dijkstraat. While Sluijter assumes this is the modern-day Dijkstraat, it could have been the St. Anthonisbreestraat, then often called Dijkstraat; Sluijter 2015, 128, 423n195. Balthasar Florisz van Berckenrode's 1625 map of Amsterdam, for instance, numbers current-day St. Anthoniesbreestraat as no. "84. *Dyck Straet*," whereas the present Dijkstraat is listed as "85. *Korte Dyck Straet*." See also Ten Cate 2008, 12.

105 Montias, "Works of Art," in Freedberg and De Vries 1991, 350–353, tables 2, 3.

106 Montias Database, 26 July 1656, no. 1262, mentions several (vanitas) still lifes and a painting of a skull retouched by Rembrandt, and a painting of (presumably dead) hares. A vanitas painting depicting "2 Mort heads with A scroll of peper and some dutch wreating

on it with some Books done on cloth and batert on wood … be Rembrant Van Ryn" is mentioned in the 1665 inventory of John Clerk of Pennycook (or Penicuik), a Scottish art dealer, for 40 lib Scots (Scottish pounds); Roscam Abbing 2006, vol. 2, 94, NRD71.

107 See CS166.

108 See Amsterdam and Cleveland 1999–2000, no. 40.

109 In 1631 Vonck was documented in Poland. On 22 May 1639, a daughter, Aeltje, was baptized in Amsterdam; Amsterdam City Archives, DTB 42 [NK], 312.

110 E.g., Elias Vonck, *Still Life with a Swan, Asparagus, Game and Vegetables*, dated by Fred Meijer to the second half of the 1630s; sale, Sotheby's, New York, 1–2 Feb. 2013, lot 545. www.sothebys.com/en/auctions/ecatalogue/2013/old-master-and-19th-century-paintings-n08953/lot.545.html (accessed 12 Jan. 2020).

111 On Weenix, see Van Wagenberg-Ter Hoeven 2018. See also Sluijter 2015, 162–165, figs. III-31, III-32, for two grisailles convincingly attributed to Weenix.

112 Qualifiable as genre paintings are *Interior with a Window and a Winding Staircase* (1632, Musée du Louvre, Paris, CS86), *The Standard Bearer* (1636, private collection, CS147), *Still Life with Peacocks* (c. 1639, CS165, pl. 150), *The Bittern Hunter* (1639, CS166, fig. 4.9), *The Polish Rider* (c. 1655, The Frick Collection, New York, CS236) and *The Slaughtered Ox* (1655, CS240, see fig. 18.4).

113 Twenty-two paintings (21 per cent of Rembrandt's total production) produced between 1636 and 1655 can be qualified as *tronies*. On *tronies* and their implications, see Hirschfelder 2008; Gottwald 2011.

114 E.g., *Portrait of Nicolaes van Bambeeck* (1641, Koninklijke Musea voor Schone Kunsten van België, Brussels, CS187a) and *Portrait of Agatha Bas* (1641, Royal Collection, London, CS187b). Followers, esp. Bol and Flinck, enthusiastically adopted this motif; see, for instance, Ferdinand Bol, *Portrait of a Man*, 1644 (Städel Museum, Frankfurt am Main).

115 Rembrandt: *Girl in a Fanciful Costume in a Picture Frame* (1641, Royal Castle, Warsaw, CS186), *A Woman in Bed* (*Sarah Awaiting Tobias*) (1647, CS194, pl. 89), *Girl Leaning on a Stone Window Sill* (1645, Dulwich Picture Gallery, London, CS200) and *Girl at a Window* (1651, Nationalmuseum, Stockholm, CS220). See also the Rembrandt School, *Girl at an Open Door* (Woburn Abbey) and Samuel van Hoogstraten, *Girl at a Half-Door* (c. 1645, Art Institute of Chicago). On the subject, see London 1993.

116 See Francisca Gottwald, "Tronies in the Work of Govert Flinck and Ferdinand Bol," in Amsterdam 2017–18, 54–57.

117 Anthony Thysz: one (Montias Database, 1634, no. 1088); Cornelis Rutgers: one (Montias Database, 1638, no. 410); Martin van den Broeck: one (Montias Database, 1647, no. 566); Johannes de Renialme: six (Montias Database, 1657, no. 180); Jan Deijman: one (Montias Database, 1668, no. 452); Herman Becker: one (Montias Database, 1678, no. 254). Some of these were clearly done before Lievens' arrival in Amsterdam.

118 Backer's *tronies* are found in several inventories: Aert Coninx: one (Montias Database, 1639, no. 161); Johannes de Renialme: one (Montias Database, 1657, no. 180); Pieter van Meldert (after Backer): one (Montias Database, 1653, no. 184); Willem van Campen: one (Montias Database, 1661, no. 1153); Gerrit Uylenburgh: one (Montias Database, 1675, no. 1357).

119 One *tronie* after Rembrandt (Reijncke Gerrits, death inventory, Montias Database, 1647, no. 234) is explicitly described as painted by the portrait painter Dirck van Santvoort. The inventory was drawn up by Hendrick Uylenburgh, who was clearly well informed. Van Santvoort might have worked with Uylenburgh and Rembrandt.

120 Sluijter 2015, 374–379.

121 Franits 2004, 175–180, esp. 176.

122 Sandrart 1675–80, vol. 2, book 3, 326.

123 See letters from Rembrandt to Huygens, 1636 and 1639, Remdoc, nos. e4428, e4429, e4458, e4459, e4460, e4461, e4462.

124 "Prince Frederick Hendrick's [Frederik Hendrik's] payment order," 29 Nov. 1646, Remdoc, no. e4545.

125 "Claude Vignon's appraisal of the painting 'The Prophet Balaam,'" Nov. 1641, Remdoc, no. e4497. *Bileam* is probably *Balaam and His Ass* (1626, Musée Cognacq-Jay, Paris, CS10).

126 See Dickey 2004, 99. Schwartz 1985, 132, suggests that Lopez had bought the *Bileam* in Amsterdam in 1628 with Uylenburgh. This, however, seems unlikely as Vignon's letter (see previous note) clearly says that Lopez bought it from Rembrandt himself ("*suo quadro del profeta Balam, che comprò da lui il sig. Lopez*"). That Rembrandt took paintings from Leiden to Amsterdam is also underlined by the intimate knowledge of Leiden period works by Amsterdam painters such as Salomon Koninck and Dirck van Santvoort; Sluijter 2015, 200, 293–296.

127 "Diego d'Andrada's [d'Andrade's] complaint regarding a true likeness," 23 Feb. 1654, Remdoc, no. e1661. D'Andrade, a Jewish merchant, refused to pay the second half, which informs us that Rembrandt demanded half prepayment, the rest upon delivery. What happened to the painting is unknown, but the work might be mentioned in 1675 as "*een Judin van Rembrant*" (a Jewess by Rembrandt) in the inventory of Gerrit Uylenburgh. See "Rembrandt paintings of a 'Jewess,' a 'little David' (or 'Danae'), and an unfinished 'Portrait of Lady' in the estate of Gerrit Uylenburgh," 27 Mar. 1675, Remdoc, no. e14095.

128 Dudok van Heel 1969; see Crenshaw 2006, 111–120.

129 "Deposition by Abraham van Wilmerdonx concerning his and his wife's portrait," 1659, Remdoc, no. e12834.

130 "Agreement with Jan Six," 5 Oct. 1652, Remdoc, no. e4602 (no longer extant but is referred to in "Cancellation of agreements between Rembrandt and Six," 13 Sept. 1658, Remdoc, no. e12788).

131 Part of a complicated agreement sworn before notary Nicolaes Listingh; Amsterdam City Archives, NA2617; "A new agreement between Rembrandt and Lodewijck [Lodewijk] van Ludick," 28 Aug. 1662, Remdoc, no. e12924.

132 Giltaij 1997; Rutgers 2003, 10–12; Magnani 2007.

133 Rembrandt's other public commissions were: *The Anatomy Lesson of Dr. Nicolaes Tulp* (1632, CS76, see fig. 1.4), *The Night Watch* (1642, CS190, see fig. 1.9), *The Anatomy Lesson of Dr. Joan Deyman* (1656, Amsterdam Museum, CS246) *The Conspiracy of the Batavians under Claudius Civilis* (c. 1661–62, CS298, see fig. 9.3) and *The Syndics of the Clothmakers' Guild* (1662, Rijksmuseum, Amsterdam, CS299).

134 See Tom van der Molen, "Painted Theatre: Flinck, Rembrandt, and Other Artists Paint Vondel's Joseph Trilogy," in Dickey 2017a, 82–97. The other contributors were Nicolaes van Helt Stockade and the Haarlem (but Amsterdam-born) artist Salomon de Bray.

135 Baldinucci in Ford 2007, 40. Baldinucci's informant was Rembrandt's former pupil Eberhard Keil, who left Amsterdam for Italy in 1651, a plausible *terminus ante quem* for the Ovid series.

136 Crenshaw 2006, 31; Peters 2010, 30; Bosman 2019, esp. 118–119. On Witsen, see Peters 2010. A patron of the arts, he lent Rembrandt 5,000 guilders in 1653. In 1659 his eighteen-year-old son Nicolaes produced a series of etchings, copied after a sixteenth-century Ovid series by Virgil Solis. How he learned printmaking is unknown, but in 1667/68, his younger brother Jonas received drawing lessons from Lievens. Was Nicolaes one of the "innumerable youths of good family" in Rembrandt's studio? Rembrandt's *Abduction of Europa* (1632, CS50, see fig. 11.1) closely relates to Solis' version of Ovid's story.

137 For instance, Keil was Rembrandt's pupil from 1642 to 1644 and afterward worked for Uylenburgh; both Rembrandt and Flinck could have sold work to Uylenburgh after their departure from his studio. See Van der Veen, "Hendrick Uylenburgh's Art Business," in London and Amsterdam 2006, 163–166, 202–203; Kok 2013, 171–172n222.

138 Montias 2002, 138–139; Dickey 2004, 99.

139 The inventory was appraised by Marten Kretzer and the painter Adam Camerarius. For *Christ and the Woman Taken in Adultery* (see fig. 9.2), see CS196.

140 *The Night Watch* cost 1,600 guilders according to "Deposition by Jan Pietersz Bronchorst concerning the 'Nightwatch,'" 1659, Remdoc, no. e12831, and "Deposition by Nicolaes van Cruijsbergen concerning the price of the 'Nightwatch,'" 1659, Remdoc, no. e12835. Not taken into account is the price of the vanitas still life in the 1665 inventory of the Scottish art dealer John Clerk of Pennycook (or Penicuik) for 40 Scottish pounds, because the exchange rate could not be determined. See Roscam Abbing 2006, vol. 2, 94, NRD71.

141 Kok 2013, 37–40; Bok, "Rembrandt's Fame and Rembrandt's Failure," in Kofuku 2004, 159–180; Crenshaw 2006.

142 For instance, by Zell 2011; Sluijter 2015, 50–55.

143 "The sixth letter to Constantijn Huygens," 13 Feb. 1639, Remdoc, no. e4461 (trans. modified); Crenshaw 2006; Zell 2011; Sluijter 2015, 50–56, esp. 54. Sluijter translates "*met goede vougen*" as "in all decency." *Voegen* in Dutch essentially means "to make fit."

144 "The sixth letter to Constantijn Huygens," ibid. Rembrandt ends politely with "I shall remain grateful for all your acts of friendship. And with my greetings to you, Sir, and to all your close friends, [I] commend you to God, [may he grant you] long-lasting health. Your obliging and affectionate servant Rembrandt."

145 "Prince Frederick Hendrick's [Frederik Hendrik's] payment order," 29 Nov. 1646, Remdoc, no. e4545.

146 Van der Veen, "Patronage," in Washington, Milwaukee and Amsterdam 2008–09, 30–31.

147 Ibid., 31.

148 Rembrandt had already graced Huygens with "his latest work" as thanks for his mediation in 1636; "The first letter to Constantijn Huygens," Feb. 1636, Remdoc, no. e4428. See the essays "Illustrious Histories" by Friederike Schütt and "A Letter from Rembrandt" by Stephanie S. Dickey in this volume.

149 Sluijter describes the two value systems in Italy, and applies them to the Dutch market: *valore di fatica* (value determined by labour expended) vs. *valore di stima* (value determined by quality and reputation); Sluijter, "Determining Value on the Art Market in the Golden Age," in Tummers and Jonckheere 2008, 9–16; Sluijter 2015, 52–59.

150 The dispute with De Graeff, for instance, is generally seen as a painful affair, whereas we really do not know both parties' initial positions nor how they accepted the judgment. Paul Crenshaw describes the case as a "symptom of a larger problem"; Crenshaw 2006, 117.

151 A complete and refreshing reassessment of the causes of Rembrandt's bankruptcy is given in Bosman 2019.

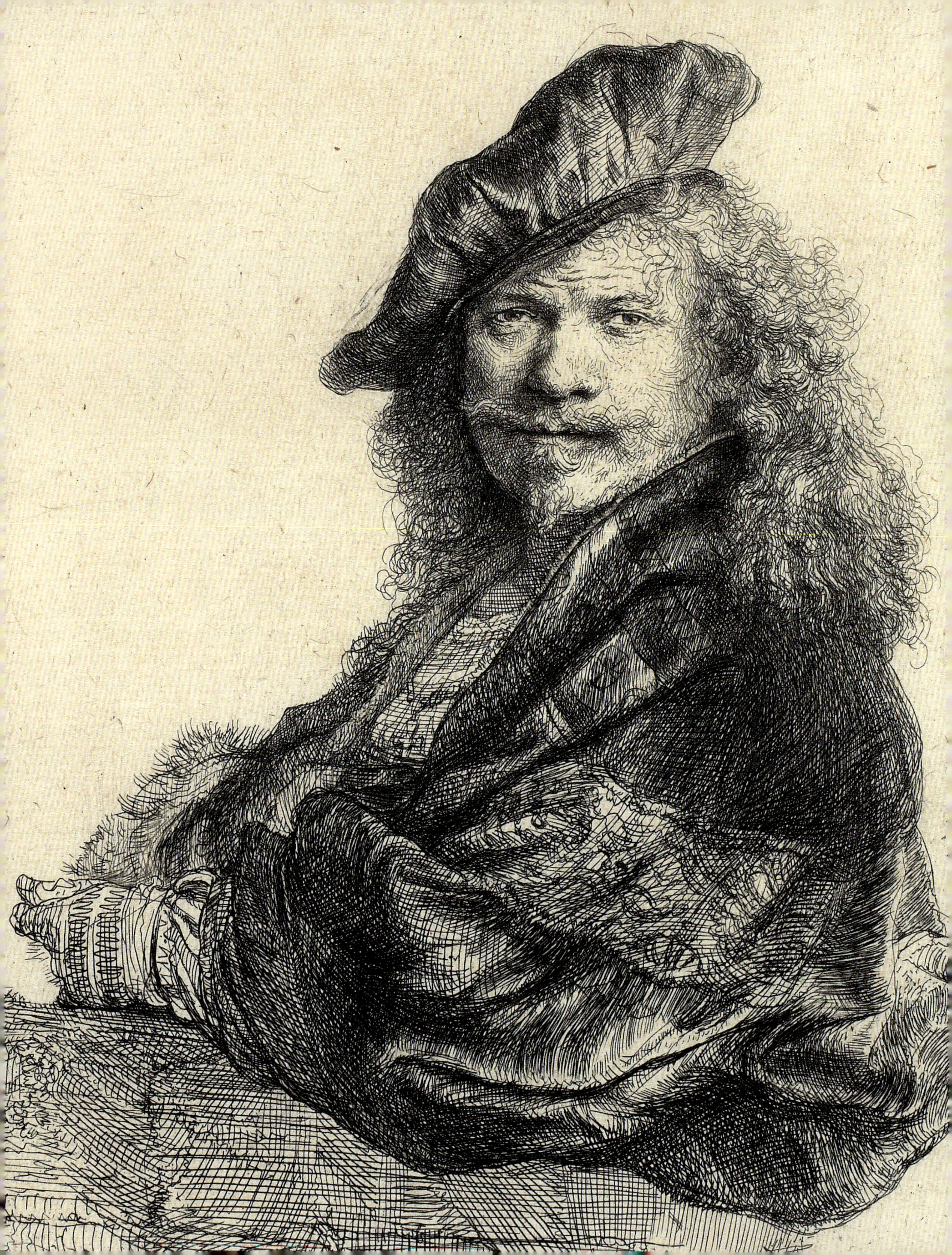

J O N A T H A N   B I K K E R

Rembrandt's International Ambitions

In 1708 the French art critic Roger de Piles composed a list of fifty-seven famous Renaissance and Baroque masters, whom he scored according to their ability in composition, drawing, colour and expression.[1] Rembrandt was conspicuously the only seventeenth-century Dutch artist included in this so-called "Balance of Painters," which also comprised such international superstars as Michelangelo, Raphael, Titian, Dürer, Holbein, Caravaggio, Guercino, Poussin, Rubens and Van Dyck. Had Rembrandt lived to read De Piles' list, he might not have been surprised to find himself the sole representative of Dutch Baroque art. Since the very beginning of his career, his work had been compared with that of the greatest artists of the past. After seeing Rembrandt's *Judas Repentant, Returning the Thirty Pieces of Silver* (see fig. 3.3) on an easel in the artist's studio in Leiden, Constantijn Huygens, secretary to Stadtholder Frederik Hendrik, enthusiastically found it worthy to "compare ... with all Italy, indeed, with all the wondrous beauties that have survived from the most ancient of days."[2] Huygens was astonished that "a youth, a Dutchman, a beardless miller, could put so much into one human figure and depict it all," all the more so because, as he noted, Rembrandt "has never ventured outside the walls of his native city."[3] This was not quite accurate – Rembrandt had spent about half

a year studying with the renowned history painter Pieter Lastman in Amsterdam – but he had never been to Italy, and, much to Huygens' chagrin, he had no intention of going there either. Nor did Rembrandt's equally youthful friend and colleague Jan Lievens, whom Huygens had also encountered in Leiden.

Lievens' and Rembrandt's reluctance to cross the Alps seems particularly odd in light of the fact that they both had studied with Lastman, who had lived in Rome and Venice from 1602 to 1607 and had been profoundly inspired by Italian Renaissance art. In addition, before his brief second apprenticeship to Lastman, Rembrandt had trained for three years with Jacob van Swanenburg, another Dutch artist who had spent many years in Italy. But perhaps it was because of the very fact that their teachers had made Italian sojourns that the young painters did not think it necessary to do the same. The early eighteenth-century artist-biographer Arnold Houbraken informs us that the Silesian painter Michael Willmann took so much pleasure in the "art, company and discourses" of Jacob Backer and Rembrandt during his stay in Amsterdam (around 1650–52) that he abandoned his plans to visit Italy.[4] It seems likely that Rembrandt and Lievens would have felt similarly toward Lastman, and that his art and teachings provided them with a more than adequate understanding of the principles

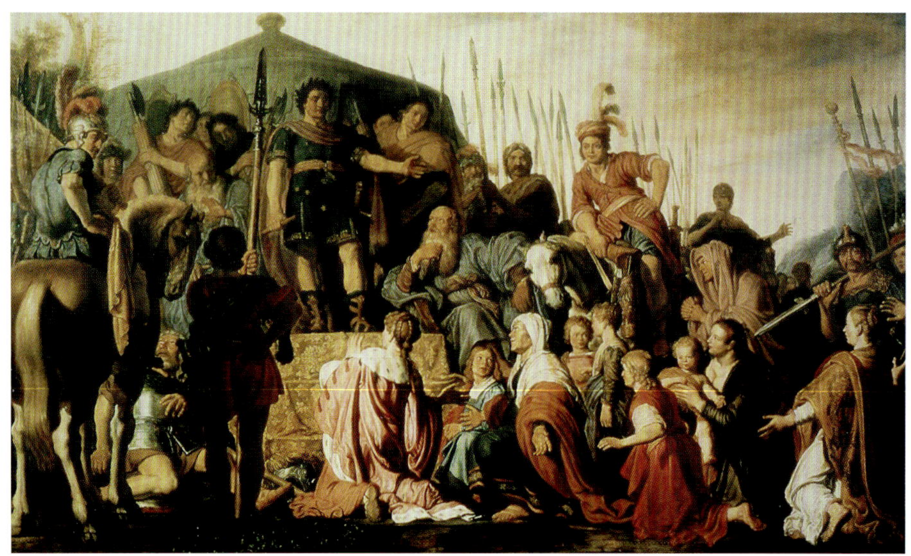

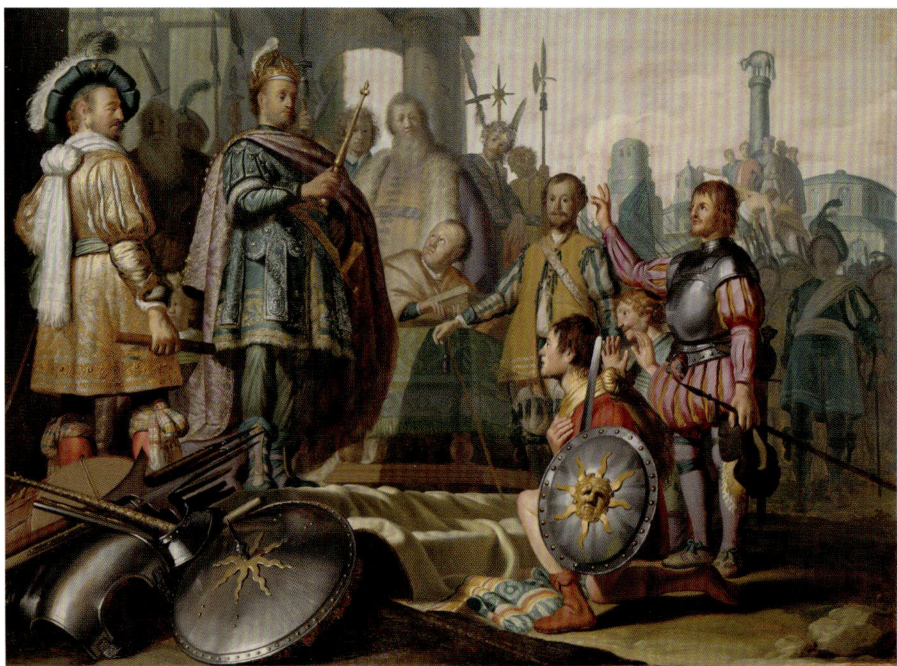

fig. 5.1 **Pieter Lastman,**
Coriolanus and the Roman
Matrons, **1625, oil on panel;**
81 × 132 cm. Trinity College,
The University of Dublin

fig. 5.2 **Rembrandt van Rijn,**
Leiden History Piece, **1626, oil on**
panel; 90 × 121 cm. Collection of
the Cultural Heritage Agency of
the Netherlands (RCE NK2615);
long-term loan to Museum
De Lakenhal, Leiden (B 564)

of Italian Renaissance art. Lastman had studied intensely the monumental frescos of Raphael and his circle when in Rome and, back in Amsterdam, went about translating their grandeur into history paintings of more modest dimensions for the Dutch market. An example is his *Coriolanus and the Roman Matrons* of 1625 (fig. 5.1), which is based on a fresco in the Vatican designed by the Raphael pupil Giulio Romano. When Rembrandt in turn based a work (fig. 5.2) on Lastman's *Coriolanus*, he was, of course, fully cognizant of the composition's famous pedigree.[5] Moreover, it was a compositional type recommended by another Dutch promoter of the principles of Italian Renaissance art, Karel van Mander, in his instruction manual for young artists, *Het Schilder-Boeck* (The Book on Painting), which had been published in 1604.[6]

So, when Lievens and Rembrandt told Huygens that they had "no time to waste on foreign travel," they may have been confident that they had learned enough about Italian art from their teacher Lastman.[7] As Huygens also noted, they were convinced that the best examples of Italian art were to be found outside of Italy, in princely collections north of the Alps.[8] Lievens and Rembrandt were undoubtedly aware of the phenomenal collections of Italian paintings that had been amassed in recent years by King Charles I of England and his courtiers Thomas Howard, Earl of Arundel, and George Villiers, Duke of Buckingham.[9] Amsterdam could also boast a few collections that included Italian paintings in this period, although none of them were on a par with those in England.[10] When Chaplain Francesco Belli visited the Dutch Republic in 1626 as part of a Venetian embassy, he marvelled at the regal splendour of two Amsterdam houses and their sumptuous furnishings, which included paintings by all the most famous "Old" and "Modern" Masters.[11] One of these houses, the so-called "house with the heads" at 123 Keizersgracht, was the property of the rich merchant Nicolas Sohier. An inventory of his collection composed after his death in 1642 reveals that he owned paintings by, among others, Palma Vecchio, Paris Bordone, Paolo Veronese, Parmigianino and Guido Reni, as well as a work that was purportedly executed by three of the greatest painters active in Venice in the early sixteenth century: Titian, Giorgione and Sebastiano del Piombo.[12] Significantly, as Huygens informs us, Sohier also owned a number of works executed by Lievens when he was still a pupil.[13]

While Lievens and, through him, Rembrandt were likely already acquainted with Sohier's Italian paintings at the beginning of their careers, Rembrandt had his own early connection to an important Amsterdam collector in this field. The earliest record of the purchase of a painting by Rembrandt dates to 15 June 1628, and can be found in the accounts of the Amsterdam citizen Joan Huydecoper, Lord of Maarseveen and Neerdijk.[14] It was a small character study, or *tronie*, perhaps the one now in the Kremer Collection (pl. 20). Huydecoper would go on to become one of the most prominent figures in the city's political and cultural life, serving six terms as burgomaster between 1651 and 1660, and acting as patron of many of the city's most eminent poets, artists and architects.[15] We know of only one Italian painting, a *Europa* by Veronese, owned by Huydecoper, but his father-in-law, Balthasar Coymans, had a deeper interest in Italian art.[16] An international banker and trader, Coymans amassed a fortune that was assessed at 400,000 guilders in 1631, making him one of the three wealthiest citizens of Amsterdam. Like Sohier, Coymans moved in later life to the Keizersgracht (no. 177), where he had a house built in 1625 in an Italianate classicizing style.[17] Unlike Sohier, however, Coymans acquired works by contemporary Italian artists whom he befriended during his business trips.

According to the German painter and artists' biographer Joachim von Sandrart, writing in 1675, one renowned acquaintance was Annibale Carracci. When Coymans met him in Rome, the Italian painter was suffering an extreme bout of melancholy brought on by a lack of payment for his ten years of work on the Farnese Gallery. Coymans, however, "took him in, and by alleviating his poverty made his desperate soul happy once more."[18] As thanks, Annibale gave Coymans a series of paintings of the Seven Acts of Mercy. Sandrart also claimed that the best place in the world to see paintings by the Caravaggio follower Bartolomeo Manfredi was in the house of "the art-loving Amsterdam citizen Coymans."[19] While this may seem implausible, it has recently been discovered that Annibale's series did in fact exist. One of the pictures, *The Young Tobias Heals His Blind Father* (fig. 5.3), now hangs in Kassel.[20] This suggests that there might be some truth to the other claim as well.

Some or all of the paintings owned by Coymans were sold in 1709. The sale advertisement mentions

one work by Manfredi and three by Caravaggio to be auctioned at that time. Others were possibly sold on another occasion. One can only imagine the impact these paintings would have had on the young Rembrandt, in particular on the development of his own unique brand of Caravaggesque *chiaroscuro*, but we can be certain that he would have been thoroughly acquainted with Coymans' collection. The advertisement also mentions Rembrandt among the artists whose work was to be sold. Furthermore, Coymans' daughter Maria married Joan Huydecoper, and his eponymous son married Maria Trip two years after

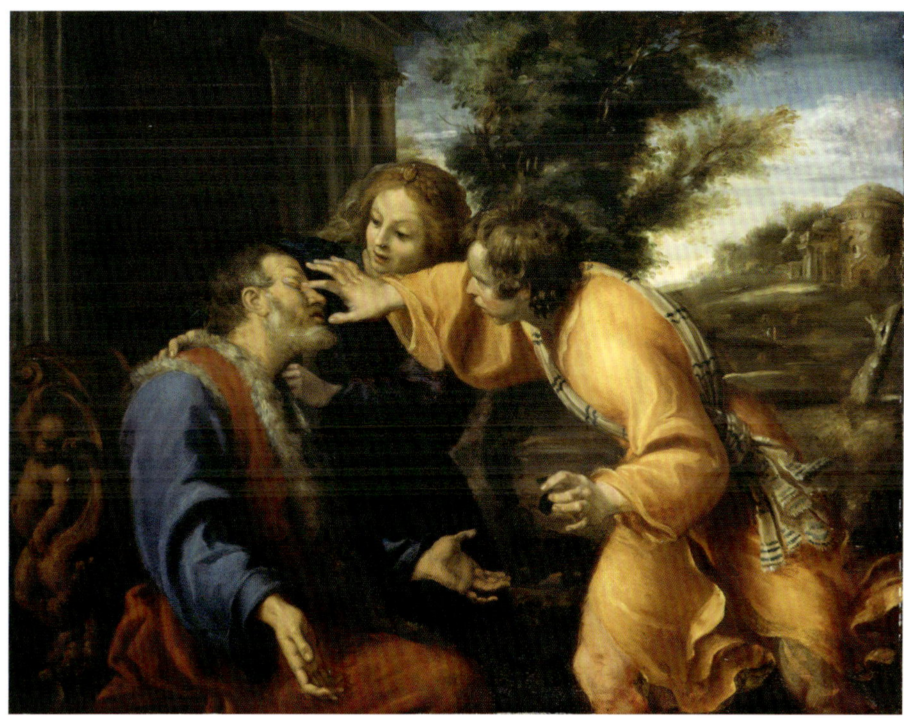

fig. 5.3 **Annibale Carracci, *The Young Tobias Heals His Blind Father*, c. 1600, oil on canvas; 52.8 × 66.5 cm. Museumslandschaft Hessen, Kassel, Gemäldegalerie Alte Meister (GK 568)**

she sat for Rembrandt in 1639 for a portrait that now hangs in the Rijksmuseum.[21]

In the 1630s, the decade Rembrandt moved to Amsterdam and became the city's foremost painter, even more outstanding collections of foreign art would join those of Sohier and Coymans on the Keizersgracht. The most spectacular was, perhaps, that of the brothers Gerard and Jan Reynst, which included about two hundred Italian paintings and three hundred antique sculptures, mostly acquired by Jan in Venice.[22] Installed in the house the brothers had built at 209 Keizersgracht in 1634, the collection was visited by numerous foreign dignitaries, including the French queen mother Marie de' Medici in 1638. The Venetian artists' biographer Carlo Ridolfi extolled its magnificence, mentioning paintings "di Raffaelo, di Gio Bellino, del Correggio, del Parmegiano [Parmigianino], di Titiano, del Tintoretto, di Paolo [Veronese]" and others in his 1648 *Le maraviglie dell'arte*, a book that was dedicated to the Reynsts.[23]

The Reynst brothers lived on the same canal as Balthasar Coymans, and their sister Wijntje was married to his nephew Isaac. Furthermore, one of Coymans' nieces married the brother of another prominent collector, Lucas van Uffelen.[24] After living many years in Venice, Van Uffelen moved back to Amsterdam, where he and his "famous cabinet of art" briefly resided at 198 Keizersgracht.[25] De Piles considered Van Uffelen "one of the greatest *curieux* (connoisseurs) that ever existed," and when his collection was auctioned by the Amsterdam Orphan Chamber in 1639 it generated the staggering sum of 59,456 guilders, equivalent to nearly 60 per cent of the total value of artworks sold at that institution in the previous forty-one years.[26] Unfortunately, no sale catalogue has survived. The astounding proceeds were noted by Rembrandt on a sketch (fig. 5.4) of the most expensive painting in the auction, which he most likely recorded while attending the sale. That picture was Raphael's *Portrait of Baldassare Castiglione* (fig. 5.5). As Rembrandt also noted, it fetched 3,500 guilders, another record price for an Orphan Chamber

auction.[27] To put this in perspective, three years later Rembrandt earned about 1,600 guilders for his monumental *Night Watch* (see fig. 1.9), containing more than a dozen life-size figures.[28]

There can be little doubt that Rembrandt, whose first documented purchase at an auction dates to 1635, would have loved to have bought Raphael's picture at the Van Uffelen sale.[29] However, 1639 was the year the artist purchased his expensive house on the St. Anthonisbreestraat, and, although he would develop a formidable reputation as a buyer at auction, his strategy – at least in the 1630s – was to make numerous small purchases, mostly of works on paper.[30] Prints and drawings by and after the great Italian masters were certainly among them, as documented in the inventory of his collection drawn up in 1658. This was known to De Piles, who attested that Rembrandt "was very curious in getting the fine Designs [i.e., drawings] that came out of Italy, and had a great Collection of them; as also of Italian Prints."[31] More costly works on panel or canvas were another matter, however. The highest recorded price Rembrandt paid for a painting was 424 guilders plus change, expended in 1637 for Peter Paul Rubens' *Hero and Leander* (pl. 46), but a scarcity of documents regarding his art purchases may skew our knowledge. If this was indeed an exceptionally

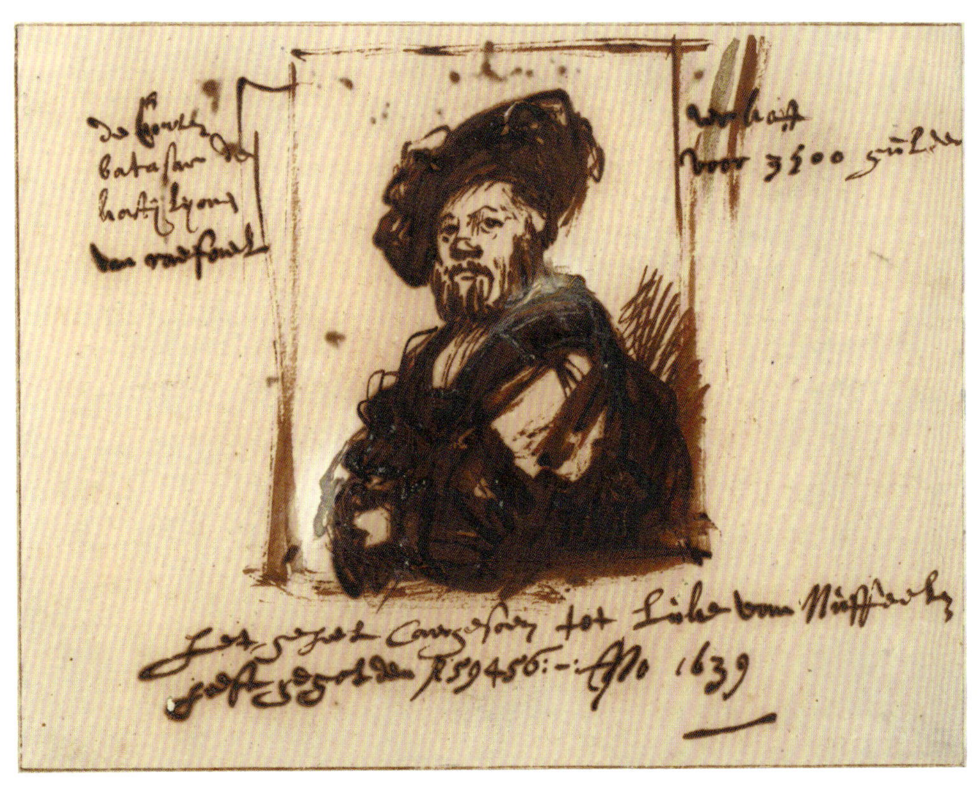

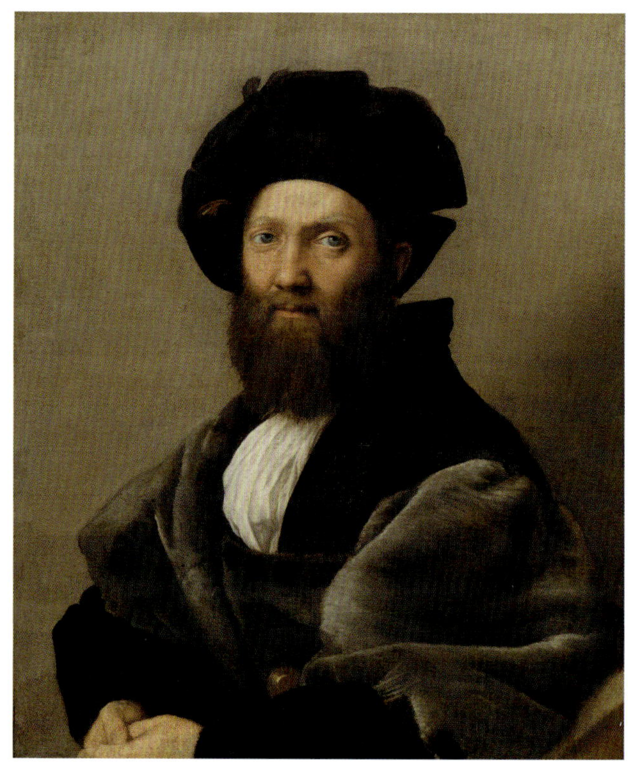

large investment for Rembrandt, he might have paid it because he intended to resell the picture, which he in fact did, in 1644, making a profit of slightly more than 100 guilders.[32]

The man who purchased Raphael's *Portrait of Baldassare Castiglione* at the Van Uffelen sale was Alphonso Lopez, a fabulously wealthy diamond merchant originally from Aragon, who set up shop in Paris in 1610.[33] He visited the Dutch Republic in 1627 and 1628, and lived in Amsterdam from 1636 to 1641, ostensibly in order to trade in jewels, but in actuality to work as an agent of the French crown, commissioned to purchase ships and armaments for Louis XIII's navy. Previously unknown is the fact that Lopez had business dealings with Balthasar Coymans' sons in 1634, at which time he was again living in Paris.[34] Lopez may have come into contact with Rembrandt through them, or possibly by way of Huygens, whom he probably met during his first trip to the northern Netherlands.[35] An early work by Rembrandt, *Balaam and the Ass* (Musée Cognacq-Jay, Paris) was in Lopez's collection by 1641, and it stands to reason that he would have purchased it from the artist closer to its execution date of 1626.[36] In addition to the paintings by Raphael and Rembrandt, Lopez owned two spectacular works by Titian: the *Flora* now in the Gallerie degli Uffizi, Florence, and the *Portrait of Gerolamo (?) Barbarigo* (which at the time was thought to portray the Italian poet Ludovico Ariosto), now in the National Gallery, London (fig. 5.7).

While Rembrandt probably did not even consider bidding for the *Castiglione*, there was another artist living in Amsterdam at the time who had the wherewithal not only to compete for the picture, but, with a bid of 3,400 guilders, to become the underbidder. That artist was Joachim von Sandrart, who had moved to Amsterdam from Frankfurt am Main in 1637.[37]

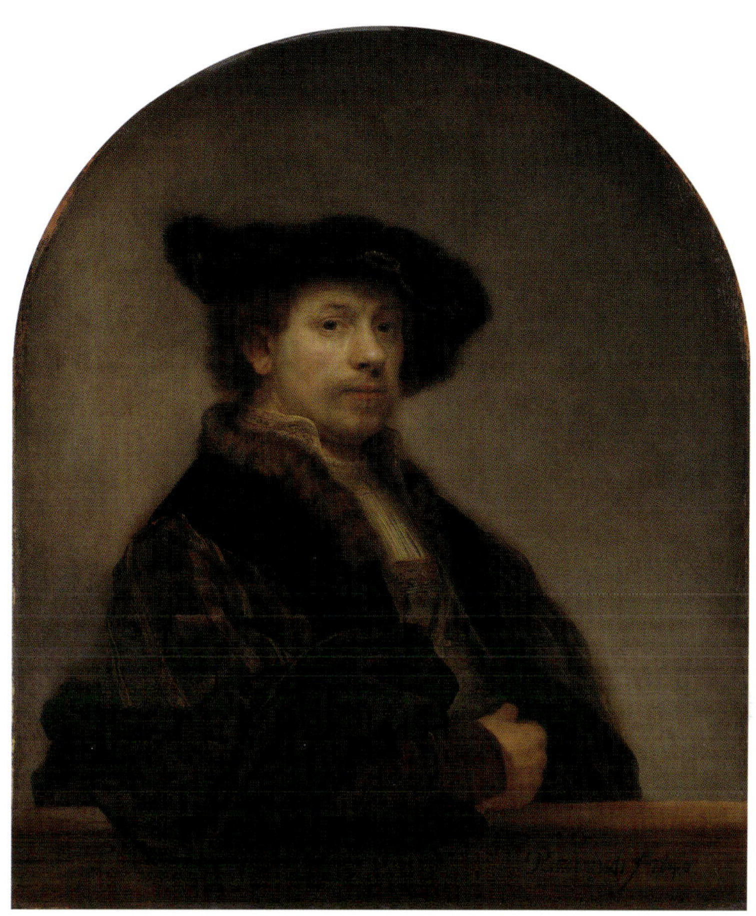

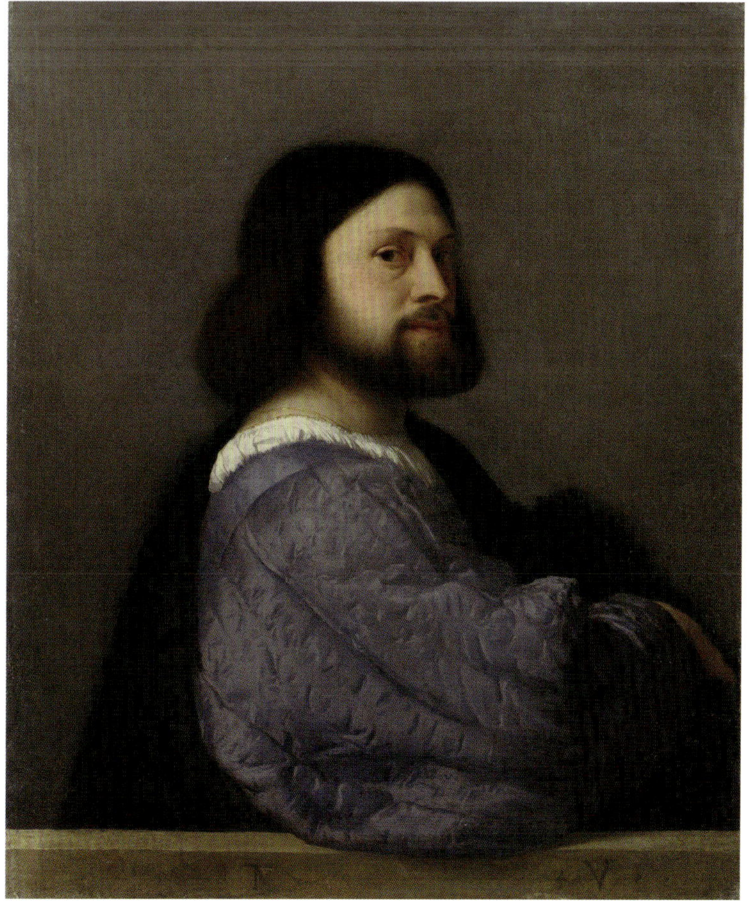

fig. 5.6 **Rembrandt van Rijn,** ***Self-portrait at the Age of 34,*** **1640, oil on canvas; 91 × 75 cm. The National Gallery, London. Bought, 1861 (NG672)**

fig. 5.7 **Titian,** ***Portrait of Gerolamo (?) Barbarigo,*** **c. 1510, oil on canvas; 81.2 × 66.3 cm. The National Gallery, London. Bought, 1904 (NG1944)**

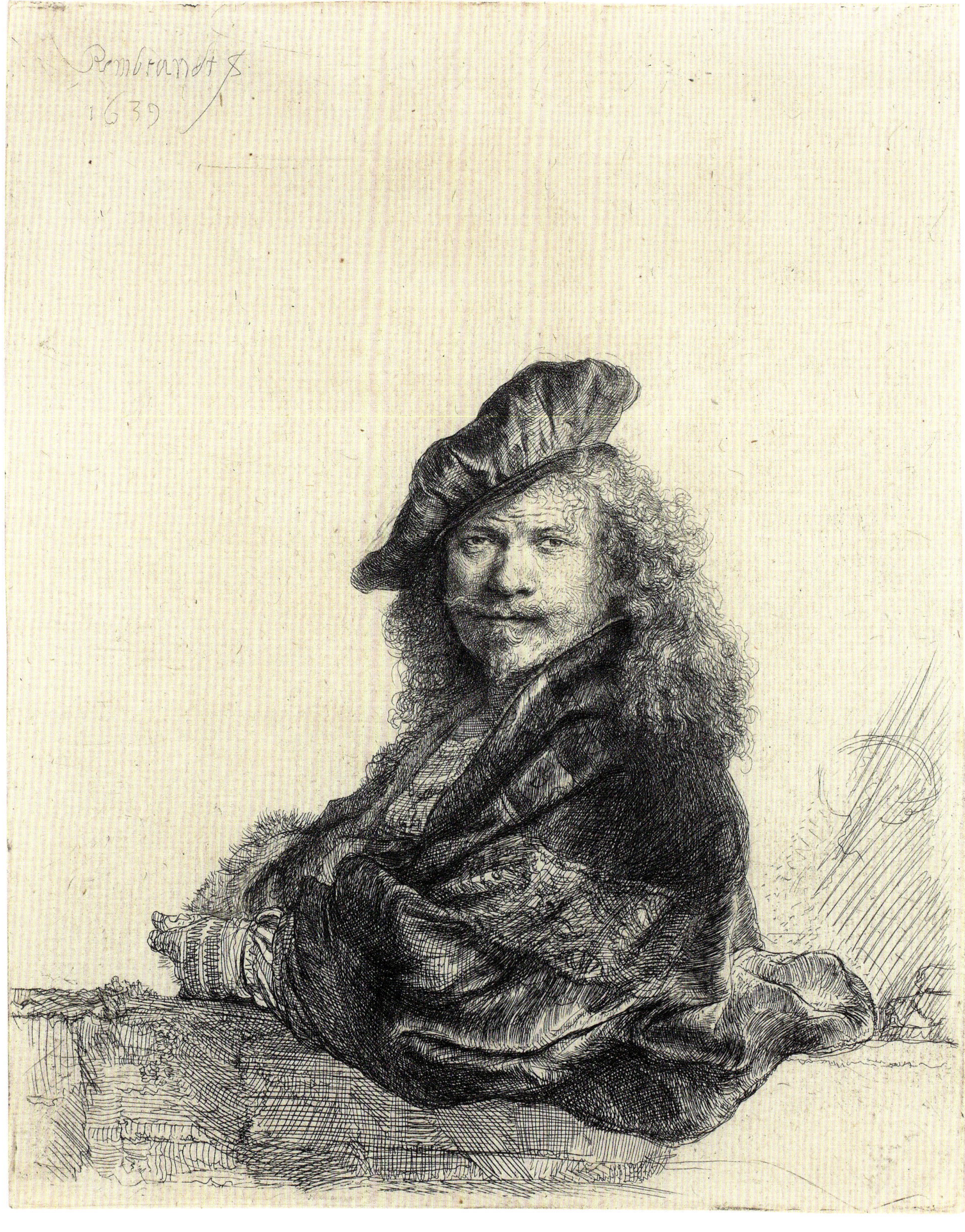

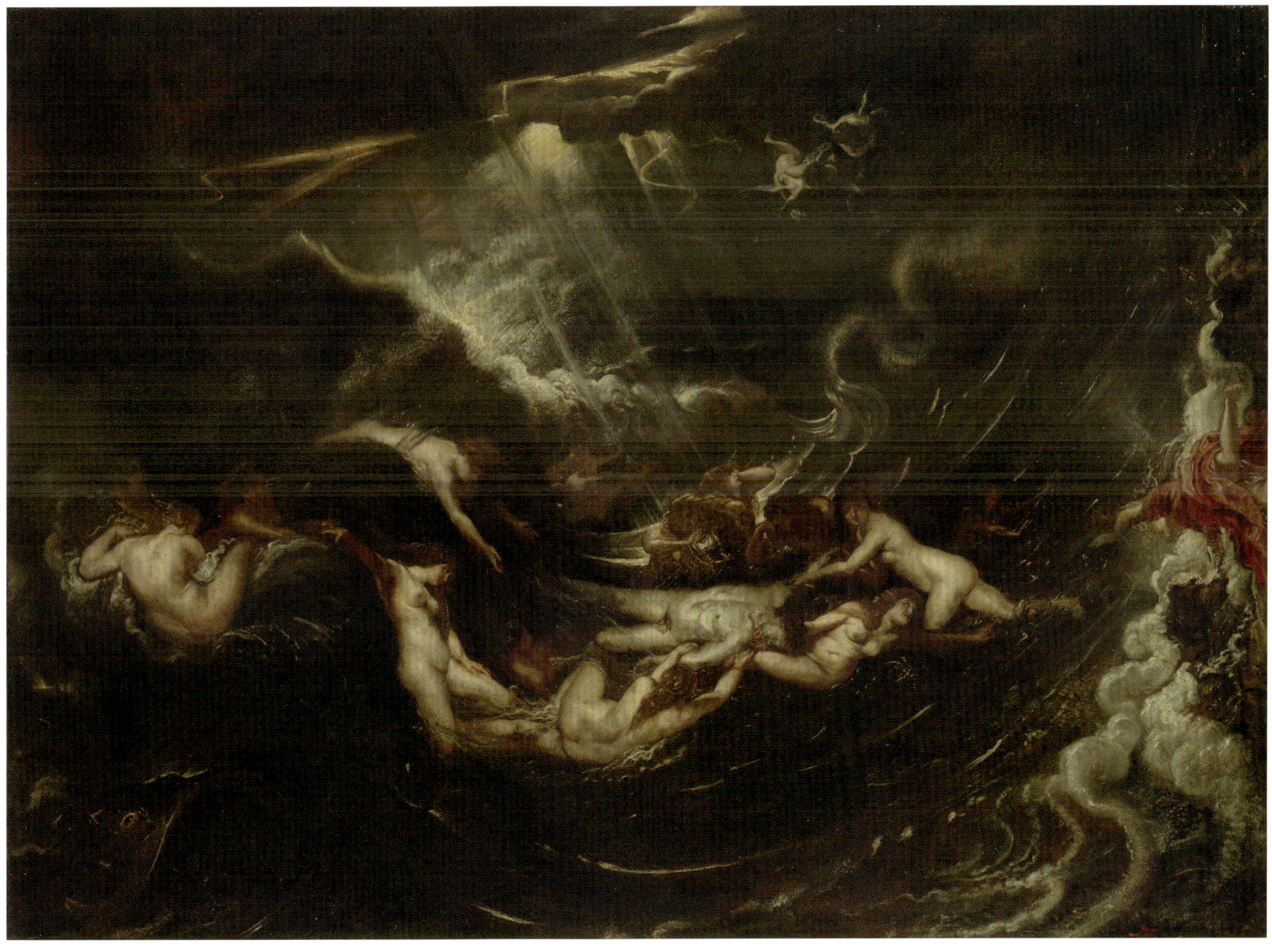

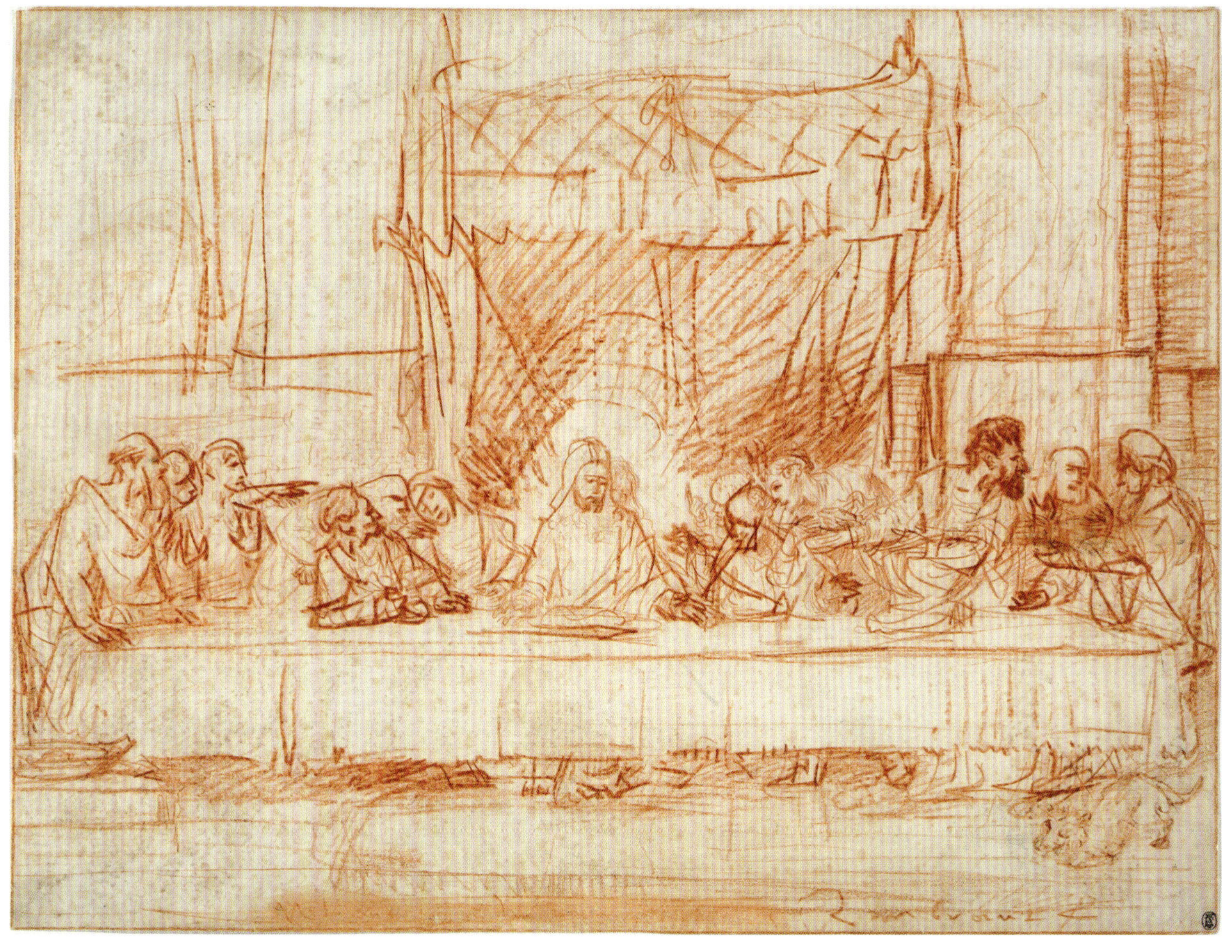

fig. 5.8 Rembrandt van Rijn (after an engraving attributed to Giovanni Pietro da Birago, after Leonardo da Vinci), *The Last Supper*, c. 1634–35, red chalk on laid paper; 36.2 × 47.5 cm. The Metropolitan Museum of Art, New York. Robert Lehman Collection, 1975 (1975.1.794)

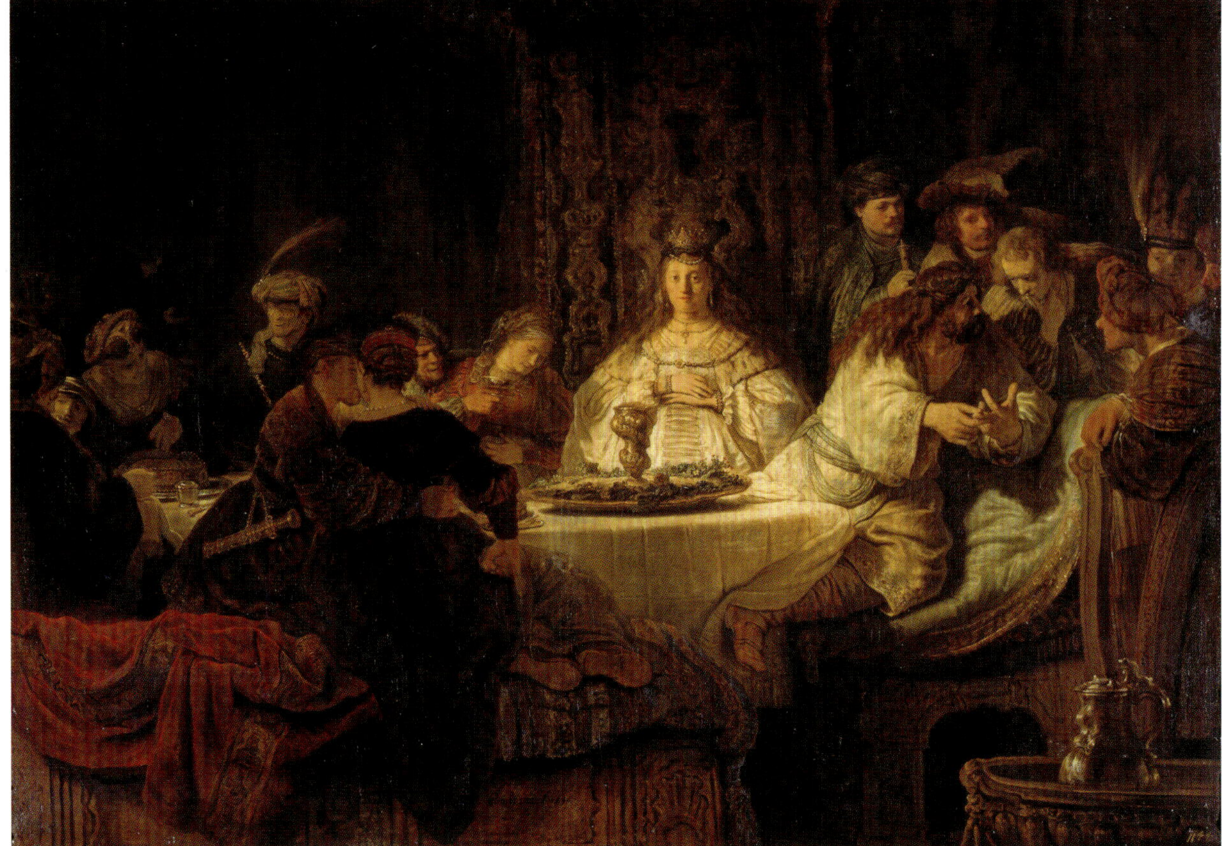

fig. 5.9 Rembrandt van Rijn, *Samson Posing the Riddle to the Wedding Guests*, 1638, oil on canvas; 126 × 175 cm. Staatliche Kunstsammlungen Dresden, Gemäldegalerie Alte Meister (1560)

Whether Rembrandt would have been jealous of Sandrart's ability to bid on the painting we cannot be certain, but there is ample reason to believe that the Dutch artist would have been wary of the artistic competition the newcomer would provide.[38] By 1639 Rembrandt had successfully cemented his reputation as the heir to the canon of great masters later listed by De Piles. Rembrandt accomplished this, in part, by emulating their compositions and motifs in his own work. A conspicuous example is a red chalk drawing he made around 1634–35 after Leonardo's *Last Supper* (fig. 5.8).[39] Rembrandt's largest surviving drawing, it is by no means a slavish copy, but an exploration of how to depict a substantial number of figures sitting at a table. He would have known the Milanese fresco from a reproductive engraving. In his *Samson Posing the Riddle to the Wedding Guests* of 1638 (fig. 5.9),

he outdid Leonardo by introducing a greater sense of movement and by giving the figures more individualized poses and expressions.[40]

Rembrandt's favourite adversary in the 1630s was Peter Paul Rubens, who was widely considered at the time to be the greatest living artist. His competition with the Flemish master reached its climax in the monumental *Blinding of Samson* of 1636 (pl. 106), which surpasses Rubens' grisly *Prometheus Bound* (fig. 5.10) as a scene of horrific violence. Rembrandt may have seen Rubens' painting in the 1620s in the collection of the English ambassador in The Hague. It has been convincingly argued that Rembrandt was also competing with other depictions of gruesome brutality present in Amsterdam collections, such as Jusepe de Ribera's paintings of Tityus, Tantalus and Ixion being tortured in Hades, all owned by Van Uffelen.[41]

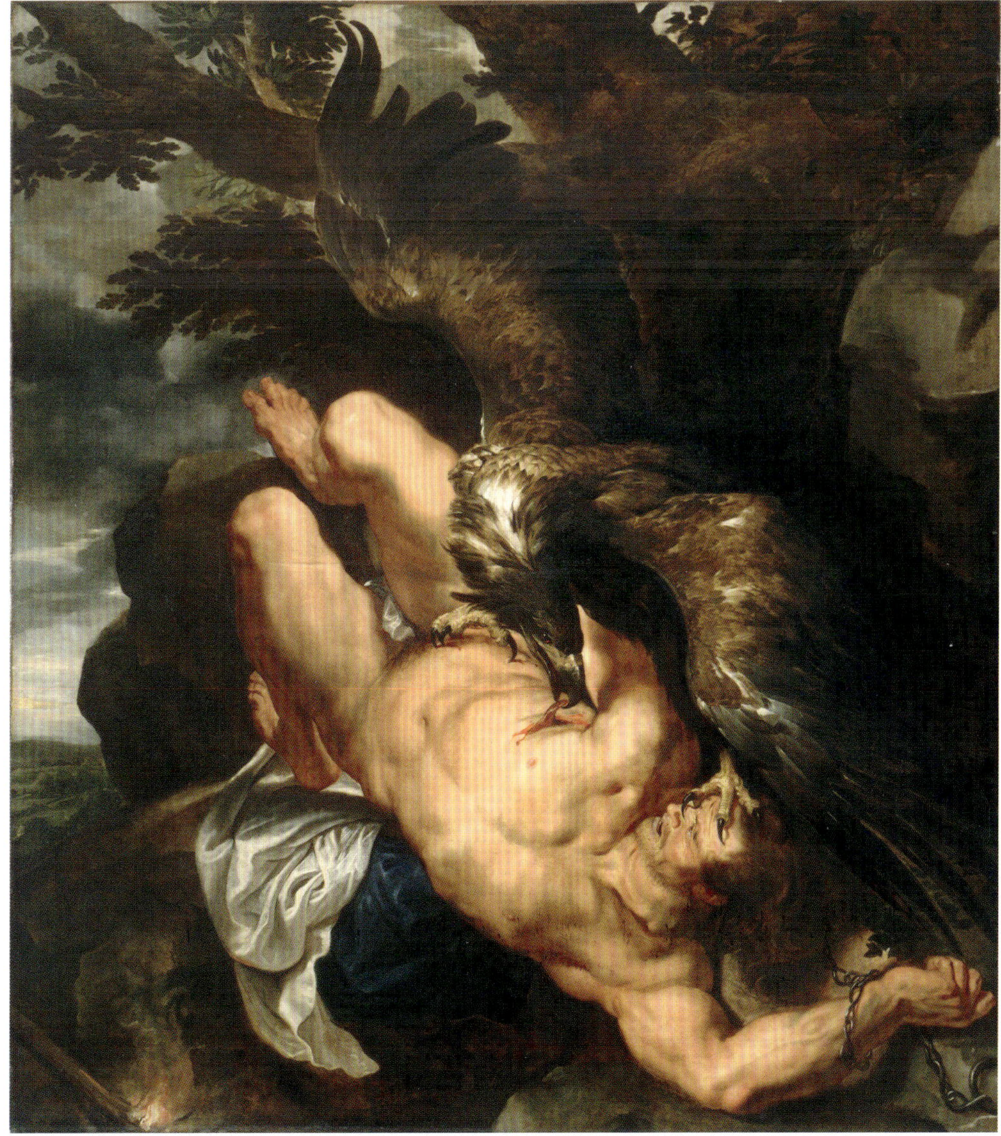

fig. 5.10 **Peter Paul Rubens,** *Prometheus Bound,* c. 1611–18, oil on canvas; 242.6 × 209.6 cm. Philadelphia Museum of Art. Purchased with the W.P. Wilstach Fund, 1950 (W1950-3-1)

The cognoscenti of the Keizersgracht[42] (as the collectors of foreign art concentrated on that canal have been aptly dubbed) would have appreciated how Rembrandt pitted himself against these other eminent contemporary artists. According to De Piles, Van Uffelen in fact once commissioned various artists, including Rubens, Guido Reni, Nicolas Poussin, Anthony van Dyck and Rembrandt, to execute a painting of the *March of Silenus* in direct competition with one another.[43]

In 1632 Rembrandt struck upon a brilliant idea to solidify his self-fashioned image as the successor to the greatest artists of the High Renaissance. In emulation of Raphael, Michelangelo, Titian and others, and unlike all other Dutch artists, he signed his works from then on with just his first name. One wonders whether some connoisseurs would have found this pretentious in light of the fact that Rembrandt had never travelled to Italy. Rembrandt's lack of international *savoir faire* would have become all the more apparent with the arrival of Sandrart in Amsterdam, for the latter had spent considerable time in Italy and had visited all the best private collections. Sandrart had been the *de facto* keeper of the collection brought together by the foremost patron in Rome, the Marchese Vincenzo Giustiniani, and befriended many of the leading artists of the day. While Rembrandt could

boast that he had clients who lived on the Keizersgracht, Sandrart himself settled there in a house (no. 236) purchased for him by his influential cousin Michel LeBlon (see fig. 1.11), a highly successful international art dealer and diplomatic agent for Queen Christina of Sweden.[44] The worldly Sandrart fit in perfectly in this culturally elite neighbourhood. As he himself later reminisced, "he was greatly esteemed, honoured, and praised by many, not only for his cosmopolitan knowledge of the arts, but also for his virtuous conduct, courteous behaviour, and elegant conversation, which few artists there had demonstrated previously."[45] Sandrart's presence in Amsterdam, next door to the cognoscenti of the Keizersgracht, and his role as underbidder for Raphael's *Castiglione*, may have played heavily on Rembrandt's mind when he decided to produce a self-portrait etching in 1639 and a painted self-portrait the following year (pl. 45, fig. 5.6) based on the *Castiglione* and Titian's *Portrait of Gerolamo (?) Barbarigo*, both by then in Lopez's collection. With these images of himself as a great Renaissance artist – the pictorial equivalent of signing with only his first name – Rembrandt claimed his place in the pantheon of artists in the vanguard of European art history.[46]

Sandrart counted several rich and powerful Amsterdam citizens among his patrons, such as the family of Jan Bicker, his neighbour across the canal at

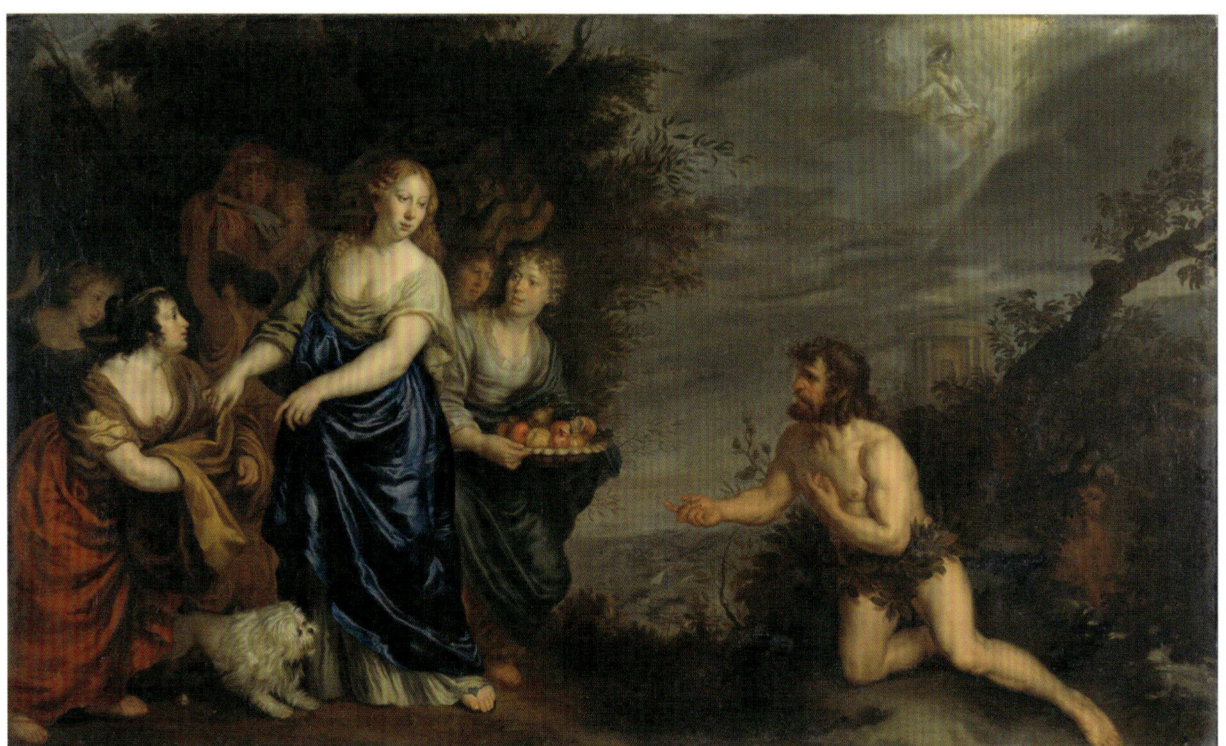

fig. 5.11 **Joachim von Sandrart,** *Odysseus and Nausicaa*, **c. 1642, oil on canvas; 103.5 × 168.5 cm. Rijksmuseum, Amsterdam. Gift of D. Franken, Le Vésinet (SK-A-4278)**

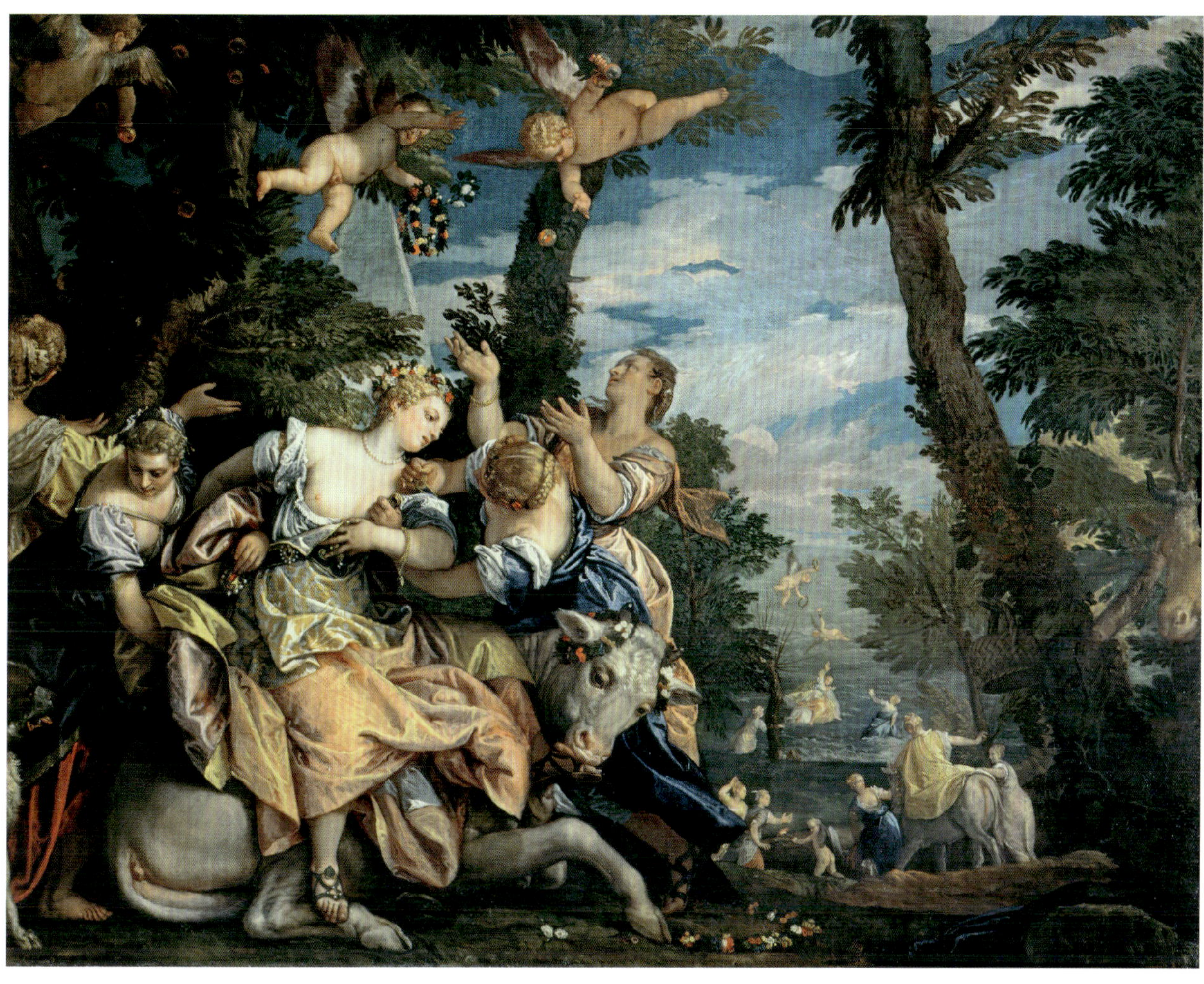

fig. 5.12 **Paolo Veronese,** *The Rape of Europa*, c. 1578, oil on canvas; 240 × 303 cm. Palazzo Ducale, Venice

221 Keizersgracht.[47] He painted portraits of Jan's cousins Hendrick Bicker and his wife Eva Geelvinck and Jacob Bicker and his wife Alida Bicker (pls. 62, 63). In 1640 his group portrait featuring Jan's brother Cornelis as captain of the civic guard was the first of seven to be hung in the Great Hall of the Kloveniersdoelen (musketeers' company headquarters).[48] Had Sandrart been unavailable or less well-connected, that commission might have gone to Rembrandt, who completed his first and only civic-guard portrait, *The Night Watch* (see fig. 1.9), for the same room two years later.

In 1641 Rembrandt's early admirer Joan Huydecoper commissioned Sandrart to execute a painting for the large reception room of his newly built house at 548 Singel in Amsterdam.[49] Mounted in the wainscoting above the fireplace, this painting of *Odysseus and Nausicaa* (fig. 5.11) may have been conceived as a direct challenge to Rembrandt's assimilation of motifs from the Italian Renaissance art owned by Amsterdam collectors. The composition of Sandrart's picture, with a group of figures on the left against a backdrop of trees, an open vista in the centre, and a tree and bushes on the right, is very similar to a painting of *The Rape of Europa* by Paolo Veronese in the Doge's Palace in Venice (fig. 5.12).[50] Rembrandt, apparently, also knew Veronese's painting, for the figure shown in extreme foreshortening on the right of his *Belshazzar's Feast* of c. 1636–38 (fig. 5.13) was surely lifted from it.[51] This suggests that Huydecoper's only known Italian picture, the *Europa* by Veronese, was a copy or version of the work in the Ducal Palace.

Huydecoper and other connoisseurs would have delighted in spotting the borrowings Rembrandt and Sandrart made from Veronese's picture, and they would have avidly discussed the seventeenth-century artists' completely opposite approaches to the legacy of the Italian Renaissance. *Belshazzar's Feast* is characterized by intense action, strong contrasts of light and dark, blurry contour lines and fanciful costumes. In *Odysseus and Nausicaa*, on the other hand, there are tranquil movements, clear and even lighting

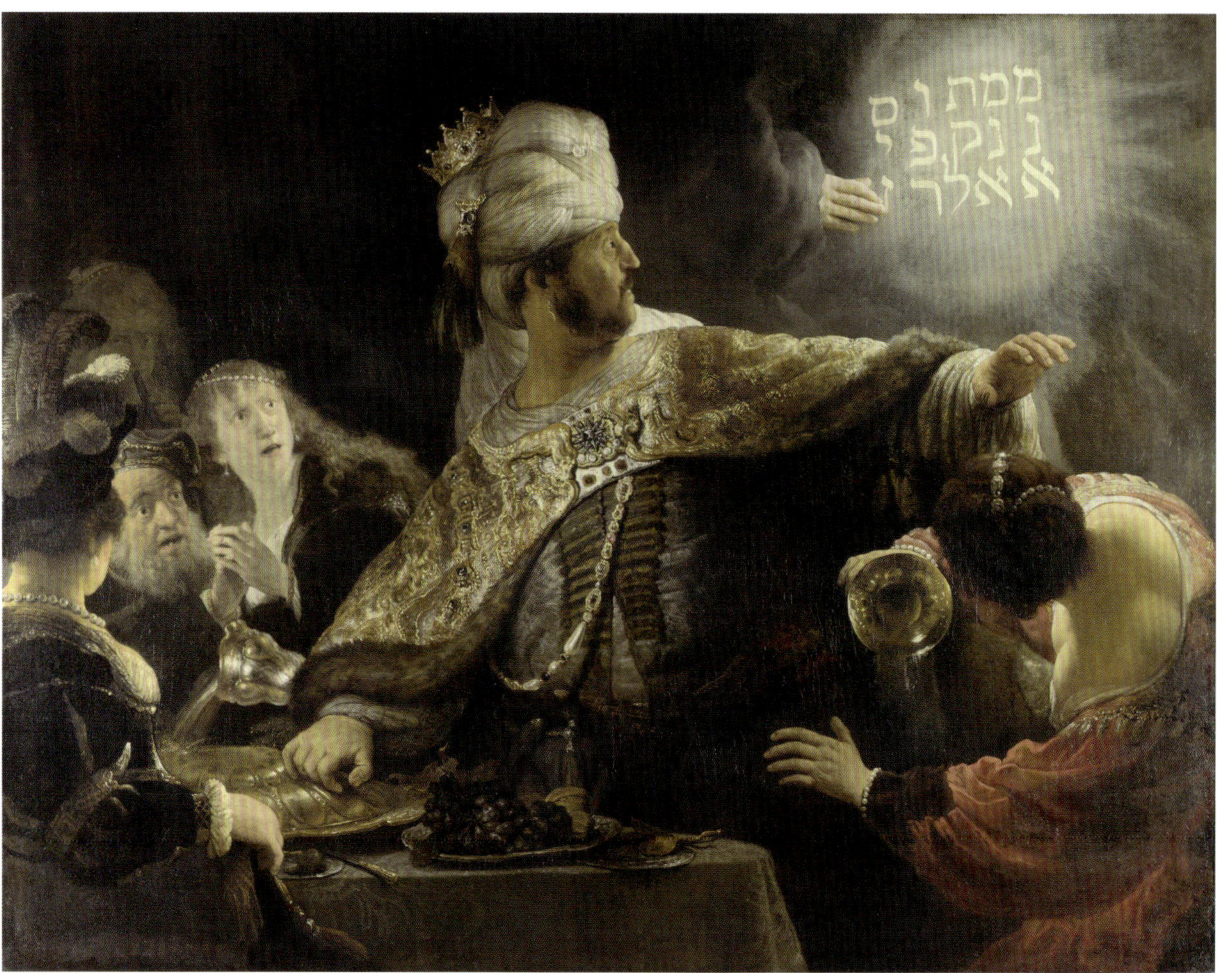

fig. 5.13 **Rembrandt van Rijn,** *Belshazzar's Feast*, **c. 1636–38, oil on canvas; 167.6 × 209.2 cm. The National Gallery, London. Bought with a contribution from the Art Fund, 1964 (NG6350)**

(now largely obscured by yellowed varnish), firm outlines and classical drapery.[52] The two modes of painting represented in these works by Sandrart and Rembrandt reflect a debate that originated in sixteenth-century Italy about whether Tuscan *disegno* or Venetian *colorito* should be considered superior.[53] In the central decades of the seventeenth century, this debate played out in the diverse tastes of Amsterdam collectors.

In the short run, Sandrart, who left Amsterdam in 1645, did not pose a serious threat to Rembrandt's client base. Yet, while the number of commissions he wrested away from Rembrandt was small, the repercussions of his presence were great. With his *Odysseus and Nausicaa* and other history paintings, Sandrart initiated a development in Amsterdam painting that Arnold Houbraken would describe in writing about the life of Rembrandt's pupil, and later rival, Govert Flinck. According to Houbraken, the importation of Italian paintings by "true connoisseurs" opened the eyes of the Dutch art world, resulting in the comeback of "clear, bright painting."[54] Foremost among those "true connoisseurs" was Huydecoper, who had the foresight to commission Sandrart's *Odysseus and Nausicaa*. In the later 1650s, as a protégé of Huydecoper, Flinck would produce monumental paintings executed in a "clear, bright" manner for Amsterdam's new town hall. While Flinck and others joined the Tuscan *disegno* camp, Rembrandt radically strengthened his allegiance to Venetian *colorito* in his later career, most dramatically through his adaptation of Titian's late, rough manner of painting. The fact that the majority of Italian paintings owned by the Keizersgracht cognoscenti, despite the developing taste for clear, bright painting, were sixteenth-century Venetian works was surely one of his prime reasons for doing so.[55] ■

NOTES

1   De Piles 1708, 494–498.

2   Huygens 1897, 79; trans. from Leiden 1991, 133; *Corpus*, vol. 6, no. 23.

3   Ibid., 133.

4   Houbraken 1718–21, vol. 2, 233.

5   Broos 1975–76.

6   Van Mander 1973, vol. 1, 139; vol. 2, 476–479.

7   Leiden 1991, 134.

8   For Rembrandt's and Lievens' reasons for not visiting Italy, see esp. Dickey 2007, 8–10.

9   For these English collections, see Brown 1995, 10–57.

10 For collections of Italian art in Amsterdam, see Golahny 1984; Henk Th. van Veen, "Uitzonderlijke verzamelingen: Italiaanse kunst en klassieke sculptuur in Nederland," in Amsterdam 1992, 102–116; Van den Berghe 1992; Bert W. Meijer, "Italian Paintings in 17th-century Holland: Art Market, Art Works and Art Collections," in Seidel 2000; Golahny 2013.

11 Meijer, "Italian Paintings," in Seidel 2000, 380.

12 On Sohier and his collection, see Jaap van der Veen, "Schilderijencollecties in de Republiek ten tijde van Frederik Hendrik en Amalia," in The Hague 1997, 92; Meijer, "Italian Paintings," in Seidel 2000, 380–381. The painting attributed to Titian, Giorgione and Sebastiano del Piombo is now in the Detroit Institute of Arts (inv. 26.107), where it is attributed to Titian alone.

13 Leiden 1991, 133.

14 Schwartz 1985, 134, 138.

15 For Huydecoper's biography and patronage of the arts, see De Balbian Verster 1932, 35–40; Kooijmans 1997, 113–121, 123–125, 130–131, 181–182, 191; Schwartz 1983; Schwartz 1985, 134–138; Ottenheym 1989, 34–45; Manuth 1993–94, 248–250.

16 The Veronese is mentioned in a 1622 list of Huydecoper's possessions; Schwartz 1985, 138.

17 On Coymans, see Jonathan Bikker, "Balthasar Coymans's Italian Paintings and Annibale Carracci's Melancholy," in Manuth and Rüger 2004, 27–33.

18 Sandrart 1675–80, vol. 2, book 2, 188.

19 Ibid., 190.

20 See Bikker, "Balthasar Coymans's Italian Paintings," in Manuth and Rüger 2004, 27–33.

21 *Portrait of a Woman* (*Maria Trip?*); *Corpus*, vol. 6, no. 184b.

22 On the Reynst brothers and their collection, see Logan 1979.

23 Ridolfi 1648, unpaginated.

24 The niece, Susanna de Haze, was married to Lucas' brother Jacomo van Uffelen.

25 Sandrart 1675–80, vol. 2, book 3, 348.

26 De Piles 1677, 142–143. On the magnitude of the Van Uffelen sale, see Montias 2002, 16.

27 Montias 2002, 16.

28 Strauss and Van der Meulen 1979, doc. 1659/16.

29 On the Van Uffelen sale and the reception of the *Castiglione*, see esp. Dickey 2004, 99–100.

30 Crenshaw 2006, 93.

31 De Piles 1706, 317. On Rembrandt's collection, see Scheller 1969; Amsterdam 1999–2000; Crenshaw 2006, 89–109.

32 Crenshaw 2006, 103.

33 For Lopez's biography and collection, see, among others, Tallemant des Réaux 1834, 226–229; Baraude 1933; Schwartz 1985, 214–215, 369–370n214c; Schnapper 1994, 99–100.

34 Rotterdam City Archives, Oud Notarieel Archief, Notary Arnout Hofflant, inv. 257, doc. 206, 24 Apr. 1634, 315; doc. 222, 8 May 1634, 340–341; doc. 247, 16 June 1634, 374; doc. 259, 20 July 1634, 392–393.

35 Gary Schwartz suggests Rembrandt came into contact with Lopez through Huygens; Schwartz 1985, 214.

36 *Corpus*, vol. 6, no. 10; Strauss and Van der Meulen 1979, doc. 1641/6.

37 As Sandrart himself later informs us: Sandrart 1675–80, vol. 1, book 3, 55.

38 On the rivalry between Rembrandt and Sandrart, see Dickey 2004, 100–104; Kok 2013, 116–117; Sluijter 2015, 71–96.

39 Carolyn Logan in New York 1995, 157–158, no. 56; Slive 2009a, 166–168.

40 *Corpus*, vol. 5, 208–209.

41 For the paintings with which Rembrandt was competing, see esp. Sluijter 2015, 42–50.

42 The term was coined by Stephanie S. Dickey; Dickey 2004, 97.

43 De Piles 1677, 142–143. De Piles' anecdote was first cited in the Rembrandt literature by Dickey 2004, 98.

44 On LeBlon, see Fontaine Verwey 1969; Badeloch Vera Noldus, "A Spider in Its Web: Agent and Artist Michel Le Blon and His Northern European Network," in Keblusek and Noldus 2011, 161–191.

45 Sandrart 1675–80, vol. 1, *Lebenslauf*, 12–13, trans. from Sluijter 2015, 74.

46 Taking the northern European models that also inform these two self-portraits by Rembrandt into consideration, Dickey concludes: "By creatively integrating these antecedents with the experience of Raphael and Titian, Rembrandt celebrates the Northern tradition, and his place within it, as equal or superior to that of Italy"; Dickey 2004, 96.

47 As pointed out in Kok 2013, 127, without, however, being aware of Jan Bicker's address on the canal. For the exact location of the house, see Amsterdam City Archives, Archief van de Schepenen, Kwijtscheldingsregisters, Transportakten voor 1811, 15 July 1718, scan no. NL-SAA-21653847.

48 Klemm 1986, 73–83, nos. 18–22, where it is mistakenly stated that Jacob and Hendrick Bicker were nephews of Jan Bicker.

49 On the commission, see Ottenheym 1989, 36.

50 As pointed out in Kok 2013, 136.

51 See esp. *Corpus*, vol. 3, 128–129.

52 For the differences between the style of Sandrart's *Odysseus and Nausicaa* and Rembrandt's paintings in general, see Sluijter 2006, 217–218; Kok 2013, 136; Sluijter 2015, 87–88.

53 Sluijter 2015, 88.

54 Houbraken 1718–21, vol. 2, 21.

55 For the preference for sixteenth-century Venetian painters, see Van den Berghe 1992, 35.

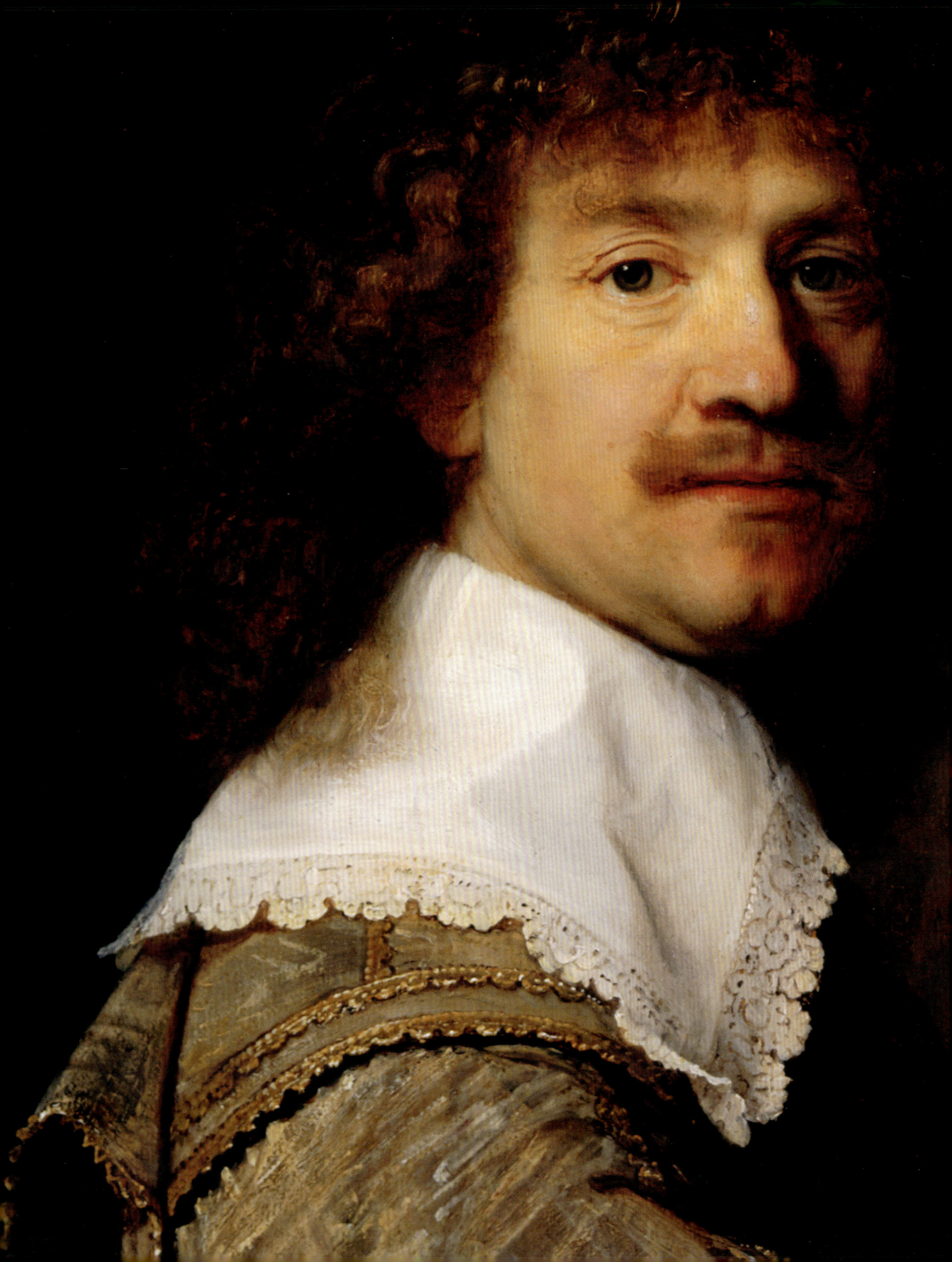

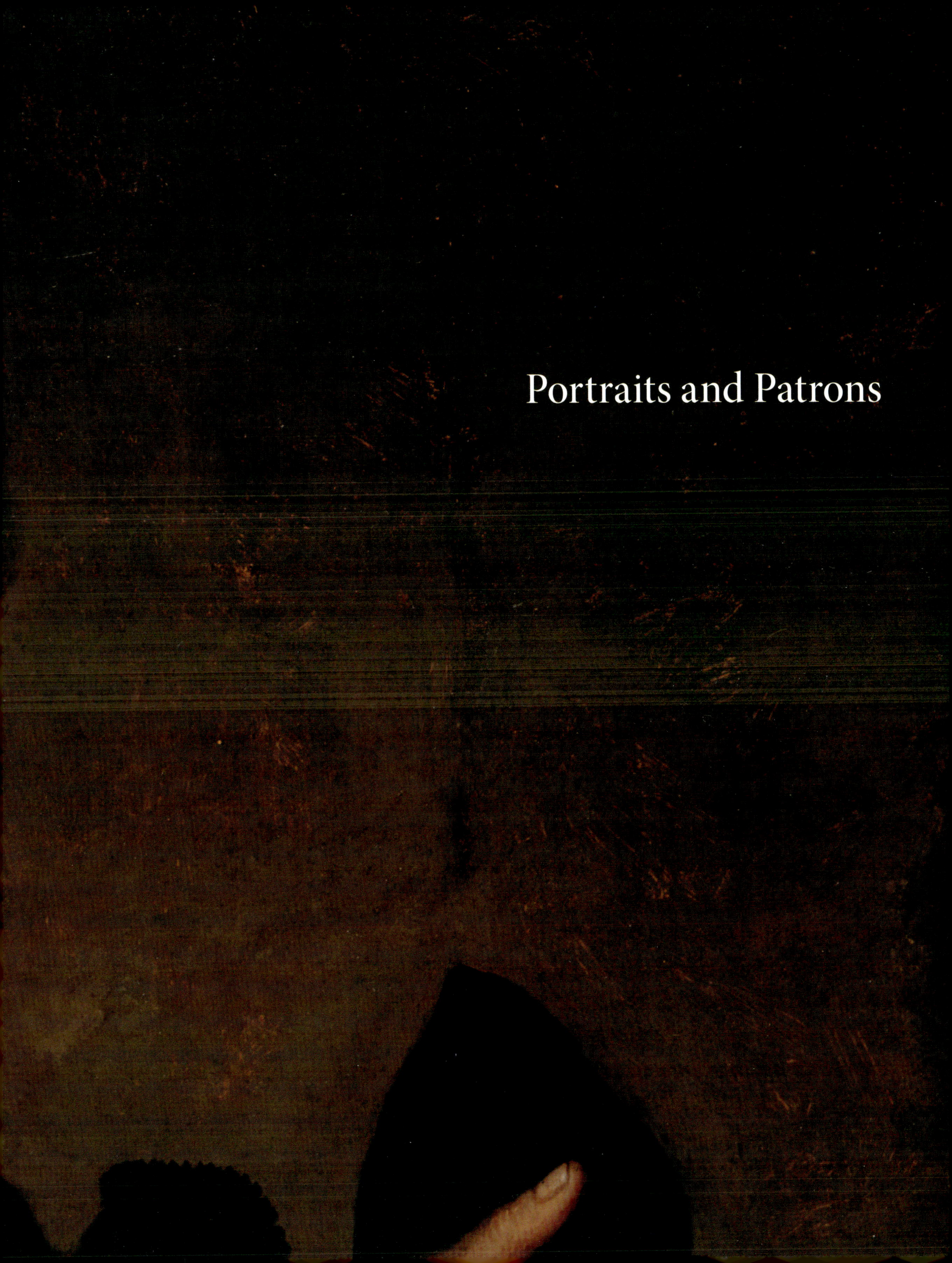
Portraits and Patrons

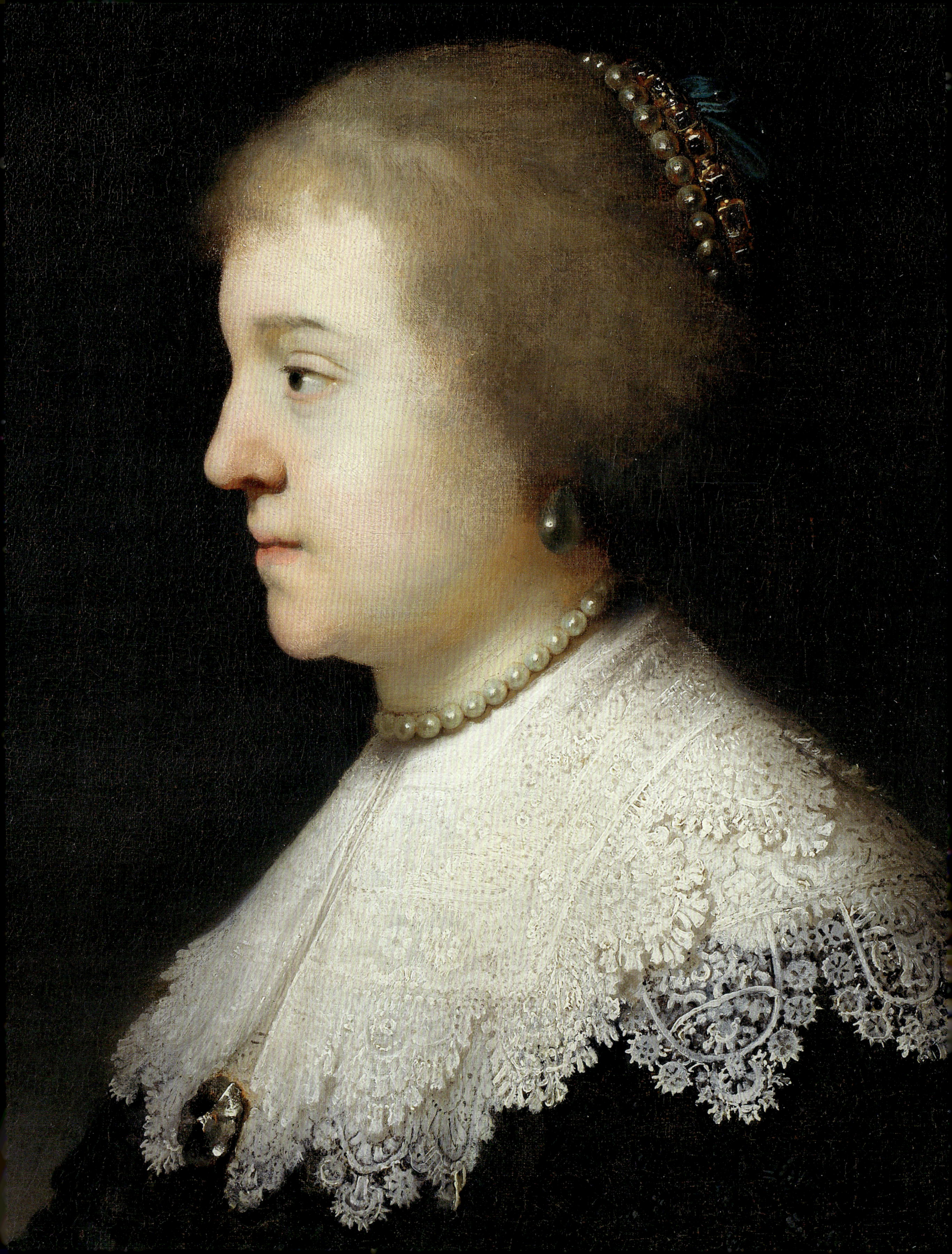

RUDI EKKART AND
CLAIRE VAN DEN DONK

Rembrandt's Portrait Commissions outside Amsterdam

Beginning in 1631, Rembrandt received a veritable stream of portrait commissions through his association with Hendrick Uylenburgh in Amsterdam.[1] It seems rather remarkable that Uylenburgh offered Rembrandt a career as a portraitist, when as far as we know the artist had yet to paint any formal likenesses; however, the state of the market provided an opportunity. The limited number of accomplished portrait painters then working in Amsterdam could not keep up with the growing demand, and a wider pool of talent was urgently needed. The prolific scale of Rembrandt's portrait production between 1631 and 1634 is matched only by that of Nicolaes Eliasz Pickenoy and to a lesser extent Thomas de Keyser. During these years, Rembrandt painted more than twenty portraits for Amsterdam patrons, in addition to the monumental group portrait for the Amsterdam Guild of Surgeons, *The Anatomy Lesson of Dr. Nicolaes Tulp*, of 1632 (see fig. 1.4). His output consisted not only of simple busts but also various life-size, full-length portraits, several double portraits, and a number of ambitious three-quarter-length likenesses. Furthermore, he was exceptional in building a portrait clientele not just in one city, but in several. This essay explores the results of these bold ambitions.

Portraits in Various Cities

While it is often assumed that Rembrandt had left Leiden definitively by mid-1631, it is more probable that he combined living in his hometown with regular periods of work in Amsterdam.[2] A document from 20 June 1631 shows that, sometime earlier, Rembrandt had loaned Uylenburgh 1,000 guilders, most likely as a business investment.[3] While commuting from Leiden to Amsterdam, he could use Uylenburgh's workshop and also stay in the dealer's home. This gave him the flexibility to accept commissions in other cities as well.

Jan Lievens – with whom Rembrandt had most likely shared a workshop in Leiden and interacted intensively in the previous few years – did not leave for London until early April 1632. Unlike Rembrandt, he had already established his name as a portraitist before his departure.[4] To obtain commissions outside of Amsterdam, Rembrandt surely used both his own network and reputation and those of his friend and *confrère*. The high reputation that Rembrandt and Lievens enjoyed in The Hague was largely due to the enthusiastic interest of Constantijn Huygens, secretary to Stadtholder Frederik Hendrik. The two artists were readily mentioned in the same breath by Huygens, whose portrait Lievens had painted around

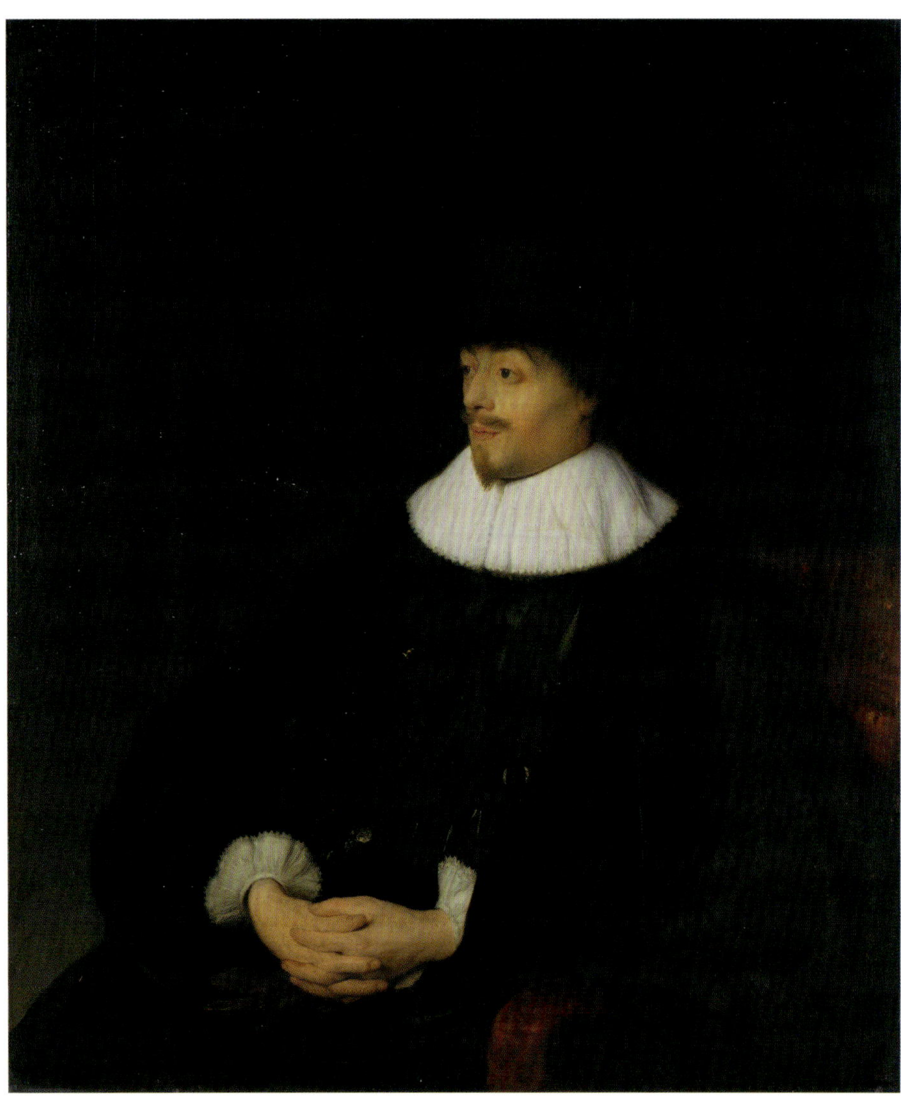

fig. 6.1 Jan Lievens, *Portrait of
Constantijn Huygens*, c. 1628–29,
oil on panel; 99 × 84 cm.
Rijksmuseum, Amsterdam.
On loan from the Musée de la
Chartreuse, Douai (SK-C-1467)

1628–29 (fig. 6.1). Although there are no indications
that Rembrandt made any portraits in the 1620s, he
did produce some for clients in The Hague in 1632
and in Leiden and Rotterdam in 1633 and 1634, while
building his reputation in Amsterdam.

This geographical range of patronage was
uncommon in the Dutch Republic as the market for
most portraitists was limited to their place of residence and immediate surroundings.[5] Clients usually
had their likenesses painted by a fellow townsman,
but naturally, there were exceptions. Sometimes an
outside portraitist was chosen because he had
immortalized close family members or other relations; or, a "celebrity" painter was enlisted whose
reputation was such that he attracted clients from
near and far. A good example is Michiel van Mierevelt
of Delft, who provided portraits to clients from all
parts of the Dutch Republic as well as to foreigners
temporarily residing there. The more fashionable
painters in The Hague, the seat of government, were
often engaged by people from elsewhere who were
stationed there as part of their administrative remit.
This was especially true of officials from smaller
cities and outlying regions, who often preferred a
popular Hague portraitist such as Jan Anthonisz van
Ravesteyn or Gerard van Honthorst to a painter in
their own hometown who may have been less familiar
with the latest trends in style and taste. When spouses
accompanied these dignitaries, they too were captured for posterity.

Occasionally, a painter based elsewhere was hired
for a larger portrait commission. This may have been
due to the fact that eligible local painters were over-
loaded with other work, or because smaller towns
often did not have a resident painter capable of carry-
ing out such major assignments. This is illustrated
by a case in Gouda, where the colonel and captains
of the civic guard turned to the Amsterdam-based
Ferdinand Bol for a group portrait in 1653.[6] That the
supply of skilled portraitists lagged behind the
demand for ambitious group portraits also manifested
itself several times in Amsterdam. For instance,
in 1616 Paulus Moreelse from Utrecht was hired to
make a civic-guard painting in Amsterdam, and in
1633 Frans Hals from Haarlem was engaged for a
similar commission, the so-called *Meagre Company*

(1633–37, Rijksmuseum, Amsterdam), which was completed by the Amsterdam painter Pieter Codde, the latter undoubtedly arranged through Uylenburgh.[7] Perhaps Uylenburgh initially approached Rembrandt solely to paint *The Anatomy Lesson of Dr. Nicolaes Tulp*. Unlike the situation with Hals, this first commission was soon followed by many more.

Ultimately, it appears that in the first half of the 1630s Rembrandt was making an ambitious attempt to forge a double career, with Amsterdam and The Hague as the key points of orientation. It is not surprising that he also received a few commissions from his native Leiden, where he was already an established artist. Meanwhile, his activities for Rotterdam clients in 1633 and especially 1634 seem to suggest an attempt to develop another market. What role could Uylenburgh, who was responsible for introducing Rembrandt to Amsterdam, have played in all this? It seems reasonable to assume that the dealer was directly or indirectly involved in the Rotterdam commissions. They came from a circle of Remonstrant patrons, and through Uylenburgh Rembrandt also established contacts with this community in Amsterdam. An important example of this is the artist's impressive portrait of the Remonstrant preacher Johannes Wtenbogaert (fig. 6.2), commissioned and painted in Amsterdam for Abraham Anthonisz Recht.

Uylenburgh's involvement in The Hague commissions, on the other hand, is improbable. Rembrandt would have had a better entrée there through Constantijn Huygens. As far as we can tell, in the early 1630s Uylenburgh had only one influential Hague relation, namely Adriaen Pauw, who became Grand Pensionary of Holland in 1631.[8] Pauw acted on behalf of his underage son, who owned the building on the corner of the St. Anthonisbreestraat and Zwanenburgwal that Uylenburgh probably rented from 1626 onward. It is doubtful whether this relationship formed an opening for obtaining commissions from court circles in The Hague. Rembrandt more likely tried to build a career in the milieu around the stadtholder's court by using the contacts that he and Lievens had previously established, such as Huygens. While this may reflect the young artist's bold ambition, it is also possible that he did this in order not to feel entirely dependant on Uylenburgh.

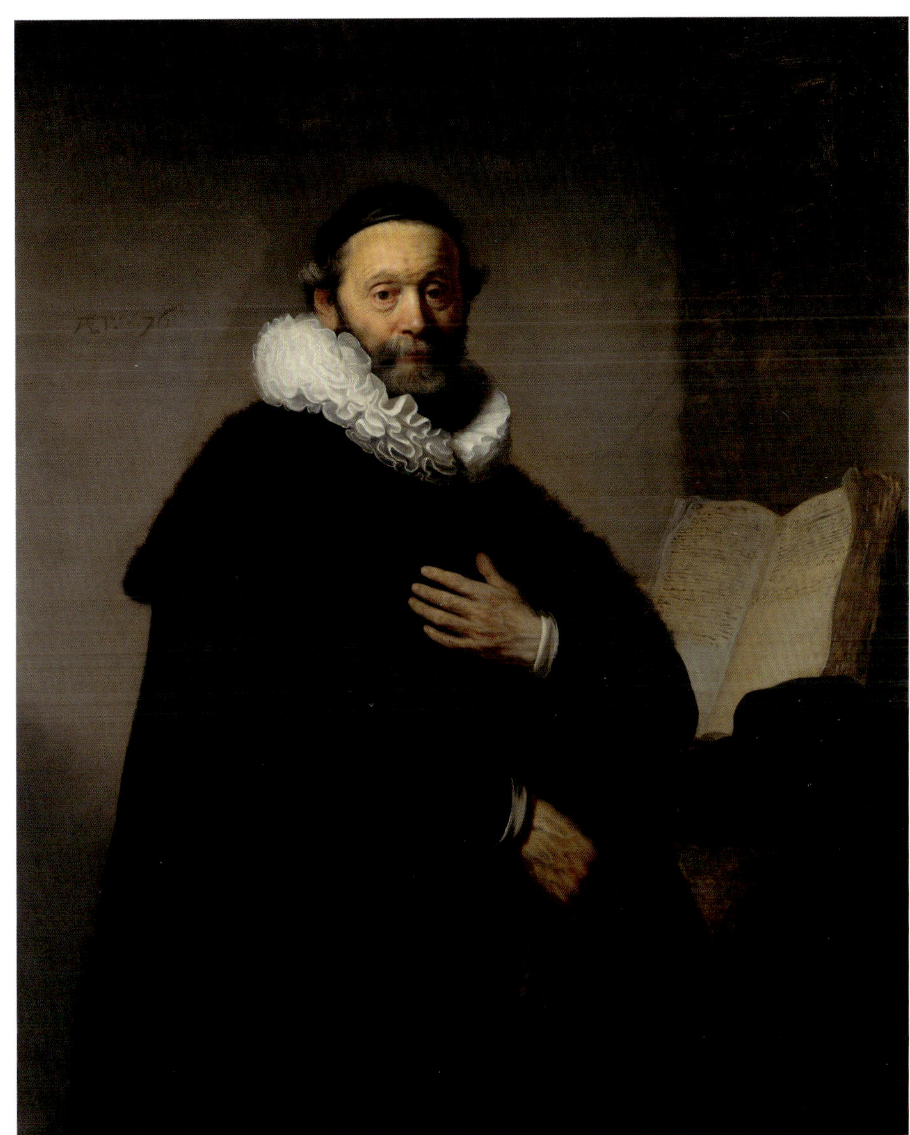

fig. 6.2 **Rembrandt van Rijn,** *Portrait of Reverend Johannes Wtenbogaert*, **1633, oil on canvas; 130 × 103 cm. Rijksmuseum, Amsterdam. Purchased with the support of the Rembrandt Association, with additional funding from the Prins Bernhard Fonds, the VSBfonds, the Rijksmuseum-Stichting, the State of the Netherlands and private collectors (SK-A-4885)**

Portraits for The Hague

Six portraits by Rembrandt, all painted in 1632, can be linked to The Hague with a fair degree of certainty. Rembrandt had already painted one or more pictures of a different nature for the stadtholder's court. There seems to be some confusion in the inventories as to which works were by Lievens and which by Rembrandt, and identification of individual pieces is unclear. In connection with Rembrandt's portrait activities of 1632, his *Simeon's Song of Praise* (1631, Mauritshuis, The Hague) is of particular importance since it is almost certainly identical to the painting of this subject mentioned in the stadtholder's inventory of 1632, "*door rembrandts of Jan Lievensz. gedaen*" (made by Rembrandt or Lievens).[9] This entry makes it clear that Rembrandt had either just recently carried out a commission for Stadtholder Frederik Hendrik and his consort Amalia von Solms or had sold them a painting made on his own initiative. This is critical, since several other and possibly earlier pieces in the same inventory are – rightly or wrongly – credited to Lievens. The same 1632 inventory also lists one painting without any hesitation as by Rembrandt, namely "*Een contrefeytsel van Haere Exce in profijl bij Rembrandts*

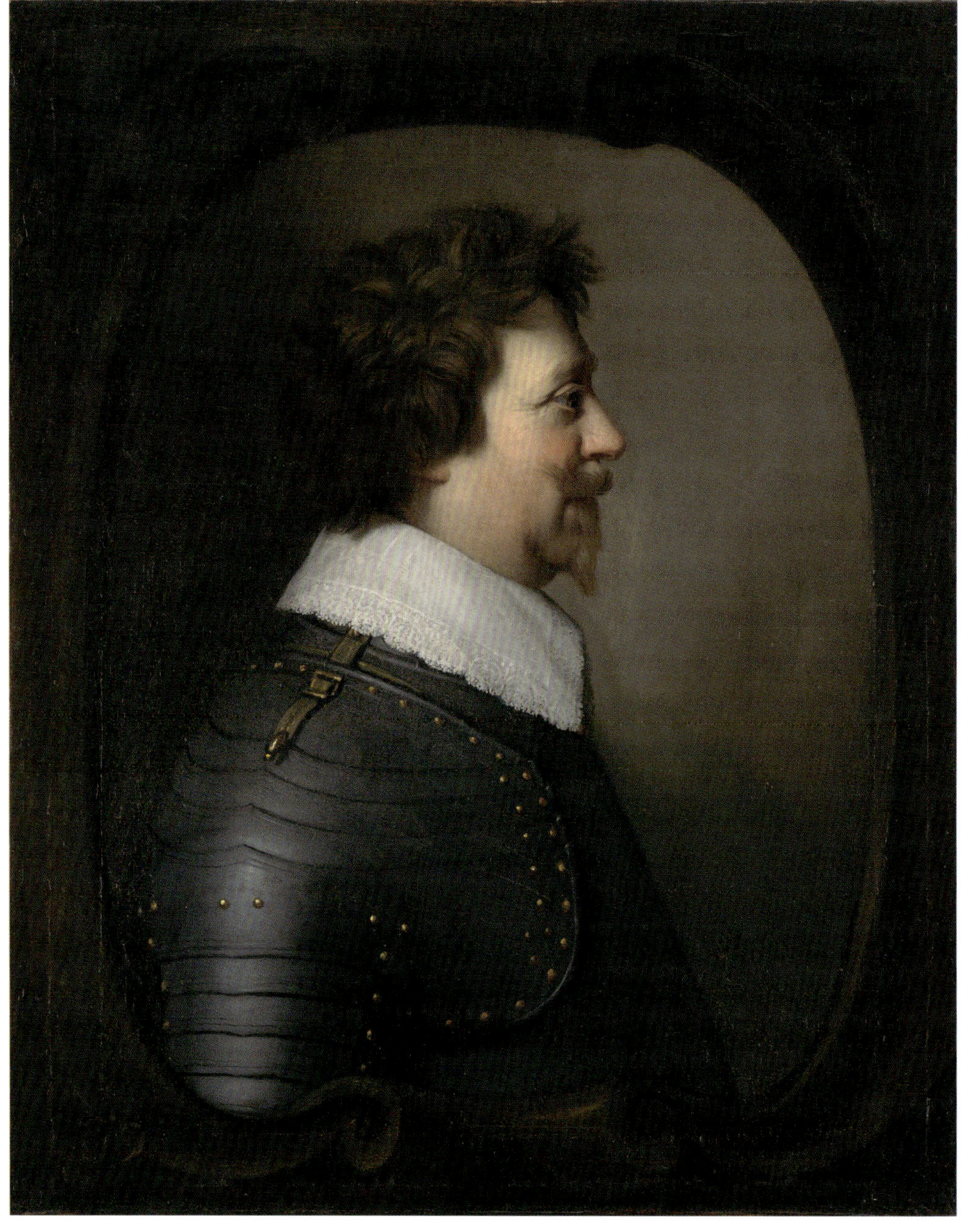

fig. 6.3 Gerard van Honthorst, *Portrait of Frederik Hendrik*, 1631, oil on canvas; 77 × 61 cm. Royal Collections of the Netherlands (SC/0010)

gedaen" (A likeness of Her Excellency in profile done by Rembrandt). The certitude with which this painting of Amalia von Solms was ascribed to Rembrandt may reflect the fact that it had just been completed.

Thanks to a restoration in 1965, a signed and dated portrait of a woman from 1632 was established as the profile portrait of Amalia inventoried in 1632 (pl. 47). The restoration revealed that the decorative cartouche framing the figure was entirely consistent with that depicted in Gerard van Honthorst's 1631 *Portrait of Frederik Hendrik* (fig. 6.3).[10] Rembrandt's choice of the pose in profile here was therefore dictated by the format of the painting for which it was meant to serve as a pendant, as was the framing cartouche. It is striking that in the same year Rembrandt painted a *tronie* in profile of a young woman, traditionally believed to be his sister Lijsbeth (1632, Nationalmuseum, Stockholm). It remains unclear whether he painted such a study head as an exercise in preparation for his depiction of Amalia, or whether it was because of such studies that he was engaged to paint the profile portrait of the stadtholder's consort. Later on, in Amsterdam, artists in his circle produced *tronies* of the same type for the open market (pl. 49).[11]

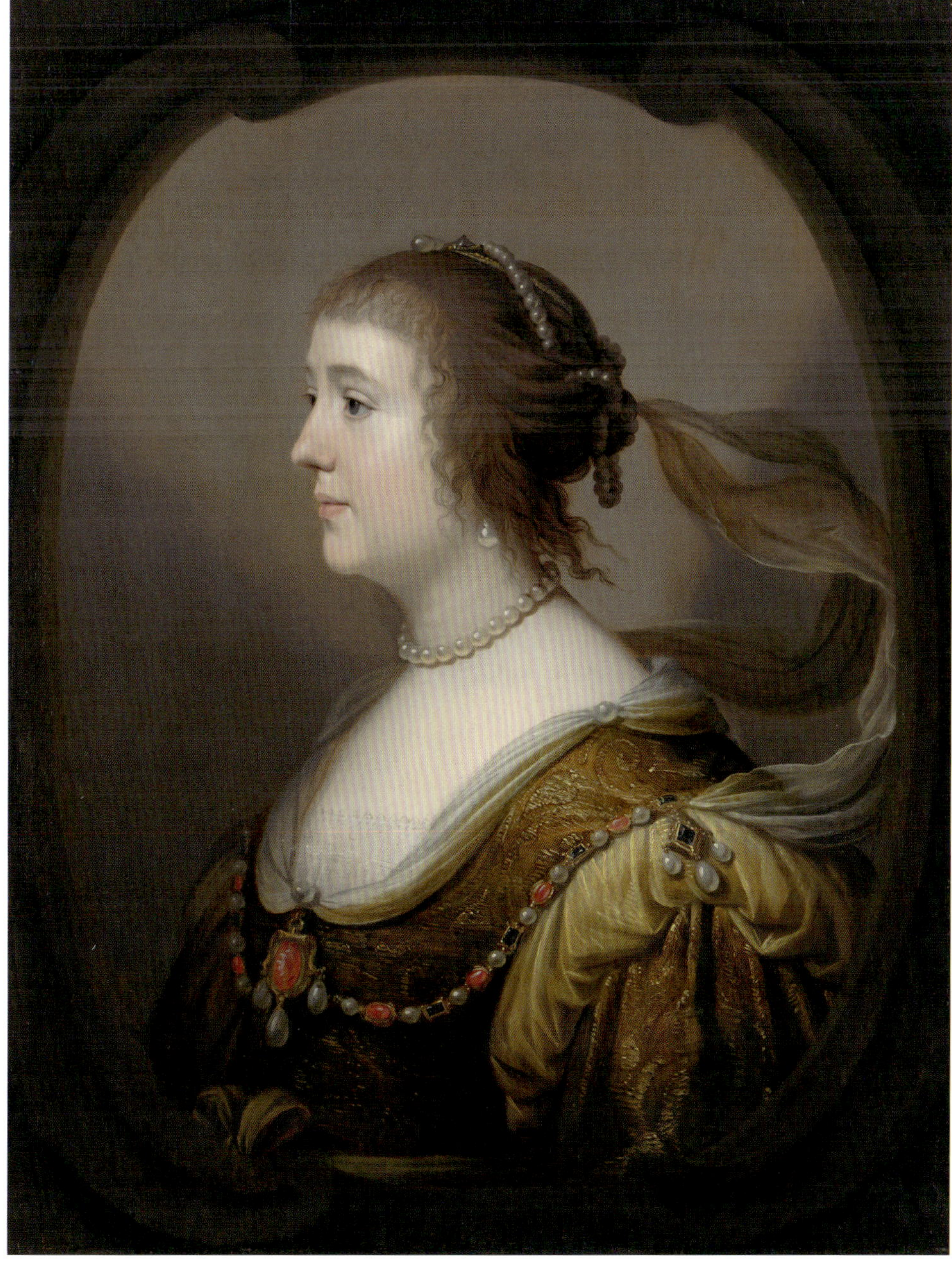

fig. 6.4 **Gerard van Honthorst,** *Portrait of Amalia von Solms,* **1630s, oil on panel; 73.4 × 60 cm. Royal Collections of the Netherlands (SC/0027)**

47 Rembrandt van Rijn, *Portrait of Amalia von Solms*, 1632. Musée Jacquemart-André, Institut de France, Paris

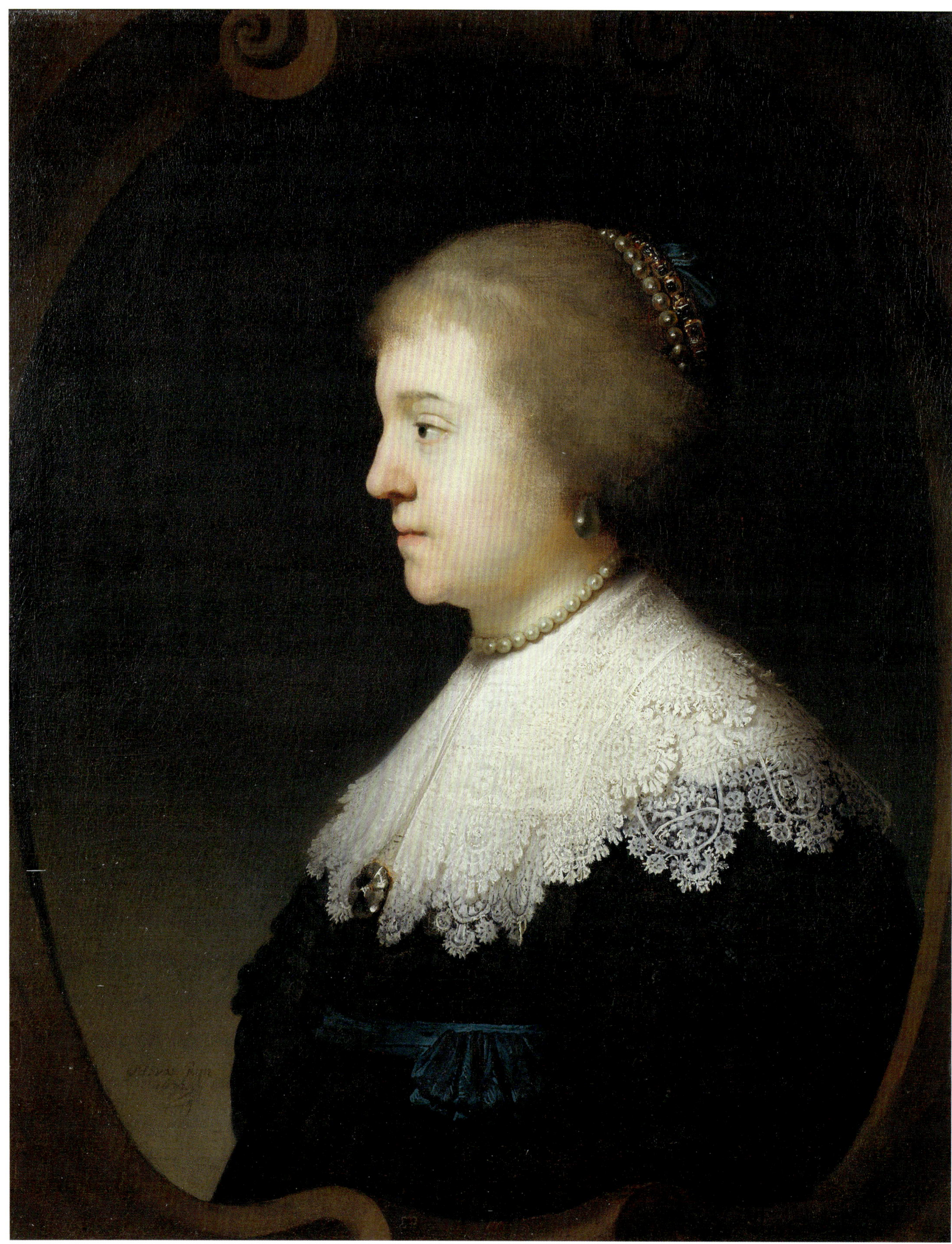

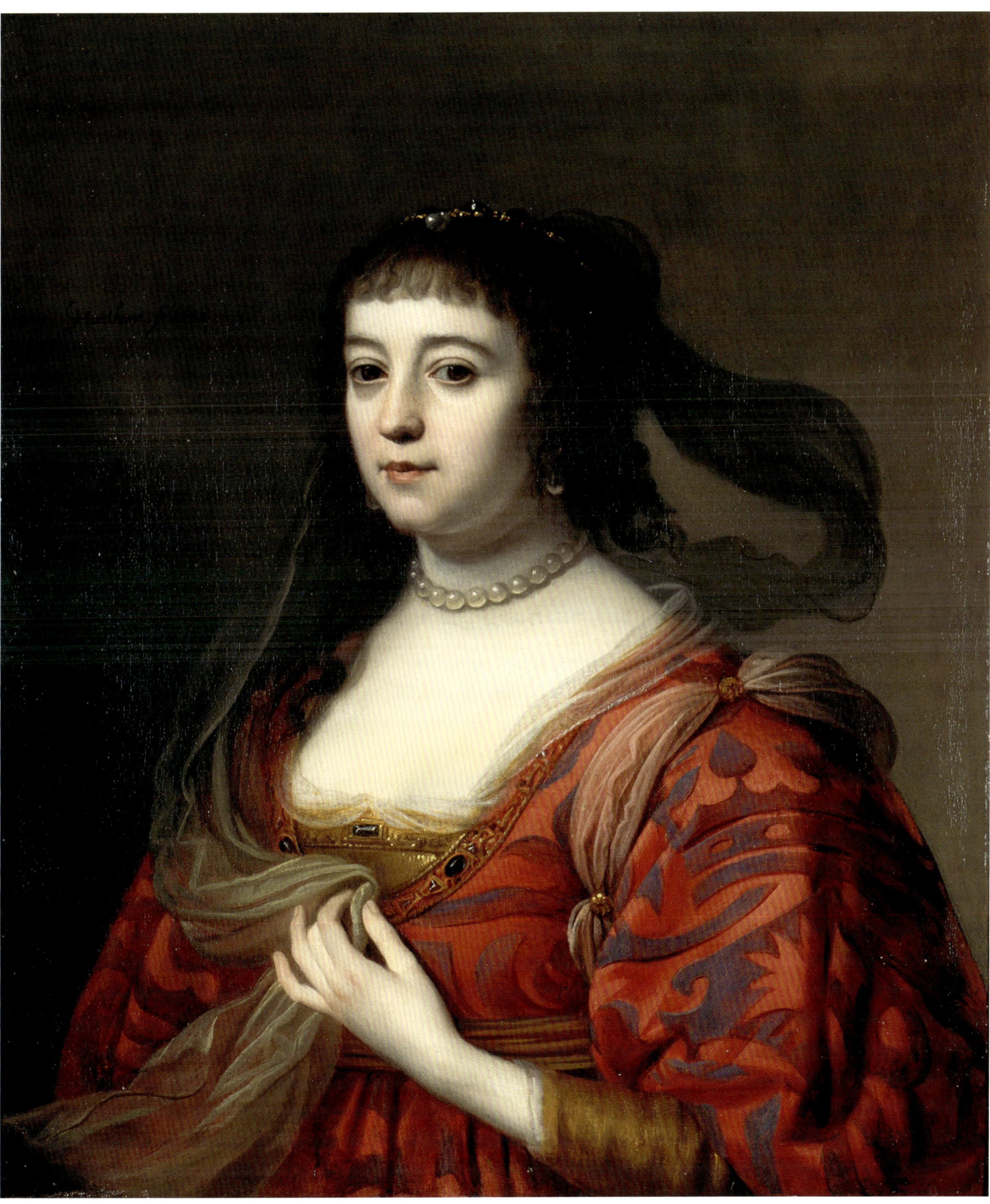

The circumstances of the commission are unclear. While it might be assumed that Rembrandt painted this likeness of Amalia by order of the stadtholder's court, it is also possible that someone else affiliated with Rembrandt and the court acted as the patron and presented the picture to her. After all, at this time the stadtholder and his wife were completely captivated by Honthorst, and they were anything but adventurous when it came to portrait commissions. Honthorst produced a profile portrait of Amalia (fig. 6.4) that seems to have replaced the one by Rembrandt, and several more glamorous images of the princess as well (pl. 48).[12] Before addressing who may have been the patron for Rembrandt's portrait of Amalia, it is useful to examine other portrait commissions carried out by the artist in The Hague in 1632.

The identities of the sitters in two other Hague portraits have been known for a long time (figs. 6.5, 6.6). This exceptional pair of paintings commemorates a friendship between Maurits Huygens (brother of Constantijn) and the draughtsman and etcher Jacques de Gheyn III, son of the painter Jacques de Gheyn II (both father and son had contacts in the stadtholder's court). The two small panels initially hung separately in the sitters' homes, but when De Gheyn III died a bachelor in 1641, his portrait went to Huygens.[13] The personal relationship between Rembrandt and the patrons is evident. Maurits Huygens knew Rembrandt at the least through his brother Constantijn, whereas De Gheyn owned – perhaps by inheritance from his father – several paintings by Rembrandt from his Leiden period, as well as works by Lievens.[14]

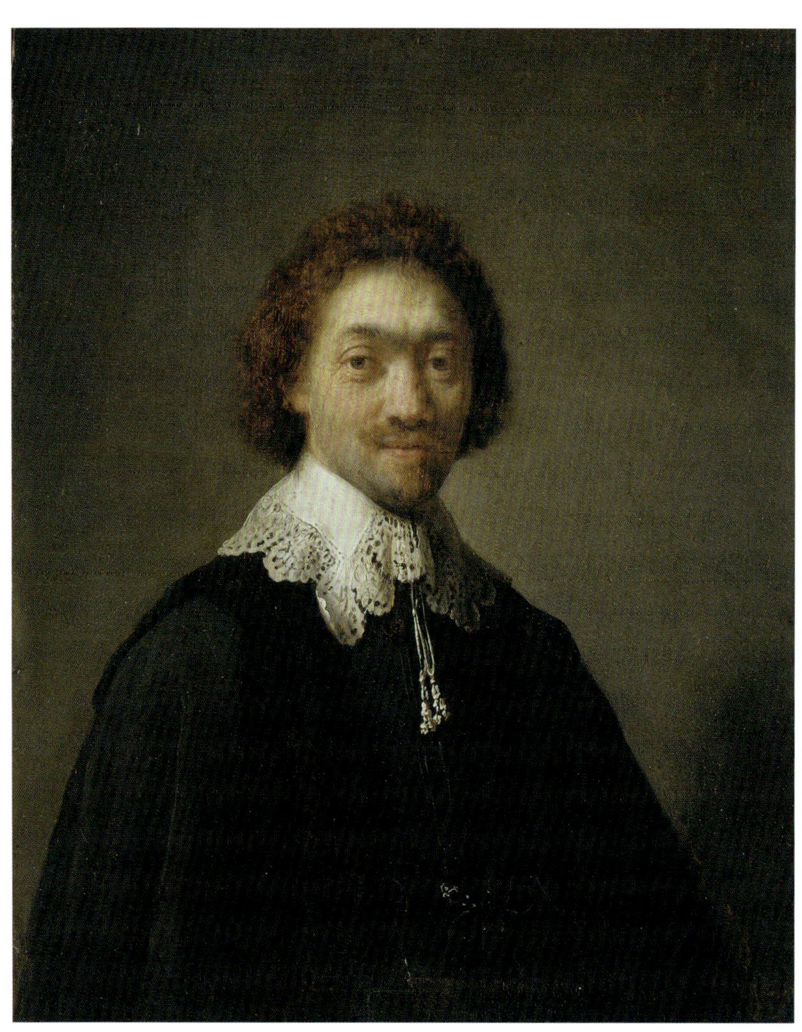

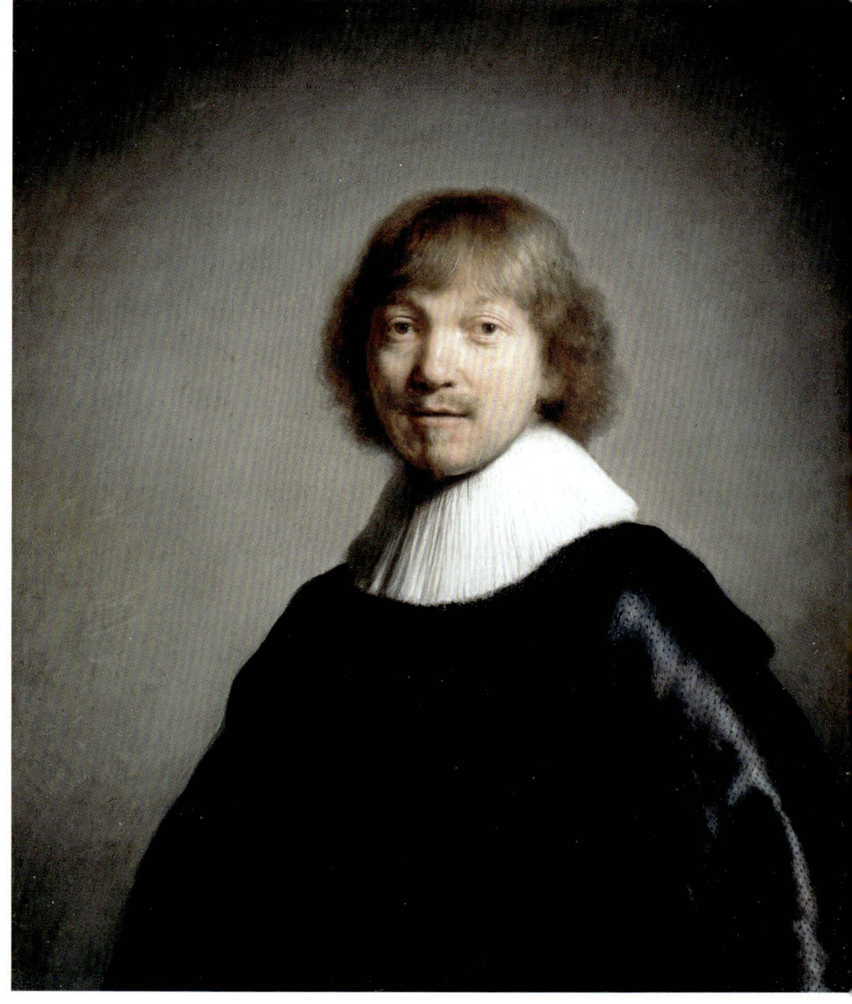

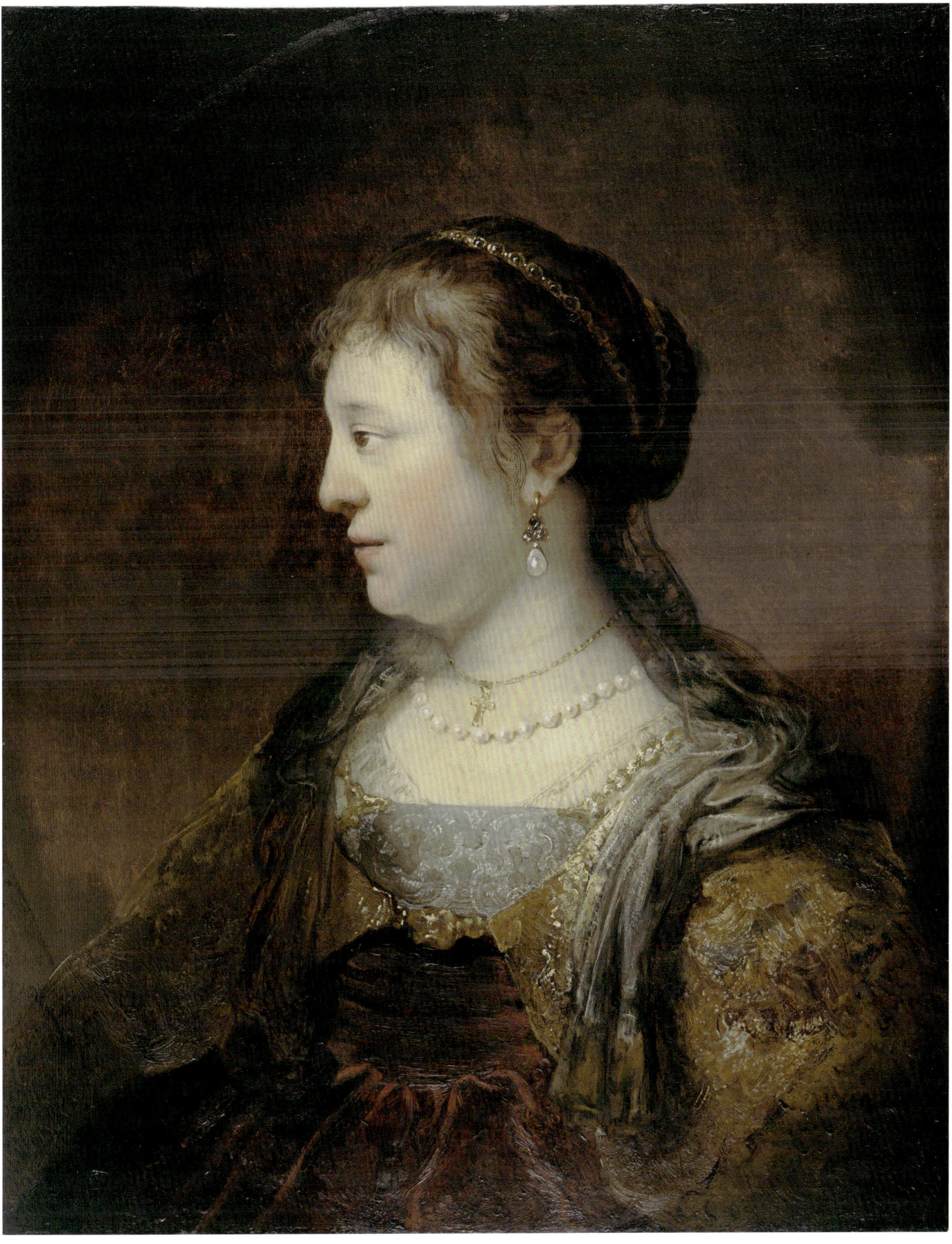

Thanks to two notarial deeds from 1654 and 1661, we know that Rembrandt painted a portrait of the sea captain, innkeeper and lieutenant of the militia Joris de Caullery, as well as one of his son Johan.[15] Since it was recorded that De Caullery was portrayed with "*het roer in de handt*" (holding a caliver), his likeness can confidently be identified as the 1632 portrait in San Francisco (fig. 6.7). De Caullery was an art-loving and apparently vain man. According to his will, he and his wife were portrayed by Anthony van Dyck (likely during one of the Flemish artist's visits to The Hague in 1628 and 1632) and by Lievens, while individual portraits of him were painted by Moyses van Uyttenbroeck and Paulus Lesire, as well as by Rembrandt. It has been suggested that there is a connection between these commissions and De Caullery's ownership of the inn "*De Grote Zwaan*" (The Great Swan), where Van Dyck and Rembrandt

may have stayed during their visits to The Hague.[16] De Caullery's portrait occupies a somewhat exceptional place in Rembrandt's oeuvre due to the sitter's rather fashionable self-presentation. Attempts to identify the portrait of his son Johan, however, have proved unsuccessful.[17] It is highly questionable whether his likeness dates from the same time as that of his father, since Johan was younger than ten years old in 1632. It seems more probable that De Caullery called on the artist much later to immortalize his son.

Two paintings in the Metropolitan Museum of Art, New York (figs. 6.8, 6.9), can be added to the four likenesses of sitters from The Hague identified above. These large, three-quarter-length paintings came from the collection of portraits of the Van Beresteyn family, once kept at Maurick Castle and auctioned in 1884. This is why they were traditionally regarded as portraits of members of the Van Beresteyn family, although without any specific identification of the individuals portrayed.[18] The discussion regarding the sitters was long overshadowed by the matter of the portraits' attribution, since in 1986, the Rembrandt Research Project rejected them as works by Rembrandt and gave them instead to an assistant, possibly Isaac de Jouderville. Today, they are once again regarded by most scholars as largely, if not entirely, painted by Rembrandt.[19]

New research on the Van Beresteyn family portrait collection in 2005–06 led to the conclusion that the sitters were most likely Thomas Brouaert and his wife Johanna van Clootwijk.[20] Their daughter Jacqueline was married to Christiaan van Beresteyn, and she bought Maurick Castle shortly after her husband's death. The pendant portraits would have entered the castle through her. Born in Brussels, Thomas Brouaert and his twin brother Johan were nursed and brought up together with the future stadtholder Frederik Hendrik. In 1622 Brouaert married Johanna van Clootwijk, daughter of a burgomaster of Geertruidenberg in Brabant, and ten years his junior. After the appointment of Frederik Hendrik as stadtholder in 1625, Brouaert became the prince's treasurer-general, a position he held until his death ten years later. The identification of the works as Thomas Brouaert and his wife Johanna is therefore reasonable as the male sitter in particular exudes a sense of grandeur befitting a courtier from The Hague. Thanks to Constantijn Huygens we know that Brouaert also collected paintings. He owned a *tronie* by

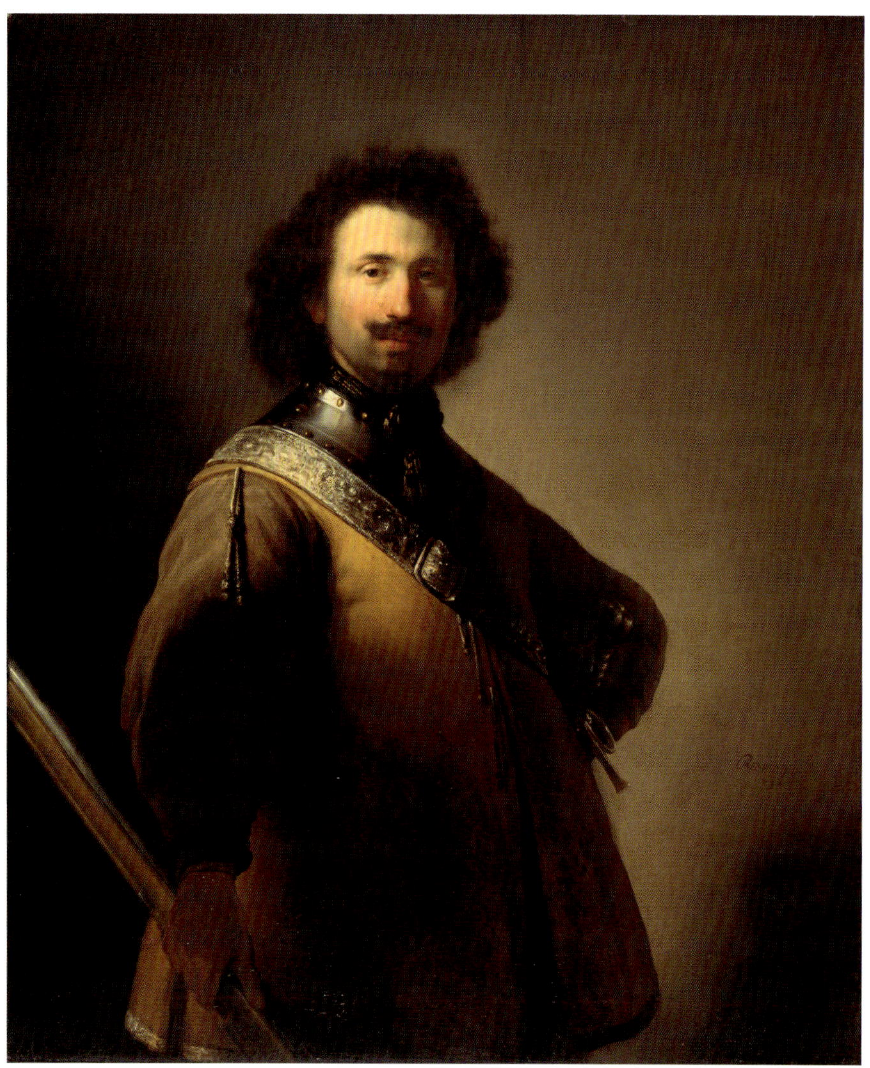

fig. 6.7 **Rembrandt van Rijn, *Portrait of Joris de Caullery*, 1632, oil on canvas mounted on panel; 102.9 × 84.3 cm. Fine Arts Museums of San Francisco. Roscoe and Margaret Oakes Collection (66.31)**

Lievens,[21] suggesting that he could have had earlier contact with Rembrandt and that Hendrick Uylenburgh was not necessarily needed as an intermediary. Brouaert's commission to Rembrandt for the portraits of his wife and himself bespeaks his confidence in the young painter. It therefore also seems quite possible that it was Brouaert, not Huygens as previously assumed, who commissioned and gifted Rembrandt's portrait of the stadtholder's wife Amalia.[22]

Even with such a small number of identifiable works, we gain the impression that in 1632 Rembrandt was busy working not only for the Amsterdam portrait market but also for a select clientele in The Hague, most of whom had clear ties to the stadtholder's court. He had already carried out other commissions for the court and would later complete his series of paintings depicting the Passion of Christ for Frederik Hendrik through the mediation of Huygens. However, there does not seem to be any continuation of his Hague portrait practice after 1632.

The few works available for comparison suggest that, while Rembrandt distinguished himself in Amsterdam by instilling his portraits with action and movement, he chose a slightly more static and dignified portrait style for his elite clientele in The Hague. Even the portrait of Joris de Caullery, whose pose at first glance seems dashing, ultimately comes across as stately and immobile. Since we cannot point to any further commissions from The Hague, it remains unclear whether this difference was a deliberate strategy or simply a coincidence. Rembrandt's success in this market was eclipsed by Gerard van Honthorst, who garnered such success at the courts of the stadtholder and his royal houseguest, Elizabeth, Queen of Bohemia, that in addition to his Utrecht studio, he opened a second one in The Hague.

fig. 6.8 **Rembrandt van Rijn,** *Portrait of a Man (probably Thomas Brouaert)***, 1632, oil on canvas; 111.8 × 88.9 cm. The Metropolitan Museum of Art, New York. H.O. Havemeyer Collection, Bequest of Mrs. H.O. Havemeyer, 1929 (29.100.3)**

fig. 6.9 **Rembrandt van Rijn,** *Portrait of a Woman (probably Johanna van Clootwijk)***, 1632, oil on canvas; 111.8 × 88.9 cm. The Metropolitan Museum of Art, New York. H.O. Havemeyer Collection, Bequest of Mrs. H.O. Havemeyer, 1929 (29.100.4)**

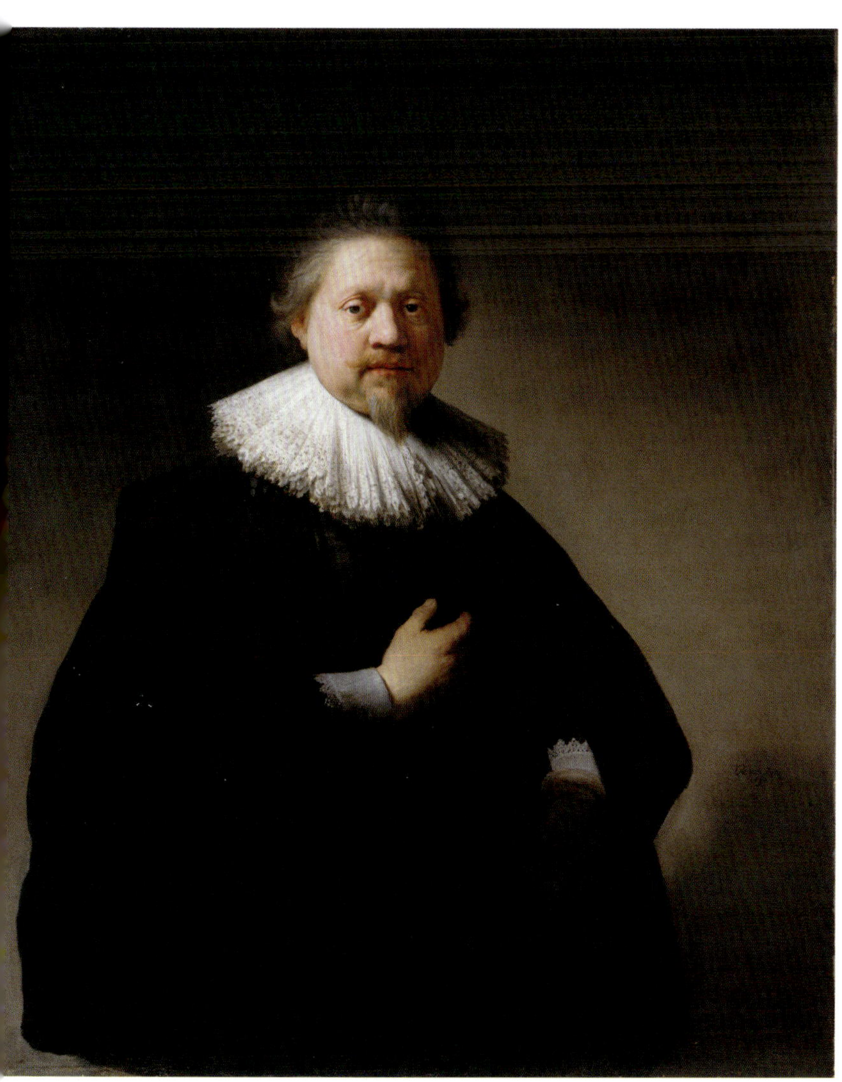

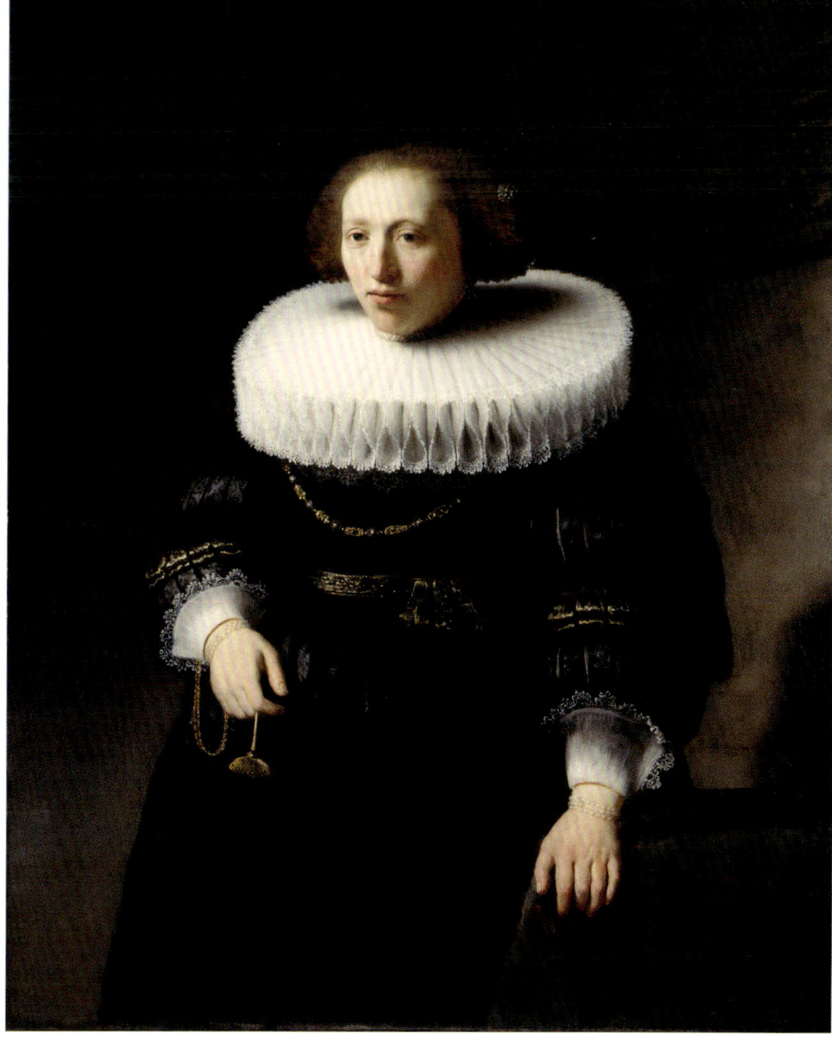

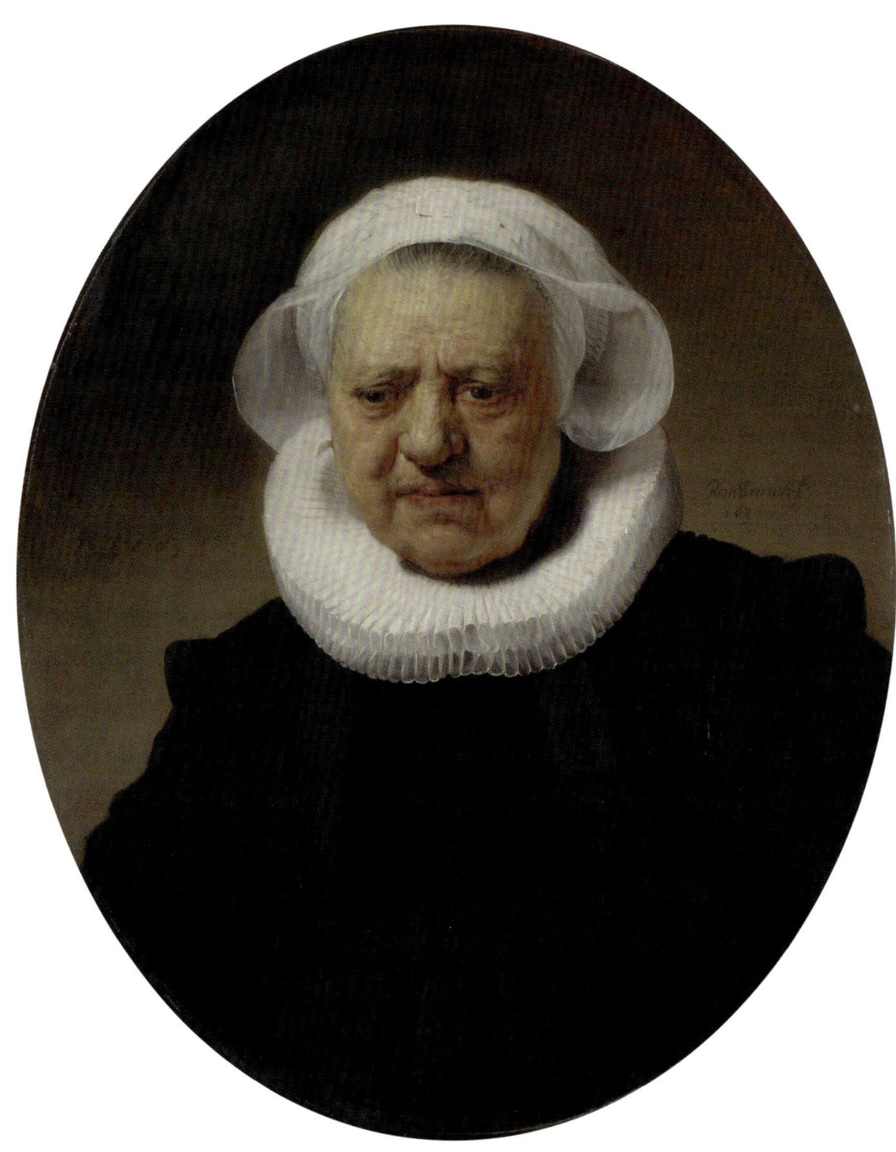

fig. 6.10 **Rembrandt van Rijn,**
Portrait of Aechje Claesdr, 1634,
oil on panel; 71.1 × 55.9 cm.
The National Gallery, London.
Bought, 1867 (NG775)

A Leiden Portrait Commission from 1633

In 1633 Rembrandt painted a bust-length portrait of a woman (pl. 44), who according to an inscription (most likely from the eighteenth century) on the back of the panel was Maertgen van Bilderbeecq, wife of the Leiden baker and grain merchant Willem Burchgraeff.[23] Because the painting was inherited by the sitter's descendants residing in Rotterdam before the end of the seventeenth century, and remained with them until the nineteenth century, it is often wrongly assumed that Maertgen also lived in Rotterdam.[24] The last word has yet to be said about whether the portrait of a man in Dresden (pl. 43) is the pendant to this painting of Maertgen, and how it relates to the 1635 portrait of a certain Willem Burchgraeff by Daniel Mijtens the Elder.[25] In the context of this essay, the key question is how Rembrandt received the commission to paint Maertgen. While the couple may have known the painter in Leiden, it is feasible that Uylenburgh played a role in this case. Maertgen's sister Neeltgen was married to the landscape painter and art dealer Pieter de Neyn, who was Uylenburgh's Leiden agent.[26]

Portraits of Rotterdam Remonstrants

A striking group of portraits by Rembrandt of non-Amsterdammers consists of five paintings from 1633–34 in which he immortalized Rotterdam Remonstrants. The sitters are the eighty-three-year-old widow Aechje Claesdr (fig. 6.10), painted in 1634; her son Dirck Jansz Pesser (Los Angeles County Museum of Art) and daughter-in-law Haesje Jacobsdr van Cleyburg (Rijksmuseum, Amsterdam), portrayed in the same year; and a pair of portraits probably depicting Claesdr's daughter Maritje Jansdr Pesser and her son-in-law Jacob Jacobsz van Couwenhoven, dated 1634 and 1633 respectively (figs. 6.12, 6.11).[27] As a leader of the Remonstrant movement, Van Couwenhoven had stayed in Amsterdam in the spring of 1633 to attend the same meeting as the elderly Hague minister Johannes Wtenbogaert that had provided the occasion for Rembrandt to paint the minister's portrait. Perhaps Van Couwenhoven also posed for Rembrandt at that time, and the artist was subsequently invited to Rotterdam to paint portraits of Van Couwenhoven's wife and elderly mother-in-law. Van Couwenhoven's brother-in-law and sister-in-law Dirck and Haesje would have sat for Rembrandt during the same sojourn in Rotterdam. From a notarial deed we know that Rembrandt was certainly in Rotterdam on 22 July 1634, only one month after his marriage to Saskia van Uylenburgh.[28]

It is remarkable that a group of Rotterdam Remonstrants chose the Amsterdam-based Rembrandt to portray them even though proficient portraitists, such as Jan Daemen Cool, who had previously recorded several of the group's family members for posterity, were available in their own city. Perhaps Van Couwenhoven's enthusiasm, and the fact that Rembrandt had portrayed the Remonstrants' revered leader Wtenbogaert, played a role in this. It seems there was a chain reaction in which an initial commission carried out in Amsterdam led to four follow-up orders probably executed in Rotterdam. This series of orders can be regarded as a direct result of Amsterdam citizen Abraham Anthonisz Recht's commission to paint a portrait of Reverend Wtenbogaert.

fig. 6.11 Rembrandt van Rijn, *Portrait of a Bearded Man in a Wide-brimmed Hat (probably Jacob Jacobsz van Couwenhoven)*, 1633, oil on panel; 69.9 × 54.6 cm. Norton Simon Art Foundation, Pasadena (M.1977.31.P)

fig. 6.12 Rembrandt van Rijn, *Portrait of a 40-year-old Woman (probably Maritje Jansdr Pesser)*, 1634, oil on panel; 69.7 × 55.9 cm. Speed Art Museum, Louisville, KY. Purchased with funds contributed by individuals, corporations and the entire community of Louisville, as well as the Commonwealth of Kentucky (1977.16)

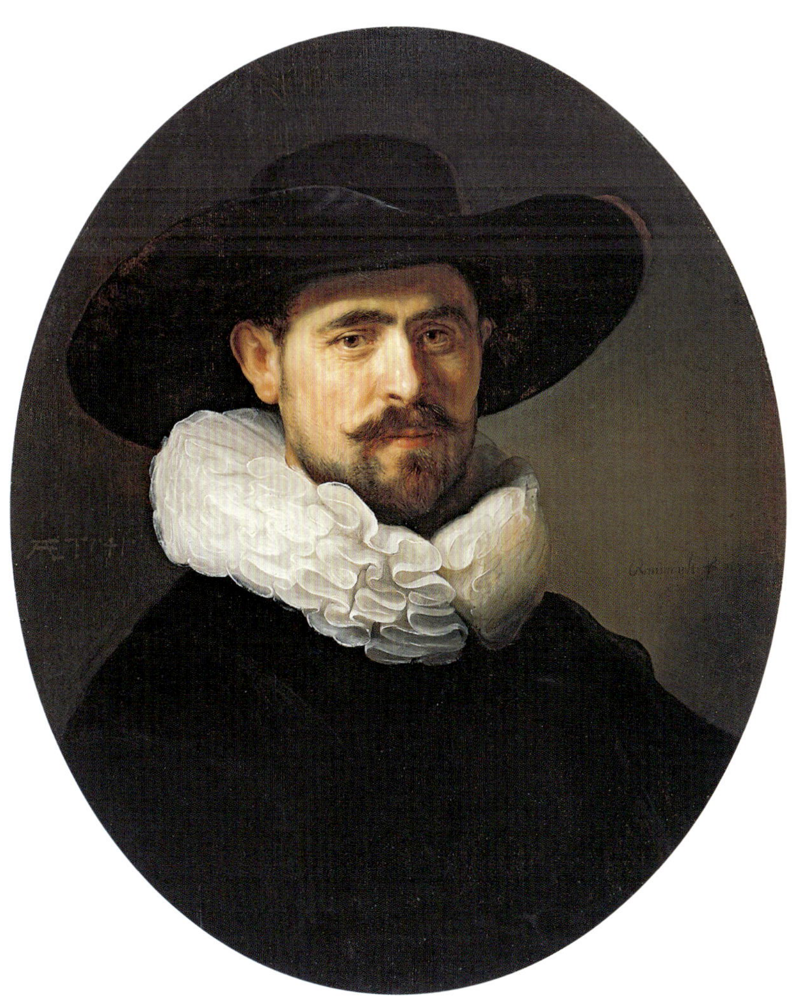

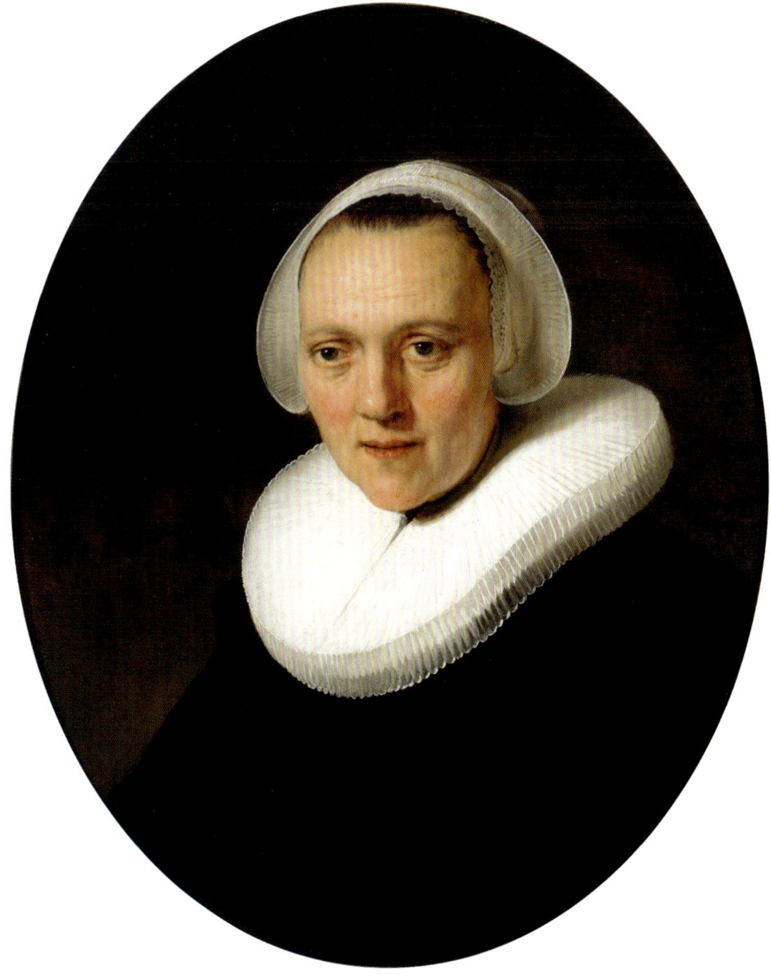

While Uylenburgh may have played a role in this commission, he seems unlikely to have had a hand in Rembrandt's Rotterdam outing. Like the portrait of Maertgen van Bilderbeecq, these four portraits, all executed as large busts, are entirely consistent with Rembrandt's work for Amsterdam sitters between 1632 and 1634. It is therefore possible that more sitters from Rotterdam or Leiden are to be found among as yet unidentified portraits from this period.

Interestingly enough, more than a decade after Rembrandt's Rotterdam "adventure," Bartholomeus van der Helst – already a firmly established, sought-after painter of the Amsterdam patriciate – also received a series of commissions from Rotterdam, and once again the Pesser family was involved. At least ten portraits by Van der Helst from 1646 and 1647 feature citizens of Rotterdam.[29] Unlike in Rembrandt's case, these efforts yielded a few later commissions for Van der Helst, notably the monumental portrait of the Visch family from around 1652 (State Hermitage Museum, St. Petersburg).[30] This success is remarkable, given that in the ten years since Rembrandt's activities there, the number of adept portraitists in Rotterdam had increased with the arrival of Hendrick Martensz Sorgh and Ludolf de Jongh. Compared with Rembrandt, Van der Helst captured a more sustainable Rotterdam clientele, although it is clear that in his case, too, his peak in the city was relatively short-lived. Like Rembrandt, he built his primary career in Amsterdam.

While Rembrandt catered to clients outside Amsterdam on various occasions after 1634, as far as we know this never involved painted portraits.[31] He carried out a number of commissions for history paintings for the stadtholder's court in The Hague, and at a later stage of his life also worked for the Italian art collector Antonio Ruffo of Messina. However, after 1634 we no longer discern any ambition to take on portrait commissions far from his place of residence. Moreover, once he established his own studio, Rembrandt's interest in portraiture began to wane as he turned his attention to making paintings and prints of other subject types and to mentoring his many students. ■

NOTES

1   On Rembrandt and Uylenburgh, see primarily London and Amsterdam 2006, 126–186, and Sebastien A.C. Dudok van Heel, "Rembrandt and Frans Hals Painting in the Workshop of Hendrick Uylenburgh," in Dickey 2017b, 17–42.

2   Dudok van Heel 2006, 195–199.

3   Strauss and Van der Meulen 1979, doc. 1631/4; "Acknowledgement of a debt owed to Rembrandt by Hendrick Uylenburch [Uylenburgh]," 20 June 1631, Remdoc, no. e4393.

4   Washington, Milwaukee and Amsterdam 2008–09, 12–13; Schneider and Ekkart 1973, 42–43.

5   London and The Hague 2007–08, 53–54.

6   Rudi Ekkart, "Govert Flinck and Ferdinand Bol: The Portraits," in Amsterdam 2017–18, 155.

7   Dudok van Heel, "Rembrandt and Frans Hals," in Dickey 2017b, 17–43.

8   London and Amsterdam 2006, 50.

9   The Hague 1997, 132–141.

10 Gerson 1969, 244–249. See also The Hague 1997, 132–141.

11 Raleigh, Cleveland and Minneapolis 2011–12, no. 22.

12 For Honthorst's portraits of Frederik Hendrik and Amalia, see Judson and Ekkart, nos. 306–312.

13 The two portraits passed by descent in the Huygens family until they were separated on the market in the eighteenth century; Van Gelder 1957, 8–9.

14 Van Regteren Altena 1983, 154–155.

15 Bredius 1893, 127–128; Strauss and Van der Meulen 1979, 313–315, 490.

16 London and Amsterdam 2006, 135.

17 Fusenig 2006, 210.

18 Van Beresteyn 1940, 135–137.

19 For a detailed discussion, see Liedtke 2007, 568–596, and most recently *Corpus*, vol. 6, no. 63a-b.

20 In his catalogue of the Dutch pictures in the Metropolitan Museum of Art, Walter Liedtke identifies the sitters as members of the Van Beresteyn family; he mentions the reference to Brouaert in his catalogue, but does not work it out further; Liedtke 2007, 568–596, esp. 576. For the identification, see Rudi Ekkart, "New Identifications: An Early Rembrandt Couple," in Madrid 2020, 152–153, nos. 36, 37.

21 Huygens 1987, 88.

22 For the suggestion that Huygens could have been the patron, see Judson and Ekkart 1999, 31–32.

23 The inscription reads "*Margaretha Hendrikse | van Bilderdijk, | Huisvrouw van | Willem Burggraaf.*"

24 On this painting and the problems surrounding the pendant, see Neumeister 2005, 380–394, referring to additional sources.

25 On this question, see also the essay by Jasper Hillegers in this volume.

26 London and Amsterdam 2006, 186.

27 Dudok van Heel 2006, 239–267; Sebastien A.C. Dudok van Heel, "Rembrandt's Portraits of Remonstrants in Rotterdam," in Madrid 2020, 129–143, esp. 137–138.

28 Strauss and Van der Meulen 1979, 112.

29 Van Gent 2011, 41–43.

30 Ibid., 225–226, no. 63.

31 There is a 1665 portrait print of the Leiden professor Jan Antonides van der Linden, who died a year earlier, which was commissioned by the Leiden publishers Daniel and Abraham van Gaesbeeck; see Dickey 2004, 159–162.

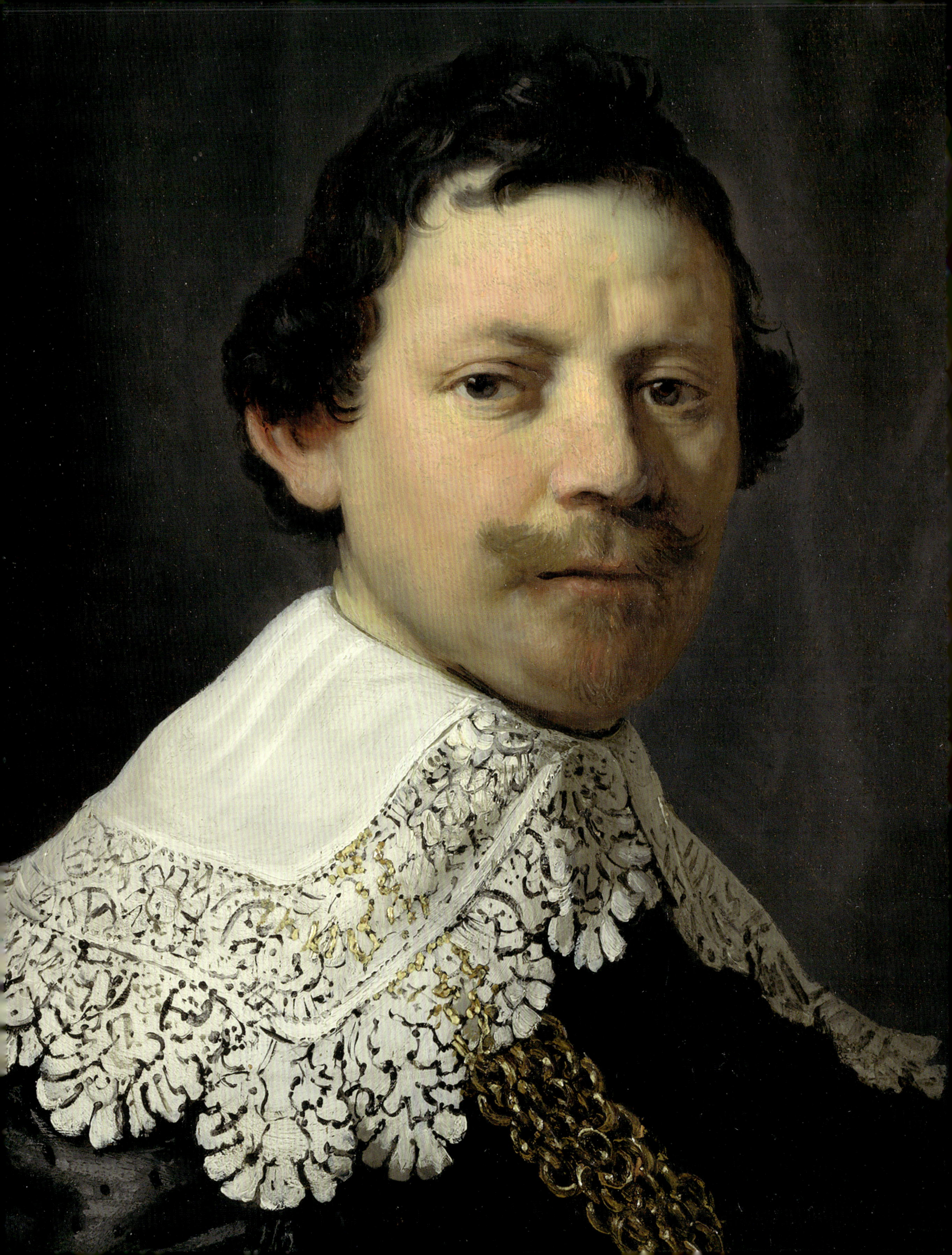

STEPHANIE S. DICKEY

Portraits of Prosperity

In Amsterdam and other cities of the Dutch Republic, art patronage was dominated by the mercantile elite. Replacing the hereditary nobility as powerbrokers and tastemakers, prosperous urban citizens adopted some of the same customs by which aristocrats had traditionally advertised their wealth and status, including portraits to commemorate accomplishments and family ties. As citizens took control of governmental and charitable organizations, their good works provided further pretexts for group portraits celebrating communal pride in social service (pls. 53, 55).[1]

Rembrandt must already have been preparing to leave Hendrick Uylenburgh's workshop for his first independent studio on the Nieuwe Doelenstraat when Philips Lucasz and his wife Petronella Buys came to pose for him in early 1635 (pls. 60, 61). Global trade was a key feature in the economic rise of Amsterdam, and this couple were among many who prospered from it. Philips, an officer in the VOC (Dutch East India Company), had met Petronella in Batavia (present-day Jakarta) in the Dutch East Indies. Her brother-in-law, Jacques Specx, had been governor general of Batavia before settling in Amsterdam in 1632, and inventory records suggest that the commission came from him. On 2 May 1635, Philips and Petronella departed Amsterdam to return to Batavia, leaving their portraits behind as vivid reminders of them for their loved ones.[2]

Specx also owned three history paintings by Rembrandt, including the brilliant *Abduction of Europa*, and, fittingly, *Christ in the Storm on the Sea of Galilee*, the artist's only known seascape (see figs. 11.1, 1.6). However, when commissioning portraits of himself and his wife in 1639, he chose Govert Flinck.[3]

Time constraints may have dictated the modest format of the Lucasz and Buys panels. Pendant portraits of husbands and wives were available in a variety of sizes, formats and price points: bust; half-, three-quarter-, or full-length; with or without contextual attributes. At first, plain backgrounds focused attention on the figure. After 1640, landscape vistas suggested the leisure of a country estate (pls. 66, 67). Many sitters opted to present themselves wearing the latest fashions, but Rembrandt and his followers created a vogue for portraits featuring antiquated dress, building on the colourful figure studies that were also a signature product of their brand (pls. 64, 65). Fantasy dress could carry biblical or mythological associations, or simply lend an air of timelessness. Other Amsterdam portraitists, especially Jacob Backer and Bartholomeus van der Helst, painted fashionable clients in pastoral guise.[4] While pendant portraits remained popular throughout the century, the more novel double portrait allowed artists to introduce allusive elements of setting and interaction.[5]

Many portraitists took liberties with observed reality in order to present sitters at their best, but they also captured accurate details that reveal the rich material culture with which urban consumers surrounded themselves. Portrait specialists such as Van der Helst and Isaack Luttichuys became adept at capturing the sheen of fabric and the sparkle of gemstones. Since textiles are so fragile, portraits are often the best remaining evidence of fashion trends. Four portraits of women shown here (pls. 68–71) suggest how an individual might dress in the latest style while customizing her look with expensive jewellery or a skirt of imported silk.[6] By the mid-1630s, many fashionable ladies had given up the millstone ruff worn by Petronella Buys (see also pls. 44, 52, 53) for flat collars composed of layers of starched linen adorned with lace. Men wore a similar style (pl. 60, fig. 7.1) or adopted simpler collars of plain linen (pls. 73, 76). In comparing portraits, one can see not only how the cut of fashionable accessories changed over time, but also the various methods for depicting them. Some artists, including Rembrandt, defined the spaces between threads of delicate lace by first blocking in the white shape of the collar or cuff and then painting black or grey lines over it. Others used white paint to draw the threads themselves (figs. 7.2, 7.3). In busy workshops, costume details were often completed by assistants. While professional techniques could be formulaic, Rembrandt took pains to capture the irregular curl of a scalloped edge or the play of light over a textured surface, turning each portrait into an exercise in acute observation and painterly virtuosity. Subtle variations of pose and expression suggest movement and personality (pls. 68, 75).

Rembrandt's portraits commanded higher prices than most, but they were not out of line with others at the top of the market. Documents indicate that burgomaster Andries de Graeff disputed the payment of 500 guilders for his portrait painted by Rembrandt in 1639, probably the life-size canvas now in Kassel (pl. 73).[7] By the 1650s, Rembrandt's younger rival Van der Helst was asking similar fees.[8] Comparison of Rembrandt's lively yet dignified likeness of De Graeff with full-length portraits of men from

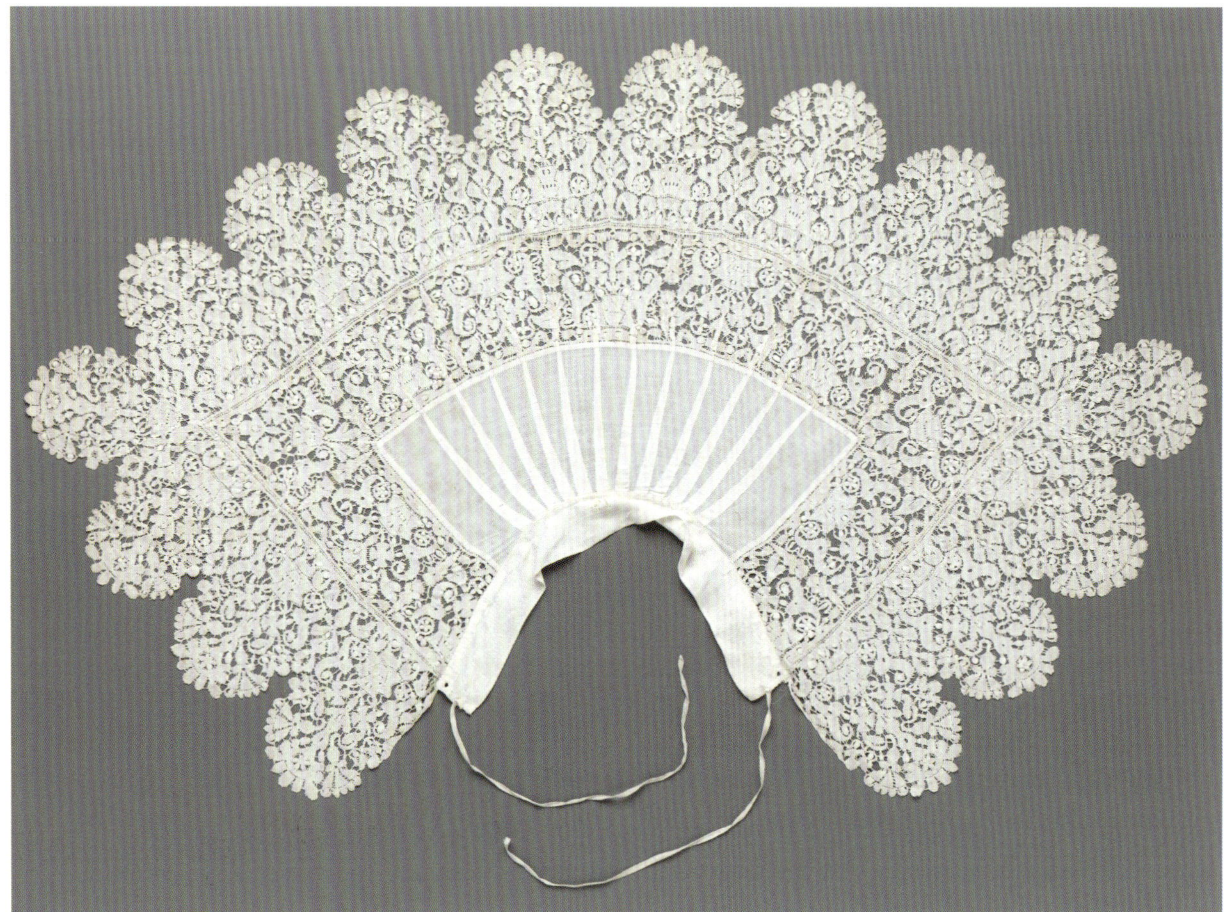

fig. 7.1 **Maker unknown, *Man's collar of linen and bobbin lace with flowerpots*, c. 1630–40, bobbin lace; 60 × 78.5 cm. Rijksmuseum, Amsterdam. On loan from the Stichting Twickel, Delden (BK-BR-934)**

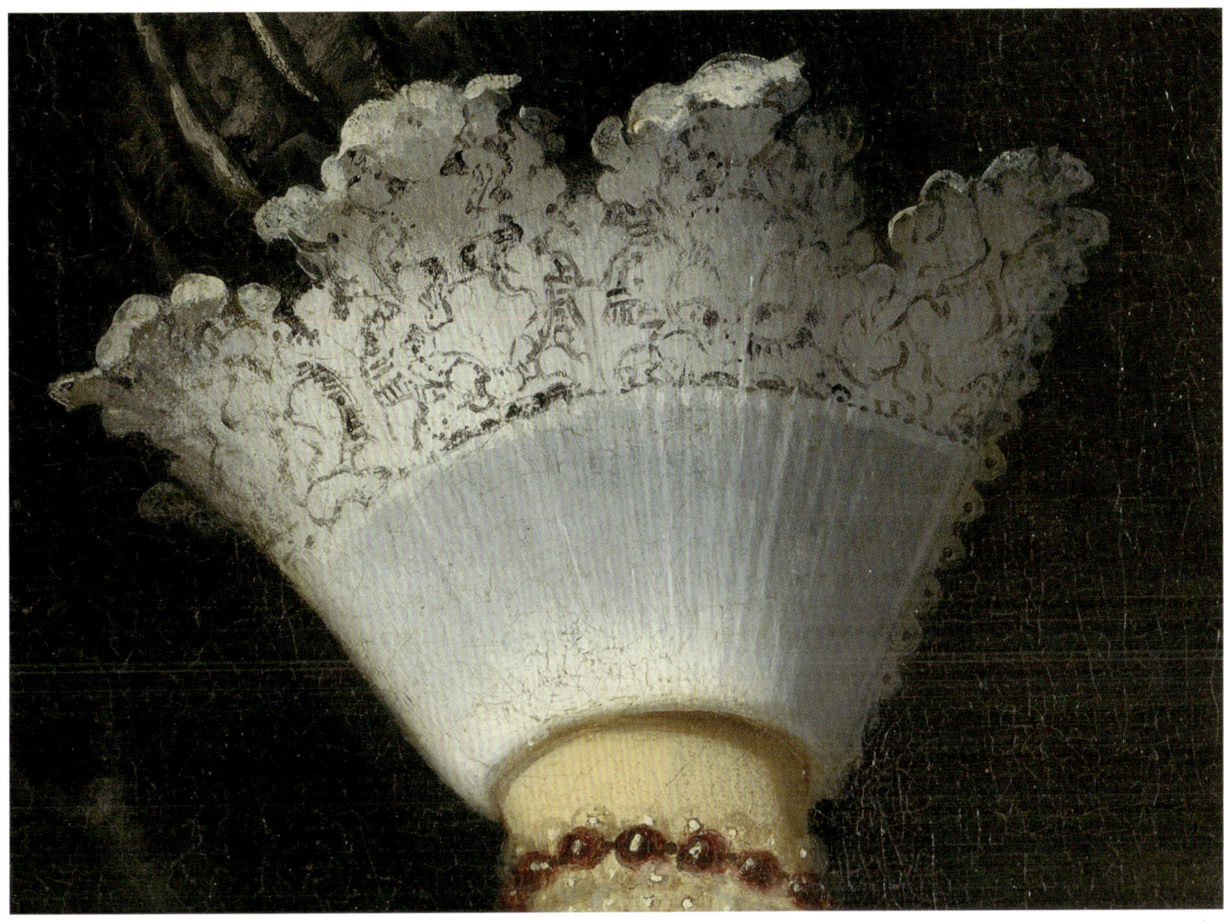

fig. 7.2 Detail of Rembrandt van Rijn, *Portrait of a Young Woman with a Fan*, 1633, plate 68

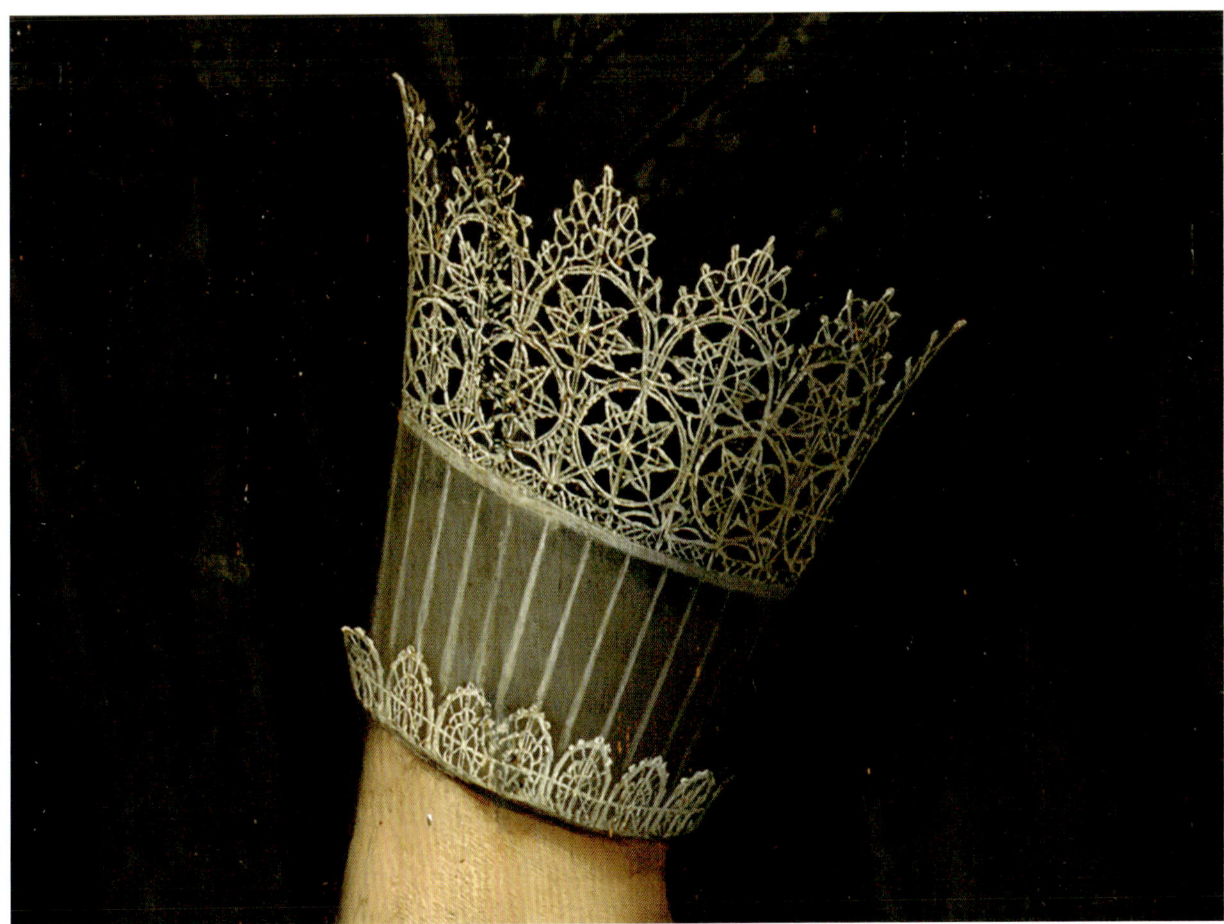

fig. 7.3 Detail of Nicolaes Eliasz Pickenoy, *Portrait of a Woman*, 1628, plate 57

1628 by Nicolaes Eliasz Pickenoy (pl. 72), the leading portraitist of the previous generation, and from 1644 by Van der Helst (pl. 74) shows progress toward greater liveliness and informality, but also marks the continuity of this imposing format, once reserved for aristocrats and heads of state, as an expensive display of prestige.[9] Thomas de Keyser reduced the full-length format to cabinet size, a variation well-suited to narrow Amsterdam town-houses (pls. 58, 59).

Rembrandt's dynamic approach to portraiture culminated in 1642 with *The Night Watch* (see fig. 1.9), the most important public commission of his middle years. Thereafter, it seems he became less interested in painting portraits, with a few exceptions for appealing models (pl. 79) or close acquaintances such as Jan Six (see fig. 1.13).[10] Meanwhile, a new generation of patrons, at ease with their prosperity, were demanding more glamour in their portraits, and a new generation of painters – including several of Rembrandt's former pupils – were prepared to serve them. *The Night Watch* was one part of an unprecedented ensemble of civic-guard group portraits ordered after the new wing of the musketeers' shooting range (the Kloveniersdoelen) was completed in 1638. Captain Frans Banninck Cocq hired Rembrandt, but other commissions went to the venerable Pickenoy, to contemporaries including Joachim von Sandrart and Backer, and to two ambitious newcomers, Govert Flinck and Van der Helst. By the later 1640s, these two had taken Rembrandt's place at the peak of portrait fashion. Inspired by the suave manner of the Flemish portraitist Anthony van Dyck, already in vogue at the stadtholder's court in The Hague, Flinck became a pioneer of the "bright style" that supplanted Rembrandt's earthy palette and rough brushwork as the choice of a newly sophisticated clientele. With his fluent technique, Backer, too, adapted easily to the demand for surface elegance and continued to find favour until his death in 1651 (pls. 51, 90).[11]

Networking was an essential strategy for Amsterdam painters, especially portraitists. It began with leveraging family ties: Flinck's first portrait commissions in the 1640s came from family and friends who shared his Mennonite religious affiliation, while Ferdinand Bol profited from connections by marriage. Artists also benefitted from networking among patrons themselves. Sitting for a portrait is an intimate and consequential experience, and many patrons took comfort in hiring artists who had also portrayed friends and relatives.[12]

Rembrandt's sombre portraits of the wealthy munitions dealer Jacob Trip and his wife Margaretha de Geer (The National Gallery, London), completed after Jacob's death in 1661, were probably commissioned by their sons, but when it came to their own portraits, the younger generation had other ideas.[13] When Rembrandt's former Leiden colleague Jan Lievens moved from Antwerp to Amsterdam in 1644, one of his first commissions was a portrait of Trip's nephew, Adriaen (pl. 76). His buff coat, bandolier and sword lend a quasi-military air, while his studied pose, with hand on hip, conveys the confidence of a swashbuckling bachelor of twenty-two; the following year, he married and joined the family firm.[14] In 1655 Adriaen's younger brother Jacob chose to present himself as a gentleman in formal black, standing before a placid landscape (pl. 77). He opted for the polished style of Van der Helst, also a favourite of the politically powerful Bicker clan, to which his wife Elisabeth belonged.[15] Each brother holds a bamboo cane, an accessory popularized through VOC trade. Around 1663, for the Trip family residence in central Amsterdam, designed in a classical style by Philips Vingboons, Bol celebrated the virtues of two female relatives with portraits *historiés* casting them as Charity and Minerva.[16] Thus, even within one family, the choice of a portraitist could reflect both market trends and personal taste. ■

NOTES

1   For surveys and key examples, see Amsterdam 2002–03; London and The Hague 2007–08; Middelkoop 2019, esp. R21, R36; Madrid 2020.

2   The couple were married on 4 August 1634 by Reverend Jan Cornelisz Sylvius (see fig. 1.17), a close relative of Rembrandt's wife, Saskia. It has been suggested that Rembrandt engaged studio assistance, perhaps to complete the portraits quickly, but recent technical study argues for the master's hand. The panels may originally have been rectangular but they were probably not substantially larger. See Lara Yeager-Crasselt, "Portrait of Petronella Buys (1605–1670)," in Leiden Collection Catalogue, with further references. It is likely that Rembrandt and Saskia took possession of their rented home on the Nieuwe Doelenstraat on 1 May 1635, the day before Philips and Petronella's departure.

3   Present whereabouts unknown; in 1655 their daughter inherited the portrait by Flinck of Specx's wife, Magdalena Doublet, dated 1639; Von Moltke 1965, 156–157, nos. 432, 433; Jaap van der Veen, "Hendrick Uylenburgh's Art Business: Production and Trade between 1625 and 1655," in London and Amsterdam 2006, 172–173.

4   Van den Brink 2016, 24–26, with further references. For Ferdinand Bol's portraits (pls. 64, 65), see Dekiert 2006, 41–43, nos. 609–610.

5   Two strong and very different examples are Rembrandt's *Portrait of Cornelis Anslo and His Wife Aeltje Schouten* (1641, Gemäldegalerie, Berlin) commissioned together with an etched portrait of Anslo in 1640 (see fig. 1.16; see among others, Dickey 2004, 30–65; *Corpus*, vol. 6, no. 183) and a double portrait by Flinck in the Staatliche Kunstalle Karlsruhe (see recently Ilona Schwägerl, "Technical Examination of Flinck's *Double Portrait of a Married Couple* [1646] in Karlsruhe," in Dickey 2017a, 154–159).

6   Despite its frontality, Rembrandt's *Portrait of a Woman* is the pendant to *Portrait of a Man* (Taft Museum of Art, Cincinnati); Liedtke 2007, no. 146; *Corpus*, vol. 6, no. 88a-b. The costume of Backer's *Portrait of a Woman* was in vogue around 1635, but Peter van den Brink dates it c. 1637/38 on stylistic grounds in Amsterdam and Aachen 2008, 38–39, no. A58. For Flinck, see Von Moltke 1965, no. 397; Cleves 2015–16, no. 5. For Van der Helst, see Van Gent 2011, no. 18.

7   Strauss and Van der Meulen 1979, doc. 1659/21. On the pricing of paintings, see Marten Jan Bok, "Pricing the Unpriced: How Dutch Seventeenth-century Painters Determined the Selling Price of Their Work," in North and Ormrod 1998, 103–111; Tummers and Jonckheere 2008; *Corpus*, vol. 6, no. 168, see also nos. 71, 167.

8   Van Gent 2011, 418, observes that Sandrart commented on Van der Helst's success and cites prices ranging from 330 guilders for two half-length portraits (1650) to 1,400 guilders for the portrait of a VOC Admiral and his family (1656).

9   Pickenoy's clientele came from among the city's wealthiest inhabitants, as shown by Kaaring 2005. His conservative style remained in favour with the regent class; in 1636 he portrayed Andries de Graeff's brother Cornelis and his wife Geertruid Overlander (Gemäldegalerie, Berlin). The portrait in the Staatliche Kunstalle Karlsruhe is unsigned, but precisely rendered details of costume and setting point to Pickenoy. Van der Helst's sitter may be Joan Hulft, one of the civic-guard members represented, perhaps with the same dog, in Van der Helst's *Militia Company of District VIII under the Command of Captain Roelof Bikker* (c. 1640–43, see fig. 1.10). A portrait of a woman and a child recorded on the London art market in 1994 is the pendant; Van Gent 2011, nos. 3, 15–16.

10   While Six's red cloak was traditional for travellers, the young lady's red dress (pl. 79) resembles a style fashionable among elite women in the 1650s, suggesting that the painting may have been made earlier than the date of c. 1665 proposed in *Corpus*, vol. 6, no. 305. Compare the costume in Gabriel Metsu, *Woman Reading a Book by a Window* (see fig. 8.4) with paintings by Isaack Luttichuys, such as *Portrait of a Woman, probably Geertruyd Spiegel* (c. 1656, private collection; Ebert 2009, 260, 263, no. Is.A55) and *Portrait of a Woman in a Red Dress* (c. 1653–55, private collection, Brussels; Ebert 2009, 283, 533–534, no. Is.A.30).

11   Arnold Houbraken coined the term "bright style" (*helder schilderen*) in his biography of Flinck, associating it with Italian painting; Houbraken 1718–21, vol. 2, 21. On its impact, see, among others, Sluijter 2006, 198, 218, 366–367; Lootsma 2007–08. On Flinck's pendant portraits in the North Carolina Museum of Art, Raleigh (pls. 66, 67), see Weller 2009, nos. 17, 18; Madrid 2020, nos. 63, 64. On Sandrart, see Klemm 1986, esp. 73–75; on Backer, see Amsterdam and Aachen 2008–09 and Van den Brink 2016.

12   Demonstrated by Erna Kok in Kok 2013; Erna Kok, "Govert Flinck, Ferdinand Bol and Their Networks of Influential Clients," in Amsterdam 2017–18, 58–79; and other publications.

13   *Corpus*, vol. 6, no. 297a-b.

14   Adriaen married into the family of his father's business partner, Louis de Geer. See Jaap van der Veen in Washington, Milwaukee and Amsterdam 2008–09, 164, no. 44.

15   Van Gent 2011, no. 83.

16   Ferdinand Bol, *Margarita Trip as Minerva, Instructing Her Sister Anna Maria Trip* (1663, Royal Netherlands Academy of Arts and Sciences, Trippenhuis, Amsterdam, on loan to the Rijksmuseum) and *Johanna de Geer with Her Children Cecelia Trip and Laurens Trip* (c. 1662–69, Rijksmuseum, Amsterdam); Blankert 1982, nos. 43, 176. Among the numerous portraits of this extended family are Rembrandt's 1639 painting of Aletta Adriaensdr, mother of Adriaen and Jacob (Museum Boijmans Van Beuningen, Rotterdam) and his 1661 *Portrait of Margaretha de Geer, Wife of Jacob Trip* (see fig. 18.3); *Corpus*, vol. 6, nos. 169, 296.

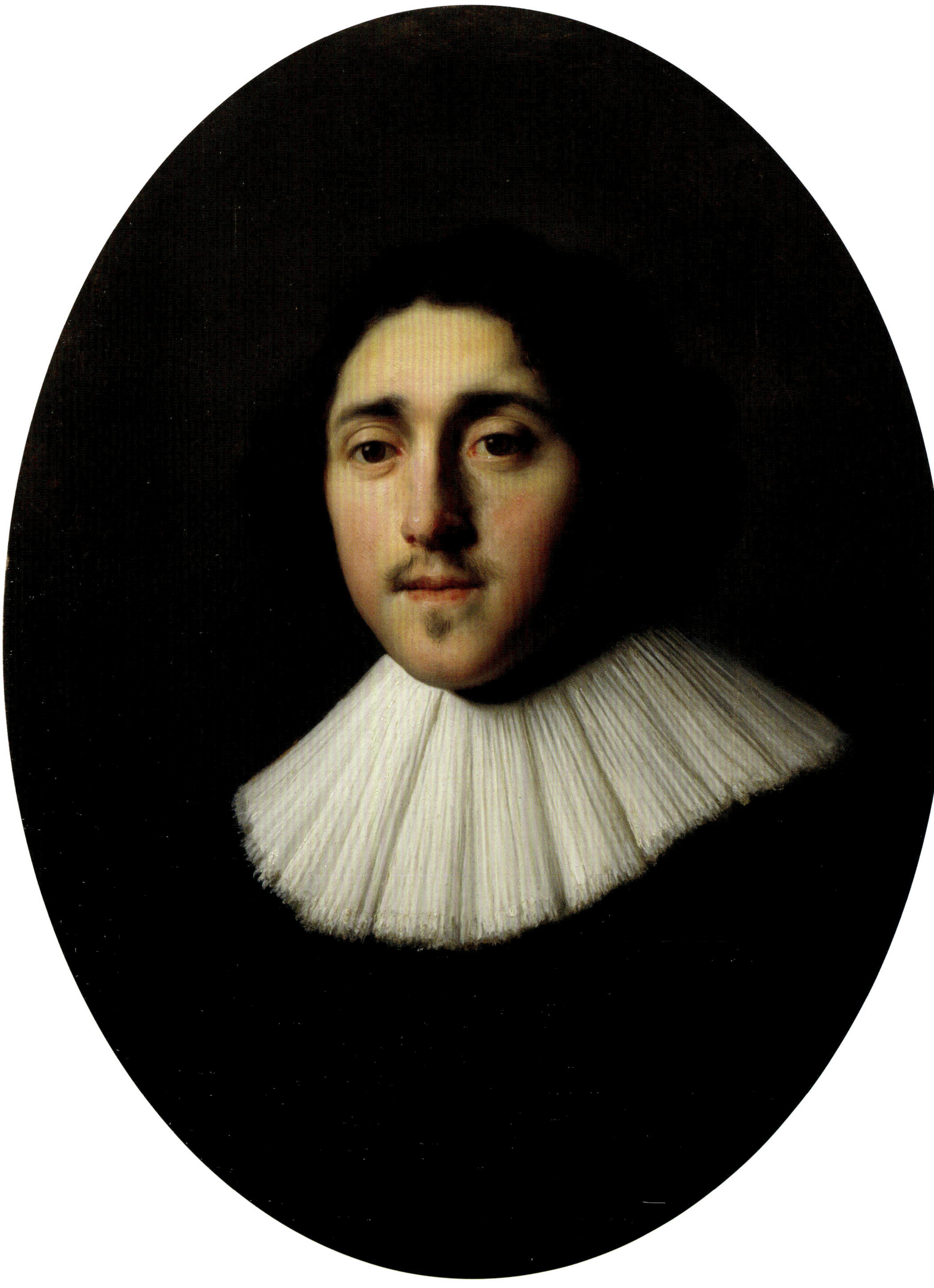

50 Rembrandt van Rijn, *Portrait of a Man*, 1632. The Peter and Irene Ludwig Foundation, Aachen

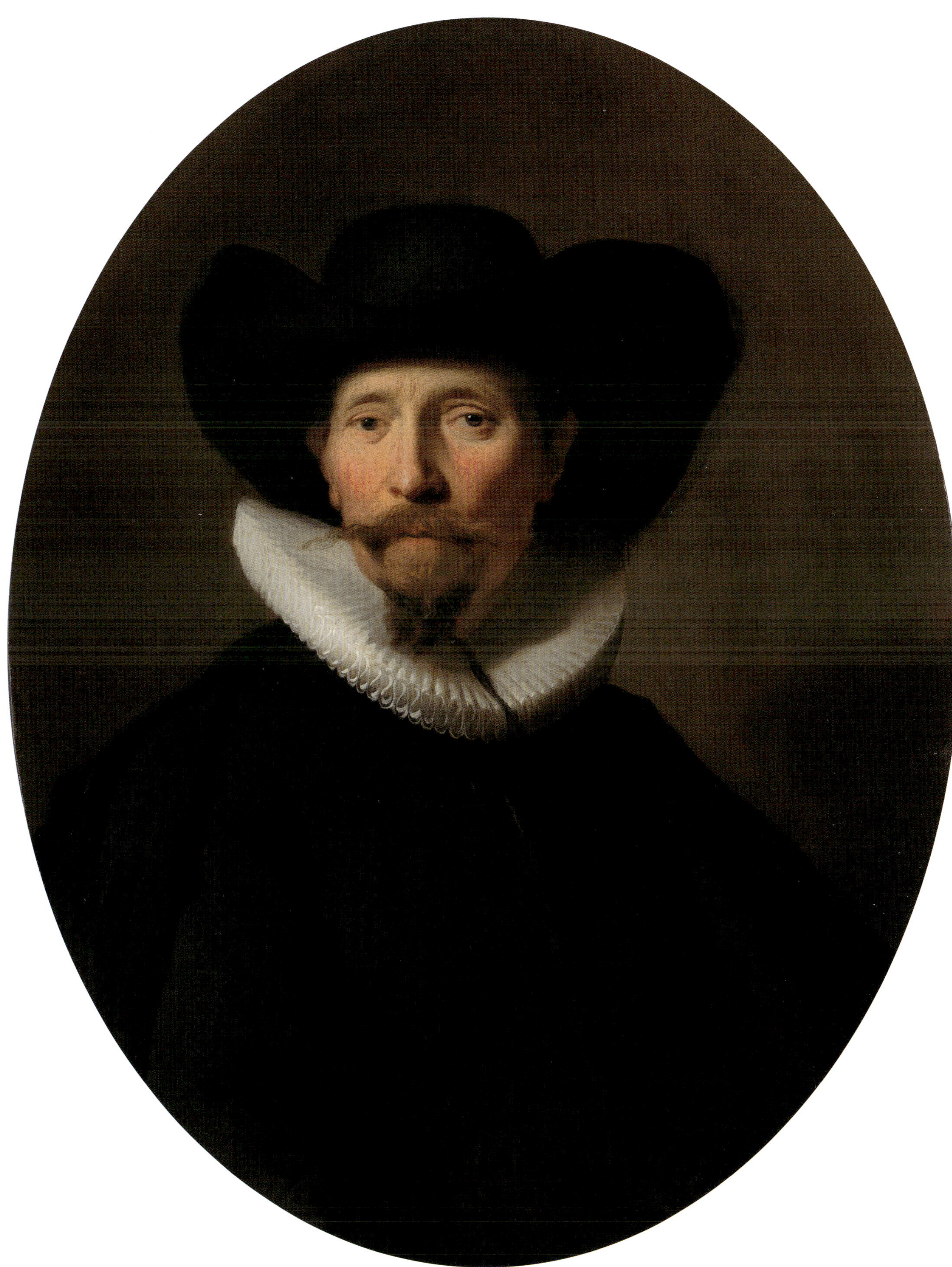

52 Jacob Backer, *Portrait of a Woman with a White Cap*, c. 1634. The Kremer Collection, Amsterdam

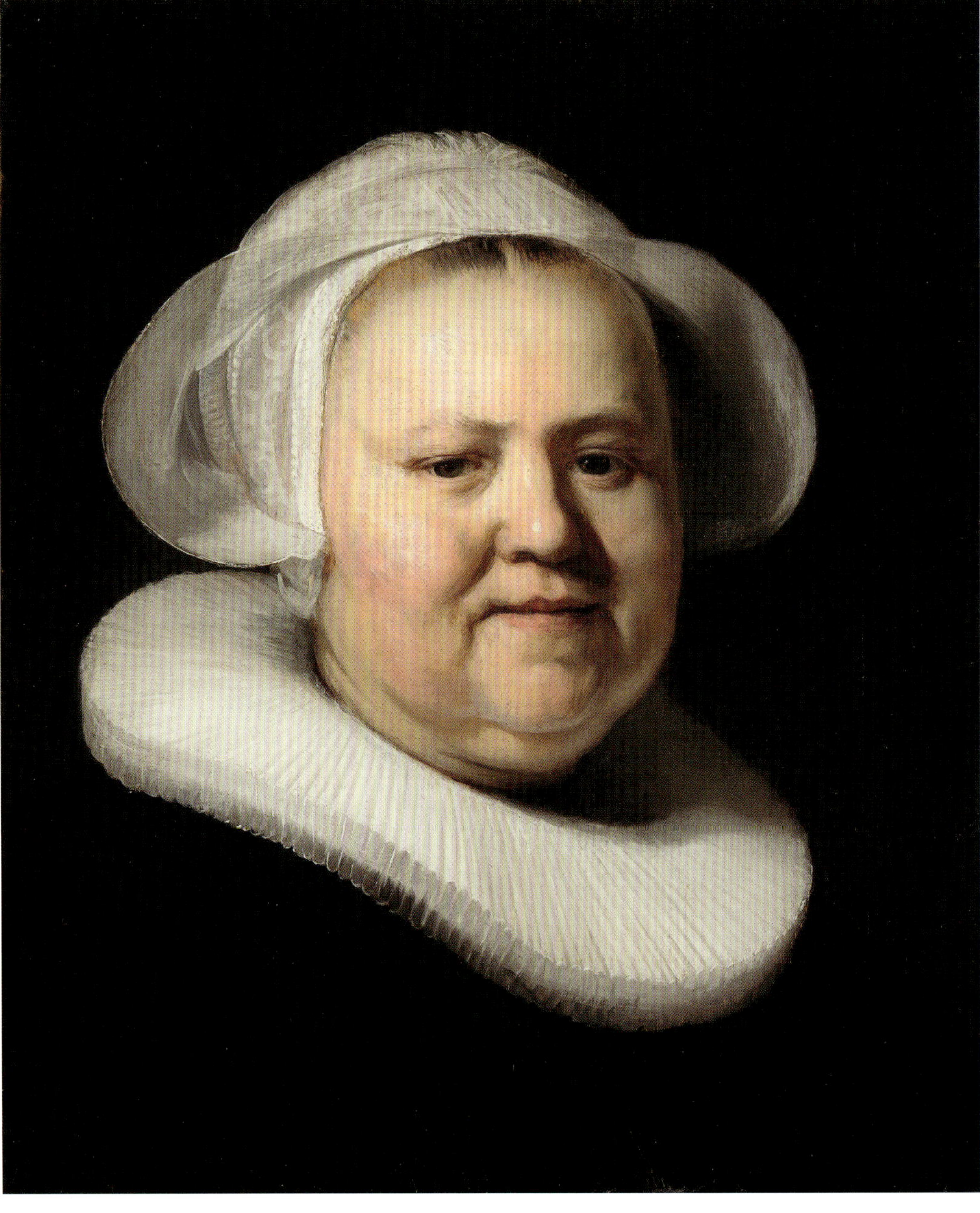

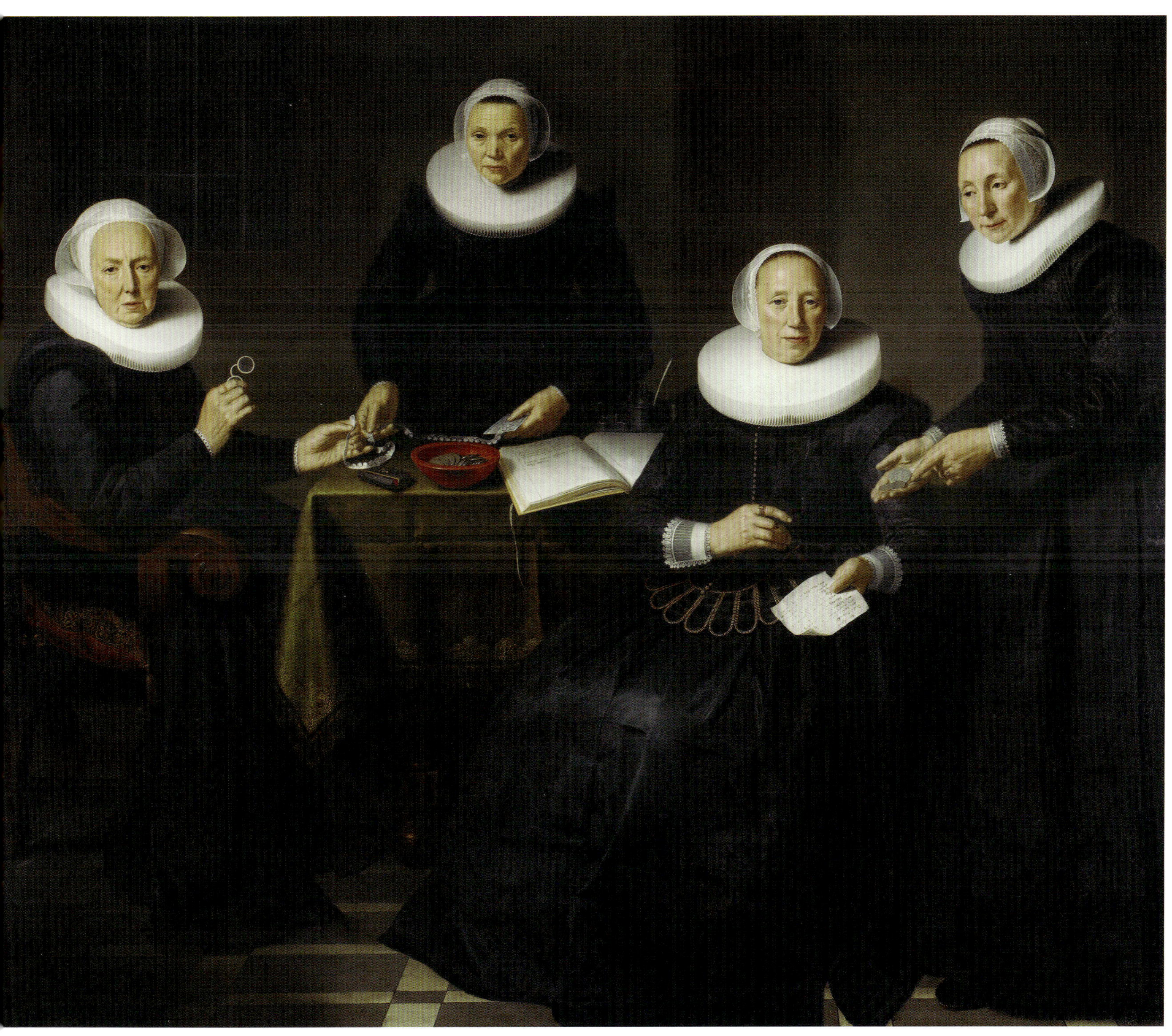

54   Govert Flinck, *Sketch for a Civic Guard Group Portrait*, 1648. Amsterdam Museum

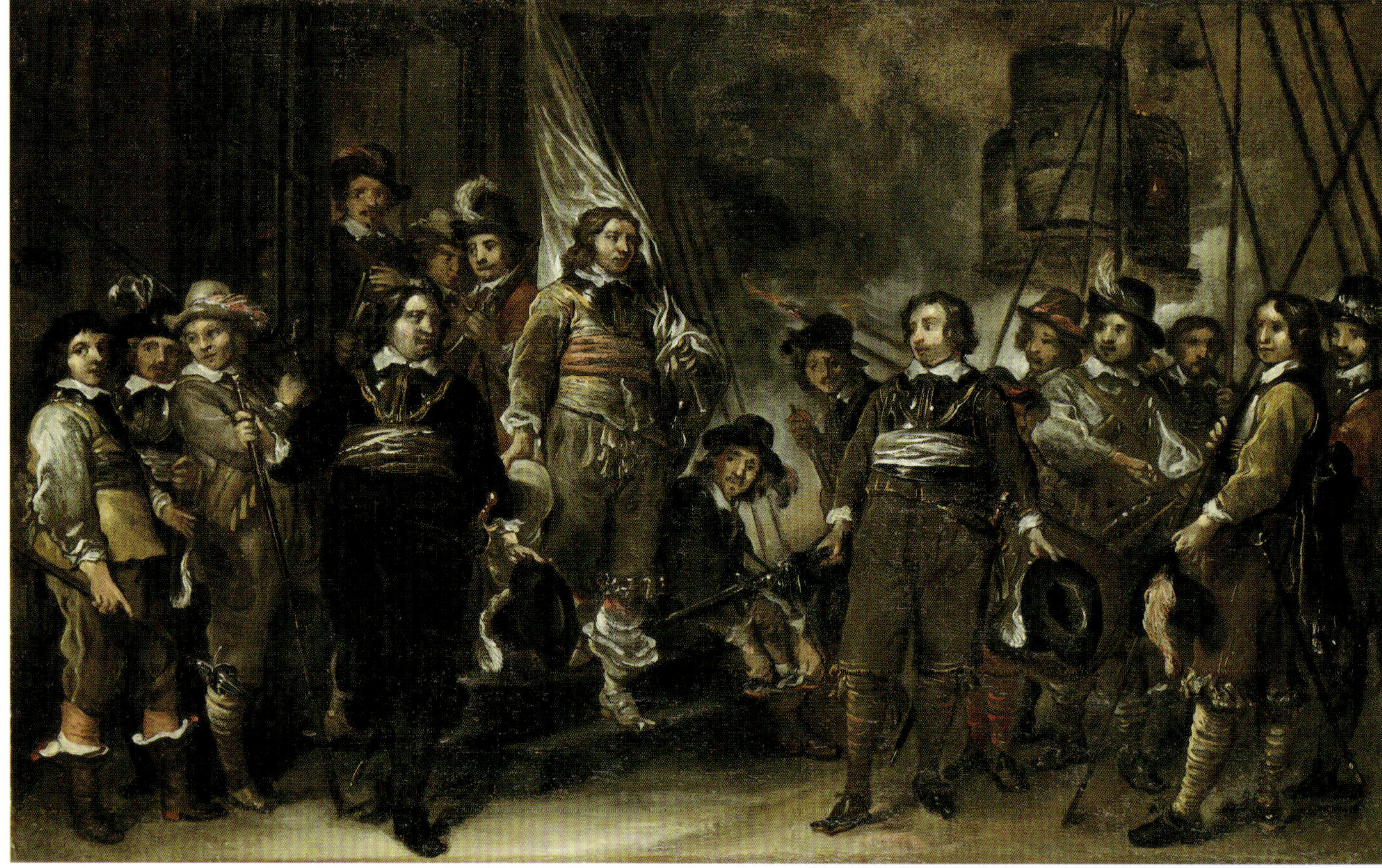

55   Ferdinand Bol, *Group Portrait of the Regents of the Leprozenhuis*, 1649. Amsterdam Museum

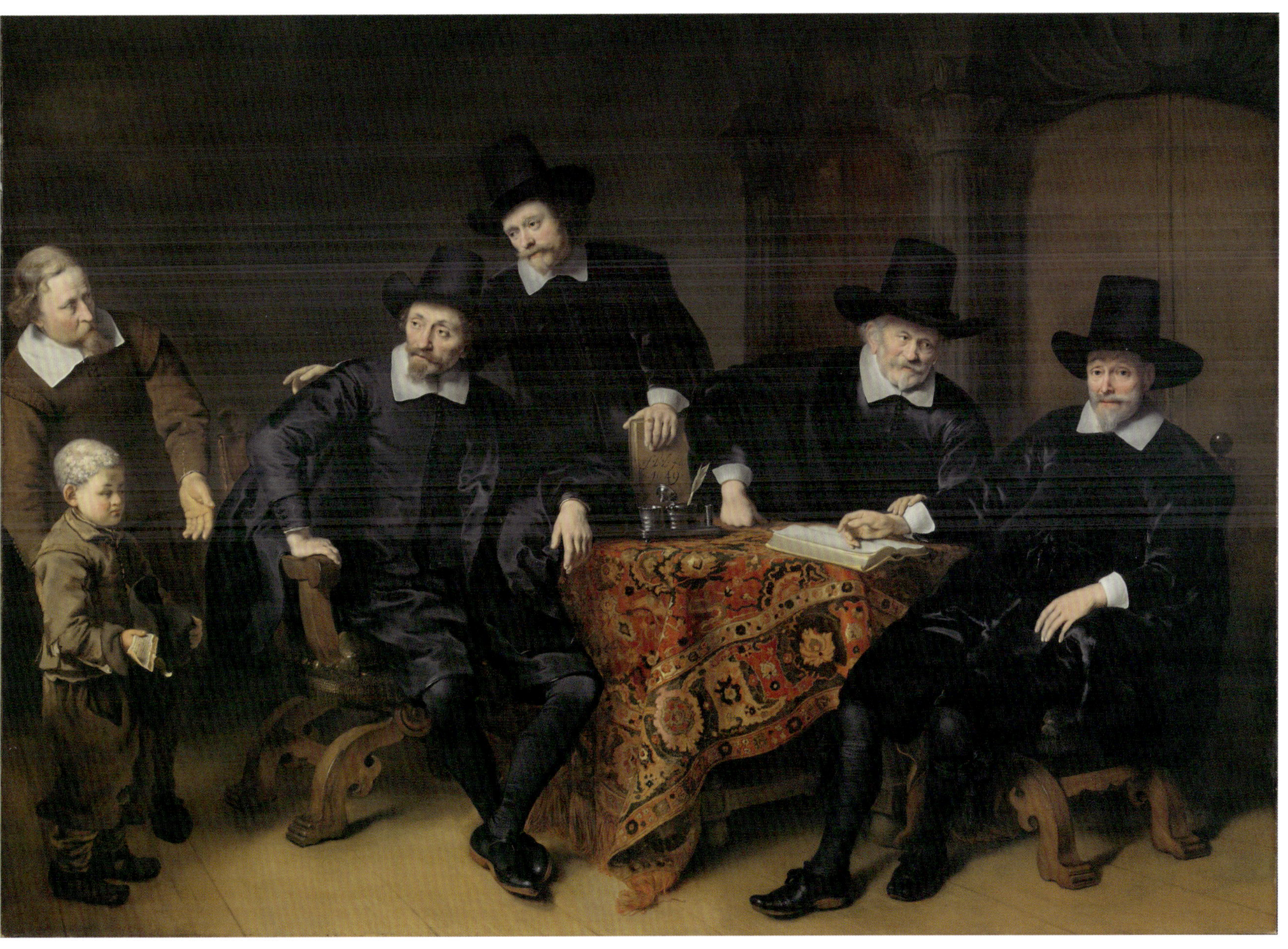

56 Nicolaes Eliasz Pickenoy, *Portrait of a Man*, 1628. Stedelijk Museum Alkmaar

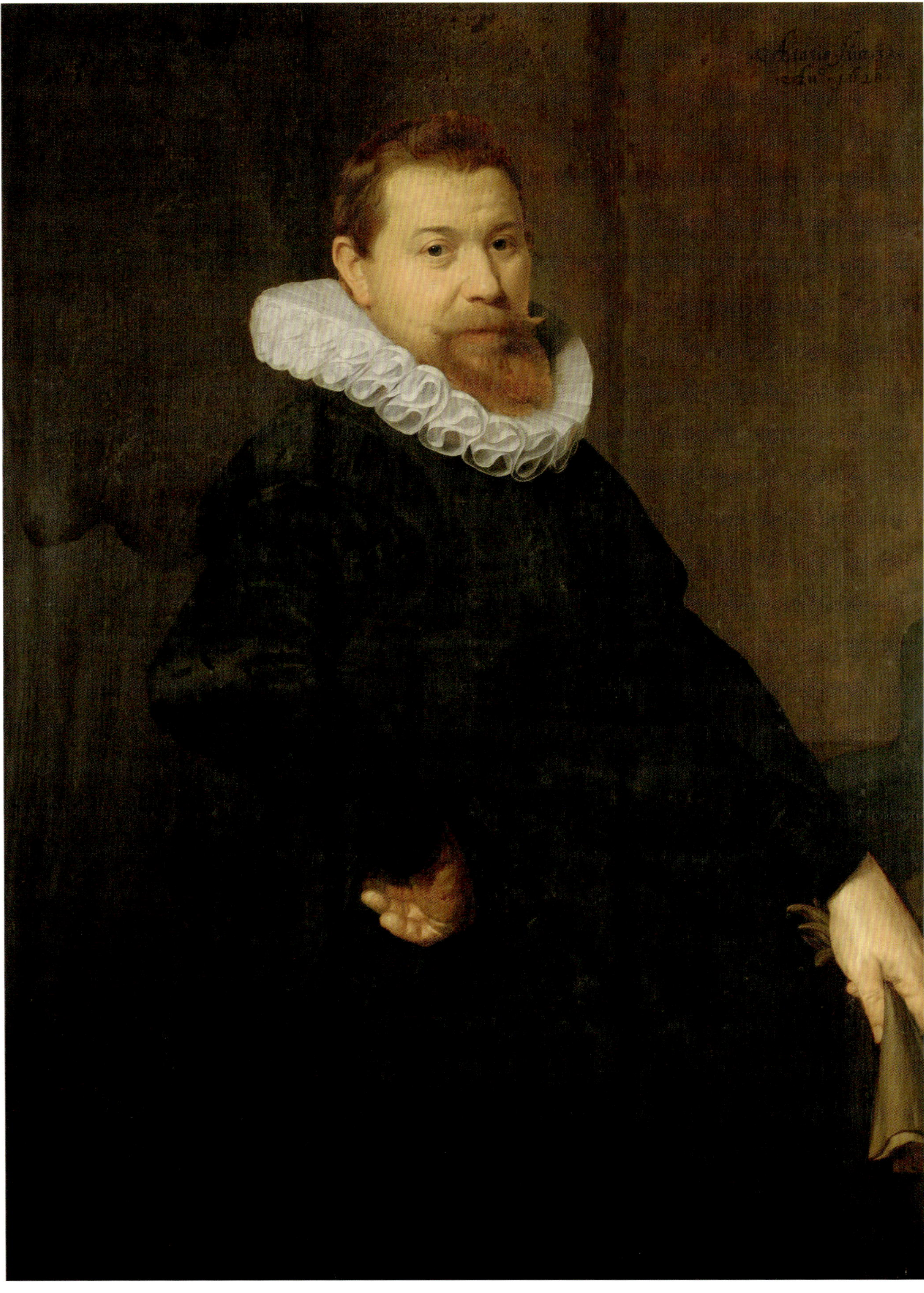

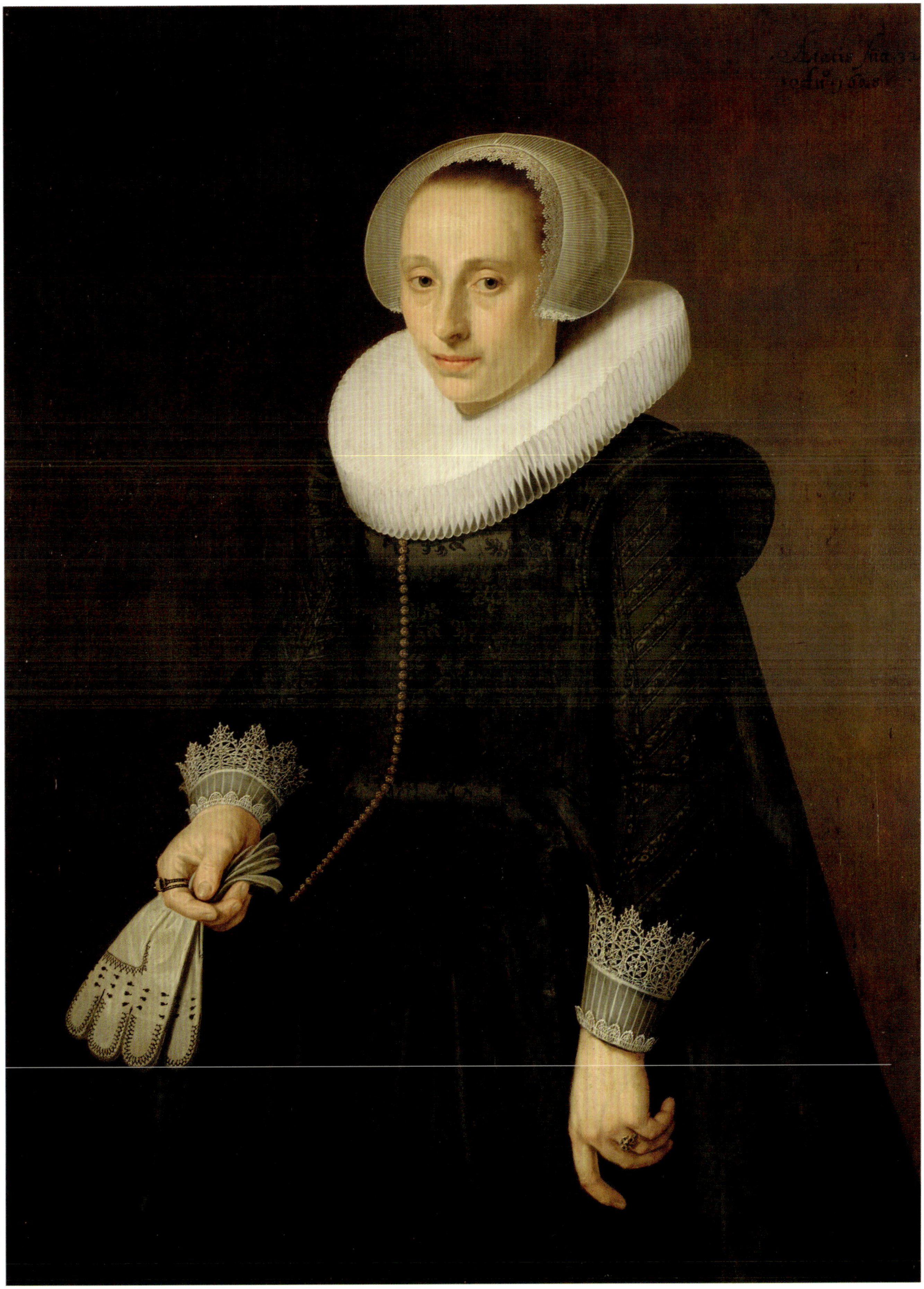

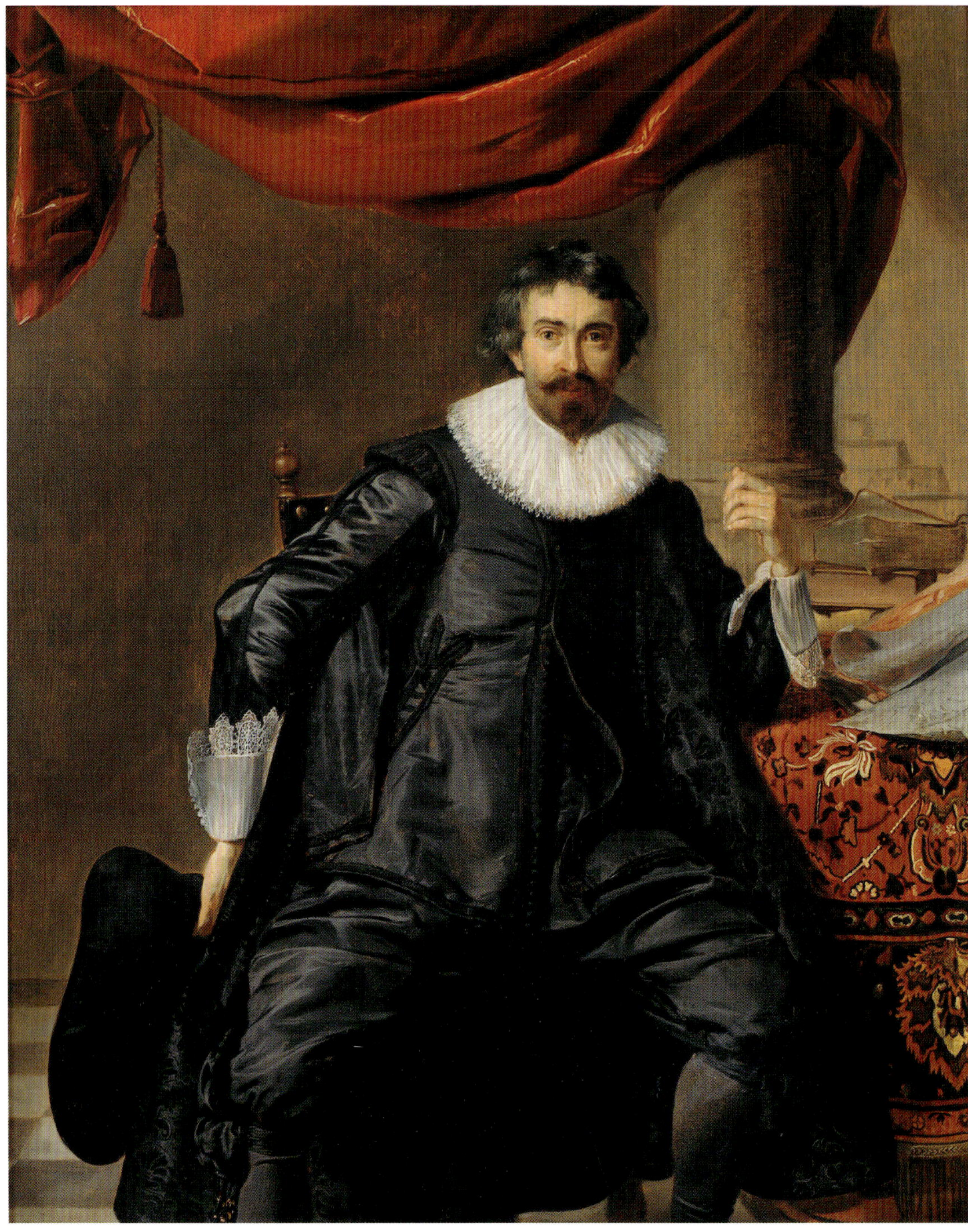

58   Thomas de Keyser, *Portrait of a Man*, 1631. National Gallery of Denmark, Copenhagen

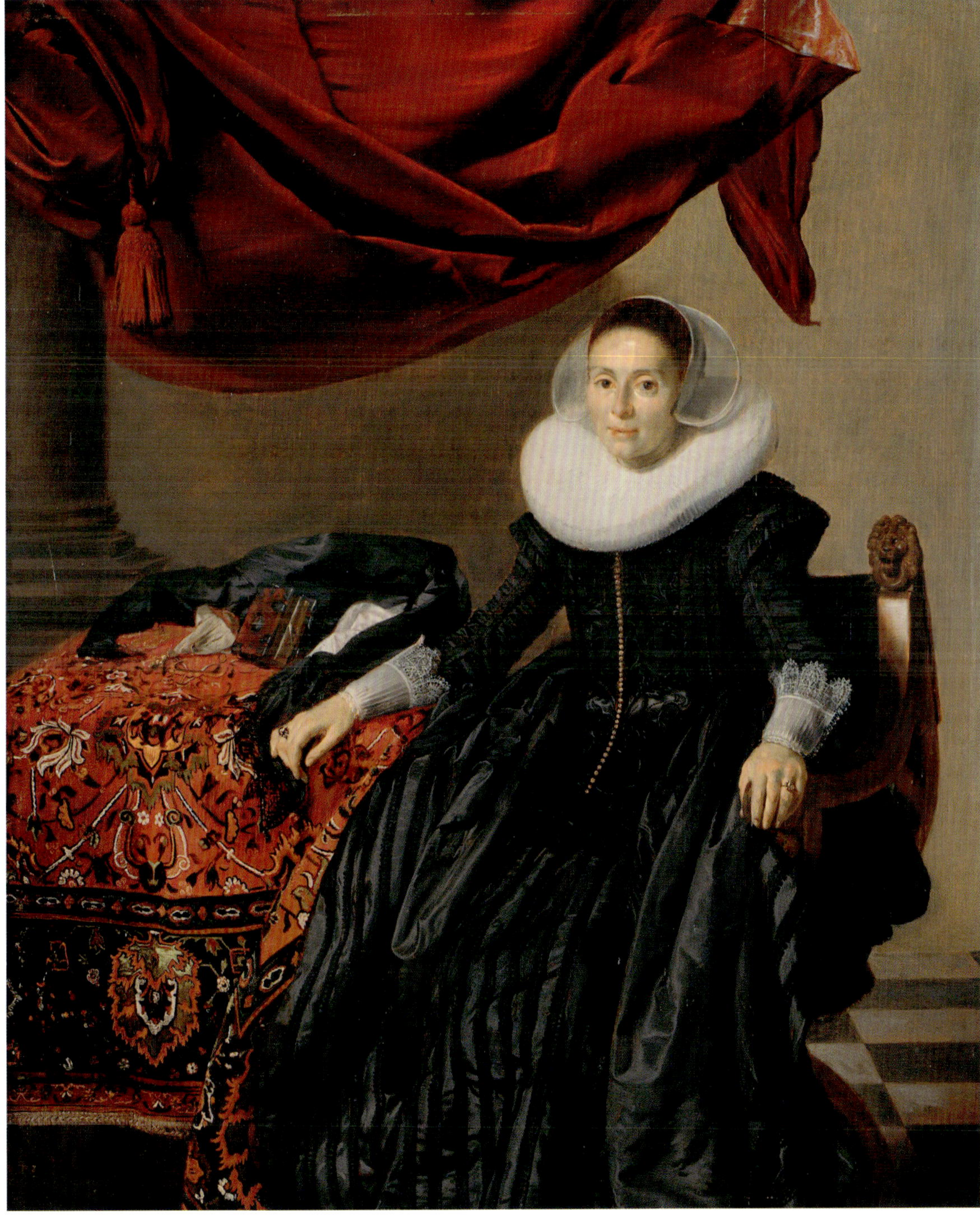

60 Rembrandt van Rijn, *Portrait of Philips Lucasz*, 1635. The National Gallery, London

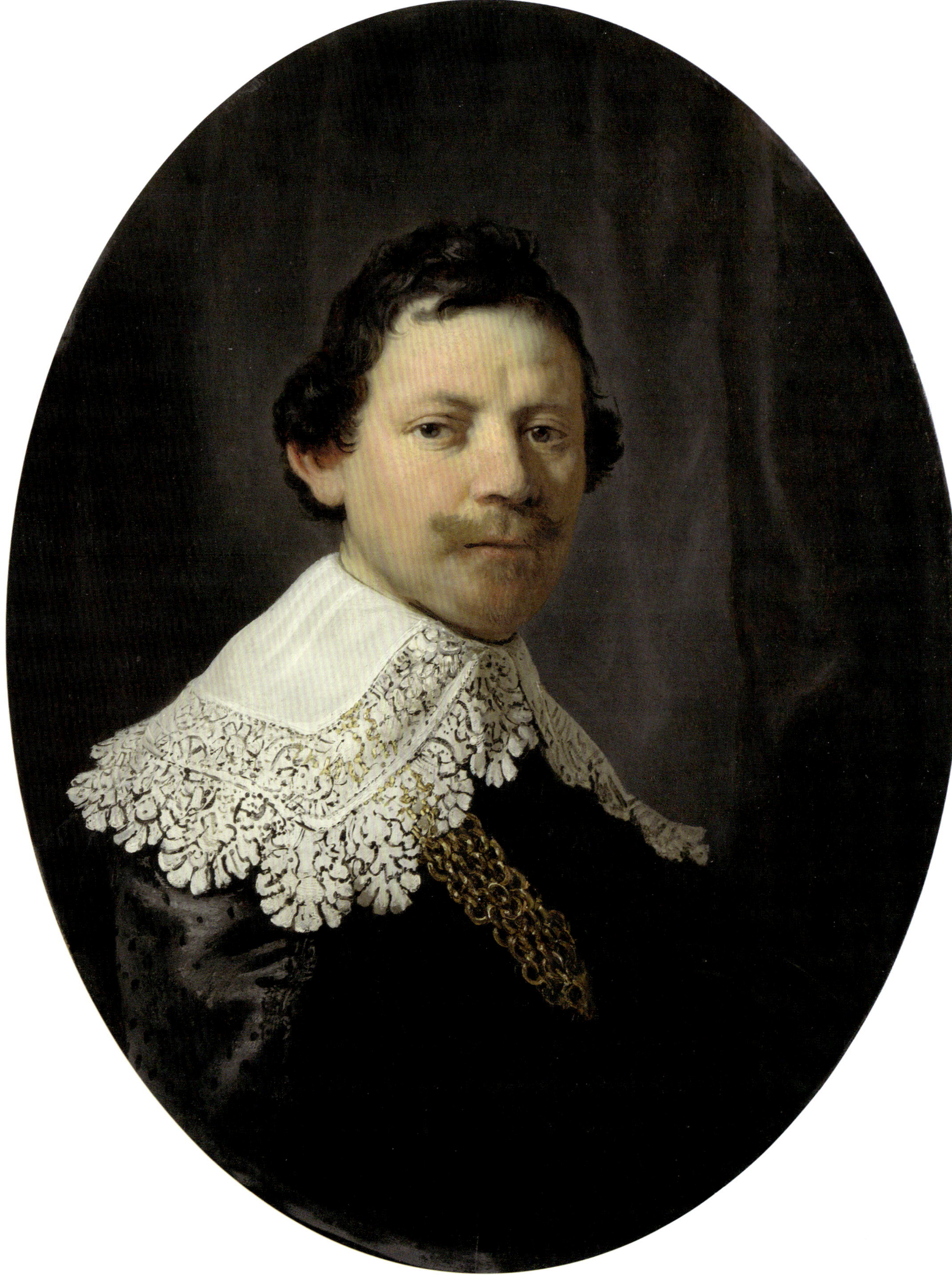

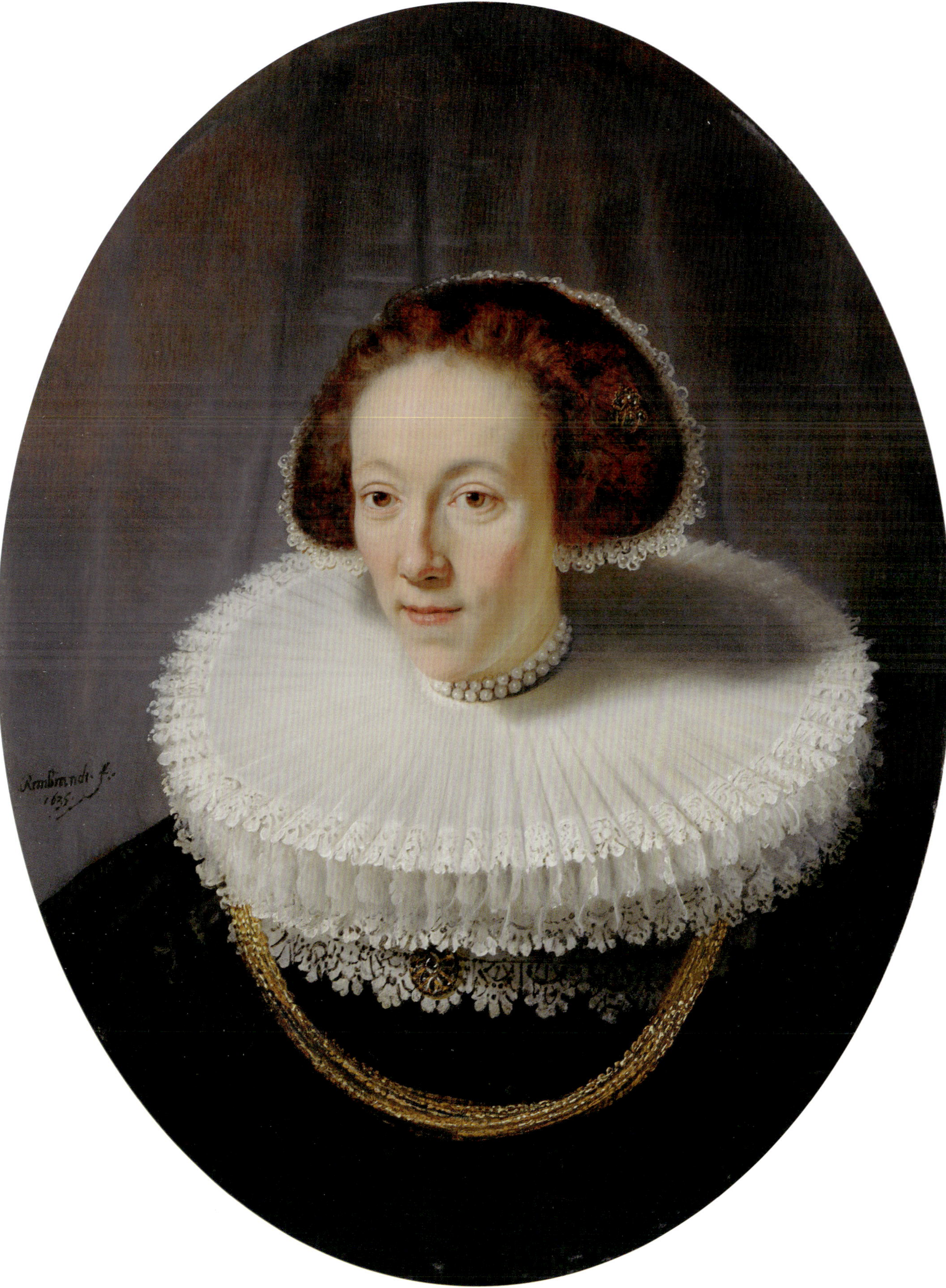

62 Joachim von Sandrart, *Portrait of Jacob Bicker*, 1639. Amsterdam Museum

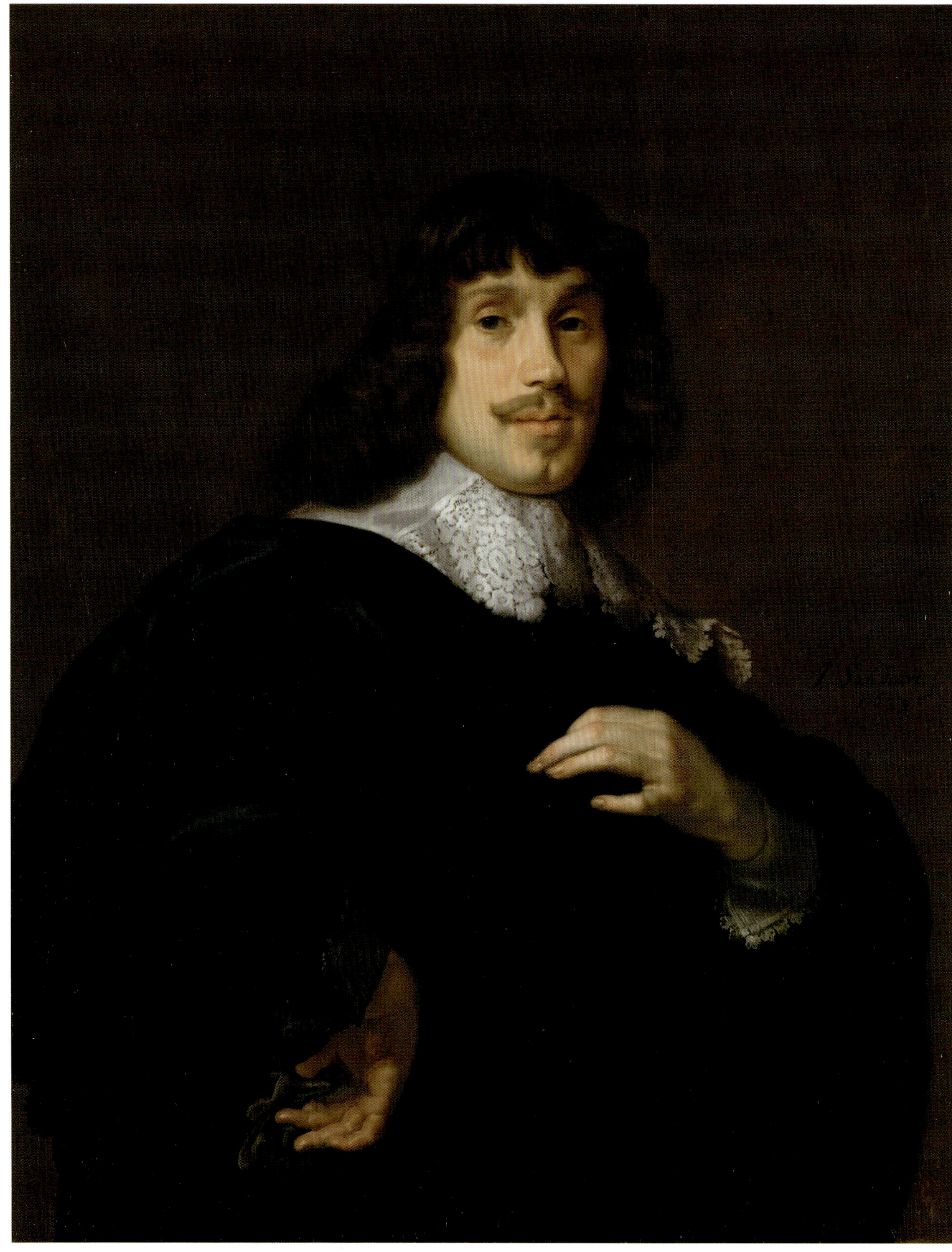

62 Joachim von Sandrart, *Portrait of Jacob Bicker*, 1639. Amsterdam Museum

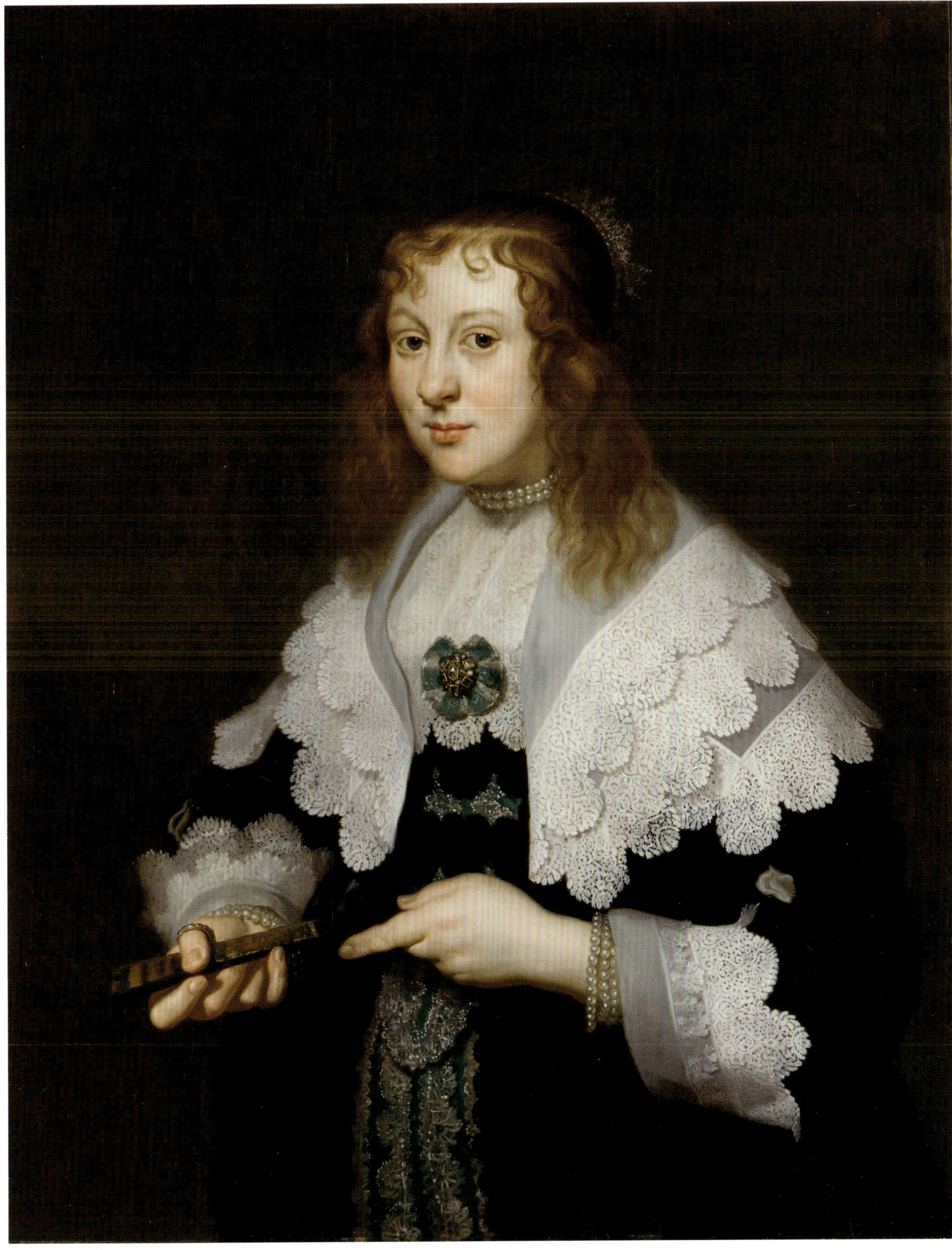

63   Joachim von Sandrart, *Portrait of Alida Bicker*, 1641. Amsterdam Museum

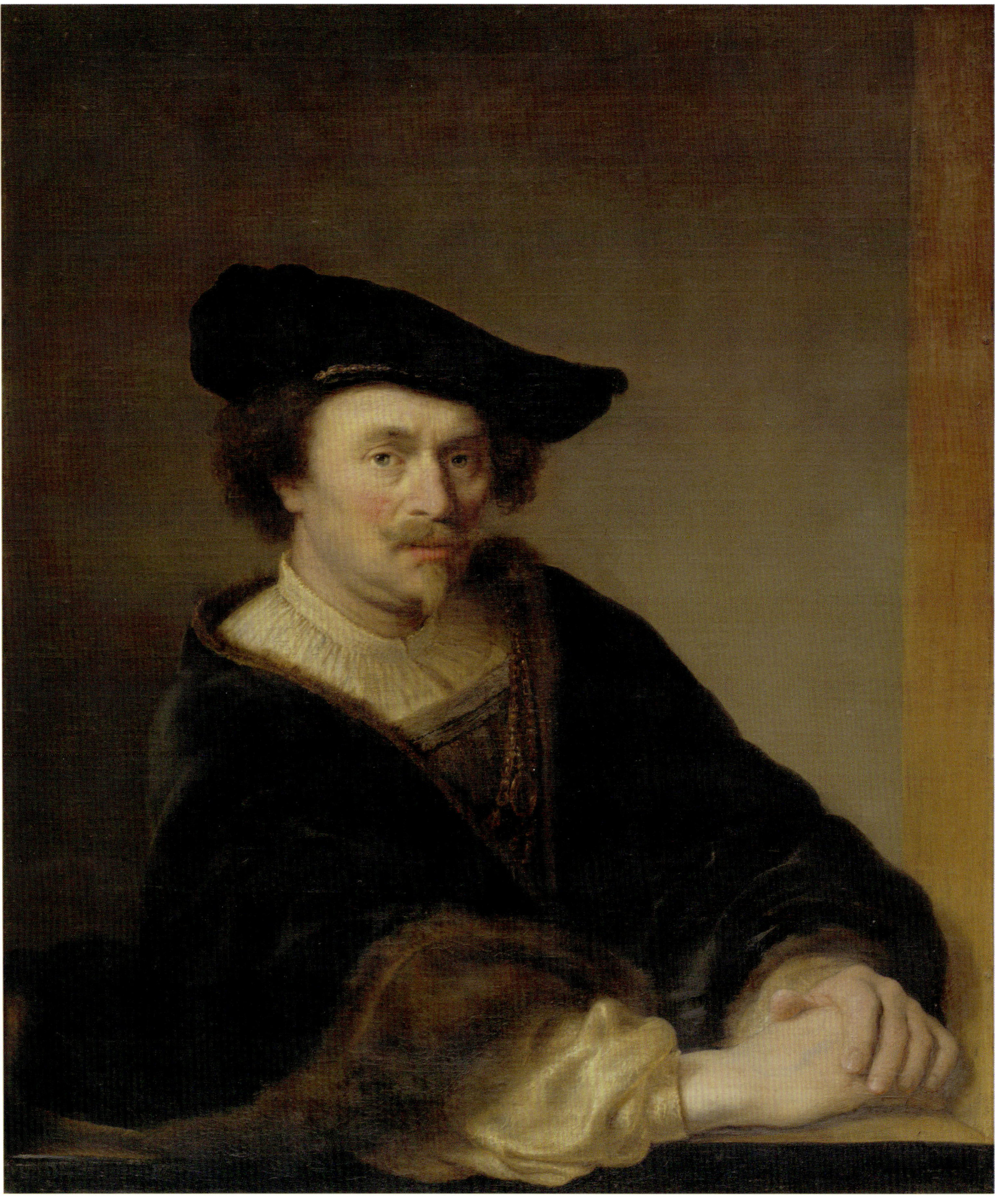

64   Ferdinand Bol, *Portrait of a Man*, c. 1645. Bayerische Staatsgemäldesammlungen, Alte Pinakothek, Munich

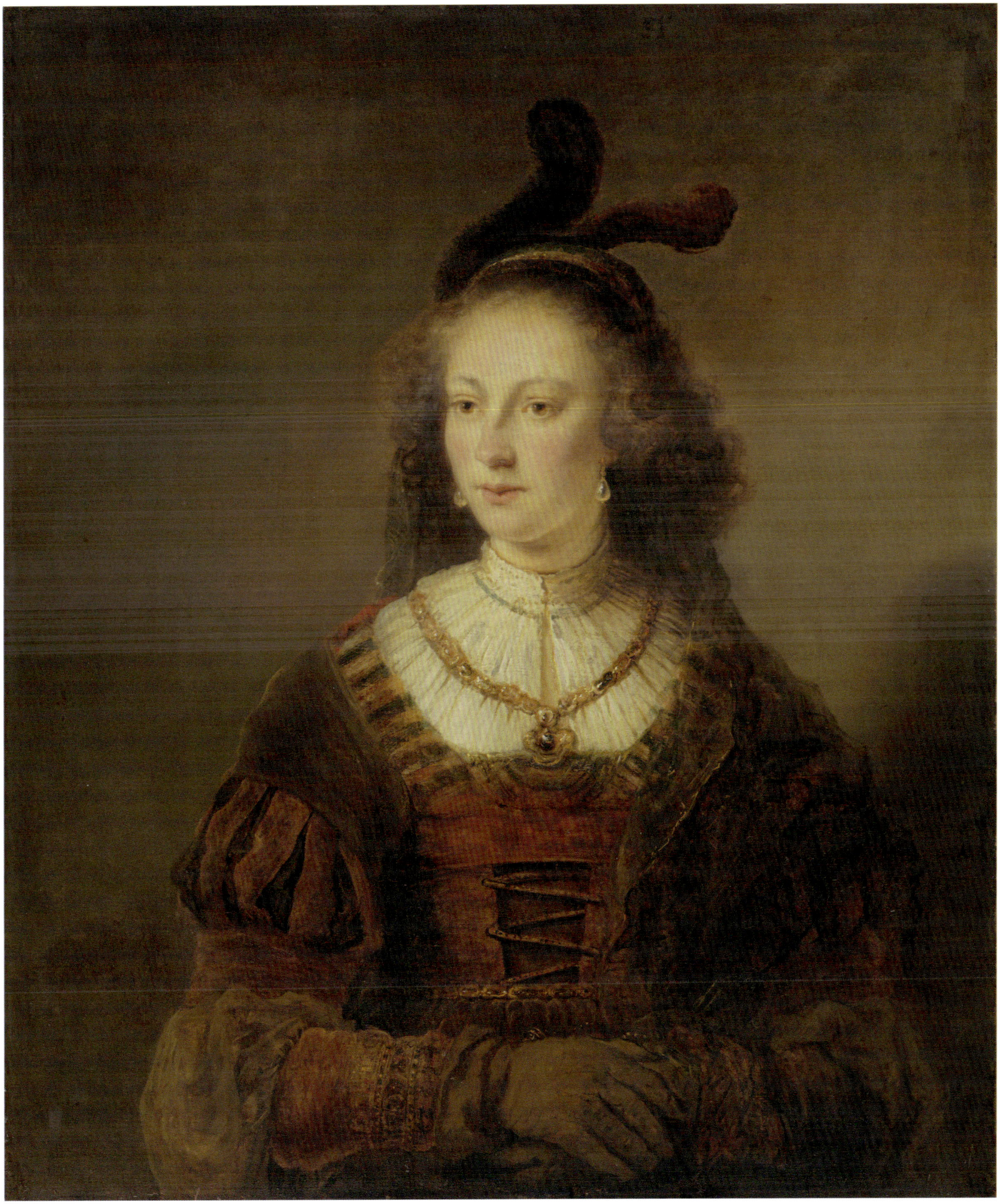

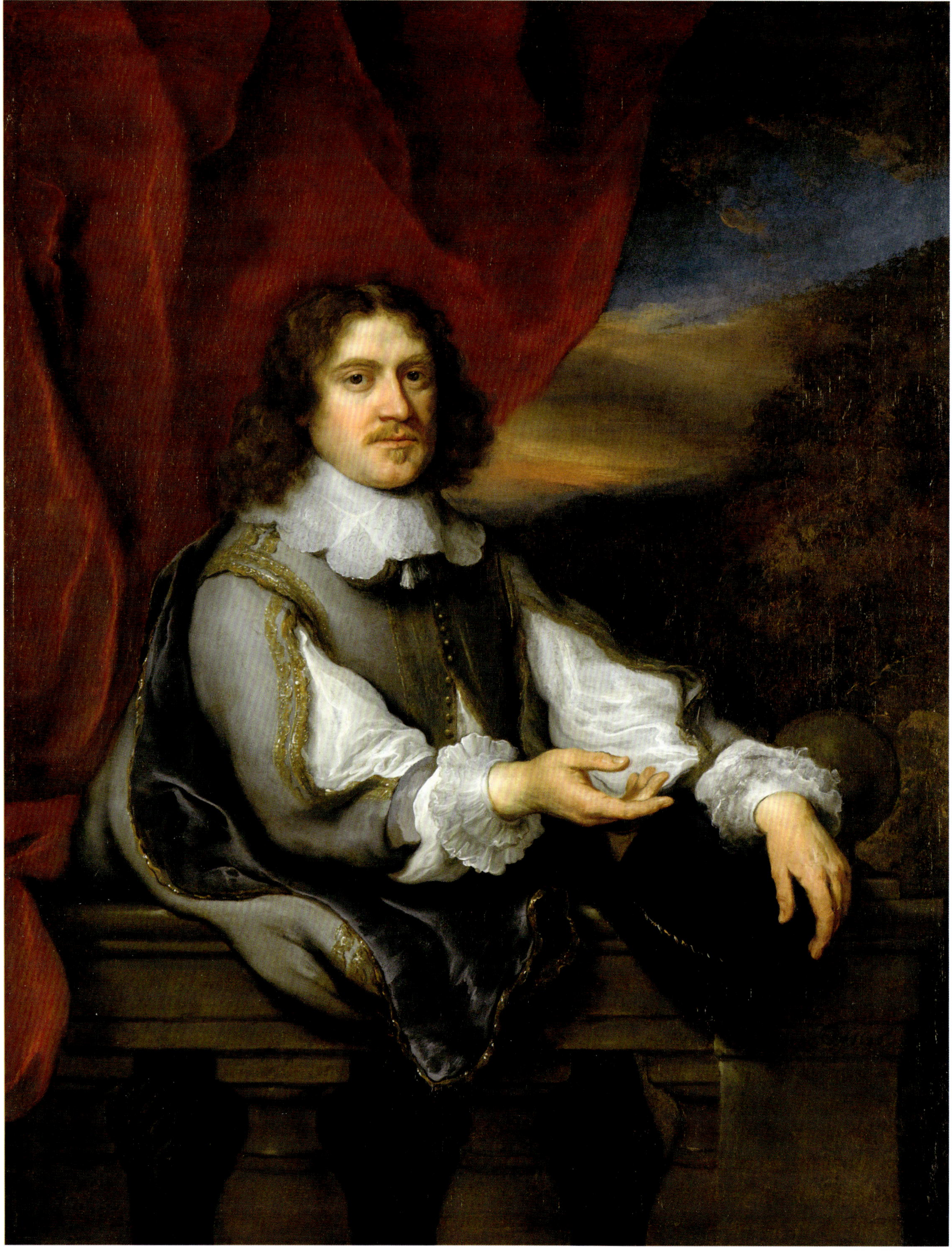

66 Govert Flinck, *Portrait of a Man (Jan van Hellemont?)*, 1646. North Carolina Museum of Art, Raleigh

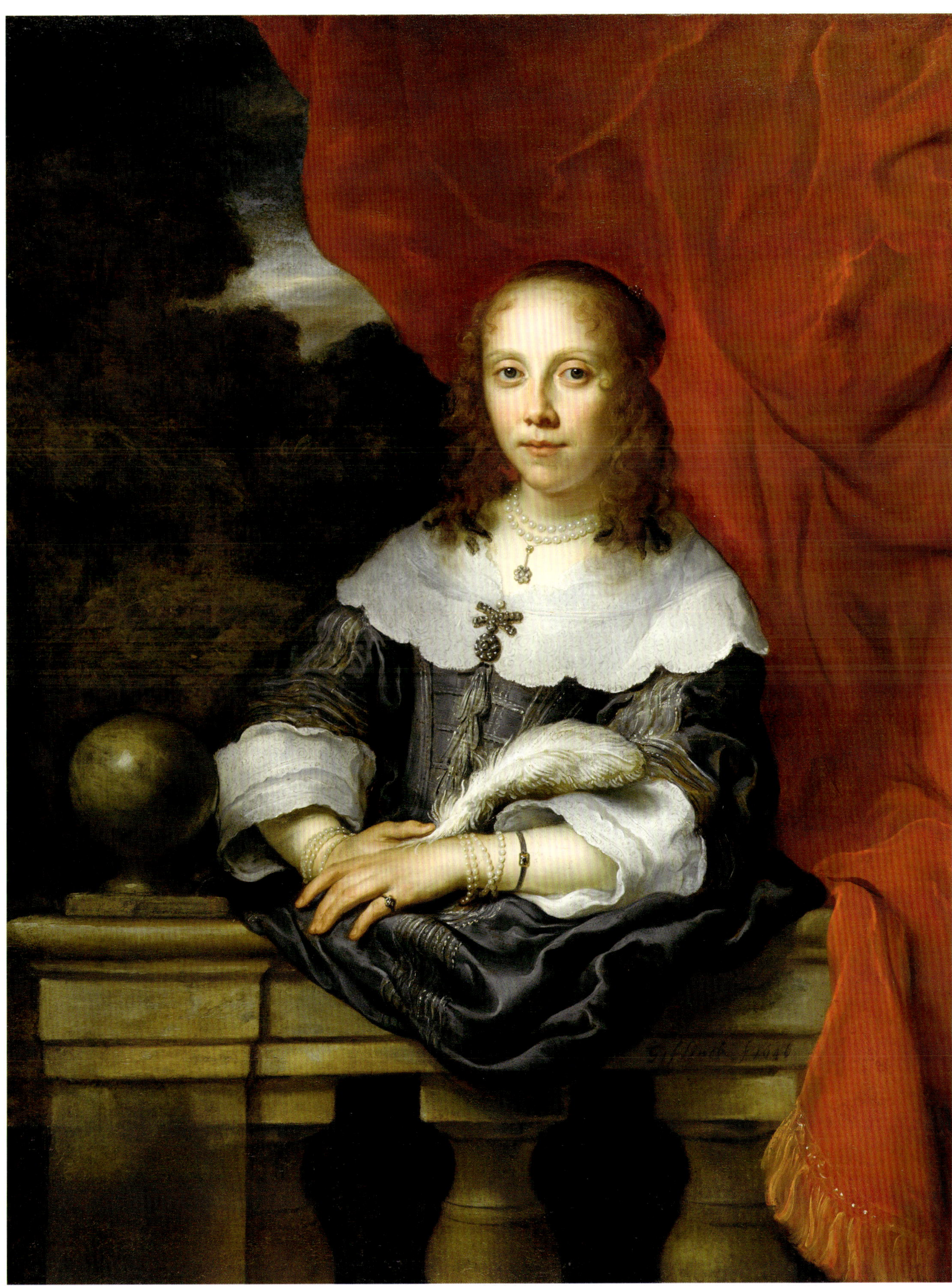

68 Rembrandt van Rijn, *Portrait of a Young Woman with a Fan*, 1633. The Metropolitan Museum of Art, New York

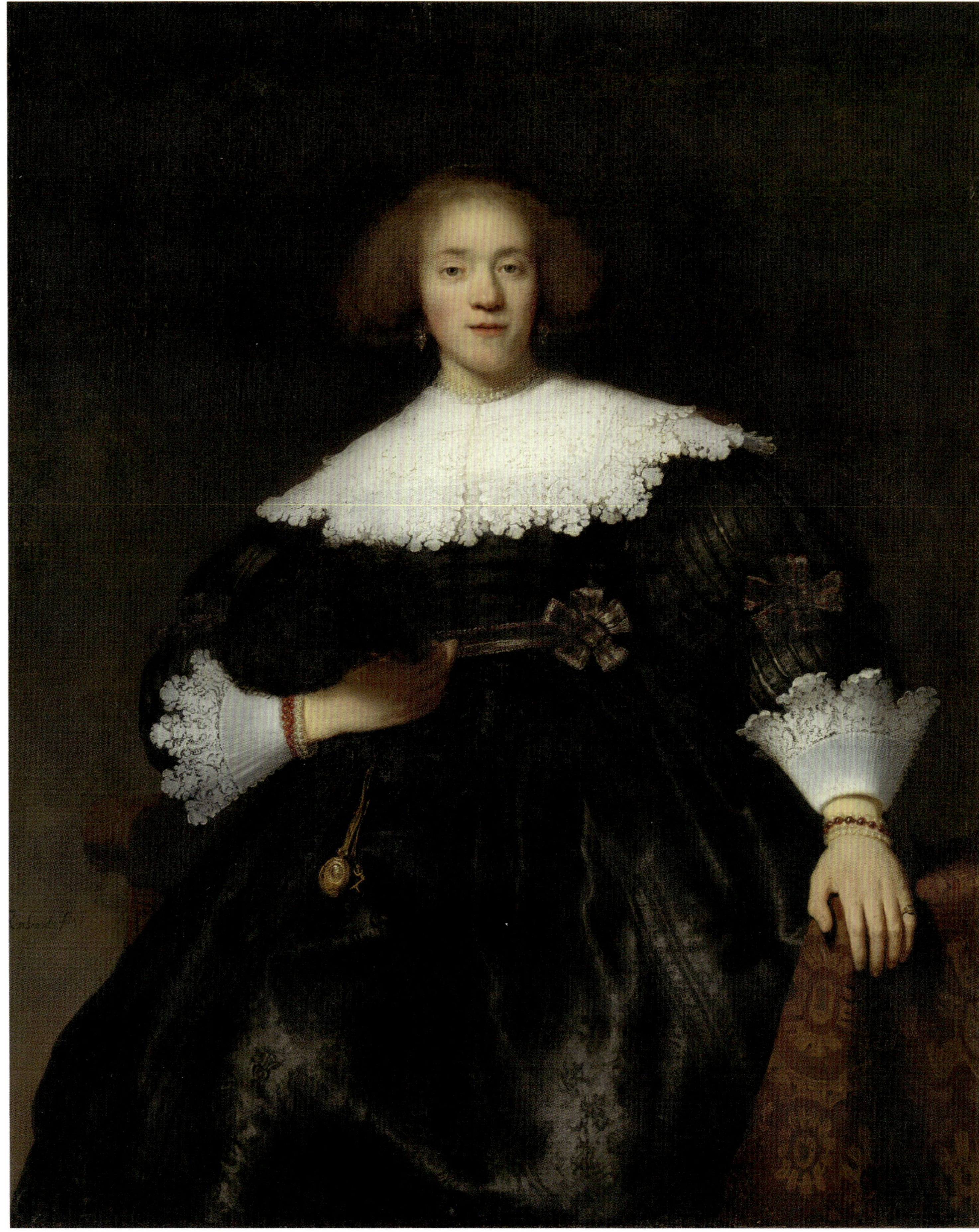

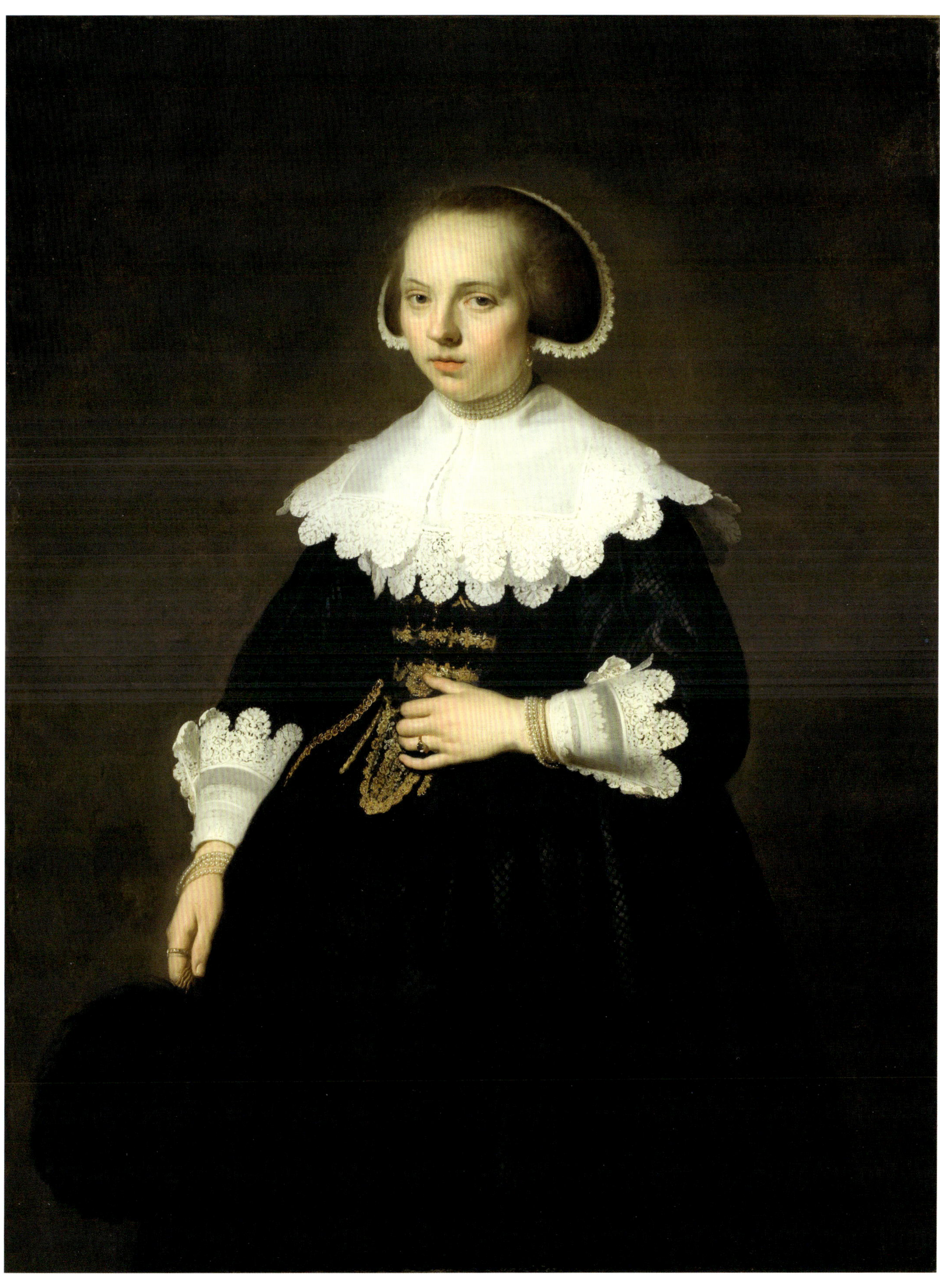

70 Govert Flinck, *Portrait of a Woman*, c. 1640. Suermondt-Ludwig-Museum, Aachen

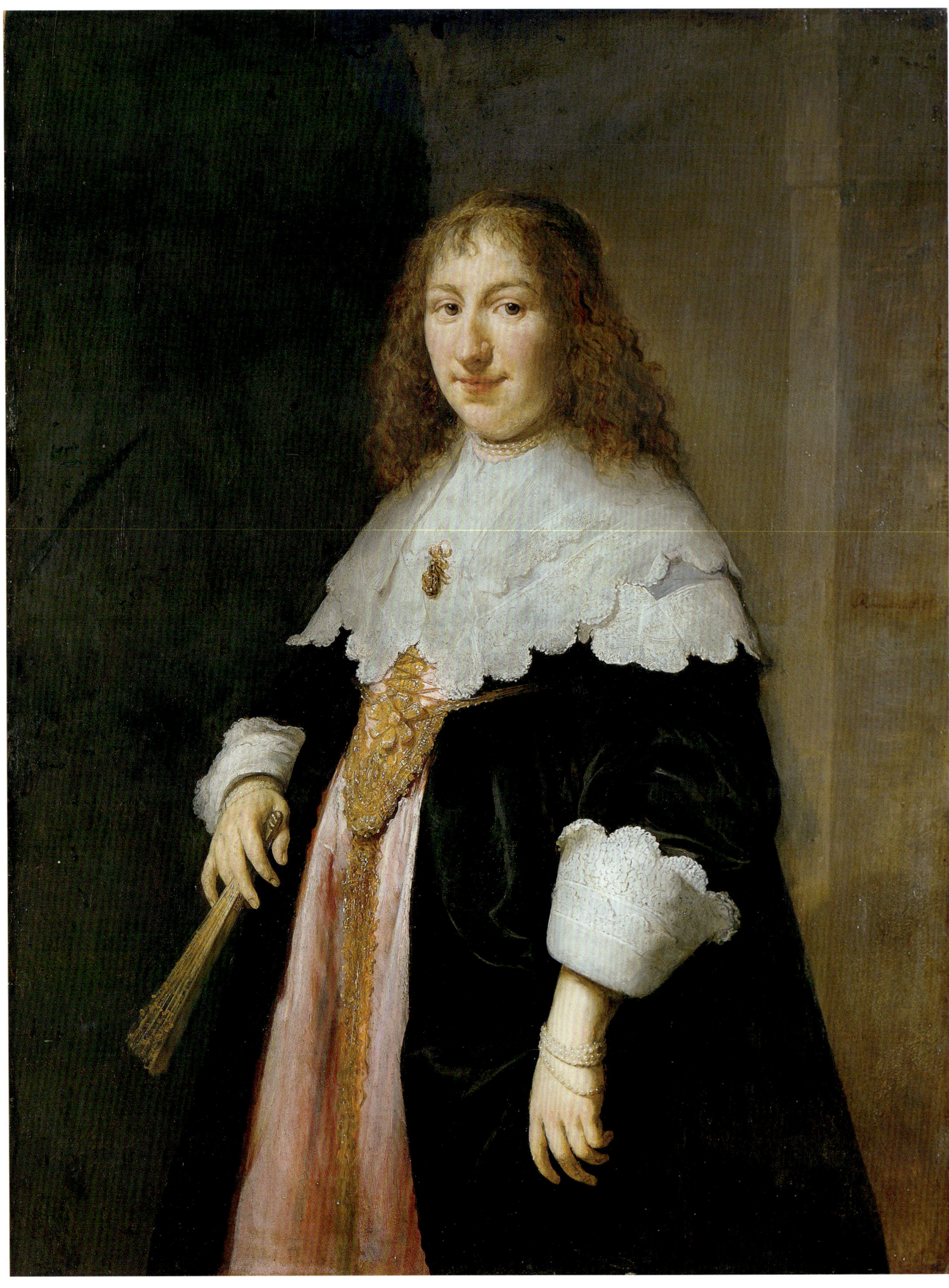

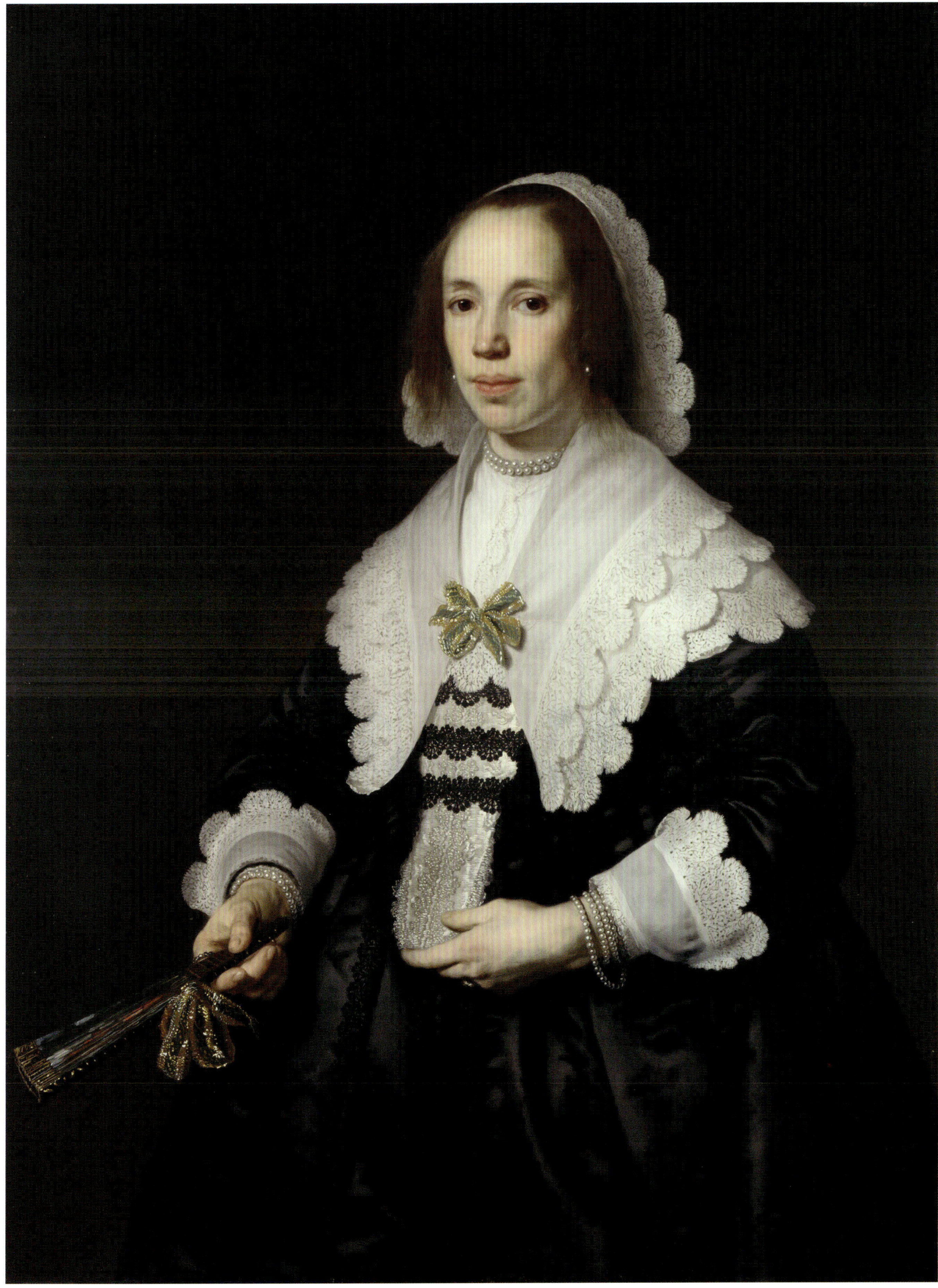

72　Nicolaes Eliasz Pickenoy, *Portrait of a Man*, 1628. Staatliche Kunsthalle Karlsruhe

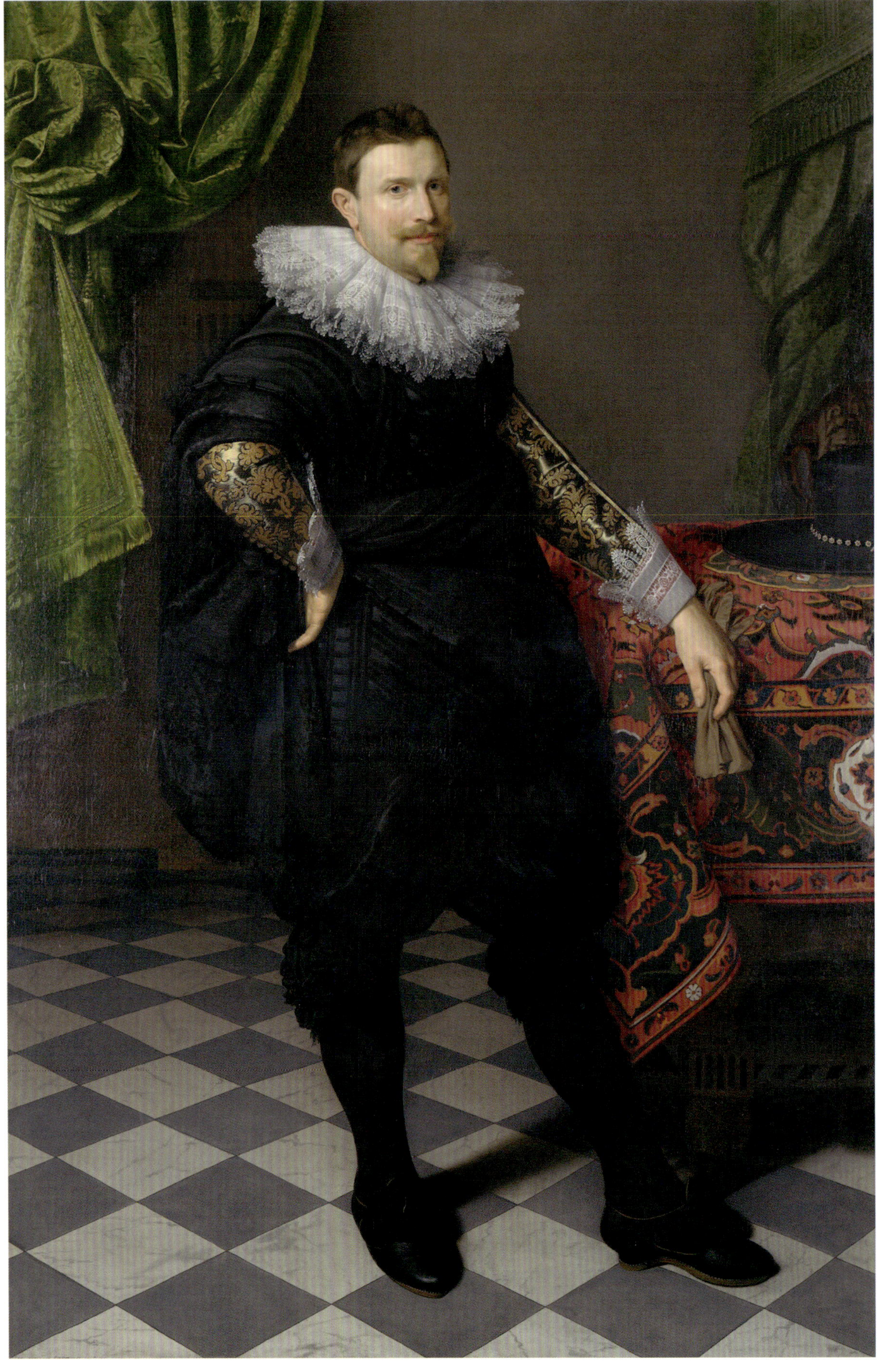

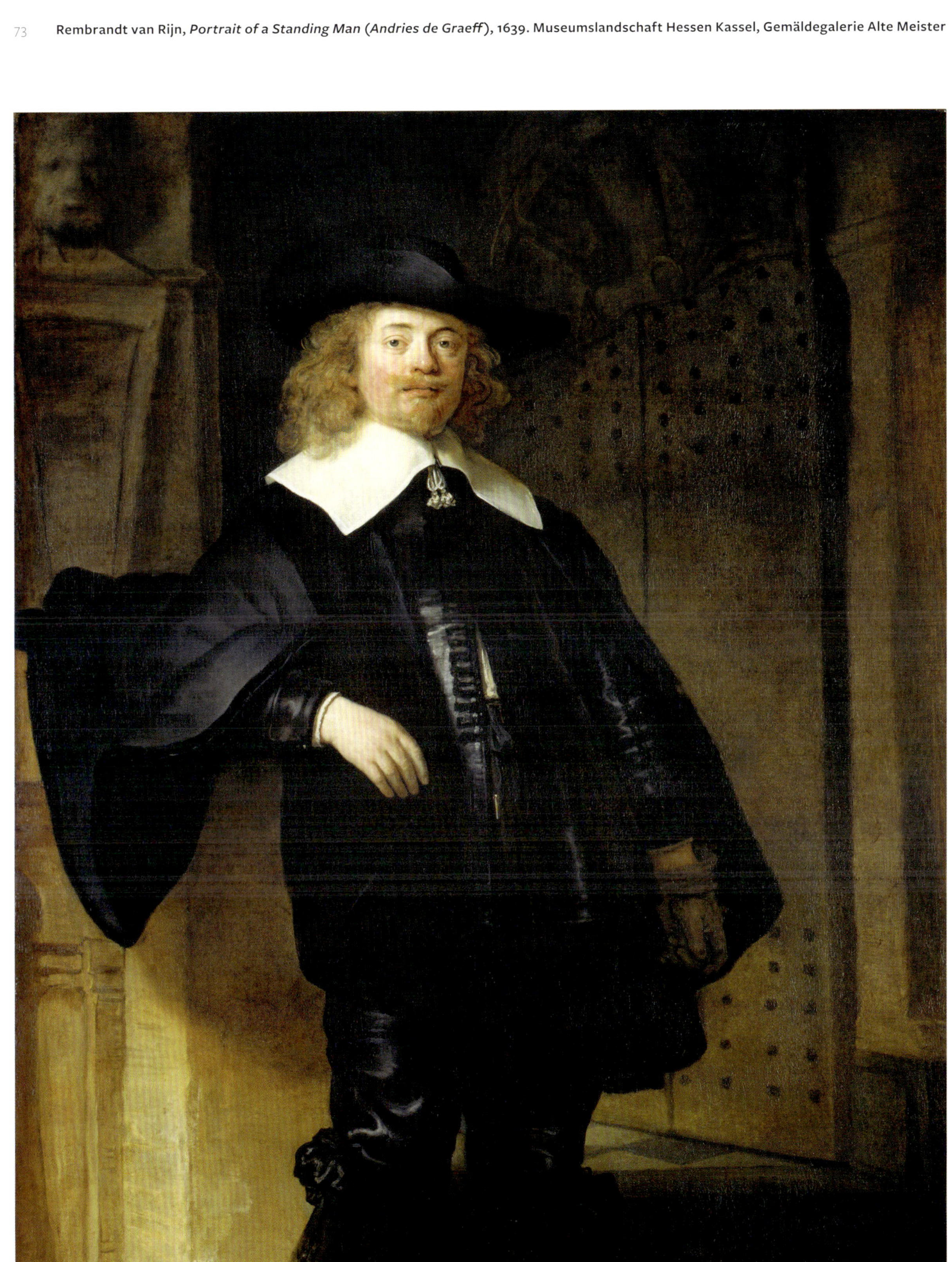

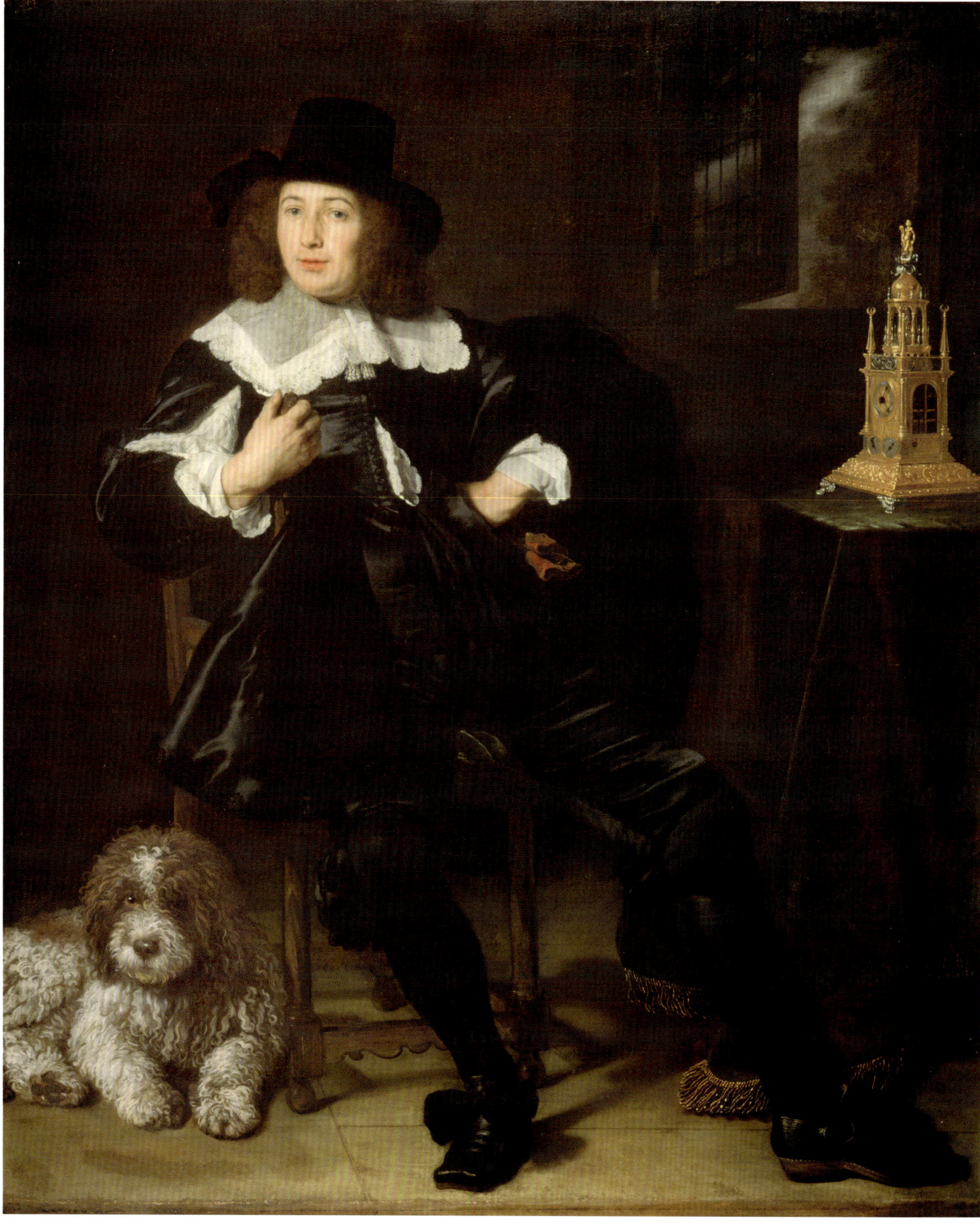

74 Bartholomeus van der Helst, *Portrait of a Man* (*Joan Hulft?*), 1644. Montreal Museum of Fine Arts

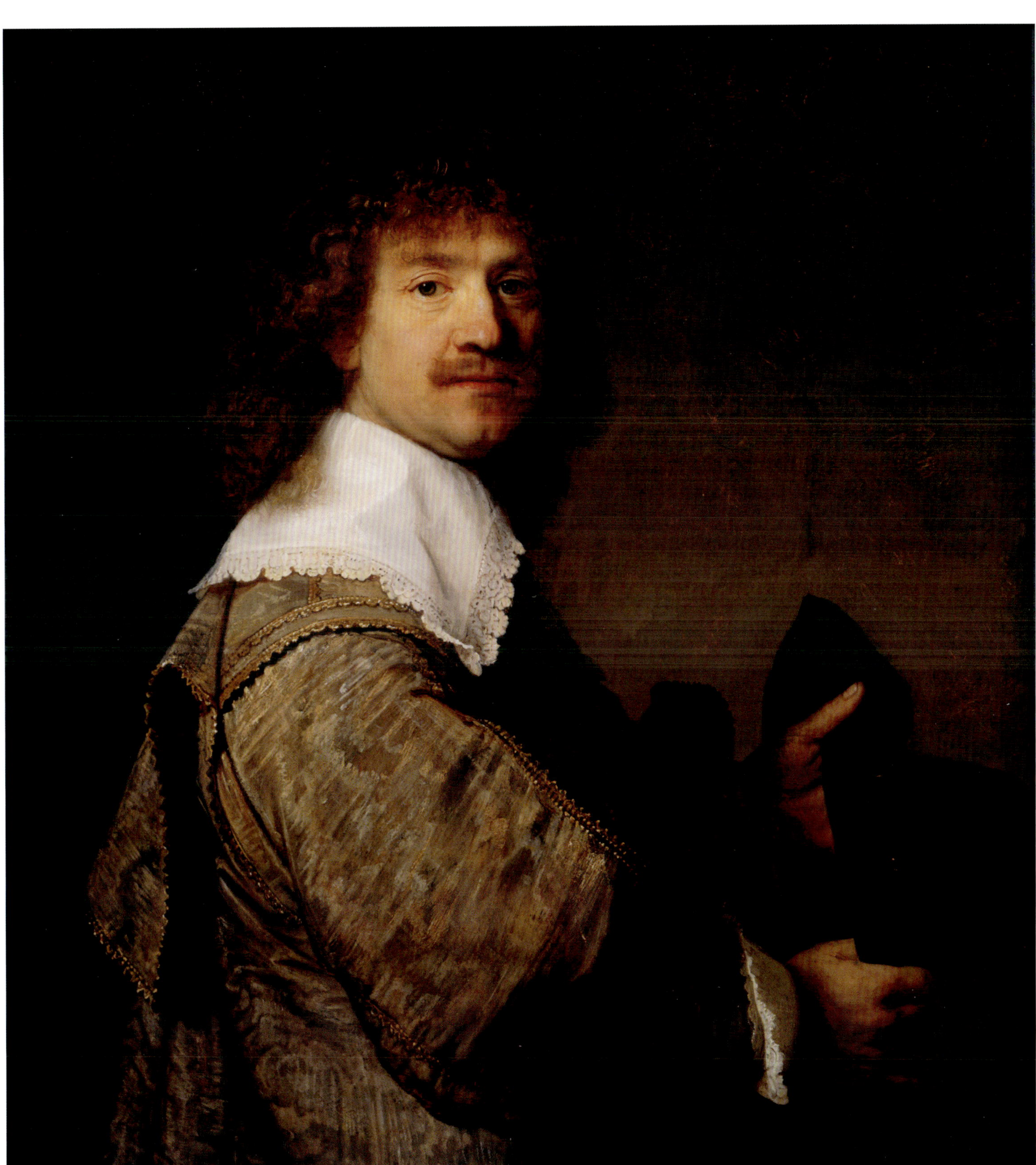

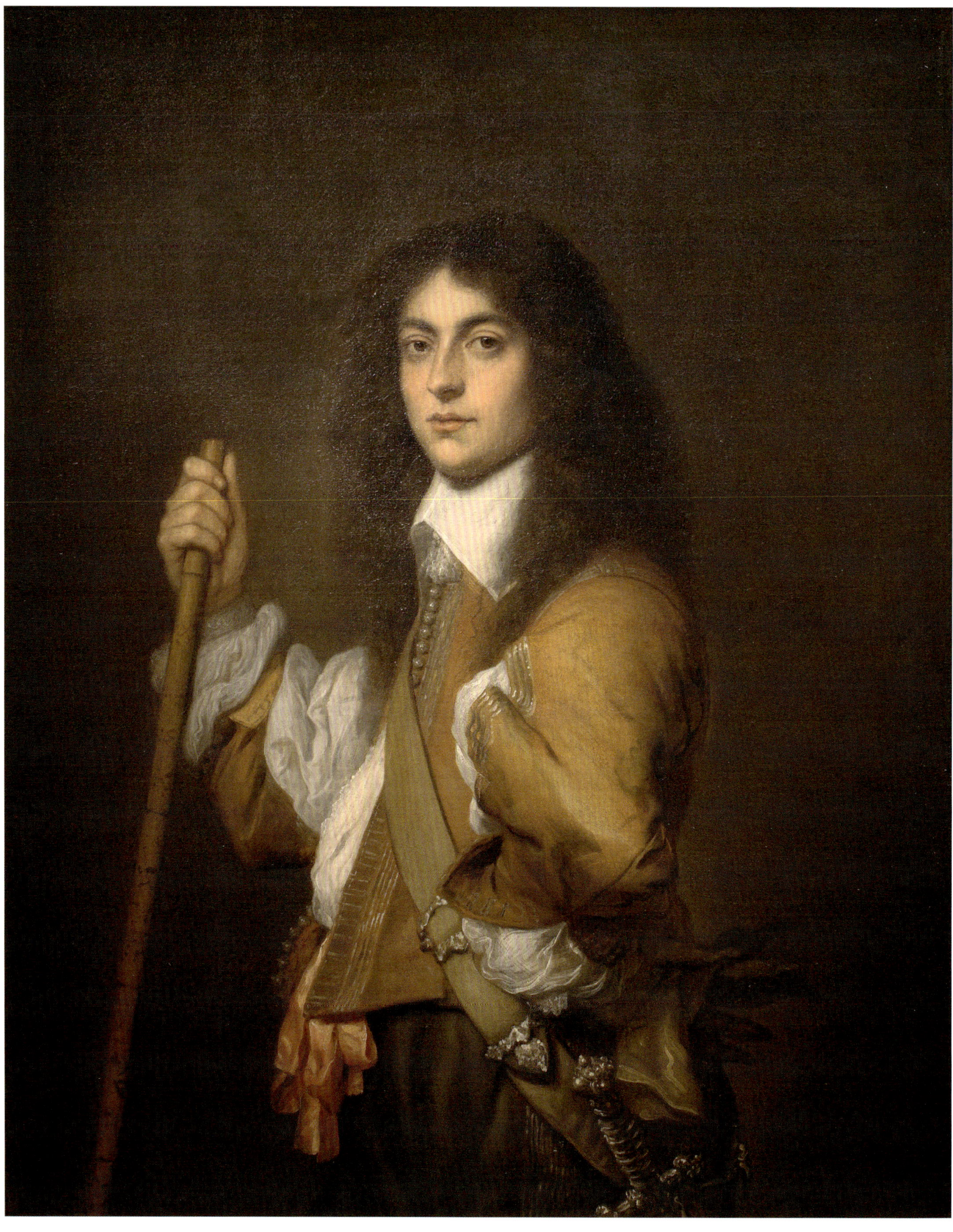

76 Jan Lievens, *Portrait of Adriaen Trip*, 1644. Rembrandt House Museum, Amsterdam

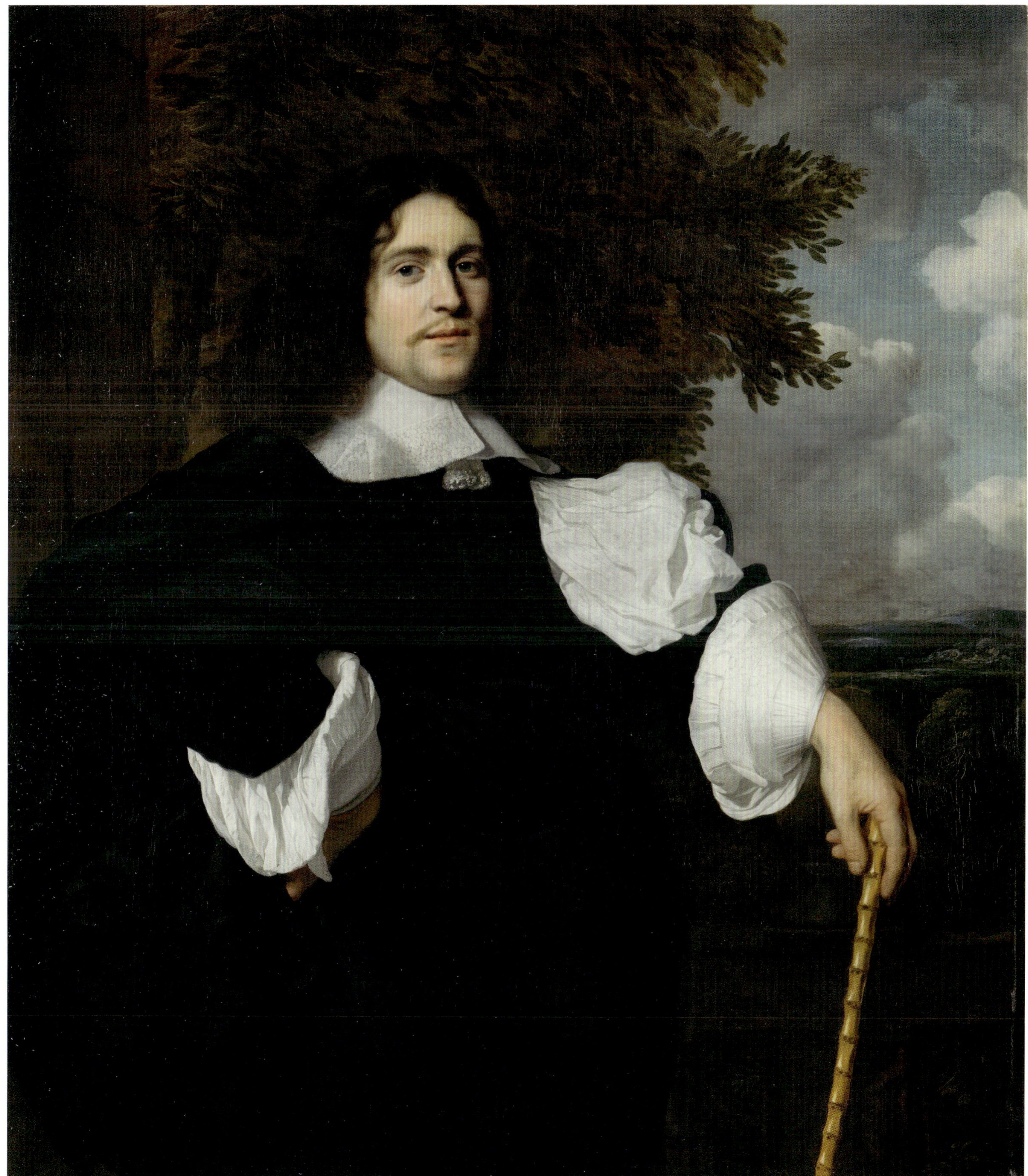

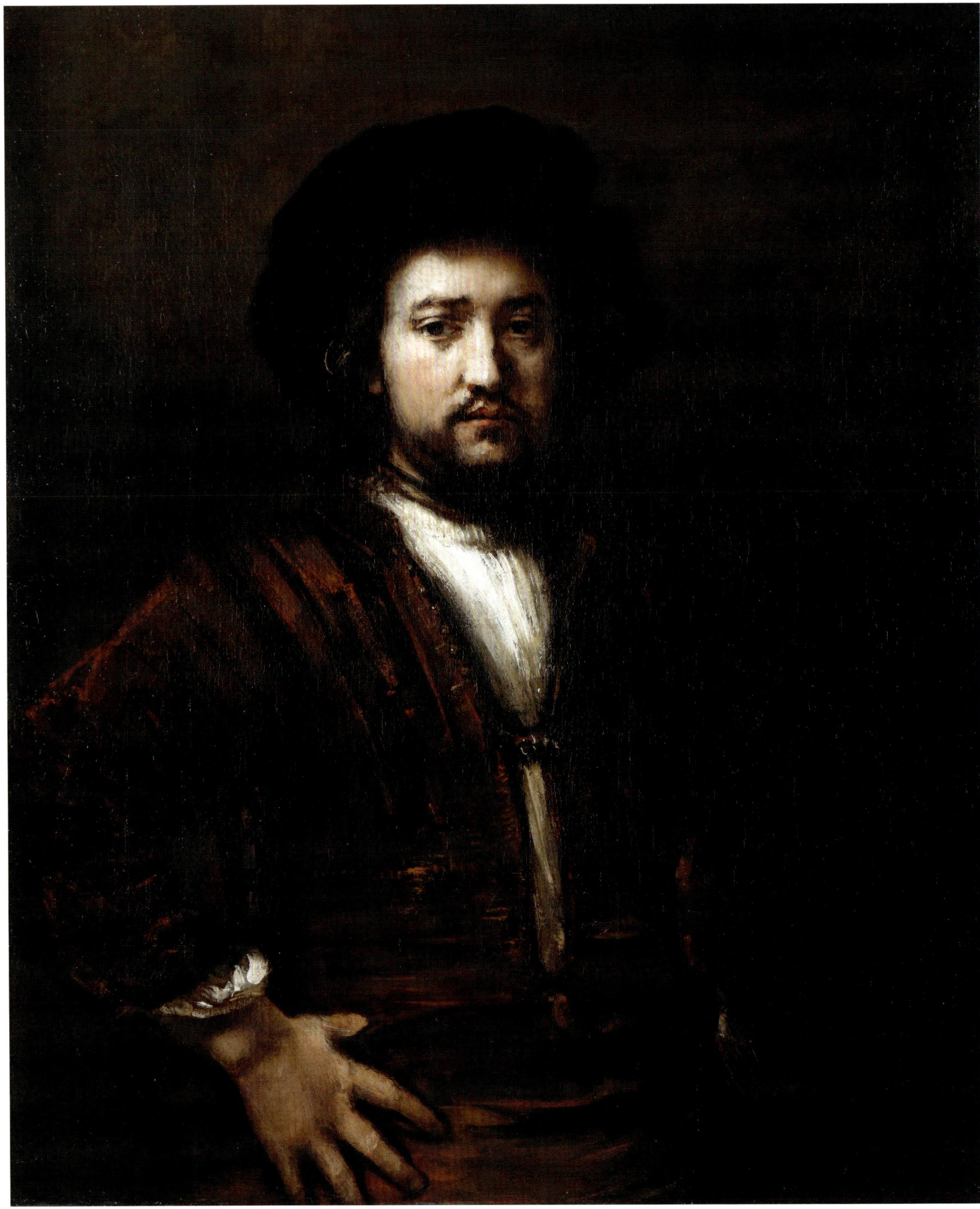

78 Rembrandt van Rijn, *Portrait of a Man with Arms Akimbo*, 1658. Agnes Etherington Art Centre, Queen's University, Kingston

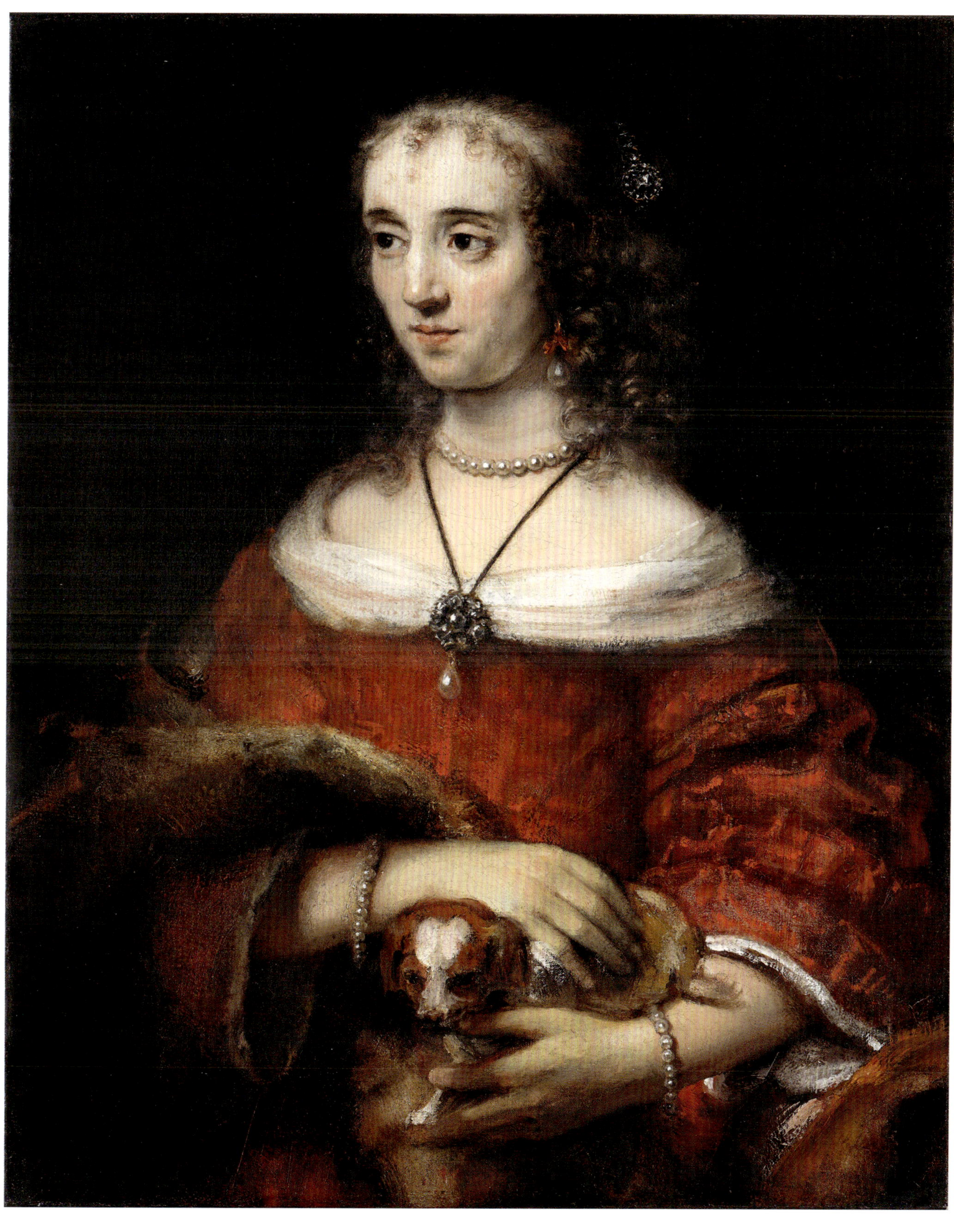

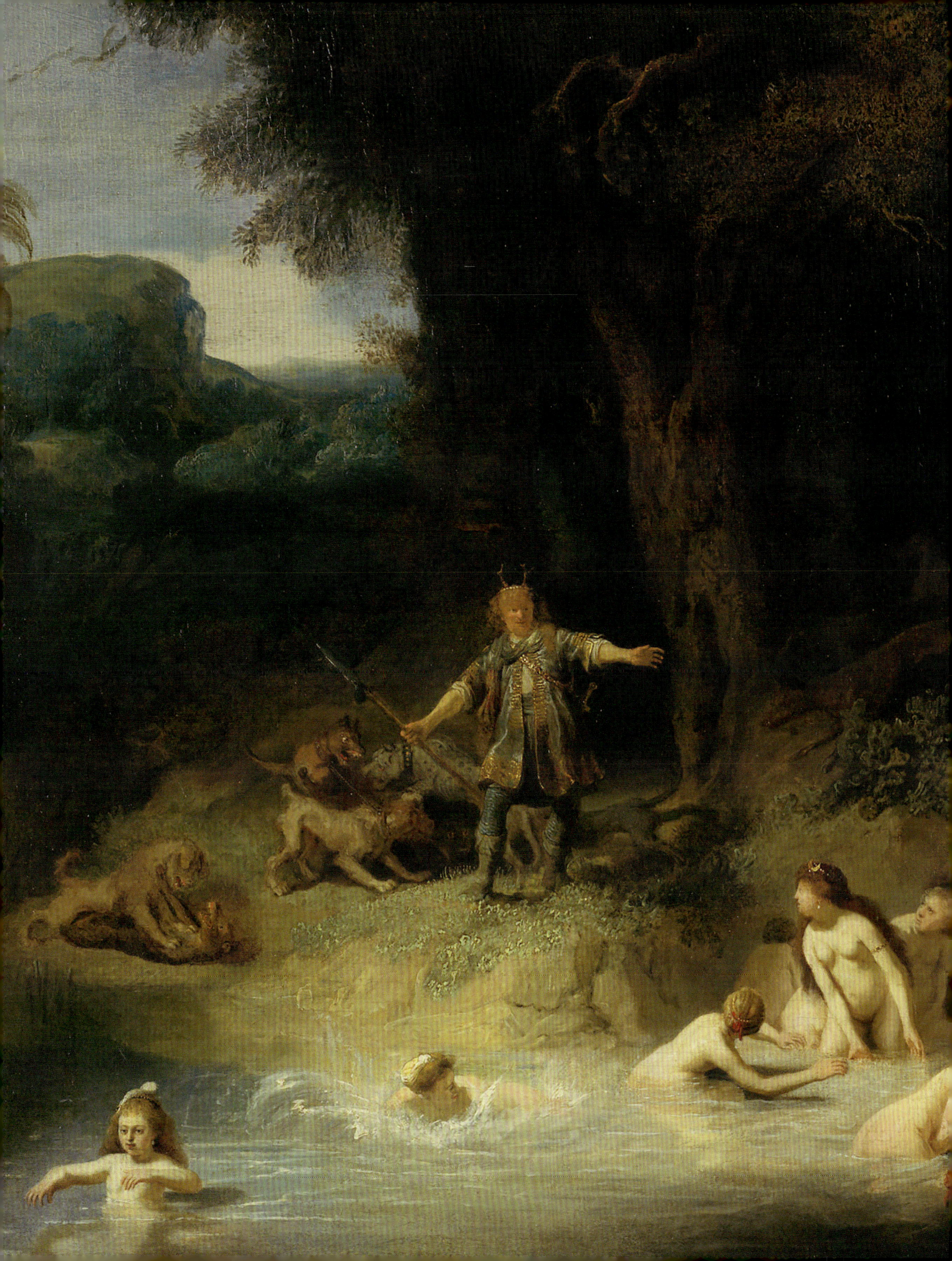

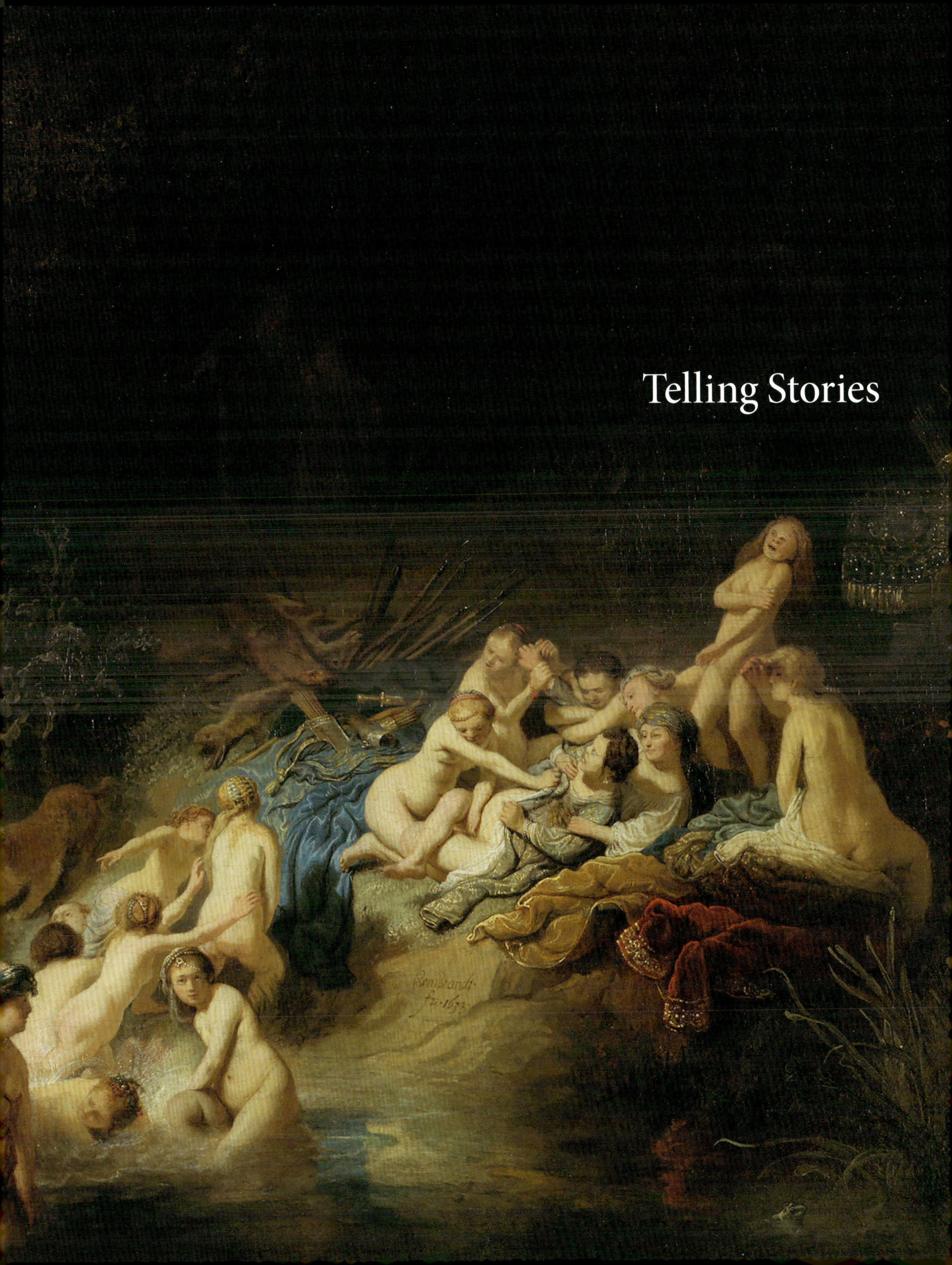
Telling Stories

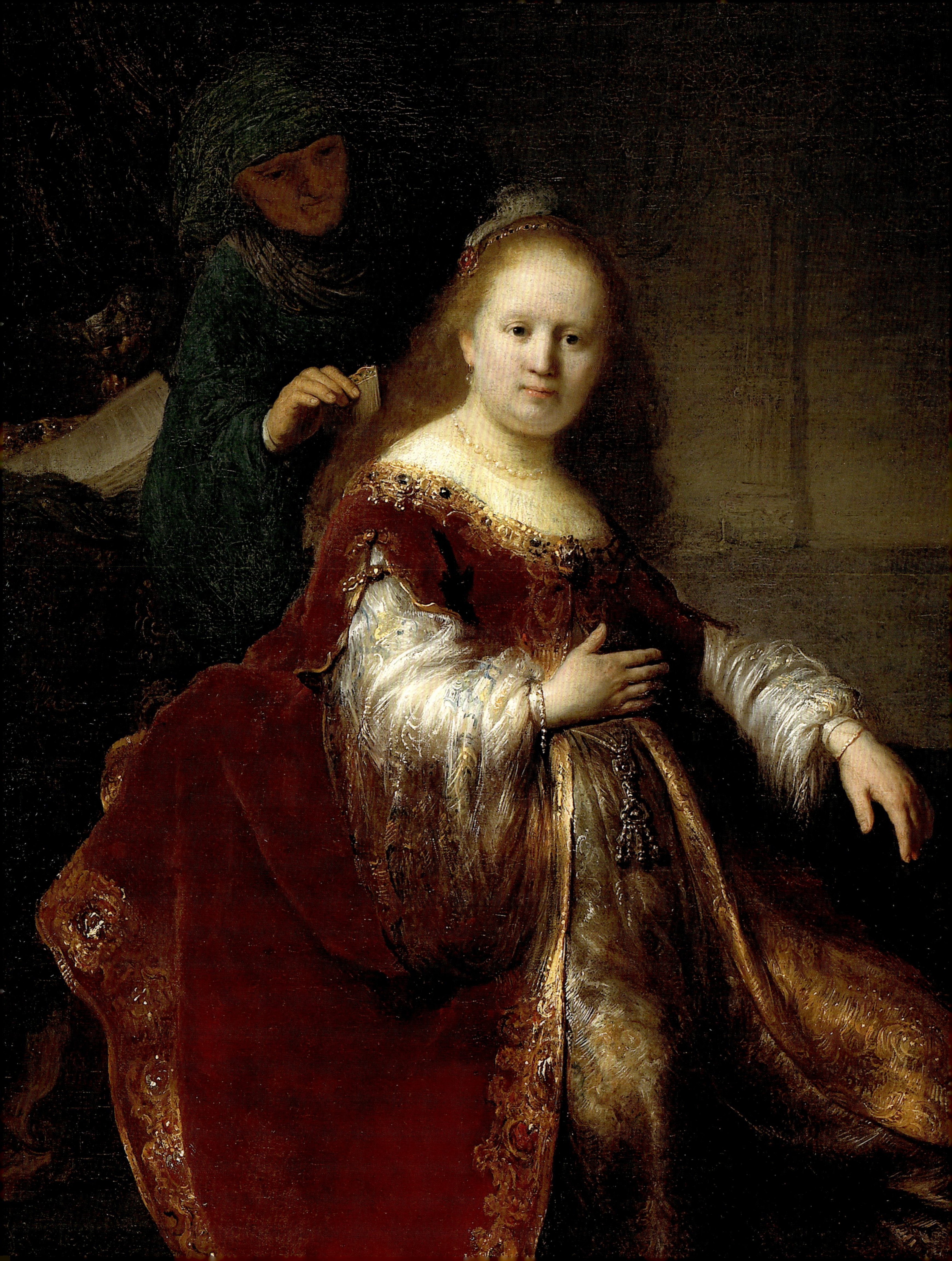

STEPHANIE S. DICKEY

Powerful Women

Rembrandt and his associates produced numerous paintings that focus on one or two figures, creatively blurring the boundaries between history, allegory, portrait and genre. Such works contributed to a thriving market for colourful character studies. Fanciful costumes blend pictorial and theatrical tradition with jewels and luxurious fabrics, imported through Dutch global trade, to evoke the antique past or add glamour to formal dress (pls. 80, 81, 83, 93).[1] Many of Rembrandt's female historical figures are exemplars of virtue, probity and courage. For instance, Bellona, goddess of war, and Minerva, goddess of wisdom, make repeated appearances in his work (fig. 8.1) and that of his followers.[2] Unlike many of his contemporaries, Rembrandt emphasized emotion and character rather than physical beauty. This approach culminated in his moving portrayal of the virtuous Roman matron Lucretia in 1666 (fig. 8.2).[3]

Saskia van Uylenburgh modelled frequently for Rembrandt after they married in 1634. The artist's affection for his young bride may have inspired two large paintings of Flora, goddess of spring (pl. 83), but this appealing subject had commercial value as well.[4] Arcadian portraiture was in vogue with fashionable women at the court in The Hague; even the stadtholder's wife, Amalia von Solms, had herself portrayed as Flora.[5] While other artists such as Jacob Backer were more successful in marketing pastoral portraits to Amsterdam matrons, visitors to Rembrandt's shop could purchase inexpensive paintings or drawings of "Flora" by pupils such as Leendert van Beijeren and Ferdinand Bol.[6]

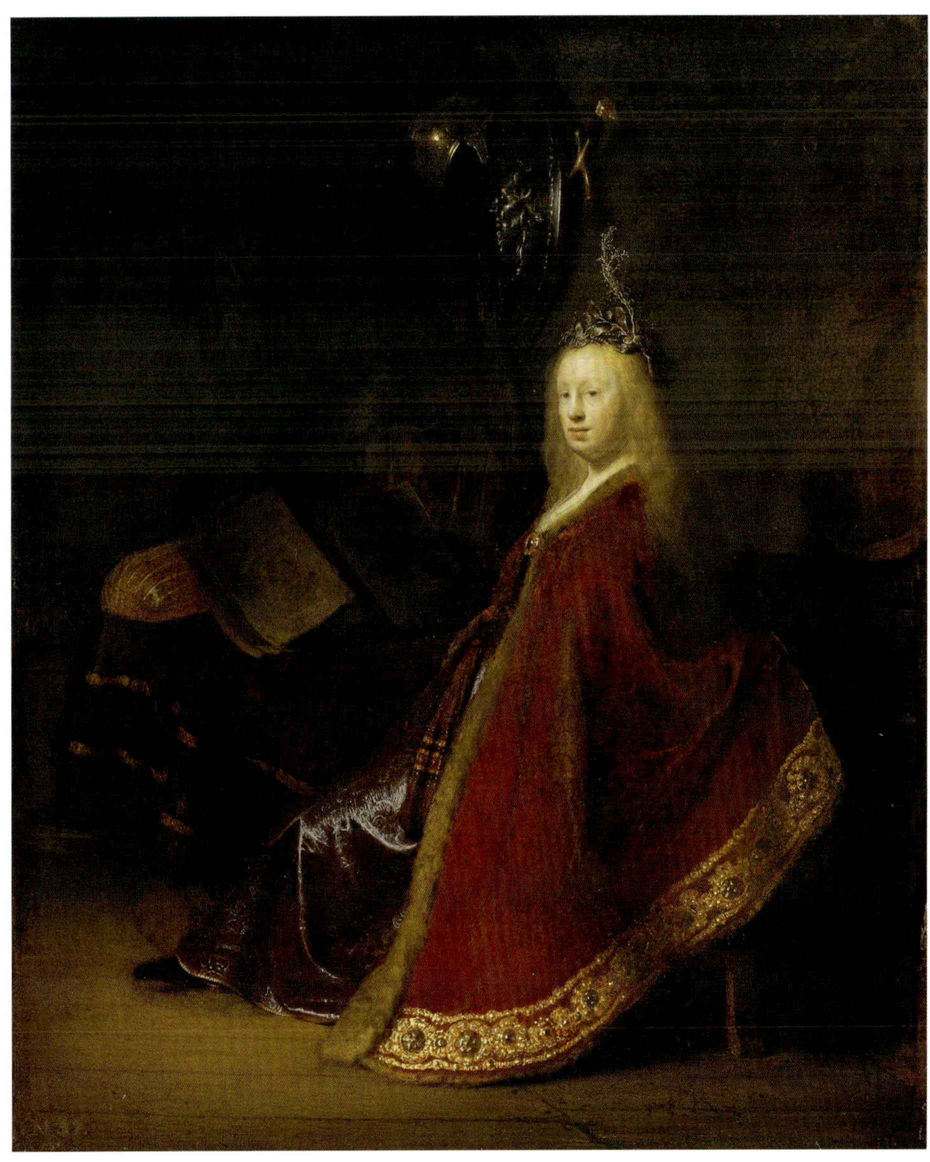

fig. 8.1 **Rembrandt van Rijn,**
Minerva in Her Study, c. 1631,
oil on panel; 60.7 × 49.3 cm.
Staatliche Museen zu Berlin,
Gemäldegalerie (828c)

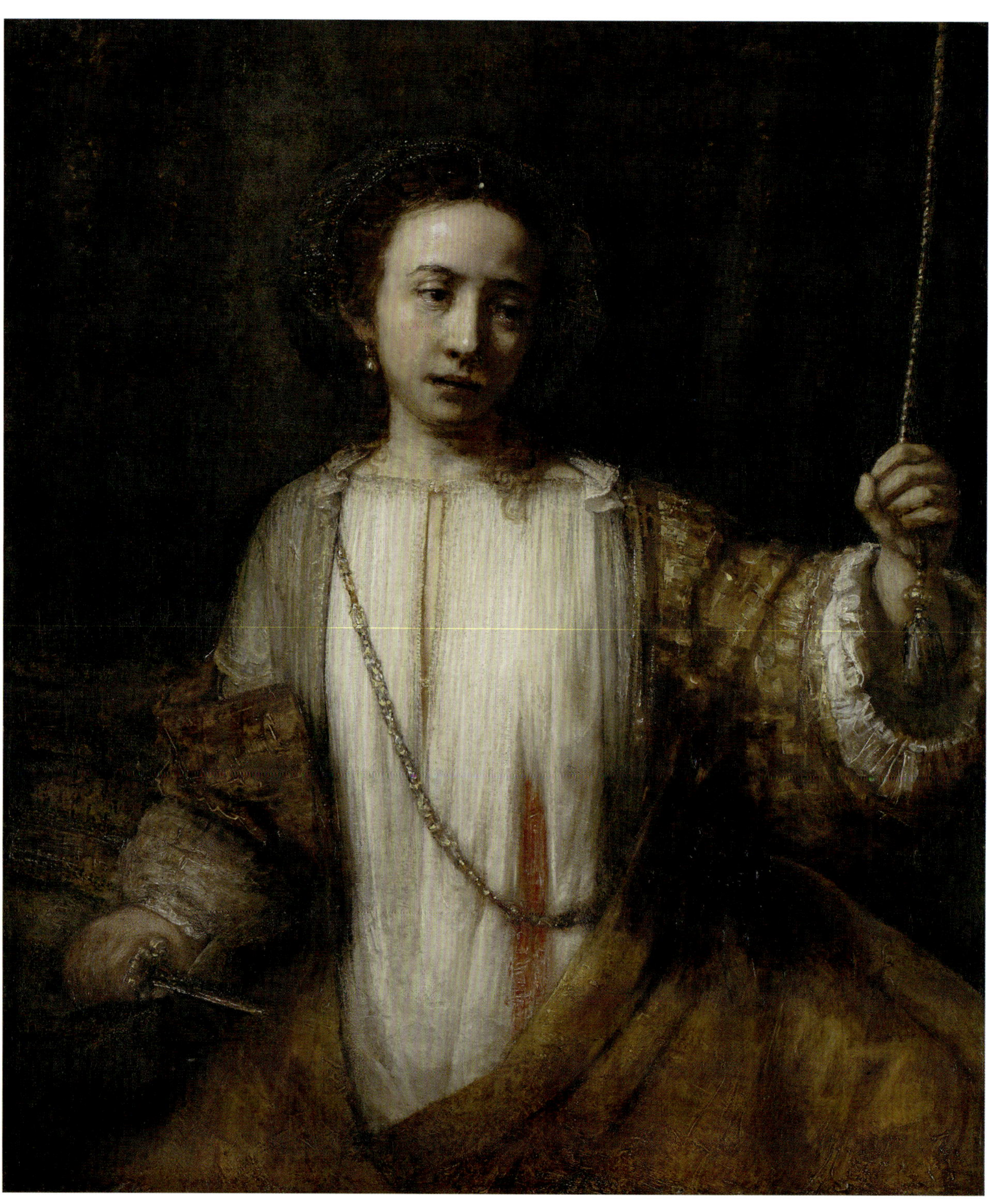

fig. 8.2 **Rembrandt van Rijn,** *Lucretia,* **1666, oil on canvas; 110.2 × 92.3 cm. Minneapolis Institute of Art. The William Hood Dunwoody Fund (34.19)**

Several gorgeously dressed figures in Rembrandt's paintings of the 1630s have resisted identification. Interpretations hinge on material clues. In a monumental canvas of 1634 (pl. 82), a girl offers her mistress a drink in a shell-shaped cup. This may point to the ancient Carthaginian noblewoman Sophonisba, who poisoned herself rather than submit to Roman captivity, or to Artemisia, ruler of ancient Caria, who honoured her deceased husband Mausolus by consuming daily doses of his ashes mixed with wine. An old woman in the background seems to be holding a cloth bag. This might be a reference to the biblical heroine Judith, who, with her maid's help, beheaded the enemy general Holofernes and escaped with his severed head concealed in a sack.[7]

Judith and other biblical heroines prepared for their encounters with powerful men by grooming themselves and dressing in their finest garments.

Esther wore royal robes when persuading her husband, the Persian King Ahasuerus, to spare his Jewish subjects from genocide.[8] For Bathsheba, the toilette itself led to a fateful affair with King David.[9] All of these identifications have been suggested for the woman in Rembrandt's painting from 1632 or 1633 now in the National Gallery of Canada, Ottawa (pl. 85), but none seems conclusive.[10] This work must have been accessible in Amsterdam for some time. Salomon Koninck, although not a member of Rembrandt's inner circle, painted several variants (pl. 84).[11] The ample figure in an etching by Rembrandt from 1635 has also been interpreted as Esther, now holding the document by which Ahasuerus would have ordered the Jews' annihilation (pl. 86). By the early eighteenth century, mystified collectors simply referred to both this figure and the Ottawa heroine as "the Jewish bride."[12]

Rembrandt twice sketched a maid tending the hair of a young woman (pl. 157). This is probably Saskia, observed in private moments following their marriage.[13] These drawings must therefore postdate the Ottawa painting, but the thematic affinity reflects the interplay between imagination and reality that informed Rembrandt's practice as an artist and teacher. In the mid-1640s, his former pupil Ferdinand Bol reimagined the motif of a woman at her toilette, richly dressed in jewels and embroidered velvet (pl. 92).[14] Looking over her shoulder to gaze at herself in a mirror, this figure may embody an allegory of vanity. Glowing colour and glimmering light reflect Bol's debt to Rembrandt while enhancing the seductive atmosphere.

In *Young Woman at a Window* (pl. 88), Jan Victors offers a creative response to the illusionism of Rembrandt's *Self-portrait at the Age of 34*, painted the same year (see fig. 5.6).[15] The motif of a girl leaning through a window proved highly successful. Bol began producing similar figures in historicizing dress (fig. 8.3), and the motif was also adopted for contemporary genre scenes by Nicolaes Maes, Carel Fabritius and others (pl. 151).[16] Rembrandt, too, continued to explore illusionistic effects.[17] In *A Woman in Bed (Sarah Awaiting Tobias)* (pl. 89), the figure's eager gaze suggests that she is Sarah awaiting her bridegroom Tobias, the hero of the Apocryphal Book of Tobit whose adventures were a favourite theme in Rembrandt's circle. The model here may be Geertje Dircks, Titus' nursemaid, whose troubled relationship with Rembrandt ended in 1649.[18]

Rembrandt may have had historical prototypes by Titian or Rubens in mind when he painted Hendrickje Stoffels, his partner in his mature years, wrapped in a soft, fur robe (pl. 91).[19] Yet, this calm, brown-eyed woman seems simply and directly herself. Her warm gaze and relaxed pose convey a quiet intimacy, enhanced by the lush impasto and broad brushwork that herald Rembrandt's late style. At this point in his career, Rembrandt faced strong competition from talented artists such as Backer and Gabriel Metsu who were producing evocative images of women, both portraits and genre subjects, in a more polished style (pl. 90, fig. 8.4).[20]

Rembrandt's fictional characters have a lifelike presence that makes them seem more real than imaginary. Yet, his commissioned portraits were not always enthusiastically received. If a portrait

fig. 8.3 **Ferdinand Bol, *Young Woman at a Window*, c. 1649, oil on canvas (transferred from panel); 100 × 84.5 cm. The State Hermitage Museum, St. Petersburg. Acquired from the Count Baudouin Collection in Paris, 1781 (ГЭ-769)**

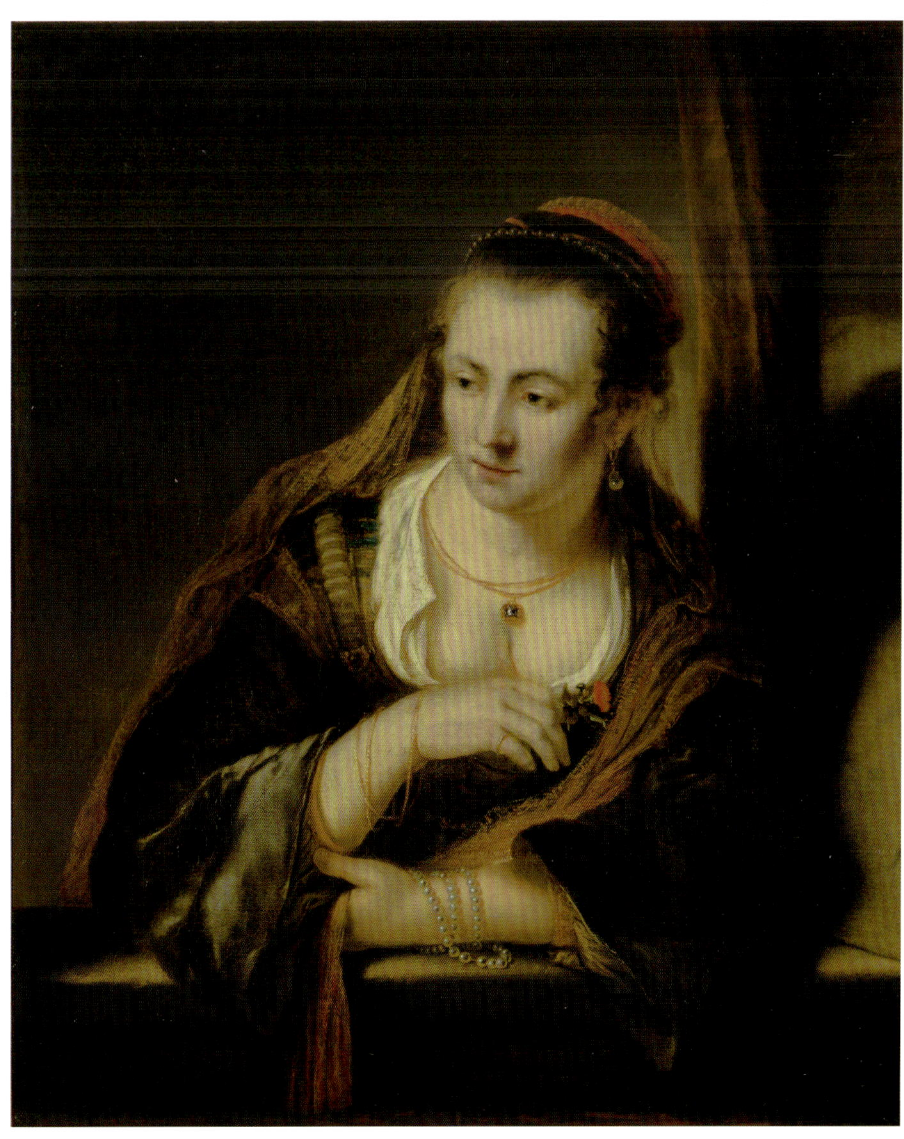

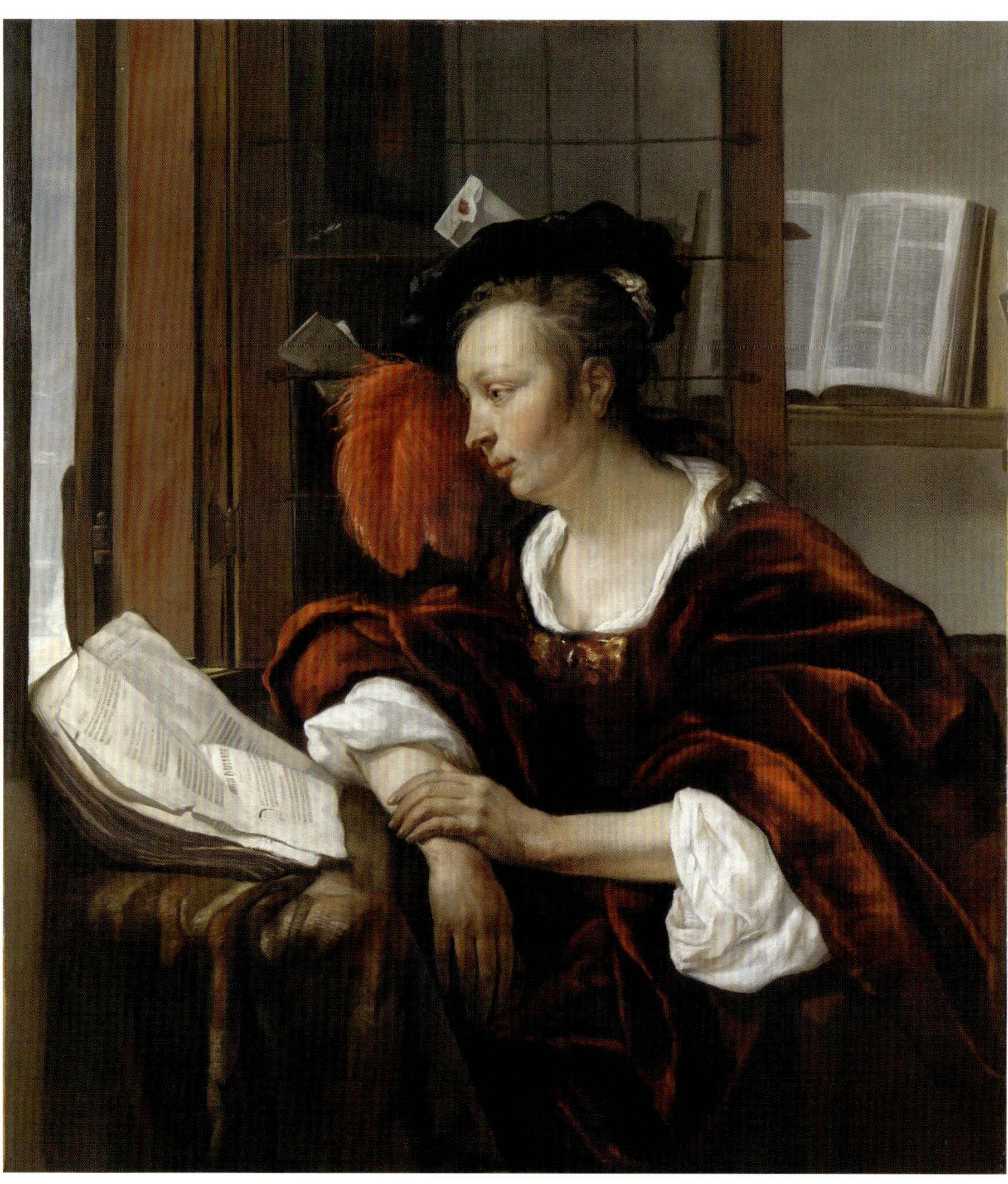

fig. 8.4 Gabriel Metsu, *Woman Reading a Book by a Window*, c. 1653–54, oil on canvas; 105 × 90.7 cm. The Leiden Collection, New York (GM-105)

was refused, he could transform it into a generic figure study for sale. This may be what happened in 1654, when Diego d'Andrade complained that the portrait of a young woman he had ordered from Rembrandt did not look anything like her.[21] The outcome is unknown, but if Rembrandt kept the painting and reworked it, the end result would most likely have been an alluring figure in fantasy dress, perhaps similar to the later *Portrait of a Young Woman (Magdalena van Loo?)* now in the Montreal Museum of Fine Arts (pl. 93). Here, however, the model is probably not a difficult client, but rather Magdalena van Loo, wife of Rembrandt's son, Titus.[22] Once

again, opulent attire transports the figure to the realm of imagination.

Joachim von Sandrart and Arnold Houbraken wrote that art collectors in Rembrandt's milieu took pleasure in visiting each other to discuss and compare their acquisitions. Rather than struggling to identify specific narratives for these images of powerful women, it may be more productive to conclude that Rembrandt and his associates cultivated an intriguing ambiguity, inviting connoisseurs to enjoy debating their meanings.[23] The stories they tell are united by themes of love, death, honour, beauty and courage. ■

NOTES

1   Raleigh, Cleveland and Minneapolis 2011–12, nos. 12, 13; Volker Manuth, "Young Girl in a Gold-trimmed Cloak," in Leiden Collection Catalogue. On costume, see esp. Marieke de Winkel, "Fashion or Fancy? Some Interpretations of the Dress of Rembrandt's Women Re-evaluated," in Edinburgh and London 2001, 55–63; De Winkel 2006.

2   For instance, *Minerva in Her Study* (1635, The Leiden Collection, New York); *Corpus*, vol. 6, no. 139; see Volker Manuth, "Minerva in Her Study," in Leiden Collection Catalogue. See also Isaac de Jouderville's *Minerva in Her Study* (c. 1631, Denver Art Museum); Kingston, Edmonton, Regina and Hamilton 2019–21, no. 13; and Rembrandt's *Bellona* (1633, The Metropolitan Museum of Art, New York); *Corpus*, vol. 6, no. 101; Edinburgh and London 2001, no. 26; Madrid 2008, no. 14. See also Vienna 2004, 176–186.

3   *Corpus*, vol. 6, no. 314; Edinburgh and London 2001, no. 141. Another version is in the National Gallery of Art, Washington; see www.nga.gov/collection/art-object-page.83.html (accessed 26 Feb. 2020). See, among others, Sluijter 2006; Dickey 2010.

4   *Flora* (1634, The State Hermitage Museum, St. Petersburg), *Corpus*, vol. 6, no. 125; *Saskia van Uylenburgh in Arcadian Costume* (1635, The National Gallery, London), *Corpus*, vol. 6, no. 138; Edinburgh and London 2001, nos. 27, 36. X-rays reveal that the London version began as Judith with the head of Holofernes. Painted a few years later, *Saskia with a Flower* (Gemäldegalerie, Dresden; *Corpus*, vol. 6, no. 181) may depict Saskia as Glycera, beloved of the ancient painter Pausias; see Stephanie S. Dickey, "Saskia as Glycera: Rembrandt's Emulation of an Antique Prototype," in Boschloo et al. 2011, 233–247.

5   Gerard van Honthorst, *Amalia von Solms as Flora* (c. 1629–30, Gotisches Haus, Wörlitz); Stephanie S. Dickey, "Rembrandt and Saskia: Art, Commerce and the Poetics of Portraiture," in Chong and Zell 2002, 17–47.

6   Rembrandt noted on the verso of a drawing from c. 1634–37 (Kupferstichkabinett, Berlin) that he sold several student works, including a "Flora" by Bol and one by Van Beijeren. Priced at only a few guilders each, they must have been copies or drawings; Strauss and Van der Meulen 1979, 594–595. On Backer, see Van den Brink 2016, 24–26.

7   Judith 13: 7–10; see esp. *Corpus*, vol. 6, no. 128; Golahny 2000, 129–133; Madrid 2008, no. 18; Cruz Yábar 2013.

8   Judith 10: 1–4; Esther 5:1. For interpretation, see esp. Kahr 1966; Perlove and Silver 2009, 137–147.

9   2 Samuel 11. See esp. Rembrandt van Rijn, *Bathsheba at Her Bath* (1654, Musée du Louvre, Paris), *Corpus*, vol. 6, no. 231. For interpretation, see esp. Adams 1998; Sluijter 2006, 341–368; Perlove and Silver 2009, 120–126.

10 *Corpus*, vol. 2, no. A64, vol. 5, 271–275, vol. 6, no. 100; Kahr 1966; Edinburgh and London 2001, no. 20; Madrid 2008, no. 11; Perlove and Silver 2009, 142–143; Paris 2016–17, no. 21; Schwartz 1985, 168.

11 Identified by Sumowski 1983–94, vol. 3, 1632, as Esther, formerly as Bathsheba; variant in North Carolina Museum of Art, Raleigh, ibid., no. 1079; see also ibid., nos. 1086, 1087. On Koninck and Rembrandt, see Sluijter 2006, 344; Sluijter 2015, 199–213.

12 NHD 154; a preparatory drawing is in the Nationalmuseum, Stockholm. See also *Saskia as St. Catherine* (1638), nicknamed "The Little Jewish Bride"; NHD 169; Edinburgh and London 2001, nos. 32–35, 74; Hinterding 2008, 573–579. For references to the Ottawa painting in early sale records, see https://rkd.nl/nl/explore/images/record?query=Rembrandt+ottawa&start=0 (accessed 29 Feb. 2020).

13 See also *A Woman Having Her Hair Combed*, pen and ink with wash (Collection Frits Lugt, Institut Néerlandais, Paris); Edinburgh and London 2001, nos. 29, 30; *Corpus*, vol. 2, 273.

14 Blankert 1982, 139, no. 127, rightly disputes the earlier identification of the figure as Saskia; see Montreal and Toronto 1969, no. 23; Judson 1969, 704.

15 Sumowski 1983–94, vol. 4, no. 1785. As argued by Sluijter 2015, 362–373, Victors must have observed Rembrandt's art from outside his studio.

16 Arthur K. Wheelock, Jr., attributes *Girl with a Broom* to Fabritius; www.nga.gov/collection/art-object-page.81.html#entry (accessed 29 Feb. 2020). See also, for instance, Nicolaes Maes, *Girl at a Window, Known as "The Day Dreamer"* (c. 1650–60, Rijksmuseum, Amsterdam); London and The Hague 2019–20, no. 6.

17 In addition to portraits, see, for instance, Rembrandt van Rijn, *Girl in a Fanciful Costume in a Picture Frame* (1641, Royal Castle, Warsaw), *Corpus*, vol. 6, no. 186; and *Girl at a Window* (*The Kitchen Maid*) (1651, Nationalmuseum, Stockholm), *Corpus*, vol. 6, no. 220.

18 *Corpus*, vol. 6, no. 194; Edinburgh and London 2011, no. 100. Scholars point to a related figure in Pieter Lastman's *Wedding Night of Tobias and Sarah* (1611, Museum of Fine Arts, Boston). For a measured account of Rembrandt's relationship with Geertje Dircks, see Sebastien A.C. Dudok van Heel, "Rembrandt: His Life, His Wife, the Nursemaid and the Servant," in Edinburgh and London 2001, 19–27. For Tobias, see the essay "Angelic Messengers" by Stephanie S. Dickey in this volume.

19 *Corpus* 6, no. 223; Edinburgh and London 2001, no. 125. X-rays show that the arms were first folded across the lap, a pose developed later in *Portrait of Hendrickje Stoffels* (c. 1659, Städel Museum, Frankfurt am Main), *Corpus*, vol. 6, no. 277. Rembrandt is unlikely to have known Peter Paul Rubens' *The Little Fur* (*Het Pelsken*) (1638, Kunsthistorisches Museum, Vienna); rather, both artists admired Titian. In 1639 both Rembrandt and Joachim von Sandrart must have seen a Titian *Flora* in the Amsterdam collection of Alphonso Lopez; Sandrart dedicated a reproductive print after it to his cousin Michel LeBlon; Dickey 2004, 100–104.

20 For Backer, see Amsterdam and Aachen 2008–09, esp. 245, no. A120. Metsu moved to Amsterdam in mid-1654; this large-format painting shows awareness of similar works by Rembrandt, Bol and Backer; see Adriaan Waiboer, "Woman Reading a Book by a Window," in Leiden Collection Catalogue, with further references.

21 Strauss and Van der Meulen 1979, doc. 1654/4. D'Andrade was probably a member of the Portuguese Jewish community in Amsterdam. See also the essay by Jasper Hillegers in this volume. There are numerous cases of generic subjects painted over portraits, for instance, *An Old Man in Military Costume* (c. 1630–31, The J. Paul Getty Museum, Los Angeles; here, Rembrandt turned the panel and started over), *Corpus*, vol. 6, no. 56.

22 *Corpus*, vol. 6, no. 318.

23 Sandrart 1675–80, vol. 1, *Lebenslauf*, 12, describes the German master's skill at artful conversation; Houbraken 1718–21, vol. 2, 23, writes of Flinck's exchange of visits with fellow art lovers including Jan Wtenbogaert and Jan Six; Dickey 2004, 75, 102. On calculated ambiguity, see also Sluijter 2006, 344.

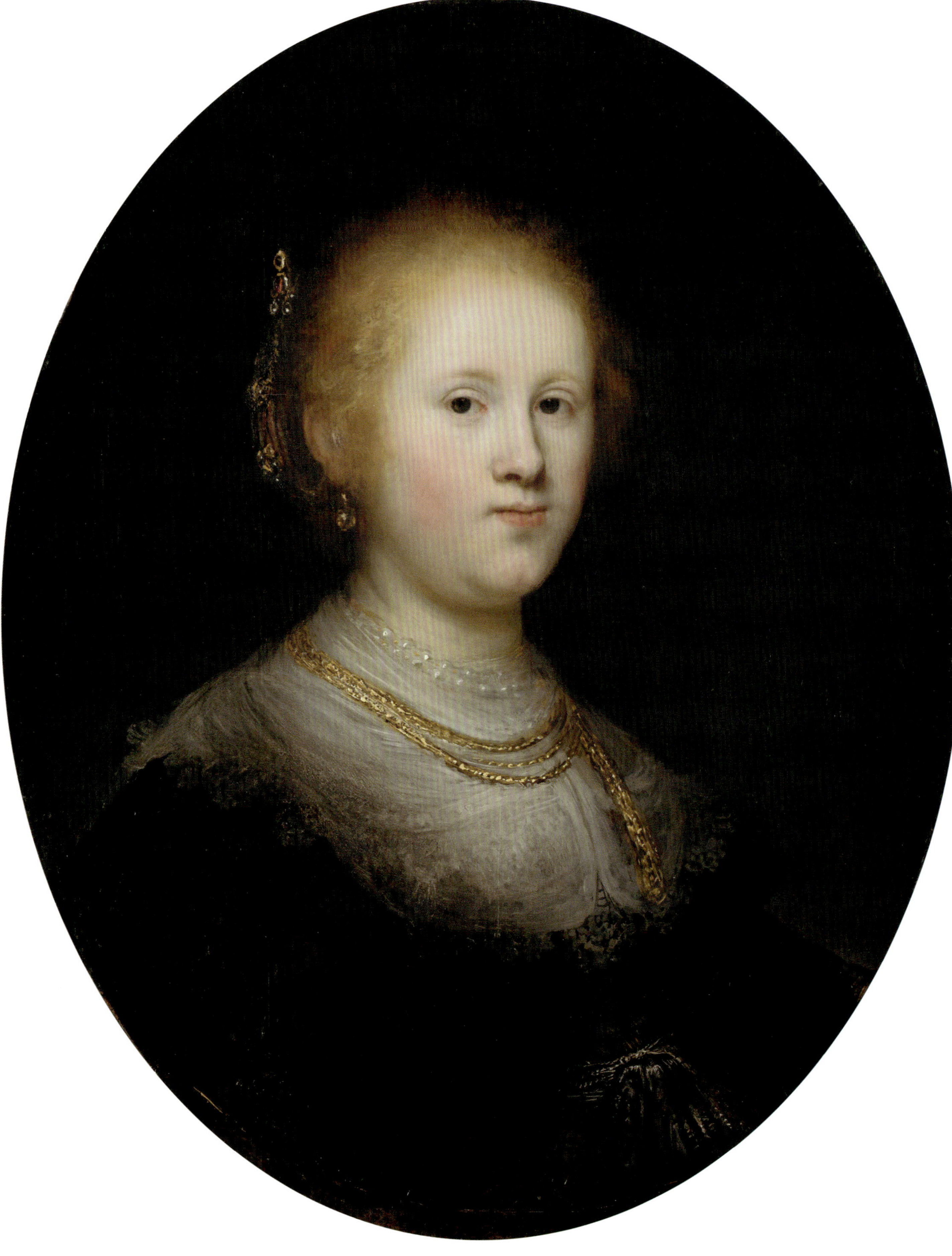

Rembrandt van Rijn, *Portrait of a Young Woman*, 1632. Allentown Art Museum

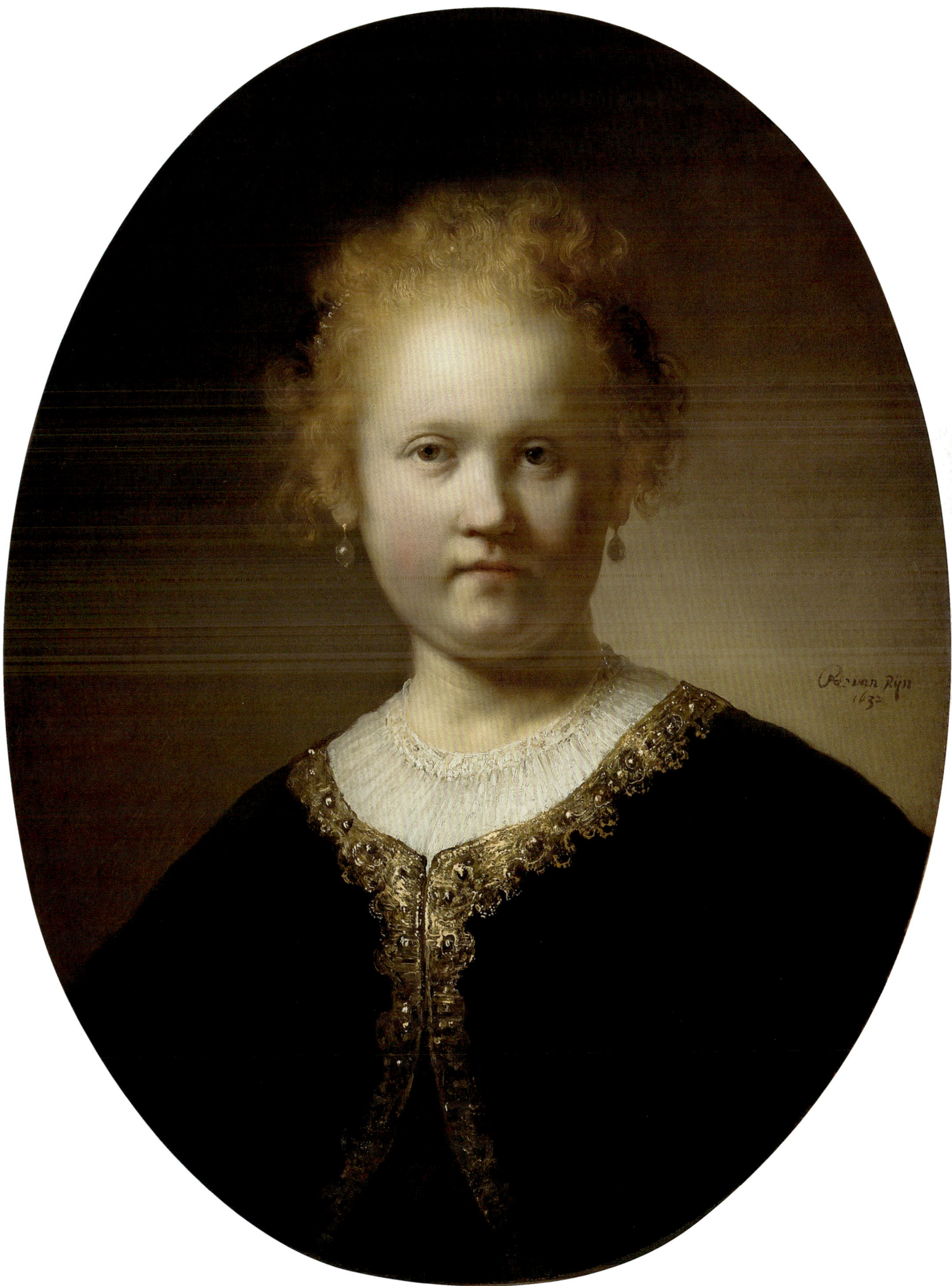

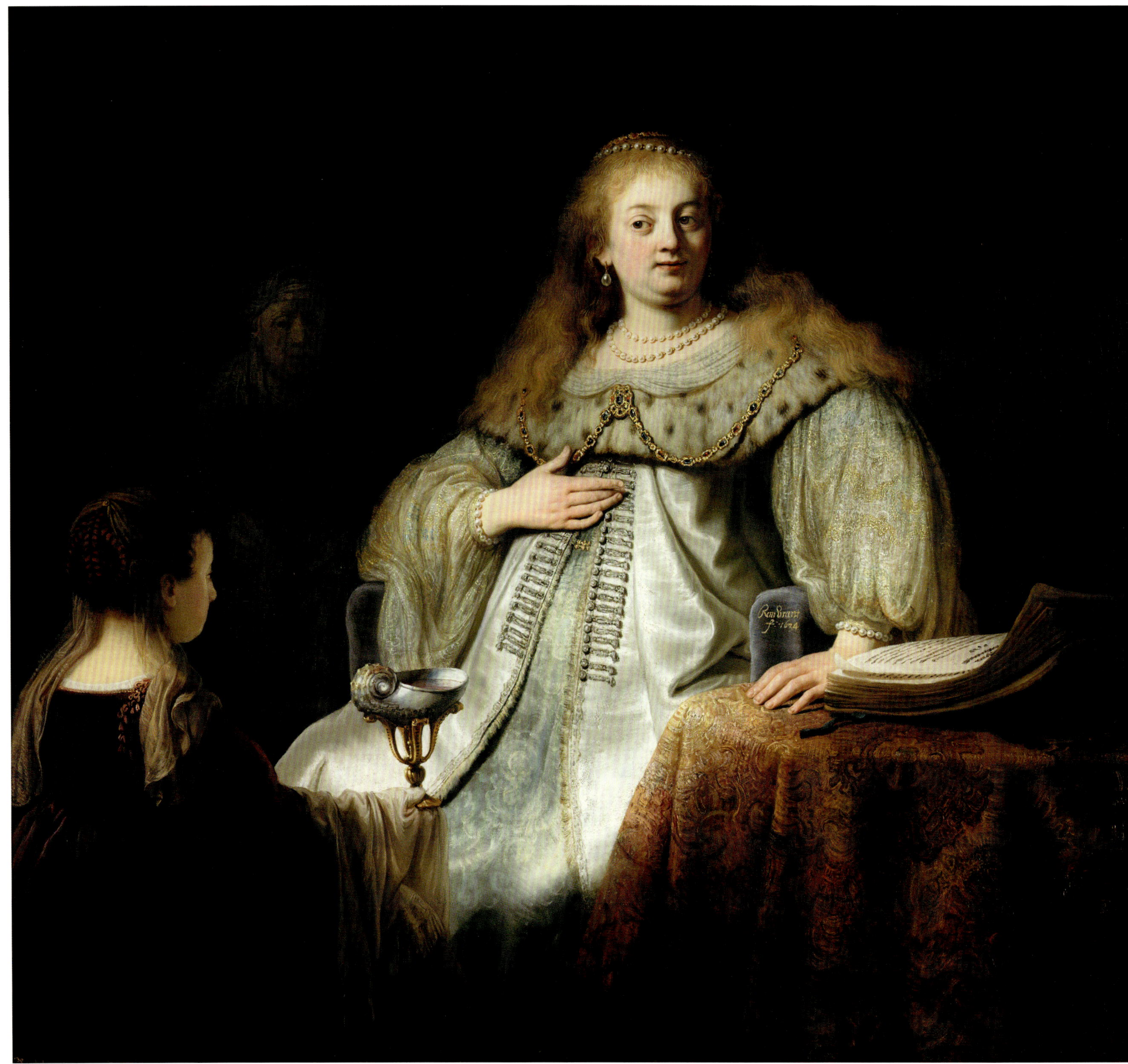

82　Rembrandt van Rijn, *Judith at the Banquet of Holofernes (formerly Artemisia)*, 1634. Museo Nacional del Prado, Madrid

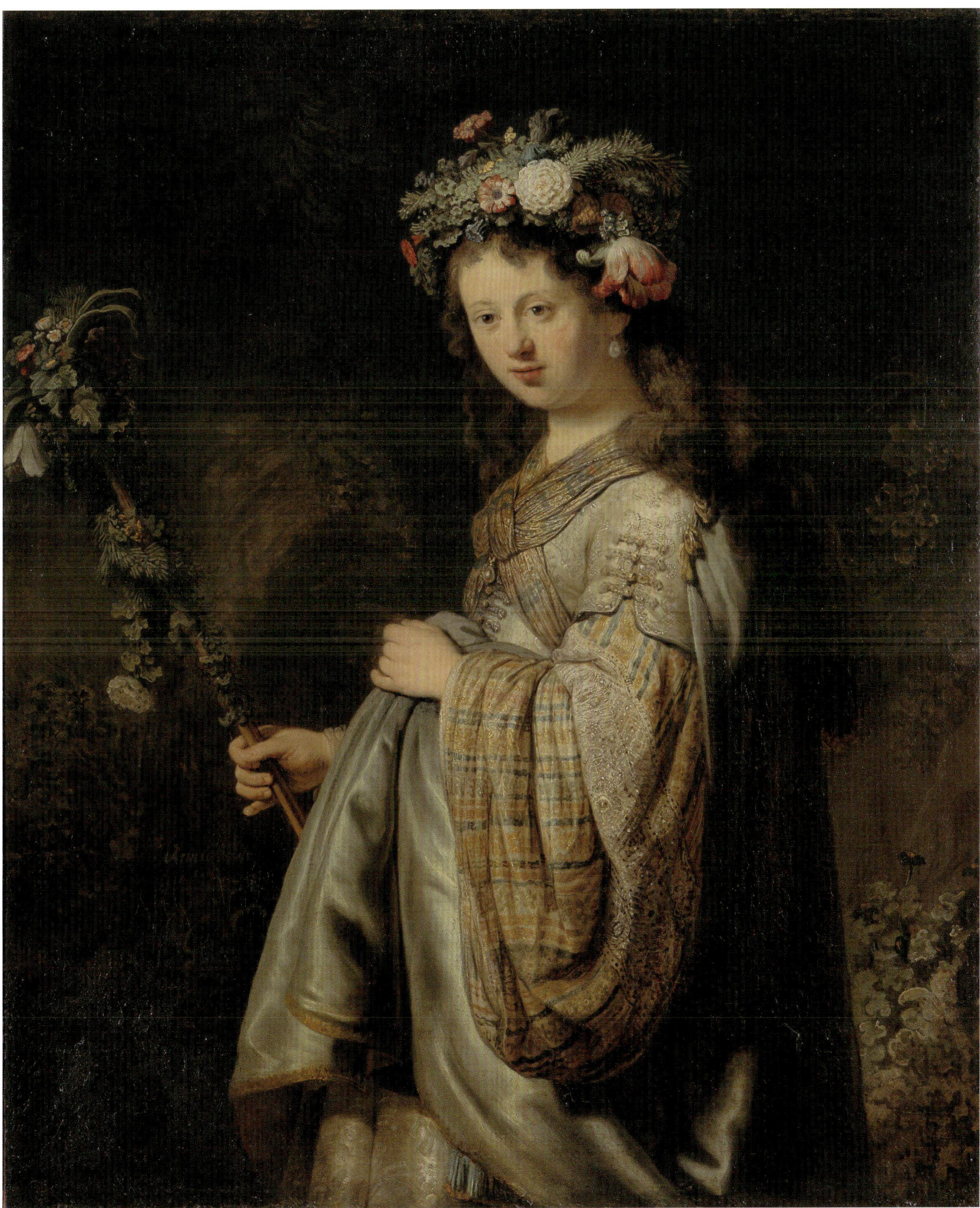

84 Salomon Koninck, *Esther Reading the Decree of the Extermination of the Jews*, 1630s. National Gallery of Denmark, Copenhagen

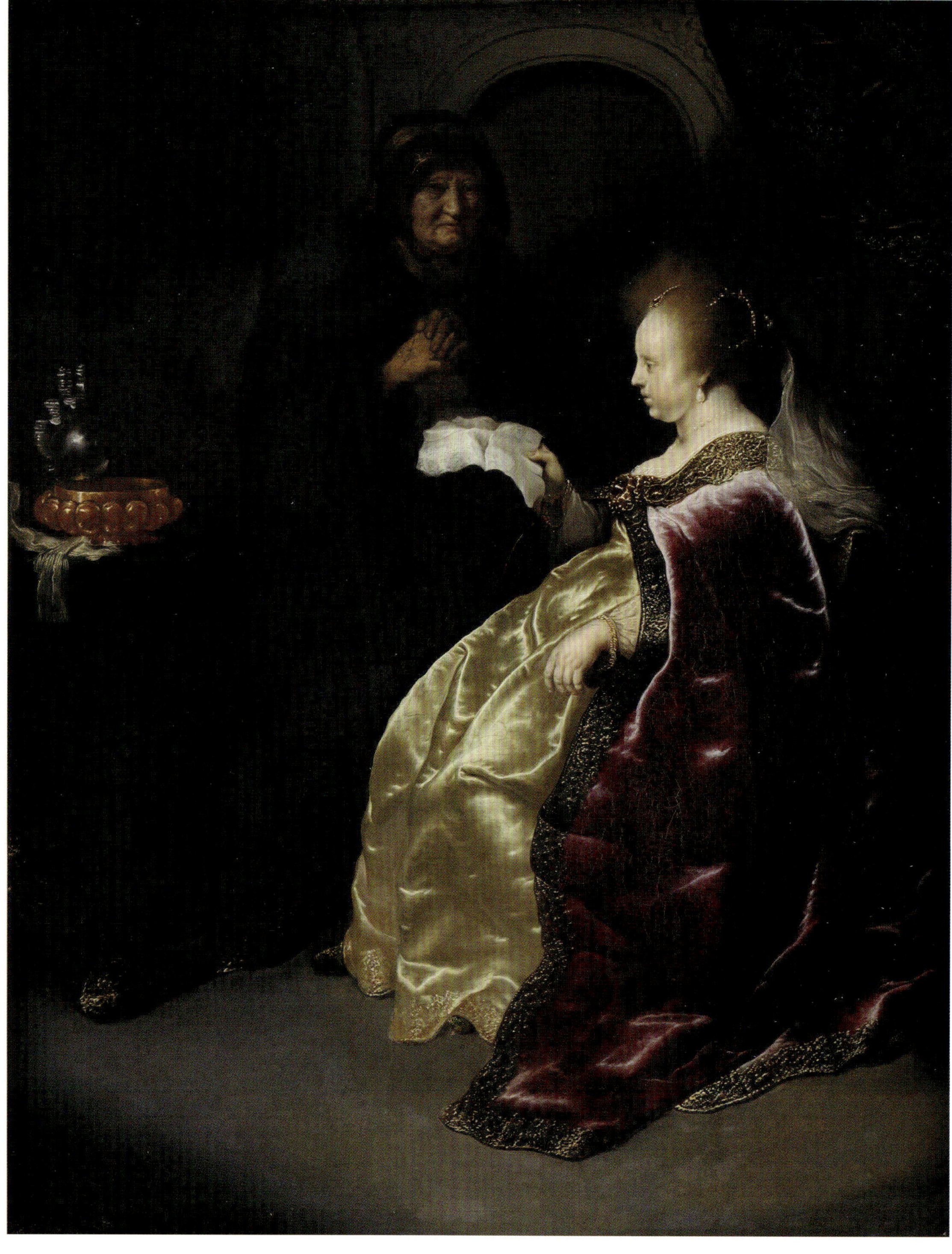

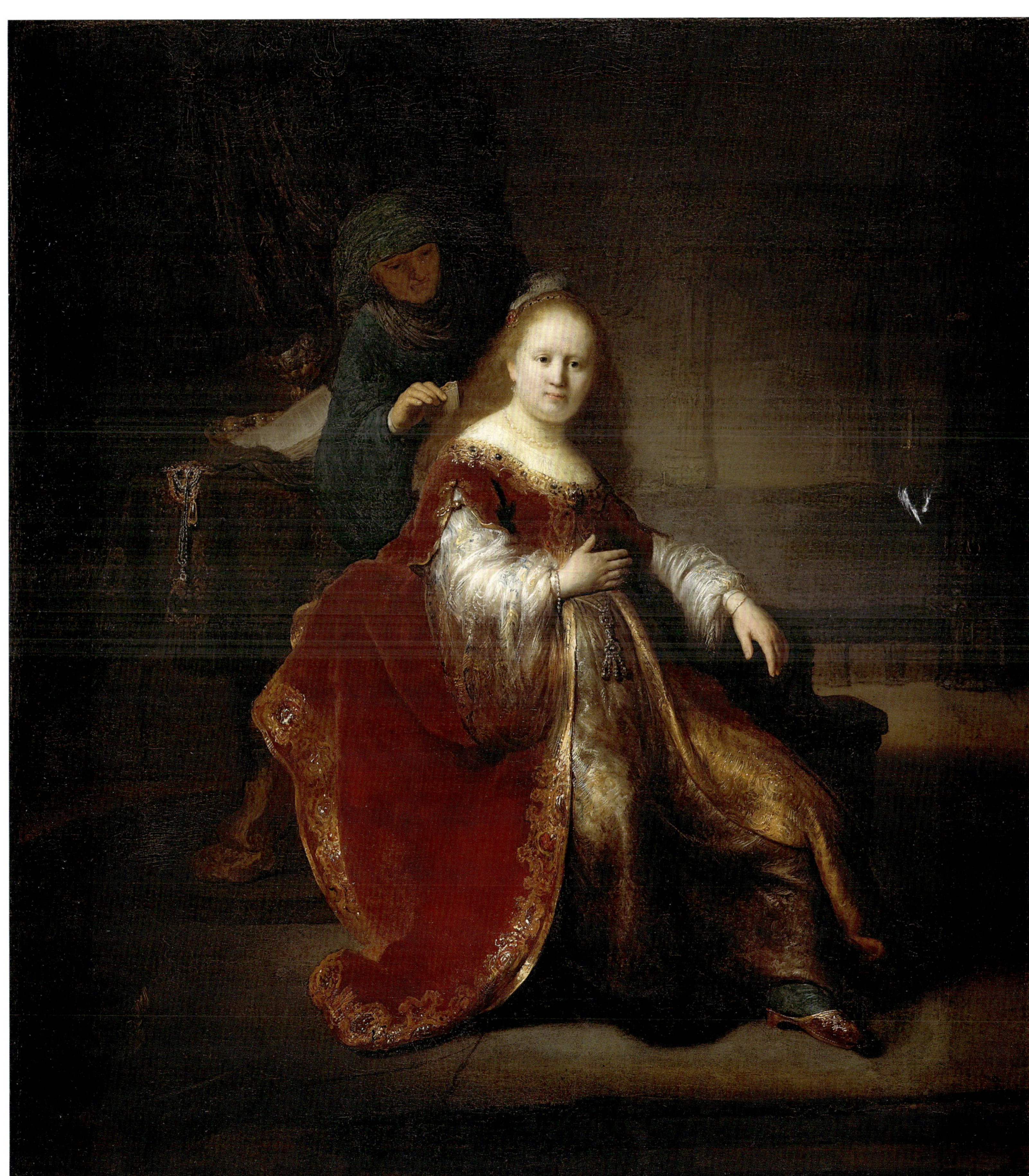

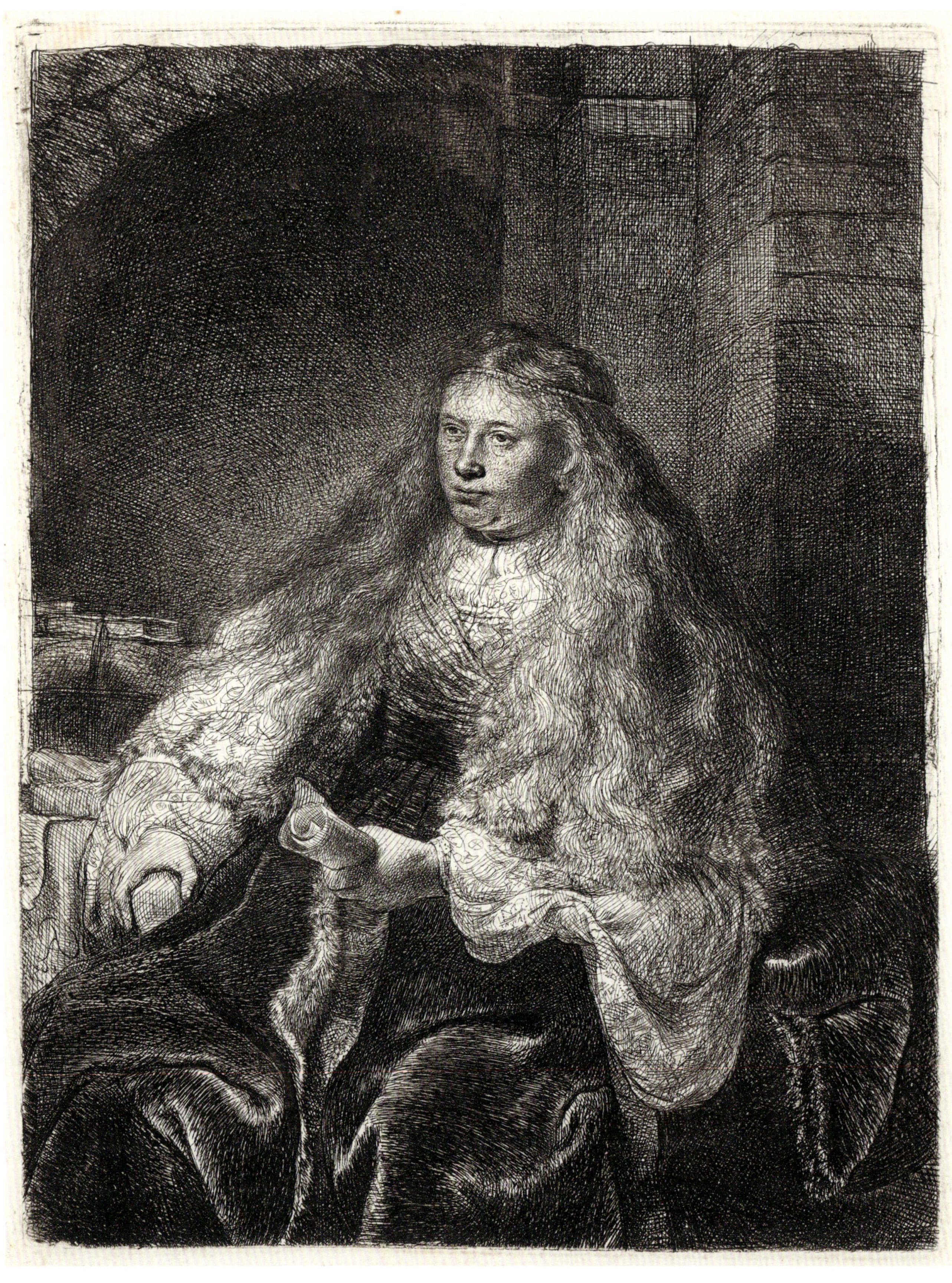

86 Rembrandt van Rijn, *The Great Jewish Bride*, 1635. Städel Museum, Frankfurt am Main

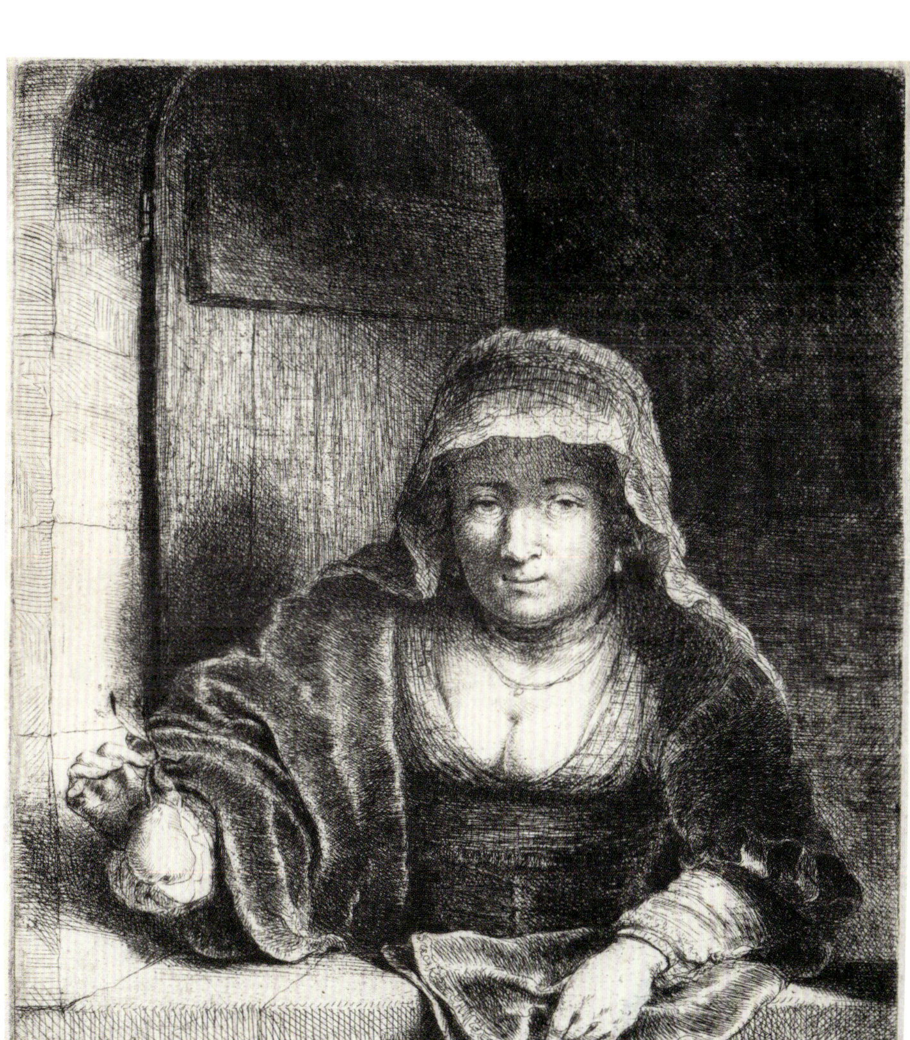

88   Jan Victors, *Young Woman at a Window*, 1640. Musée du Louvre, Paris

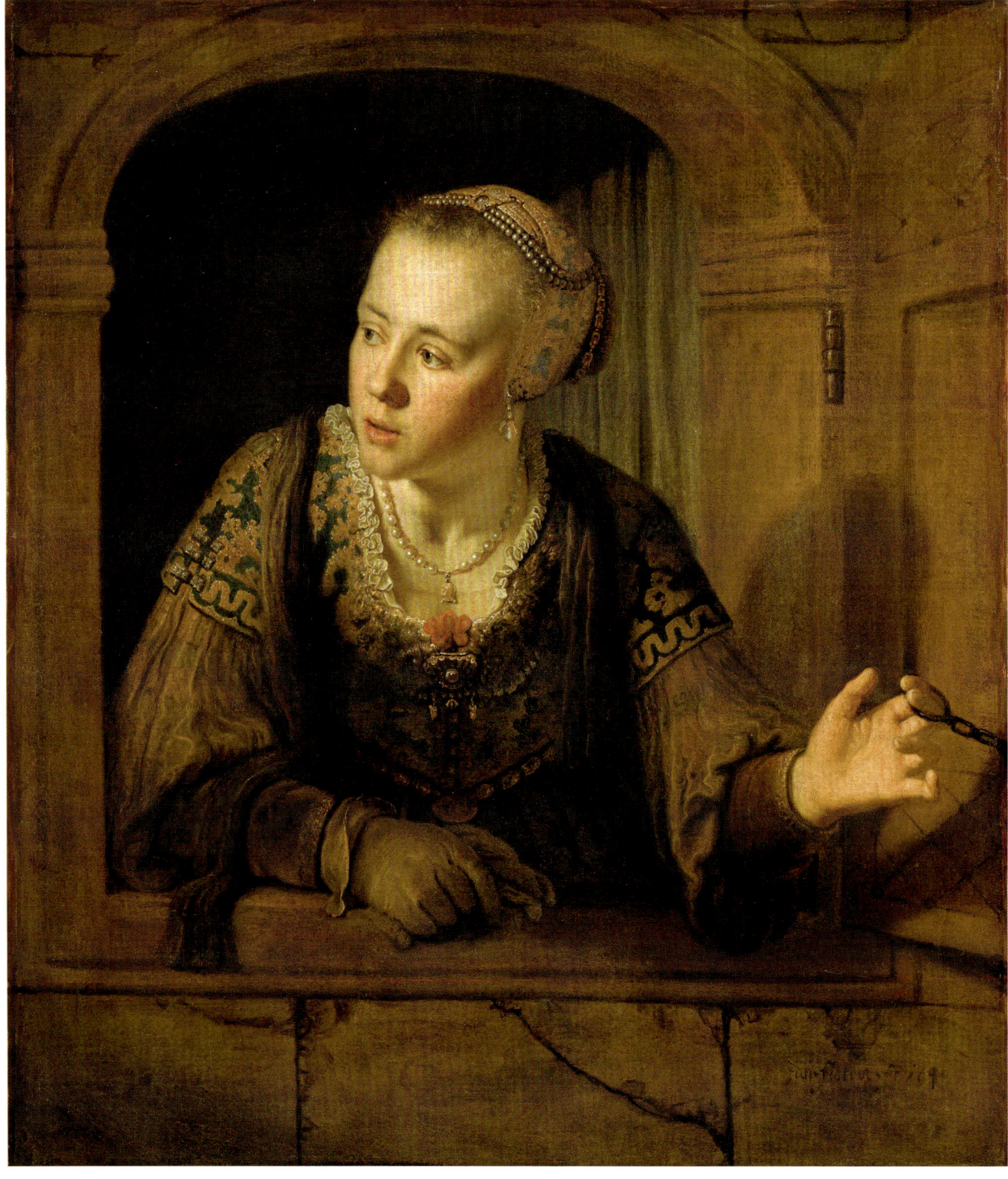

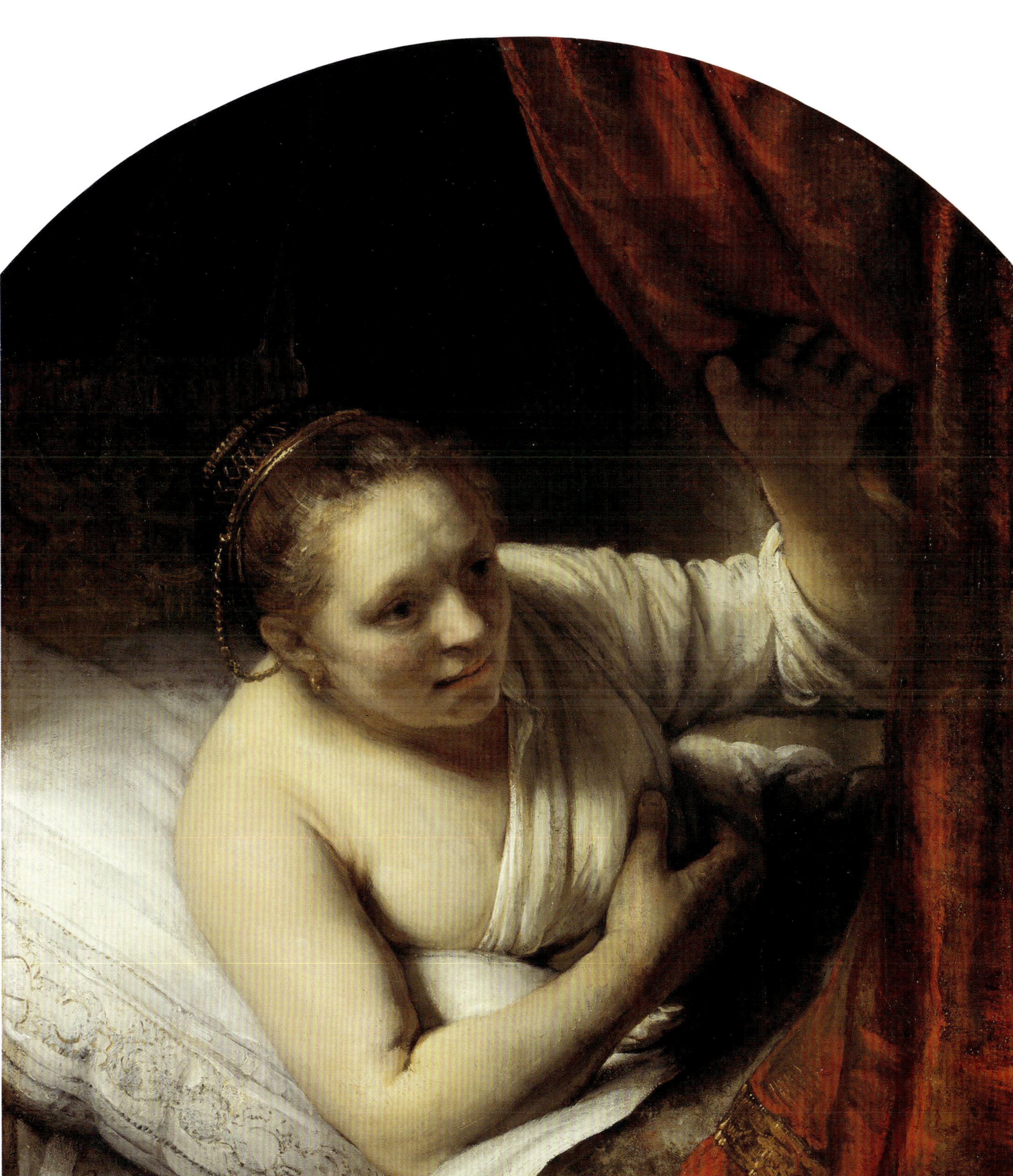

90   Jacob Backer, *Portrait of a Woman*, c. 1647. The J. Paul Getty Museum, Los Angeles

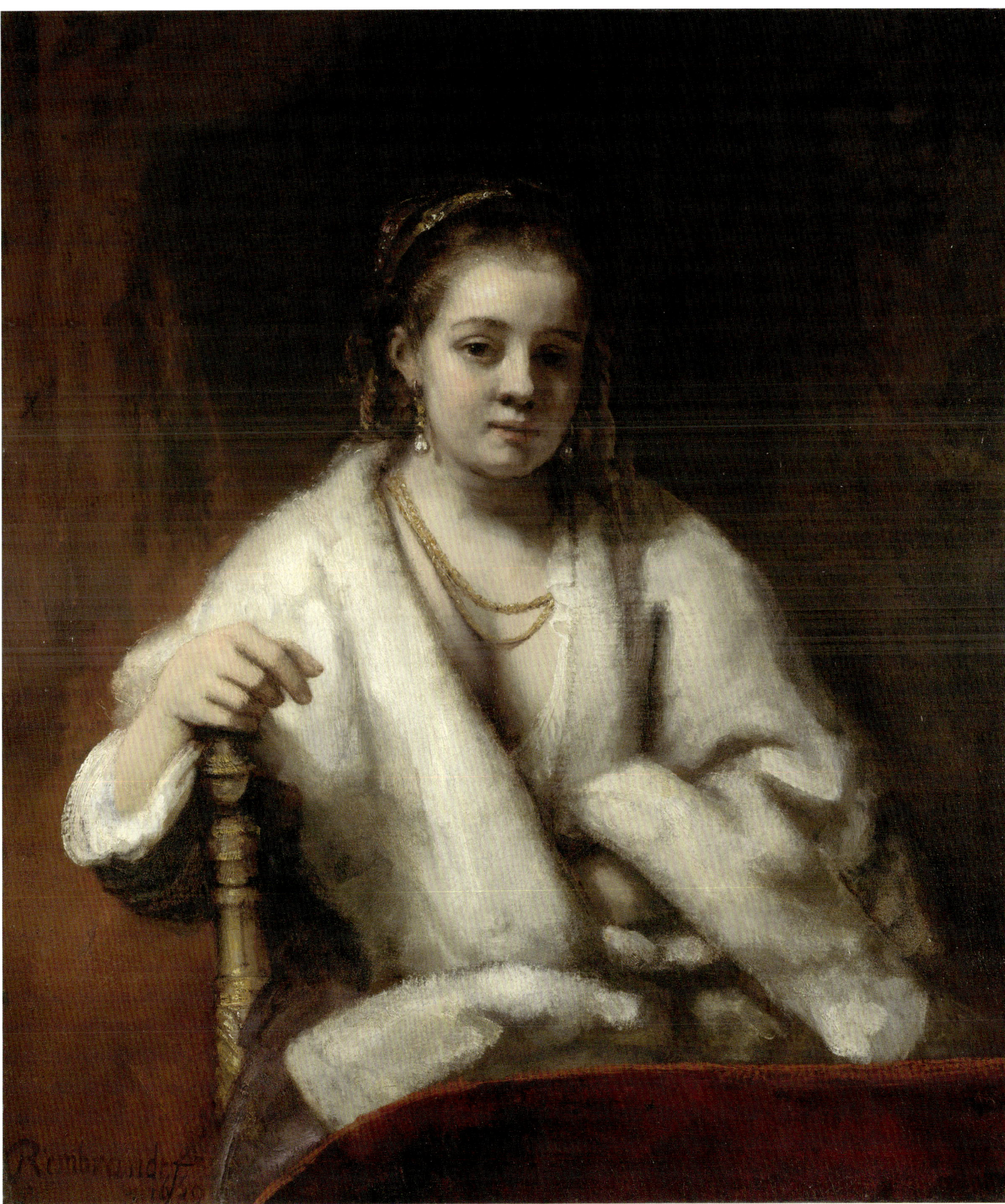

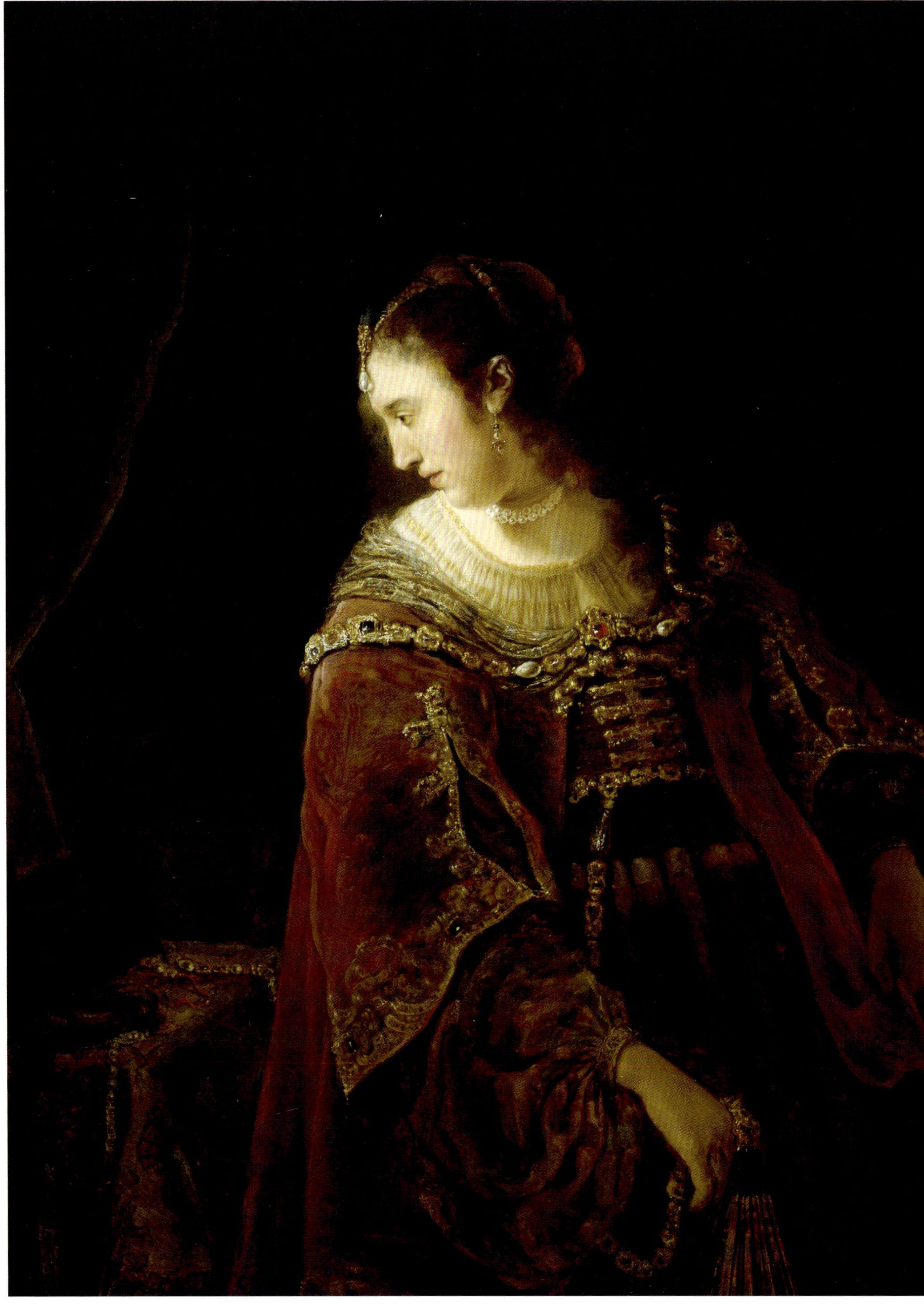

92　Ferdinand Bol, *Woman at Her Dressing Table*, c. 1645. The Museum of Fine Arts, Houston

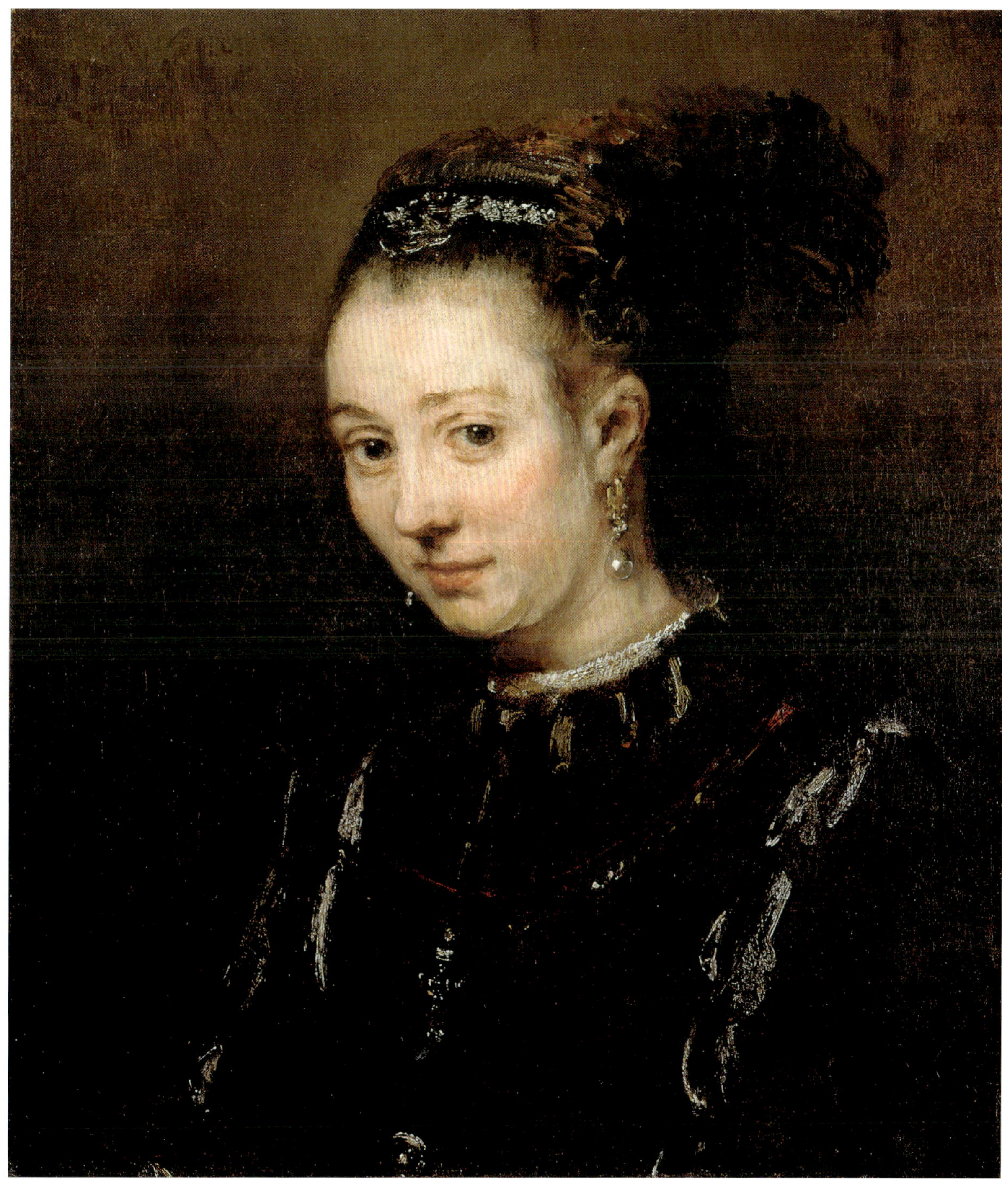

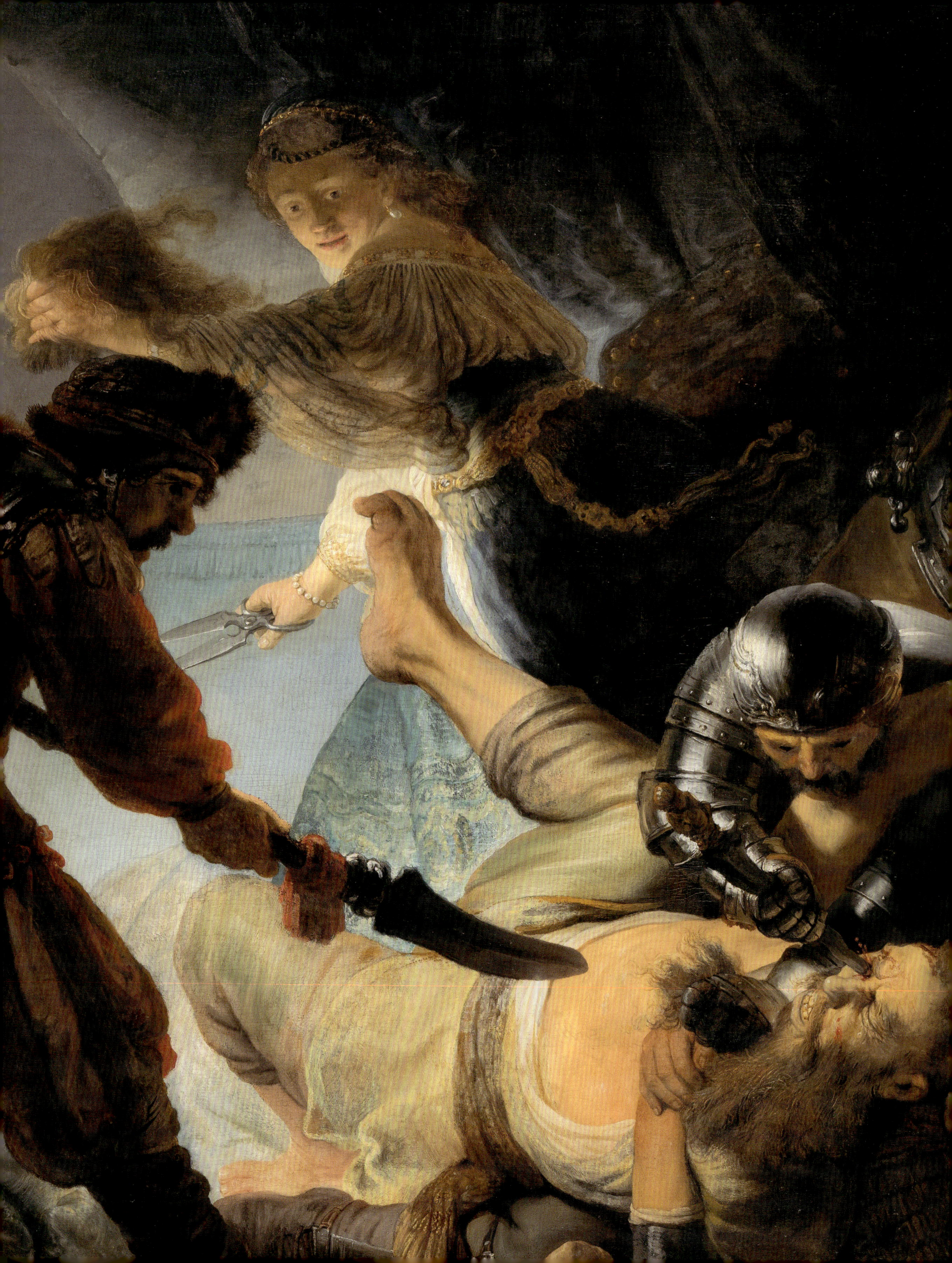

F R I E D E R I K E   S C H Ü T T

Illustrious Histories

After leaving Hendrick Uylenburgh's workshop in 1635, Rembrandt set portraiture aside for several years, refocusing on history painting, which he had already pursued successfully during his time in Leiden.[1] He had previously demonstrated his skills and ambition in this most prestigious of genres with outstanding cabinet pictures, as well as two paintings for a series on the Passion of Christ for Stadtholder Frederik Hendrik. Adopting elements from these earlier works, but heightening the emotional pitch, Rembrandt created scenes with life-size figures and dramatic chiaroscuro. He measured himself not just against the many highly skilled history painters in Amsterdam but also against renowned international artists such as Anthony van Dyck and Jusepe de Ribera, whose works he could study in Amsterdam collections.[2]

At this time, the history paintings of Rembrandt's former teacher Pieter Lastman, who had died in 1633, were regarded as highly innovative. After returning from Rome to Amsterdam in 1607, Lastman had laid the foundation for the development of this genre, to which he contributed many paintings.[3] Distilling decisive moments from well-known and less familiar stories from the bible, classical mythology and history, his compositions compressed the narrative into a readily accessible pictorial form, often with numerous, dramatically gesturing figures (pl. 19). Artists in Lastman's circle, such as Claes Moeyaert, who would later be known as "Pre-Rembrandtists," continued working in Lastman's style until the 1650s, offering popular alternatives to the history paintings created in Rembrandt's workshop (fig. 9.1).[4] For Rembrandt and the following generation of artists, Lastman's works continued to be important models that stimulated emulation and advancement.[5]

Following the rules of rhetoric, visual representations of familiar stories should stir the viewer, give pleasure and provide moral instruction.[6] Effective pictorial narrative depended above all on convincing representation of figures and their emotions. Artists could best convey the development and essence of a story by focusing on a turning point in the narrative when emotions reached a climax. A novel source of inspiration for Rembrandt and others was contemporary theatre with its dramatic staging and colourful costumes.[7]

Throughout the Dutch Republic, the market for historical subjects was declining in favour of accessible themes such as landscape, but both the demand for history painting and the number of artists producing it were especially high in Amsterdam.[8] The city became a magnet for artists seeking commissions and fame in this field.[9] History paintings were even mass-produced, so that by 1678 Samuel van Hoogstraten noted that "illustrious histories are a dime a dozen."[10] His observation offers an insight into the quantity and diversity of paintings that potential buyers could choose from, including those who could not afford the work of distinguished masters such as Rembrandt, nor even the copies and variants sold from his workshop.[11]

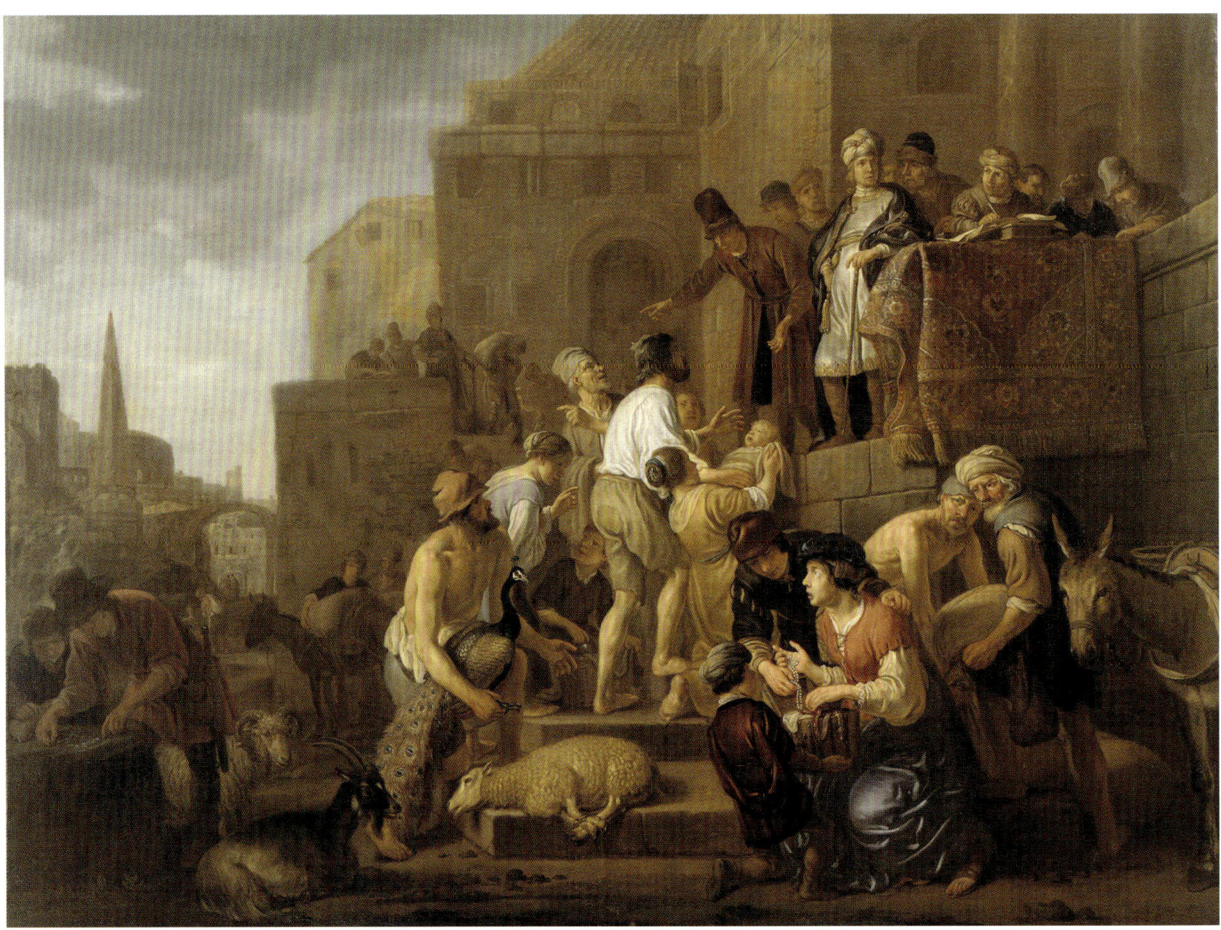

fig. 9.1 **Claes Cornelisz Moeyaert,** *Joseph Selling Grain in Egypt,* 1650, oil on canvas; 136 × 179 cm. Agnes Etherington Art Centre, Queen's University, Kingston. Gift of Dr. and Mrs. Alfred Bader, 1980 (23-038)

The market for history painting reflected considerable variation in price and quality. At the bottom end of the market, history paintings could be purchased for under four guilders.[12] While Rembrandt occupied the very top bracket, prices for his works varied considerably. In the 1657 estate inventory of the prominent art dealer Johannes de Renialme, for instance, Rembrandt's luminous *Christ and the Woman Taken in Adultery* (fig. 9.2) was valued at 1,500 guilders, far higher than any other painting in stock, yet a "Mary and Joseph by Rembrandt van Rijn" was valued at only 136 guilders. However, the latter may well have been a workshop product completed by a student and sold under the Rembrandt brand.[13] Joachim von Sandrart in turn received 280 guilders for an impressive chimney piece depicting Odysseus and Nausicaa (see fig. 5.11), painted around 1642 for the future burgomaster Joan Huydecoper.[14]

There is no strict correlation between subject preferences and the religious denomination of the artist or buyer, especially at the upper end of the market, where aesthetic appreciation would have balanced devotional interest. Many biblical themes were appreciated across denominations. While some artists such as Jan Victors, Gerbrand van den Eeckhout, Ferdinand Bol and Bartholomeus Breenbergh produced primarily Old Testament scenes, Rembrandt's body of prints and paintings is stronger in New Testament subjects. Potential buyers seem to have known from which artist they could purchase paintings that were appropriate for their faith.[15]

The popularity of Old Testament scenes in Amsterdam is striking compared to other European centres of the time. This may be linked to new ways of interpreting biblical stories, which were no longer read primarily as prefigurations of the life and Passion of Christ. Instead, focus shifted to the fates of the protagonists depicted and how their stories conveyed moral values and a framework of guidance for everyday situations and experiences. Furthermore, to understand them did not require a humanist education.[16] Artists often focused on heroines such as Judith or

Esther (pls. 82, 84), or moments of divine intervention featuring angelic messengers.[17] Painted in cabinet size, these depictions were desirable, decorative and collectible objects for wealthy burghers.[18]

Old Testament and historical scenes could also be found in public spaces, where they alluded to political events or the function of the room in which they were placed. The fierce competition between Amsterdam history painters can be seen clearly in public commissions for the adornment of government or other public buildings.[19] Rembrandt reached the peak of his success in 1642 with his famous group portrait known as *The Night Watch* (see fig. 1.9), created for the Kloveniersdoelen (musketeers' civic-guard hall). In the mid-1650s, two of his former pupils, Govert Flinck and Ferdinand Bol, were commissioned to decorate the most prestigious rooms of the new Amsterdam town hall. Their manner of history painting, shaped by Rembrandt in the 1630s, initially imitated the master's approach to colour and form with great success, but over the following years they increasingly adopted a more Italianate style. Their palette became lighter and brighter, and their figures, poses and gestures more reminiscent of Lastman's narrative visual language.[20] In some respects, however, their depictions still owed a debt to Rembrandt. For example, Bol's monumental chimney piece for the Council Chamber in the town hall, worked out in a lively *modello* (pls. 94, 95), features costumes and character types that resemble those in Rembrandt's biblical paintings (pls. 34, 106).

Based on a story told by the ancient historian Plutarch, Bol's painting shows a moment during the peace talks between King Pyrrhus of Epirus and the Roman Consul Gaius Fabricius Luscinus, who had lost the war against Pyrrhus. After Fabricius had rejected the terms demanded by Pyrrhus and could not be bribed with offers of gold, Pyrrhus threatened him with an elephant, a frightening beast unknown to Fabricius. When Fabricius remained steadfast, Pyrrhus released the Roman prisoners. In the painting, the Roman Consul points at the elephant, visibly unimpressed. Bol designed the composition with a low vantage point, directing the viewer's gaze up the stairs to the figures recoiling from the elephant, and finally to the hero of the story. In the town hall, this painting served as a warning against corruption and an example of virtuous leadership.[21]

By the mid-1650s, the emotional intensity and rough brushwork of Rembrandt's late style did not

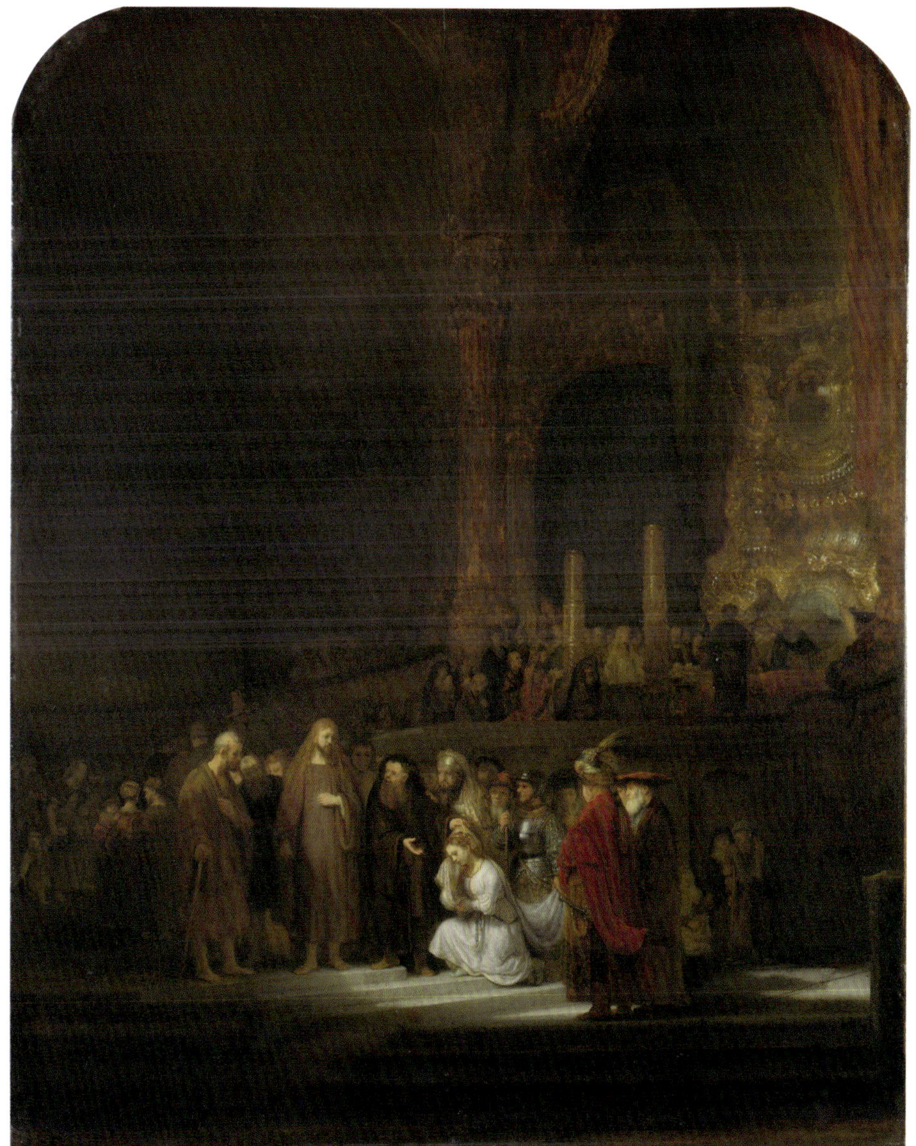

fig. 9.2 **Rembrandt van Rijn,** *Christ and the Woman Taken in Adultery,* 1644, oil on panel; 83.8 × 65.4 cm. The National Gallery, London. Bought, 1824 (NG45)

make him the most suitable artist for such commissions. He was only asked to decorate one lunette of the gallery of the town hall after Flinck died suddenly in 1660, leaving unfinished the most important commission of his career: the cycle of paintings honouring the Batavian ancestors of the new Dutch Republic. And even as a substitute, Rembrandt had to compete with several other painters hired to succeed Flinck, including Rembrandt's friend and colleague Jan Lievens, Flinck's pupil Jürgen Ovens, and the Flemish master Jacob Jordaens. Rembrandt's painting *The Conspiracy of the Batavians under Claudius Civilis* (fig. 9.3) was rejected and removed in 1662, but the works of his rivals have remained in the building (now the Royal Palace) on Dam Square to this day.[22]

Having completed prestigious works for Stadtholder Frederik Hendrik and the Kloveniersdoelen, Rembrandt seems to have had little further interest in obtaining high-profile public commissions. It appears that he always regarded history painting as an artistically as well as economically profitable endeavour in which he could experiment with new techniques, measure himself against renowned international artists, and develop his own characteristic idiom to appeal to a select group of wealthy connoisseurs and collectors. ■

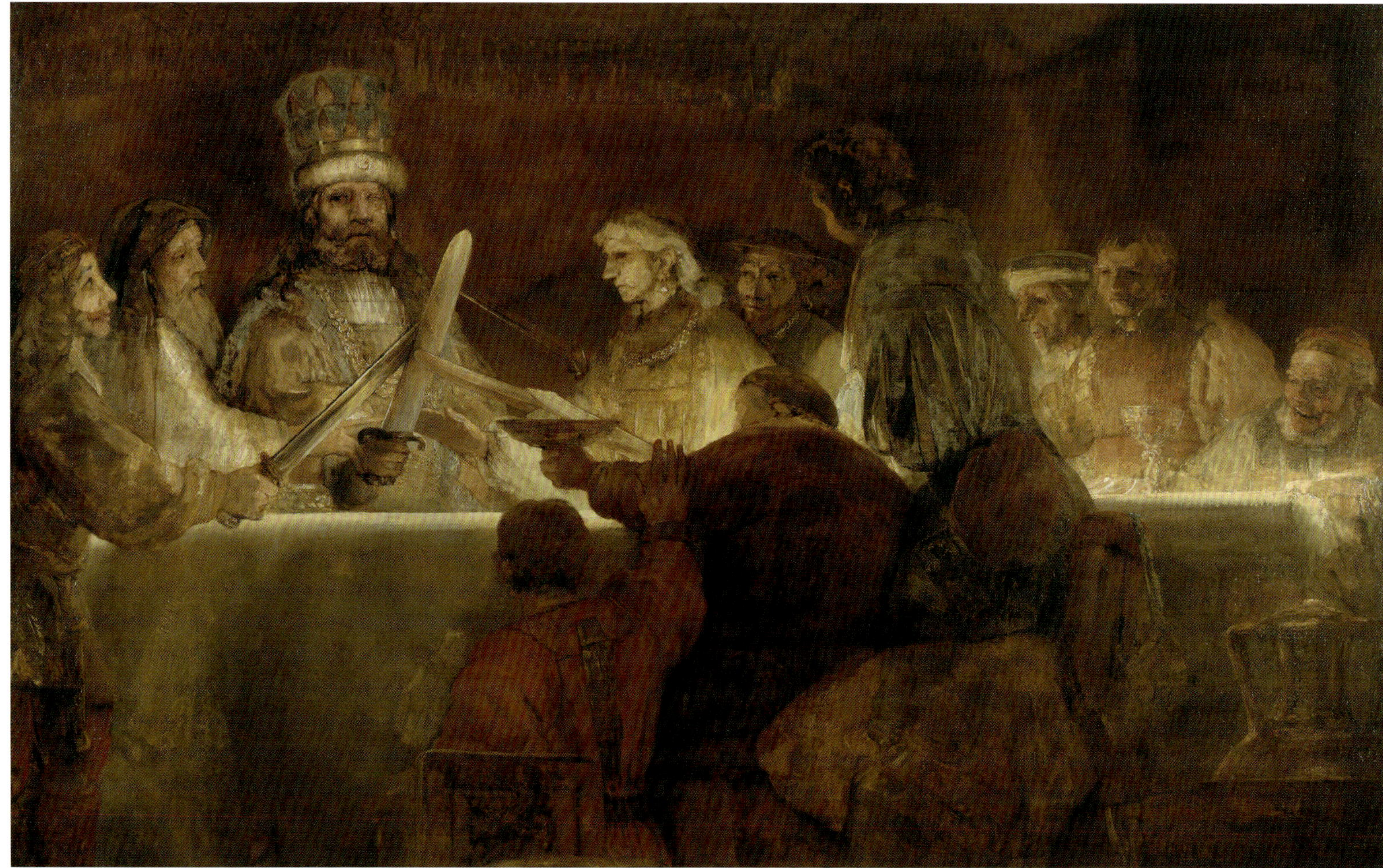

fig. 9.3 **Rembrandt van Rijn,**
The Conspiracy of the Batavians
under Claudius Civilis, **c. 1661–62,**
oil on canvas; 196 × 309 cm.
Nationalmuseum, Stockholm.
On long-term loan from
The Royal Swedish Academy
of Fine Arts (NM 578)

NOTES

1   Sluijter 2015, 27, 35–38.

2   See the essay by Jonathan Bikker in this volume.

3   See Christian Tico Seifert, "Pieter Lastman. 'Constrijcken history Schilder tot Amsterdam' – kunstreicher Historienmaler zu Amsterdam," in Hamburg 2006, 14–23; Martina Sitt, "Lastman und Rembrandt am Beispiel der 'Verstoßung der Hagar,'" in Vienna 2004, 292–294.

4   See Christian Tümpel, "Die alttestamentliche Historienmalerei im Zeitalter Rembrandts," in Münster, Amsterdam and Jerusalem 1994, 12–13.

5   See Martina Sitt, "Pieter Lastman und Rembrandt – von der stummen Sprache des Körpers zur Verdichtung von Emotion," in Hamburg 2006, 73.

6   See Büttner 2014, 65–66.

7   See Kassel 2005–06, 27–32.

8   Sluijter 2015, 14–16.

9   Ibid.; Franz Wilhelm Kaiser, "Die Geburt des Kunstmarkts?," in Hamburg 2017–18, 106.

10 Van Hoogstraten 1678, 87.

11 See Kaiser, "Geburt des Kunstmarkts," in Hamburg 2017–18, 106.

12 See Jager 2015, 1.

13 A *Raising of Lazarus* by Rembrandt was valued at 600 guilders. Secular subjects were less expensive, from a self-portrait at 250 guilders to a "Moor" at only 12 guilders; Strauss and Van der Meulen 1979, doc. 1657/2, items 291, 399, 294, 300. See also Sluijter 2015, 29, 58–64, 396–398.

14 See Sluijter 2015, 87–88.

15 See Pastoor, "Biblische Historienbilder," in Münster, Amsterdam and Jerusalem 1994, 123–124; Sluijter 2015, 395–396.

16 See Stechow 1998, 17–18; Volker Manuth, "Religious History Paintings in the World of Rembrandt," in Kofuku 2004, 56–65; Kassel 2005–06, 22.

17 See the essays "Powerful Women" and "Angelic Messengers" by Stephanie S. Dickey in this volume.

18 See Tümpel, "Die alttestamentliche Historienmalerei," in Münster, Amsterdam and Jerusalem 1994, 8–10, 22; Pastoor, "Biblische Historienbilder," in ibid., 122–123; Sluijter 2015, 373.

19 See Kassel 2005–06, 16.

20 See Eric Jan Sluijter, "Out of Rembrandt's Shadow: Govert Flinck and Ferdinand Bol as History Painters," in Amsterdam 2017–18, 116–120.

21 See Eric Jan Sluijter, "In Focus: Govert Flinck and Ferdinand Bol in the Burgomasters' Cabinet," in Amsterdam 2017–18, 138–141; Eymert-Jan Goosens, "The Biblical and Roman Republican Heroes of Amsterdam," in Cleves 2015–16, 46–47.

22 The reasons for the rejection of Rembrandt's painting, of which the existing canvas is just a fragment, are still unclear. See, among others, *Corpus*, vol. 6, no. 298; Büttner 2014, 199–200.

94   Ferdinand Bol, *Pyrrhus and Fabricius* (modello), c. 1655. Herzog Anton Ulrich-Museum, Kunstmuseum des Landes Niedersachsen, Braunschweig

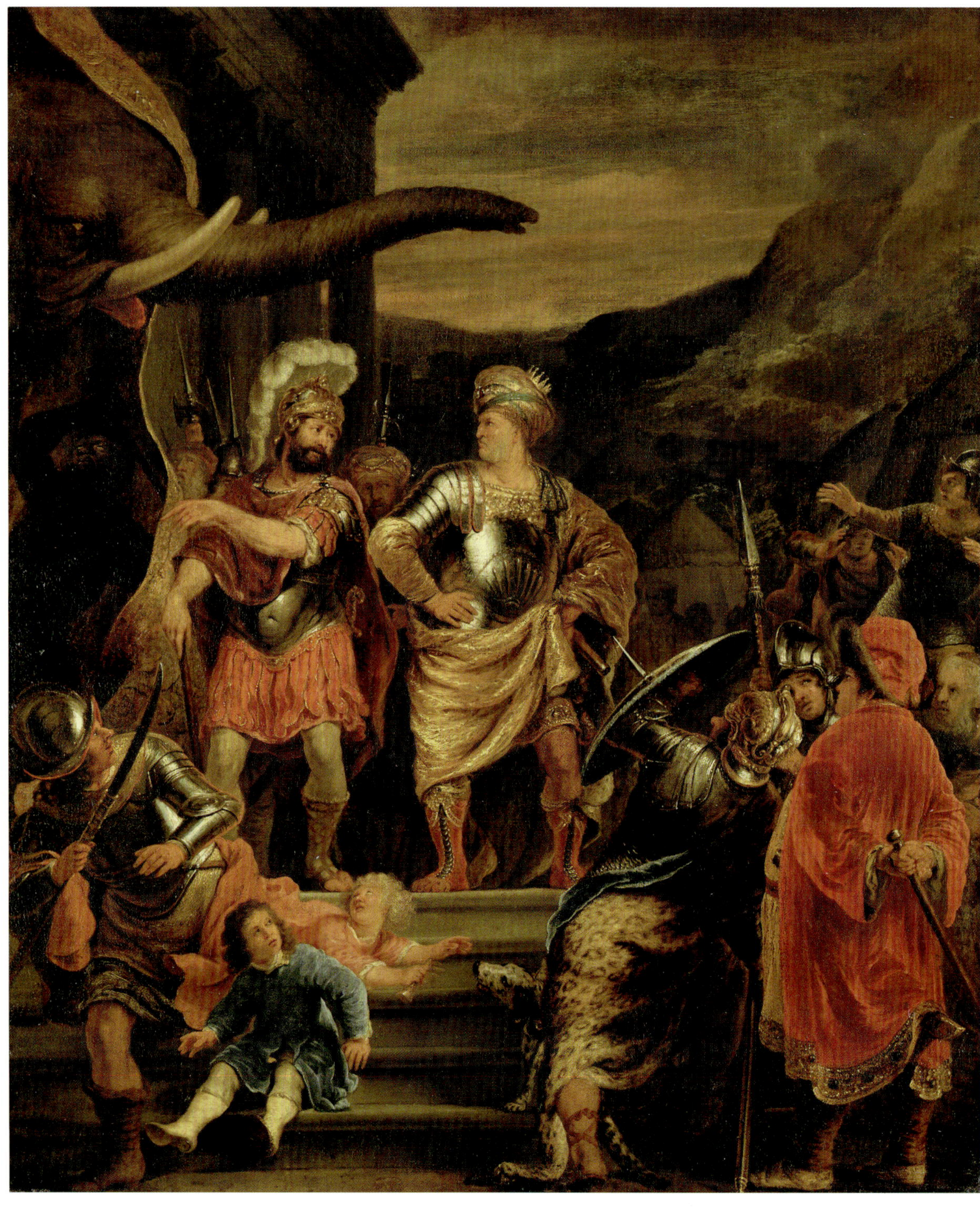

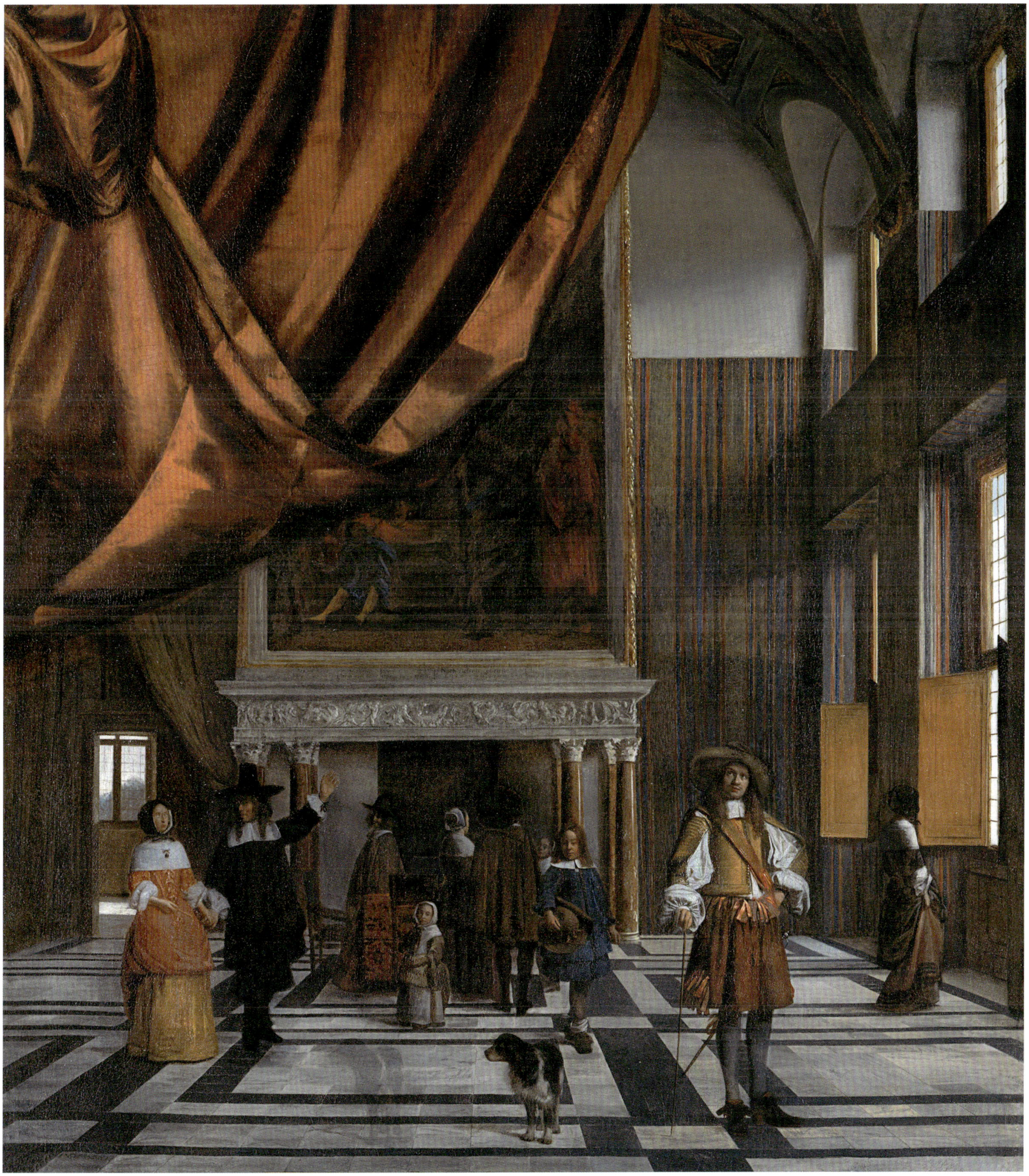

A Letter from Rembrandt

STEPHANIE S. DICKEY

My lord

Because of the great pleasure and devotion I have exercised in executing well the two pieces His Highness commissioned me to make, these being the one in which the dead body of Christ is being laid in the grave and the other in which Christ rises from the dead to the great consternation of the guards, and as a result of studious diligence, these two pieces have now been completed as well, so that I am now disposed to deliver them for the pleasure of His Highness, for it is in these two pictures that the greatest and most natural motion and emotion have been observed. That is also the main reason why they have taken so long to execute. Therefore I ask my lord to be so kind as to inform His Highness of this, and whether it would please my lord that these two pictures should first be delivered to your house, as was done before. Concerning this, I shall first await a note in reply.

And because my lord has been troubled with these matters for the second time, as a token of gratitude, a piece shall be added measuring ten feet long and eight feet high, that my lord shall find a worthy gift to display in his house. Wishing you all happiness and the blessing of salvation, Amen.

Your lordship's obliging and devoted servant
Rembrandt

This 12 [day of] January
1639

[In the margin] My lord: I reside on the Binnen-Amstel. The house is called the "Sugar Bakery."

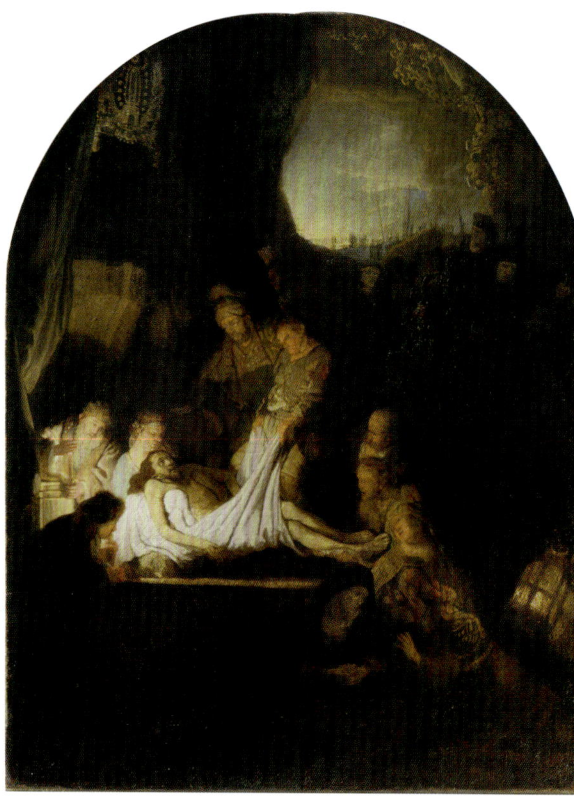

fig. 10.1 **Rembrandt van Rijn,** *The Entombment of Christ,* **1635–39, oil on canvas; 92.6 × 68.9 cm. Bayerische Staatsgemäldesammlungen, Alte Pinakothek, Munich (396)**

fig. 10.2 **Rembrandt van Rijn,** *The Resurrection of Christ,* **1635–39, oil on canvas; 91.1 × 67 cm. Bayerische Staatsgemäldesammlungen, Alte Pinakothek, Munich (397)**

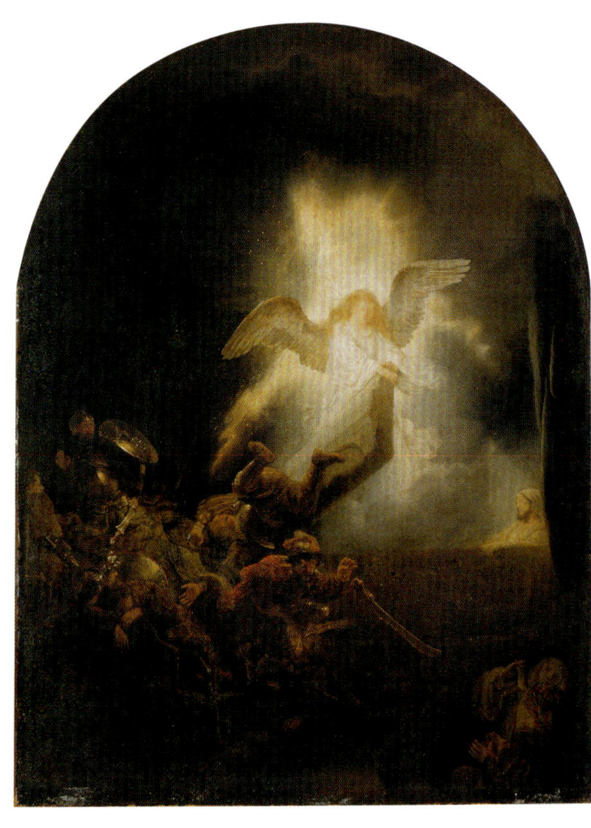

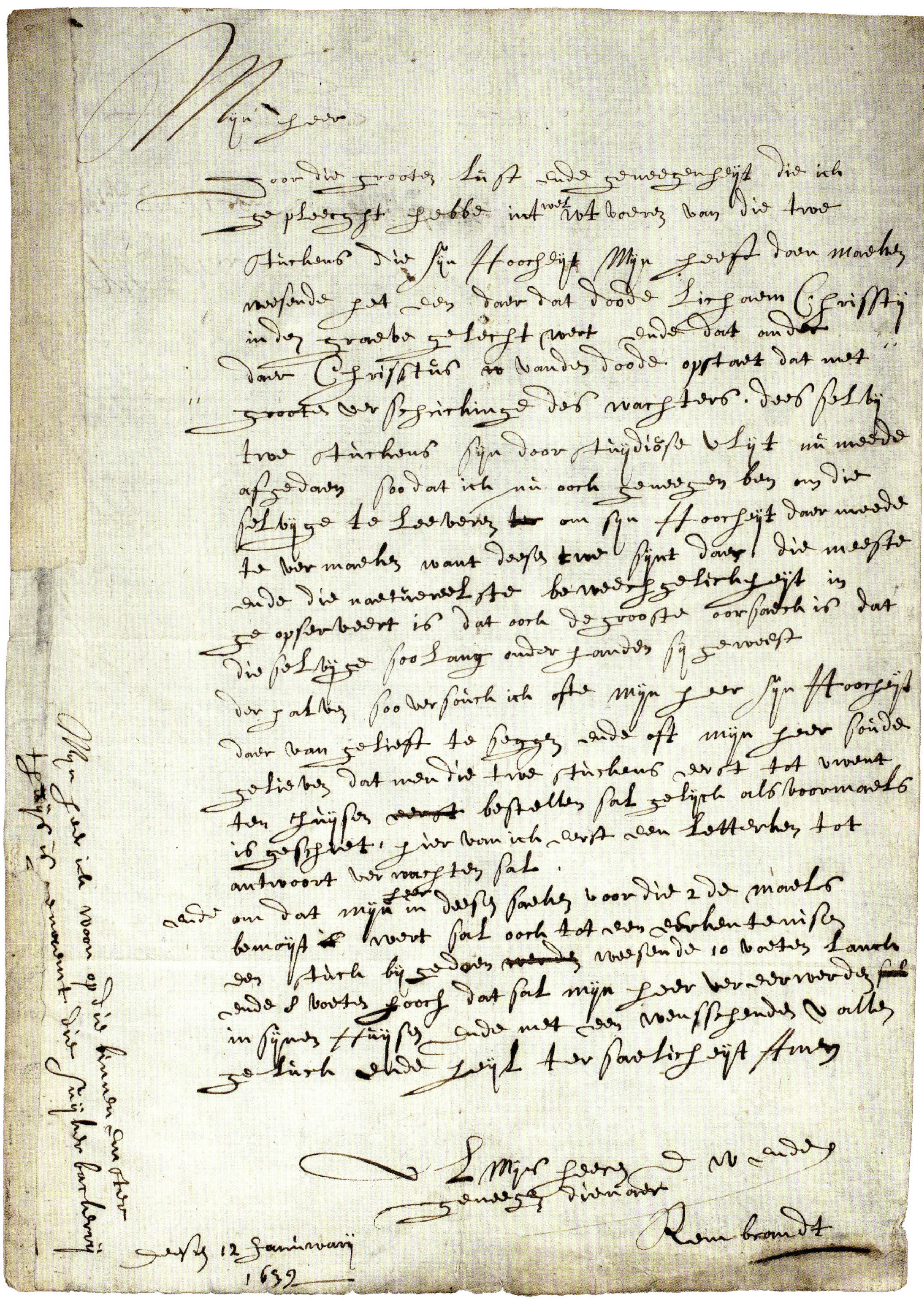

Of the rare documents that reveal Rembrandt's thinking about art, none are more precious than seven letters he wrote to Constantijn Huygens, Secretary to Stadtholder Frederik Hendrik, concerning a commissioned series of paintings on the Passion of Christ. In the third letter, dated 12 January 1639, Rembrandt informs Huygens that he has just completed *The Entombment of Christ* and *The Resurrection of Christ* (figs. 10.1, 10.2), working diligently to depict *"die meeste ende die naetuereelste beweechgelickheijt."*[1] The precise meaning of this phrase has prompted much debate, but there is no doubt that it encapsulates a central goal of Rembrandt's art. *Beweeglijkheid*, to use the modern spelling, means liveliness of body and spirit: motion and emotion combined. In history paintings and prints of the 1630s, Rembrandt sought to convey profound and sometimes violent passions through physical movement, often choosing a dramatic moment of reversal or revelation. Later, he turned to inward emotions expressed through stillness and introspection. The binding principle throughout was to capture the pathos of human experience.[2]

After inviting Huygens to take delivery of the stadtholder's canvases, Rembrandt thanks him for his help with a remarkable offer: a painting ten feet wide and eight feet high (3 × 2.5 metres).

The extant work that best fits this description is *The Blinding of Samson*, painted in 1636 (pl. 106). As a connoisseur of the arts, Huygens should surely have welcomed this extravagant gesture, but a later letter suggests he rejected it.[3] Why did this happen? Confronted some years earlier with a horrific *Head of Medusa* by Peter Paul Rubens in the collection of the Amsterdam merchant Nicolas Sohier, Huygens had admired the artist's skill but observed: "I would prefer to eulogize this [painting] in the house of friends than in my own."[4] Perhaps he found Rembrandt's imagery overly gruesome as well, but social convention provides a more likely answer: to accept such a generous gift would have placed him under too great an obligation to the painter.[5]

A postscript finds Rembrandt living on the Binnen-Amstel (pl. 31), where he had moved in 1637, in a house called the "Sugar Bakery."[6] Situated beside the Amstel River, this was the second rented accommodation he occupied after joining the Guild of Saint Luke in 1634 as an independent master. A few months later, Rembrandt and his wife Saskia moved into their grand home on the St. Anthonisbreestraat, next door to where Rembrandt had worked for Saskia's cousin, Hendrick Uylenburgh.[7] Did they take *The Blinding of Samson* with them? Its original buyer remains unknown.[8]

NOTES

1   *Corpus*, vol. 6, nos. 162, 163; Strauss and Van der Meulen 1979, doc. 1639/2; see also doc. 1636/1, 1636/2, 1639/3, 1639/4 1639/5, 1639/6. On the reverse, Rembrandt addresses the letter to Huygens as Lord of Zuylichem, a manor Huygens purchased in 1633. On the Passion series, see the essay "The Life of Christ" by Stephanie S. Dickey in this volume. The translation here is based largely on Gerson 1961, 38, with thanks to Jasper Hillegers and Eric Jan Sluijter for consultation.

2   See Thijs Weststeijn, "Rembrandt and Rhetoric: The Concepts of *Affectus, Enargeia* and *Ornatus* in Samuel van Hoogstraten's Judgement of His Master," in Van den Doel et al. 2005, 111–130, esp. 119; Schwartz 2006, 155–157; Sluijter 2006, 99–111; Sluijter 2010; Sluijter 2014.

3   Strauss and Van der Meulen 1979, doc. 1639/4.

4   Trans. from Heinen 2010, 151. The description in Huygens' autobiography of c. 1629–30 probably refers to a studio version of Rubens' *Head of Medusa* (c. 1617, Kunsthistorisches Museum, Vienna). On Sohier, see also the essay by Jonathan Bikker in this volume.

5   Zell 2011; on social reciprocity, see also Kok 2013; Sluijter 2015, 50–52.

6   A document of 17 December 1637 places him on the Binnen-Amstel; Strauss and Van der Meulen 1979, doc. 1639/1. On the "Sugar Bakery," see Strauss and Van der Meulen 1979, 147; Sebastien A.C. Dudok van Heel, "Rembrandt van Rijn (1606–1669): A Changing Portrait of the Artist," in Berlin, Amsterdam and London 1991–92b, 55.

7   Rembrandt signed the purchase contract on 3 January 1639; Strauss and Van der Meulen 1979, doc. 1637/1. It is often suggested that financial exigency impelled him to complete the two paintings for the stadtholder; later letters press Huygens to help arrange payment. On Rembrandt's debts, see Crenshaw 2006.

8   On *The Blinding of Samson*, see Manuth 1990; Neumeister 2005, 395–420; *Corpus*, vol. 6, no. 148; and the essay "Desire and Enchantment" by Friederike Schütt in this volume.

Desire and Enchantment

FRIEDERIKE SCHÜTT

In Rembrandt's time, biblical and mythological stories featuring seduction and desire, passion and love made up a large portion of the themes chosen for history paintings. They offered an opportunity to depict nude bodies but also served as moral warnings about the consequences of sensual (visual) pleasure.

A popular source for mythological representation was Ovid's *Metamorphoses*. Rembrandt drew inspiration from these tales for numerous works; for example, his 1632 painting *The Abduction of Europa* (Metamorphoses II, 833–875), which hung in the Amsterdam house of Jacques Specx, the former governor general of Batavia in the Dutch East Indies (fig. 11.1).[1] In 1634 Rembrandt proved his pictorial inventiveness with a painting that for the first time combined Ovid's myth of Diana and Actaeon (Metamorphoses III, 155–252) with the tale of the unchaste nymph Callisto (Metamorphoses II, 401–465) (pl. 99). Diana, goddess of the hunt, punishes Actaeon for gazing at her naked without permission by transforming him into a stag that is torn to pieces by his own hounds, and she bans her favourite nymph Callisto from her retinue of virgins after finding out about Callisto's pregnancy. Despite this rather grim plot, the imagery is quite idyllic. In this regard, Rembrandt's painting recalls the peaceful depictions of nymphs by Cornelis van Poelenburch, whose cabinet pieces were held in high esteem at the stadtholder's court (fig. 11.2).[2] Yet, it also contains more dramatic elements, such as the scene at right where Callisto's pregnancy is revealed amid much laughter and squabbling.

Rembrandt's nymphs are small and agile. Brightly lit against the dark forest, their movements look spontaneous and natural while concealing their feminine charms. As Diana turns to splash Actaeon, thus initiating his transformation, other nymphs rush into the water or clamber up the riverbank to escape his gaze. A nymph in the left foreground wades on undeterred, while another at right provocatively exposes her companion's naked bottom as she pushes her under the water. Eroticism and humour, pleasure and warning (watch where you are looking!) go hand in hand in this depiction, which is both sensual and candid. Rembrandt has also included some more ambiguous elements – such as the couple in the forest and the frog at bottom right – which, now as then, encourage conversation in front of the picture.[3] Yet, neither instruction nor eroticism supersede the sheer joy of artistic storytelling.

A slightly later painting by Nicolaes Eliasz Pickenoy (pl. 98) conveys this moral message about desire and unchastity in a much more explicit manner.

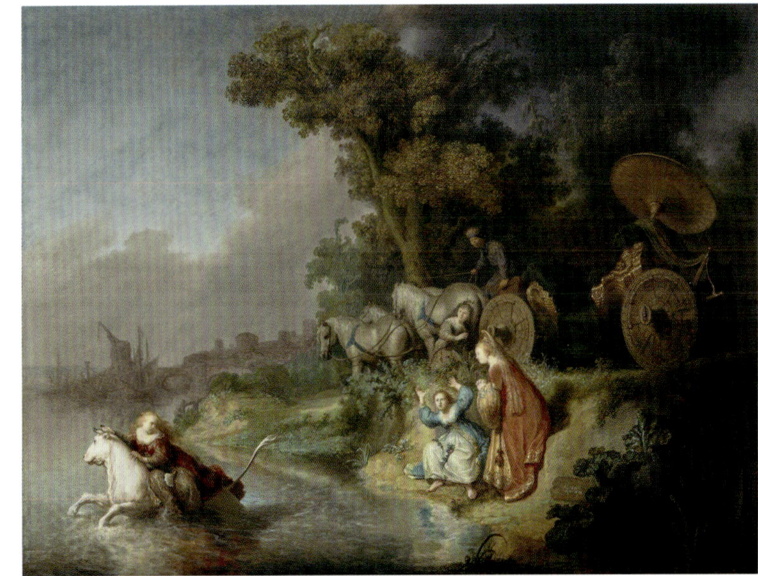

fig. 11.1 **Rembrandt van Rijn, *The Abduction of Europa*, 1632, oil on panel; 64.6 × 78.7 cm. The J. Paul Getty Museum, Los Angeles (95.PB.7)**

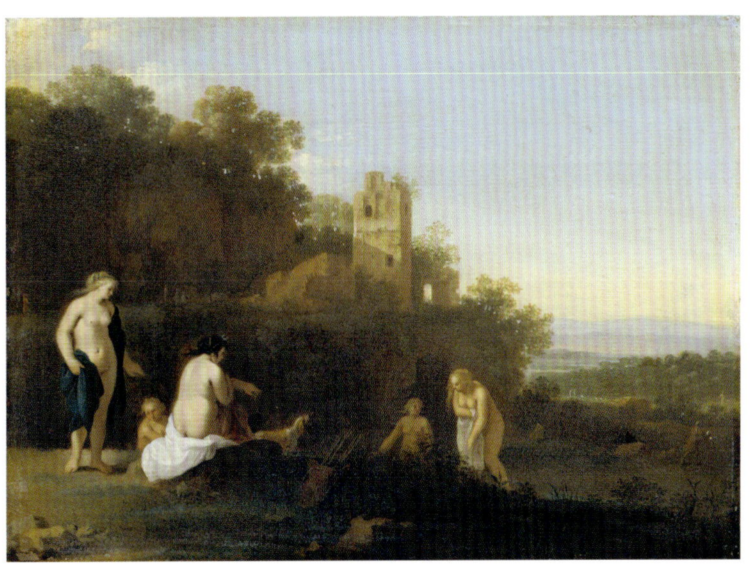

fig. 11.2 **Cornelis van Poelenburch Workshop, *Landscape with the Discovery of Callisto's Pregnancy*, c. 1630–40, oil on panel; 16.8 × 22.7 cm. Städel Museum, Frankfurt am Main (625)**

Here, the nymphs express their outrage with theatrical gestures, while Diana points admonishingly toward Actaeon.[4] In contrast, in a painting of 1654, Jacob van Loo presents Diana's ideally proportioned naked body in contrapposto in the centre (pl. 100), blurring the boundary between seduction and instruction. The market value of this work clearly derives from its classicist rendering of the figures. Thanks to the proliferation of French academic art and theory in the Netherlands, classicist principles were increasingly gaining favour over Rembrandt's realistic treatment of nature and the human form.[5]

Rembrandt's often earthy, humourous treatment of classical literary themes, which he passed on to his pupils, is evident in his drawing *Venus and Mars Caught in Vulcan's Net* (pl. 102), as well as in the painting *Mercury, Argus and Io* (pl. 103) by his pupil Carel Fabritius. Rembrandt focuses his drawing on the climatic moment in Ovid's tale (Metamorphoses IV, 170–189). Through the faces and postures of the figures, he shows how the gods react with mockery and derision to Vulcan's attempt to expose his wife's infidelity. Fabritius depicts the story of the hundred-eyed Argus (Metamorphoses I, 601–688, 713–724). While Argus guards Io – who has been turned into a white heifer – from Jupiter's lustful advances, Mercury lulls Argus to sleep with his enchanted flute and will shortly cut off his head. The sketchy brushwork and decidedly unidealized figures are indebted to Rembrandt's realistic treatment of mythological themes. Amusingly, Mercury leans close to Argus to check whether all of his victim's eyes are indeed shut before proceeding with his cruel deed.

In his 1635 painting *The Abduction of Ganymede* (pl. 97), Rembrandt depicts the myth of the most beautiful youth on earth, who was chosen to be the cupbearer of the gods and carried to heaven by Jupiter in the form of an eagle (Metamorphoses X, 155–161). Rembrandt focuses attention on Ganymede, caught up in the clutches of the eagle, and again shows his sense of humour. Rather than depicting an attractive youth, as might be expected, like the one in Nicolas Beatrizet's widely disseminated etching after Michelangelo's drawing (which Rembrandt certainly would have known),[6] he presents a stout, feisty toddler who urinates, kicks and wails. Just how vividly Rembrandt has captured the child's terror and defiance, confronting the viewer with Ganymede's powerful emotions, is evident if we compare the painting to the preparatory drawing (fig. 11.3), which shows the desperate parents trying to prevent the abduction.[7]

The infantile figure of Ganymede draws inspiration from contemporary emblems and Karel van Mander's interpretation of the figure as the incarnation of the pure soul.[8] Yet, despite these references to visual and literary culture, Rembrandt's treatment is unique. The painting would have pleased potential buyers with its bold directness as well as its ambiguous iconography, which has invited numerous interpretations

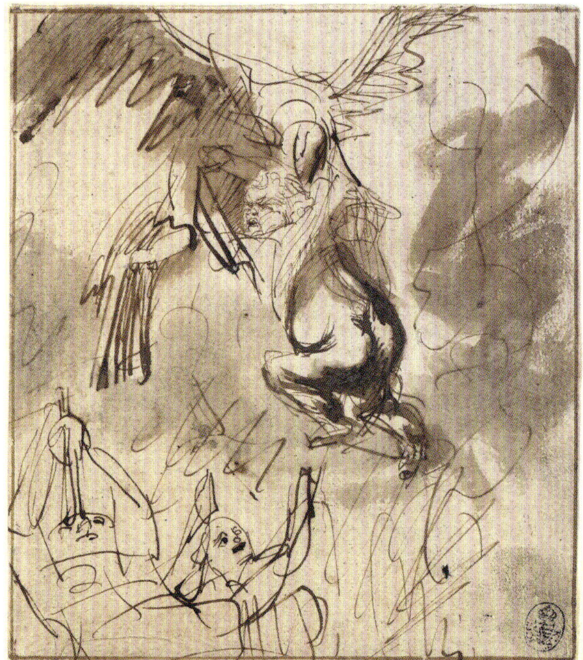

fig. 11.3 **Rembrandt van Rijn,** *Preparatory Sketch for "The Abduction of Ganymede,"* **c. 1635, pen and ink on laid paper; 18.5 × 16.1 cm. Staatliche Kunstsammlungen Dresden, Kupferstich-Kabinett (C 1357)**

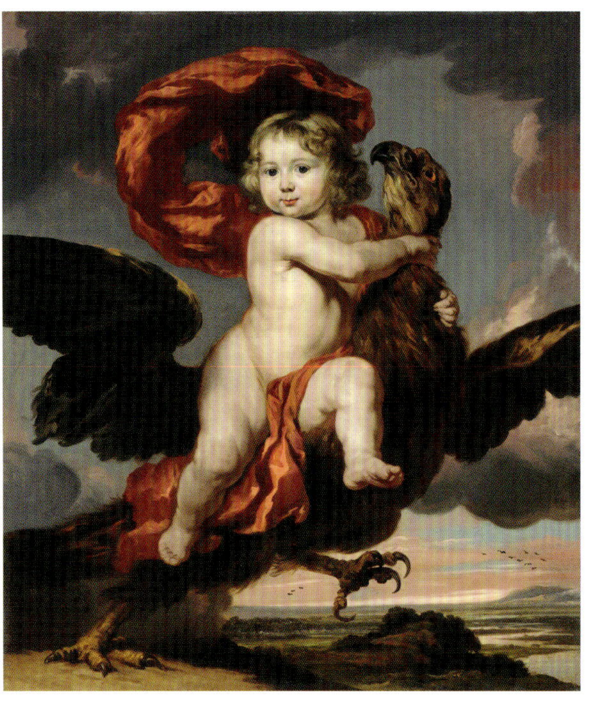

fig. 11.4 **Nicolaes Maes,** *Portrait of George Bredehoff de Vicq as Ganymede,* **1681, oil on canvas; 99 × 84.5 cm. Harvard Art Museums / Fogg Museum, Cambridge, MA. Kate, Maurice R., and Melvin R. Seiden Purchase Fund in honour of Lisbet and Joseph Leo Koerner (1993.250)**

to this day.[9] Subsequent depictions of Ganymede by Rembrandt's pupil Nicolaes Maes were aimed at a very diffcrcnt clicntclc. From thc 1670s Macs drcw upon this mythological story to create memorial portraits of children who had died young, presenting each in the role of Ganymede as a sweet child carried by the eagle to heavenly salvation (fig. 11.4).[10]

Rembrandt's career as a history painter reached an indisputable high point in 1636 with *The Blinding of Samson* (pl. 106). Yet, this painting, unique in its emotional power and monumentality, at first proved difficult to sell. Its original format corresponds to the measurements – "ten feet in length and eight feet in height" – of a painting that Rembrandt offered as a gift to Constantijn Huygens in 1639 to thank him for arranging the commission of Passion scenes for Stadtholder Frederik Hendrik.[11] It seems that Huygens did not accept the gift.

Rembrandt shows how Samson is punished by being blinded for giving in to the enemy Philistine Delilah and revealing the secret of his superhuman strength. Contrary to the visual tradition to which he and Jan Lievens still adhered in paintings completed in Leiden between 1625 and 1630,[12] Rembrandt does not depict Delilah's deceitful seduction of Samson (fig. 11.5). Instead, he chooses a moment that can hardly be surpassed in its brutality and violence: blood spurts from Samson's eye, his foot cramps up in pain and he balls his hand into a fist.[13]

How much thought Rembrandt put into his treatment of this Old Testament story (Judges 16) is documented by a drawing from 1636–40 (pl. 105), in which the constellation of figures might have been inspired by Anthony van Dyck's *Samson and Delilah* of c. 1618–21 (pl. 104).[14] Rembrandt may have encountered Van Dyck's work during the latter's stay at the court in The Hague or through an Amsterdam collection.[15] Van Dyck's composition, with Samson's heroic body theatrically positioned in the foreground and the diagonal forward surge of the other figures, seems to have been a source of inspiration for Rembrandt. While Van Dyck's modelling of muscles and breasts heightens the erotic tension between Samson and Delilah, Rembrandt depicts his figures without emphasizing the story's erotic aspects.

With his *Blinding of Samson* Rembrandt sought competition and recognition on an international scale – as can also be seen from his often cited references to Peter Paul Rubens (see fig. 5.10)[16] – and he

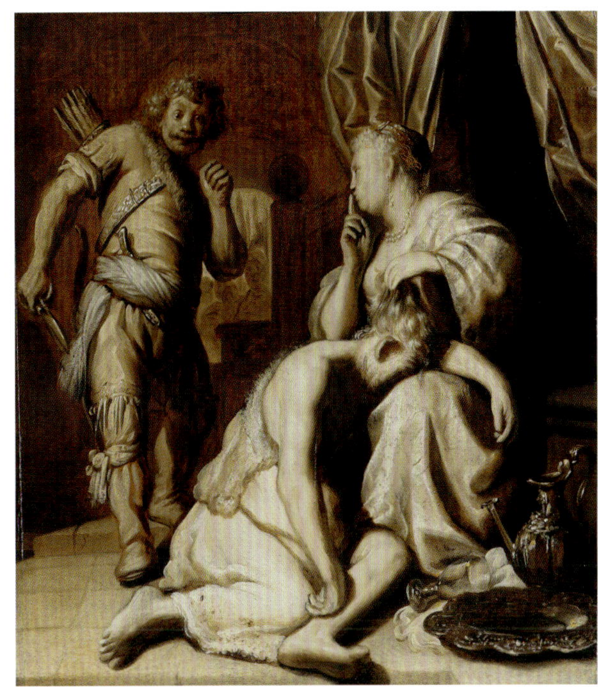

fig. 11.5 **Rembrandt van Rijn, attributed to,** *Samson and Delilah*, **c. 1626–30, oil on panel; 27.5 × 23.5 cm. Rijksmuseum, Amsterdam. Purchased with the support of the Stichting tot Bevordering van de Belangen van het Rijksmuseum (SK-A-4096)**

provided a model and a challenge for the next generation of artists. Thus, in Cornelis Holsteyn's large-format *Venus and Cupid Lamenting the Dead Adonis* (pl. 101), for example, the diagonal arrangement of Adonis' body seems to draw some inspiration from Rembrandt's *Blinding of Samson* and its models.[17] Yet, Holsteyn's idealized bodies and muted emotions could hardly be more different from Rembrandt's narrative approach. The unusual format of this painting, which can be dated stylistically to the mid-1650s, may be due to the fact that it was commissioned for the mantelpiece of a house in Haarlem, where Holsteyn was born and trained. However, it was probably painted in Amsterdam, where the artist registered as a citizen in 1652. Around the same time, he also contributed a ceiling painting and a chimney piece to the decoration of the new Amsterdam Town Hall.[18] His restrained classicist style offered patrons a clear alternative to Rembrandt's dramatic naturalism.[19]

With Venus and Adonis, Holsteyn chose a mythological story that was as widely represented as Diana and her nymphs.[20] Rembrandt and his contemporaries drew their motifs from the same fund of well-known, popular tales. What made Rembrandt's paintings so innovative was not his chosen themes but rather the emotional power and intensity with which he rendered each story. What he had to offer – and what set him apart from his colleagues – were exceptional paintings created for a select clientele. ■

NOTES

1   See *Corpus*, vol. 2, no. A47; Manuth, De Winkel and Van Leeuwen 2019, no. 97.

2   See Grohé 1996, 199; Sluijter 2006, 182.

3   On Rembrandt's thematization of the gaze and other interpretations of this painting, see Busch 1989; Grohé 1996, 208–211; Cologne and Prague 2019–20, 224–227.

4   Pickenoy emulated a print by Antonio Tempesta on the same subject; Sluijter 2015, 292.

5   See Grohé 1996, 30; Sluijter 2015, 374–378.

6   See Müller 2015, 188–191.

7   See Uta Neidhardt, "Rembrandts 'Ganymed' – fremd und vertraut," in Dresden 2006–07, 11; Thomas Ketelsen, "Ein Körper von Gewicht. Rembrandts 'Ganymed'-Zeichnung in Dresden," in ibid., 21–32.

8   See Ketelsen, "Ein Körper von Gewicht," in ibid., 29; Werner Busch, "Die Entblößung des Mythos als die Freilegung der Natur. Rembrandts 'Ganymed' jenseits der Ikonographie," in ibid., 34–35.

9   Sluijter 2015, 41, has proposed that Lucas van Uffelen might have commissioned this painting; for different interpretations, see Grohé 1996, 103–117; Prater 2015, 157–159.

10 See Busch, "Die Entblößung des Mythos," in Dresden 2006–07, 35; Krempel 2000, 98.

11 "The third letter to Constantijn Huygens," 12 Jan. 1639, Remdoc, no. e4458; see the essay "A Letter from Rembrandt" by Stephanie S. Dickey in this volume; Manuth 1990, 171–172; Neumeister 2005, 395–422; Büttner 2014, 130–131; Sluijter 2015, 42, 50–52.

12 Jan Lievens, *Samson and Delilah* (c. 1625–26, Rijksmuseum, Amsterdam); Rembrandt van Rijn, *Samson and Delilah* (1628, Gemäldegalerie, Berlin); Rembrandt van Rijn, attributed to, *Samson and Delilah* (fig. 11.5). See recently Leiden and Oxford 2019–20, 190–194.

13 See Manuth 1990, 172–179; Kassel 2005–06, 57.

14 The Dresden Kupferstich-Kabinett lists this drawing as "Rembrandt School," see https://skd-online-collection.skd. museum/Details/Index/883082 (accessed 24 Jan. 2020); see also Dresden 2019, 63, 65 (attributed to Jan Victors). Martin Royalton-Kisch, in his online catalogue of Rembrandt's drawings, attributes the work to Rembrandt himself; Royalton-Kisch 2012 (Benesch 0093). The same attribution is supported by Schatborn and Hinterding 2019, no. D47, who add that the drawing is a sketch for the 1636 *Blinding of Samson* (pl. 106). On Van Dyck's *Samson and Delilah*, see Bergvelt and Jonker 2020. I would like to thank Ellinoor Bergvelt for kindly sharing her unpublished text on this painting.

15 Since works by other Amsterdam artists also draw upon Van Dyck's *Samson and Delilah*, it is possible that the painting was in an Amsterdam collection from the 1630s. Sluijter has suggested Lucas van Uffelen as a possible owner; see Sluijter 2015, 43, 45–47; Stephanie S. Dickey, "Lievens in Antwerp: Three Rediscovered Works," in Dickey 2017b, 152.

16 Numerous scholars have discussed the relationship between Rembrandt's *Blinding of Samson* and works by Rubens. See, for example, Neumeister 2005, 416–420; Kassel 2005–06, 47–57; Toshiharu Nakamura, "Rembrandt's *Blinding of Samson*: A Work for Artistic Emulation with Rubens?," in Kofuku 2004; Sluijter 2015, 43–51.

17 Like Rembrandt, Holsteyn probably used an etching by Antonio Tempesta as a source of inspiration for Adonis' body. See Rotterdam and Frankfurt 1999–2000, 234.

18 See ibid., 232–234; Athens and Dordrecht 2000–01, no. 35.

19 Albert Blankert, "Classicism in Dutch Painting, 1614–1670," in Washington, Detroit and Amsterdam 1980–81, 188, names Holsteyn's *Venus and Cupid Lamenting the Dead Adonis* as a typical example of Amsterdam classicism.

20 See Erik Hinterding, "Rembrandt's Etchings of Biblical and Mythological Subjects: Associations with His Painting," in Kofuku 2004, 141.

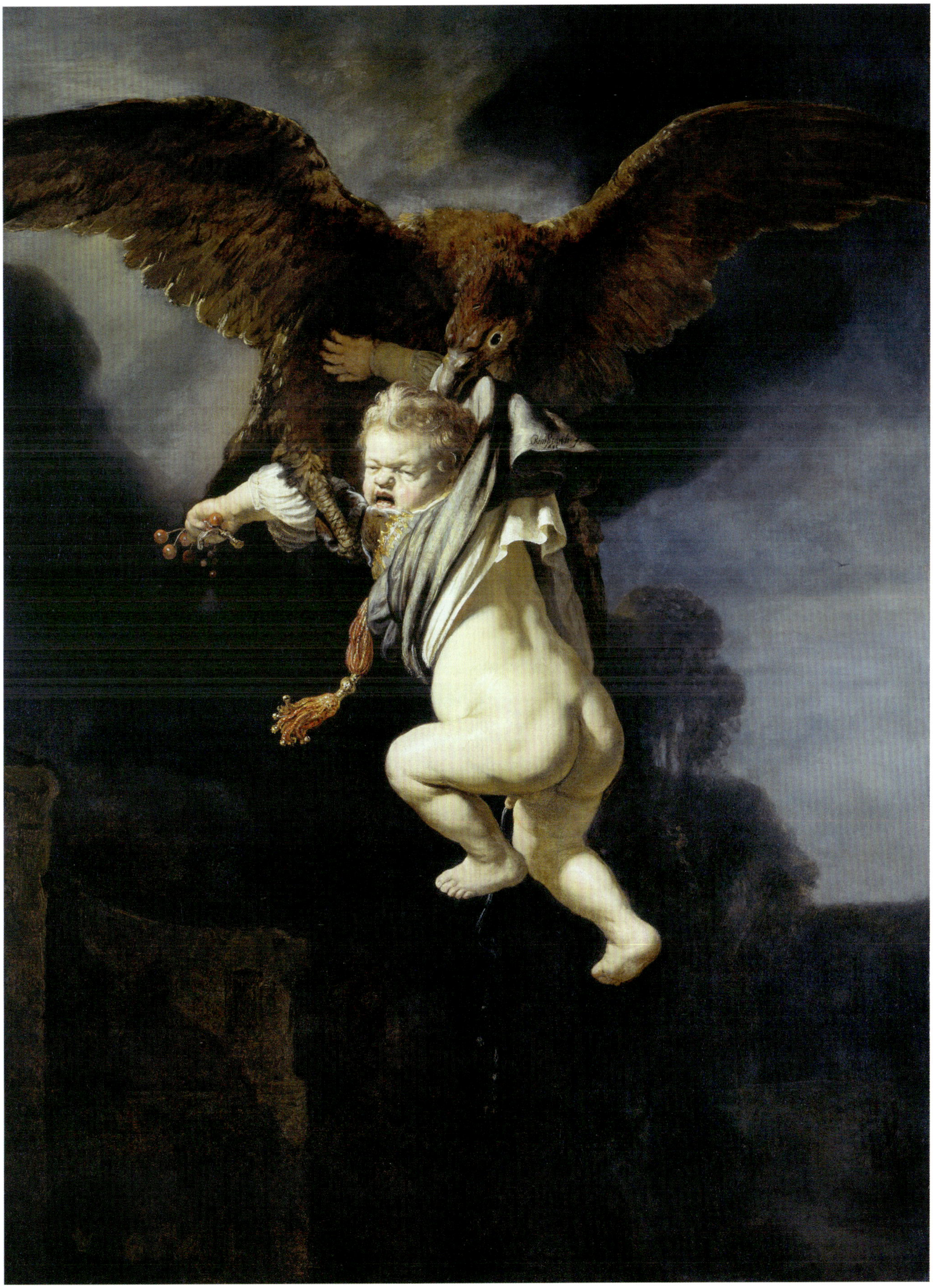

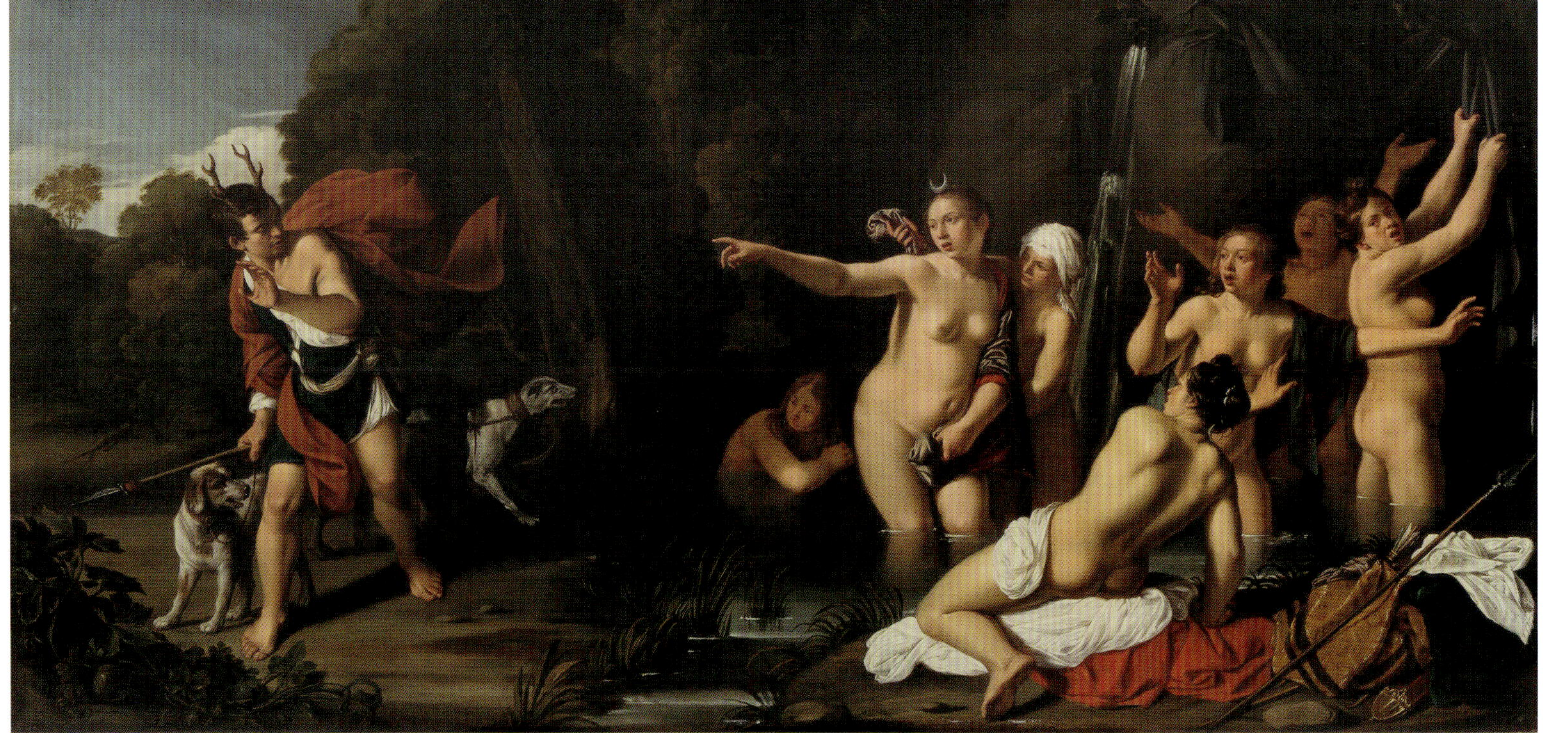

98 Nicolaes Eliasz Pickenoy, *Diana and Actaeon*, c. 1640. Herbert F. Johnson Museum of Art, Cornell University, Ithaca

99 Rembrandt van Rijn, *Diana and Her Nymphs Bathing, with the Stories of Actaeon and Callisto*, 1634.
Sammlung der Fürsten zu Salm-Salm, Museum Wasserburg Anholt, Isselburg

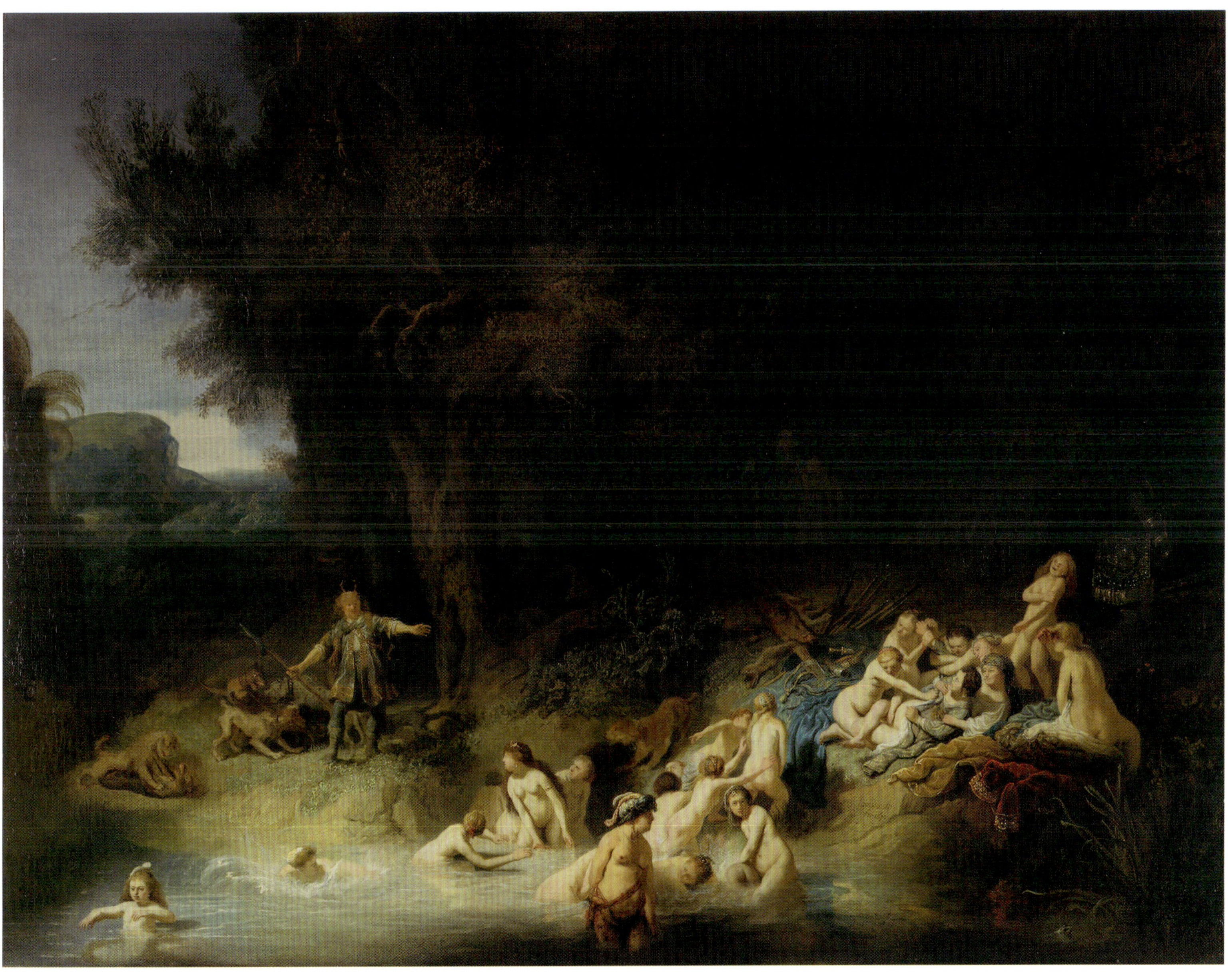

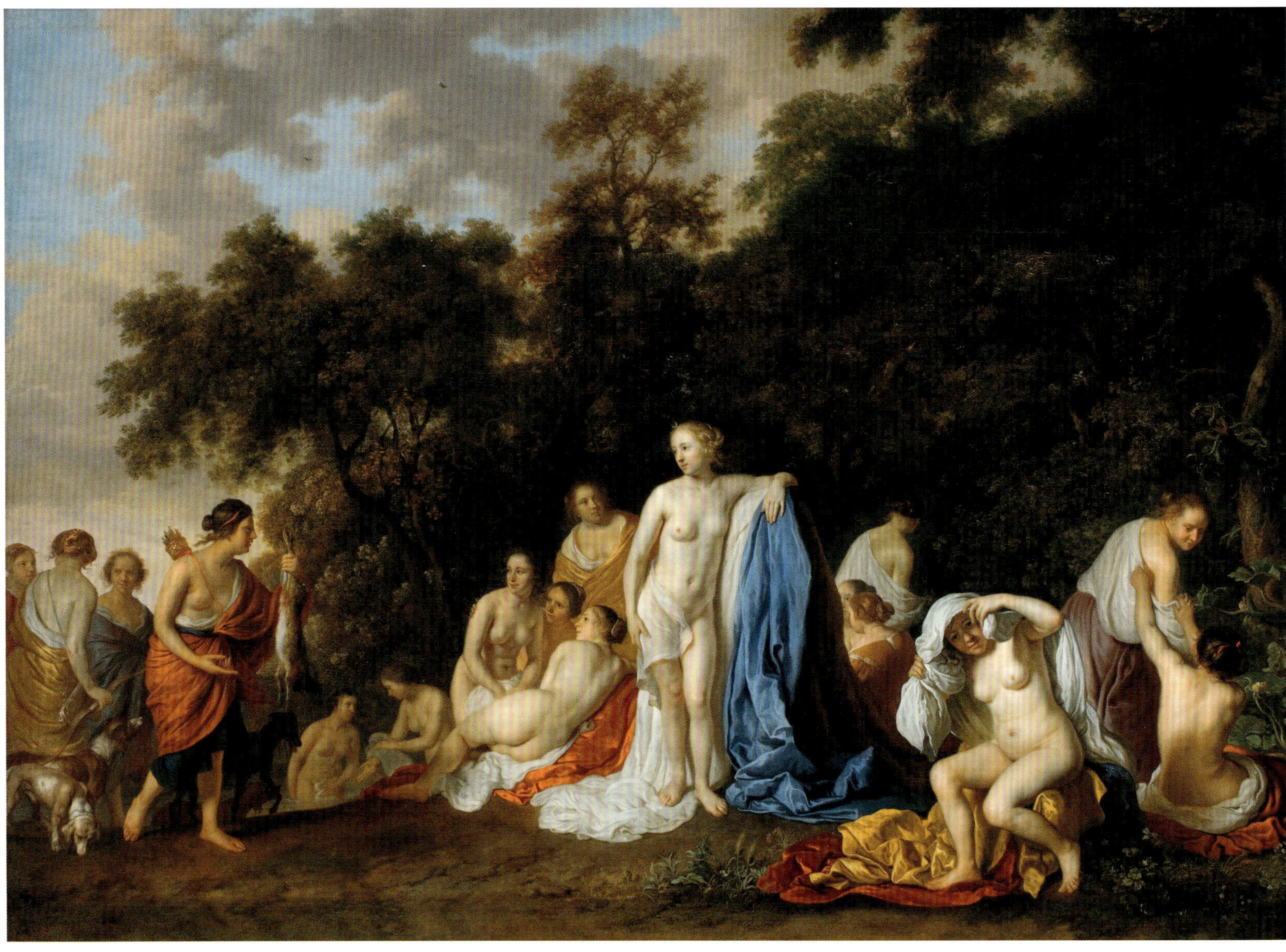

100 Jacob van Loo, *Diana and Her Nymphs*, 1654. National Gallery of Denmark, Copenhagen

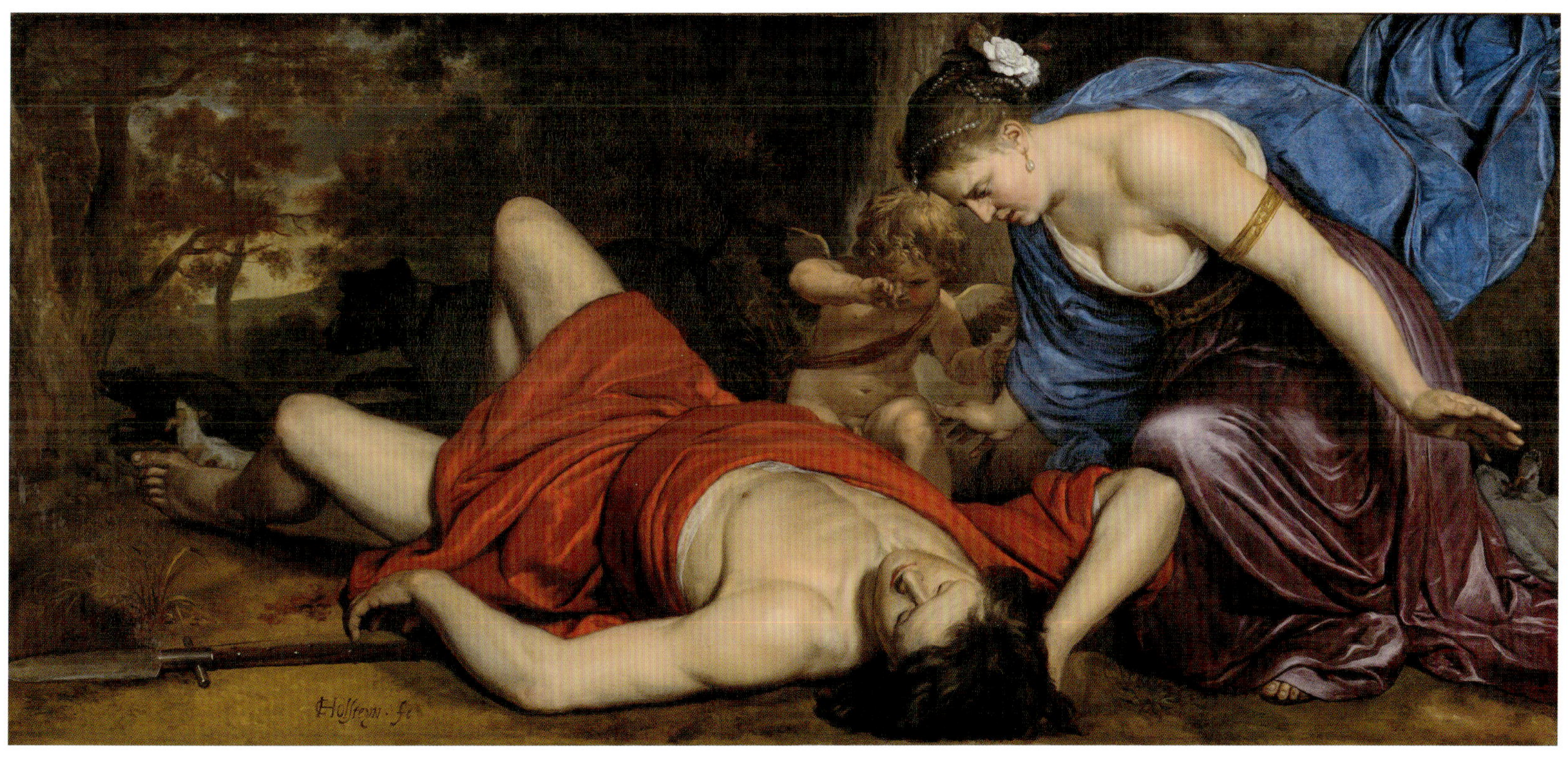

102   Rembrandt van Rijn, *Venus and Mars Caught in Vulcan's Net*, c. 1633–38. Amsterdam Museum

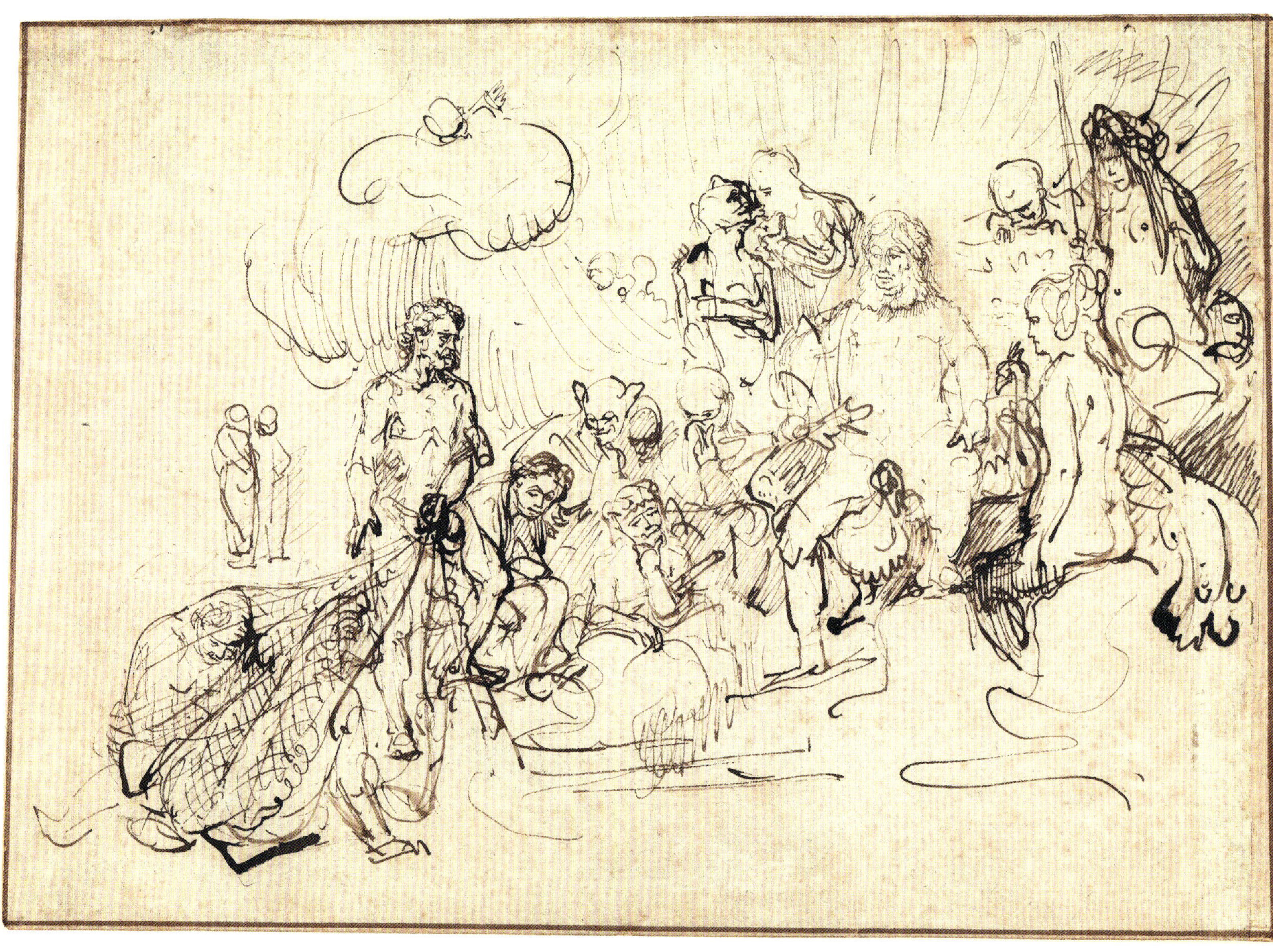

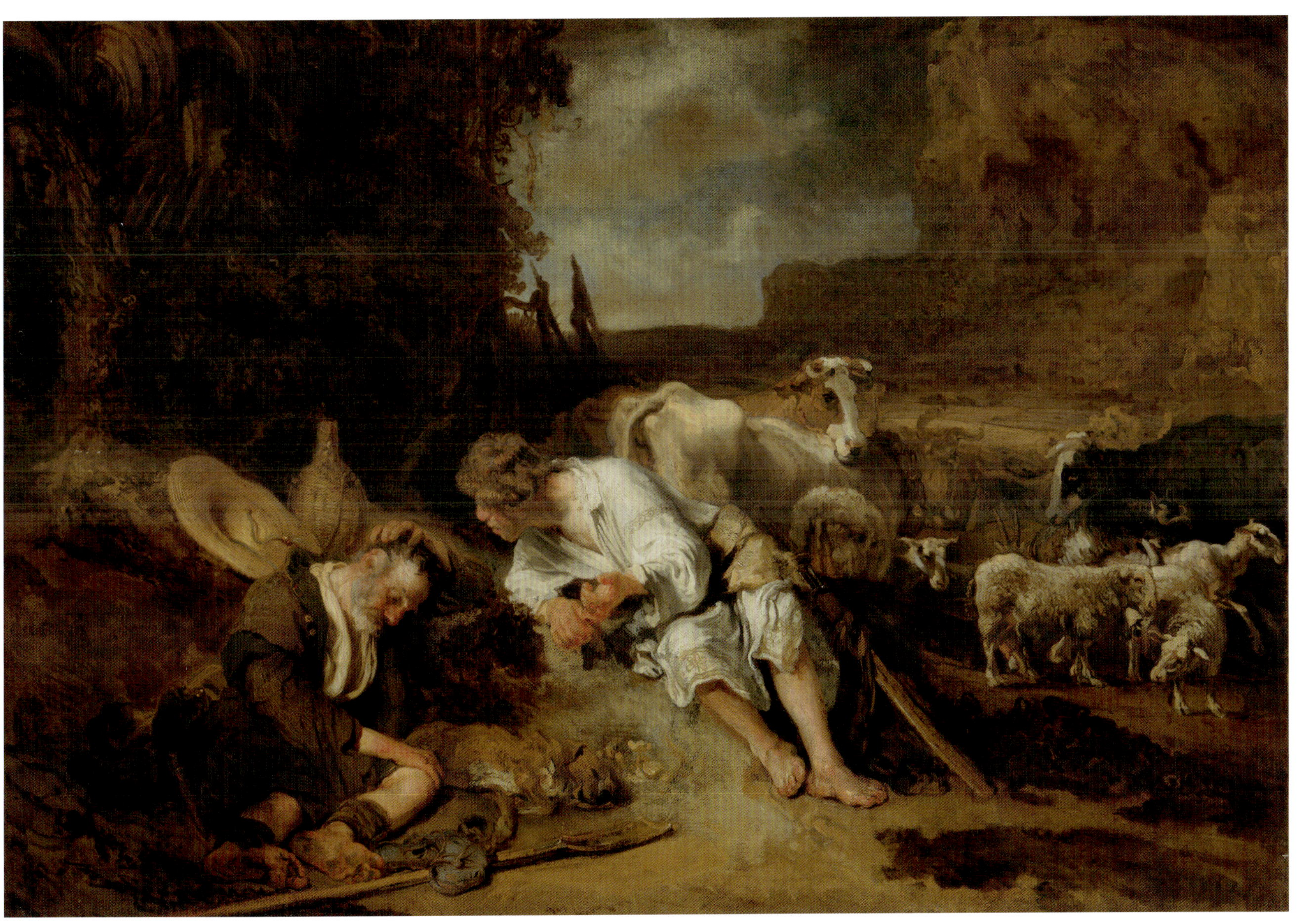

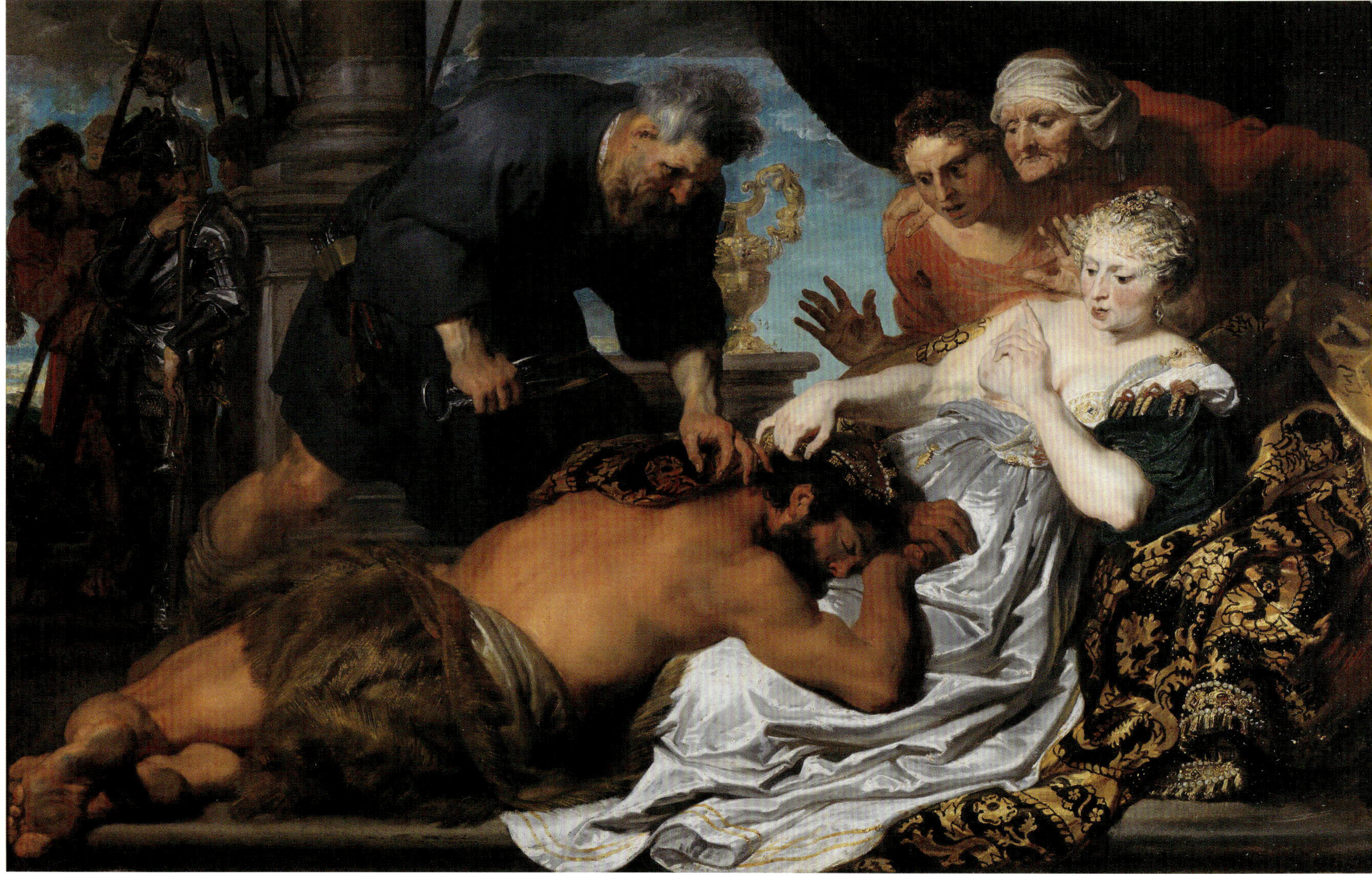

104   Anthony van Dyck, *Samson and Delilah*, c. 1618–21. Dulwich Picture Gallery, London

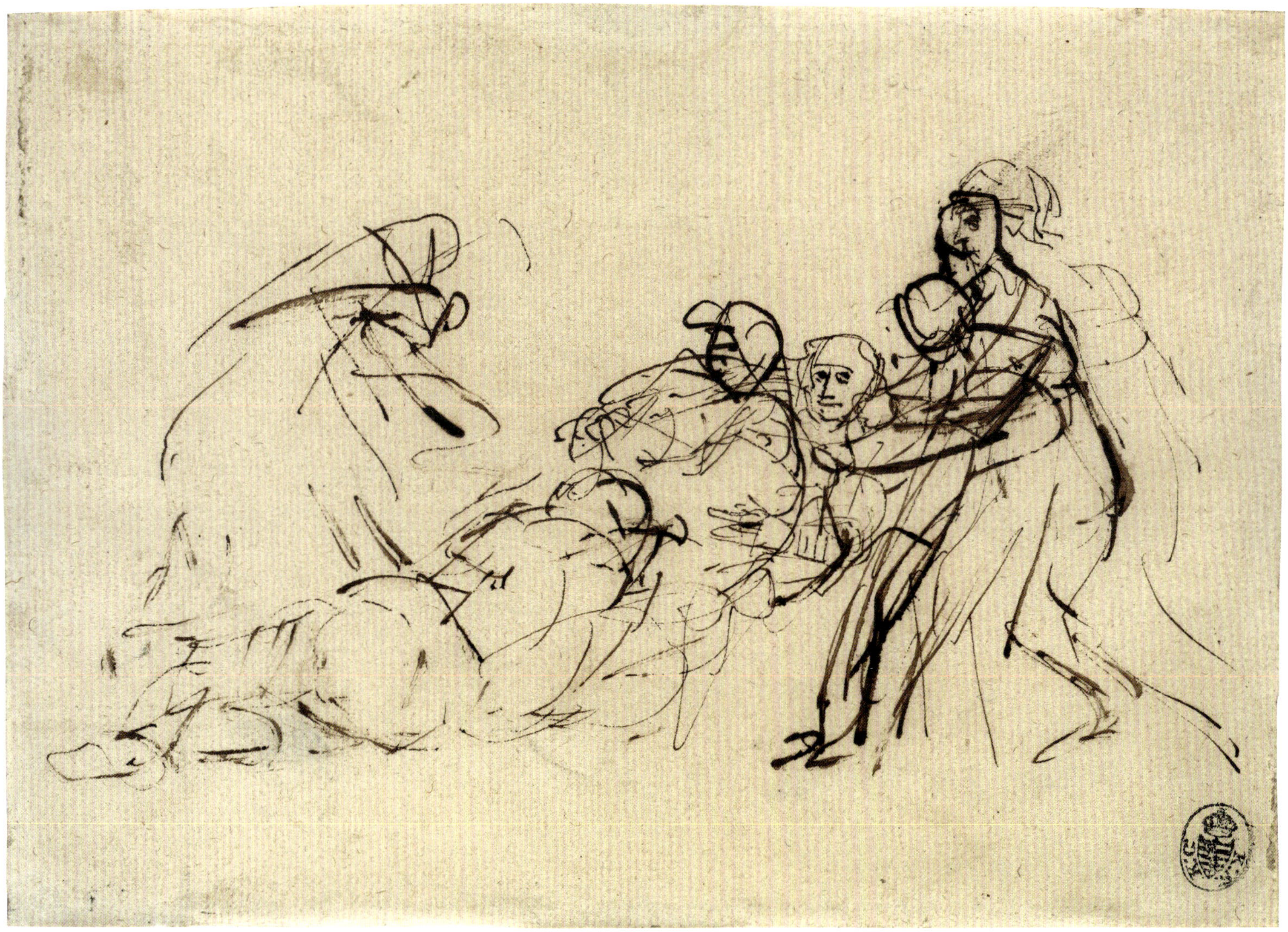

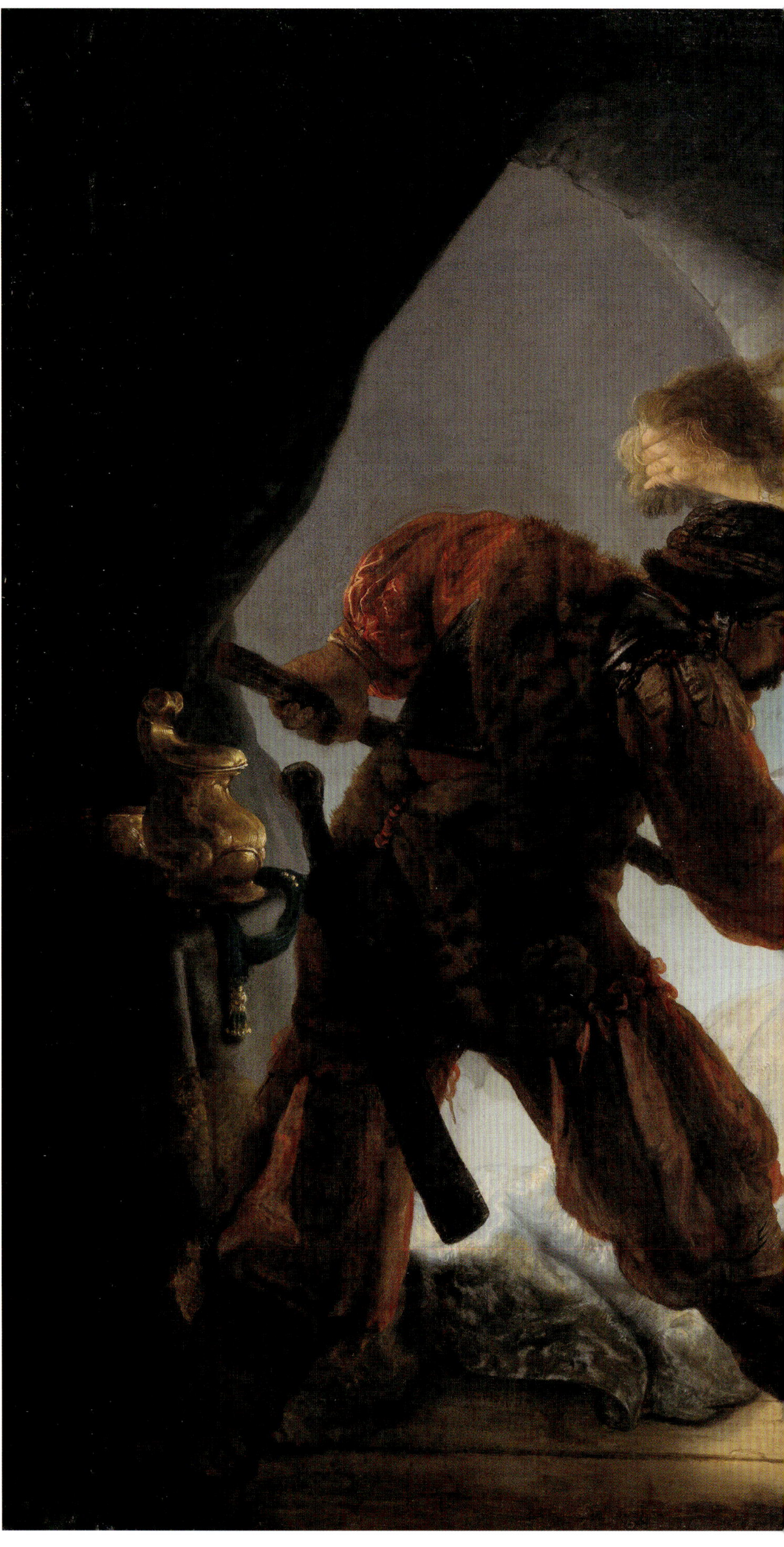

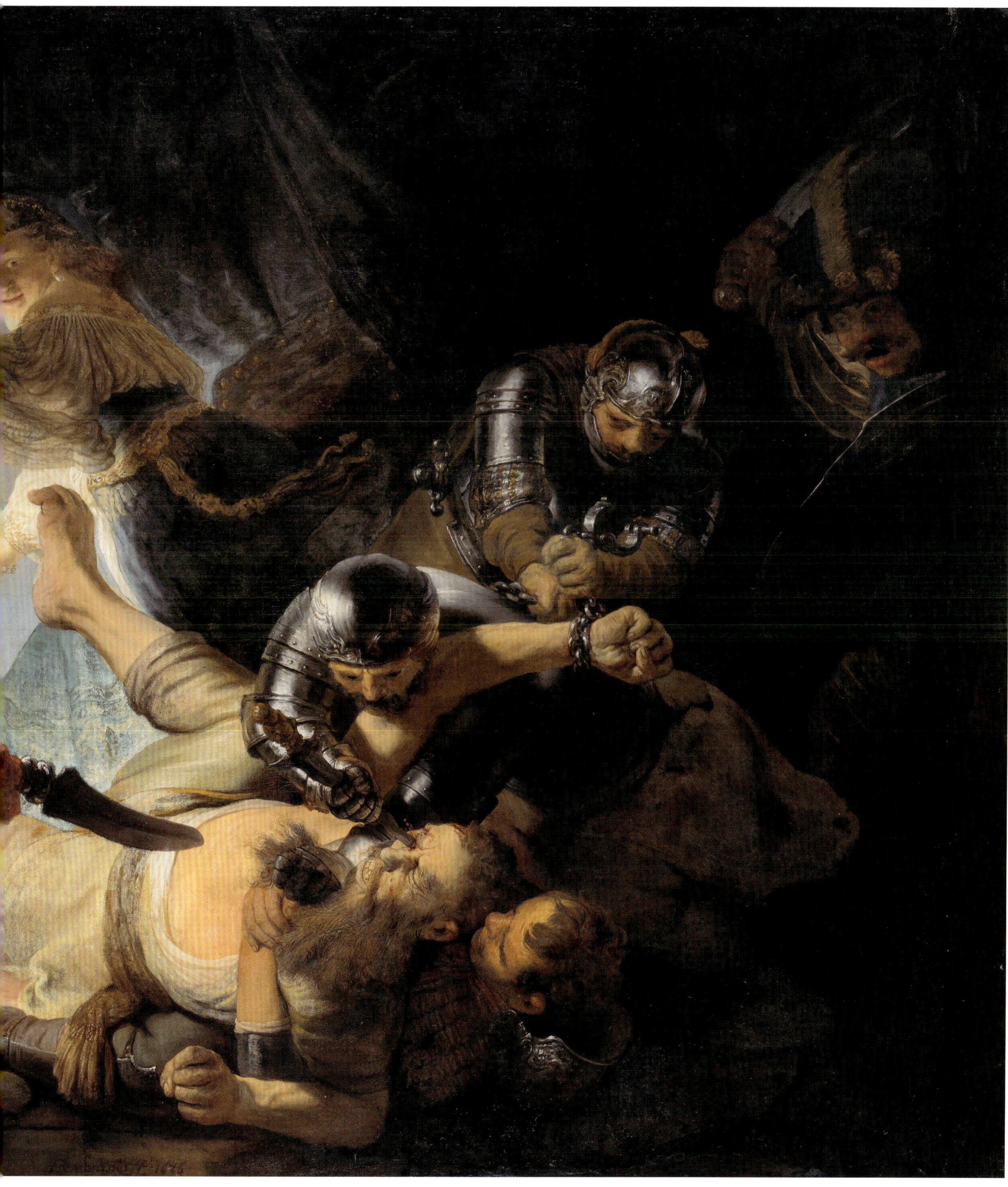

The Expulsion of Hagar

FRIEDERIKE SCHÜTT

For several decades, the expulsion of Hagar was one of the most popular religious subjects portrayed in the studios of Rembrandt and his contemporaries and sold on the Amsterdam art market for a range of different prices.[1] We know from inventories that paintings of this theme, typically small in scale, adorned interiors such as the living and reception rooms of wealthy merchants and regents.[2] Its popularity hinged on both the moral values and the profound human passions and conflicts conveyed in the biblical passage and its pictorial representation.[3]

According to Genesis 21:9–14, since Abraham and Sarah had remained childless for a long time, Sarah asked their Egyptian maidservant Hagar to bear Abraham's child; a son was born, whom they named Ishmael. When Sarah later gave birth at a very advanced age to a child of her own, Isaac, she urged Abraham to cast out Hagar and Ishmael. God would later call upon Abraham to sacrifice Isaac in a heart-rending test of faith (pls. 114–116). Protestant theologians associated Ishmael with Judaism and Isaac with the advent of Christianity.[4]

The story concerns love and grief, jealousy and doubt. It thematizes questions of tolerance and faith in God, as well as family values and challenges. In the Netherlands, a country enduring the separation of its northern and southern provinces, the theme also held particular social and political relevance. The pictorial narratives created from the 1630s onward aroused sympathy for the conflicted patriarch and the powerless maidservant.[5]

Many of these works drew upon a 1612 painting by Pieter Lastman (pl. 107).[6] His rendition must have been accessible in Amsterdam for at least the next forty years, as evidenced by Rembrandt's c. 1637 drawn copy (pl. 108), Barent Fabritius' painting from the 1650s (pl. 111) and no fewer than 150 other variants of the subject.[7]

Focusing on the interaction between the protagonists, Lastman shows Abraham and Hagar facing each other before a landscape that offers, on the left, a view of family life on the farm and, on the right, the path that Hagar must now take. Standing between them, Ishmael wipes tears from his face.

Abraham lays a hand on his son's head, at once blessing and reassuring him, and touches Hagar's arm, while Hagar expresses her farewell with an expansive gesture.

Rembrandt's drawing concentrates on the same constellation of figures. With loose yet precise lines, he captures the emotional dynamics of the parting.[8] Almost two decades later, the continued impact of Lastman's motif, mediated by Rembrandt's drawing, manifested itself in Fabritius' painting. Fabritius takes over the figure of Abraham but changes the palette, lighting and background details, and equips the youthful Hagar with a handkerchief to dry her tears. Especially striking is Fabritius' revised conception of the figure of Ishmael. He probably emulated two drawings by Rembrandt that show the boy from the back with quiver and staff, thus shifting the focus to Abraham and Hagar (pls. 109, 110).[9]

Rembrandt returned to the subject in an etching from 1637 (pl. 112), in which he positions Abraham between Sarah and Hagar and their sons, showing great sensitivity to the patriarch's inner conflict. Abraham stands with arms outstretched, one foot on the house steps and the other on the path.[10] Rembrandt must have been keenly aware of the market value of this popular theme, since he sold the copperplate to a Portuguese merchant but kept a few impressions of the print for himself to profit from their sale.[11] Although he depicted several moments in the story of Abraham over the course of his career, there is no indication that he ever painted this scene.[12]

Further evidence of the diverse creative approaches to this theme is Govert Flinck's painting from around 1642 (pl. 113). Depicting three half-figures in close-up and linking them through their gazes and gestures (a formula he learned in Lambert Jacobsz's Leeuwarden studio), Flinck emphasizes the emotional exchange between Abraham and Hagar. Sarah and Isaac are nowhere to be seen.[13] To gratify his affluent clientele's taste, Flinck opted for a smooth application of colour and a brighter palette[14] – a style that could hardly have been more different from the one favoured by his former master, Rembrandt. ■

NOTES

1 Sluijter 2015, 261–263; Netty van Kamp, "Die Genesis. Die Urgeschichte und die Geschichte der Erzväter," in Münster, Amsterdam and Jerusalem 1994, 30. See also the essay by Jasper Hillegers in this volume. On the popularity of this theme in the lower price range, see Jager 2015, 10–12.

2 See Sellin 2006, 3.

3 See Van Kamp, "Die Genesis," in Münster, Amsterdam and Jerusalem 1994, 30; Sellin 2006, 156. Martina Sitt points out that Hagar "as a fascinating woman and mother [embodied] a clear alternative to the mariological tradition of the Catholic Habsburgs in Spain"; Martina Sitt, "Lastman und Rembrandt am Beispiel der 'Verstoßung der Hagar,'" in Vienna 2004, 293.

4 Perlove and Silver 2009, 76–77, 82.

5 See Sellin 2006, esp. 156.

6 Lastman's depiction is based on an iconography established in the sixteenth century with works such as Lucas van Leyden's engravings of 1506 and 1516; see Hamann 1936, 475–479; Martina Sitt, "Pieter Lastman und Rembrandt – von der stummen Sprache des Körpers zur Verdichtung von Emotion," in Hamburg 2006, 82.

7 See Sitt, "Lastman und Rembrandt," in Vienna 2004, 292; Seifert 2011, 229–230. See also the essay by Jasper Hillegers in this volume.

8 See Hamann 1936, 474.

9 See ibid., 484–486; Hadjinicolaou 2016, 277–278; Jonathan Bikker, "Imitation and Originality in the History Paintings of Rembrandt's Pupils," in Kofuku 2004, 78; Peter Schatborn, "Rembrandt van Rijn, *Expulsion of Hagar and Ishmael*, Amsterdam, c. 1650," in Turner 2017.

10 See Sitt, "Lastman und Rembrandt," in Vienna 2004, 292; Perlove and Silver 2009, 76–92, esp. 82–86; Englard 2018, 284.

11 "Rembrandt's sale of the plate of his etching 'Abraham's Dismissal of Hagar and Ishmael,'" 17 Dec. 1637, Remdoc, no. e4445; Strauss and Van der Meulen 1979, doc. 1637/7; this is the first known instance in which he sold one of his copperplates.

12 On representations of Abraham, see also Sellin 2006, 109–113; New York 2017; Perlove and Silver 2009, 76–92.

13 As for the absence of Sarah and Isaac, a precedent is Lucas van Leyden's engraving of 1516, for which see, among others, Perlove and Silver 2009, 83.

14 See Eric Jan Sluijter, "Govert Flinck's Historical Paintings in Artistic Context," in Cleves 2015–16, 67–70; Erna E. Kok, "Prosperous Friends and Distinguished Gentlemen: The Patrons of Govert Flinck," in ibid., 24–25, 28–29; David de Witt, "Govert Flinck Learns to Paint like Rembrandt," in Amsterdam 2017–18, 37–39.

107 Pieter Lastman, *The Expulsion of Hagar and Ishmael*, 1612. Hamburger Kunsthalle, Hamburg

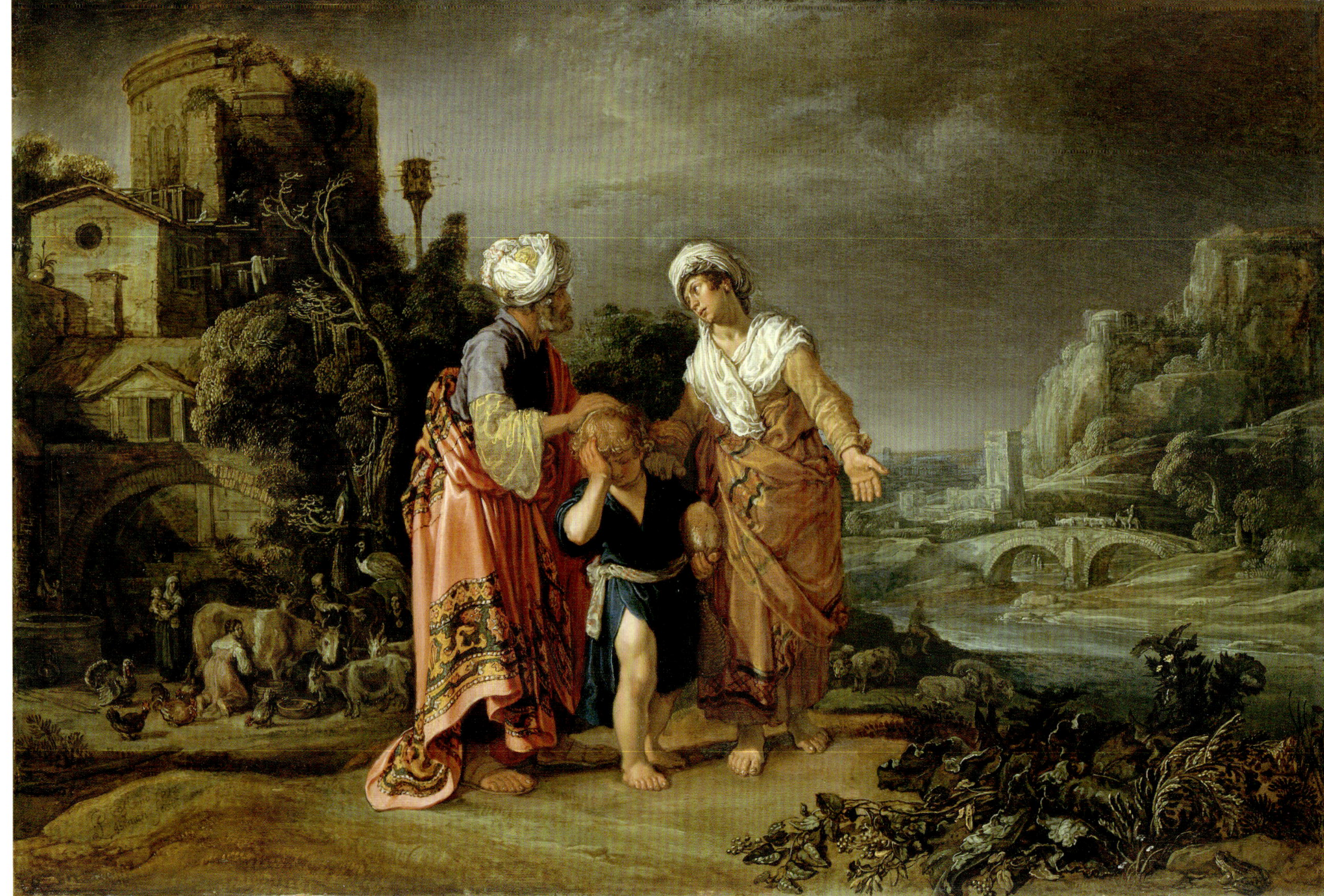

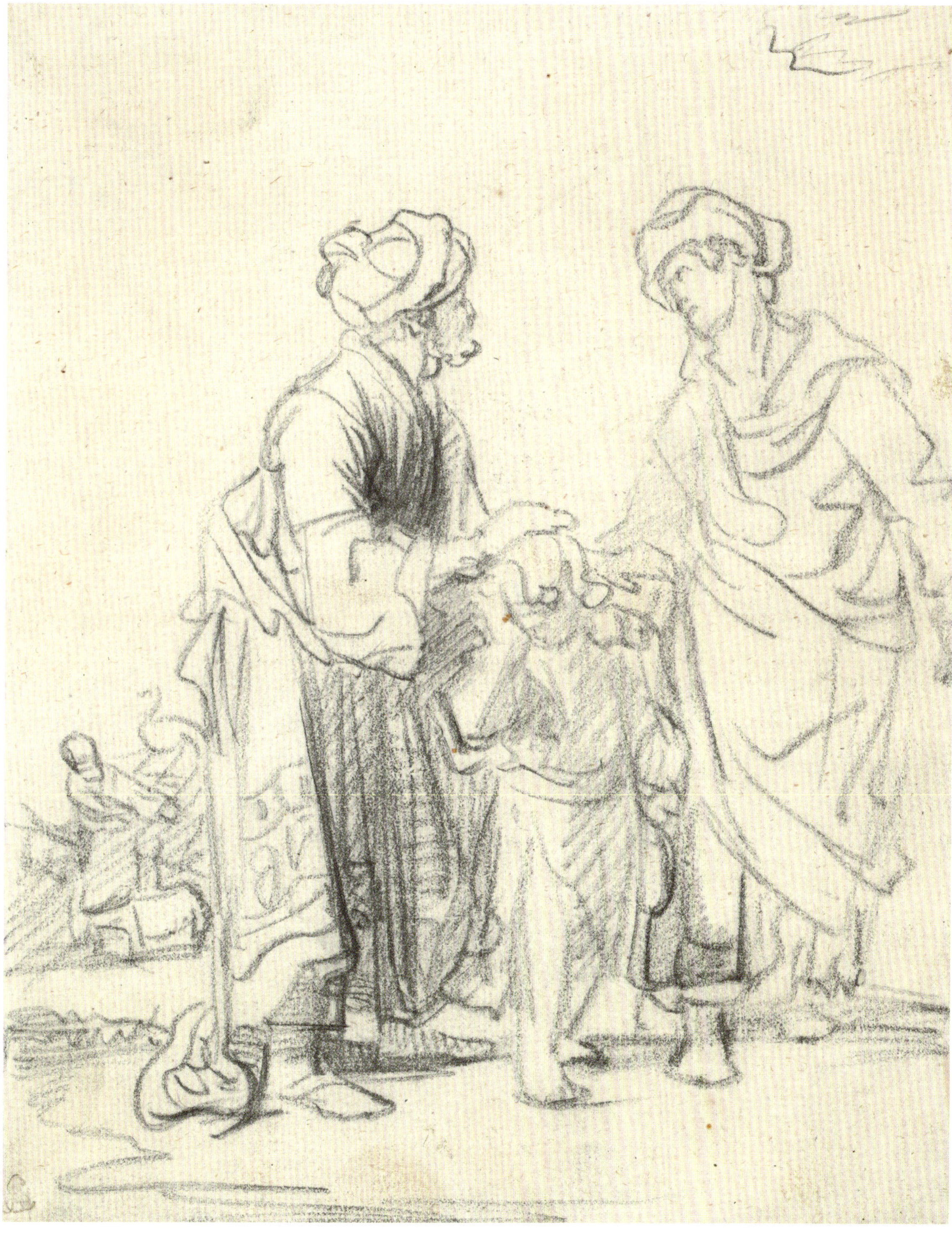

109   Rembrandt van Rijn, *The Expulsion of Hagar and Ishmael*, c. 1650. Rijksmuseum, Amsterdam
110   Rembrandt van Rijn, *The Expulsion of Hagar and Ishmael*, c. 1642–46. The British Museum, London

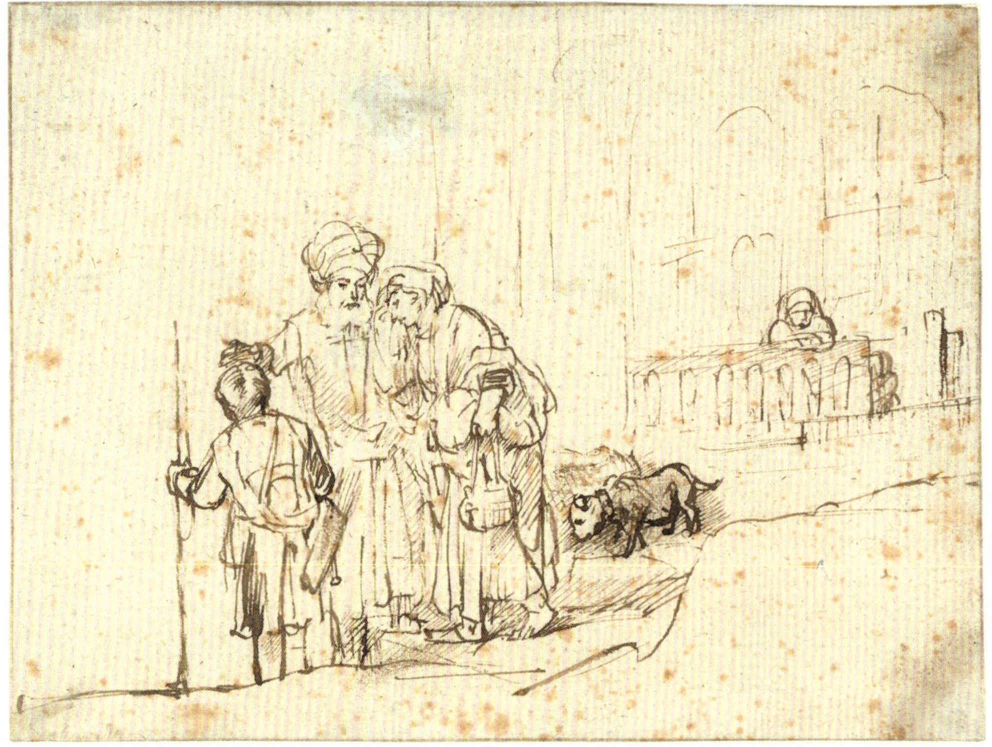

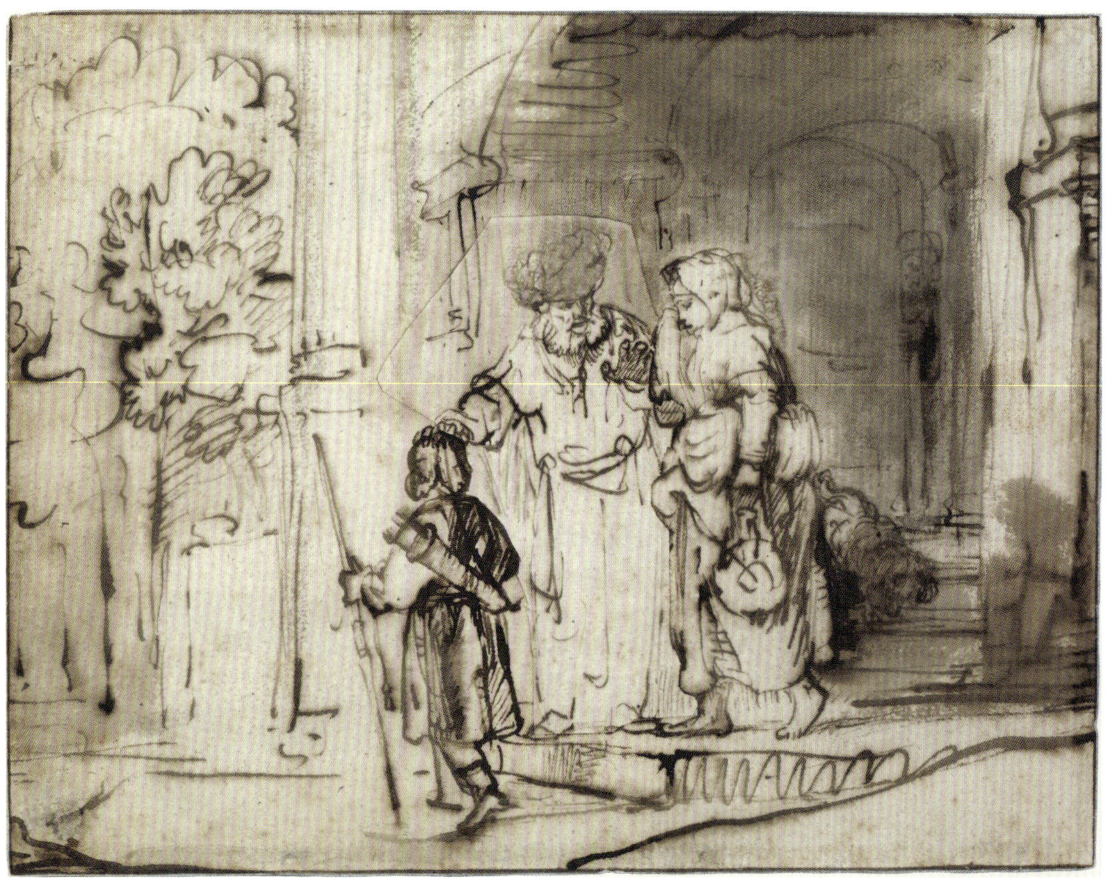

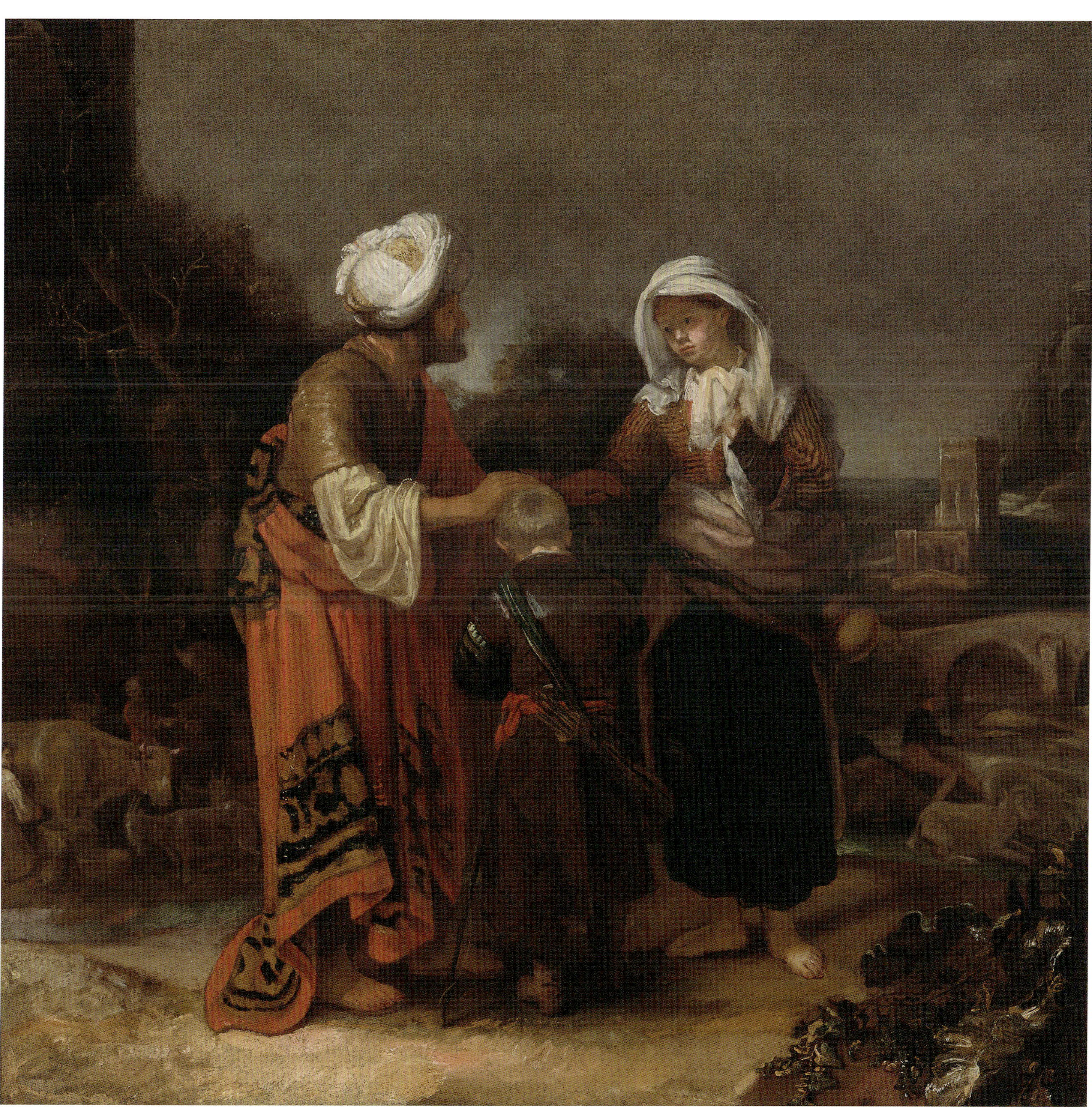

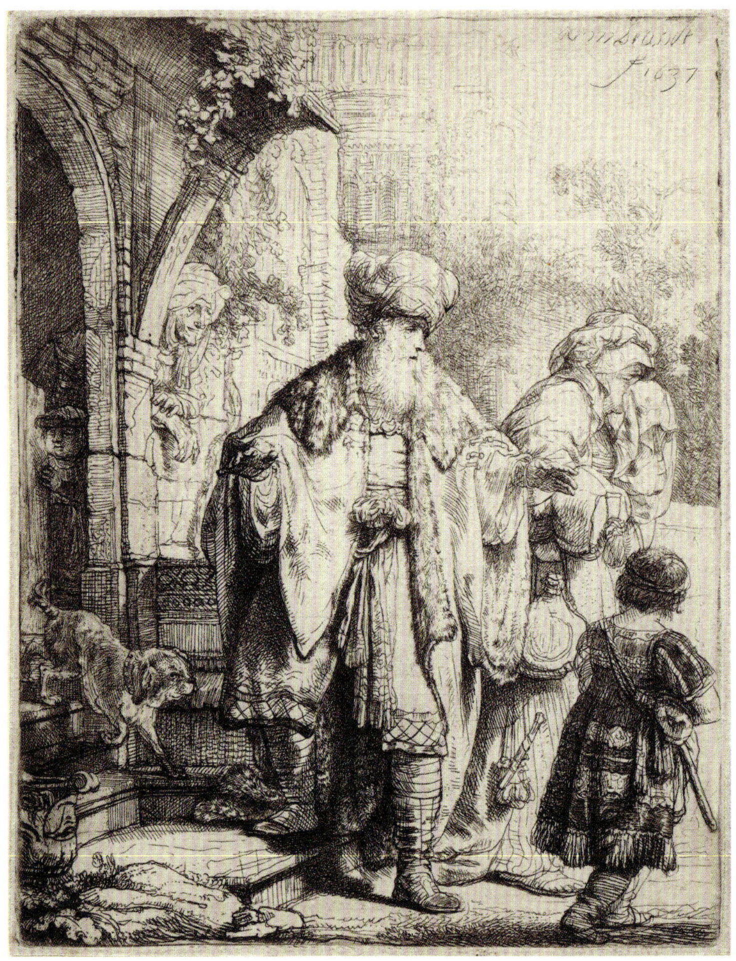

112 Rembrandt van Rijn, *The Expulsion of Hagar and Ishmael*, 1637. Städel Museum, Frankfurt am Main

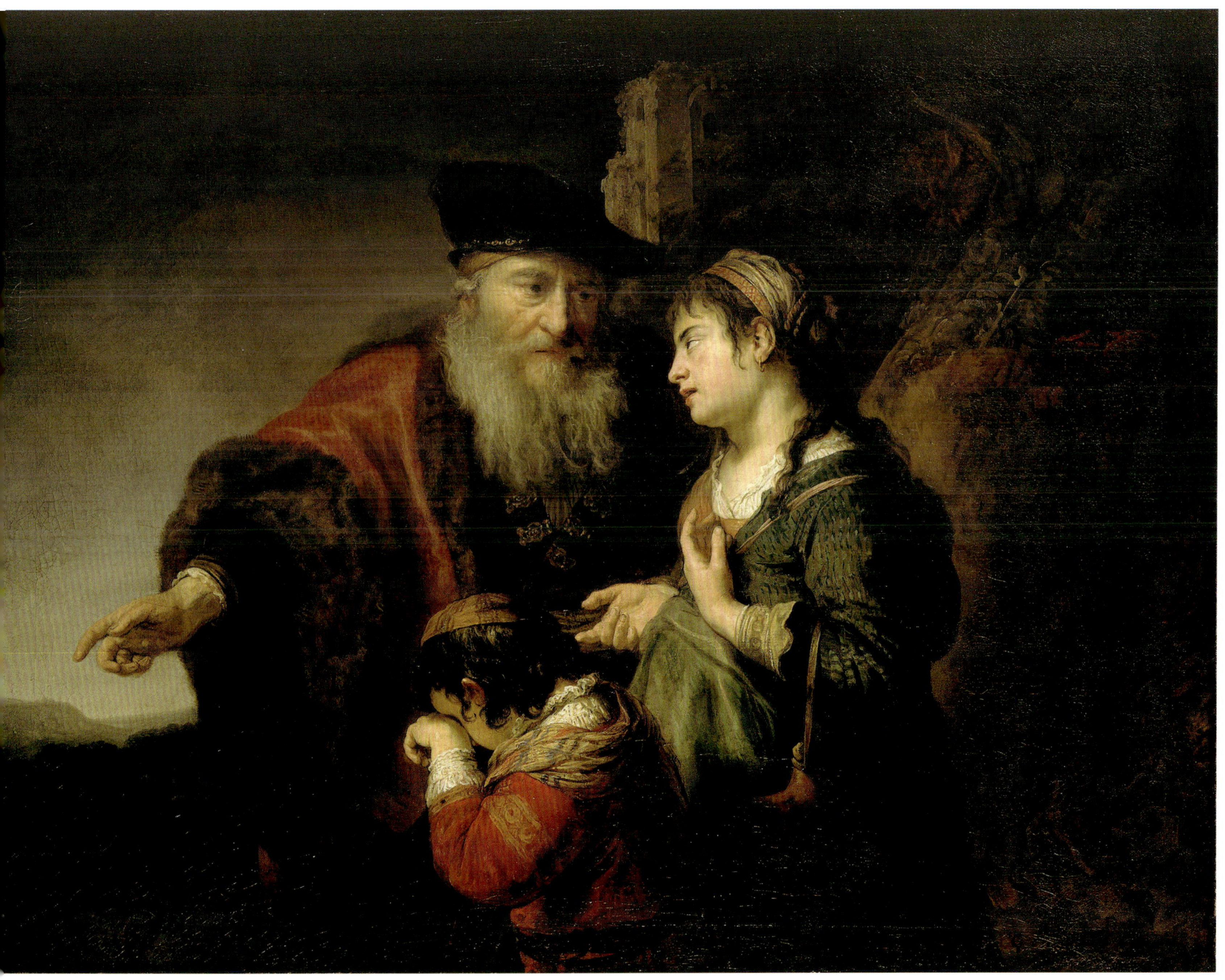

Angelic Messengers

STEPHANIE S. DICKEY

Some of the most gripping tales in the Bible depend on angelic intervention at crucial moments in human experience, and seventeenth-century artists took full advantage of the opportunity to depict dramatic scenes of reversal and revelation.[1] Arnold Houbraken remarked on Rembrandt's talent for continually reinventing familiar themes, and Rembrandt passed on this skill by encouraging his students to produce creative variants of his compositions.[2] Originals, variants and copies could all be sold as part of the workshop's stock in trade. Before Rembrandt became independent in 1635, Hendrick Uylenburgh would have taken a cut of the profits, but after that the artist made a substantial income from workshop production.[3] For Dutch Protestant theologians, angelic messengers in the stories of Abraham, Manoah, Gideon, Elijah and other patriarchs manifested God's presence on Earth, linking the Old Testament with the Christian promise of salvation (pl. 120).[4] These dramatic scenes became a staple of the Rembrandt brand.

A well-known case is his *Abraham's Sacrifice of Isaac* of 1635 (fig. 12.1), depicting the angel's arrival just in time to save Abraham from sacrificing his son Isaac in a brutal test of faith.[5] An inscription shows that Rembrandt retouched a second version, probably painted by Govert Flinck (fig. 12.2). A drawing by Rembrandt suggests that he consulted with his pupil on the one substantial change: the sharp foreshortening of the angel.[6] Years later, the composition still resonated in Ferdinand Bol's etching of the subject (pl. 115), where Isaac actively witnesses his salvation, and in a monumental painting Bol completed in 1646 for the home of a wealthy Amsterdam merchant.[7] Nicolaes Maes showed greater independence in a version painted soon after leaving Rembrandt's studio in 1651, depicting the psychologically charged moment just before Abraham draws his knife (pl. 114).[8] In 1655 Rembrandt returned to the scene in a masterful etching, now wrapping Abraham in a redemptive angelic embrace (pl. 116).[9]

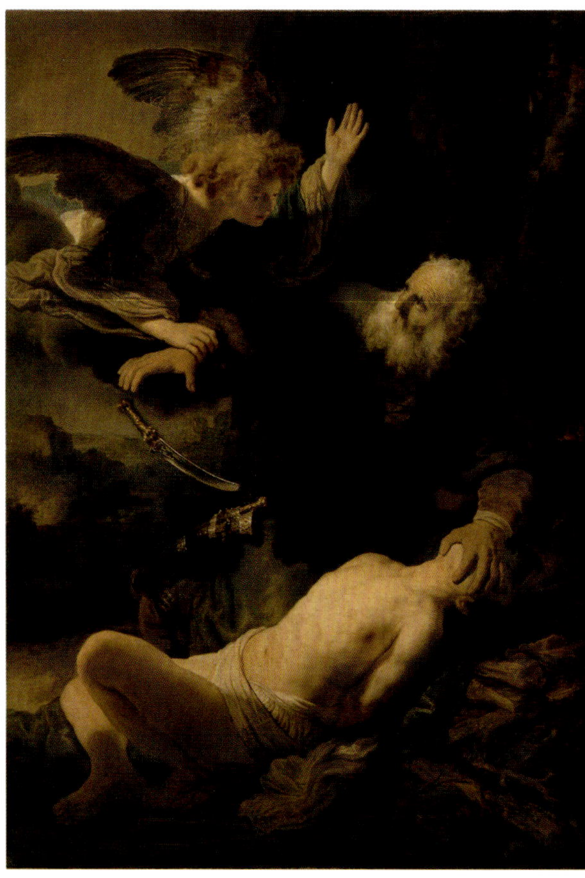

fig. 12.1 **Rembrandt van Rijn,** *Abraham's Sacrifice of Isaac,* 1635, oil on canvas; 193 × 132 cm. The State Hermitage Museum, St. Petersburg (ГЭ-727)

fig. 12.2 **Rembrandt Workshop, attributed to Govert Flinck, retouched by Rembrandt van Rijn,** *Abraham's Sacrifice of Isaac,* 1636, oil on canvas; 195 × 132.3 cm. Bayerische Staatsgemäldesammlungen, Alte Pinakothek, Munich (438)

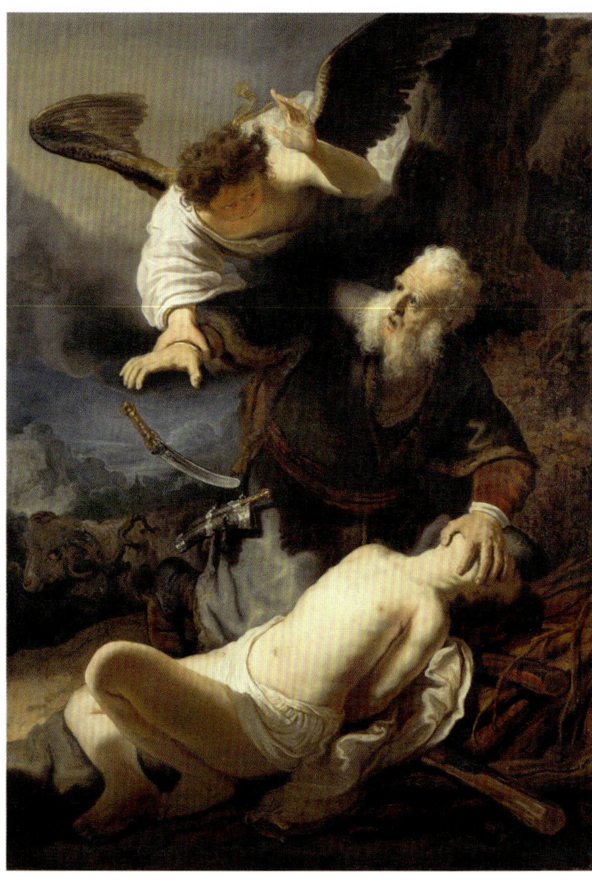

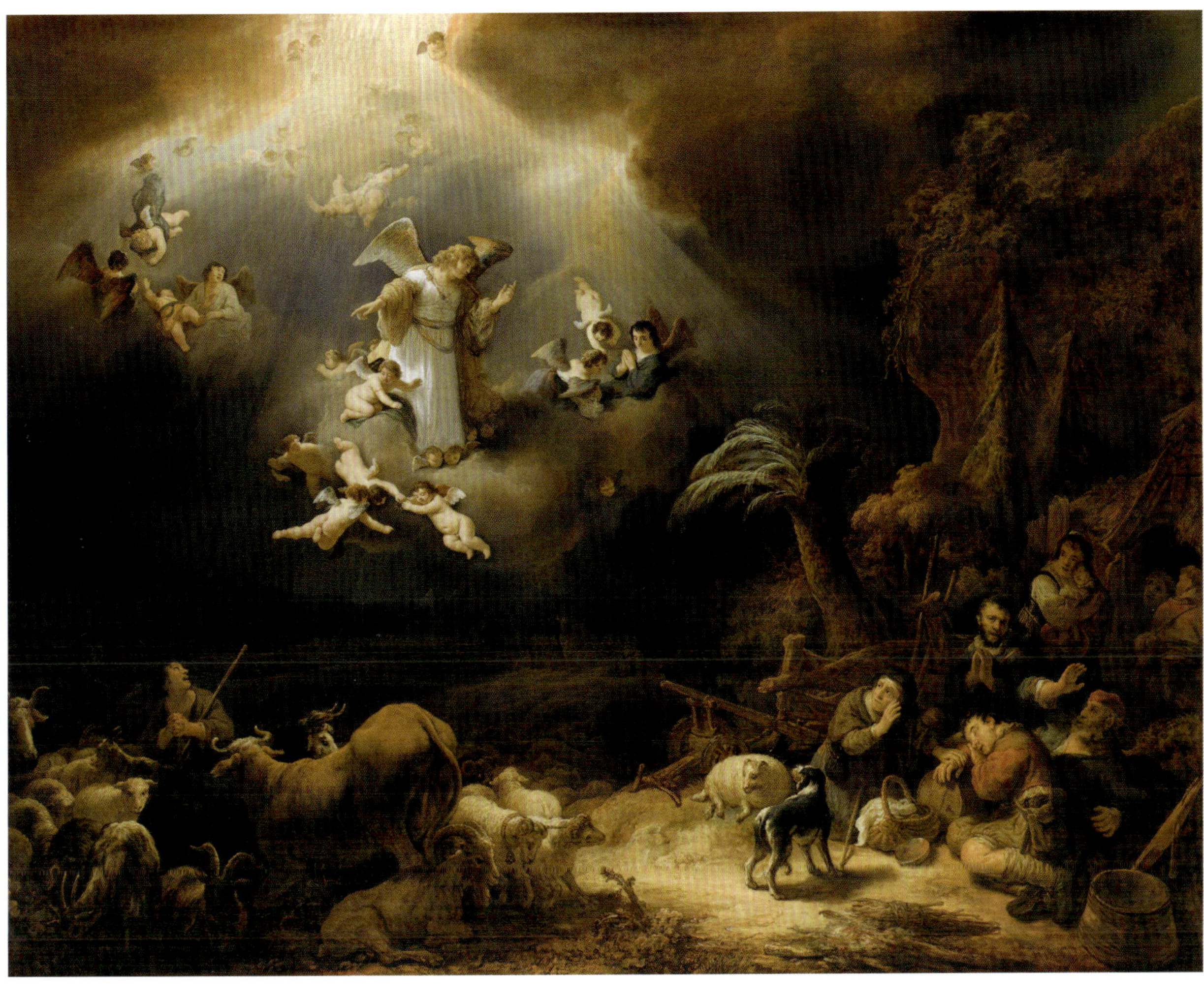

fig. 12.3 Govert Flinck,
The Angel Appearing to the
Shepherds, 1639, oil on canvas;
160 × 196 cm. Musée du Louvre,
Paris (1291)

Rembrandt's lessons echoed long after followers left his workshop. Flinck may have owned an impression of Rembrandt's *Angel Appearing to the Shepherds* (pl. 126), created in 1634 while both artists were working for Uylenburgh. In 1639 Flinck adapted the composition for a large painting that ambitiously blends admiration and rivalry (fig. 12.3). It was purchased by Uylenburgh himself.[10]

A whole sequence of images features an airborne angel seen from behind. This figure has been traced to a single source, a woodcut from a series of scenes from the Book of Tobit designed around 1548 by Marten van Heemskerck (fig. 12.4). It must have been available for study in Rembrandt's extensive print collection.[11] This motif became a focal point for Rembrandt's students to compete with each other and with the master himself, perhaps to the delight of collectors who enjoyed comparing their acquisitions.

Around 1635 Rembrandt borrowed Heemskerck's angel for a drawing depicting a moment of revelation from the Book of Judges, where an angelic messenger disappears after instructing Manoah and his wife on how to bring up their miracle child, Samson (fig. 12.5).[12] For a painting of 1640, Flinck adapted the angel and the couple's reverent poses (pl. 117). The unusually wide format may have been commissioned for a hidden Catholic church in Gouda.[13]

Numerous artists depicted the adventures of Tobit's son Tobias, accompanied by the Archangel Raphael in disguise, in search of a cure for his father's blindness. Heemskerck's woodcut shows the final moment when the angel disappears after announcing his identity. In 1637 Rembrandt borrowed the angel for his painting of the same scene (fig. 12.7). It must have been a commercial success, since the composition was repeated by Ferdinand Bol and others in his workshop, with creative variations including a hovering angel who now faces forward (pl. 119).[14]

It is unlikely that Jan Victors, a native of Amsterdam, worked directly in Rembrandt's studio; the decisive clarity of his manner differs from Rembrandt's nuanced treatment of light, colour and composition.[15] Yet, he clearly sought to emulate both

Rembrandt and Pieter Lastman, borrowing subjects, figure types, costume details and narrative strategies. His work is thus an intriguing indicator of Rembrandt's broader impact on the Amsterdam market. In Victors' large painting of 1649 *The Angel Departing from the Family of Tobias* (pl. 118), strong colours and clear daylight mark his stylistic independence from Rembrandt, yet the familiar angel once again ascends into the sky. The animated figures each react differently to the revelation, a rhetorical technique perfected by Lastman. While no documentation for Victors' early patronage is known, the large number of extant portraits, histories and genre paintings suggests that his precise rendering and lucid story-telling found a ready market.[16]

One etching of 1641 stands apart from the competition. Here, Rembrandt situates us at ground level, watching with Tobias and his parents as Raphael departs (fig. 12.6).[17] The angel's rather stocky bare legs are all that is visible as he vanishes in a blaze of light off the corner of the plate. Below, the donkey pricks its ears in amazement, while the little dog, companion of Tobias' adventure, turns his back on the action. These witty details bring divine revelation squarely down to earth. ■

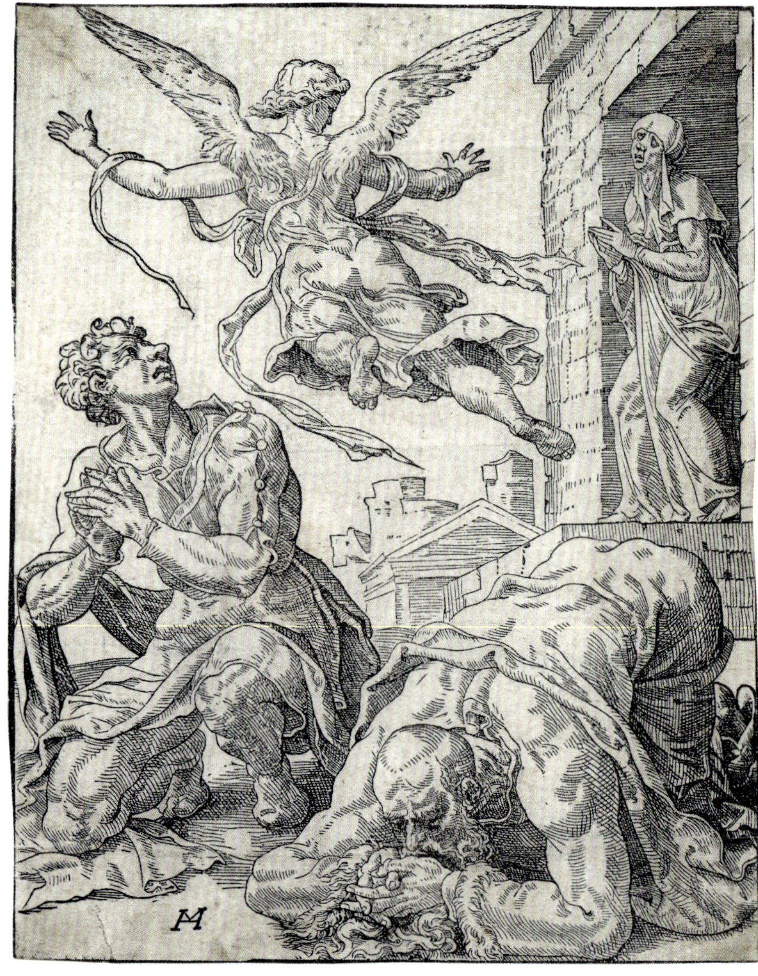

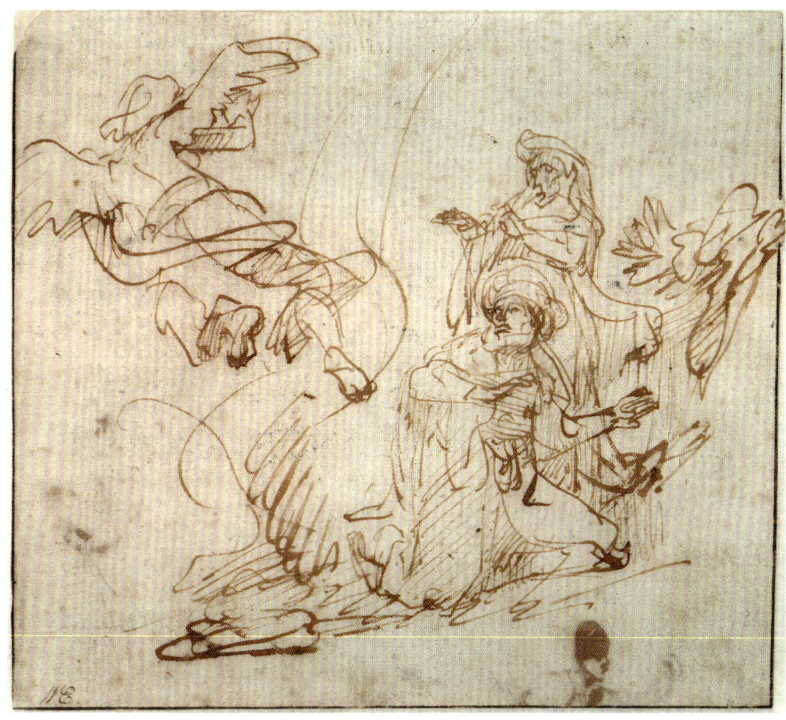

fig. 12.4 **Dirck Volckertsz Coornhert (after Marten van Heemskerck),** *The Angel Departing from the Family of Tobias*, 1548, woodcut on laid paper; 24 × 17.7 cm. Agnes Etherington Art Centre, Queen's University, Kingston. Purchase, Bader Acquisition Fund, 2010 (53-046.018)

fig. 12.5 **Rembrandt van Rijn,** *The Angel Departing from Manoah and His Wife*, c. 1635–38, pen and ink on laid paper; 17.4 × 19 cm. Staatliche Museen zu Berlin, Kupferstichkabinett (KdZ 3774)

fig. 12.6 **Rembrandt van Rijn,** *The Angel Departing from the Family of Tobias*, 1641, etching and drypoint on laid paper; 10.3 × 15.4 cm. National Gallery of Art, Washington. Rosenwald Collection (1943.3.7188)

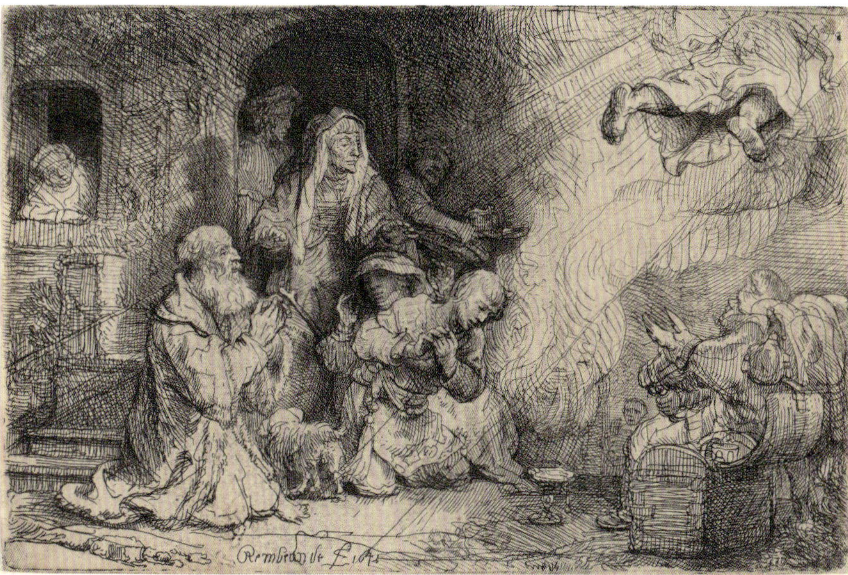

fig. 12.7 **Rembrandt van Rijn,** *The Angel Departing from the Family of Tobias*, 1637, oil on panel; 66 × 52 cm. Musée du Louvre, Paris (1736)

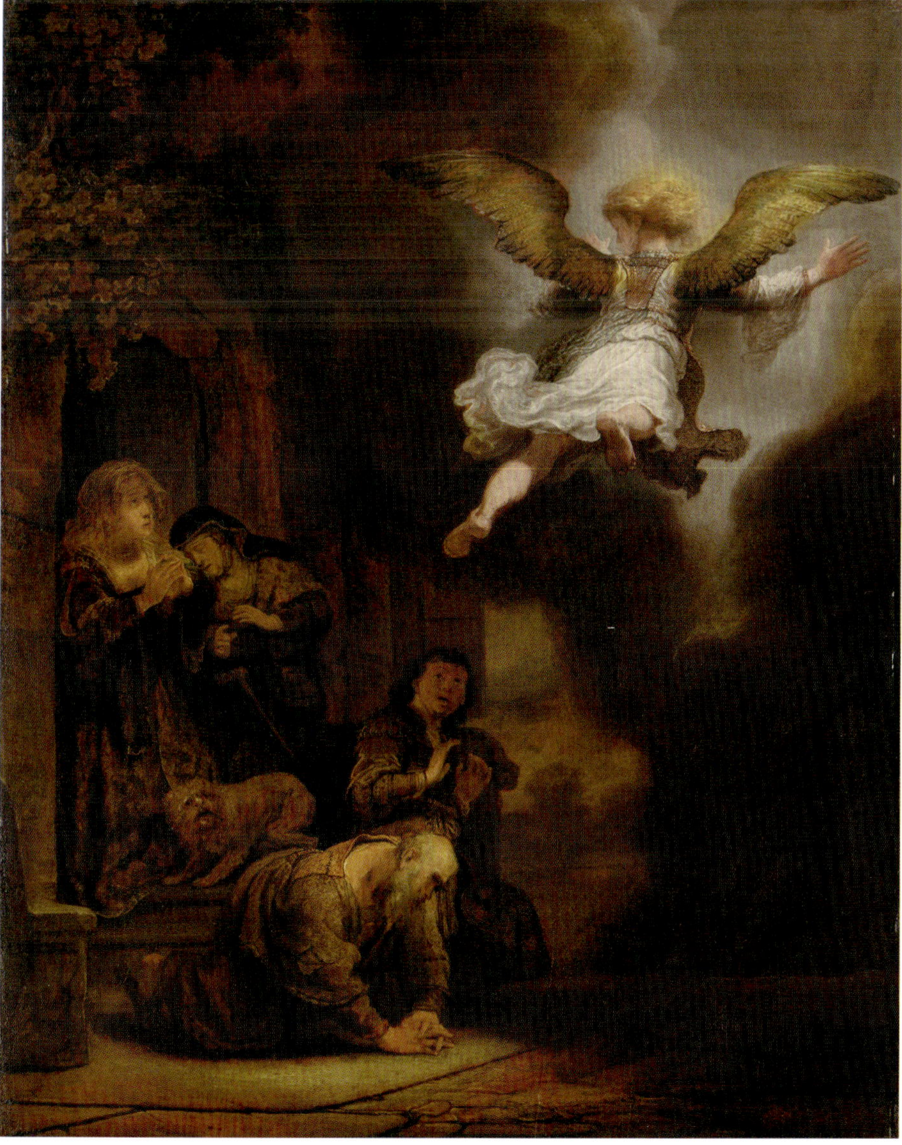

NOTES

1   On narrative strategies, inspired in part by dramatic theory, see, among others, Sluijter 2010; Sluijter 2014. On Rembrandt's angels, see also New York 2017.

2   Houbraken 1718–21, vol. 1, 257–258.

3   Sandrart 1675–80, vol. 2, book 3, 326, states that Rembrandt charged tuition of 100 guilders per year and made between 2,000 and 2,500 guilders from the sale of his pupils' work; Sluijter 2015, 76.

4   Perlove and Silver 2009, 352–358, 367. See also New York 2017. On Fabritius, see Sumowski 1983–94, vol. 2, no. 583.

5   Genesis 22: 1–15; on the role of this subject in Dutch theology, see Perlove and Silver 2009, 86–92.

6   Rembrandt van Rijn, *The Sacrifice of Isaac* (The British Museum, London, inv. 1897,1117.5); Royalton-Kisch 2010, no. 10; Schatborn and Hinterding 2019, no. D43. A now lost painting by Pieter Lastman, later recorded in a print by Jan van Somer, may have suggested this change. In a grisaille of c. 1612 (Rijksmuseum, Amsterdam), Lastman in turn borrowed an angel from Caravaggio.

7   Now in Museo Nazionale di Palazzo Mansi, Lucca; see Amsterdam 2017–18, 100–104.

8   De Witt 2014, no. 32; London and The Hague 2019–20, no. 3. A preparatory drawing for the figure of Isaac is in the Victoria and Albert Museum, London.

9   NHD 287. Abraham's life furnished other subjects as well; for the Expulsion of Hagar, see pls. 107–113.

10   NHD 125; on Flinck's painting, see recently Amsterdam 2019–20, 32–33; Stephanie S. Dickey, "Introduction: Rising Stars in Rembrandt's Amsterdam," in Dickey 2017a, 6–18, esp. 6–8.

11   Rembrandt's collection as of 1656, about which much has been written, is listed in the inventory taken at his bankruptcy; Strauss and Van der Meulen 1979, doc. 1656/12.

12   Schatborn and Hinterding 2019, no. D34. Judges 13: 1–24, the first chapter in the story leading to *The Blinding of Samson* (pl. 106); see Perlove and Silver 2009, 107–115, esp. 109–110.

13   De Witt 2008, no. 75.

14   Here again, Heemskerck offers an antecedent; see unknown engraver (after Marten van Heemskerck), *The Departure of the Angel*, NHD Heemskerck 198. For Rembrandt's painting and variants, see esp. Golahny 2007; *Corpus*, vol. 6, no. 150; Amsterdam 2017–18, 46–50; Dickey, "Introduction," in Dickey 2017a, 6–12; and the essay by Jasper Hillegers in this volume.

15   Sluijter 2015, 362–373, argues convincingly that Victors could not have learned his lucid style from Rembrandt and discusses the likelihood of Calvinist and Jewish patronage.

16   Sumowski 1983–94, vol. 4, no. 1742; variant in the Alte Pinakothek, Munich, no. 1750. Sumowski's catalogue lists one hundred paintings by Victors.

17   NHD 189; Dickey, "Introduction," in Dickey 2017a, 11; for analysis, see also Hinterding 2008, 98–100.

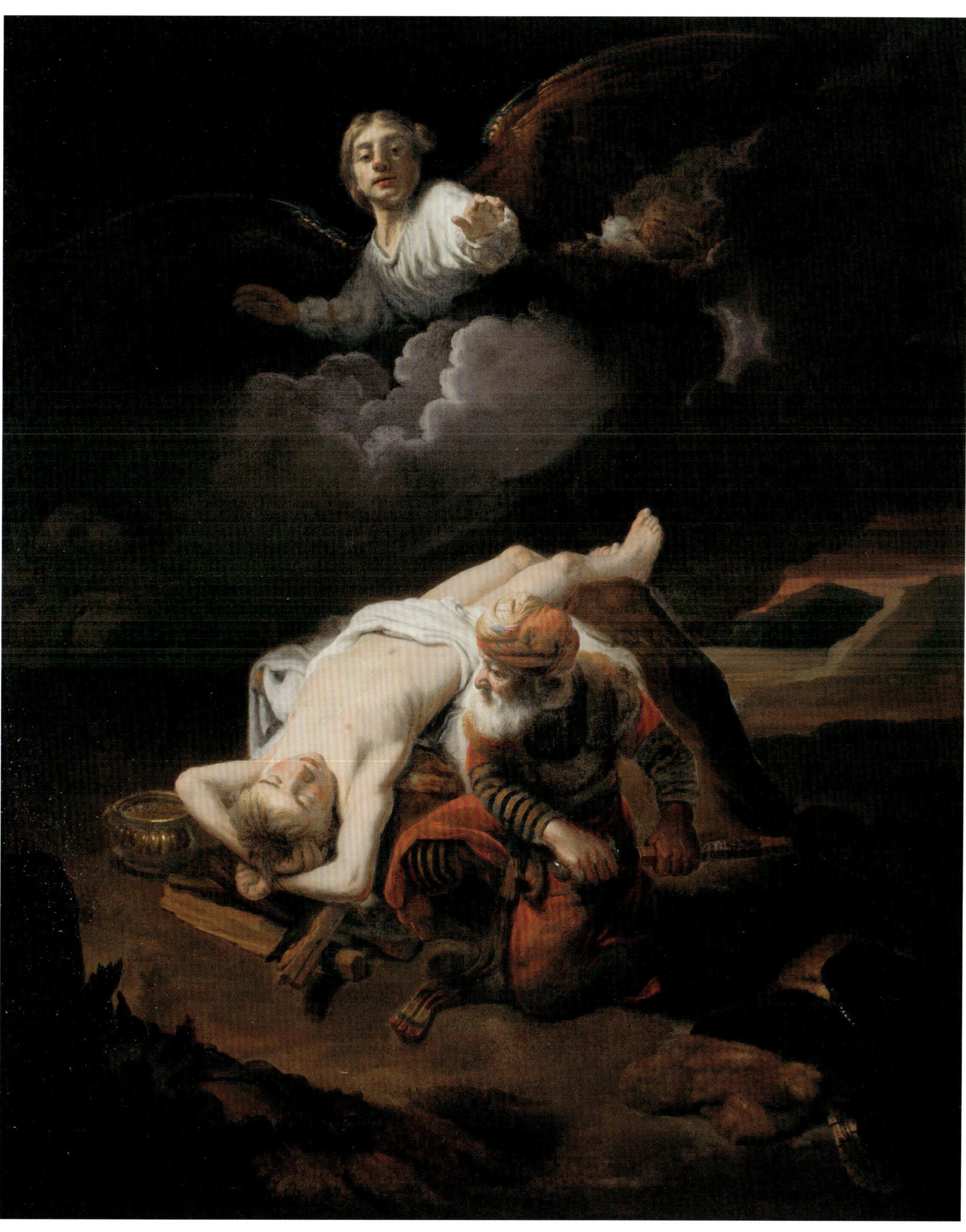

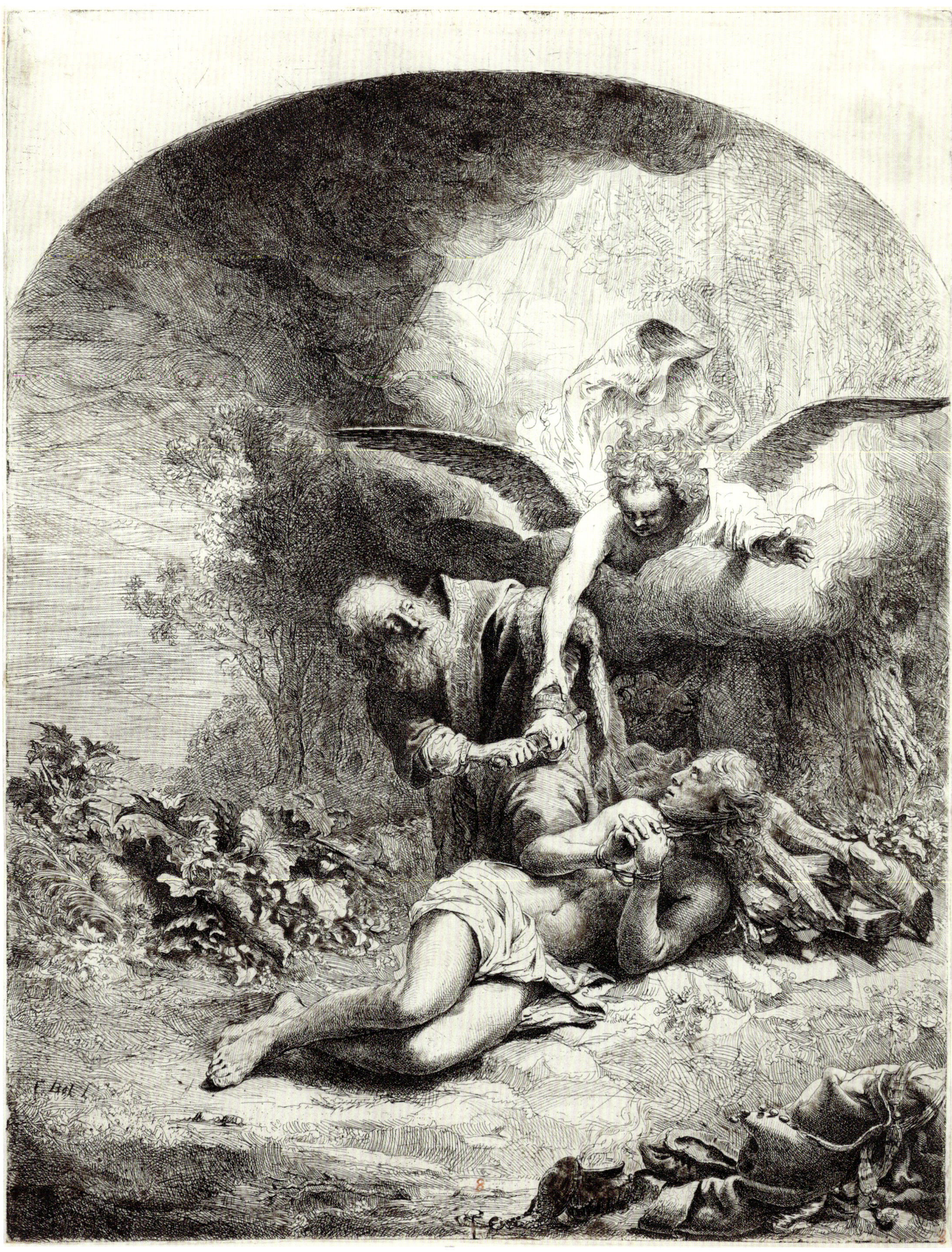

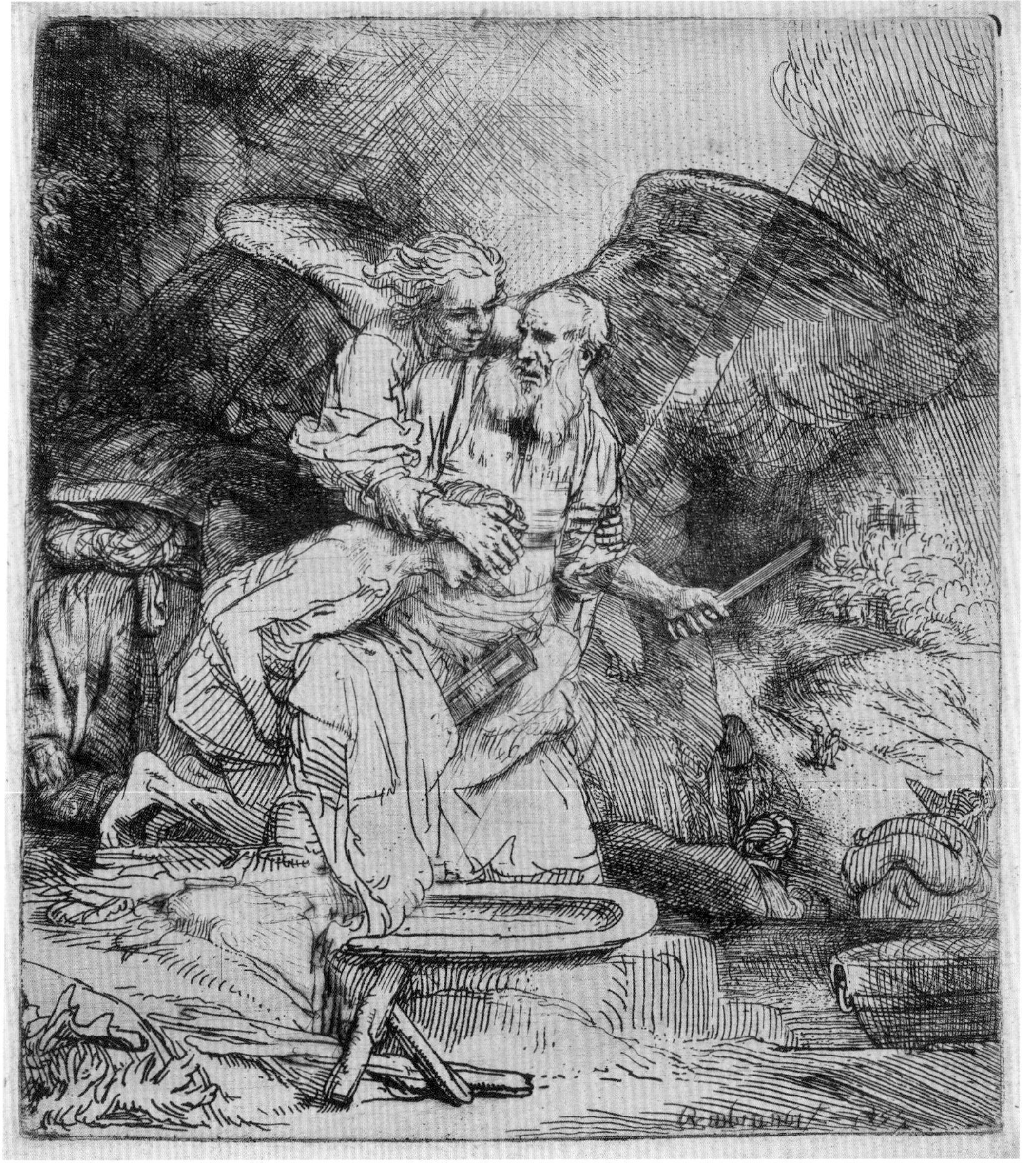

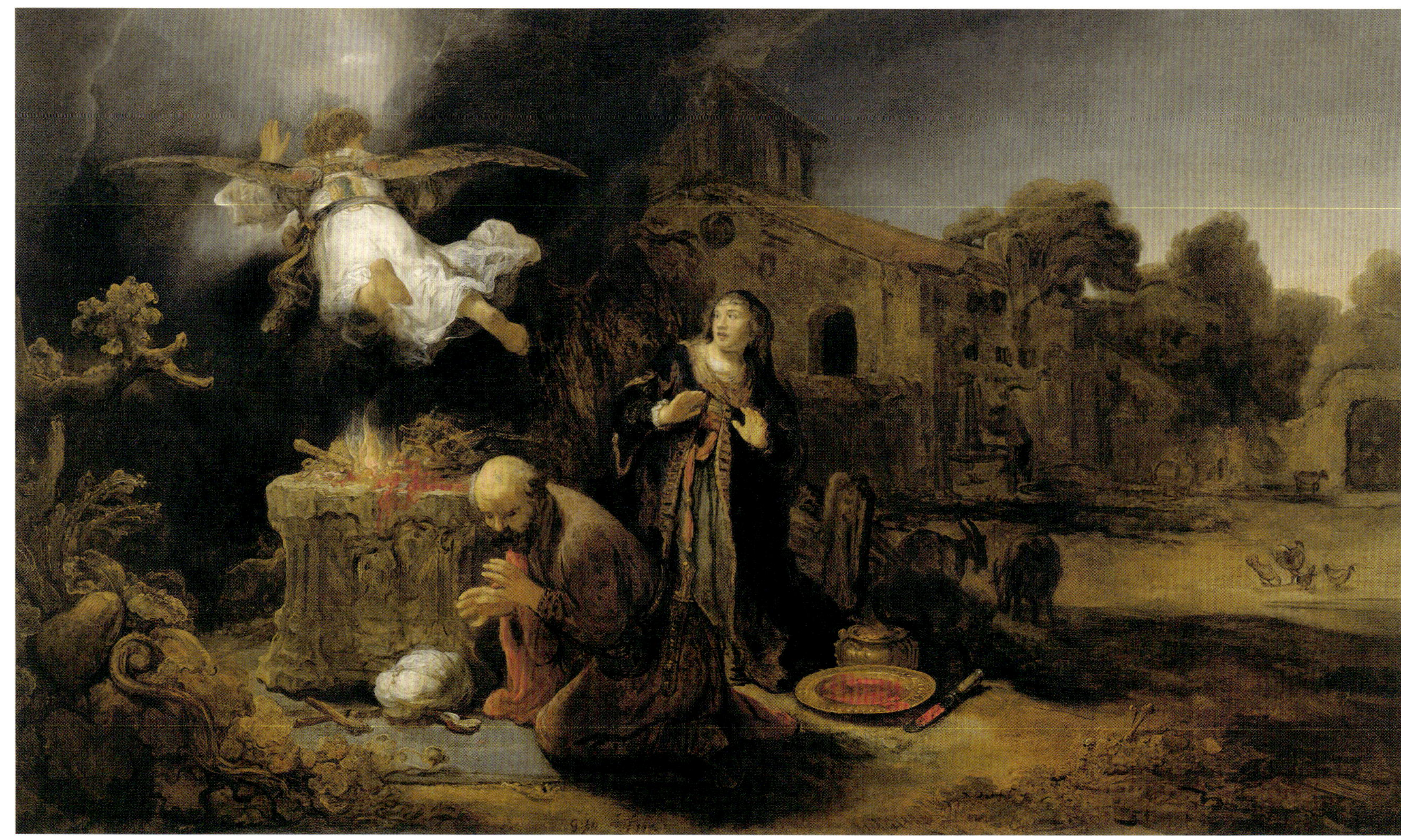

117 Govert Flinck, *The Sacrifice of Manoah*, 1640. Agnes Etherington Art Centre, Queen's University, Kingston

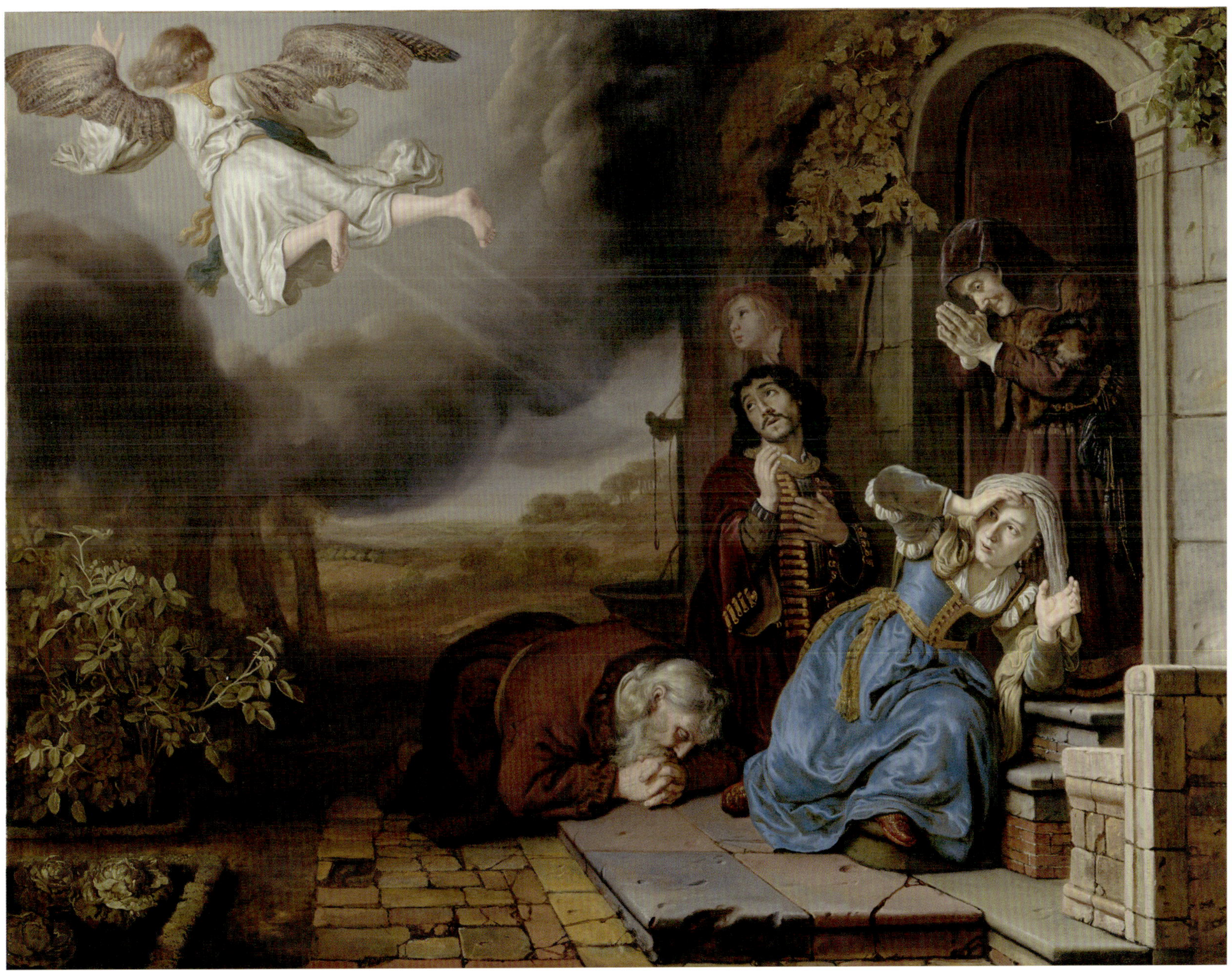

119 Rembrandt Workshop, here attributed to Ferdinand Bol, *The Angel Departing from the Family of Tobias*, c. 1637–40. Private collection

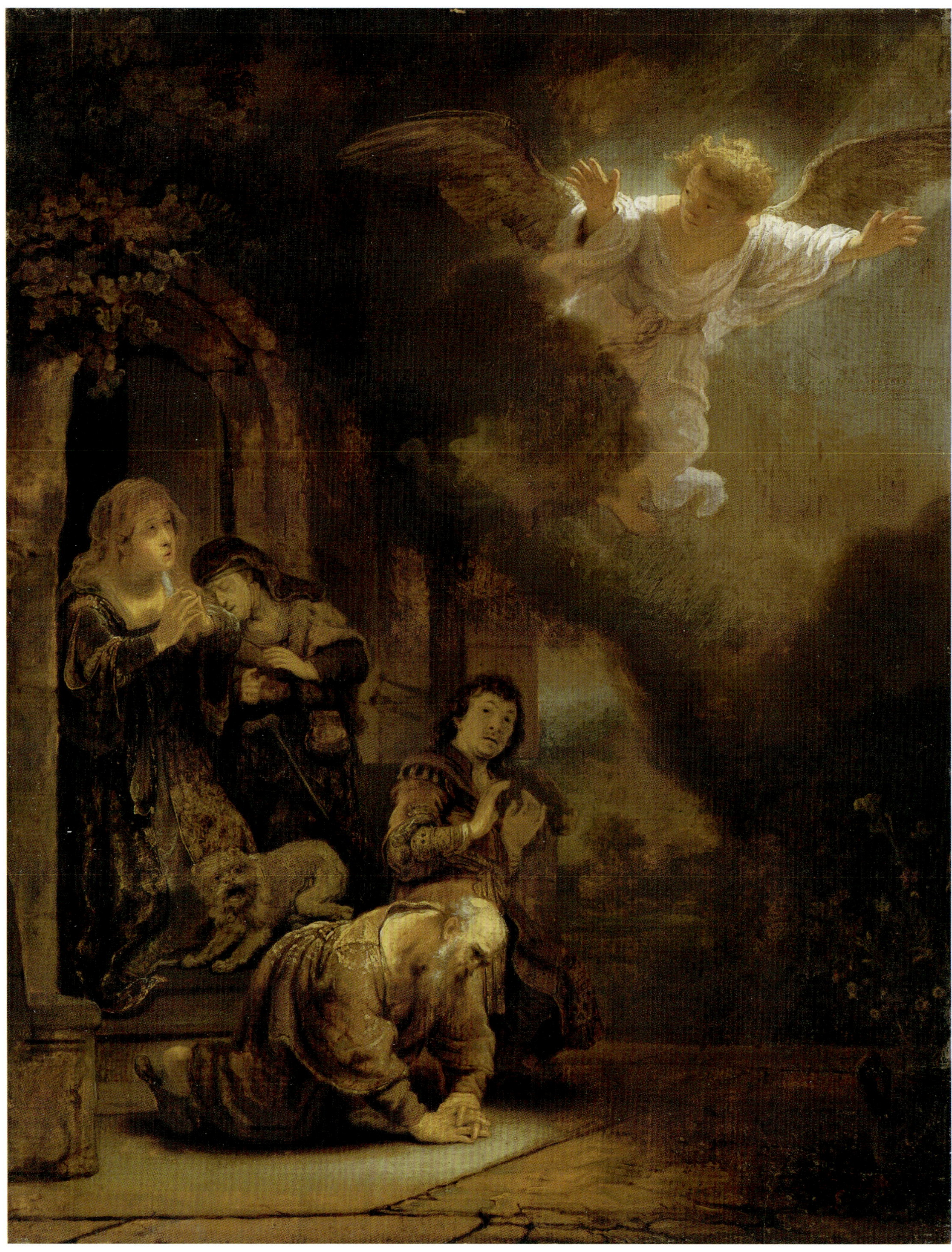

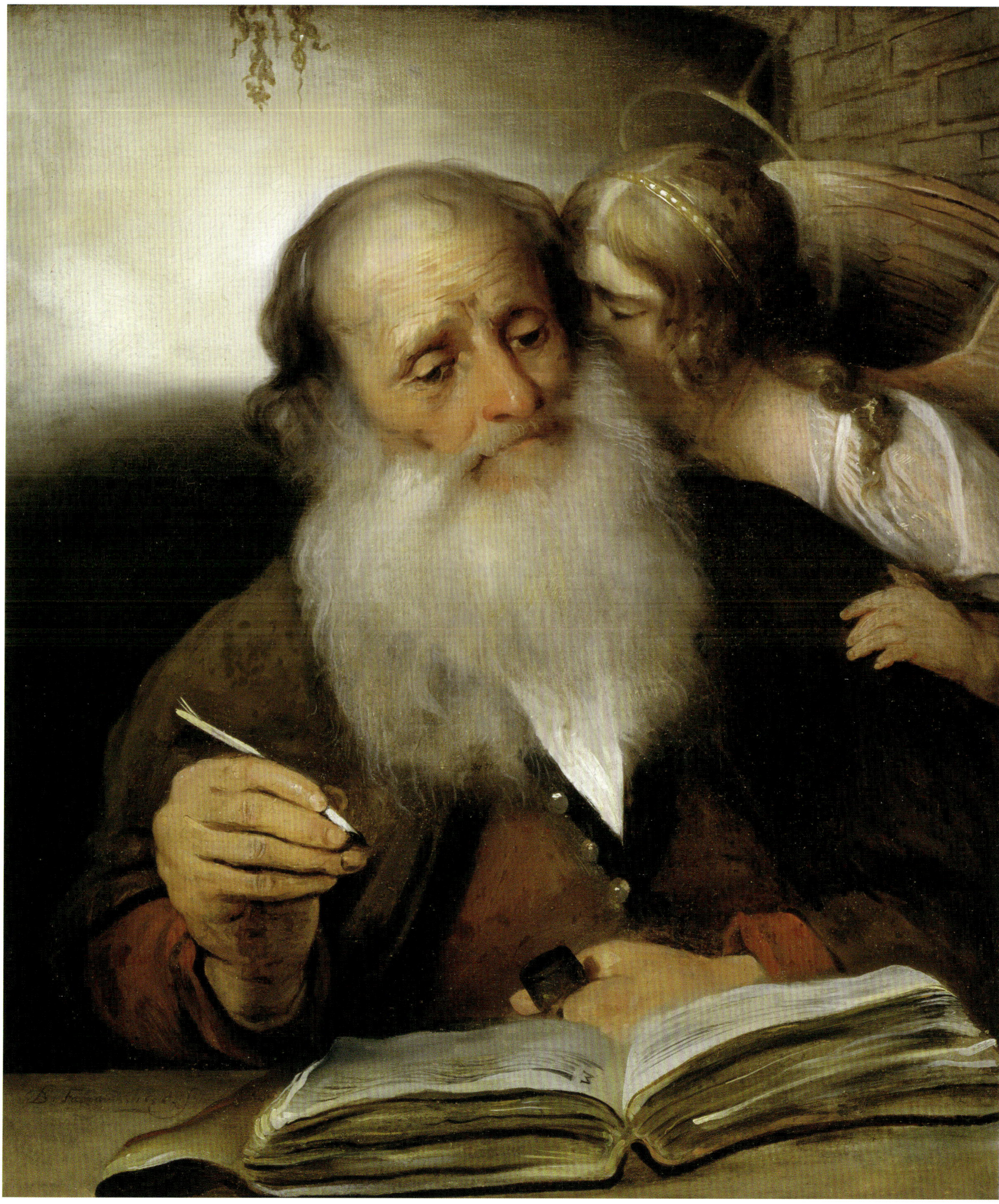

The Life of Christ

S T E P H A N I E   S .   D I C K E Y

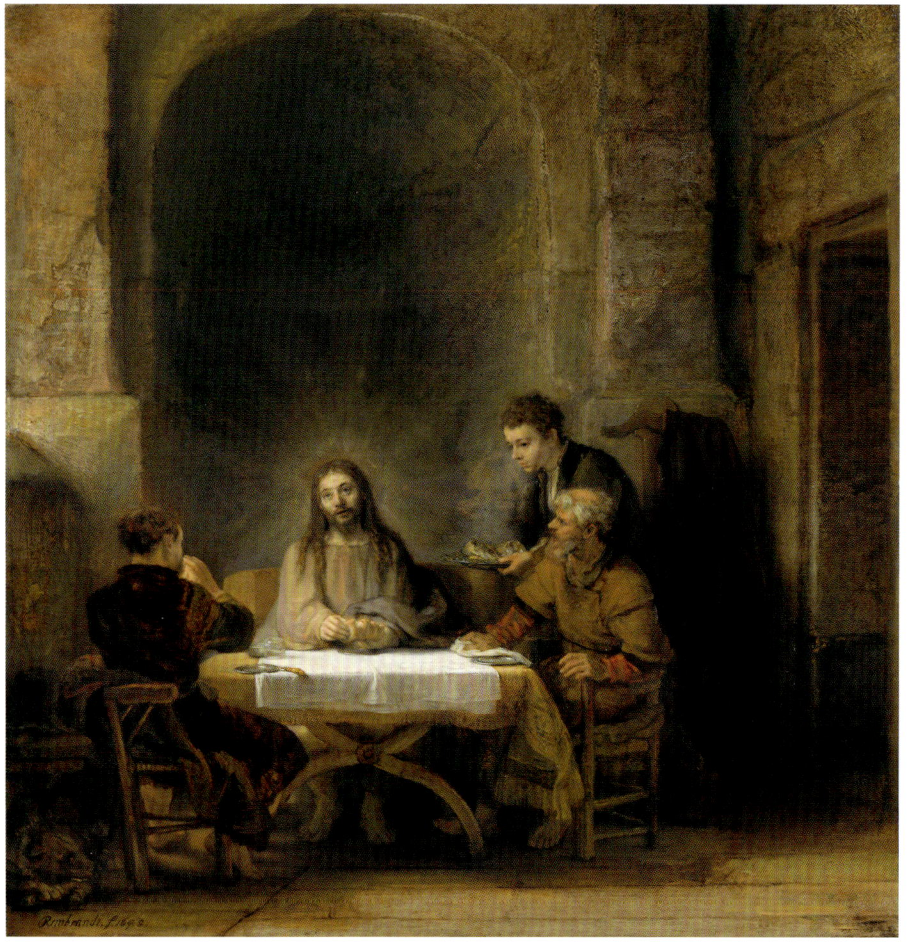

fig. 13.1 **Rembrandt van Rijn,**
***The Supper at Emmaus**, 1648,
oil on panel; 67.8 × 65 cm. Musée
du Louvre, Paris (1739)

The religious climate of the Dutch Republic, while exceptionally diverse compared to other parts of Europe, was dominated by Calvinism, and with it a hearty skepticism toward iconic devotional imagery. Inventory records suggest that many Protestant collectors preferred morally instructive Old Testament stories such as the Expulsion of Hagar or Abraham's Sacrifice of Isaac.[1] Rembrandt and artists in his circle excelled at bringing these riveting tales to life. Yet, throughout his career, Rembrandt was more deeply engaged with the New Testament, especially the life of Christ.[2] Here, too, narrative themes could reach across confessional lines. Scenes of revelation such as *Christ and Mary Magdalene at the Tomb* (1638, Royal Collection, London) and *The Supper at Emmaus* (fig. 13.1) and parables from Christ's teaching ministry offered life lessons in historical guise.[3] The market offered versions of these themes for buyers at all levels. In the 1657 inventory of the art dealer Johannes de Renialme, history paintings "by Rembrandt" (probably including studio copies) are valued between 120 and 1,500 guilders each.[4]

While still in Leiden, Rembrandt was invited to paint *The Descent from the Cross* and *The Raising of the Cross* (figs. 13.2, 13.3) for Stadtholder Frederik Hendrik's quarters at the Binnenhof in The Hague. Rembrandt was then actively competing with his friend and rival Jan Lievens for commissions from the court. It was probably Constantijn Huygens who selected Rembrandt as the winner of this plum assignment.[5] By the time the two panels were delivered to The Hague in 1633, Lievens had moved to London and Rembrandt to Amsterdam.

For *The Descent from the Cross*, Rembrandt may well have studied Lucas Vorsterman's print after Peter Paul Rubens' grand altarpiece in Antwerp, but his depiction of the sagging, broken body of Jesus contrasts poignantly with Rubens' muscle-bound hero (see fig. 17.2). While the Flemish master's idealizing approach reflected Counter-Reformation theology, Rembrandt's emphasis on the humanity of Christ had an ecumenical appeal. Rubens profited from

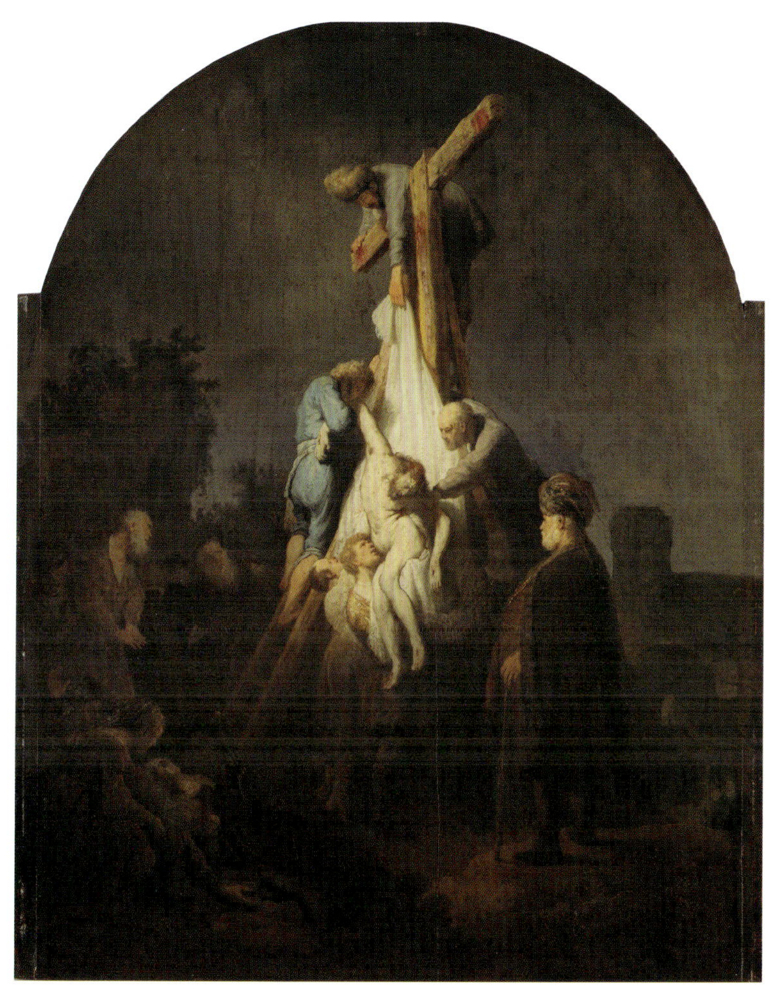

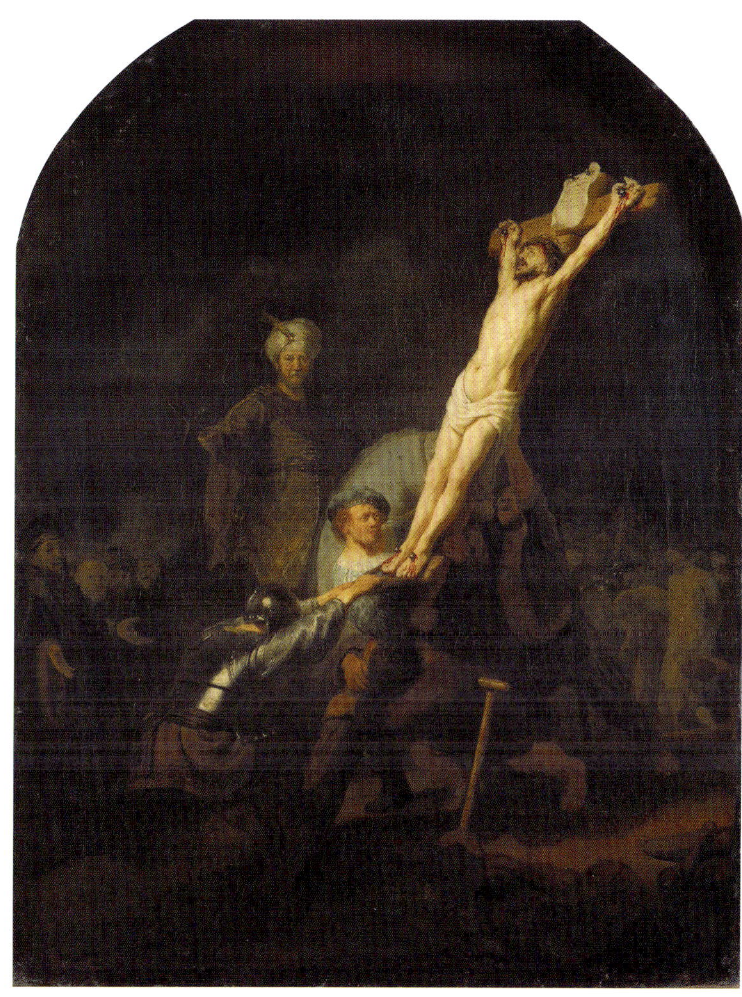

reproductive prints to build his reputation, and Hendrick Uylenburgh's publication of a print after Rembrandt's *Descent from the Cross* marks a parallel effort (pl. 166). While this venture was not repeated, Rembrandt produced dozens of etchings on Old and New Testament themes, culminating in the celebrated *Hundred Guilder Print* (pl. 168) – nicknamed for its exceptionally high market value – and the magisterial drypoints *Christ Presented to the People* and *The Three Crosses* (pls. 128, 129).[6] Within his lifetime, his prints circulated throughout Europe, contributing to a venerable tradition of biblical illustration by masters such as Albrecht Dürer and Lucas van Leyden. Of Rembrandt's followers, Ferdinand Bol was the only

accomplished printmaker. His *Holy Family in an Interior*, based on an elaborate preparatory drawing, emulates Rembrandt's intricate hatching to create rich tonality (pls. 122, 123). To enhance this effect, he also picked up Rembrandt's practice of printing on Asian paper.[7]

The commission from The Hague developed into a series of seven scenes from the life of Christ, of which the last two were not completed until 1646.[8] Numerous students thus watched and learned as the project developed. Rembrandt encouraged them to devise their own interpretations of related subjects while continuing to ponder them himself. In 1634 he reimagined *The Descent from the Cross* with weightier

fig. 13.2 **Rembrandt van Rijn,** ***The Descent from the Cross*,** **c. 1632–33, oil on panel;** **89.4 × 65.2 cm. Bayerische** **Staatsgemäldesammlungen,** **Alte Pinakothek, Munich (395)**

fig. 13.3 **Rembrandt van Rijn,** ***The Raising of the Cross*, 1633, oil on** **canvas; 95.7 × 72.2 cm. Bayerische** **Staatsgemäldesammlungen,** **Alte Pinakothek, Munich (394)**

figures and warmer light, creating a new prototype to which several followers responded (pl. 127, fig. 13.4).[9] This was both an effective teaching strategy and a means to capitalize on the prestige of the court commission. Students absorbed the master's evocative treatment of colour, light and brushwork and strove to meet the central goal expressed in a letter from Rembrandt to Huygens (pl. 96): to depict the strongest and most natural movement and emotion.[10] Numerous extant copies and variants testify that their works found a ready market.

Rembrandt's final paintings for Frederik Hendrik shifted the focus from Jesus' final years to his infancy, a theme that had occupied Rembrandt since his early years in Leiden. In Amsterdam, one of his first large-scale history paintings was *The Holy Family* of around 1634 (fig. 13.5), purchased by wealthy portrait clients Marten Soolmans and Oopjen Coppit.[11] His Dordrecht followers Samuel van Hoogstraten and Nicolaes Maes adopted the glowing colour and hushed atmosphere of his nativity scenes both for religious subjects (pl. 124) and for genre scenes that find sacredness in contemporary domesticity.[12] In contrast, talented competitors such as Bartholomeus Breenbergh and Jan Baptist Weenix brought clear daylight and Italianate staging to their depictions of themes such as the Rest on the Flight into Egypt (pls. 121, 125).[13] Their works offered buyers a distinctively different option. ■

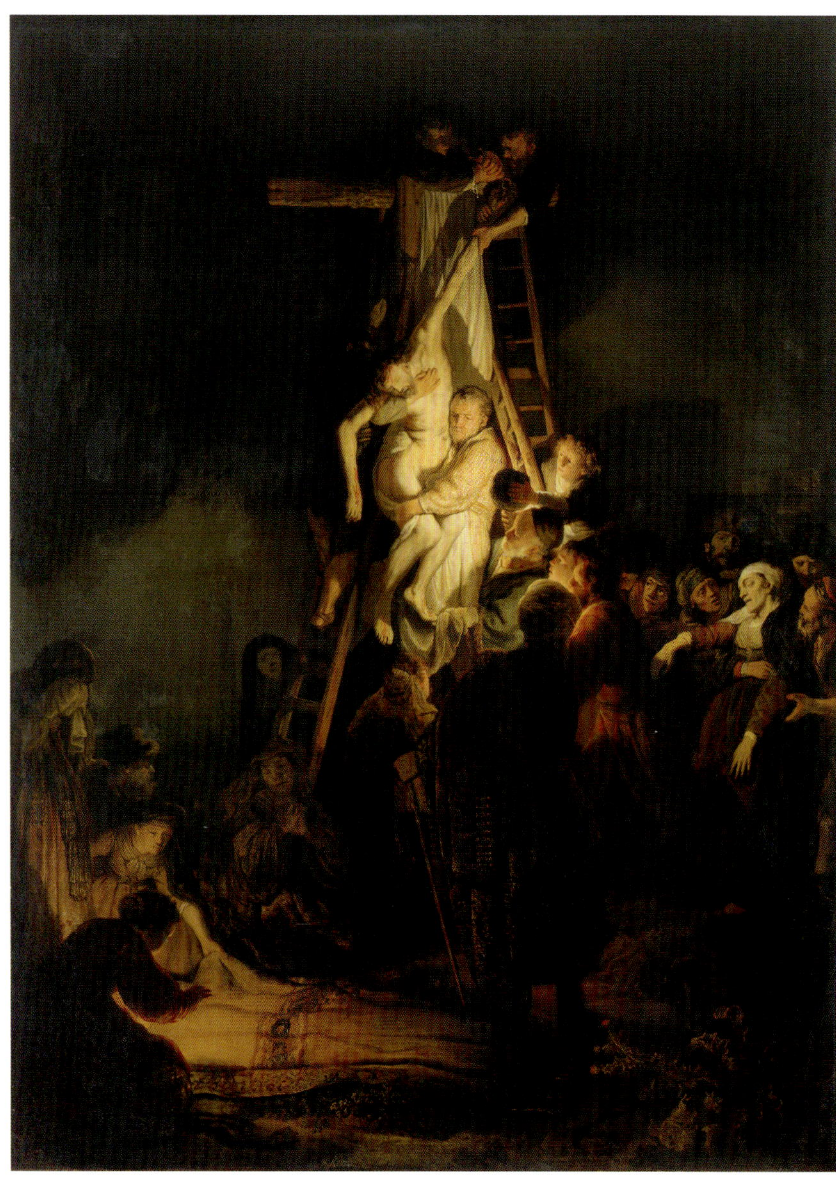

fig. 13.4 **Rembrandt van Rijn,** *The Descent from the Cross*, 1634, oil on canvas; 158 × 117 cm. The State Hermitage Museum, St. Petersburg (ГЭ-753)

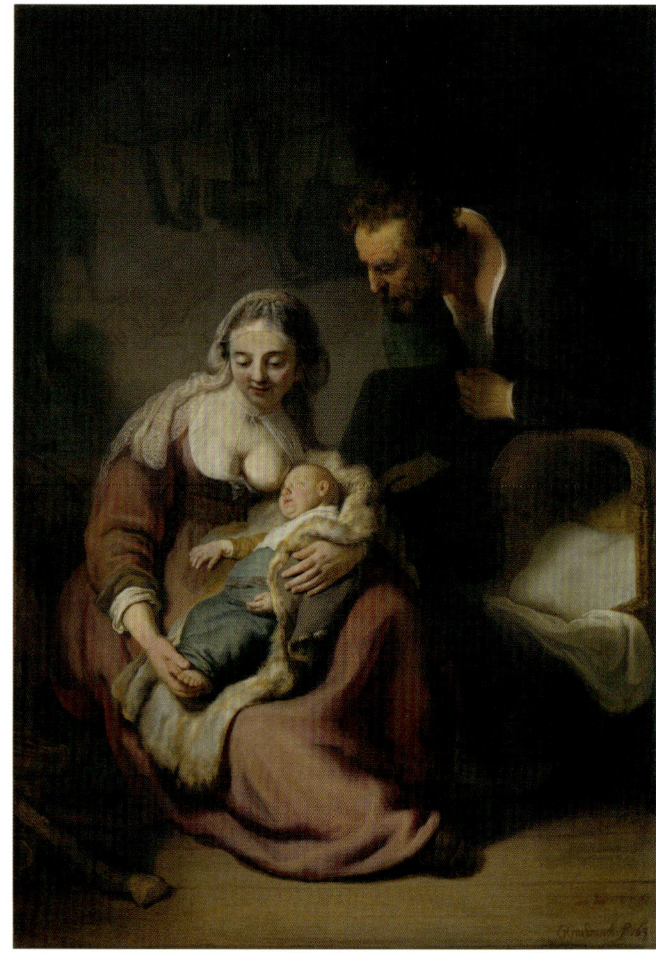

fig. 13.5 **Rembrandt van Rijn,** *The Holy Family*, c. 1634, oil on canvas; 183.5 × 123.5 cm. Bayerische Staatsgemäldesammlungen, Alte Pinakothek, Munich (1318)

NOTES

1   John Michael Montias, "Works of Art in Seventeenth-century Amsterdam: An Analysis of Subjects and Attributions," in Freedberg and De Vries 1991, 331–372, esp. 337–340, figs. 6a–7b.

2   Rembrandt etched only seventeen prints of Old Testament subjects, compared with forty-seven from the life of Christ and sixteen of other New Testament themes. Manuth, De Winkel and Van Leeuwen 2019 count twenty-nine Old Testament paintings and forty-six New Testament. For Rembrandt's biblical imagery, see esp. Perlove and Silver 2009; for the life of Christ, see also Paris, Philadelphia and Detroit 2011–12; Glasgow 2012; for New Testament themes in Dutch printmaking, see Rotterdam 2006a.

3   *Corpus*, vol. 6, nos. 158, 218. On the market, see, among others, Marten Jan Bok, "Rembrandt's Fame and Rembrandt's Failure: The Market for History Paintings in the Dutch Republic," in Kofuku 2004, 159–178; Sluijter 2015, 395–396; Jager 2015.

4   Strauss and Van der Meulen 1979, doc. 1657/2; Sluijter 2015, 397.

5   In 1631 both artists painted small panels of the Crucifixion, perhaps as trial pieces for the competition. Rembrandt's painting is in the Church of St. Vincent in Le Mas d'Agenais; *Corpus*, vol. 6, no. 52. Lievens' panel is in the Musée des Beaux-arts, Nancy; Paris, Philadelphia and Detroit 2011–12, nos. 9, 10.

6   On prints, see also the essay by Robert Fucci in this volume.

7   See Leonore van Sloten, "Ferdinand Bol, the Etcher," in Amsterdam 2017–18, 206–221, esp. 213–214.

8   *The Descent from the Cross* (c. 1632–33, fig. 13.2; the only work in the series on panel, not canvas, suggesting it came first), *The Raising of the Cross* (1633, fig. 13.3), *The Ascension* (1636), *The Entombment of Christ* (1635–39, see fig. 10.1), *The Resurrection of Christ* (1635–39, see fig. 10.2) and *The Adoration of the Shepherds*

(1646) are still together in the Alte Pinakothek, Munich. *The Circumcision* (1646) is lost but recorded in a copy in the Herzog Anton Ulrich-Museum, Braunschweig; *Corpus*, vol. 6, nos. 107, 106, 145, 162, 163, 211a-b.

9   For a discussion of attribution and impact, see *Corpus*, vol. 6, no. 126. On prototypes and "satellite" versions of small-scale history paintings in Rembrandt's workshop, see Ernst van de Wetering in *Corpus*, vol. 5, 239–282.

10 Strauss and Van der Meulen 1979, doc. 1639/2. See the essay "A Letter from Rembrandt" by Stephanie S. Dickey in this volume. For emotion as a central principle in Rembrandt's work, see esp. Sluijter 2006, Sluijter 2014 and Sluijter 2015.

11 *Corpus*, vol. 6, no. 131; Sluijter 2015, 28–29n34, with further references. For early works, see recently Leiden and Oxford 2019–20, 170–175. Rembrandt's *Portrait of Marten Soolmans* and *Portrait of Oopjen Coppit* (see figs. 3.1, 3.2) are jointly held by the Musée du Louvre, Paris, and Rijksmuseum, Amsterdam; *Corpus*, vol. 6, no. 120a-b.

12 For instance, Nicolaes Maes, *Young Woman at a Cradle* (1652–62, Rijksmuseum, Amsterdam); see recently London and The Hague 2019–20, 76–79, no. 7.

13 Dekiert 2006, 50, no. 1647. For Breenbergh and Amsterdam history painting, see Sluijter 2015, 127–148. Weenix was born in Amsterdam in 1621; from 1640 to 1642 he studied with Pieter Lastman's associate Claes Moeyaert, and his early history paintings show awareness of Rembrandt. Before settling in Utrecht, he was in Rome from 1643 to 1647 and then in Amsterdam for a year or two; this is likely when *Rest on the Flight into Egypt* was painted. See Van Wagenberg-Ter Hoeven 2018, vol. 2, 86–88, no. 11.

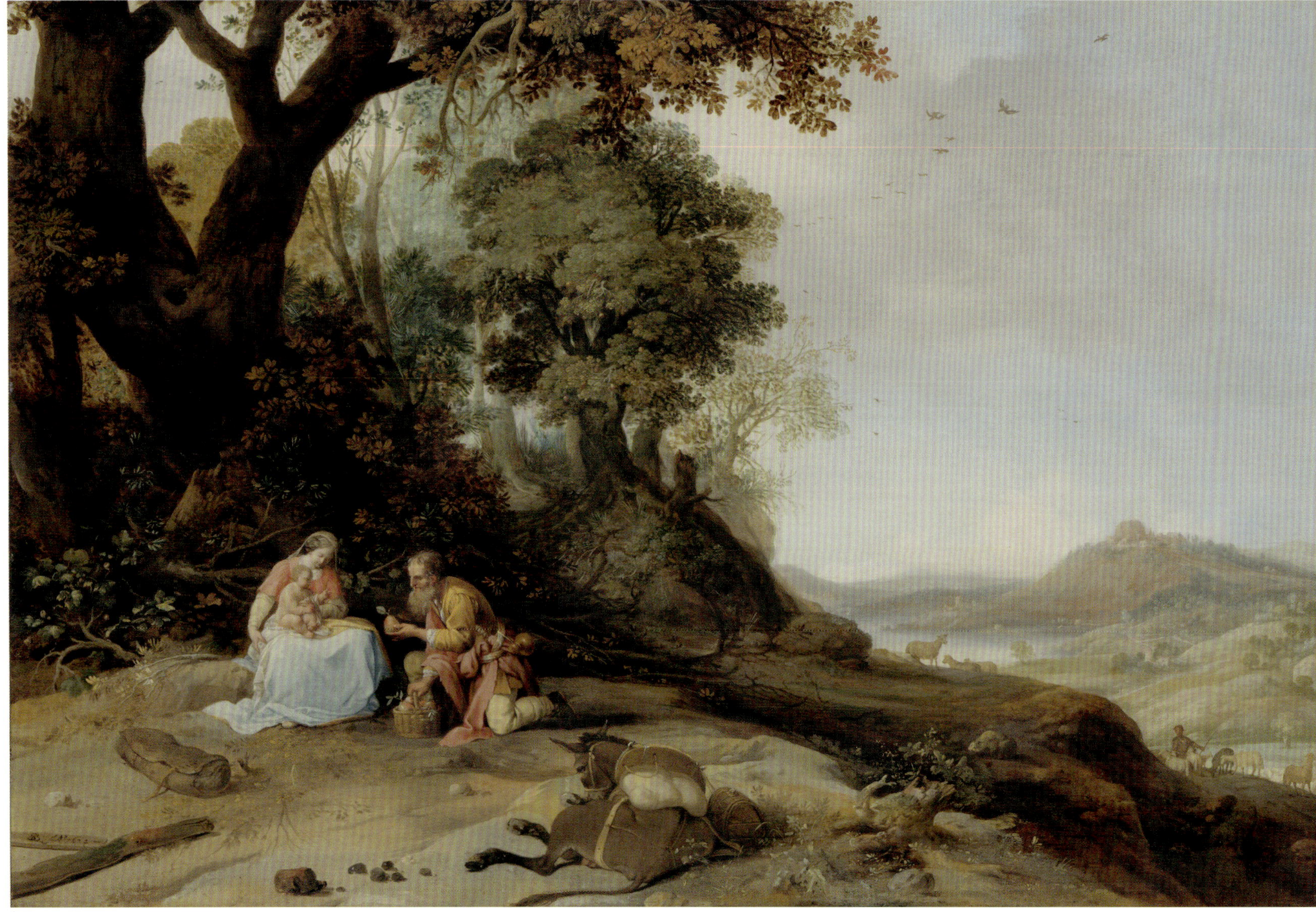

 121 Bartholomeus Breenbergh, *Landscape with the Rest on the Flight into Egypt*, 1634. Bayerische Staatsgemäldesammlungen, Alte Pinakothek, Munich

122   Ferdinand Bol, *The Holy Family in an Interior*, c. 1635–42. The British Museum, London

123   Ferdinand Bol, *The Holy Family in an Interior*, 1643. Rijksmuseum, Amsterdam

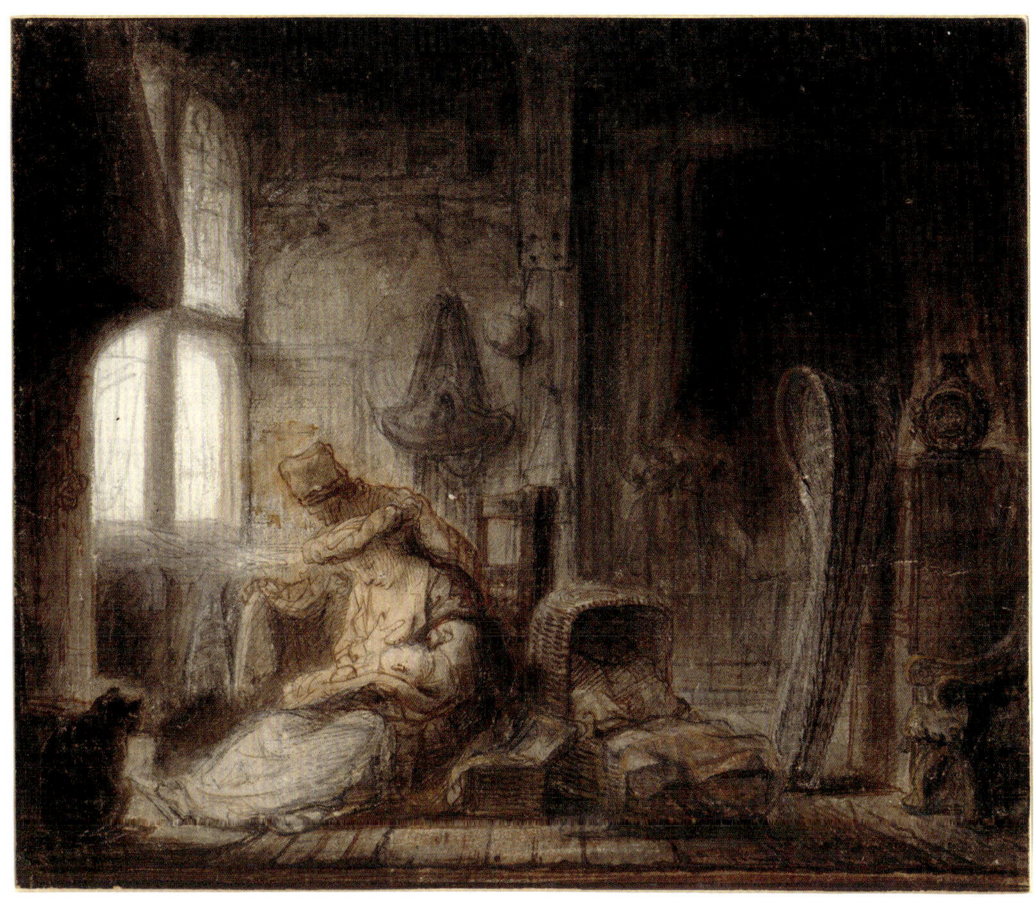

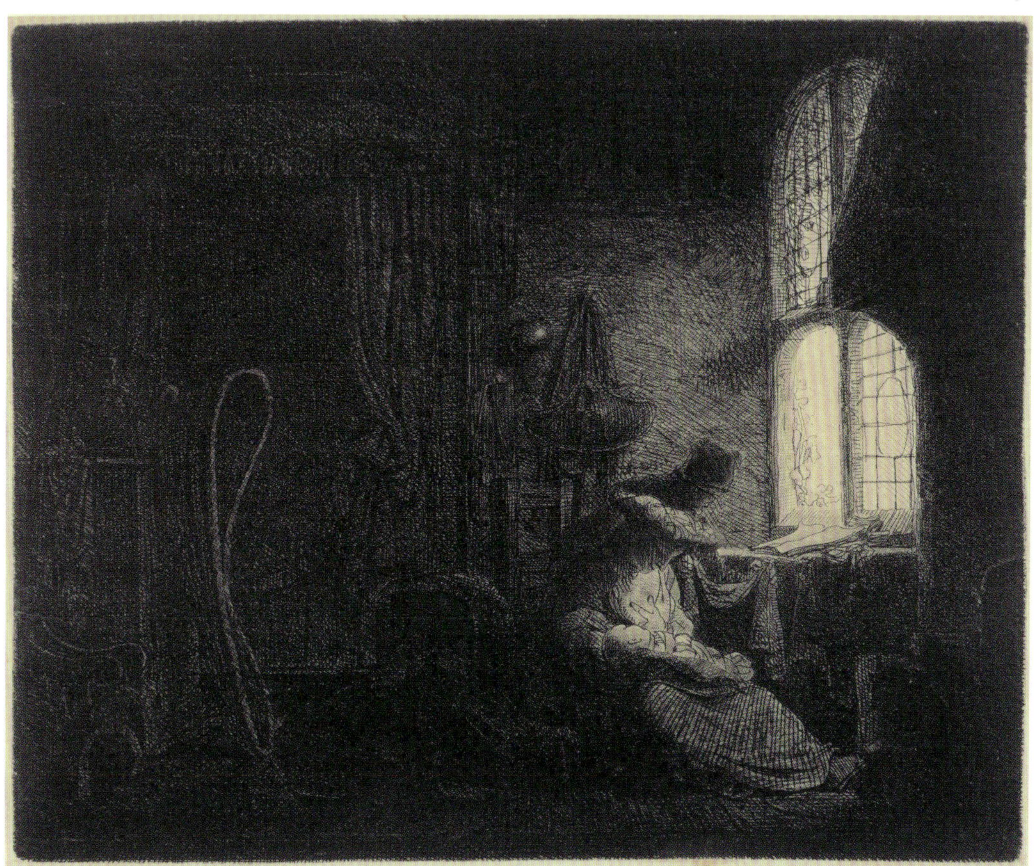

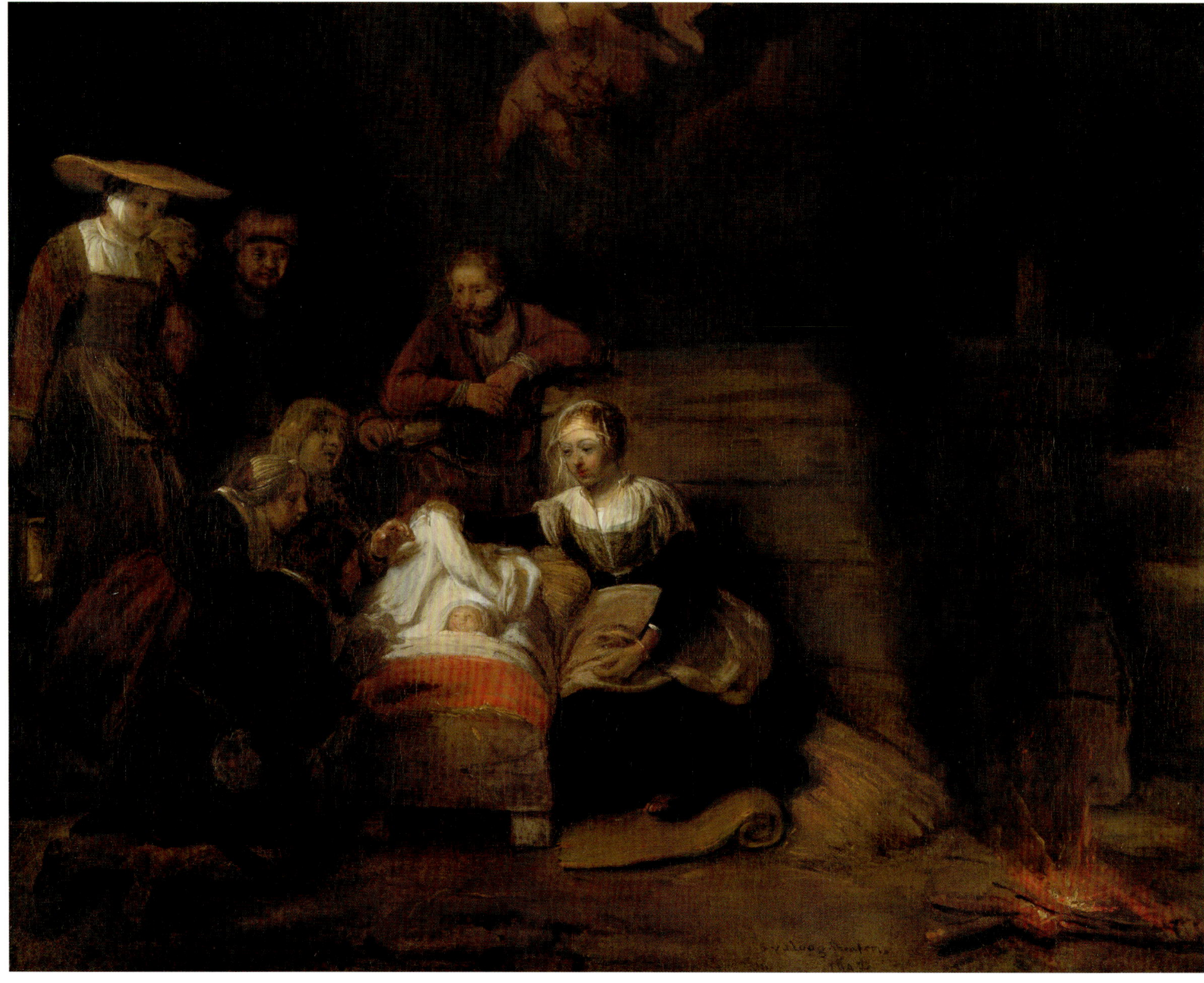

124 Samuel van Hoogstraten, *Adoration of the Child*, 1647. Dordrechts Museum, Dordrecht

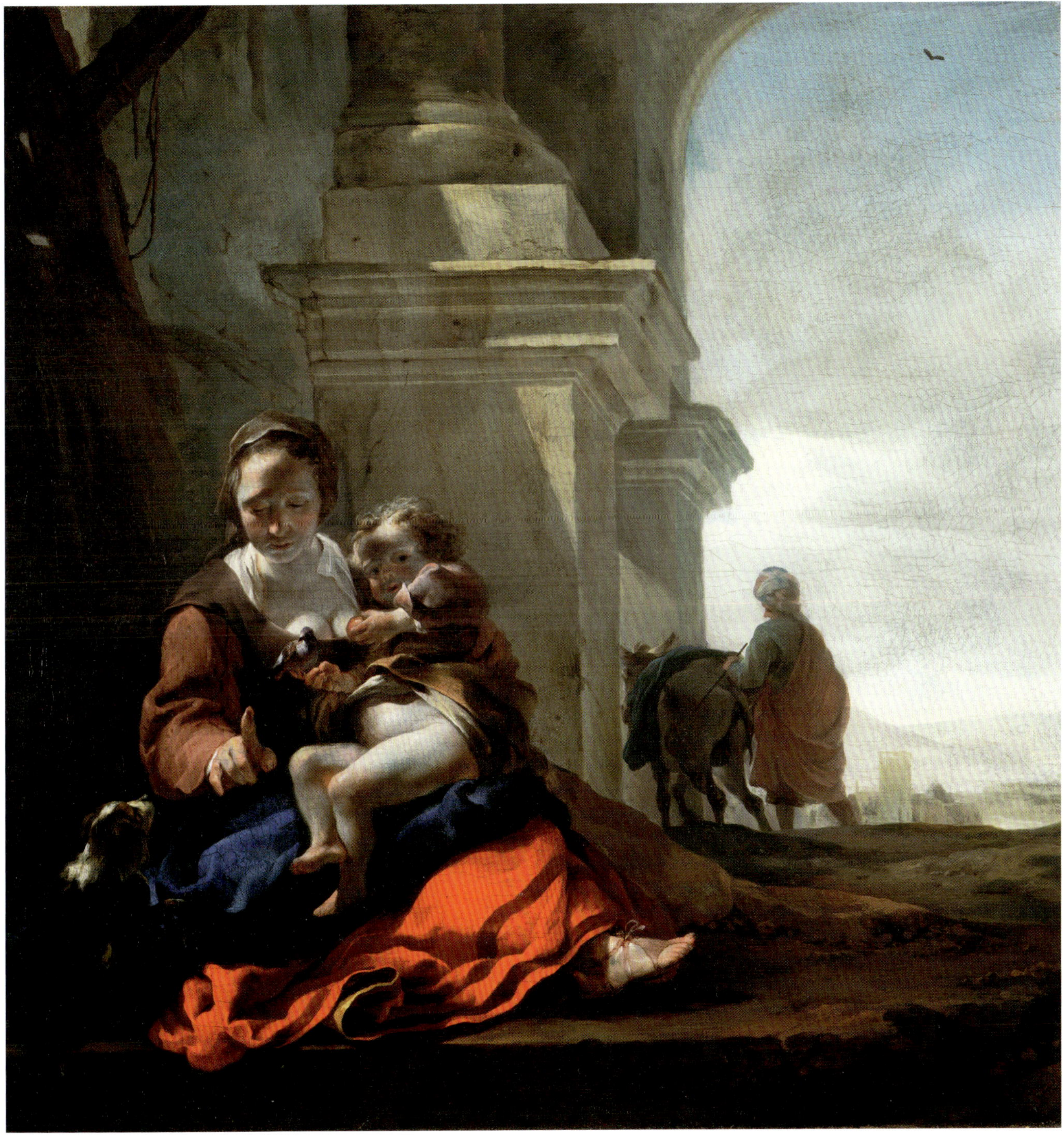

126   Rembrandt van Rijn, *The Angel Appearing to the Shepherds*, 1634. National Gallery of Canada, Ottawa

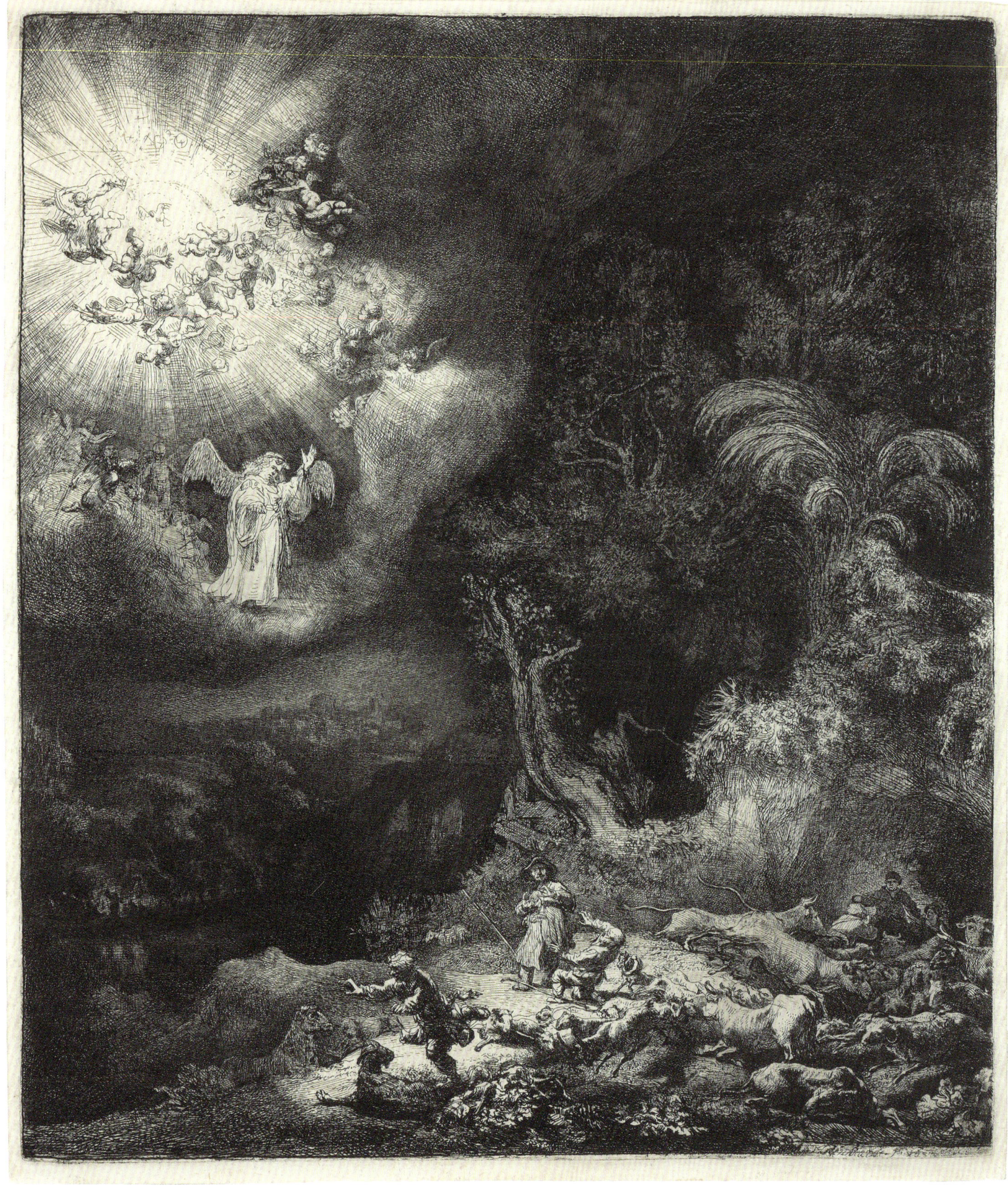

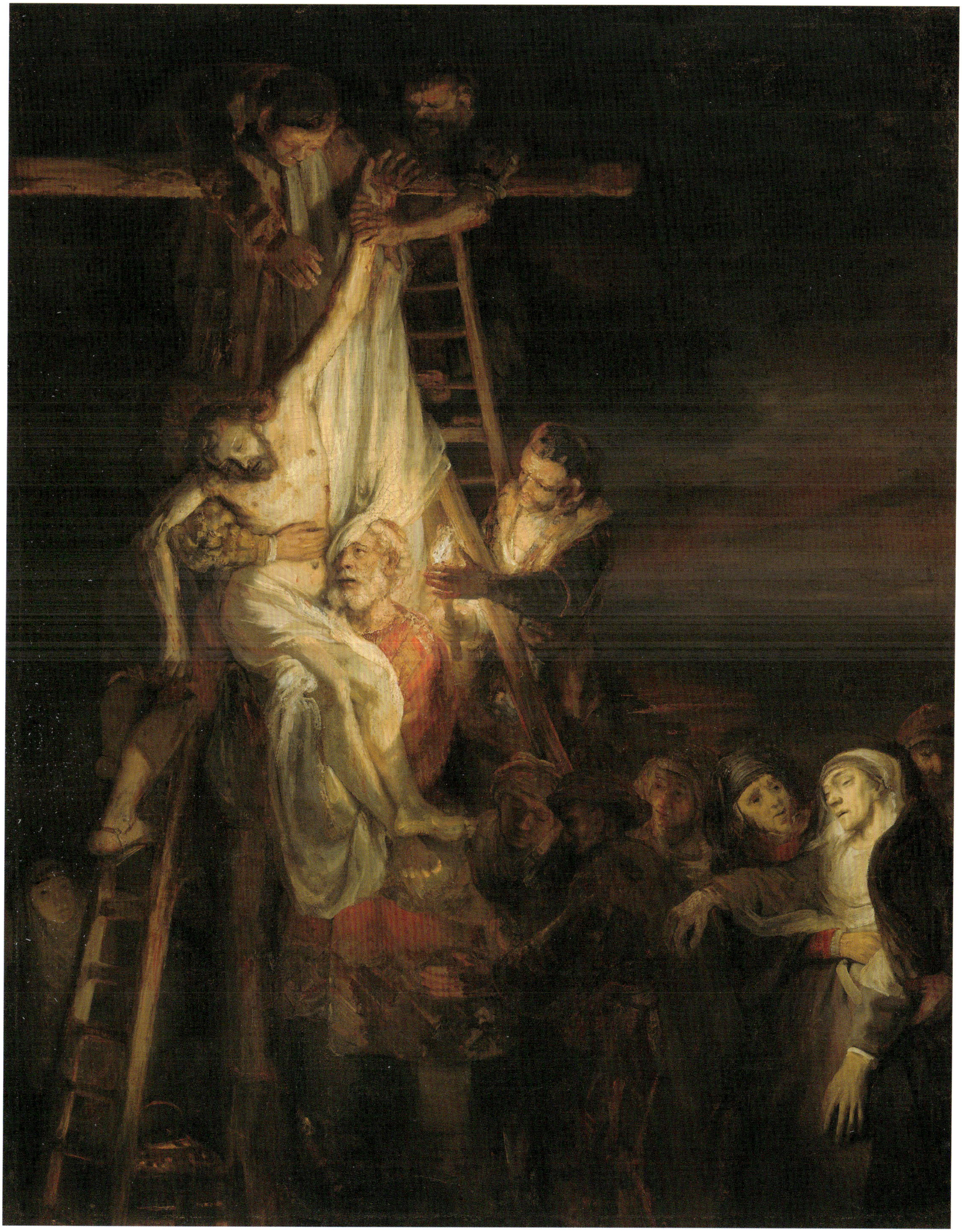

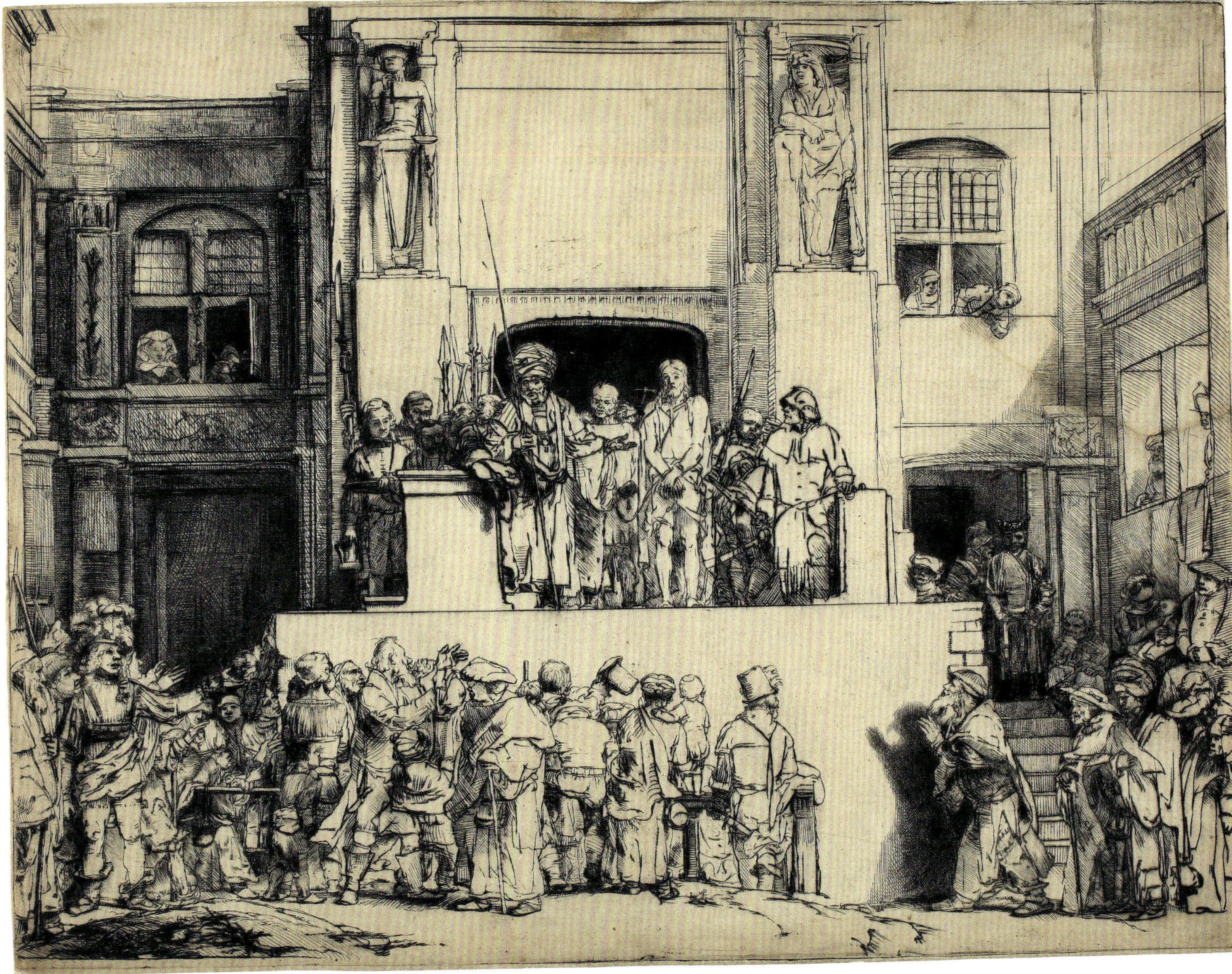

128 Rembrandt van Rijn, *Christ Presented to the People: Oblong Plate*, 1655. National Gallery of Canada, Ottawa

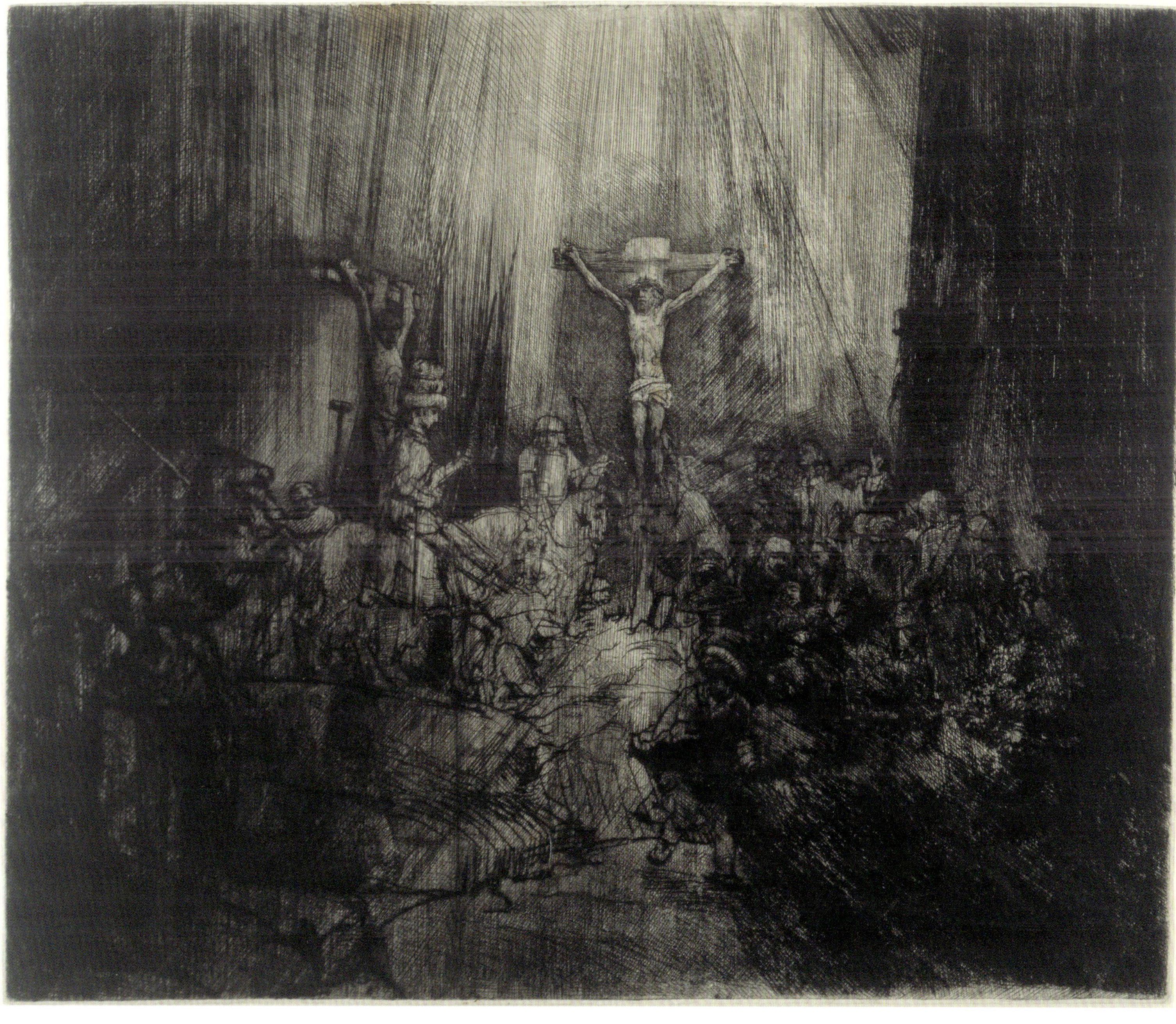

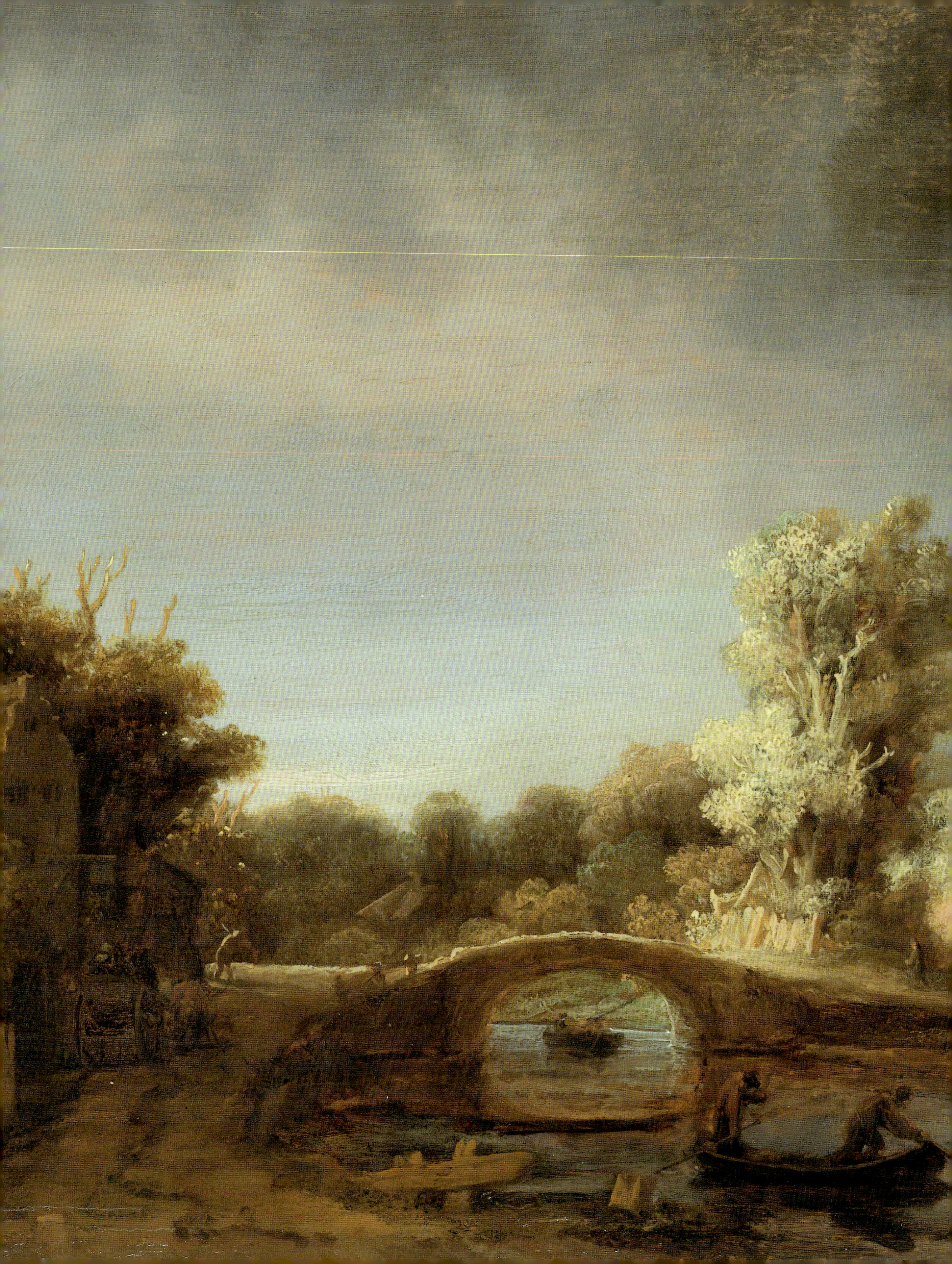

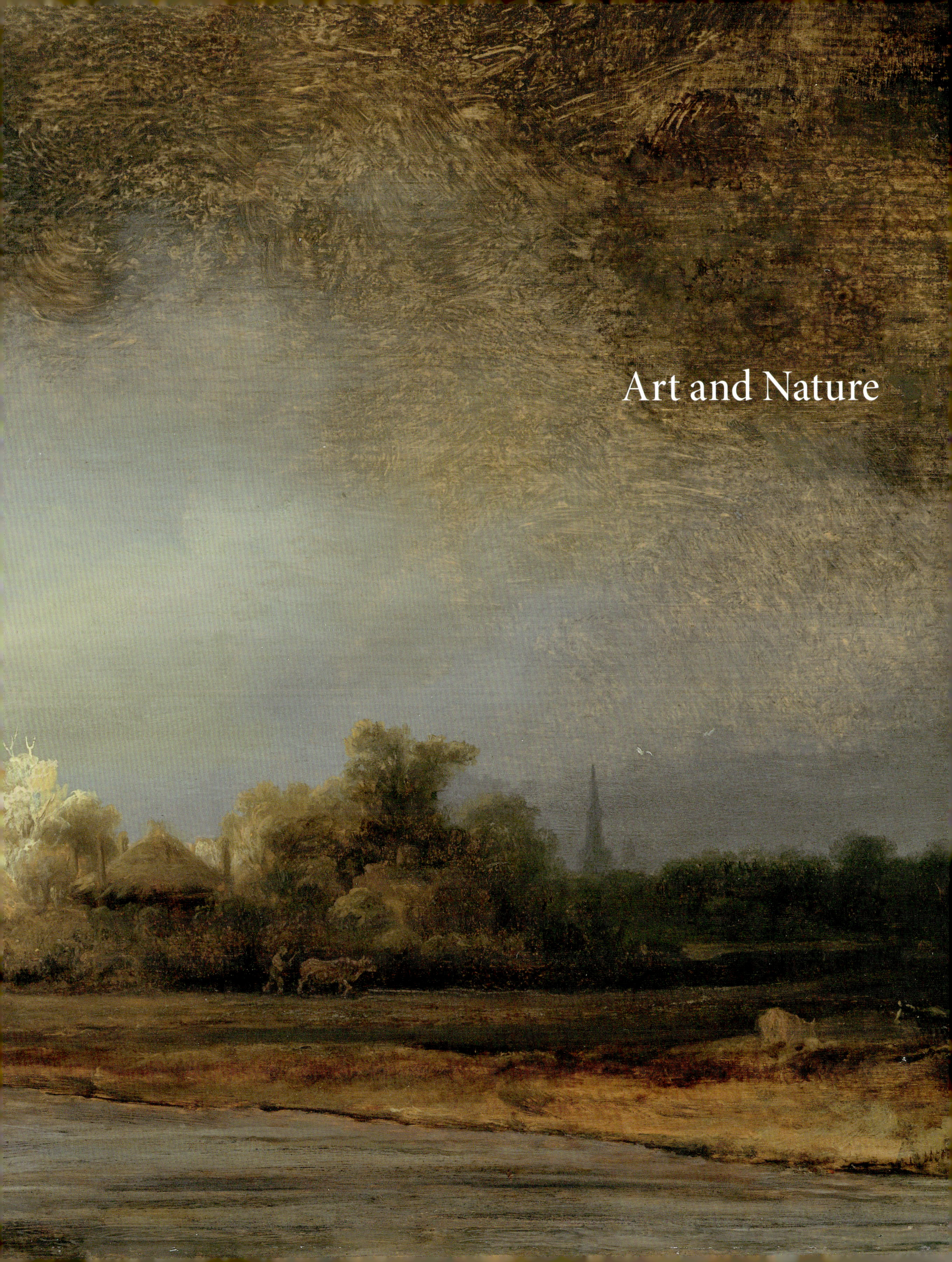

Art and Nature

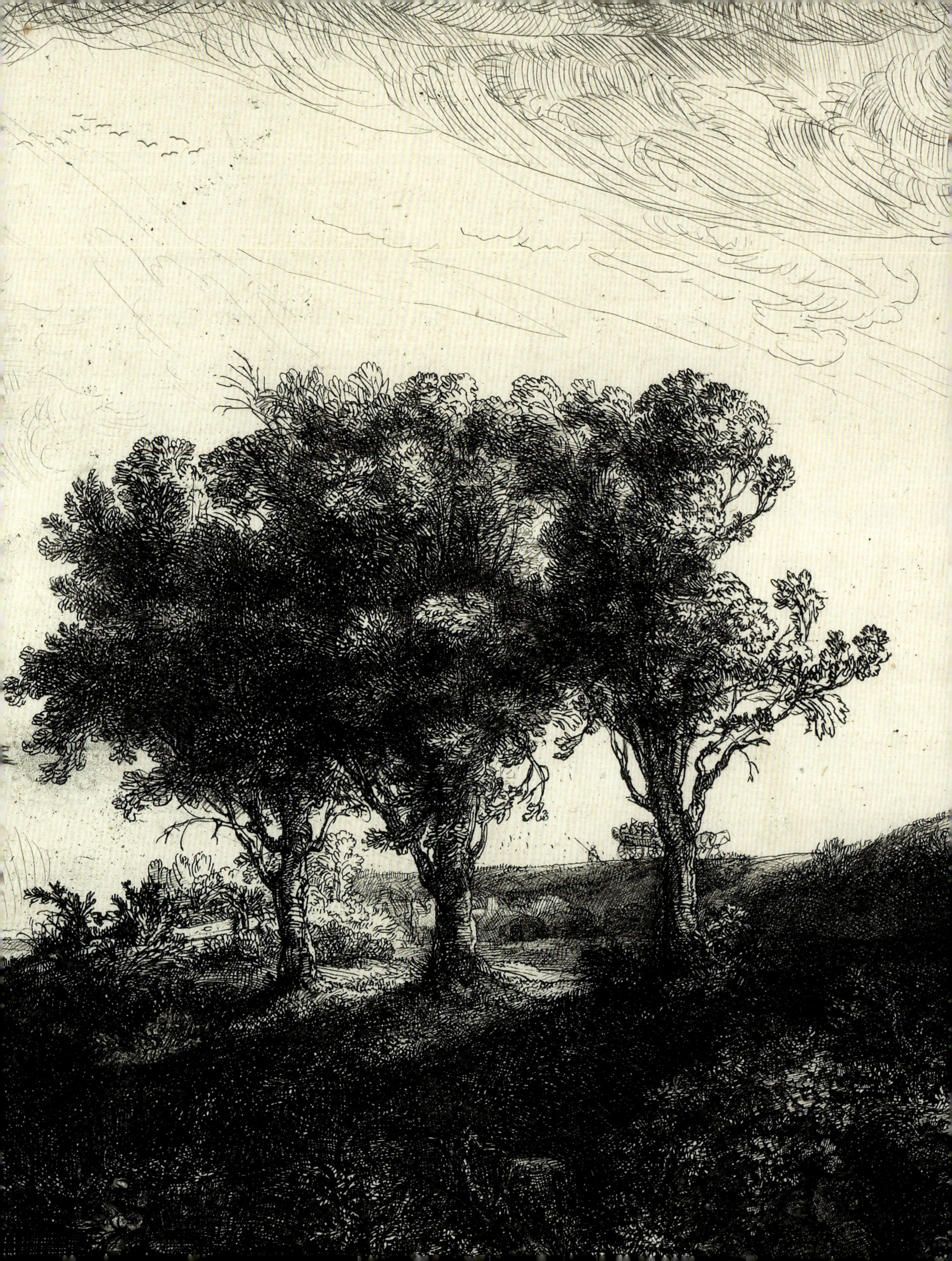

M A R T I N   S O N N A B E N D

Rembrandt and Landscape

During the seventeenth century, landscape painting flourished in the Netherlands. Specialist painters created views of local or Mediterranean landscapes, topographically realistic or imaginary scenes, seascapes, winter landscapes, and atmospheric nightscapes. Through these paintings, viewers could experience nature in a way that spoke to their emotions and unburdened their souls; they could admire an artist's virtuosity, find symbolic meaning or feel a sense of patriotic pride. There are a number of reasons for this efflorescence of art: for instance, the long struggle for Dutch independence, increasing connoisseurship among the prosperous bourgeoisie, interest in geography, and not least, religion. The followers of the Calvinist faith, for example, rejected representations of God and the saints, but found it permissible and desirable to depict nature as God's creation entrusted to humankind.[1]

Rembrandt is celebrated primarily for his history paintings and portraits, rather than for his landscapes. Yet, he embraced this genre as an artistic challenge and contributed to the growing market for landscape imagery, especially with his etchings. In the early 1630s, the landscape backgrounds in his history paintings and etchings started to play an active part in the pictorial narrative. In the nocturnal *Angel Appearing to the Shepherds* (pl. 126), an etching from 1634 that demonstrates his masterful rendering of subtle gradations of light and shade, a sleepy landscape bathed in pale moonlight forms a powerful narrative contrast to the dramatically illuminated divine message in the foreground. Rembrandt's first autonomous landscape paintings date from the end of the 1630s; from then on he applied himself assiduously to this genre, and by 1652 he had created about a dozen paintings, nearly thirty etchings and numerous drawings.[2]

Rembrandt's few known painted landscapes are mostly small in size and executed with bold, experimental brushwork. They depict motifs typical of Dutch paintings of the time – such as riverbanks and farmsteads – or imaginary views cast in dramatic light. Often they reflect the work of his precursors, such as the "world landscapes" of Joachim Patinir and Pieter Bruegel the Elder or the paintings and etchings of Hercules Segers (pl. 130, see fig. 1.7). Rembrandt's small but deeply expressive *Landscape with a Stone Bridge* (pl. 131), completed around 1638, combines both aspects – Dutch imagery and dramatic intensity. Although it may look like a local scene, it does not depict a specific location and takes its inspiration from an engraving by Jan van de Velde (fig. 14.1). While contemporary viewers might have interpreted the figures travelling on foot, on horseback or by boat as allusions to the poetic theme of life as a pilgrimage or journey, Rembrandt's artistic interest lay primarily in the dramatic staging of chiaroscuro. Strong light striking the tree in the centre, balanced against the darkness on the right, gives the otherwise tranquil scene a sense of foreboding that imbues nature with pathos. This approach may be linked to Rembrandt's notion of himself as a history painter.

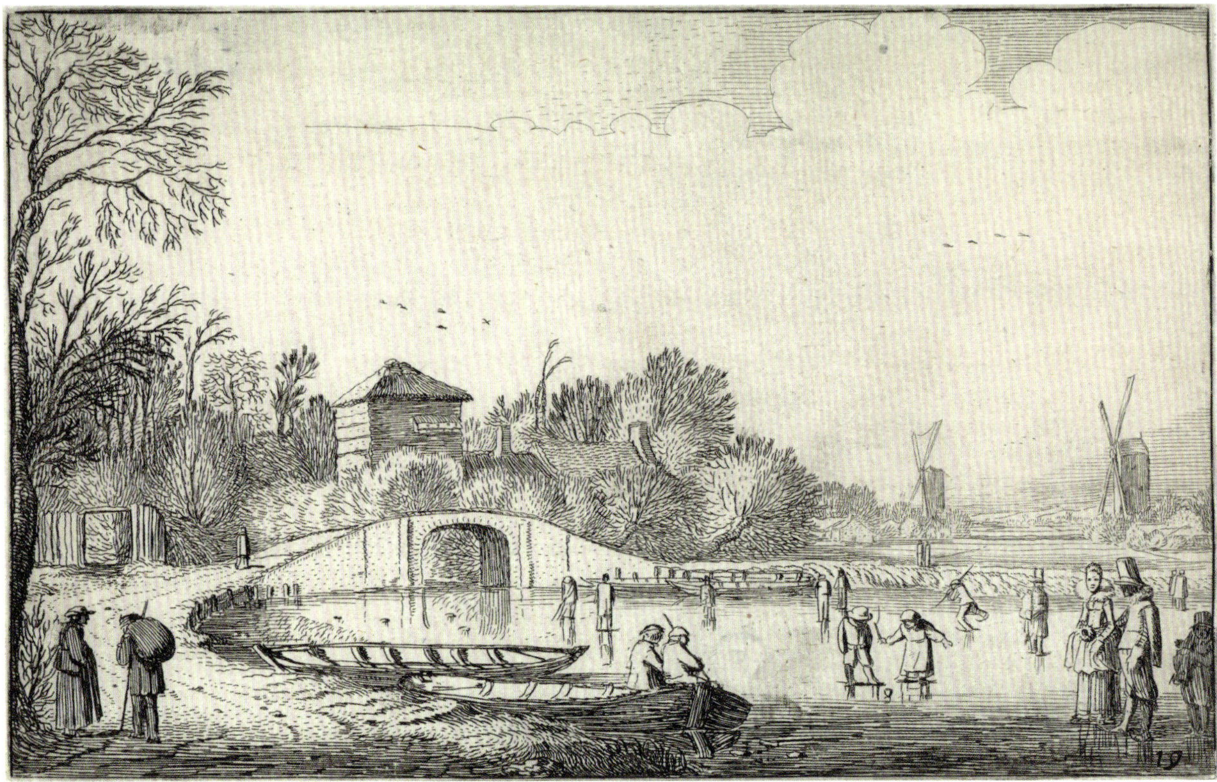

fig. 14.1 **Jan van de Velde, *Winter Landscape with Ice Skaters near a Bridge*, 1616, etching on laid paper; 12 × 19 cm. Rijksmuseum, Amsterdam. D. Franken Bequest, Le Vésinet (RP-P-1898-A-20393)**

Rembrandt certainly made no great effort to market his landscape paintings; only three of them were documented in collections in Delft and Amsterdam before he declared insolvency in 1656. The inventory taken on that occasion shows that most of his landscapes were still in his house at that time; some of them were hung in the front rooms where paintings were displayed for sale to visitors.[3] Even after his possessions were auctioned off, it was mostly collectors with a direct personal or artistic link to Rembrandt who seem to have taken an interest in these canvases.[4] Jan Lievens, who turned to landscapes at the same time as Rembrandt, was considerably more active on the art market with his paintings.[5]

Around 1640 Rembrandt began sketching on walks in the countryside outside Amsterdam (pl. 135). Many of the locations where he found his motifs can still be identified today.[6] In these masterful sketches, he explored the organization of space, the depiction of light, and the rendering of natural and artificial textures. He often drew picturesque, weather-beaten farmhouses that seem to have returned to a state of nature (pls. 135, 163, see fig. 16.3). But unlike Lievens (pl. 164), he rarely finished his drawings to a degree that would suggest they were meant for sale. Even the relatively large-format *Cottages under a Stormy Sky* (pl. 163), a nature study that he may have reworked in his studio, does not look like a finished product destined for the art market. Some of Rembrandt's landscape drawings served instead as studies for etchings executed in the studio and distributed on the market. One example is *Landscape with Cottages and Haybarn* (pl. 138), in which he combined disparate topographical elements into one cohesive composition.[7]

In *The Three Trees* (pl. 140), Rembrandt's most accomplished landscape etching of the early 1640s, a seemingly endless expanse of space is rendered on a minute scale. Pastures scattered with people and animals stretch toward a city on the far horizon. Just as in *Landscape with a Stone Bridge*, dark storm clouds are set against radiant light, but the contrast is created this time solely by the juxtaposition of inked lines and bare paper. The trees form an arcade through which light seems to flow like animate matter. *The Three Trees* is a "world landscape" composed from local nature studies. On the hill on the right the artist himself is visible, a tiny draughtsman in a vast universe. Rembrandt's landscapes bring together the small and the large, the everyday and the extraordinary. They constitute an exploration – no doubt grounded in the painter's religious faith – of the magnificence of Creation.[8]

The study of landscape was closely bound up with theories of artistic practice. Dutch art theorists from Karel van Mander to Rembrandt's pupil Samuel van Hoogstraten emphasized the importance of studying nature for the training of artists.[9] Van Mander considered working "*naer het leven*" (from life, from nature) as being at least as important as "*uit den gheest*" (from imagination).[10] But for Rembrandt, his walks in the countryside around Amsterdam were more than mere exercises in nature study; with his landscape paintings, drawings and etchings he also placed himself within the tradition of the "universal" artist.[11] This art-theoretical concept, which dates back to the Renaissance, can be interpreted in different ways; in the Netherlands it referred not just to an artist who was at home in all genres but also to the ability to represent everything, including immaterial phenomena.

To draw from nature means to work without a preconceived model. Thus, artists not only have boundless possibilities to choose from but must also translate their diverse observations into the medium of drawing, and then print or painting, including phenomena they would not encounter in the same way in the studio, such as the effects of weather, light or atmosphere. Painting responds to this challenge by making use of colour; etching must rely entirely on expressive line. Rembrandt solved this problem with an experimental technique quite different from other artists: rather than labouring over details, he omitted or merely hinted at them. Thus, *The Three Trees*, despite the limitations of a monochrome medium and small scale, conveys a powerful suggestion of space and light as well as weather and atmosphere. An extreme example of this technique of omission and allusion is the etching known as *Six's Bridge* (fig. 14.2), in which the wide expanse of a Dutch landscape and the mood of a sunny summer's day are rendered with just a few lines.

One reason why Rembrandt decided to produce more landscape prints for sale than paintings might well have been that etchings required less effort, especially given the fierce competition in landscape painting in Amsterdam. But would that really have deterred him? A more important reason was probably that etched landscapes encouraged him to experiment in order to do justice to the visual experience of nature. In addition, it seems there was a market for such works among wealthy collectors who prized originality as well as quality.[12] Even in the case of Rembrandt's smaller, more incidental etchings, the number of impressions produced is too large to assume that he did not intend them for sale, but not large enough for broad distribution.[13] In the later group of etched

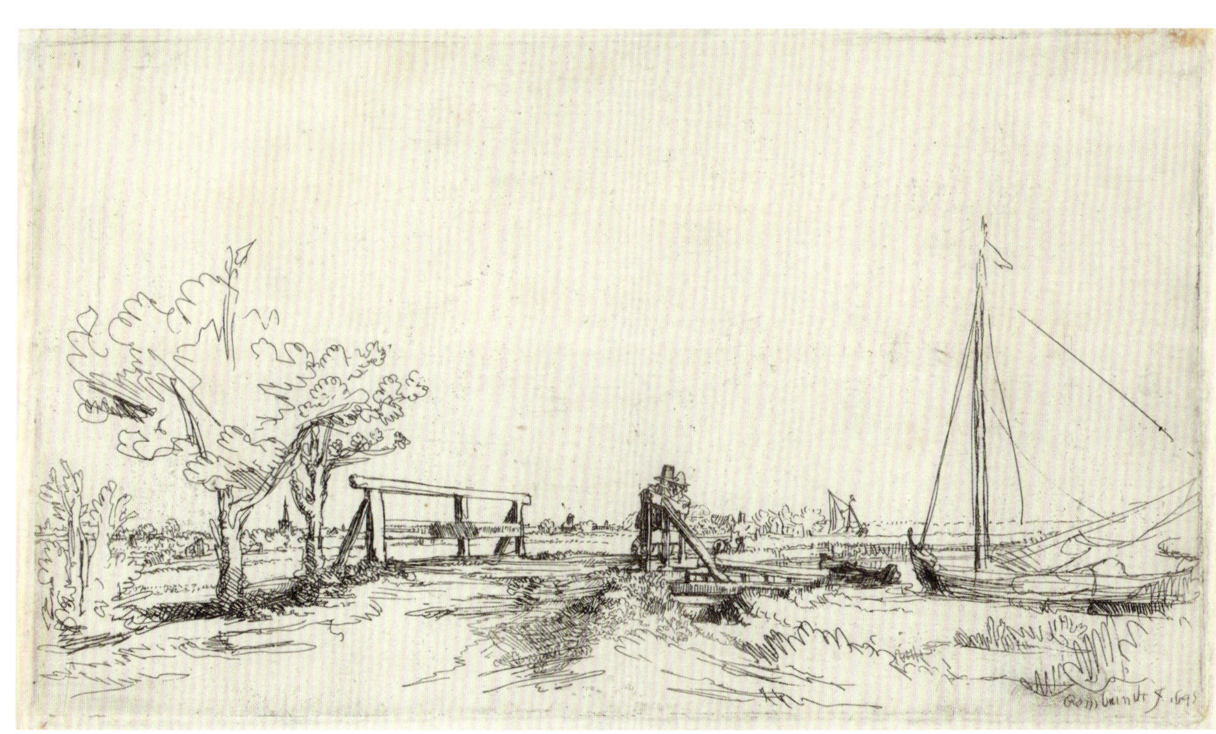

fig. 14.2 **Rembrandt van Rijn,** *Six's Bridge*, **1645, etching on laid paper; 12.9 × 22.4 cm. Städel Museum, Frankfurt am Main (5946)**

landscapes, executed between 1650 and 1652, Rembrandt increasingly adopted the more fugitive drypoint technique, which he would continue to use in his most accomplished prints of the 1650s (pl. 139).[14] His mastery in capturing fleeting "impressions" of light and weather in his etchings and drypoints is underscored by the fact that, in the nineteenth century, his landscape prints were not just held in high esteem but also regarded as modern and topical.

Rembrandt's landscape paintings found few followers. One reason for this might be that he treated these canvases more like exercises or contributions to art-theoretical discourse in his circle. Some of his pupils, such as Govert Flinck, Ferdinand Bol and Carel Fabritius, who in the 1630s and 1640s took part in discussions in his studio, as well as artists close to him, such as Jan Lievens and Philips Koninck (pl. 132), created a few related works and used elements that drew upon Rembrandt's painted landscapes. Perhaps Rembrandt's idea of the grandeur, drama and pathos of Creation could not easily be emulated by others.

His etchings, on the other hand, were influential and often imitated. Yet, among innumerable attempts to create pictorial effects by graphic means in the seventeenth century, they have remained unrivalled in the assured economy with which details of spatial organization and tonal quality are rendered.[15] Jacob van Ruisdael, for example, created several etchings with gnarled trees and decaying cottages whose motifs may be based on Rembrandt's works, but whose linear structures follow their own experimental paths (pl. 137).

Rembrandt and the artists of his circle seem to have regarded landscape as an important and topical theme in the late 1630s, perhaps because the genre was gaining prominence in the art market. Engaging with landscape not only offered new motifs and products to these artists but also led to fundamental discussions about art theory and artistic self-conception. Rembrandt explored this theme in a small number of landscapes, but more intensely in drawings after nature created for his own use and in etchings that, despite being intended for the market, were more direct and intimate than paintings in their small scale and monochromy.

Landscape art has been linked to emotional experience since long before the era of Romanticism.[16] Rembrandt's walks beyond the city gates of Amsterdam from 1640 onward, as well as the attentive and contemplative nature of his drawings done outdoors, were certainly informed by contemporary artistic and theoretical ideas. These sketches may also have had a more personal dimension. For such a deeply reflective artist, it is possible that the death of three newborn children between 1636 and 1640 and the illness of his wife Saskia, who would die in 1642, could have prompted him – after many years of professional success – to find in sketching the landscape a means to reconsider the fundamental tenets of his artistic practice. ◼

NOTES

I would like to thank Stephanie Dickey, Joachim Jacoby, Friederike Schütt and Mona Stocker for their careful reading of my text and their insightful comments.

1   For Rembrandt's landscape painting and its reception, see Jacquelyn N. Coutré, "Painted Landscapes by Lievens and Rembrandt: The View from Seventeenth-century Amsterdam Collections," in Dickey 2017b, 122–150, esp. 126–128.

2   For the pictorial narrative in *Angel Appearing to the Shepherds*, see Frankfurt 2003b, 21–22, 62, no. 14. As for Rembrandt's landscape paintings, there are eight documented paintings (of which six are securely attributed to Rembrandt), all executed between around 1637/38 and 1647. The inventory drawn up at Rembrandt's bankruptcy in 1656 lists eleven landscape paintings by his hand. On Rembrandt's landscapes, see esp. Schneider 1990; Washington 1990; Amsterdam and Paris 1998–99; Kassel and Leiden 2006–07; Hinterding 2006, vol. 1, 104–108; Bakker 2012; Boudewijn Bakker, "Rembrandt and the Humanist Ideal of the Universal Painter," in Dickey 2017b, 67–98; Coutré, "Painted Landscapes," in Dickey 2017b, 122–150.

3   Coutré, "Painted Landscapes," in Dickey 2017b, 129, see also 134–135.

4   Ibid., 122–150, esp. 130–132, 139–140, and 149n69 (Delft collection). Coutré also mentions a case in which Rembrandt seems to have used a landscape painting as security in a business transaction; ibid., 131.

5   Ibid., 128–130, 132.

6   Lugt 1915; Amsterdam and Paris 1998–99.

7   Amsterdam and Paris 1998–99, 284; Hinterding 2006, vol. 1, 104. For the marketing of landscape drawings by Rembrandt and Jan Lievens, see also the essay by Sonia Del Re in this volume.

8   On Rembrandt's faith, see Jürgen Müller, "Homer and the Pharisees – A New Aspect of Rembrandt's Hundred Guilder Print," in Dresden 2019, 45–57; Bakker 2012.

9   This has been explored especially by Boudewijn Bakker; see, for example, Boudewijn Bakker, "Nature or Art? Rembrandt's Aesthetics and the Netherlandish Tradition," in Kassel and Leiden 2006–07, 145–171; Bakker 2012.

10   Van Mander 1973, vol. 1, 102–105 (chap. 2, fol. 9-9v); on drawing outdoors from nature, see also vol. 1, 202–203 (chap. 8, fol. 34). On Van Hoogstraten and other theorists, see Weststeijn 2008, esp. 102–113.

11   See Bakker, "Rembrandt and the Humanist Ideal," in Dickey 2017b, 67–98.

12   See the essay by Robert Fucci in this volume.

13   See the landscape etchings in NHD, as well as Hinterding 2006, vol. 1, e.g., 51–54, 59–65, 104–108, 119–121. It is striking that neither the plates of the landscape etchings nor any reprints are documented after the mid-1650s (an exception is *The Omval*, NHD 221) – as if Rembrandt had removed these plates from circulation before his insolvency.

14   Rembrandt's first works executed entirely in drypoint, produced shortly before *The Three Crosses*, were landscapes (NHD 272, 273).

15   See Boston and St. Louis 1980–81.

16   On contemporary accounts of the "therapeutic" effects of landscapes on viewers, see Coutré, "Painted Landscapes," in Dickey 2017b, 126; Zell 2003.

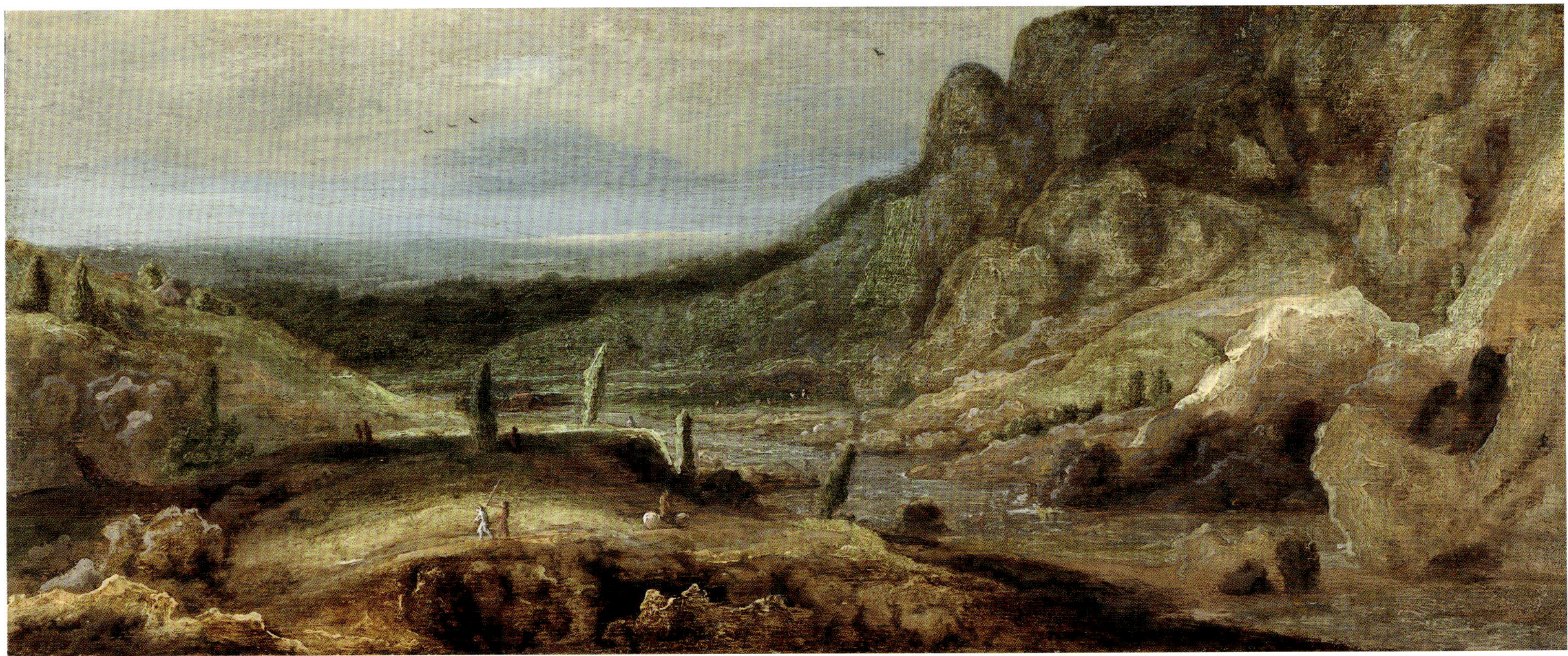

130 Hercules Segers, *River Valley*, c. 1620. Mauritshuis, The Hague

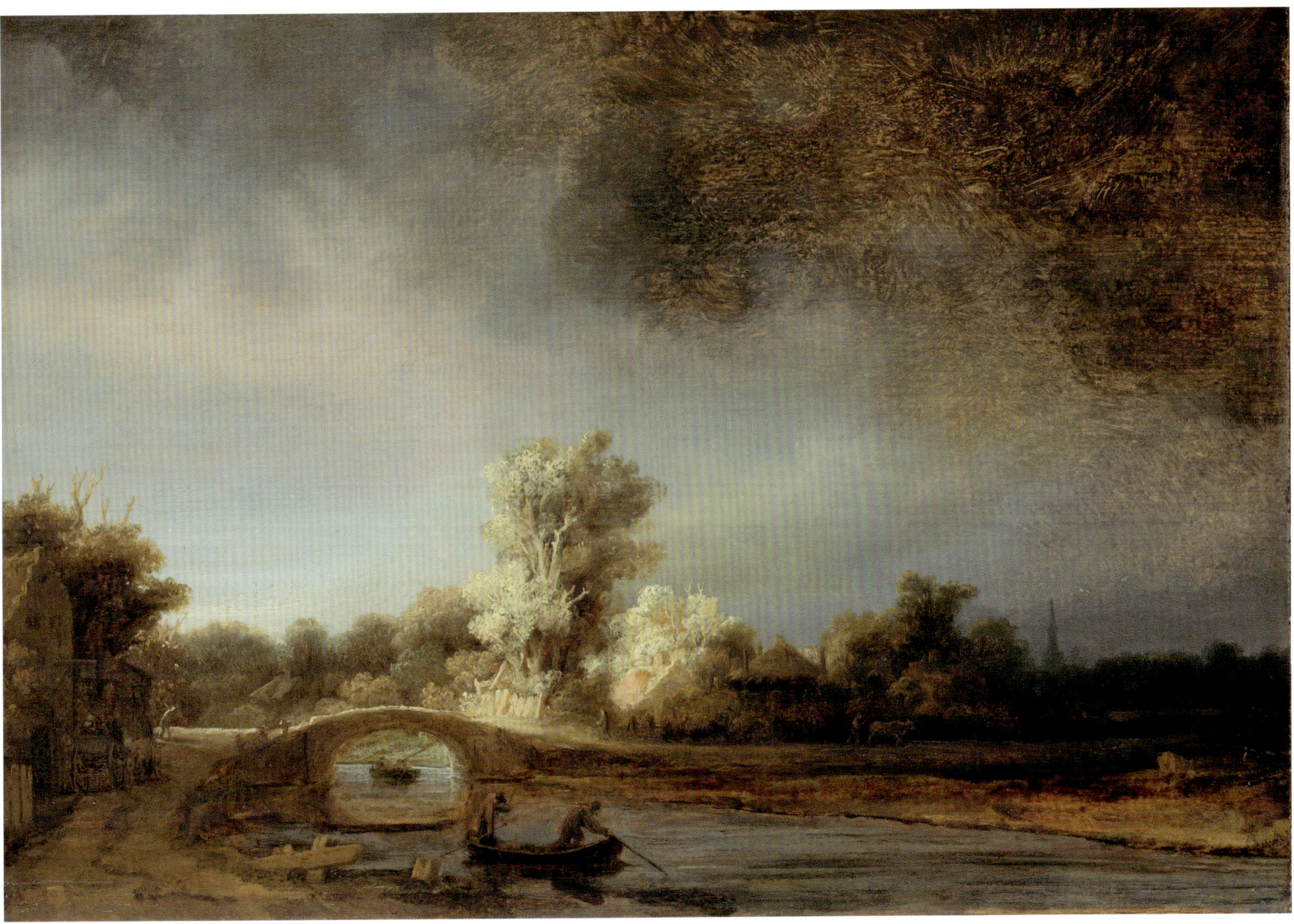

132   Philips Koninck, *Panoramic Landscape with a Village*, c. 1648–49. Los Angeles County Museum of Art

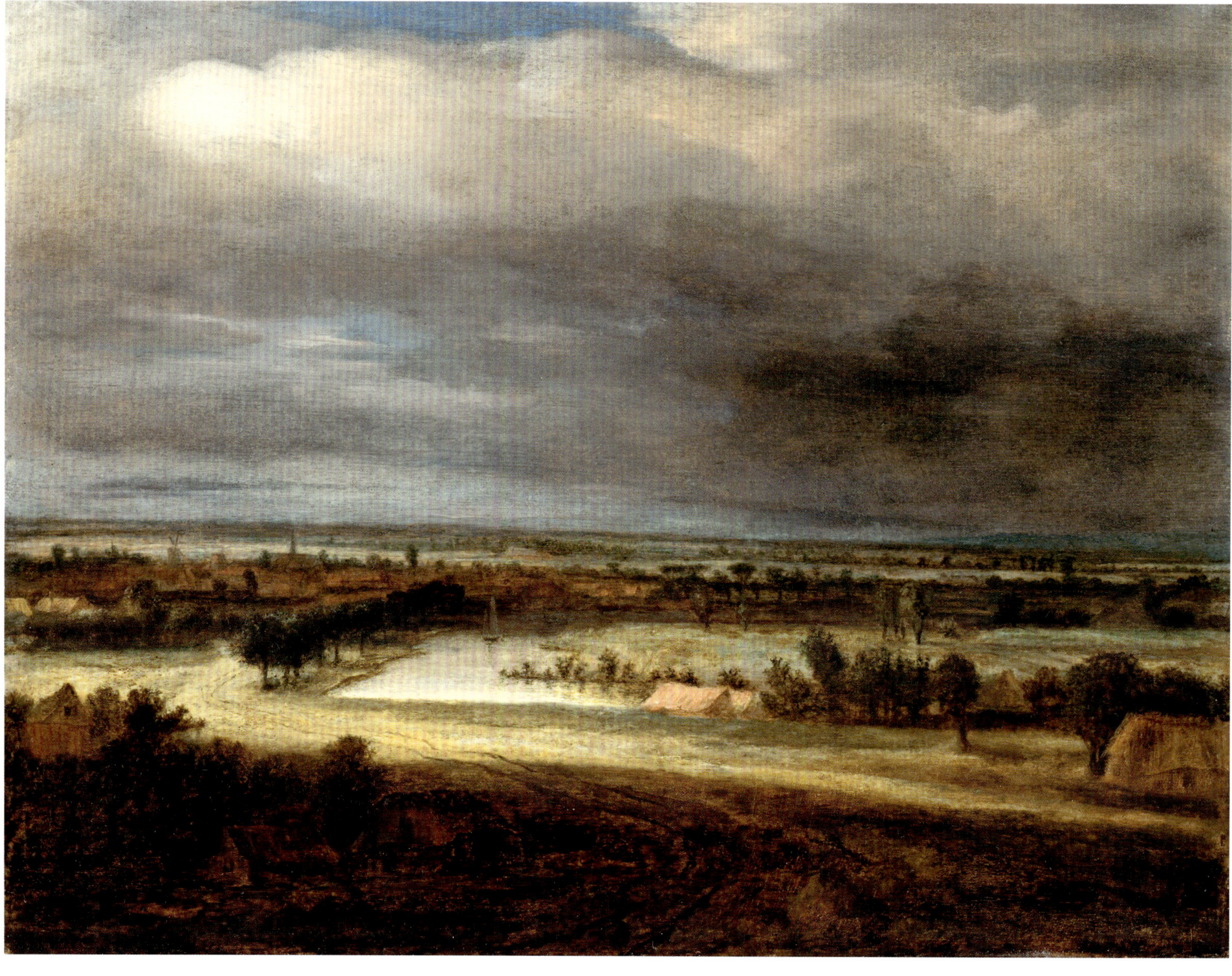

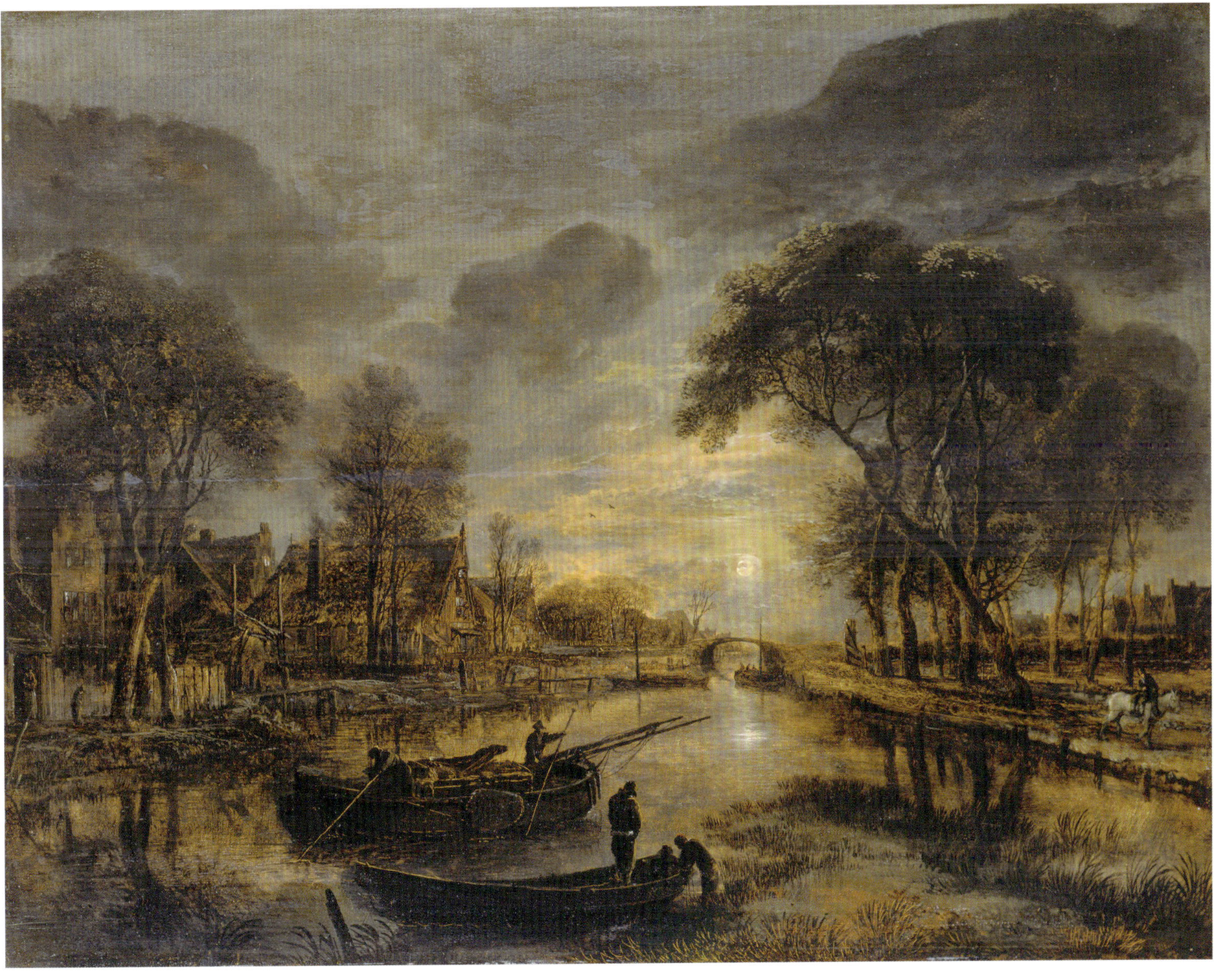

134   Jan Asselijn, *The Tiber River with the Ponte Molle at Sunset*, c. 1650. National Gallery of Art, Washington

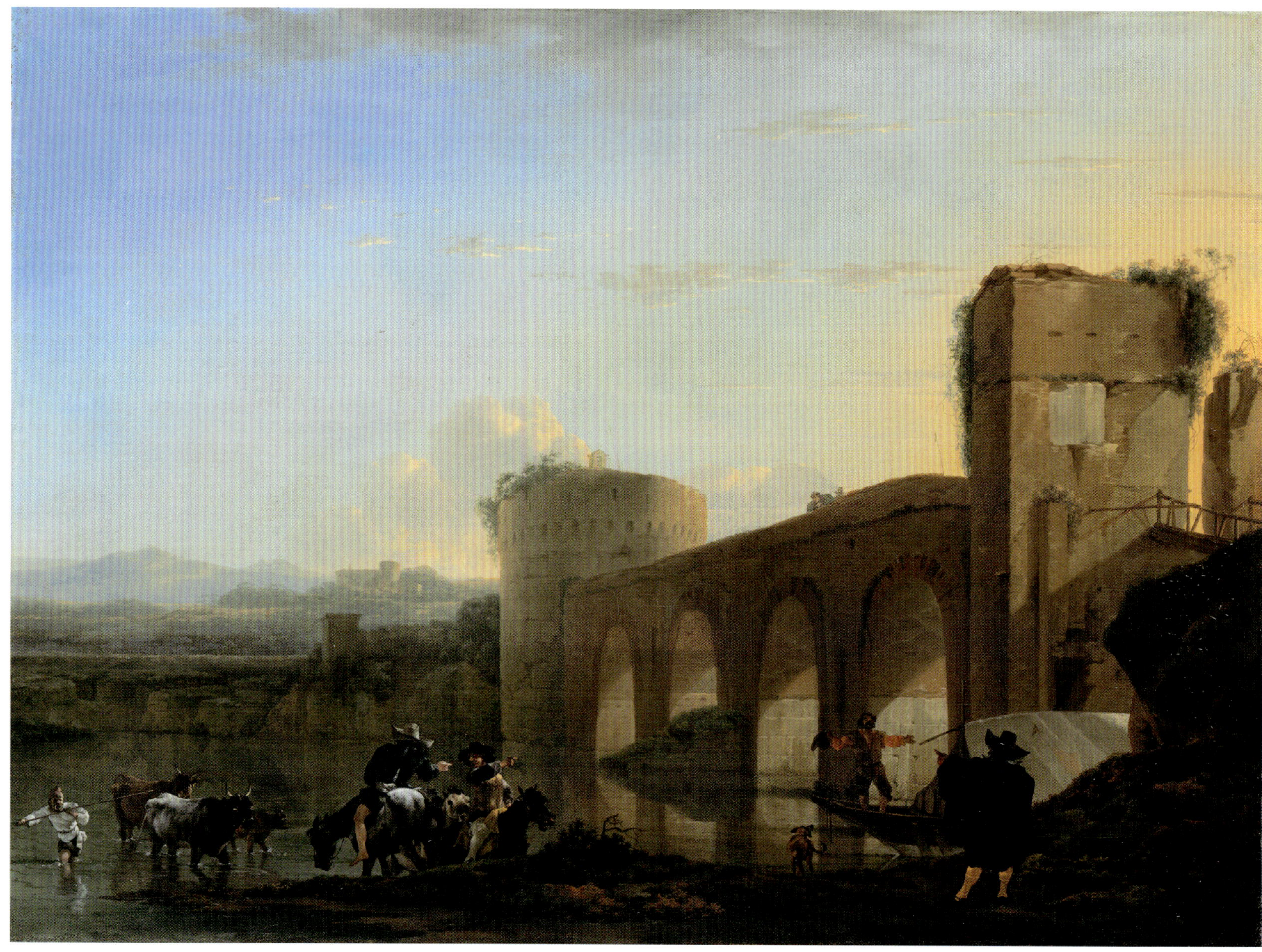

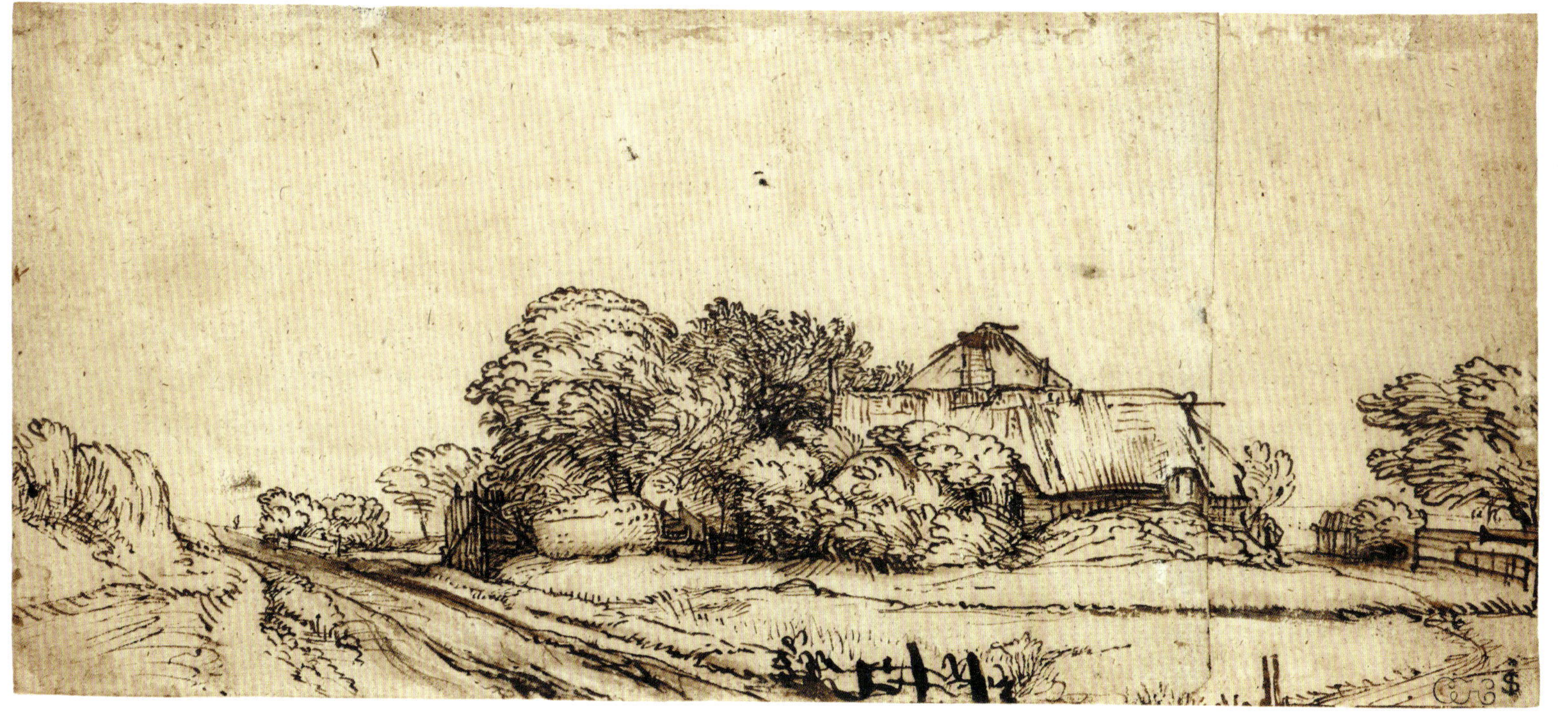

136 Rembrandt van Rijn, *Landscape with Cottages and Farm Buildings and a Man Sketching*, c. 1645. Städel Museum, Frankfurt am Main

137 Jacob van Ruisdael, *The Little Bridge*, c. 1650–55. Rijksmuseum, Amsterdam

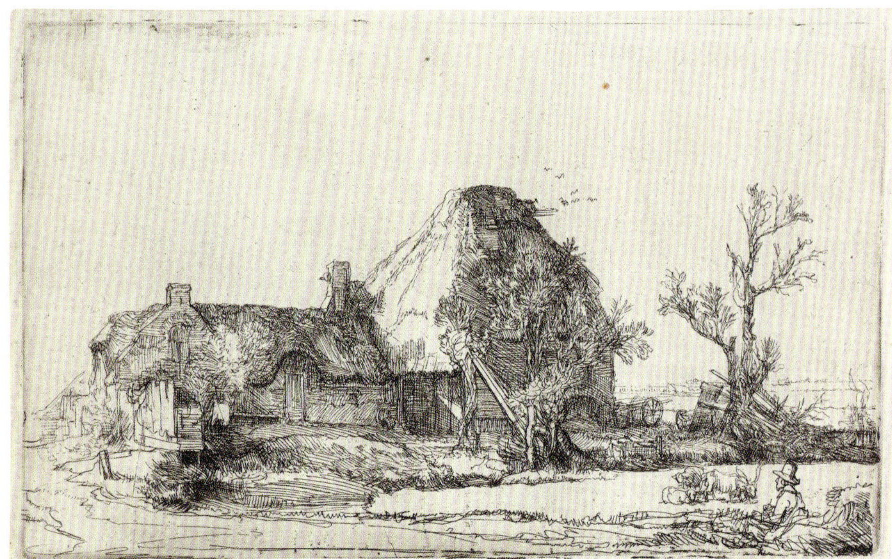

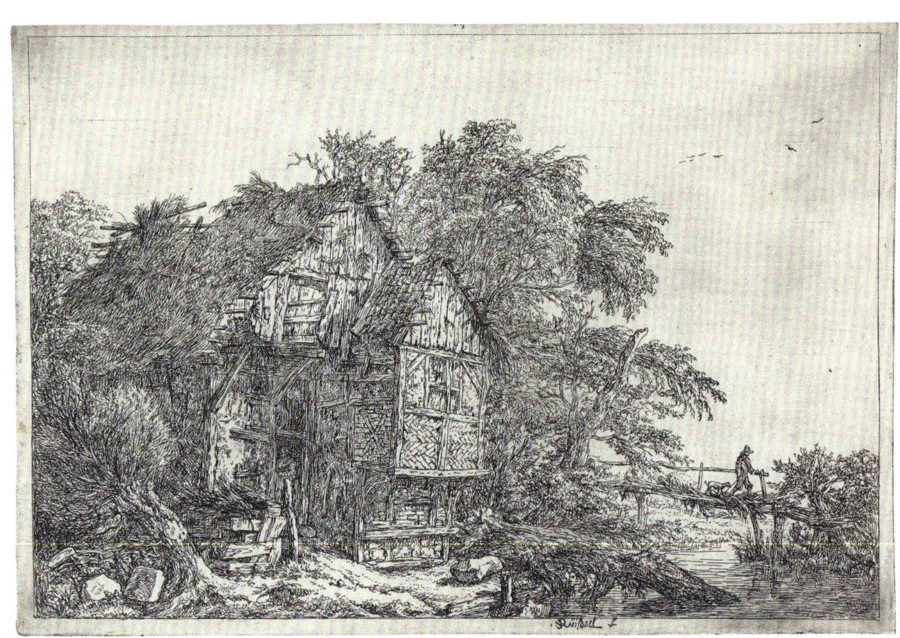

138   Rembrandt van Rijn, *Landscape with Cottages and Haybarn*, 1641. Städel Museum, Frankfurt am Main
139   Rembrandt van Rijn, *Three Gabled Cottages,* 1650. Städel Museum, Frankfurt am Main

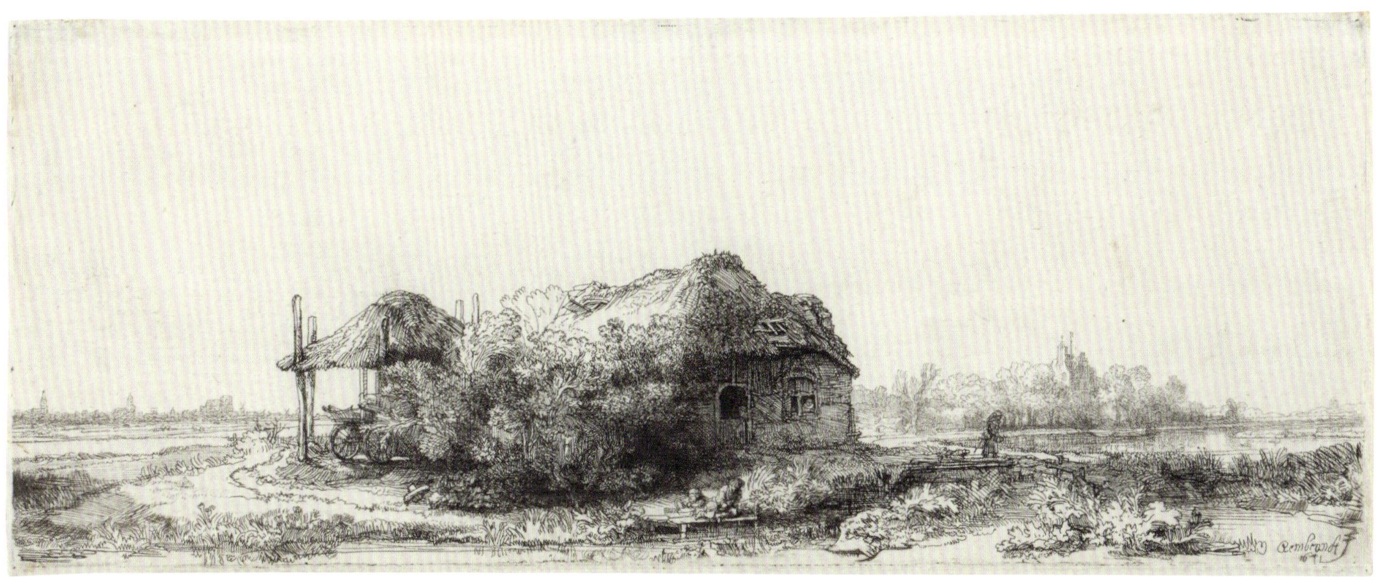

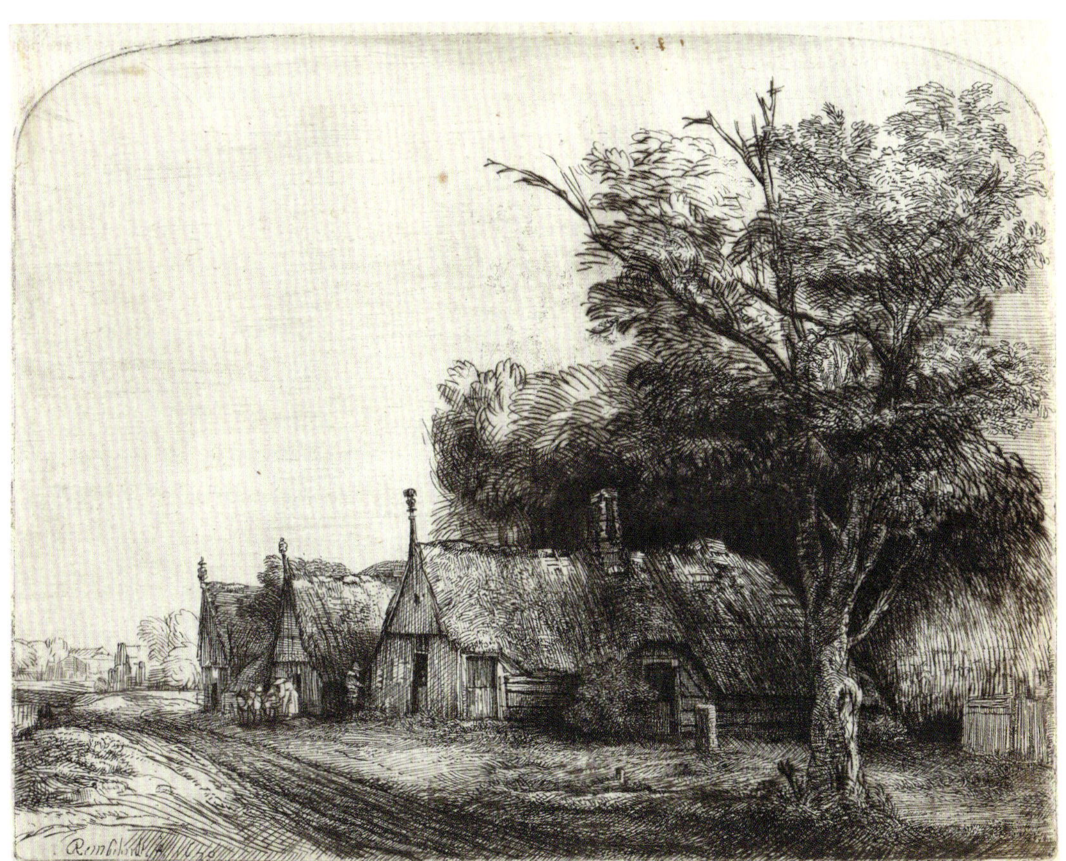

140   Rembrandt van Rijn, *The Three Trees*, 1643. National Gallery of Canada, Ottawa

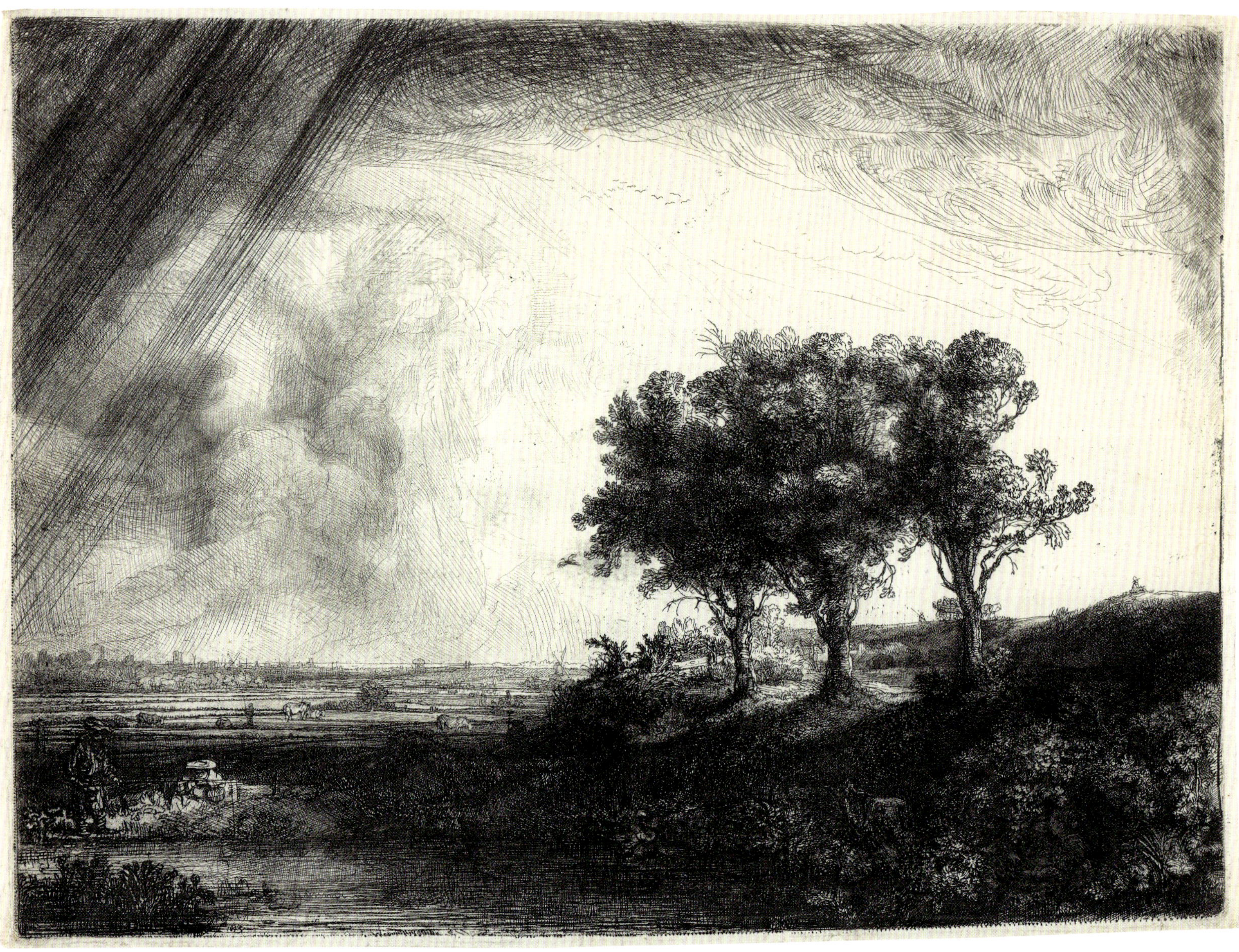

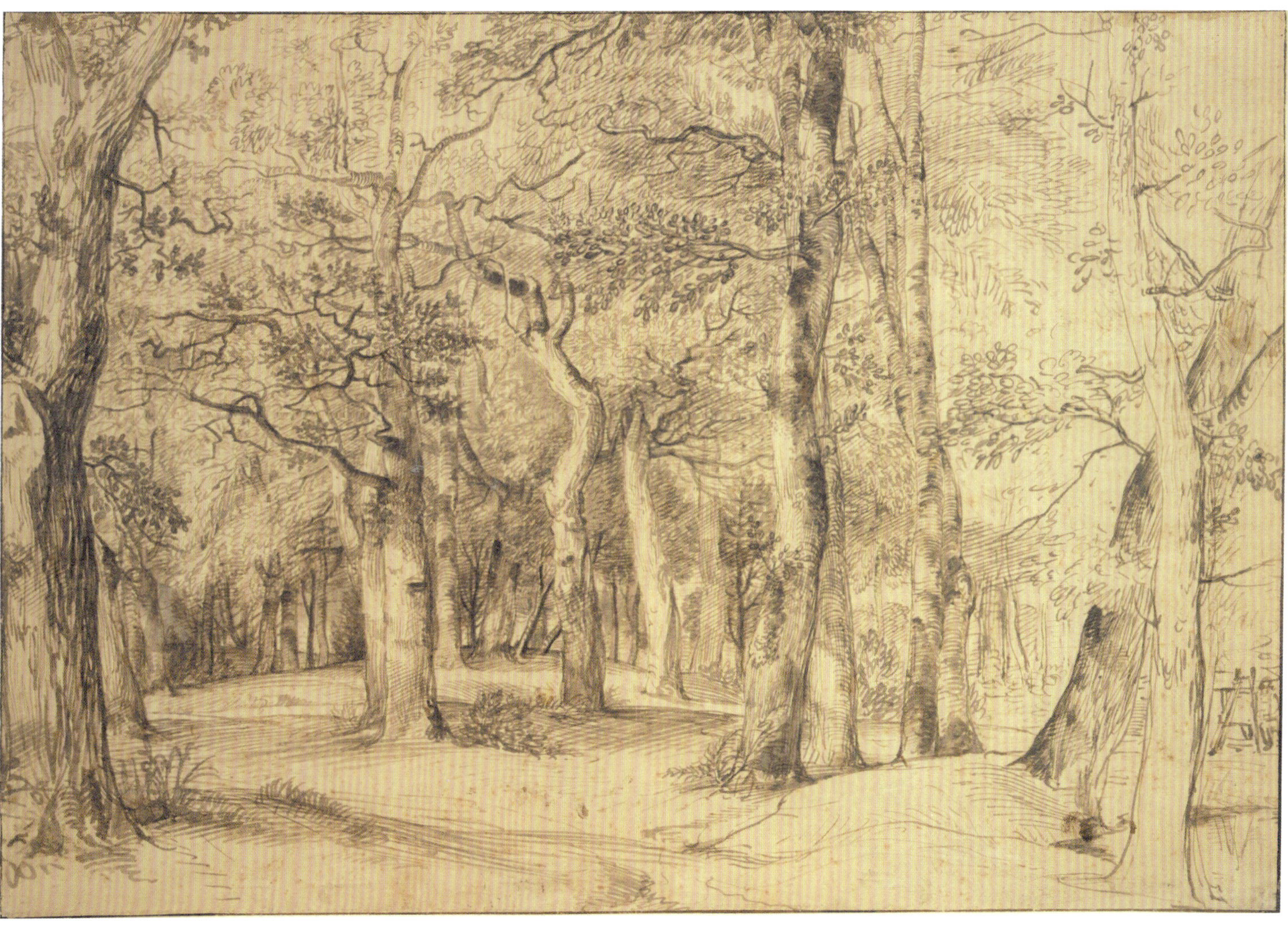

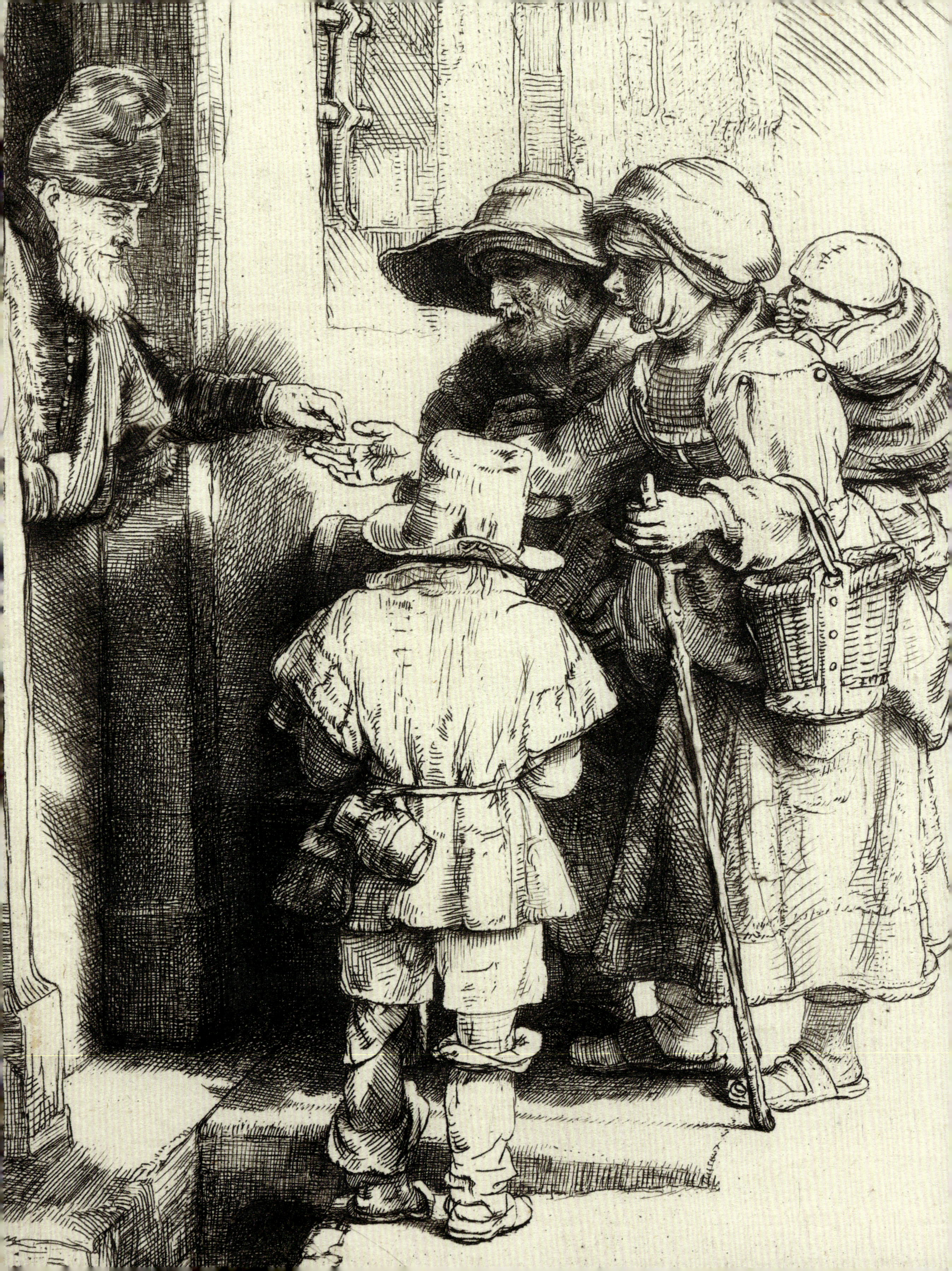

S T E P H A N I E   S .   D I C K E Y

Art and Life

The representation of contemporary life was an exceptionally fertile and innovative feature of art in the
Dutch Republic. Accessible and entertaining, genre
painting became increasingly popular with private
collectors, while ponderous history painting declined.[1]
Rembrandt took an early interest in this trend: a number of paintings from his first years in Leiden depict
genre themes, including an allegory of the five senses
imagined as a sequence of humorous interactions
between tricksters and buffoons (fig. 15.1).[2] These
pictures synthesize acerbic commentary on human
nature with awareness of pictorial and iconographic
conventions as established in comic theatre and in
the work of artists such as Lucas van Leyden and
Albrecht Dürer. A similar sensibility later informed
the paintings of Haarlem genre specialists Jan Miense
Molenaer (pl. 142) and Judith Leyster, who lived in
Amsterdam from 1637 to 1648.[3]

While only a few of Rembrandt's mature paintings
address genre themes, numerous drawings and prints
reflect his attentive observations of daily life. His
sketches feature beggars, models, lovers, vendors,
performers, sportsmen, musicians, neighbours, farm-
ers, animals and more. The 1680 estate inventory of
the wealthy seascape painter Jan van de Cappelle lists
more than five hundred drawings by Rembrandt,
including two albums of landscapes and one with 135
studies of women and children (pl. 144). These most
likely included sketches of family members: private
documents released onto the market when Rembrandt
died in 1669, or earlier, when bankruptcy forced him to
sell many of his possessions around 1656 (pls. 155, 156).[4]
Among his dozens of etchings of genre themes, one

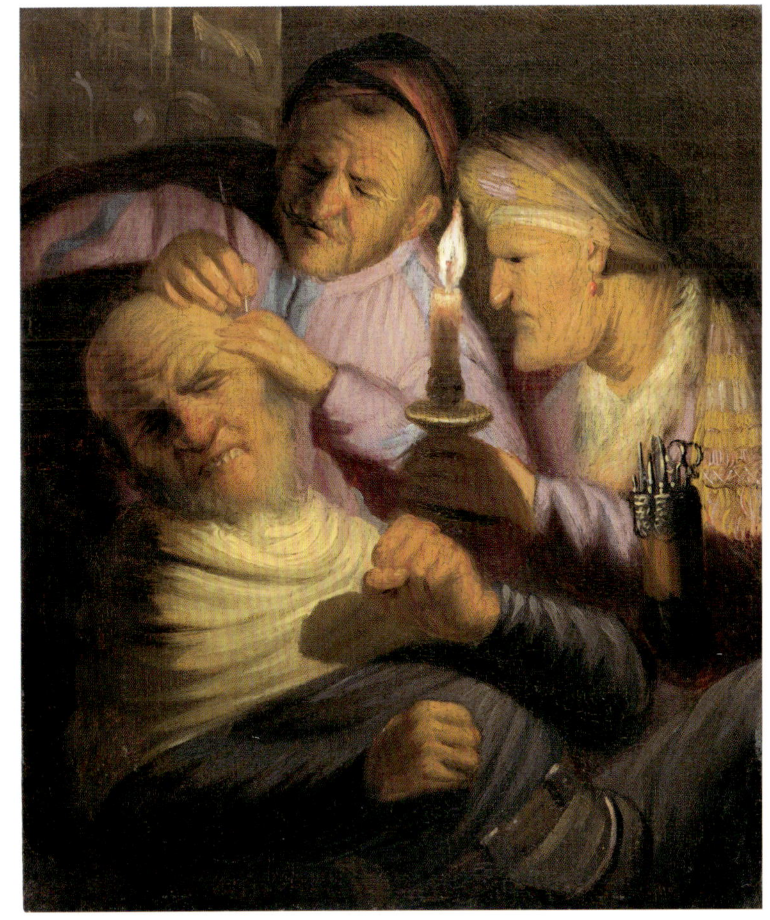

fig. 15.1 **Rembrandt van Rijn,**
The Stone Operation (Allegory
of Touch), **c. 1624–25, oil on**
panel; 21.5 × 17.7 cm. The Leiden
Collection, New York (RR-102)

studio scene nicknamed *The Walking Trainer* (see fig. 16.2) reflects the intimate fusion of work and home life: like a toddler learning to walk, Rembrandt's students must learn to draw from the model before they can graduate to painting.[5] Etchings and drawings of street scenes capture the fabric of urban life with wit and empathy (pls. 144, 146, 147, 148, see fig. 1.2).

The spontaneity of Rembrandt's etching style contrasts markedly with the polished engravings of Cornelis Visscher, a talented younger printmaker from Haarlem. The third state of Visscher's *Pancake Woman* (pl. 149) was published in Amsterdam by Clement de Jonghe, who also owned many plates by Rembrandt. Visscher made drawings on vellum that, like Rembrandt's etchings, were luxury collectibles, but his large prints might have appealed to modest buyers who could display them as inexpensive substitutes for paintings.[6]

Rembrandt painted *Still Life with Peacocks* (pl. 150) around 1639, the year he purchased his grand house on the St. Anthonisbreestraat (now the Rembrandt House Museum). Part still life and part genre, this work is unique in his oeuvre. The artist was clearly fascinated by the rich hues and textures of the birds' feathers, rendering them with bold, linear strokes of unblended colour. The innocent child seems to share this fascination. She has not yet noticed the congealing blood, a slick reminder of mortality. In 1660 the Amsterdam author Tobias van Domselaer inherited this painting from his parents; the same year, he edited an anthology of occasional verse that included seven poems praising Rembrandt.[7]

Several talented artists in Rembrandt's circle became experts in genre painting, extending the reach of his brand into this rising segment of the market. Gerrit Dou, his first pupil, founded a multigenerational school of painters in Leiden who specialized in precisely rendered genre scenes.[8] Dou's *Tooth Puller* (fig. 15.2) echoes Rembrandt's *Stone Operation* (*Allegory of Touch*), recording a fascination with the visible traces of human suffering.[9] The cringing pose of the patient, with clenched fists and curled toes, recurs in Rembrandt's gruesome *Blinding of Samson* (pl. 106).

fig. 15.2 **Gerrit Dou, *The Tooth Puller*, 1630–35, oil on panel; 32 × 25 cm. Musée du Louvre, Paris (1220)**

fig. 15.3 **Nicolaes Maes, *The Lacemaker*, 1655, oil on panel; 57.1 × 43.8 cm. National Gallery of Canada, Ottawa. Purchased 1954 (6189)**

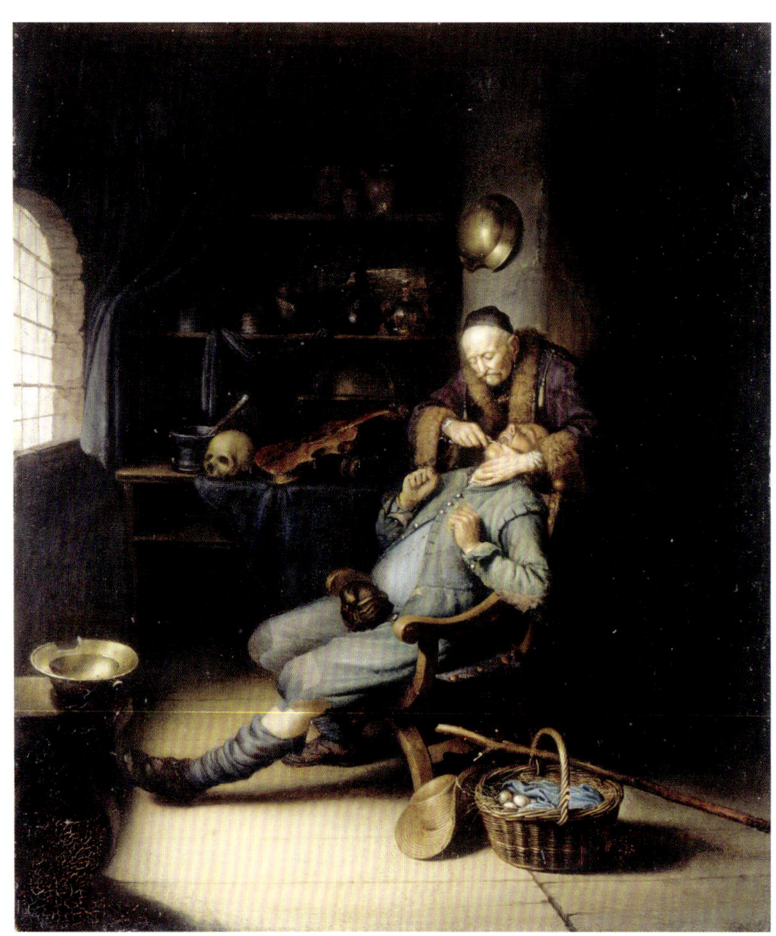

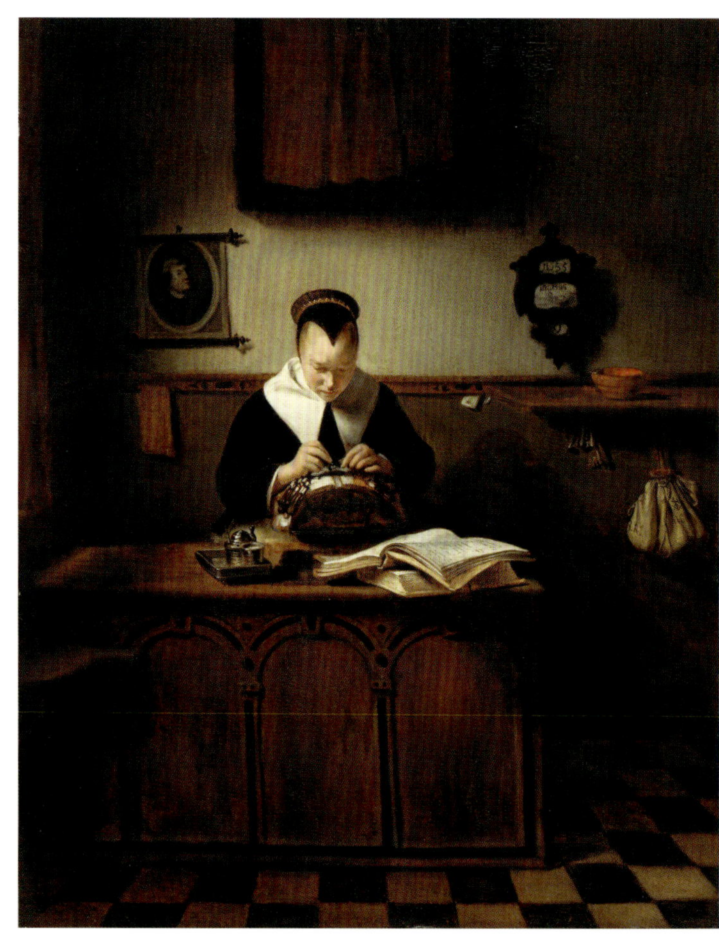

A productive dialogue between historical and genre imagery also informs the work of several of Rembrandt's Amsterdam associates, including Nicolaes Maes, Jan Victors, Gerbrand van den Eeckhout, Carel Fabritius and others (pls. 88, 151).[10] Maes learned to paint biblical scenes in Rembrandt's workshop (pl. 114) but took up genre painting around the time he returned to his native Dordrecht (fig. 15.3).[11] In the 1650s, along with Jacob van Loo, Van den Eeckhout revived the vogue for elegant merry company scenes first pioneered in Amsterdam by Pieter Codde (figs. 15.4, 15.5).[12] Van Loo worked in a cooler, more classical idiom (fig. 15.6), offering buyers an elegant alternative that may well have inspired Johannes Vermeer and other artists of the Delft school, including Pieter de Hooch, who moved to Amsterdam around 1661 (pl. 95). Amsterdam collectors also bought genre paintings by artists from other cities, strongly increasing the competition.[13] ■

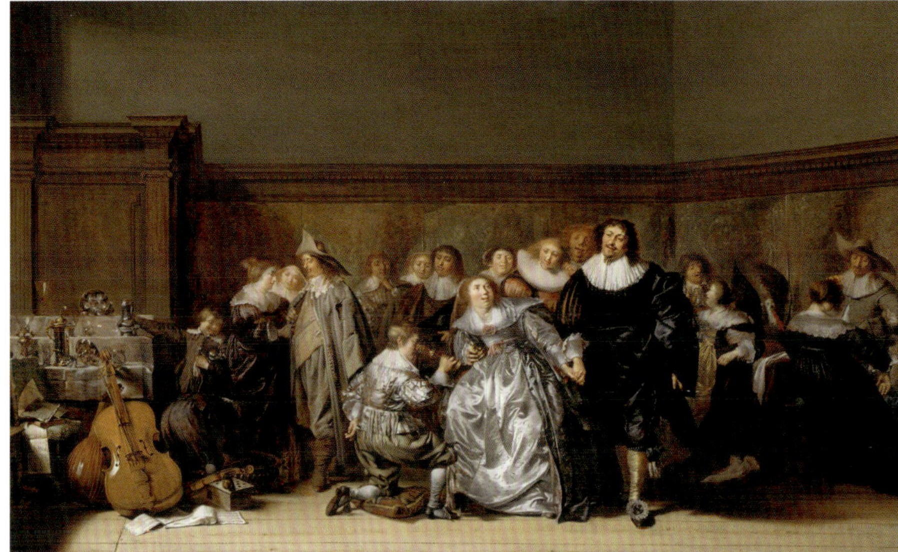

fig. 15.4 Pieter Codde, *An Elegant Company*, 1632, oil on panel; 58.8 × 92.7 cm. Art Institute of Chicago. Mr. and Mrs. Martin A. Ryerson Collection (1993.1069)

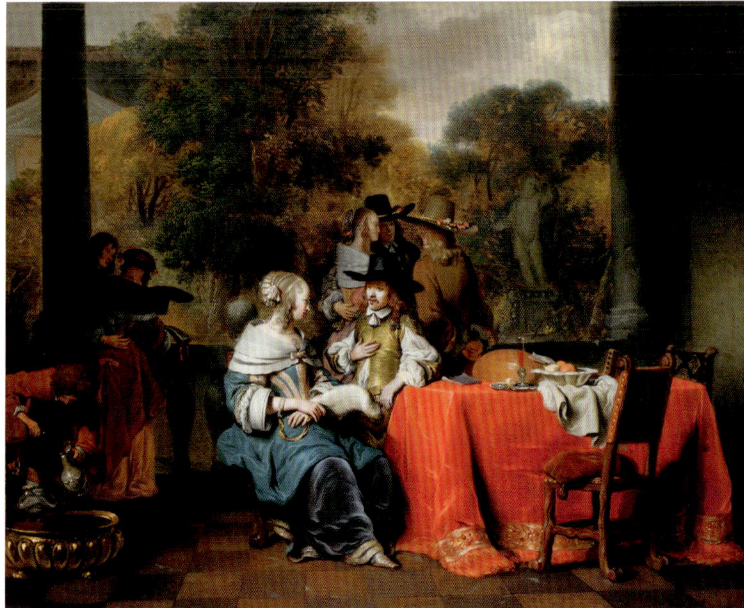

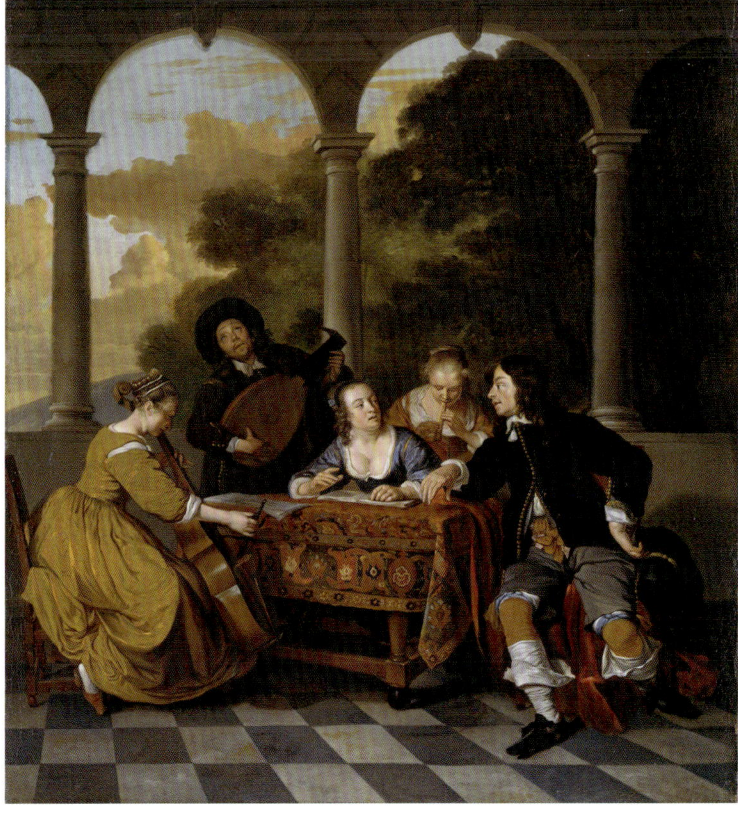

fig. 15.5 Gerbrand van den Eeckhout, *Party on a Terrace*, 1652, oil on canvas; 51.4 × 62.2 cm. Worcester Art Museum. Museum purchase (1922.208)

fig. 15.6 Jacob van Loo, *The Concert*, 1650–52, oil on canvas; 73.3 × 55 cm. Museo Nacional Thyssen-Bornemisza, Madrid (225 / 1930.47)

NOTES

1   See, among others, John Michael Montias, "Works of Art in Seventeenth-century Amsterdam: An Analysis of Subjects and Attributions," in Freedberg and De Vries 1991, 331–372. For an overview of Dutch genre painting, see Franits 2004.

2   *The Stone Operation* (*Allegory of Touch*), *Three Musicians* (*Allegory of Hearing*) and *The Unconscious Patient* (*Allegory of Smell*) are in The Leiden Collection, New York; *The Spectacles Seller* (*Allegory of Sight*) is in the Museum De Lakenhal, Leiden; the presumed fifth panel (*Allegory of Taste*) is lost. See Alexandra Libby, Ilona van Tuinen and Arthur K. Wheelock, Jr., "Allegory of Hearing, Allegory of Smell, Allegory of Touch, from the Series of the Five Senses," in Leiden Collection Catalogue; Leiden and Oxford 2019–20, 139–142, no. 46.

3   Franits 2004, 43–51. Rembrandt's old friend Jan Lievens rented a room from Molenaer and Leyster when he returned from Antwerp in 1644; see Schneider and Ekkart 1973, 7; Arthur K. Wheelock, Jr., "Jan Lievens: Bringing New Light to an Old Master," in Washington, Milwaukee and Amsterdam 2008–09, 1–27, esp. 18–19.

4   Schatborn and Hinterding 2019, nos. D324, D362; Edinburgh and London 2001, no. 38; Vienna 2004, no. 37. "Works by Rembrandt in the estate of the late Amsterdam painter, architect Jan van de Cappelle," 4 Jan. 1680, Remdoc, no. e14075; first published by Bredius 1892. For an overview of themes in Rembrandt's drawings, see Slive 2009b.

5   NHD 233. For interpretation and connection to workshop drawing practice, see, among others, Emmens 1968, 154–159; Dickey 1986, 255; Holm Bevers, "Drawing in Rembrandt's Workshop," in Los Angeles 2009–10, 1–29, esp. 10–19.

6   See Hollstein (Visscher), no. 52. A drawing of the central figure in black chalk on vellum was sold at Sotheby's, New York, 25 Jan. 2012, lot 151. Visscher portrayed a variety of prominent Amsterdammers and lived there for several years before he died at only thirty-eight. For Rembrandt and De Jonghe, see the essay by Robert Fucci in this volume.

7   Van Domselaer 1660; see, among others, Dickey 2004, 14, 113, 162–167. For provenance, see *Corpus*, vol. 2, 97; *Corpus*, vol. 3, no. A134. For game still lifes on the Amsterdam market, see the essay by Jasper Hillegers in this volume.

8   Franits 2004, 115–134, with further references.

9   See also Rembrandt van Rijn, *The Foot Operation* (1628, Kunst Museum Winterthur); Leiden and Oxford 2019–20, no. 47.

10 *Girl with a Broom* is one of numerous illusionistic portraits and genre studies produced in Rembrandt's circle between c. 1640 and 1655; Arthur K. Wheelock, Jr., has proposed an attribution to Carel Fabritius. See www.nga.gov/collection/art-object-page.81.html (accessed 27 Feb. 2020).

11 For a recent survey of Maes' career, see London and The Hague 2019–20, *The Sacrifice of Isaac*, no. 3. For Maes' relationship to other genre painters of the 1650s, see also Paris, Dublin and Washington 2017–18, no. 15.2.

12 Franits 2004, 57–64, 177–180.

13 See recently Piet Bakker, "Painters of and for the Elite: Relationships, Prices and Familiarity with Each Other's Work," in Paris, Dublin and Washington 2017–18, 85–99, esp. 95, and 267, for statistics on paintings in Amsterdam collections.

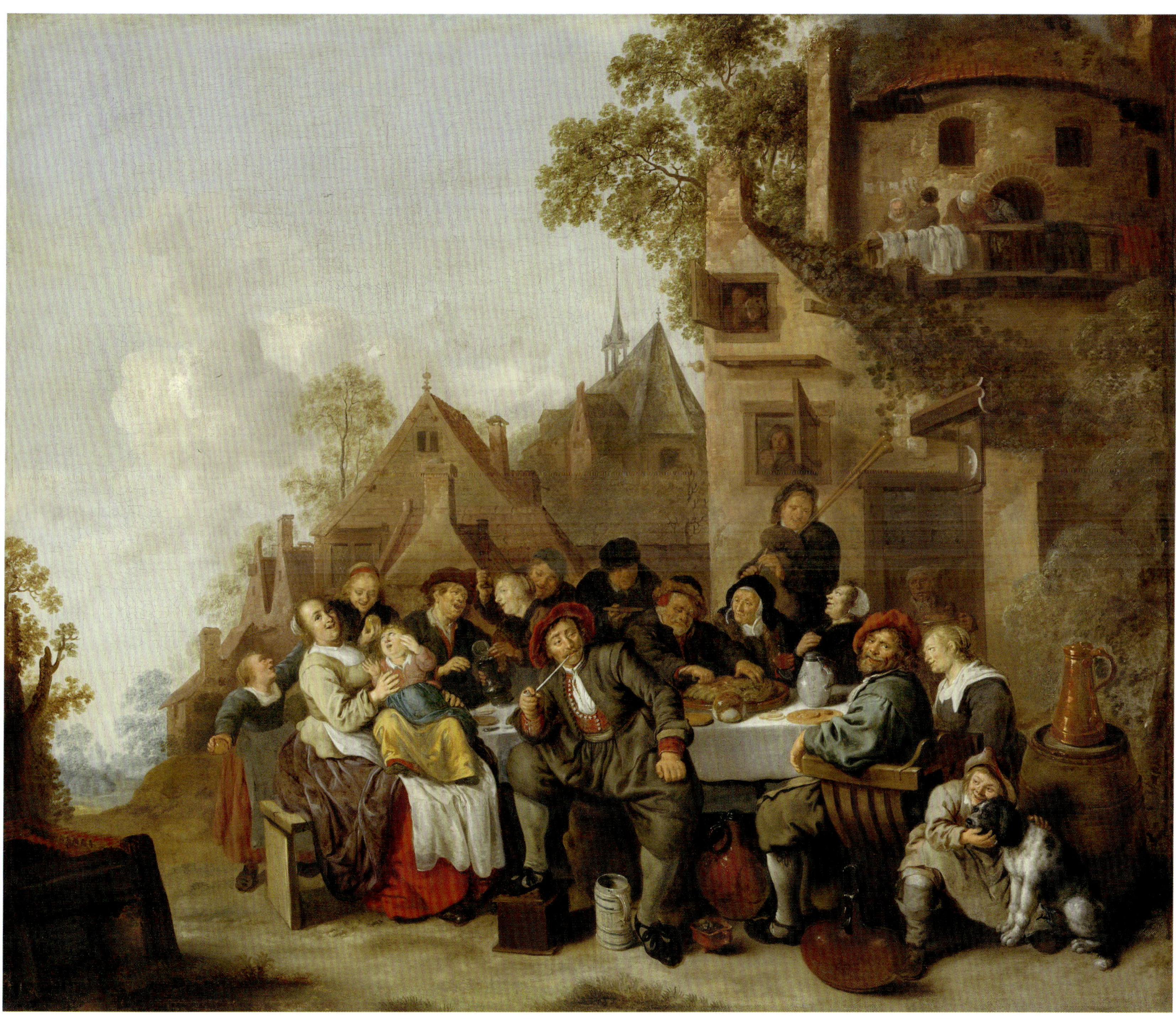

143　Rembrandt van Rijn, *Two Studies of a Woman Reading*, c. 1638. The Metropolitan Museum of Art, New York

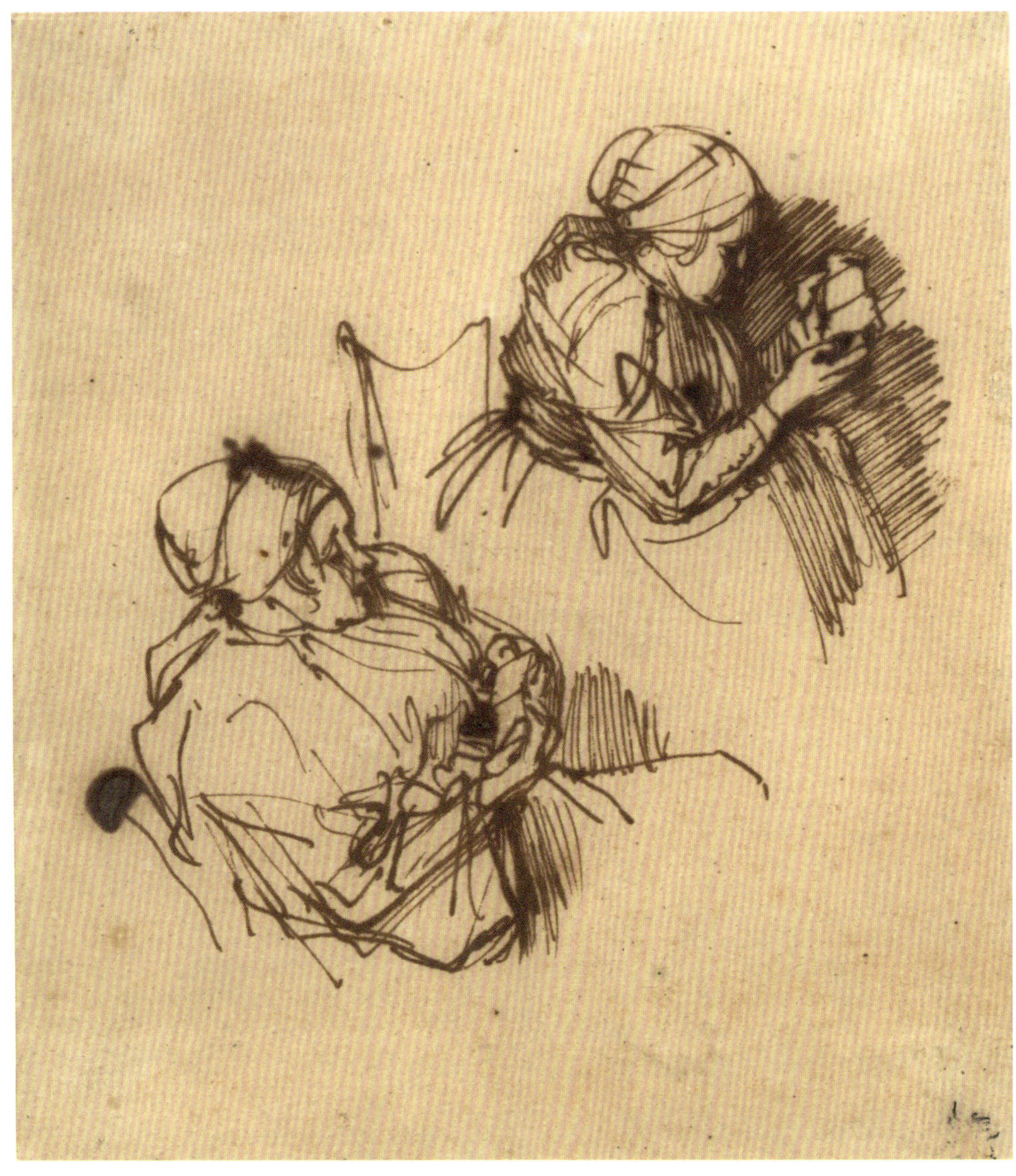

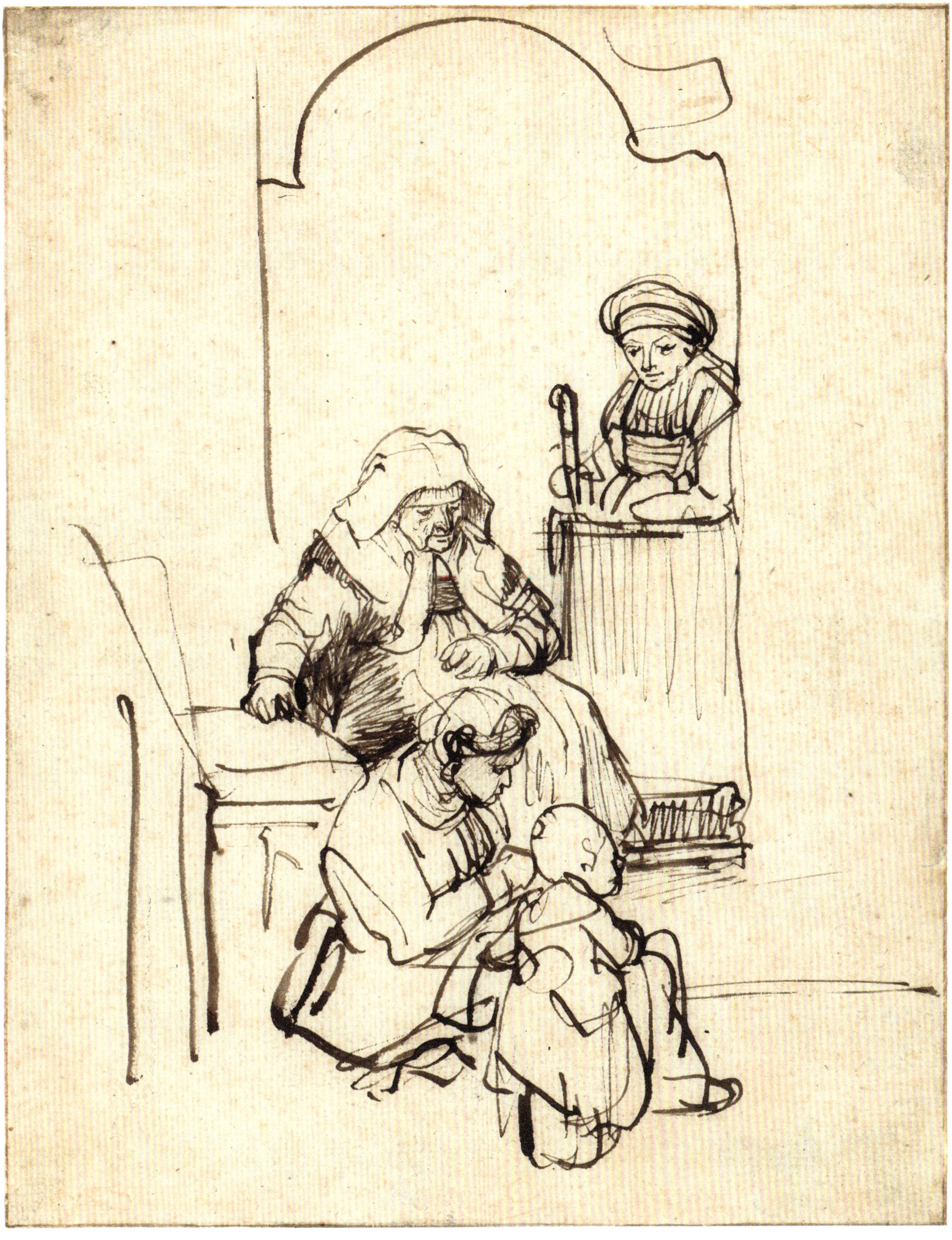

145 Rembrandt van Rijn, *The Hog*, 1643. Städel Museum, Frankfurt am Main

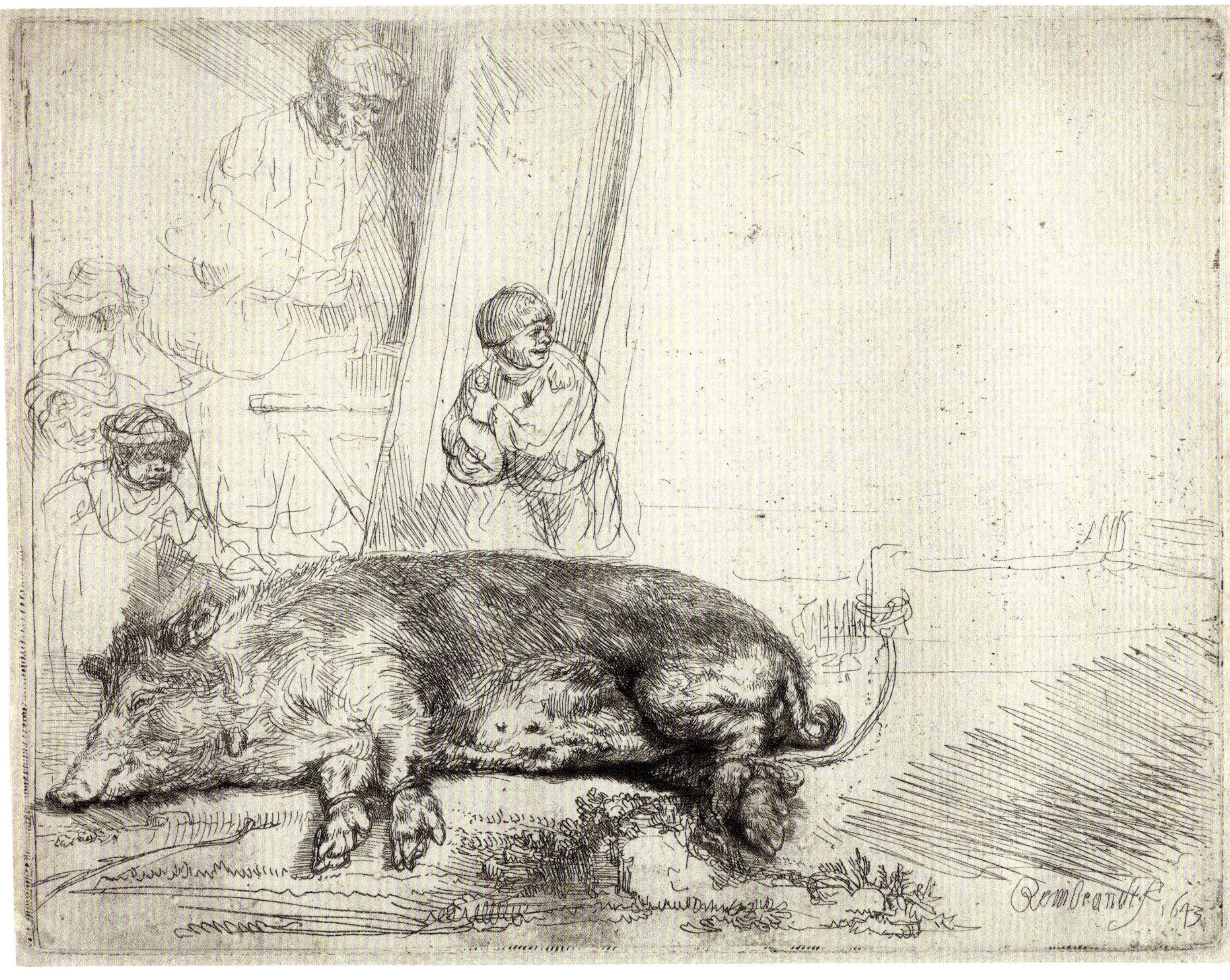

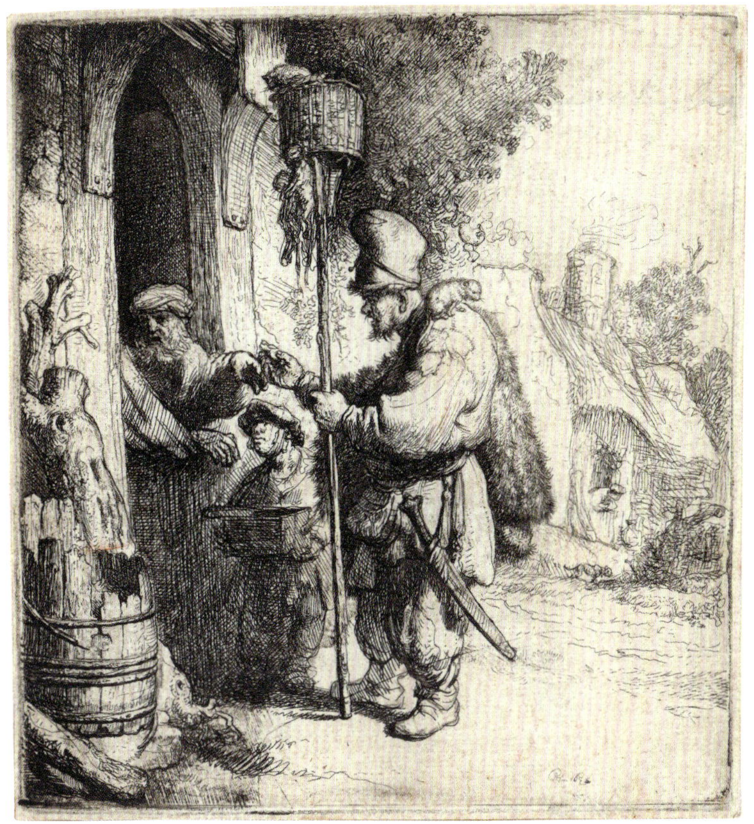

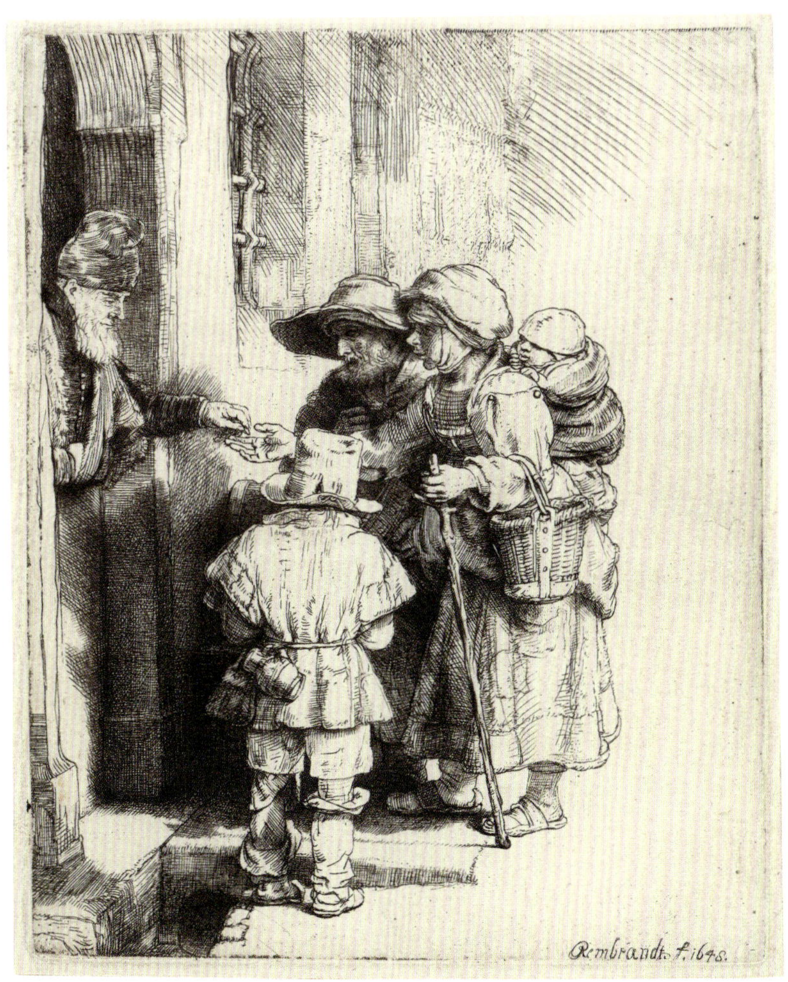

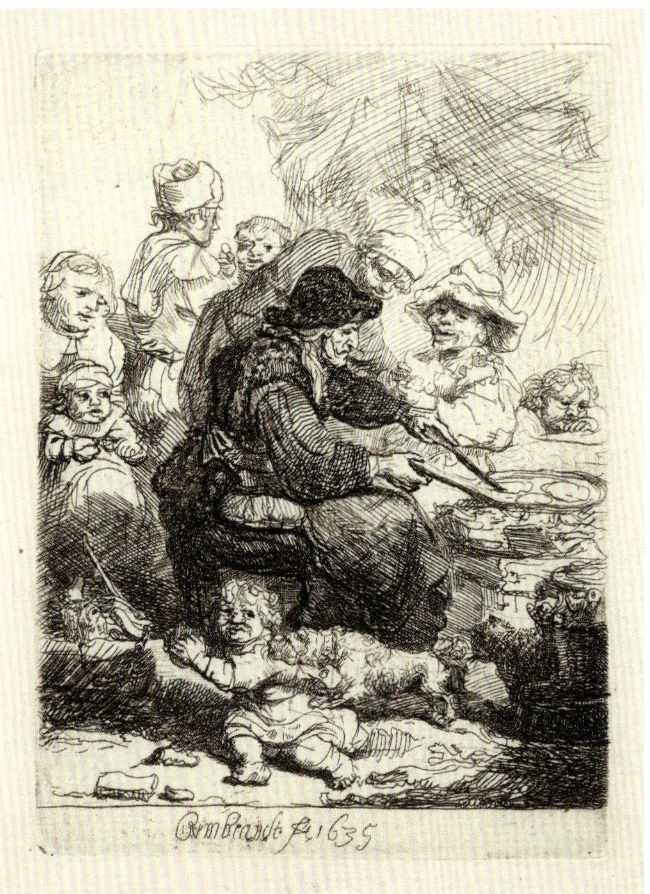

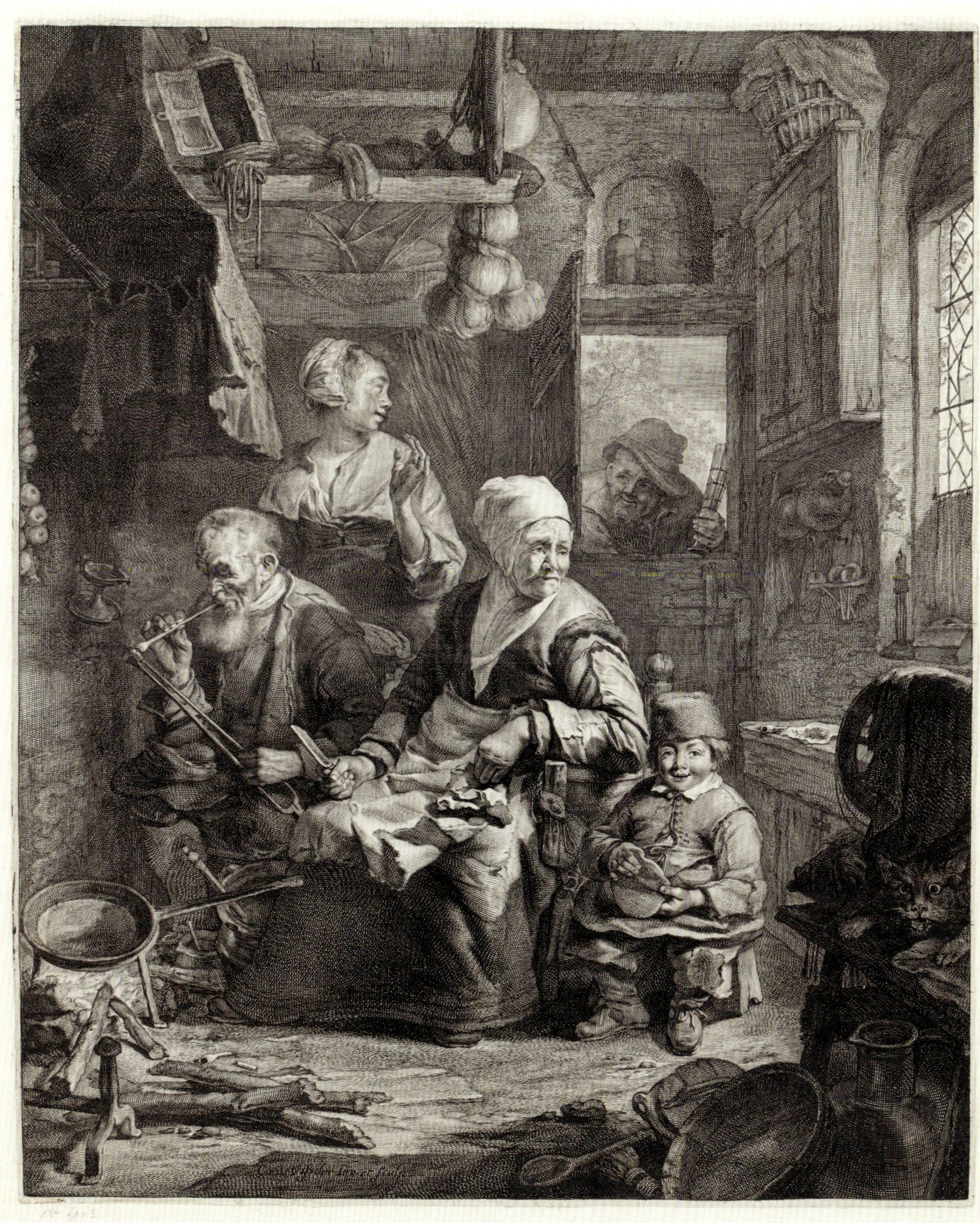

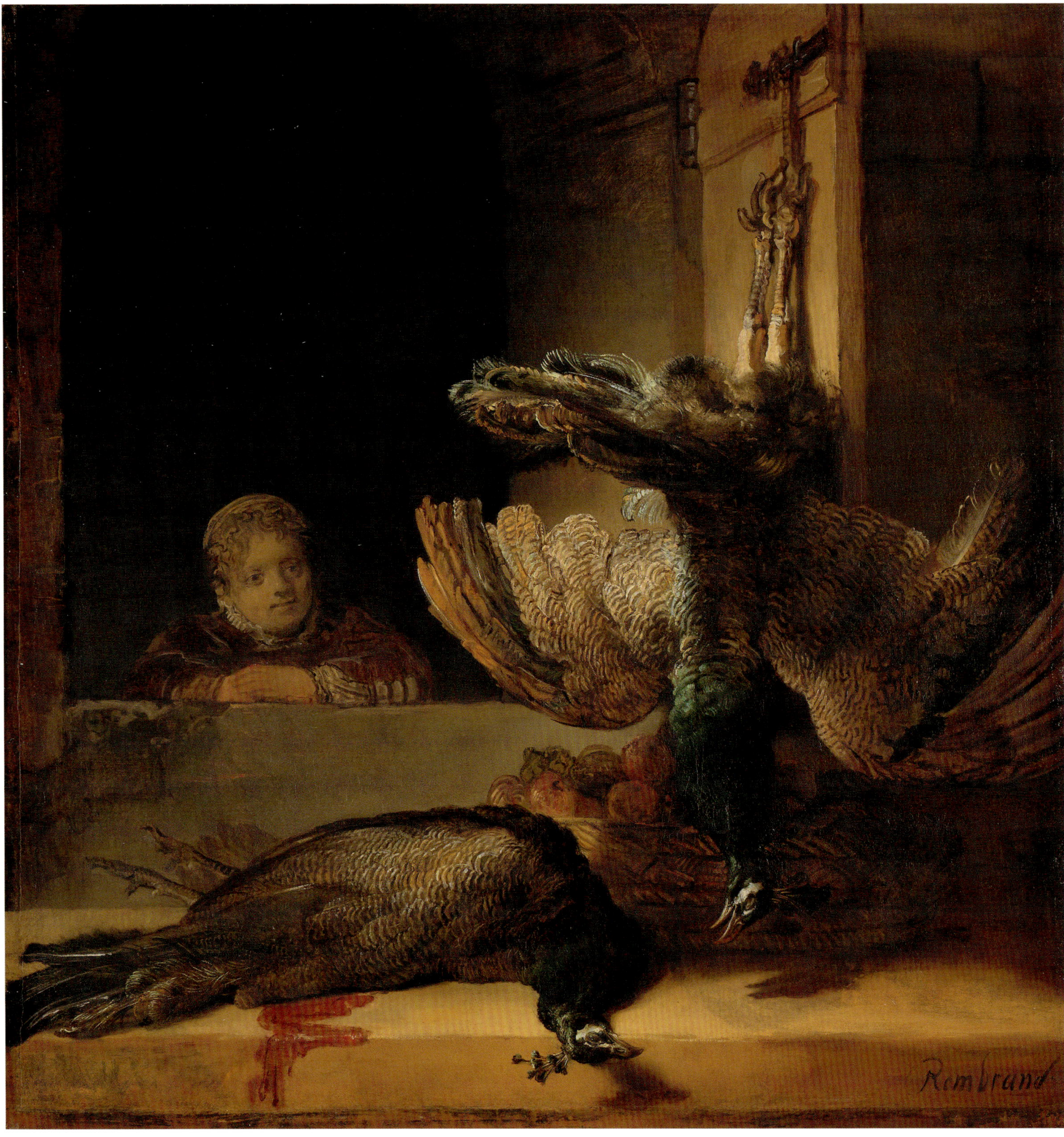

150   Rembrandt van Rijn, *Still Life with Peacocks*, c. 1639. Rijksmuseum, Amsterdam

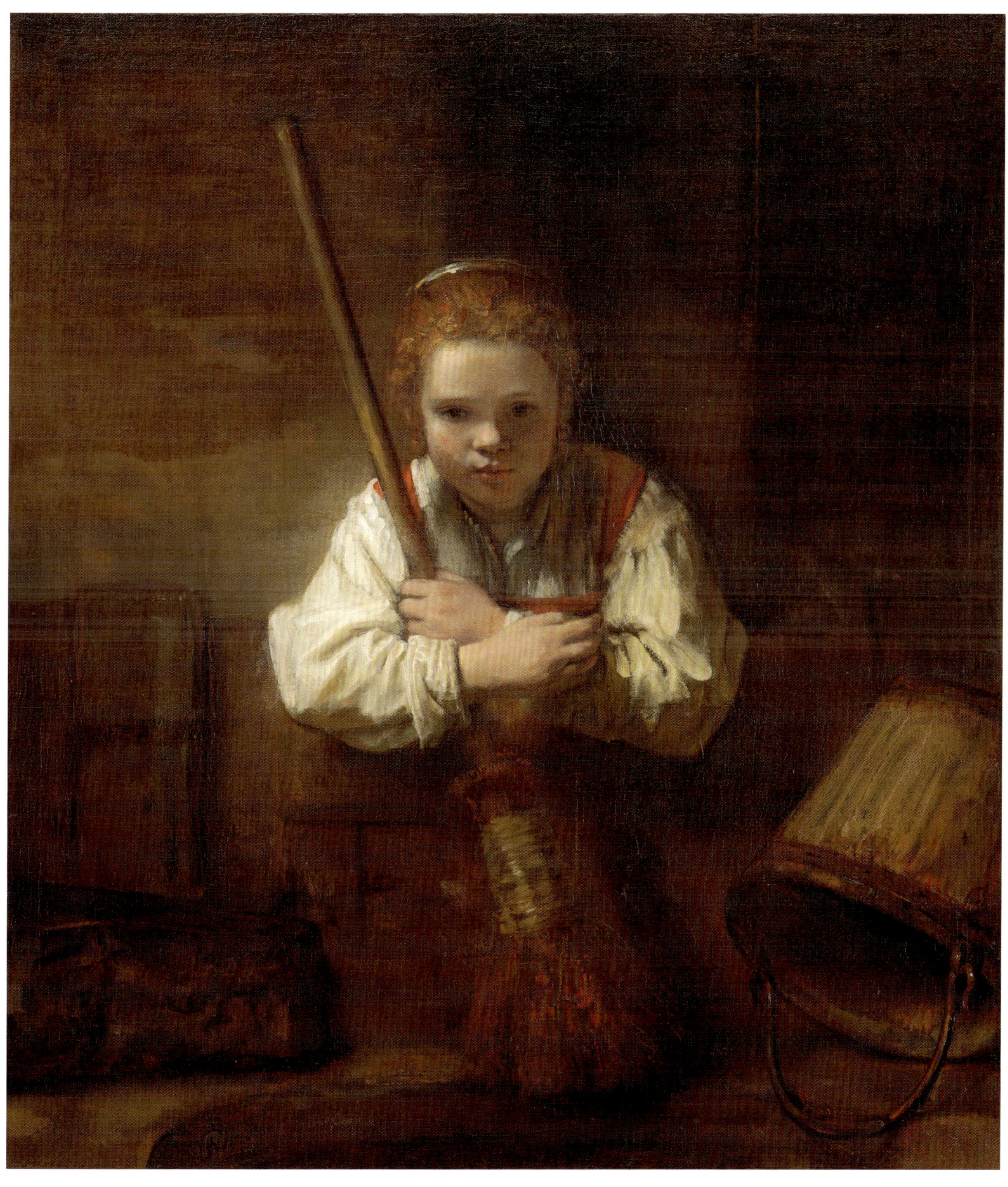

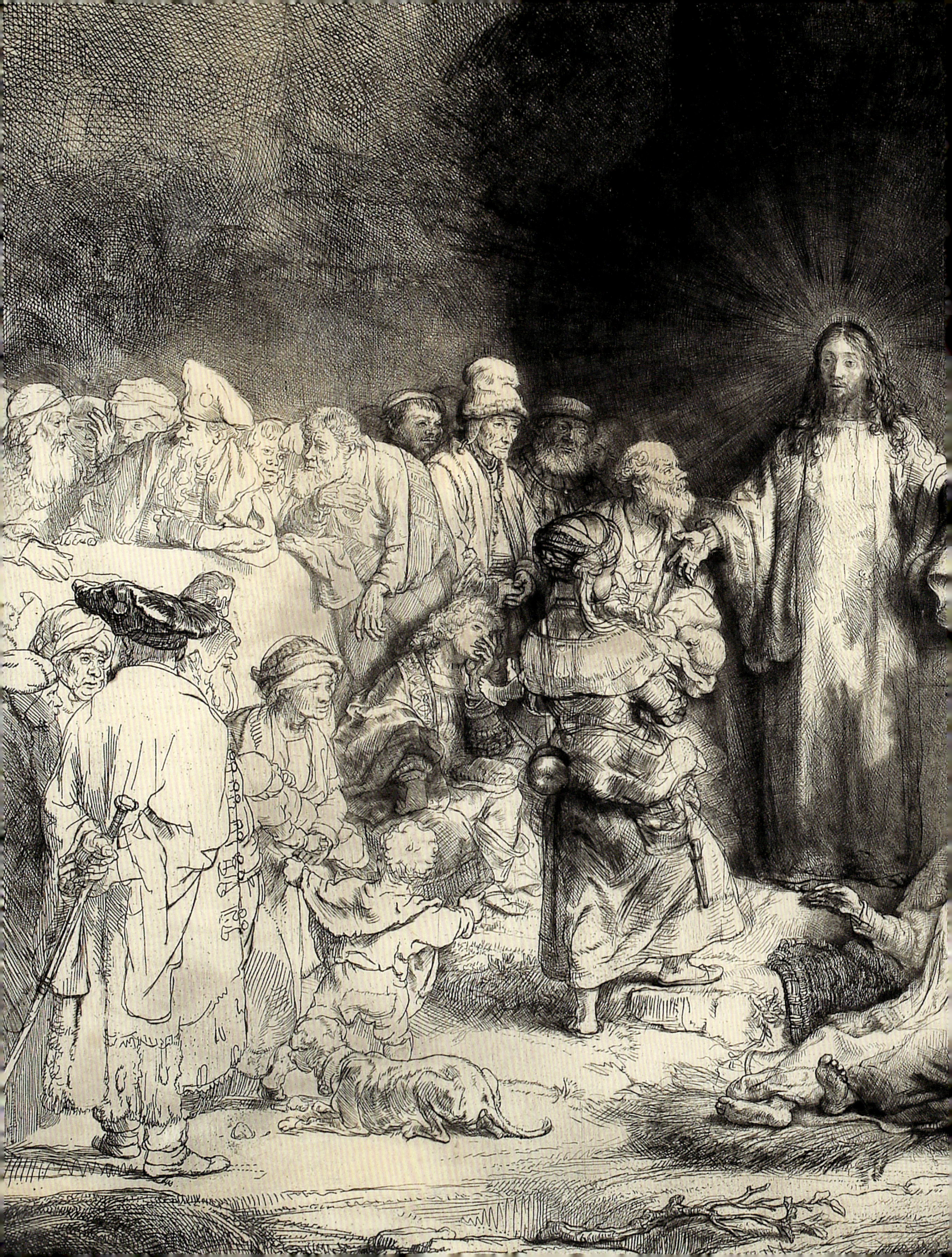

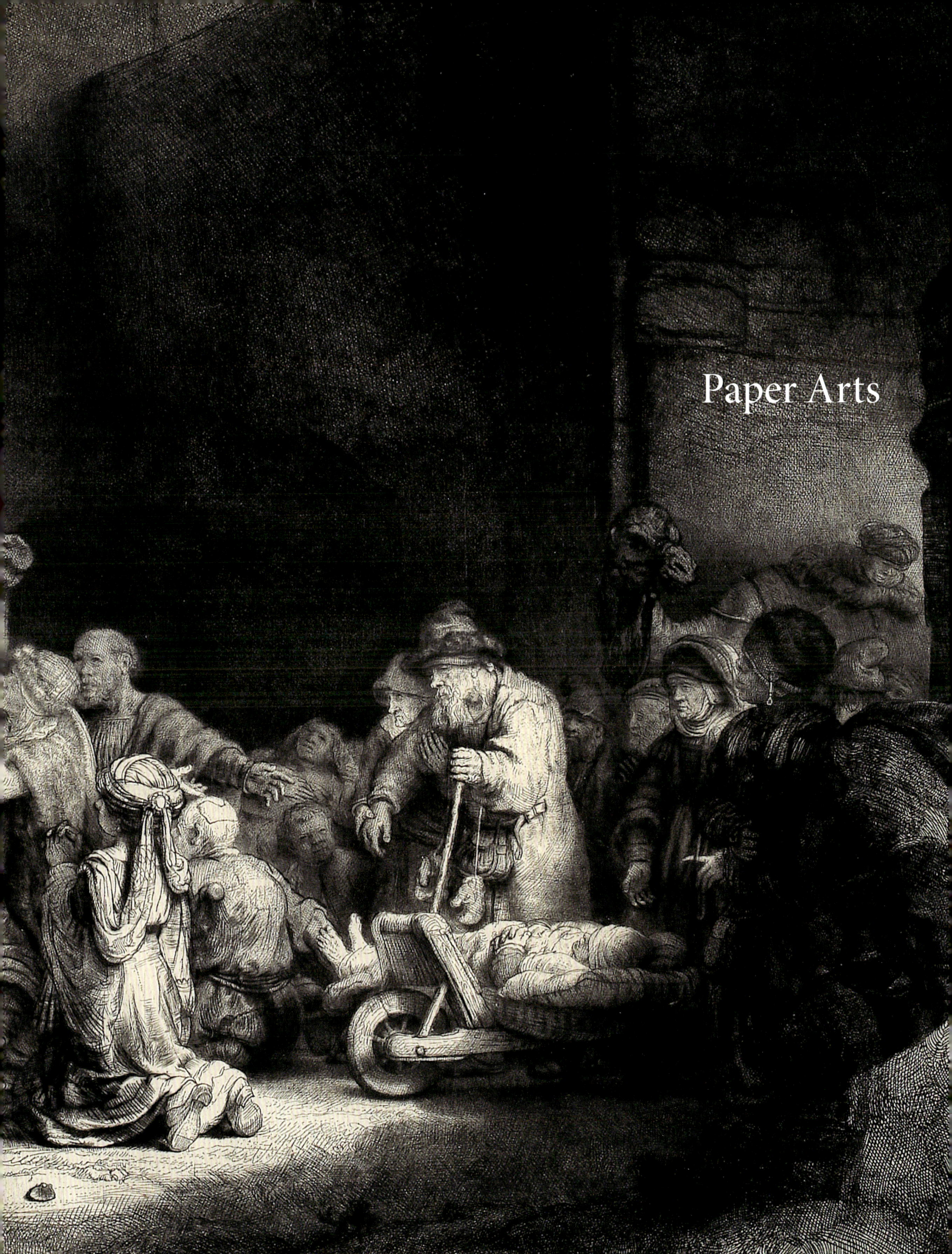
Paper Arts

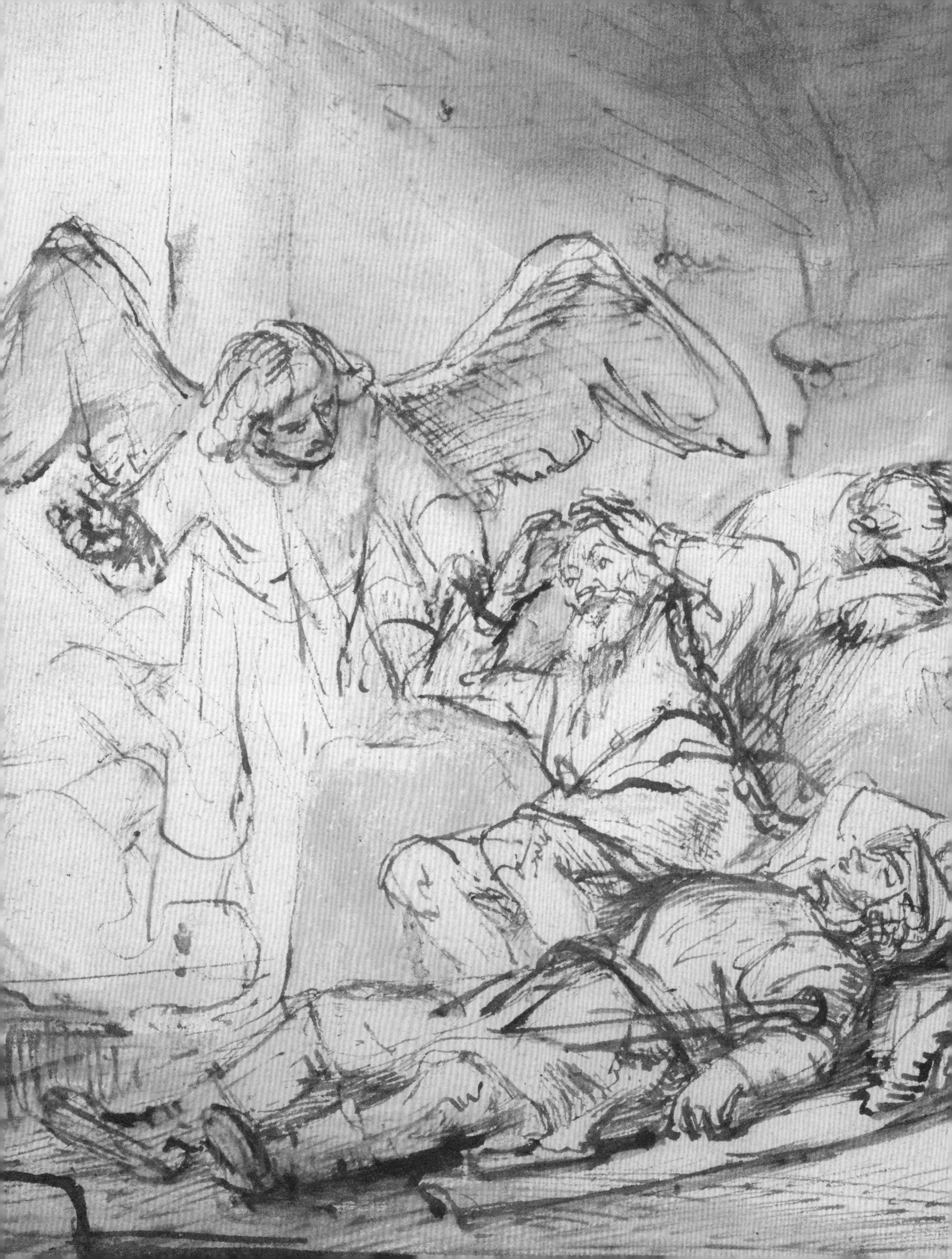

SONIA DEL RE

Drawings in and out of Rembrandt's Studio

By and large, Rembrandt's activities – painting, print-making, teaching and art dealing – were a lucrative enterprise. However, drawing, as central to his art practice as it was, occupied a very different role in his business model. Hundreds of sheets by his hand survive, countless more by his pupils. Yet, unlike his prints and paintings, they were not devised as commodities for sale.[1] On the contrary, an estimated 1,500 to 2,000 drawings, likely including many by his students, remained in his studio until 1655–56, when he declared insolvency and was forced to sell his collection.[2] Set apart from the rest of the studio's production, the drawings were kept in albums alongside some seventy books in which he collected and stored a precious 8,000 or so prints and drawings by other artists.[3]

The 1656 inventory for the room in Rembrandt's home designated as the "art chamber" lists, in addition to two packets of drawings, twenty-four albums and books of studio sheets "by Rembrandt" organized by category, including: "a book filled with drawings by Rembrandt of nude men and women"; "one full of landscapes drawn by Rembrandt from nature"; "one filled with drawings by Rembrandt of animals done from life"; "a packet of drawings from the antique by Rembrandt"; "one filled with figure sketches by Rembrandt"; "one full of drawings of statues by Rembrandt done from life"; as well as the enticing "book bound in black leather with the best sketches by Rembrandt."[4]

As an artist and collector, Rembrandt was immersed in the fastest growing art market in Europe, one with an appetite for drawings of varying degrees of finish.[5] "It was a culture," writes Ger Luijten, "in which people appreciated the quality of drawings as much as of paintings."[6] Yet, while a handful of Rembrandt's sheets are documented as the property of other Amsterdammers or Leidenaars prior to his insolvency, most of his sketches, along with those of his pupils, only made it onto the market after 1655.[7] Lambert Doomer, a topographical draughtsman and pupil of Rembrandt who, on the contrary, made a living from his drawn landscapes, purchased several of his teacher's albums of drawings at auction at this time.[8]

If not for financial gain and self-promotion, then why did Rembrandt and his pupils draw so much? To prepare and work through compositions for his prints

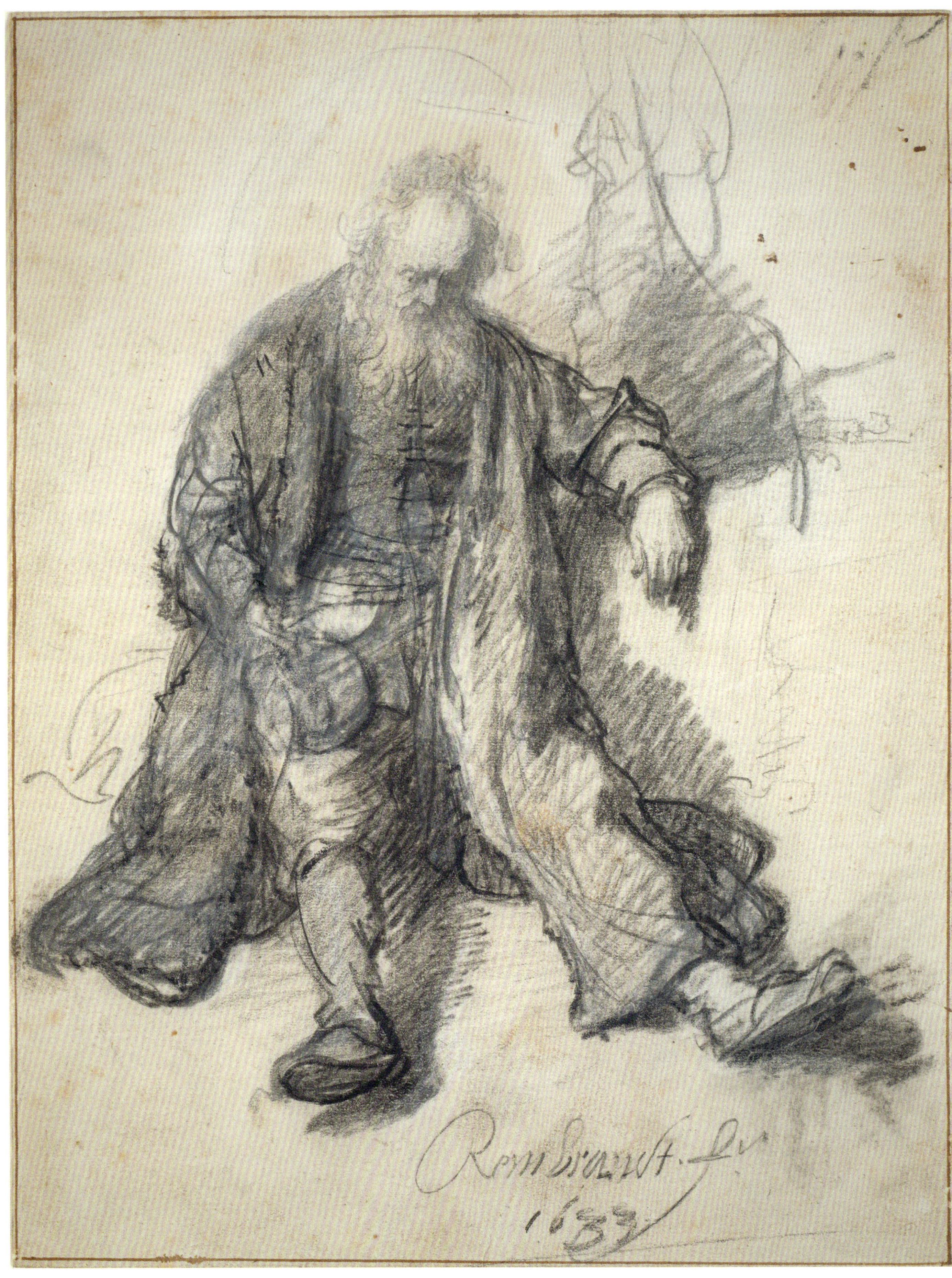

and paintings, in turn devised for the market or commissioned by patrons? Rarely.[9] Rembrandt preferred to draft directly onto the copper plate to conceive etchings, and right into the ground laid on a canvas to outline a painting.[10] Therefore, most of his drawings are unrelated to his production in other media.[11]

Rembrandt's drawing of an old bearded man known as *The Drunken Lot* (pl. 152) and his *Farmhouses by the Diemerdijk* (pl. 135) are two of the rather scarce pieces that are compositionally linked to other works: respectively, Jan van Vliet's *Lot and His Daughters* and Rembrandt's *Landscape with a Fisherman* (*The Milkman*), two etchings destined for the art market (pl. 165, fig. 16.1).[12] Thought to have been done in preparation for Rembrandt's lost painting *Lot and His Daughters,* known through Van Vliet's reproductive print mentioned above, *The Drunken Lot* is all the more unusual in that it is signed and dated; only twenty other sheets considered to be by Rembrandt bear a signature or monogram.[13] As such, his drawings stand in direct contrast to his etchings and paintings, which he often signed. Customarily, this would indicate their status as finished works for sale.

Hence, the signature on *The Drunken Lot* is particularly intriguing. The old bearded figure is a model who appears in other works from Leiden by both Rembrandt and Jan Lievens (pls. 21, 22). Yet, the sheet bears the date of 1633 and the signature "Rembrandt" that the artist adopted that year while living in Amsterdam. It is possible that he signed and dated the sheet sometime after its initial creation with the intent to sell or give it to someone in the city.[14] Thus, in this case at least, we can infer that a preparatory sketch became a collector's item.

The Draw of the Big City

Rembrandt's gradual move to Amsterdam, and more precisely, the opportunity it provided to establish a large studio where he could train several budding artists at once, is key to understanding the prevailing purpose of drawing in his studio. When Rembrandt left Hendrick Uylenburgh's workshop to start his own in 1635, he found himself in need of teaching materials and strategies; he suddenly devoted much more of his efforts to drawing than he had before.[15] Concurrently, he diversified his repertoire to become the most versatile Dutch draughtsman of the seventeenth century.[16]

The drawings made in Leiden, such as *The Drunken Lot*, were primarily figure studies, but as an independent master in Amsterdam Rembrandt also passionately ventured into the realms of history, landscape and, to a lesser extent, portraiture, as well as studies of animals. His representations of elephants, lions, pigs, etc. are as psychologically penetrating as those of his human sitters. Even the most quotidian activities became subjects for sketching and for acute observation of life. *Two Butchers at Work* (pl. 153) bears the unpleasant inscription "the skin on it and furthermore the rest trailing," documenting the artist's careful attention to detail.[17] In Rembrandt's hands, snapshots of everyday life like this one pulsate with tension.

This renewed and ever more intense drawing practice is bracketed in time by the other important juncture in Rembrandt's career: his bankruptcy in 1656 and the sale of his belongings. After this, his production of drawings waned once more, never to regain the frantic pace of his middle years in Amsterdam.[18]

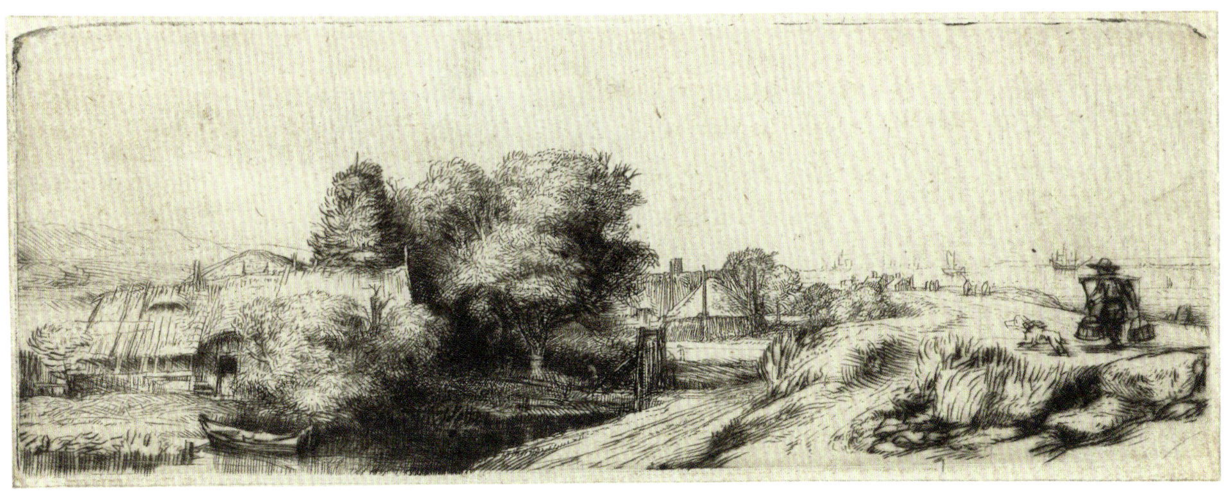

fig. 16.1 **Rembrandt van Rijn,** *Landscape with a Fisherman* (*The Milkman*), **1648–52, etching on laid paper; 6.5 × 17.4 cm. Rijksmuseum, Amsterdam (RP-P-OB-445)**

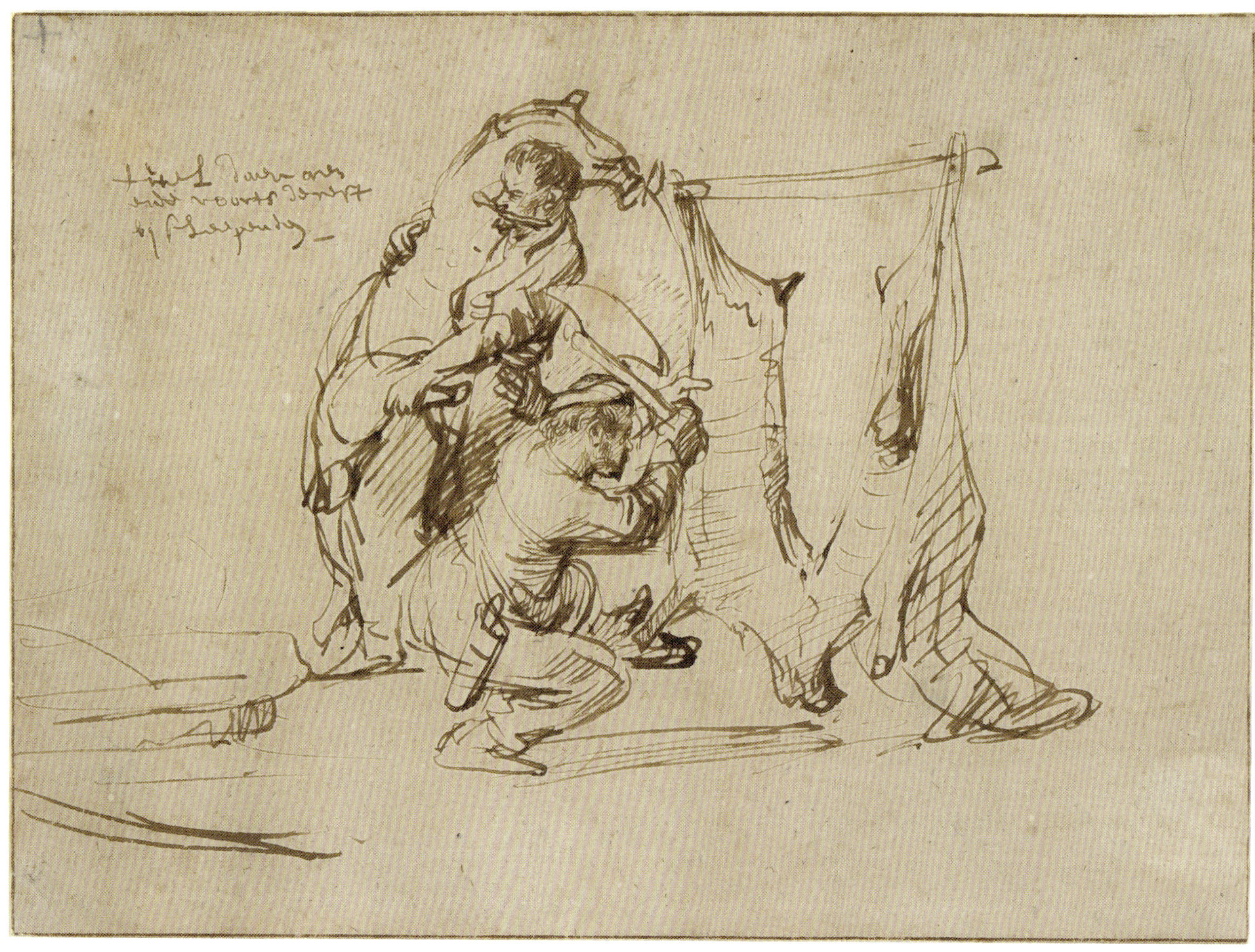

153   Rembrandt van Rijn, *Two Butchers at Work*, c. 1636–39. Städel Museum, Frankfurt am Main

Private Becomes Public

Whether sketching indoors or out, Rembrandt appears to have worked sometimes alone and at other times with a group of fellow artists. Some of his most intimate sketches – those depicting women, children and the interactions between the two – were kept in a separate album. These domestic scenes were sold at the insolvency auctions. One purchaser was the Amsterdam seascape painter Jan van de Cappelle, who owned more than five hundred drawings from Rembrandt's studio. One of five albums on which Van de Cappelle successfully bid contained "135 drawings of women and children," according to his 1680 inventory.[19]

Van de Cappelle's acquisitions must have included some of Rembrandt's heartbreaking portrayals of his wife Saskia lying in bed, possibly recovering from one of her four childbirth experiences between 1635 and 1641, or suffering from the illness that would take her life in 1642, months after the arrival of Titus, their only surviving child. Two sensitive studies executed in pen and ink shaded with wash (pls. 155, 156) afford us a glimpse into the life of Rembrandt's household. These expressive yet contemplative sketches are rendered with a vivacity that contrasts with the subdued subject matter. In the sketch of Saskia now in the Morgan Library & Museum, New York (pl. 156), Rembrandt has drawn essentially the same pose twice, capturing two variations of her semi-clutched right hand, as if recording a slight movement in his wife's slumber. In the eighteenth century, the work made its way into the collection of Jan van Rymsdyk, an Amsterdam portrait painter and engraver living in London. The inscription "Rymsdyk's M.[useum]" in the lower-left corner serves as a reminder that even a private sketch documenting an intimate moment, stored in an album with like images and meant to be seen only by those closest to the artist, could eventually become an object for consumption on the art market.[20]

In another ink drawing from around 1637, a young woman, probably Saskia, is shown having her hair coiffed (pl. 157).[21] Dark wash engulfs the seated young woman and her older standing attendant in the quiet stillness of a domestic interior. The tonal contrast calls attention to the luxuriant tumble of hair the maidservant diligently attempts to arrange. This drawing may be a spontaneous record of daily life, but it also resonates with several of Rembrandt's historical compositions from the 1630s, including the earlier painting *Heroine from the Old Testament* and the etching *The Great Jewish Bride* (pls. 85, 86).

In *Three Women and a Child by a Door* (pl. 144), an old woman now takes the seated position, surrounded by younger women at the threshold between private and public spaces.[22] Here, an everyday scene gives form to an allegorical representation of the Four Ages of [Wo]man: Childhood, Youth, Maturity and Old Age. A middle-aged woman looks out from behind a half-door or balustrade to the exterior pavement, where a young sister or mother tends to a child under the watchful eye of an elderly matriarch. Whereas Rembrandt often employs brush and wash – here absent – to construct space and depth in his drawings, this allegory of sorts gains instead its architectonic quality from the fluidity and sinuosity of his penstrokes as he builds his composition as a sculptural group.

In later drawings, such flowing gestural penmanship is supplanted by sharp, short, heavy lines of the kind that make up *Girl Asleep in a Window* from around 1655 (pl. 158).[23] If the subject of this sheet lends itself well to stillness, so does the discontinuous, jagged application technique, which has the effect of reducing three-dimensionality and movement.[24] Paradoxically, the flatness in this case conveys immediacy rather than remoteness as the figure emerges from the darkness of the room behind her. Close cropping heightens the composition's great sense of intimacy, further accentuated by the idea that this is a likeness of Rembrandt's late-life partner, Hendrickje Stoffels (pl. 91).[25] If this is so, her moment of repose at the window places her, like her counterparts in the previously discussed drawing, on the edge of private and public worlds.

The Artistic Touch

As personal as some of Rembrandt's sketches are, drawing in his studio was often a team effort. Whether the master and his pupils were picturing the same model in the same sitting or producing more than a hundred paper variations on the theme of the Expulsion of Hagar, sketching could be very much a group sport, with each draughtsman contributing his own play to the game.[26] In drawing together from live models in the studio as well as

154   Rembrandt van Rijn, *Abraham's Sacrifice of Isaac*, c. 1652–54. Staatliche Kunstsammlungen Dresden, Kupferstich-Kabinett

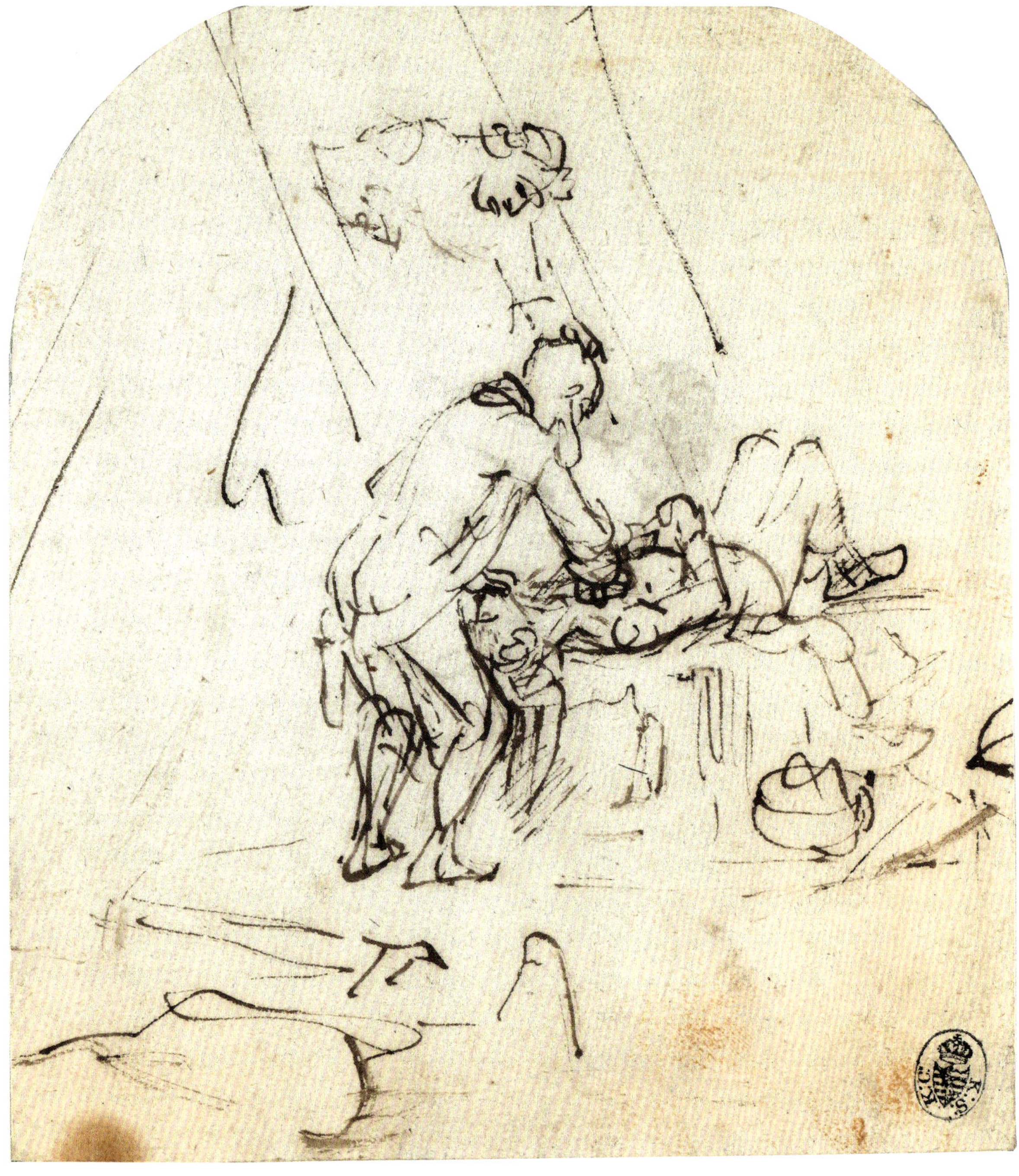

sketching landscapes *en plein air*, and in crafting strings of compositions on the same historical subject to which the master might make corrections, Rembrandt and his school created a joint drawn oeuvre of a complex nature.[27]

Studies of a live model provide evidence of a group sketching session in Rembrandt's studio in the 1640s. The master and at least three pupils (Samuel van Hoogstraten, Carel Fabritius and one unidentified artist) must have gathered together in front of a young man dressed in just a loincloth, his left arm propped up on a structure onto which he leaned his hip, for he – with his distinct physiognomy, hair and loincloth – appears in that position in four works by different hands, including an etching by Rembrandt (fig. 16.2).[28]

Connections between drawings done from imagination can also be established. In the same way that paintings and prints featuring celestial beings illustrate the creative linkages of biblical scenes, so do a cluster of sheets by Rembrandt and his circle involving angelic messengers. In a swiftly executed *Abraham's Sacrifice of Isaac* from the early 1650s (pl. 154), Rembrandt signifies with a few parallel oblique lines the abrupt arrival of a heavenly body to prevent a horrific human sacrifice.[29] Abraham's tense, thickly drawn hands, holding a knife to his son's throat and stifling the young man's screams, echo the impassioned touch of the ghostly half-angel on the patriarch's bent head. Despite the importance of touch between the three characters in this scene in interpretations by Rembrandt and his circle (pls. 115, 116, see figs. 12.1, 12.2), independent thinkers such as Nicolaes Maes could do away with these types of conventions (pl. 114).

On the other hand, the motif of momentous contact between an angelic messenger and a distressed man could be transferred to other religious tales such as the Liberation of Saint Peter. In a sheet by an unidentified artist in Rembrandt's circle (pl. 159), the touch of an angel's hand on the saint's shackled right wrist unexpectedly awakens him, while the surrounding slumbering guards remain oblivious.[30] Delicate parallel lines around the wings suggest both light and hovering motion.

Saint Peter's dramatic reaction made this a choice subject in Rembrandt's studio, where students were encouraged to explore expressions of bewilderment. Willem Drost, who likely apprenticed

with Rembrandt around 1650, chose a novel approach by omitting the celestial creature that comes to Peter's rescue. In Drost's *Liberation of Saint Peter from Prison* (pl. 160), the vivid light that shines onto Peter – composed of just four long and assured penstrokes – effectively conveys divine intervention without resorting to physical embodiment. Such ensembles of like sheets may share the same materials, technique and subject, but each artist brings inventiveness to the mix.

The leitmotif of touch is equally vital to representations of *The Baptism of the Ethiopian Chamberlain* by Rembrandt and Van Hoogstraten (pls. 161, 162). This subject occupied the master at several points in his career, including in an etching of 1641.[31] Rembrandt's drawing seems to show the apostle Philip dabbing water with the tip of his heavily contoured fingers on the head of the kneeling chamberlain or eunuch. The scene takes place on the bank of a river along the road from Jerusalem to Gaza. Perhaps, having studied his teacher's example, Van Hoogstraten placed his apostle in a near-identical bended-knee pose on the edge of the riverbank in a setting analogous to that of Rembrandt. However, Van Hoogstraten depicts a baptism by immersion:

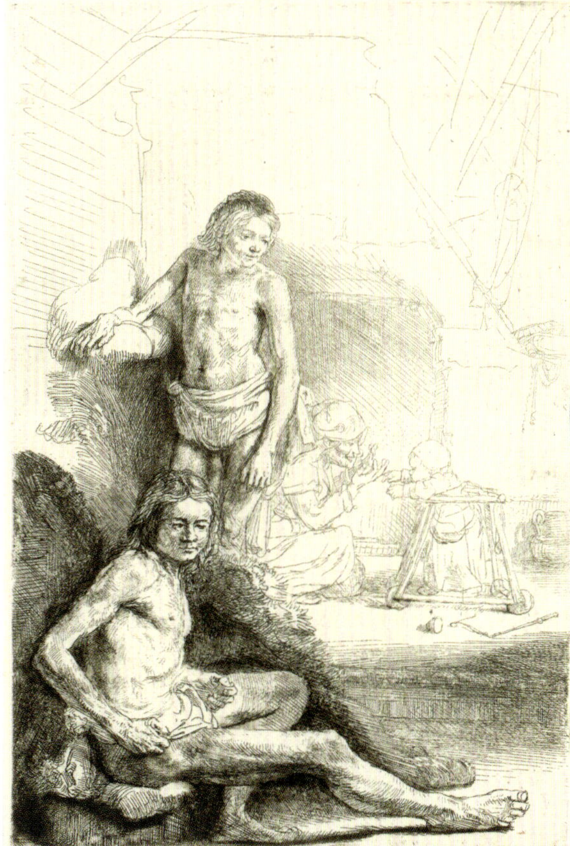

fig. 16.2 **Rembrandt van Rijn,** *Nude Man Seated and Another Standing* **(***The Walking Trainer***), c. 1644–48, etching on laid paper; 19.5 × 13 cm. Rijksmuseum, Amsterdam (RP-P-OB-251)**

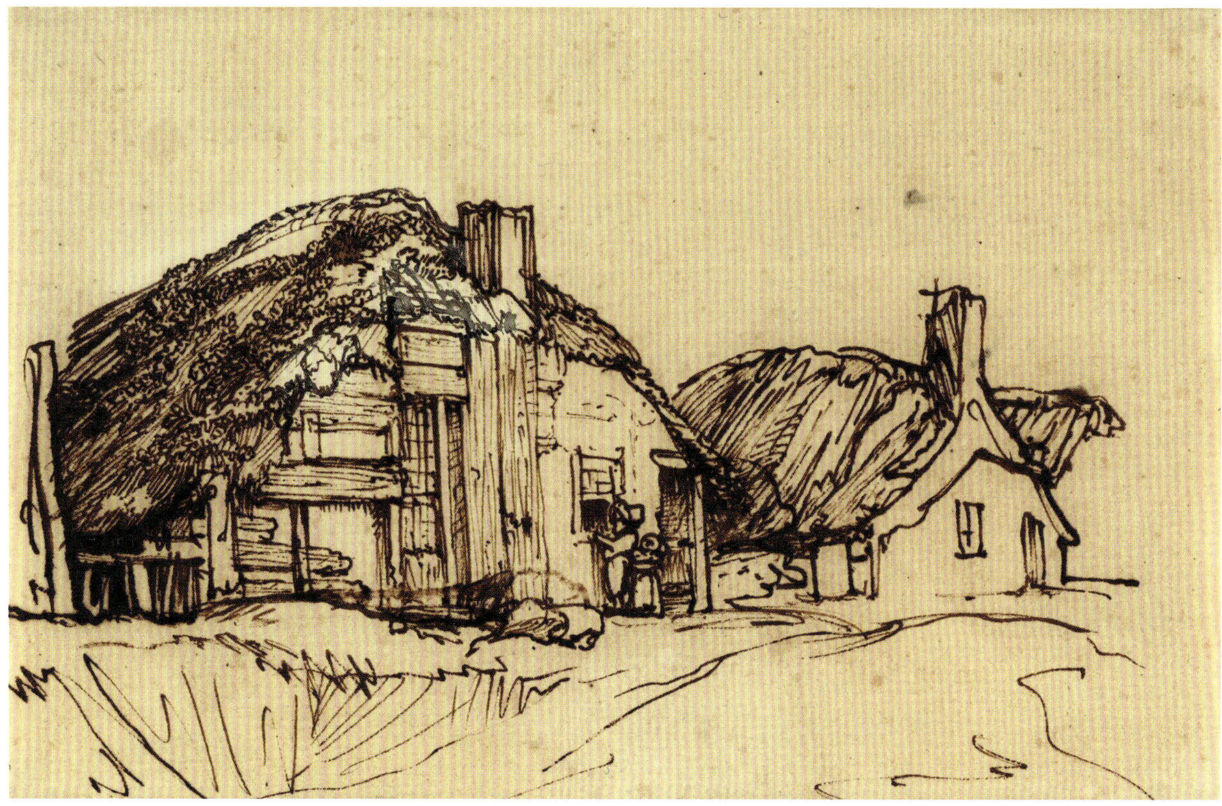

fig. 16.3　**Rembrandt van Rijn,**
Two Thatched Cottages with
Figures at a Window, **c. 1640,**
pen and ink, corrected with white,
on laid paper; 13.3 × 20.2 cm.
The J. Paul Getty Museum,
Los Angeles (85.GA.93)

Philip presses his hand onto the eunuch's head as the latter folds his upper body into the water, in which he stands thigh-high.[32] In both drawings, the contact between the hand of one figure and the head of the other is placed physically and metaphorically at the centre of the narrative.

The Shape of Landscape

The human figure – the most commonly depicted motif in Rembrandt's drawings – takes a back seat in his landscapes, letting the natural and built environment assume centre stage instead.[33] Even city views are seemingly under-populated. The scenery itself, however, is rendered with personality, acquiring a character of its own.

Around 1640 Rembrandt portrayed the distinctive motif of two thatched cottages along a country road at least five times. In a sheet in the J. Paul Getty Museum, Los Angeles (fig. 16.3), the houses occupy the middle picture plane; clear sky and bare earth do not distract from the monumentality of the rustic dwellings.[34] The artist defines the moss-covered thatched roof through dense, textural curlicues confidently executed with a quill pen. Bold but succinct short strokes outline two small figures at a

window, but their watchful presence refutes any narrative content.

The four or five figures in *Cottages under a Stormy Sky* (pl. 163) are likewise peripheral to the singularity of this landscape.[35] Here, Rembrandt emphasizes the dramatic effects of light and weather. The brewing tempest engulfs the virtually indistinguishable figures, two standing at the fence at the far right, and two, perhaps even a third (a child?) under the trees on the left-hand side. This dazzling drawing shines a light on Rembrandt's virtuoso draughtsmanship: lines are both vivacious and skilful, executed in a dynamic variety of thicknesses, while a selectively applied, richly coloured wash contrasts brilliantly with areas of paper left in reserve, such as the tree foliage at the far left and parts of a thatched roof. In this way, Rembrandt sweeps even the viewer into the storm.

Highly atmospheric scenes such as this set Rembrandt apart from his local contemporaries. After settling in Amsterdam in 1644, his fellow Leidenaar and colleague Jan Lievens also produced numerous landscape sketches, usually in pen and ink. In *Farm Buildings behind a Fence, and Cows* (pl. 164), for instance, the fine, crisp style suggests a finished work intended for sale, unlike Rembrandt's sketchier *Cottages under a Stormy Sky.*[36] Lievens' pan-oramic view of an enclosed complex of structures foregrounded by a small herd of tranquil animals shows much subtler variations of light, gently under-lined by the characteristic warm tint of the Asian paper on which it was drawn.[37] In contrast to Rembrandt's fascination with dramatic effects of weather, Lievens delivers clear skies over an orderly countryside for the enjoyment of removed specta-tors.[38] Also characteristically, the Asian paper absorbs the ink in an even, flat way, which confers a sense of polish to the sheet, further emphasized by the sheen of the paper's surface.

Rembrandt used similar Asian papers for print-making from about 1647, but few other artists in Amsterdam did the same. Thus, it may well be that Rembrandt supplied Lievens with a stack of these sheets so that his old friend could create finished, saleable landscapes, of which at least twenty have survived.[39] Despite differences in their material and representational strategies, for Rembrandt and his contemporaries, including also the landscape spe-cialist Jacob van Ruisdael (pl. 137), rustic farm build-ings represented a bucolic antidote to the crowded city life of Amsterdam, providing the same solace we seek today in cottage country.

Indelible Mark

Within Rembrandt's workshop, inventions on paper stored in albums formed a stock of motifs that could be consulted for inspiration or copied by students in training. By then, this was a well-established feature of studio practice. Accordingly, the frequency with which Amsterdam artists put pen to paper meant that drawing materials were readily available in the city.

Be that as it may, Dutch papers were not of the writing, drawing or printing quality artists sought until about half a decade after Rembrandt's death.[40] If the Dutch were not great papermakers in Rembrandt's time, they were, however, active import-ers and distributors: fine paper was brought from Italy, Switzerland, Germany and France. Most of it was of a make known as laid paper, based on the ribbed texture imparted by the rectangular mould's wire sieve onto the pulp, which was made from linen rags. While a few of Rembrandt's drawings were

executed on papers produced in the Asian tradition – that is from tree fibres – even fewer were drawn on vellum, a membrane of calfskin.[41]

A dark purple-black ink made by extracting gallotannic acid from oak galls and mixing it with water, iron sulfate and gum arabic (the so-called iron-gall ink) was ideal for sketching with a pen. Drawing implements could easily be crafted from reeds, which grew plentifully everywhere. Quill pens could be purchased ready-made.[42]

For a more fluid application with a brush, a trans-lucent brown ink called bistre could be manufactured by boiling the wood soot. Finally, white plaster paint served to highlight details that Rembrandt or the artists in his entourage wanted to emphasize. That same plaster paint came in handy when changes were required, in the same way correction fluid is used today. Remnants of it are visible, for instance, in the area of the Getty Museum sheet where the roof of the large cottage meets the chimney (fig. 16.3).

Resolute and adaptable, Rembrandt embraced strategies to salvage a spoiled drawing.[43] In addition to white corrections, the artist sometimes pasted down patches of blank paper to cover up blotches or messes, which he might have cut out beforehand. In this way, the figure of Abraham in *The Expulsion of Hagar and Ishmael* (pl. 110) was drawn on a piece of paper with a watermark different from that of the rest of the composition and then inserted, leaving an unintentional gap by Hagar's right foot.[44] In *Farmhouses by the Diemerdijk* (pl. 135), Rembrandt added a broad-ening strip at the right to enlarge the support out-grown by his evolving composition.[45]

Rembrandt's drawings were often transformed by his own hand during the process of creation, but have also changed with time. Because iron-gall ink fades to a brown closer to the coloration of bistre, a majority of the artist's sheets look quite different today than they did when he first sketched them. Still, the drawings of Rembrandt and his school have lost none of their graphic power. As a collaborative activity independent from painting and printmaking, they have generated their own enduring legacy. It is nevertheless paradoxical that the hundreds of draw-ings Rembrandt and his pupils fashioned as studio tools for creative use have left an indelible mark on art history. ◼

NOTES

1 Peter Schatborn, "Dans l'atelier de Rembrandt," in Brussels 2005, 8, 15.

2 As listed in Rembrandt's 1656 inventory; see Strauss and Van der Meulen 1979, doc. 1656/12. In his original six-volume standard reference *The Drawings of Rembrandt*, Otto Benesch ascribed 1,400 sheets to the master himself; Benesch 1954–57.

3 Strauss and Van der Meulen 1979, doc. 1656/12.

4 Ibid., nos. 239, 244, 249, 251, 257, 261, 236.

5 Ger Luijten, "Reasons for Drawing in Seventeenth-century Holland," in Washington and Paris 2016–17, 47. The author adds that in seventeenth-century Holland, people "valued and collected drawings on a large scale"; ibid., 49–50. For more on collecting drawings in the seventeenth century in the Netherlands, see Michiel Plomp, "L'art de collectionner les dessins en Hollande jusqu'à 1730 environ," in Haarlem and Paris 2001–02, 17–40, esp. 34–36 on collecting Dutch drawings.

6 Luijten, "Reasons for Drawing," in Washington and Paris 2016–17, 49–50.

7 Two are listed in the inventory of Maria Rutgers of 1653 (7 Feb. 1653, Remdoc, no. e4630), one in the inventory of Dirck Thomasz Molengraeff of 1654 (13 Jan. 1654, Remdoc, no. e4646) and one in the inventory of Alethea Talbot, Countess of Arundel, of 1655 (10 Apr. 1655, Remdoc, no. e4673), while three more had been sold in Leiden in 1645 by Dr. Gerrit Aelbertsz van Hoogeveen to Hendrick van der Stock (3 May 1645, Remdoc, no. e4533), all cited in Schatborn 2011, 321n9.

8 Schatborn, "Dans l'atelier de Rembrandt," in Brussels 2005, 10 (auction dates listed as 1656–57).

9 For a discussion on drawings by Rembrandt related to paintings and prints, see Schatborn 2011, 302–319.

10 Peter Schatborn, in Washington and Paris 2016–17, 157.

11 See, for instance, Royalton-Kisch 2011, 98.

12 Schatborn and Hinterding 2019, nos. D13, D529. Martin Royalton-Kisch, "The Role of Drawings in Rembrandt's Printmaking," in Amsterdam and London 2000–01, 72. For more on the Frankfurt sheet and its connection to the reproductive print by Van Vliet, see Frankfurt 2000, 136, no. 55; Martin Sonnabend, "Rembrandt Harmensz van Rijn: Model Studies and Melancholy," in Frankfurt 2015–16, 232–235; Schatborn 2011, 298; Dresden 2019, no. 29.2.

13 Count taken from Royalton-Kisch and Schatborn 2011, 325–345.

14 Schatborn 2011, 298–299. The author offers a second, and by his own admission less plausible, explanation: could Rembrandt have kept his studio in Leiden after transferring to Amsterdam, and featured the same model when revisiting an earlier subject in 1633?

15 Holm Bevers, "Drawing in Rembrandt's Workshop," in Los Angeles 2009–10, 2; Schatborn and Hinterding 2019, 17, 25, 143.

16 Schatborn and Hinterding 2019, 17, 18.

17 Schatborn and Hinterding 2019, no. D245; Annette Strech in Frankfurt 2000, 140–141, no. 58. The inscription, in Rembrandt's handwriting reads: "'*t vel daer aen | ende voorts de rest | bysleepende.*" Trans. from Schatborn and Hinterding 2019. Seymour Slive translates it as "Its skin is still attached, but it is dangling"; Slive 2009b, 101.

18 Schatborn and Hinterding 2019, 20.

19 See "Works by Rembrandt in the estate of the late Amsterdam painter, architect Jan van de Cappelle," 4 Jan. 1680, Remdoc, no. e14075, no. 17. Schatborn and Hinterding 2019, nos. D267, D268; Edinburgh and London 2001, no. 42.

20 Schatborn and Hinterding 2019, no. D268. For more on Rymsdyk and his "museum," see Tonkovich 2005.

21 Schatborn and Hinterding 2019, no. D298; Edinburgh and London 2001, no. 30; Vienna 2004, no. 75.

22 Schatborn and Hinterding 2019, no. D362; Edinburgh and London 2001, no. 101.

23 Magnusson 2018, no. NMNH 2084/1863; Schatborn and Hinterding 2019, no. D444; Edinburgh and London 2001, no. 123.

24 Courtright 1996, 485.

25 *Corpus*, vol. 5, 526; *Corpus*, vol. 6, 614.

26 Bevers, "Drawing in Rembrandt's Workshop," in Los Angeles 2009–10, 10–11, 19.

27 Peter Schatborn, "Aspects of Rembrandt's Draughtsmanship," in Berlin, Amsterdam and London 1991–92a, 11, 13–14; Schatborn, "Dans l'atelier de Rembrandt," in Brussels 2005, 13; Bevers, "Drawing in Rembrandt's Workshop," in Los Angeles 2009–10, 22; Royalton-Kisch and Schatborn 2011, 324.

28 The other works are Samuel van Hoogstraten, *Standing Male Nude* (Musée du Louvre, Paris); Carel Fabritius, *Standing Male Nude* (Albertina, Vienna); unknown artist, *Standing Male Nude* (The British Museum, London). See recently Judith Noorman, "On Truth and Beauty: Drawing Nude Models in Rembrandt's Time," in Amsterdam 2016, 32–37; Dresden 2019, nos. 40.1–42.2.

29 Schatborn and Hinterding 2019, no. D106.

30 For more on this sheet, see Frankfurt 2000, 142, no. 58. In a written communication from January 2011, Peter Schatborn attributed the drawing in the Graphische Sammlung of the Städel Museum (inv. 858) to Samuel van Hoogstraten.

31 See NHD 186. The Baptism of the Ethiopian Chamberlain is one of the first historical subjects Rembrandt addressed in two early history paintings (1626, Museum Catherijneconvent, Utrecht, and a lost painting recorded in a 1631 etching by Jan van Vliet); see also a black chalk drawing in the Staatliche Graphische Sammlung, Munich. See also Los Angeles 2009–10, nos. 24.1, 24.2; Van Straten 2005, 112; Leiden and Oxford 2019–20, 144–151.

32 Los Angeles 2009–10, nos. 24.1, 24.2; Schatborn and Hinterding 2019, no. D118. Van Hoogstraten's interpretation may reflect his own Mennonite baptism by immersion in Dordrecht on 12 Apr. 1648. See Odilia Bonebakker in Ottawa 2004, 112–113. For baptismal imagery, see also Bonebakker 1999; Perlove and Silver 2009, 20–23, 239, 268–269; Schwartz 2020.

33 Schatborn and Hinterding 2019, 143. See, among others, Washington 1990, esp. no. 22; Jaco Rutgers, "Rembrandt's Landscapes on Paper," in Kassel and Leiden 2006–07, 173–202.

34 Schatborn and Hinterding 2019, no. D483; Boston and Chicago 2003–04, no. 116; Slive 2009b, 148–149, 243.

35 Schatborn and Hinterding 2019, no. D487; Vienna 2004, no. 151.

36 Washington, Milwaukee and Amsterdam 2008–09, no. 131. See also the essay by Martin Sonnabend in this volume.

37 While the tree fibres used to make Asian papers – in Rembrandt's case usually *gampi* (*diplomorphasikokiana* or *wikstroemia sikokiana*) – are partly responsible for its yellowish tint, the Japanese method of colouring paper and making it less translucent by adding a yellow clay to the paper pulp can also be partly responsible for its warm glow, which is distinct from Western paper. See Stijnman 2015.

38 For more on this drawing, see Washington, Milwaukee and Amsterdam 2008–09, no. 131.

39 Stijnman 2015, 21–22.

40 Rather, the papers manufactured in the Netherlands at this time were of a grade suitable for wrapping and packaging; that is, of a coarse texture and dark colour. See Antoinette Owen, "Paper in the Netherlands," in Chicago 2019–20, 323, 325.

41 As Owen notes, the VOC (Dutch East India Company) is known to have imported to Amsterdam supplies of paper from Japan in 1643 and 1644; ibid., 323.

42 Schatborn and Hinterding 2019, 20, 26, suggest the artist favoured reed pens for biblical sketches in the 1650s.

43 Schatborn, "Aspects of Rembrandt's Draughtsmanship," in Berlin, Amsterdam and London 1991–92a, 14.

44 See Royalton-Kisch 2010, no. 75.

45 Martin Royalton-Kisch suggests Rembrandt expanded the sheet while preparing the related etching; Martin Royalton-Kisch, "The Role of Drawings in Rembrandt's Printmaking," in Amsterdam and London 2000–01, 72.

155 Rembrandt van Rijn, *Saskia Asleep in Bed,* c. 1640–42. Ashmolean Museum, University of Oxford

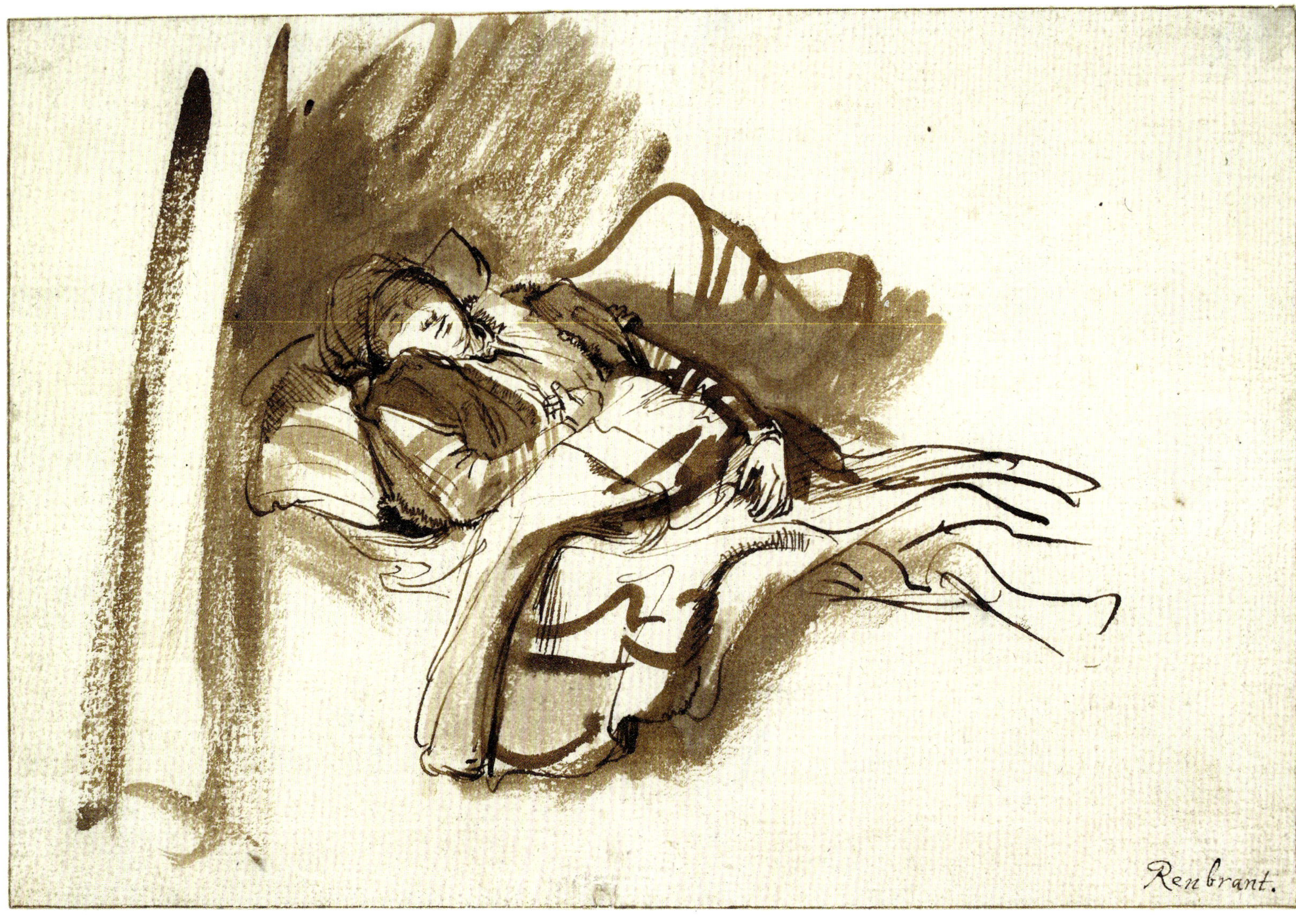

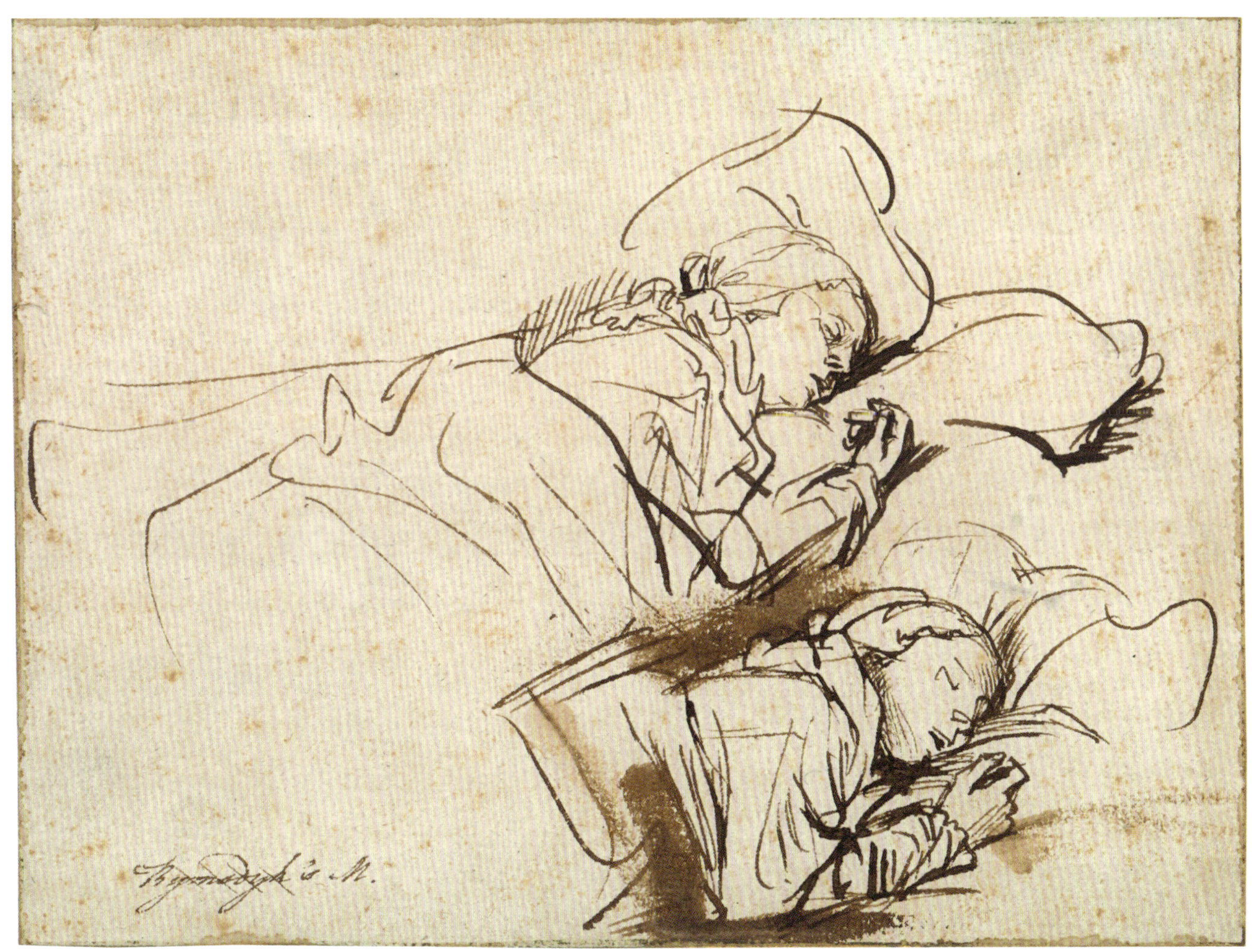

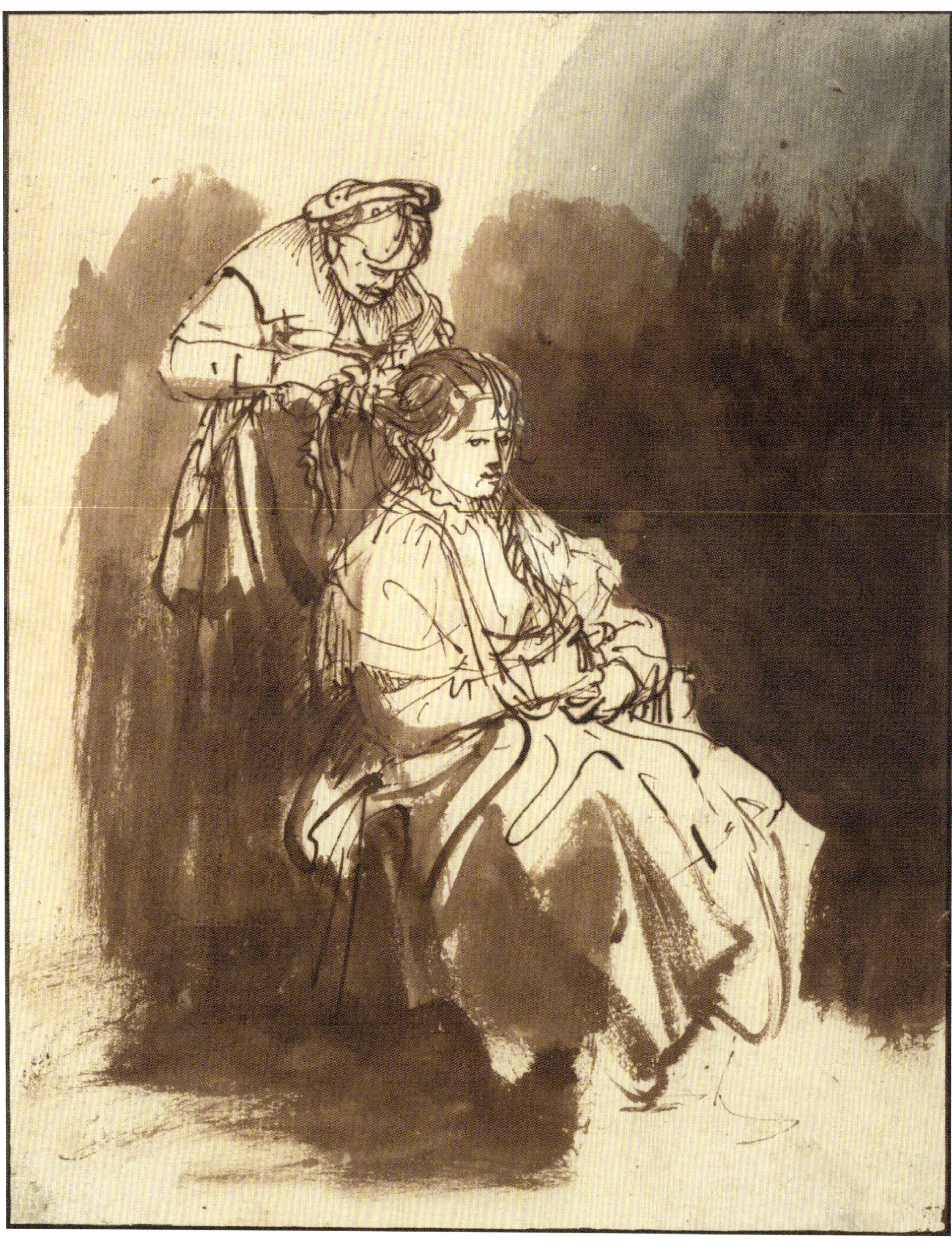

157 Rembrandt van Rijn, *A Young Woman (the Artist's Wife, Saskia?) being Coiffed*, c. 1637. Albertina, Vienna

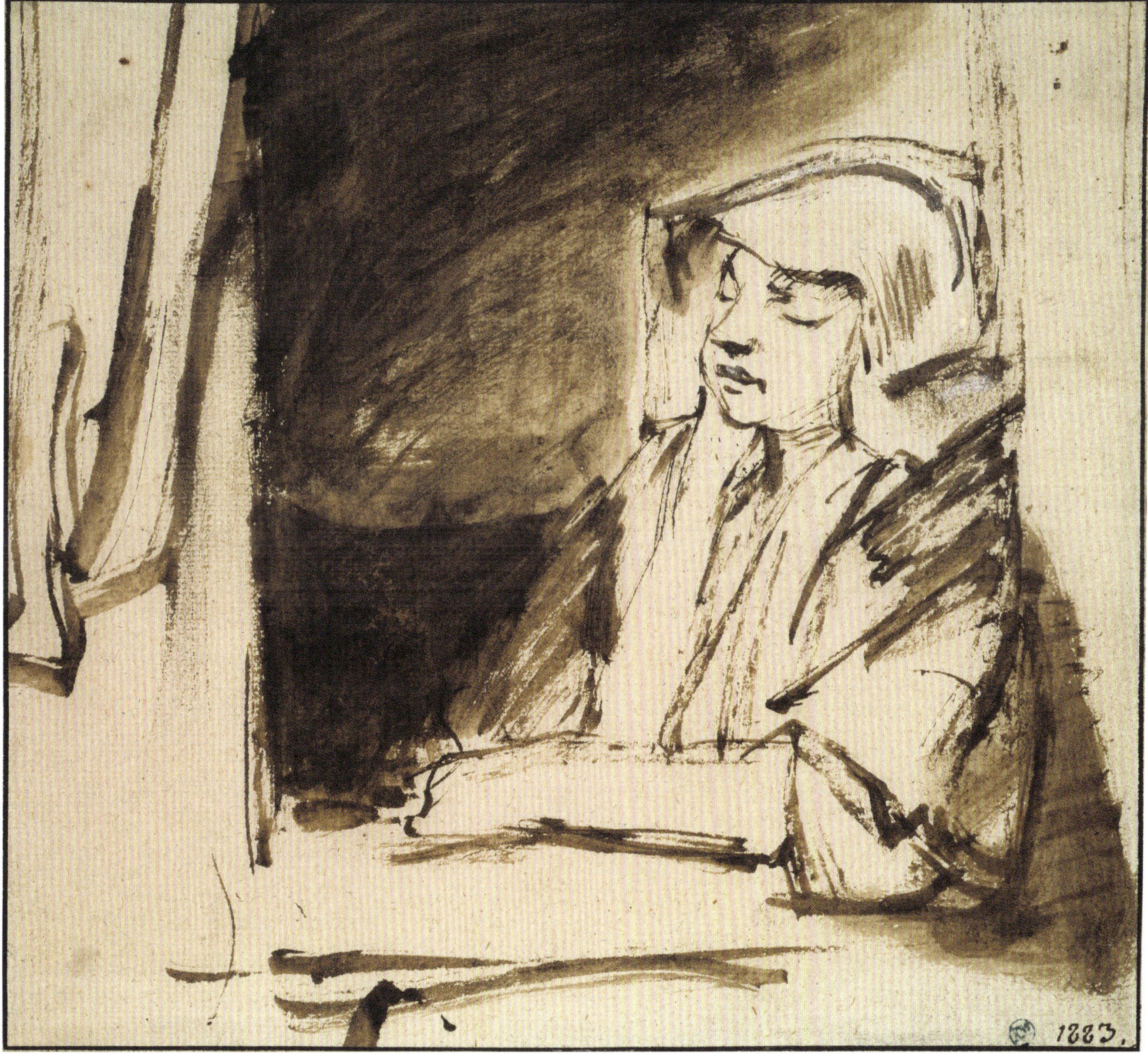

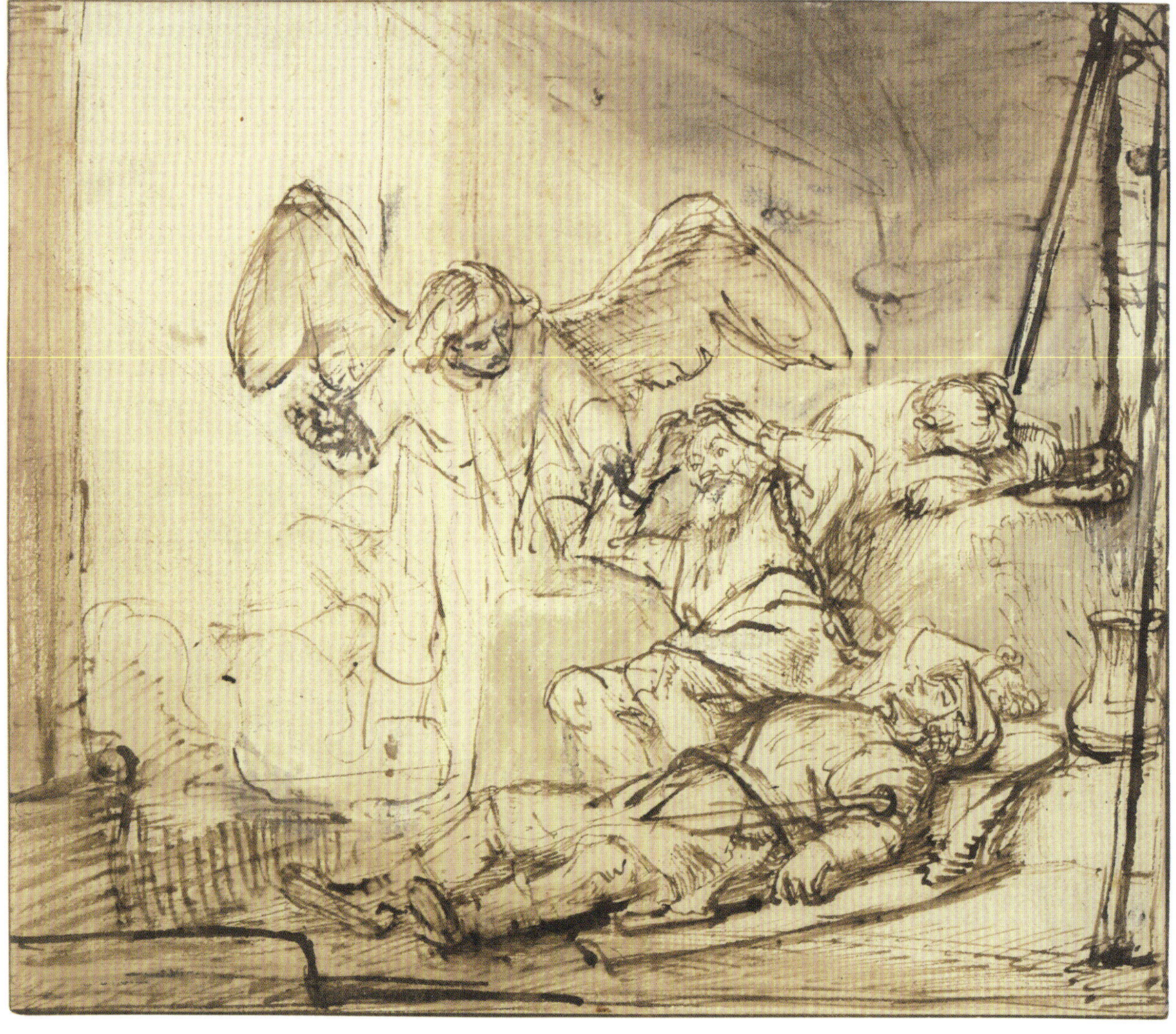

159　Rembrandt Workshop, *The Liberation of Saint Peter from Prison*, c. 1640–50. Städel Museum, Frankfurt am Main

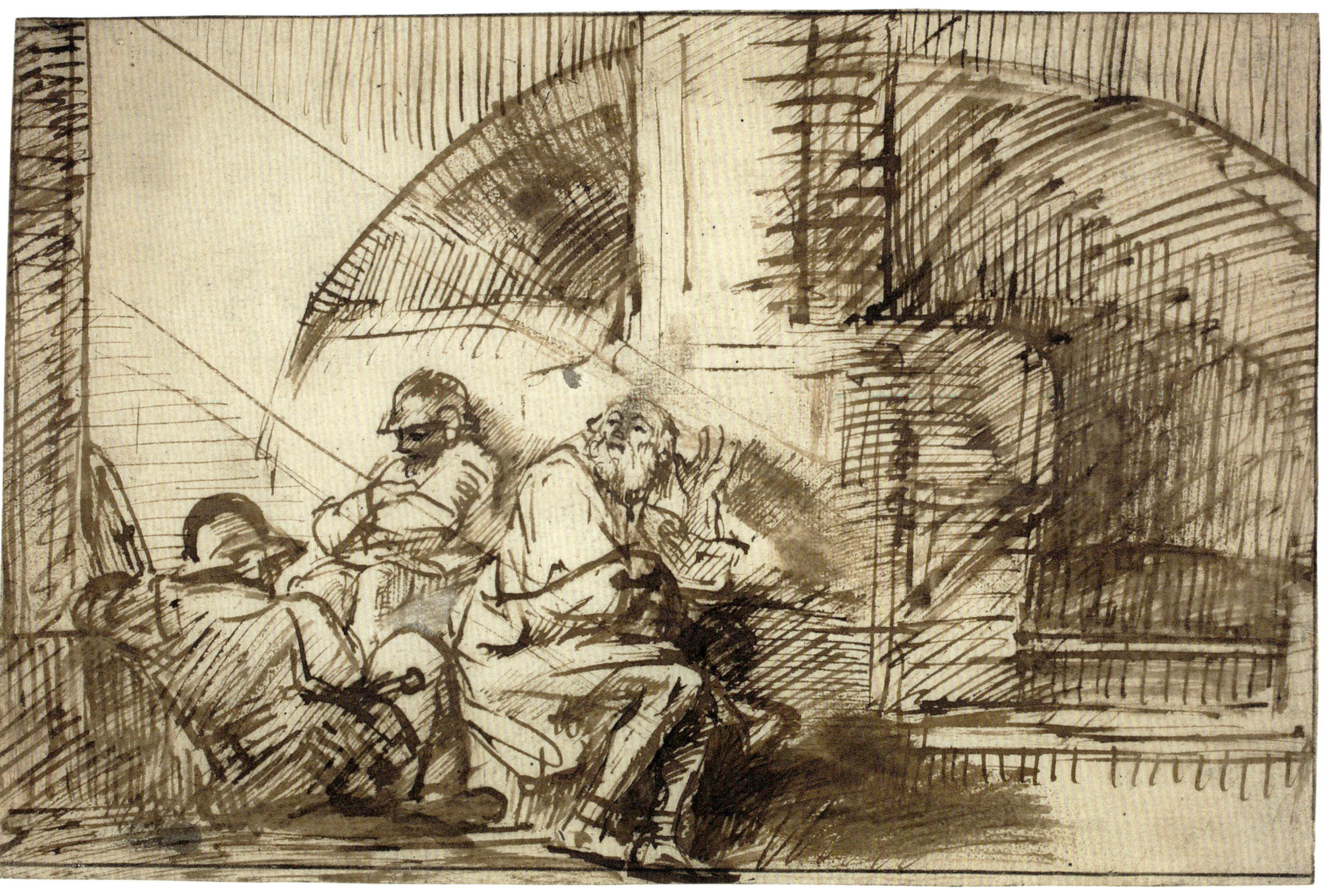

161　Rembrandt van Rijn, *The Baptism of the Ethiopian Chamberlain*, c. 1652. National Gallery of Canada, Ottawa

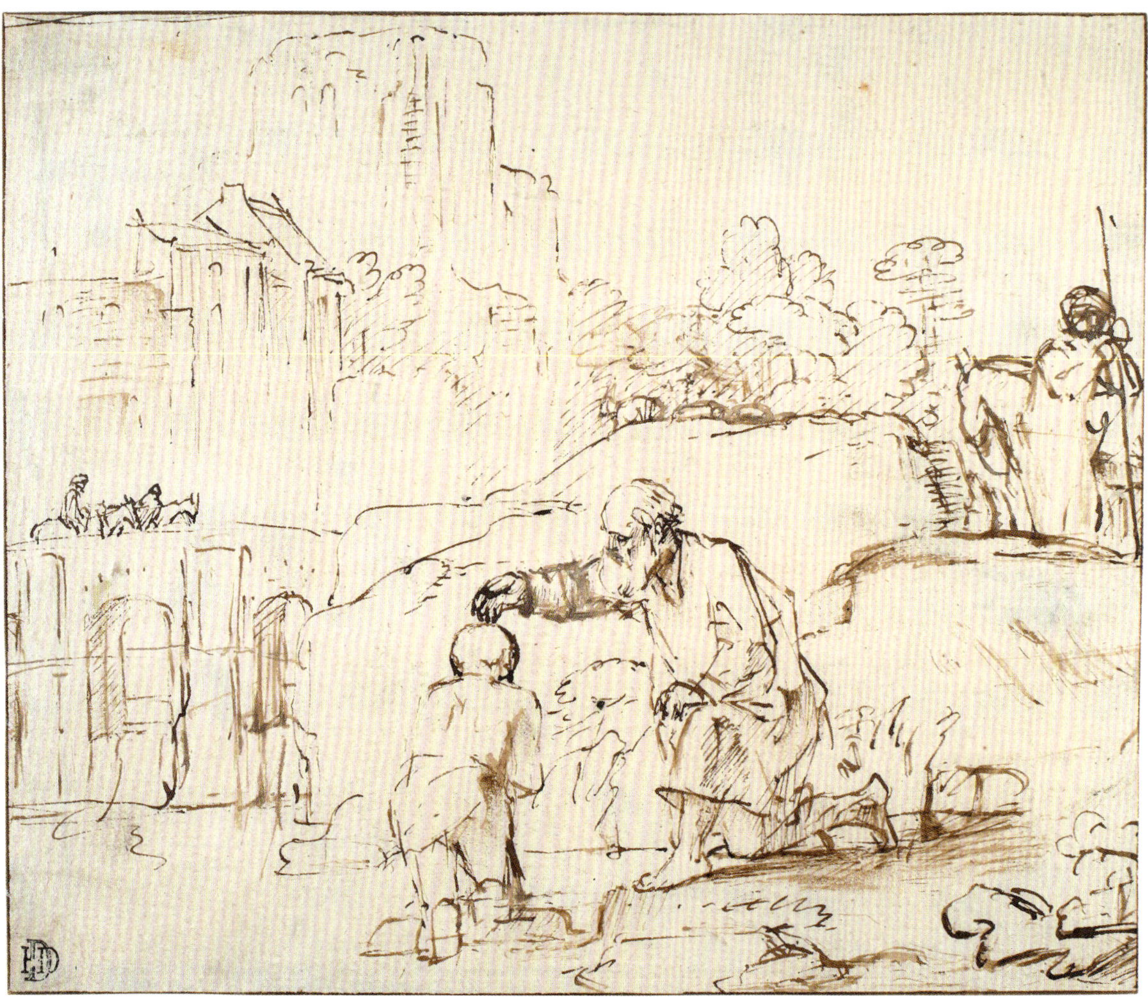

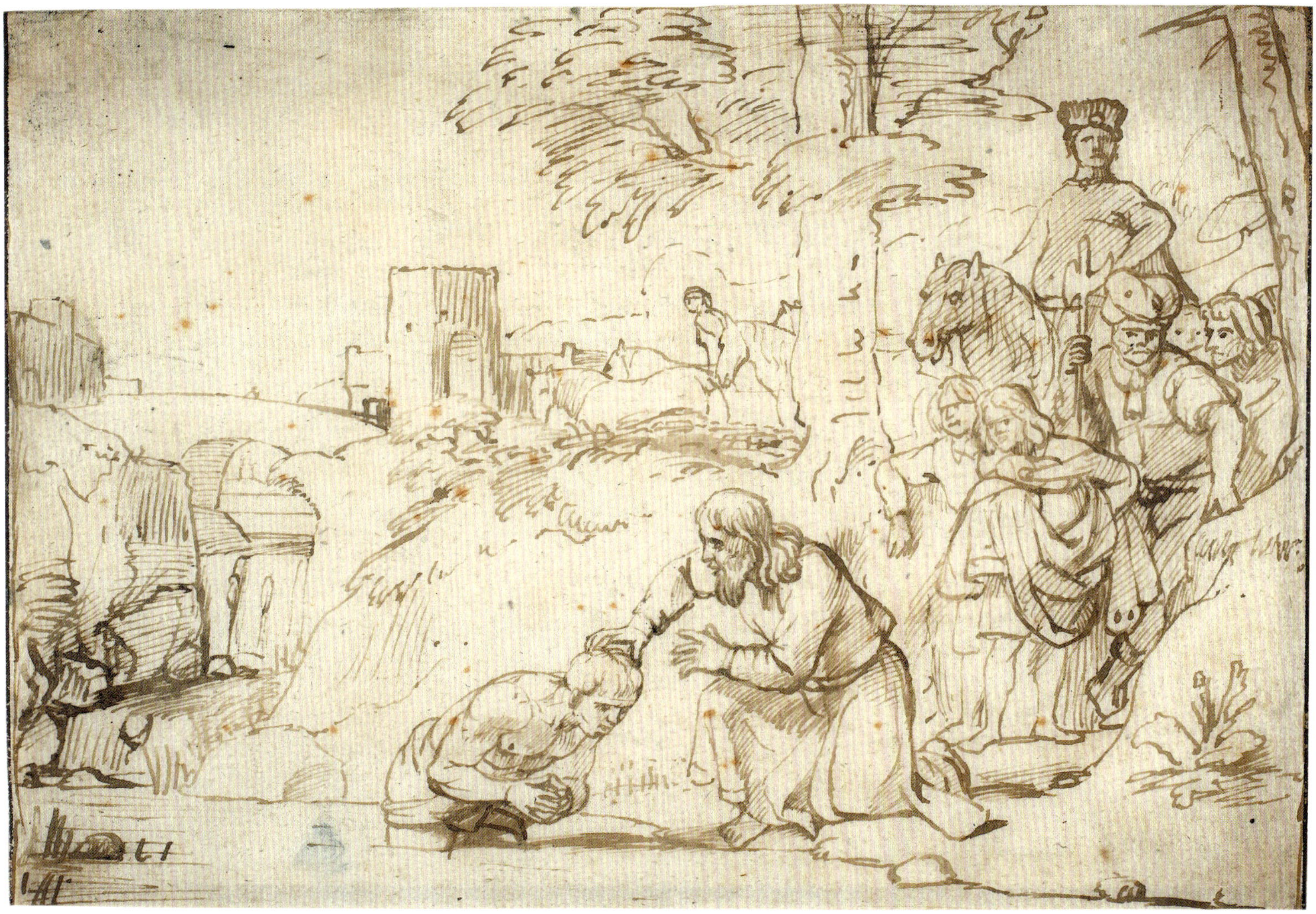

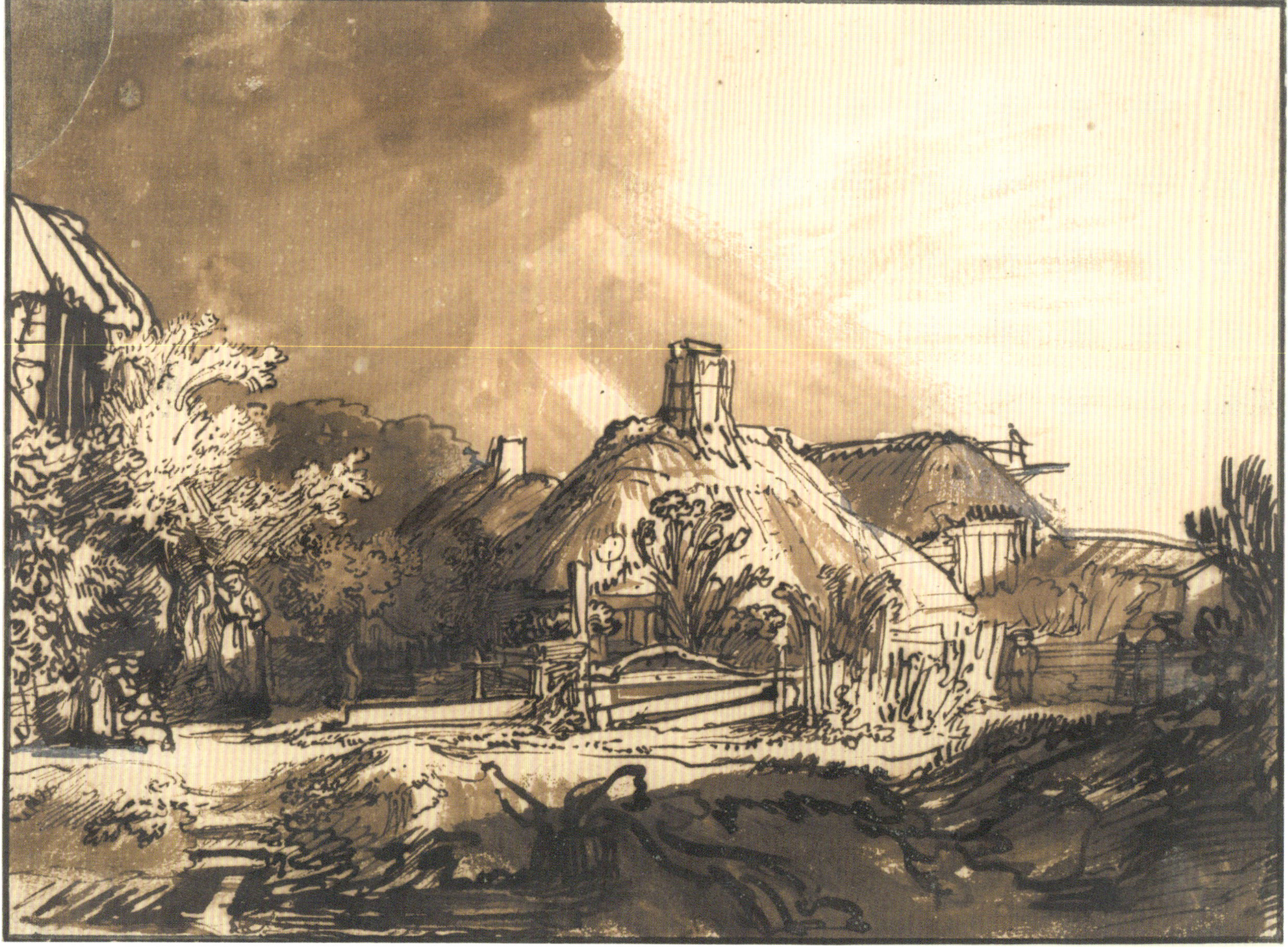

163 Rembrandt van Rijn, *Cottages under a Stormy Sky*, c. 1640. Albertina, Vienna

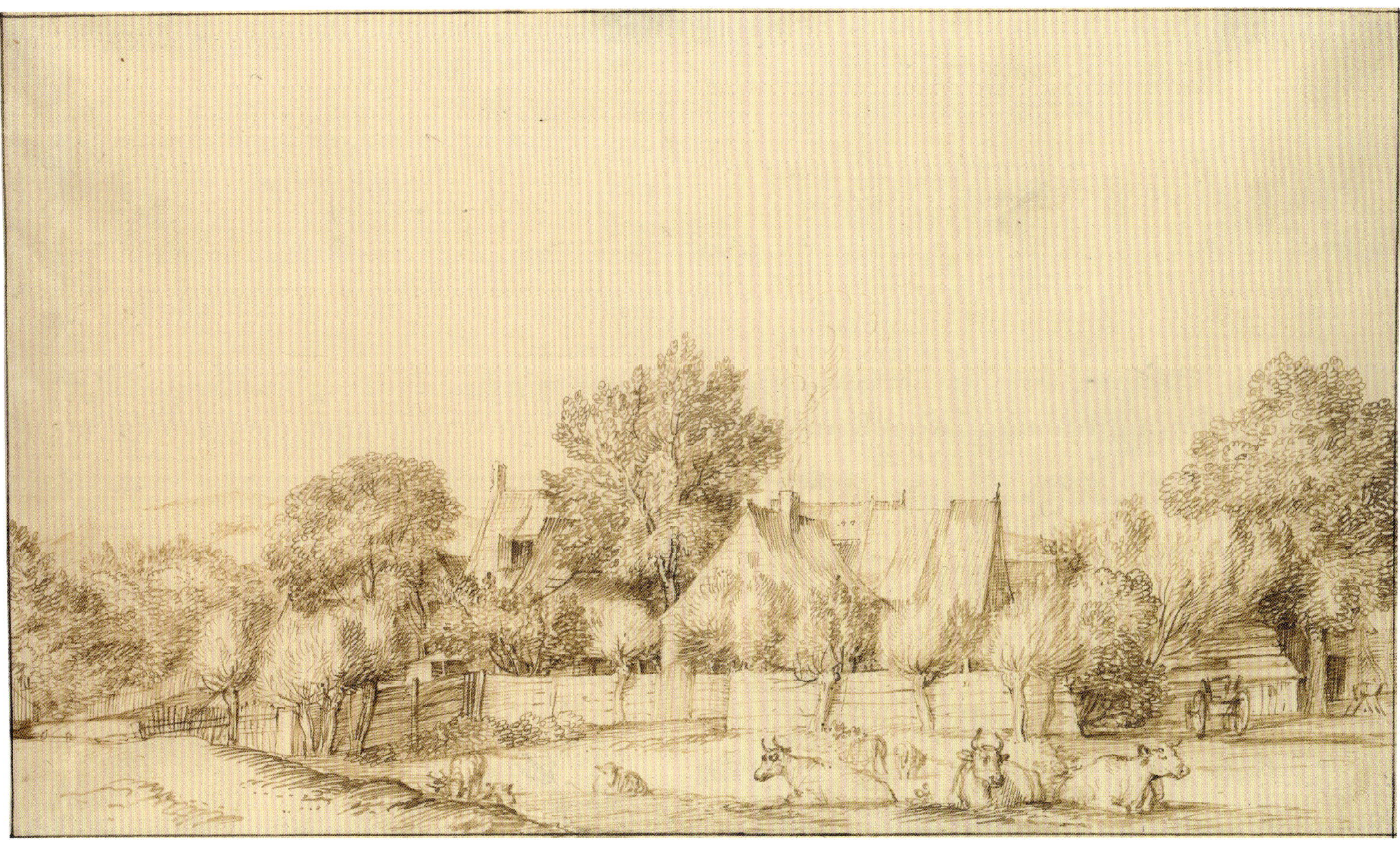

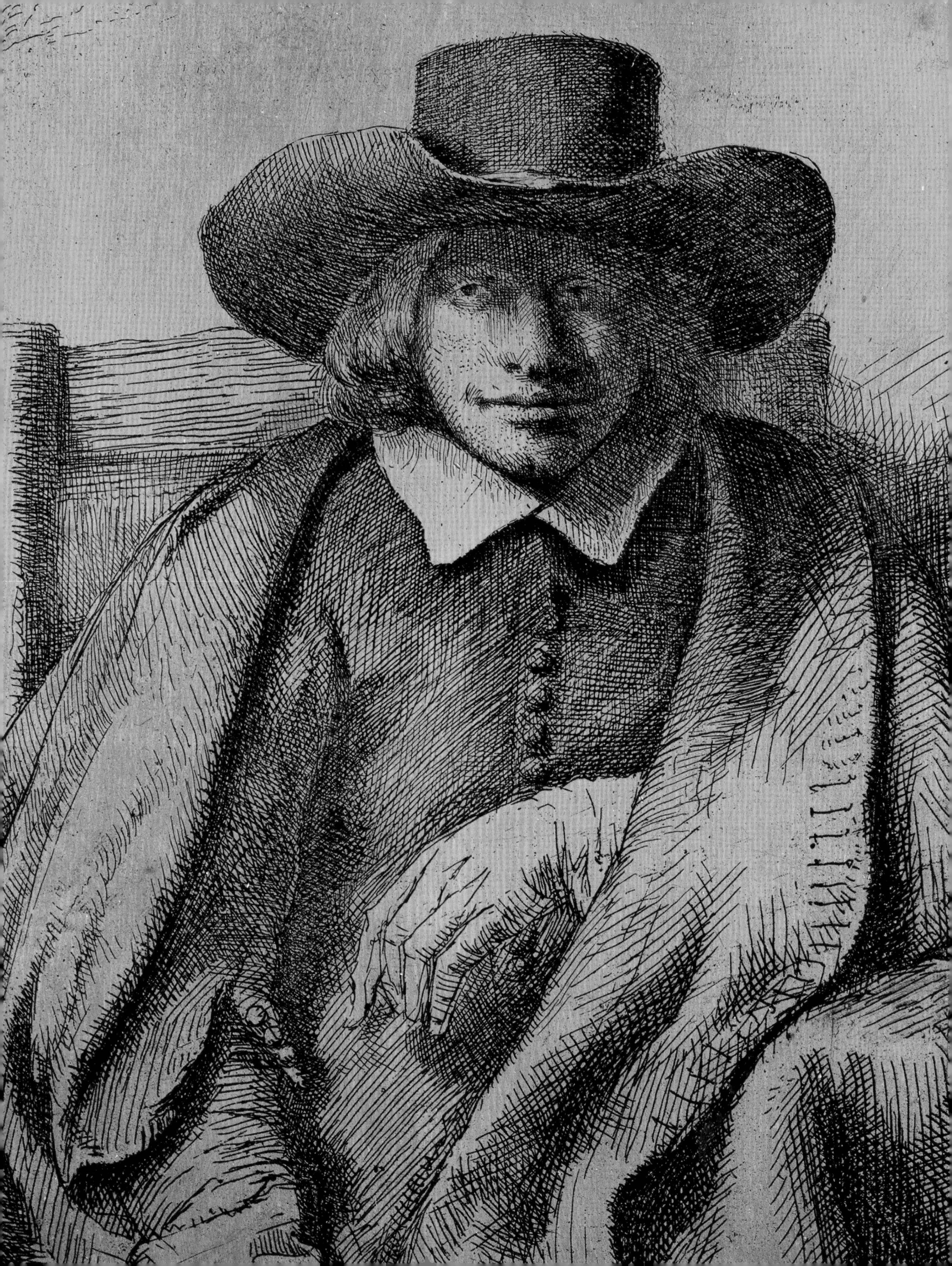

ROBERT FUCCI

Rembrandt and the Business of Prints

In addition to this he etched many and various things in copper, issued in print from his own hand, through which it can be seen that he was a very industrious and indefatigable man.

– Joachim von Sandrart, *Teutsche Academie*, 1675[1]

By the time Rembrandt moved to Amsterdam in the early 1630s, the city had already established itself as one of the most substantial and attractive market-places for printmakers, print dealers and print collectors in northern Europe. The commerce in single-sheet printed works of art, or *constprenten*, went hand in hand with Amsterdam's enormous book and map trades.[2] One found prints not only by and after contemporary artists from across Europe, but also by esteemed Old Masters such as Albrecht Dürer and Lucas van Leyden. Many of Amsterdam's print, map and book-related businesses gravitated to Dam Square, the centre of commercial activity in the city (fig. 17.1).[3] Several of the most notable establishments, including the shop of Clement de Jonghe, were located just off the square at the opening of the Kalverstraat. De Jonghe is the one print dealer we can be sure knew Rembrandt personally, since the artist produced a portrait of him in 1651 (pls. 170, 171) – appropriately enough, as a print instead of a painting.[4] The inventory made after De Jonghe's death included an extraordinary number of the artist's copperplates: seventy-four out of the slightly more than three hundred that he executed over the course of his career.[5]

While it might be tempting to think that De Jonghe served as one of Rembrandt's main print dealers, much as a gallerist works with an artist today, this reflects neither the usual practice in the seventeenth century, nor Rembrandt's own approach to the business of prints. The variety of means through which prints were traded was strikingly broad. Print publishers or other individuals might have commissioned prints and sold the resulting works, or printmakers might have taken the initiative to copy or invent designs themselves. Some publishers held enormous stocks of plates by artists past and present, from which they printed and sold thousands of impressions, while others traded in a more limited selection or dealt in prints as a side activity. Prints could be purchased from dealers' shops or artists' ateliers, at daily marketplaces, annual fairs, or periodic auctions, from an international network of travelling art dealers who catered to elite connoisseurs, or from itinerant print sellers who accommodated every level of society.[6] While some of Rembrandt's business practices might seem exceptional, they should be seen through the lens of this large and fluid marketplace.

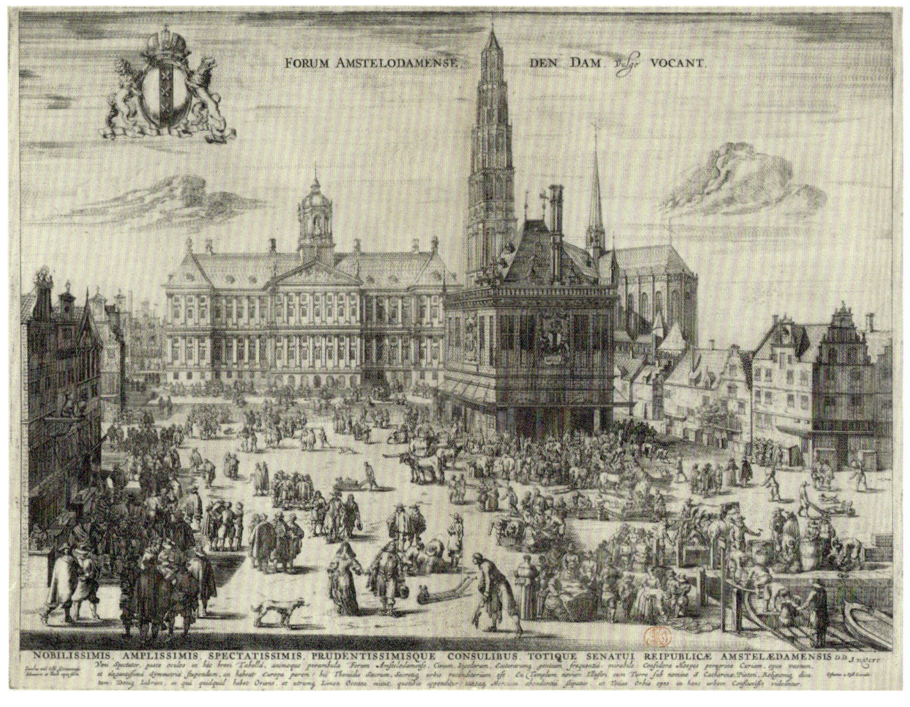

fig. 17.1 **Jacob van der Ulft,**
View of Dam Square, Amsterdam,
c. 1654, etching on laid paper;
41.5 × 54.1 cm. Rijksmuseum,
Amsterdam (RP-P-AO-21-24)

Rembrandt's output of prints was extraordinary for a painter. Many professional printmakers (called *plaatsnijders* or "plate cutters") were more prolific, but they formed a separate profession, generally working on commission to translate designs by others into print. Professional training in the art of engraving could take years to master. Rembrandt, like most painters who chose to try their hand at printmaking (later categorized by critics as *peintres-graveurs*), favoured the more fluent medium of etching, a technique that resembled drawing in its practical application and could be mastered more easily. Whereas engraving was more durable in terms of the number of impressions that could be pulled from a plate, etching afforded painters a chance to offer their own prints without the help of specialists.[7]

Rembrandt was not just a casual etcher; he was arguably the most committed practitioner of printmaking among the painters of his day. Even the most enthusiastic of his painter colleagues who tried their hand at making prints, such as Jan Lievens and Nicolaes Berchem, produced only a fraction of Rembrandt's total output.[8] The German painter, printmaker and author Joachim von Sandrart was not always kind in his comments about Rembrandt's art, but he was struck by the remarkable number of prints that issued "from his own hand."[9] Rembrandt's evident passion for etching provided him not just extra income, but also a chance to develop his innovative technique in a medium that complemented his painting and circulated internationally, promoting his fame. His success in this regard can be measured by the high desirability of his prints among the cognoscenti of his day. From a practical standpoint, this also meant that, in addition to the painting aspect of his business, he had to contend with the production, printing and sale of an immense number of works on paper.

Today, several thousand impressions of Rembrandt's prints still exist that were made during his lifetime. His total output must have been even greater.[10] To what degree Rembrandt handled the creation, printing and sale of these prints himself, instead of relying on help from others, remains unclear, but we can bring to light a number of aspects of his approach to the business of printmaking through a study of documentary sources and the works themselves.

For Fame and Profit

Rembrandt's former pupil Samuel van Hoogstraten, in his treatise of 1678, noted that Dürer and Van Leyden were famous painters in their day, but became best known through their prints.[11] Even early in his career, Rembrandt was keenly aware of the transformative impact that prints could have on an artist's reputation. One of his great models was certainly the Flemish master Peter Paul Rubens, who actively commissioned reproductive printmakers to make his painted compositions more widely known and to profit from them.[12] For a few years early in his career, Rembrandt similarly worked with the Leiden printmaker Jan van Vliet to publish etchings after his paintings.[13] Why he engaged an etching specialist rather than an engraver remains an open question; perhaps Van Vliet was the most convenient choice, or perhaps Rembrandt preferred the fluid character of etching.[14] Some of Van Vliet's prints document now lost paintings by Rembrandt, such as *Lot and His Daughters* from 1631 (pl. 165).[15] Rembrandt himself had already begun experimenting with etching around 1625, but his earliest prints do not match this level of scale and complexity.

Even larger and more technically challenging was *The Descent from the Cross* from 1633 (pl. 166).[16] There is some scholarly disagreement over whether Van Vliet helped with the plate or whether Rembrandt actually managed to execute it himself, the latter

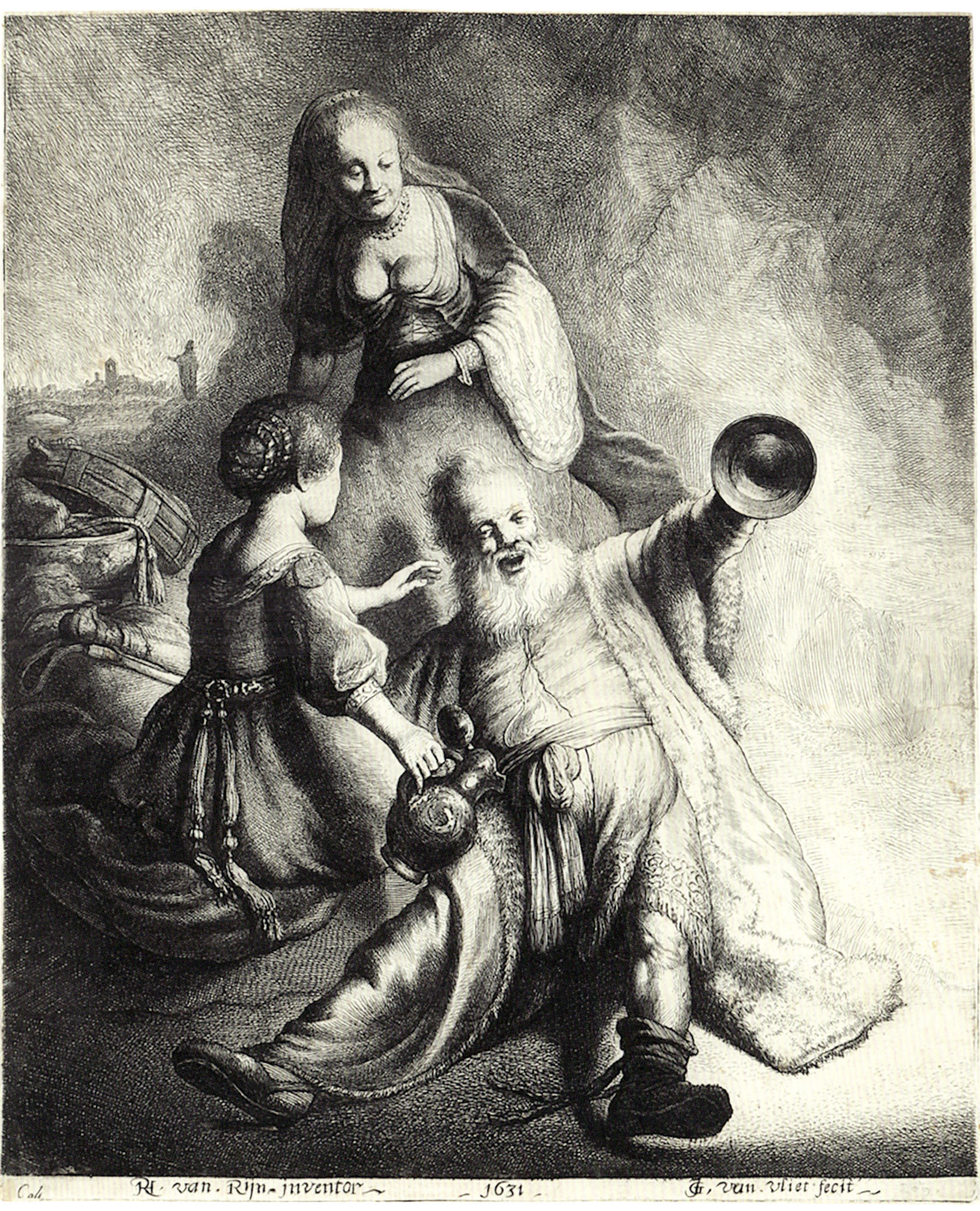

RL. van Rijn. inventor
1631
F. van Vliet fecit

166   Rembrandt van Rijn, *The Descent from the Cross*, 1633, fourth state (with address of Hendrick Uylenburgh). Städel Museum, Frankfurt am Main

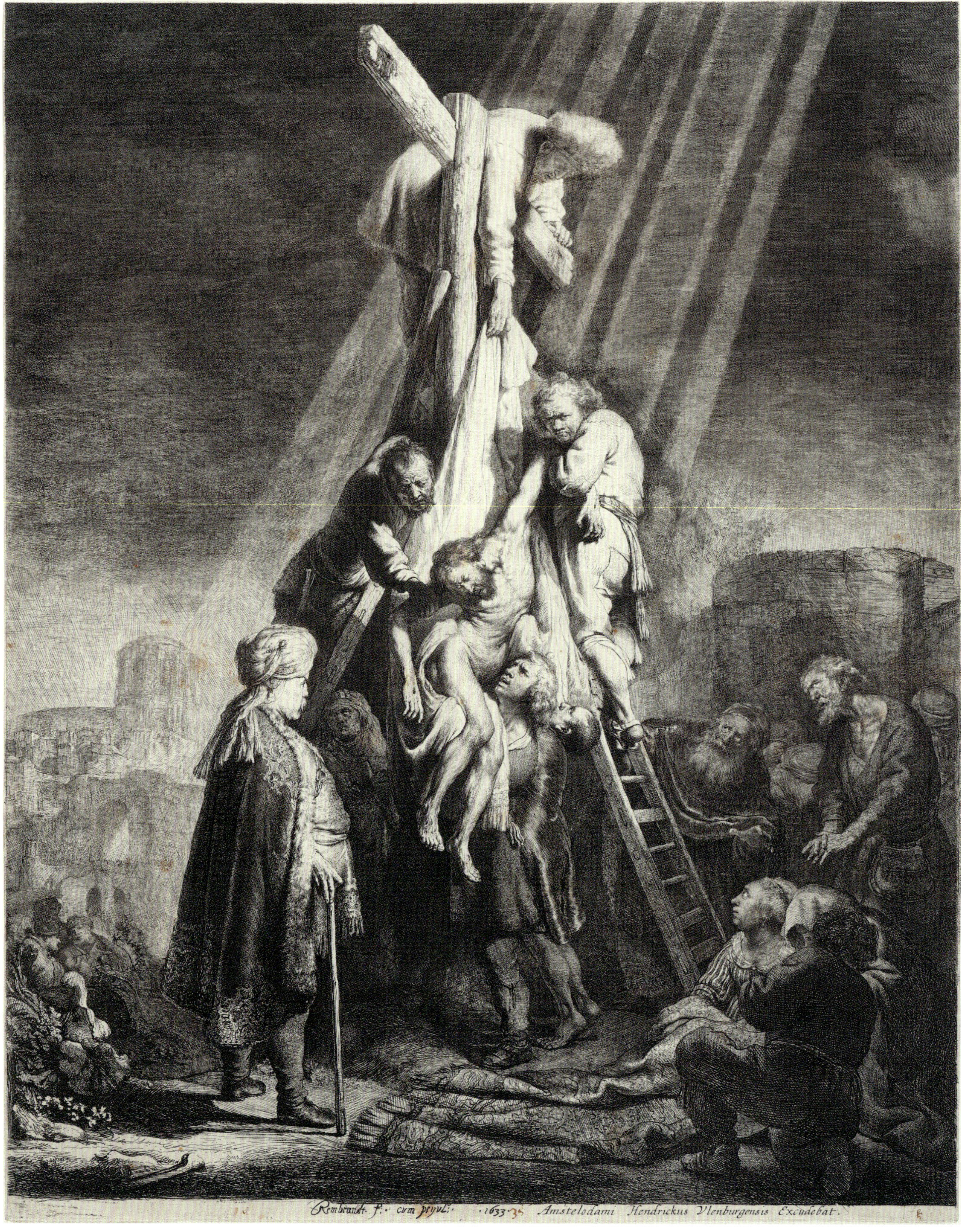

recently argued convincingly as a distinct possibility.[17] This ambitious plate reproduces a painting commissioned by Stadtholder Frederik Hendrik, and it makes sense that Rembrandt would have wanted to promote this prestigious commission. Striking in this case is the compositional similarity with an engraving after Rubens by Lucas Vorsterman from 1620 (fig. 17.2), and we can assume that Rubens' design provided inspiration for Rembrandt's painting in the first place.[18] Two inscriptions hew to established conventions of reproductive printmaking. One asserts a "privilege" (*cum privilegio*), indicating that Rembrandt sought copyright protections. This is a rare instance of the artist going through legal channels to protect the investment of time and labour that went into a major plate such as this. Securing a privilege meant that anyone making or selling unauthorized copies would be fined.[19] The other inscription is a "publisher's address," indicating the owner of the plate.

This was Hendrick Uylenburgh, whose workshop Rembrandt joined when he moved to Amsterdam, and whose cousin, Saskia, he married. While it might be tempting to assume that Uylenburgh commissioned the plate from Rembrandt, this remains uncertain since his name appears only on later impressions (perhaps from the late 1630s onward).[20] It is possible that Rembrandt may have tried to market the print himself before eventually selling the plate to Uylenburgh, who would have then had the sole right to print impressions and profit from their sale. It has been suggested that Uylenburgh and Rembrandt ambitiously planned an entire series of large-scale prints, for which *The Descent from the Cross* and *Christ before Pilate* (fig. 17.3) were the only two completed; however, since Uylenburgh's name only appears on later impressions of *The Descent from the Cross* (and not at all on *Christ before Pilate*), this conjecture should be treated with caution.[21]

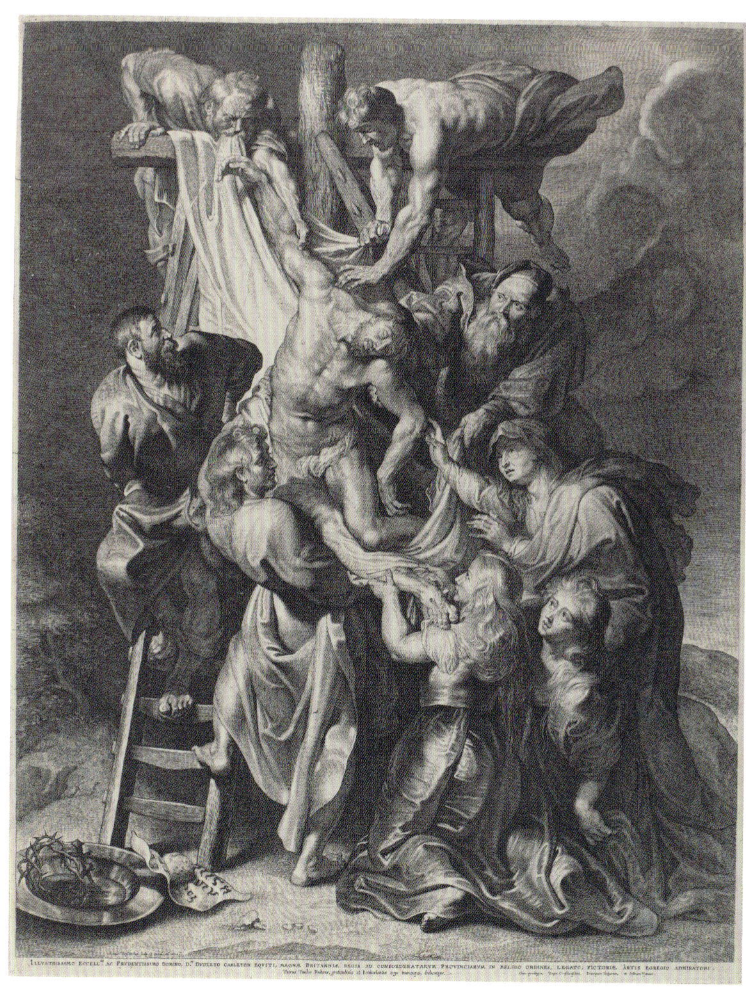

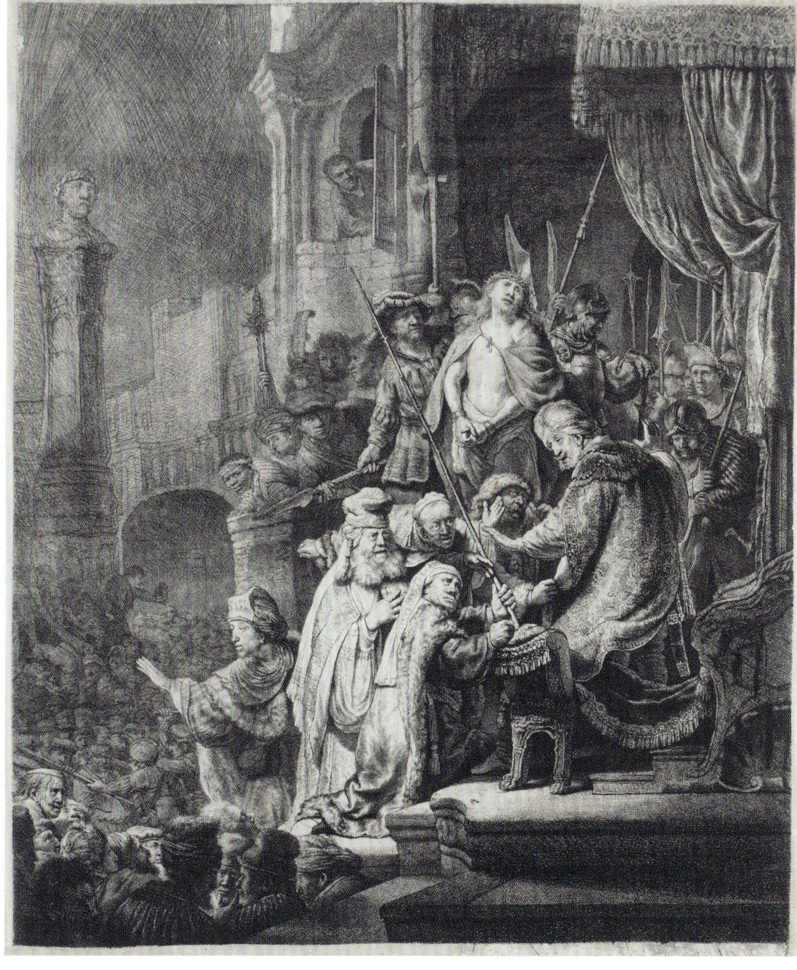

fig. 17.2 **Lucas Vorsterman (after Peter Paul Rubens),** *The Descent from the Cross*, 1620, engraving on laid paper; 58.5 × 43.5 cm. Rijksmuseum, Amsterdam (RP-P-OB-4591)

fig. 17.3 **Rembrandt van Rijn,** *Christ before Pilate: Large Plate*, 1636, etching on laid paper; 54.7 × 44.5 cm. Rijksmuseum, Amsterdam (RP-P-OB-614)

Unlike Rubens and most other artists, Rembrandt quickly began to take a more direct role in producing his own plates. By the time he arrived in Amsterdam, he had already begun to fully master the art of etching. In 1632 he executed the large plate for *The Raising of Lazarus*, cleverly adding a fictional frame to reinforce its status as the record of a painting (see fig. 18.2).[22] One of the most remarkable etchings by his own hand from these years is the dramatic night scene *The Angel Appearing to the Shepherds* from 1634 (pl. 126), an early display of the complex chiaroscuro effects that would frequently mark his later oeuvre.[23] We have evidence that some of Rembrandt's prints were already highly valued at this point in his career. At a 1637 auction, an unknown buyer purchased an impression of *The Descent from the Cross* for 1 guilder and 12 stuivers (1 guilder = 20 stuivers).[24] At the time, most *constprenten* generally sold for one to three stuivers apiece. In 1636, at the height of the so-called Tulip Mania, the painter Jacob de Wet made a wager in which he stood to gain a valuable bulb, the "Lyon." For his part, de Wet put up 24 Carolus guilders in cash and sweetened the deal by including "one small print by Albrecht Dürer … as well as two prints by Rembrandt" valued at 3 guilders and 10 stuivers (he lost both the wager and the prints).[25]

After 1636 Rembrandt no longer engaged the services of another printmaker, nor sought to have his painted compositions issued as prints. Printmaking became a separate creative activity, one almost entirely independent of his painted inventions. Moreover, he developed a broader range of pictorial themes in print than in painting. For instance, some of his most remarkable genre imagery can be found in etchings such as *The Hog* from 1643 and *Beggars Receiving Alms at the Door of a House* from 1648 (pls. 145, 147). Instead of the conventional business relationship in which the painter hires a printmaker, or a publisher hires them both, Rembrandt chose to explore the medium of etching as an expressive component of his own practice.

The Practicalities of Print

It is likely that Rembrandt had a printing press in his house on the St. Anthonisbreestraat (the present-day Rembrandt House Museum), where he lived from 1639 until 1658.[26] This is suggested by the many novel aspects of his working style. Frequent access to a printing press would have made it easier to experiment with wiping the ink from the plate differently for certain impressions, or printing multiple proof states.[27]

In these flourishing years, Rembrandt could have easily afforded to set up a print studio in his house. The press itself might have cost around fifty to sixty guilders; paper might have run two to four guilders per ream depending on size and quality (each ream containing about five hundred sheets, as it does today); copperplates might have cost one to three guilders apiece depending on their size and level of finish (hammering and polishing); and costs for equipment such as basins, chemicals and ink would have probably been incidental by comparison.[28] Rembrandt could have printed editions himself or enlisted the help of studio assistants. For larger print runs, or ones in which he did not feel the need to experiment, he could also have sent the plate to a commercial printer, who might have charged somewhere in the range of one to two guilders per one hundred impressions for the labour of printing.[29]

Rembrandt was certainly aware of the economic advantage of making his own etchings, without the outlay of costs for the long hours of labour for the printmaker and publisher. Since even highly appreciated *constprenten* generally sold for stuivers rather than guilders, turning a profit in commercial printmaking might have easily required the sale of more than a hundred impressions before expenses could be recouped.[30] Rembrandt faced only the cost of materials. Furthermore, if Rembrandt kept his finished plates on hand, he could periodically print small editions as needed. There is evidence that he did this, based on the watermarks found on his papers. For example, *The Three Trees* (pl. 140) is dated 1643, but watermarks indicate that it was printed on at least eight different types of paper dating to his lifetime, some certainly coming after 1650.[31]

The original sizes of Rembrandt's print runs are impossible to estimate accurately.[32] His etched plates might generally have yielded a few hundred impressions before needing reworking to strengthen lines worn down from the pressure of printing. The more delicate drypoint technique, which he increasingly used in combination with etching, would have yielded fewer good impressions, perhaps only a few dozen before showing wear.[33] One of the most fascinating aspects of Rembrandt's printmaking was his tendency to slightly or even significantly transform an image on the plate after he had already printed a standard run of impressions. A dramatic example of this can be found in the early and late states of *Christ Presented to the People*

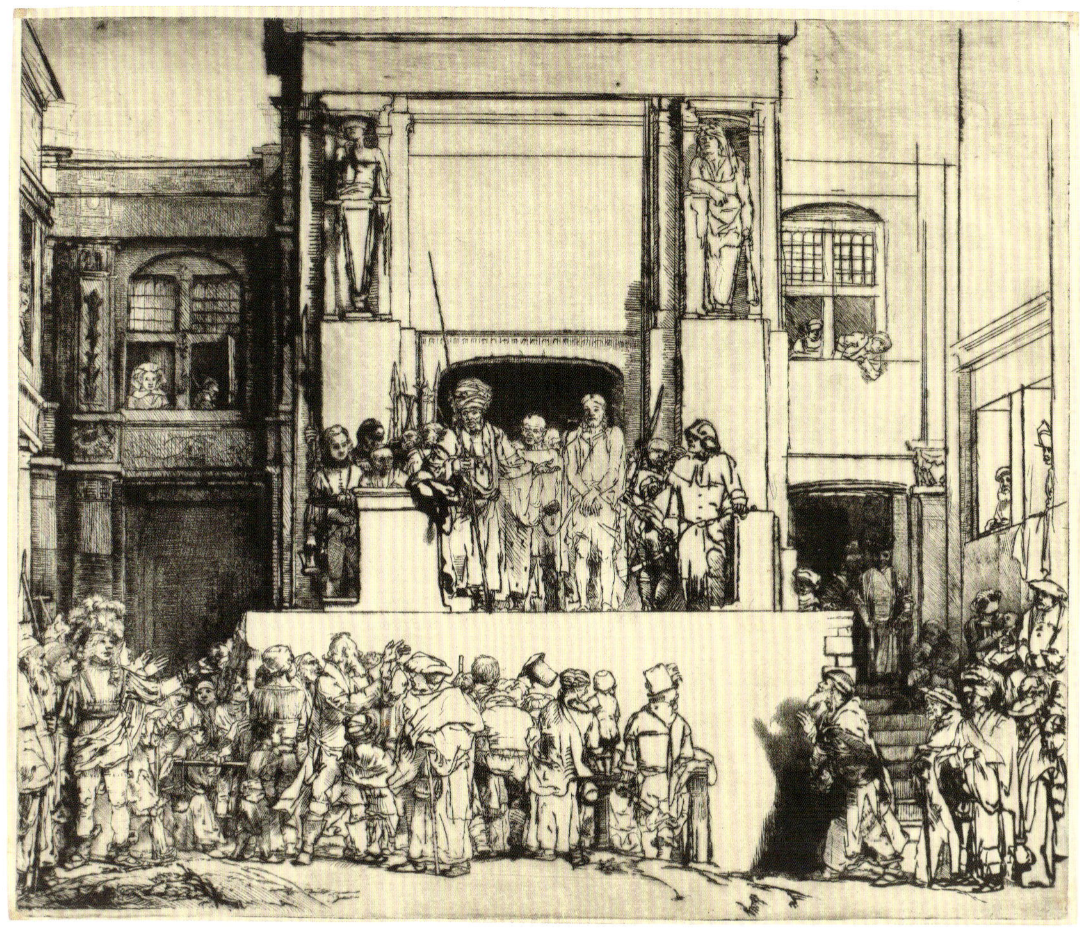

fig. 17.4 Rembrandt van Rijn, *Christ Presented to the People: Oblong Plate*, 1655, drypoint on Asian paper, third state; 38.7 × 45.4 cm. Rijksmuseum, Amsterdam. Purchased with the support of the Stichting tot Bevordering van de Belangen van het Rijksmuseum (RP-P-1975-1)

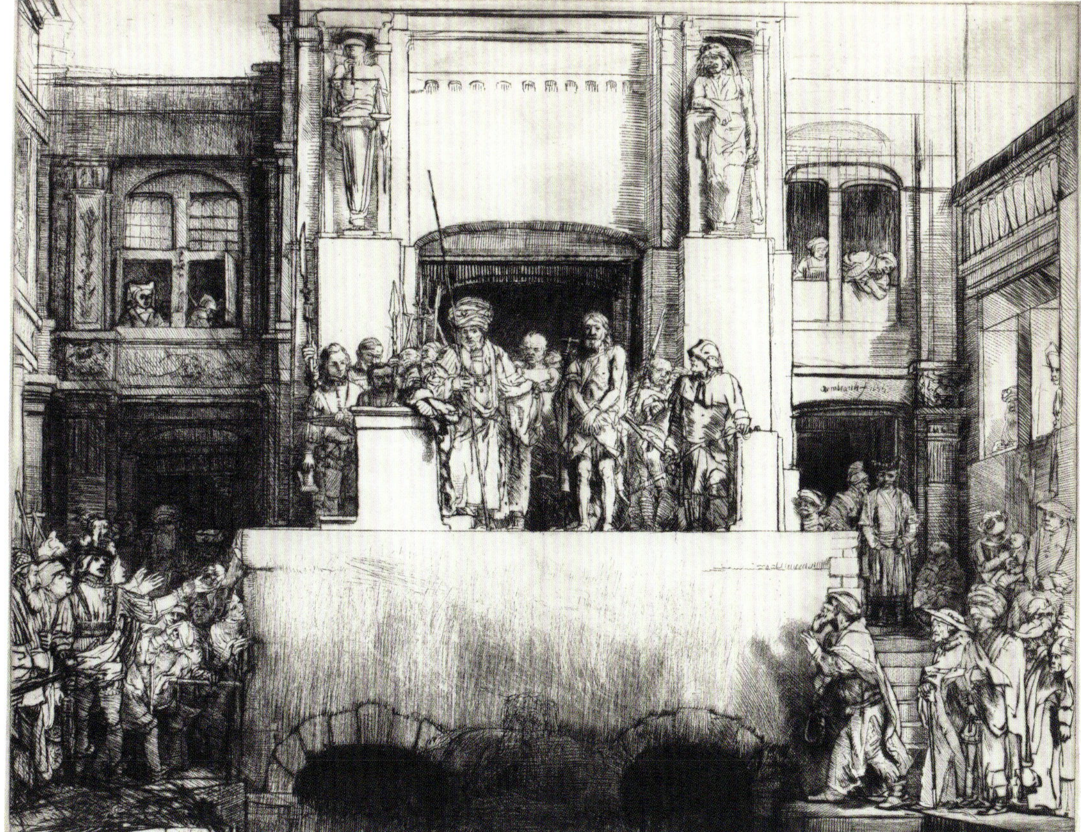

fig. 17.5 Rembrandt van Rijn, *Christ Presented to the People: Oblong Plate*, 1655, drypoint on laid paper, eighth state; 38.3 × 45.5 cm. Rijksmuseum, Amsterdam. Mr. and Mrs. De Bruijn-van der Leeuw Bequest, Muri, Switzerland (RP-P-1962-121)

from 1655, in which he removed much of the crowd in the foreground, ultimately leading to a more iconic focus on the scene taking place on the podium (figs. 17.4, 17.5).[34] While the need for reworking may have inspired him to rethink an image once he laid his hands on the plate again, this practice led Rembrandt's early biographer Arnold Houbraken to accuse him of making changes in order to lure collectors into buying more than one impression of the same print, a charge that will be discussed further below.[35] No other printmaker of his time so regularly transformed his prints "mid-edition."

Selling and Distribution

It seems likely that Rembrandt sold many prints directly from his home, in tandem with his paintings, likely with the help of family members or studio assistants.[36] There is evidence that Titus van Rijn (once he was old enough) even brokered print commissions for his father.[37] Given the large number of surviving lifetime impressions, Rembrandt's self-operated print dealership was clearly not small-scale. Already by the middle of his career, his prints were widely known and appreciated throughout Europe, and there must have been some means of distribution. In 1641 the painter Claude Vignon wrote to the French dealer François Langlois, asking him to give his regards to Rembrandt in Amsterdam and to bring back something from him. This suggests that the dealer was restocking directly from Rembrandt.[38] The Parisian dealer Pierre Mariette II was also acquiring Rembrandt prints by the late 1640s, likely by visiting Amsterdam himself.[39] Rembrandt's prints were known in England, Denmark, Germany and Italy during his lifetime as well.[40] He may have thus made certain bulk sales straight from his atelier, or even sent shipments to distributors on request, although there is no direct evidence of either. We do know that in 1669 he sent a set of 189 etchings to the Sicilian collector Antonio Ruffo in Messina.[41] Bulk sales might therefore have consisted of sets of individual impressions of separate subjects, rather than multiple impressions of the same subject. Another "complete set" of Rembrandt's printed oeuvre remained with his daughter-in-law Magdalena van Loo after he and Titus died.[42] This may have been Rembrandt's personal collection of his own prints, but it is tempting to suppose that he had a few other sets like this on hand that might have been available to collectors for the right price.

There is good evidence to suggest that Rembrandt sold many (or even most) of the copperplates in his possession around 1656 during his financial crisis. This would explain how the dealer Clement de Jonghe came into possession of so many of them. Watermark research demonstrates that certain impressions bear watermarks matching those found on prints by other artists that De Jonghe was printing and selling from his shop between the mid-1650s and Rembrandt's death in 1669.[43] Rembrandt therefore probably witnessed someone else printing and profiting from his plates during his lifetime, and not only De Jonghe. The plate for *The Descent from the Cross* was acquired by Dancker Danckerts after it left Uylenburgh's shop.[44] The plate for *The Expulsion of Hagar and Ishmael* (pl. 112) was acquired by the Portuguese merchant Samuel d'Orta soon after its completion in 1637. Notably, he accused Rembrandt of withholding more impressions than the "two or three for his own use" that had been agreed upon.[45] Although no such complaint is known from De Jonghe, one imagines that Rembrandt withheld a certain number of impressions from those plates as well, especially since he had enough stock years later to sell large sets to collectors like Ruffo.

A Mania among Collectors

Several extraordinary aspects of the market reflect a singular passion for Rembrandt among contemporary print connoisseurs. Rembrandt's prints reached unprecedented prices for a living artist at the time.[46] The archetypal example is his masterpiece, *Christ Preaching* of c. 1648, nicknamed *The Hundred Guilder Print* (pl. 168).[47] Already by 1654, in a letter from the Antwerp print dealer Johannes Meyssens to the print collector Karel van den Bosch, Bishop of Bruges, there is a reference to impressions selling for "one hundred guilders and more."[48] This was an extraordinary sum for a print at the time, on par with paintings of good quality, and matched only by the most desired impressions of prints by famous Old Masters. Houbraken, for example, reported that Nicolaes Berchem paid 60 guilders for a rare Raphael print.[49] Rembrandt also collected prints after Raphael.[50] He even traded an impression of *The Hundred Guilder Print* for Marcantonio Raimondi's famous engraving *Plague among the Trojans* (*Il Morbetto*) after Raphael from 1515–16 (pl. 167).[51] One of the highest recorded prices for a print at the time was actually for one purchased by Rembrandt himself; he reportedly paid 179 guilders for what was then considered the ultimate Lucas van Leyden rarity, the engraving called

Uylenspiegel or *The Beggar's Family* from 1520 (fig. 17.6).[52] The tax collector Jan Wtenbogaert, a friend of Rembrandt and a fellow art collector, paid a similar price for his own impression.[53]

Rembrandt was clearly one of the most seasoned and cultivated print collectors of his day. The inventory taken during his insolvency proceedings in 1656 records an enormous collection of prints by and after famous artists that covered nearly the full range of the history of the medium.[54] As a collector, Rembrandt intimately understood the print market, and his evident sensitivity to the appeal of *rarity* must have played a role in the marketing of his own oeuvre.[55] To create special impressions that would appeal to collectors for both rarity and artistic effect, Rembrandt printed on a wider variety of supports than any other printmaker up to that point.[56] Beginning in the late 1640s, he was the first to popularize the use of Asian papers, which offered a wide range of tone and weight.[57] On occasion he also used vellum, which had less absorbency and could convey deeper tones. By printing the same etching or drypoint on a range of supports, he offered collectors unprecedented possibilities for comparing and appreciating subtle nuances of inking and tone. While we do not have an inventory of individual impressions of Rembrandt's prints in a collection from the seventeenth century, documents from the early eighteenth century confirm that serious collectors would often possess two or more impressions (sometimes as many as four or six) of Rembrandt's individual subjects because of their multiple variations in image, elaborated through a sequence of states, and support.[58] Rembrandt was not just a prolific printmaker; he was also unmatched, especially from the late 1640s onward, in producing individually variable impressions.

The passion for collecting these rarities was no doubt the source of Houbraken's damning statement that Rembrandt intentionally manipulated the market for his prints by making slight changes to them. Writing in 1718, he claimed:

> Doing this brought him great fame, and no little profit, especially the little trick of making a slight change or a small and trifling addition to his prints which would allow him to sell them again a second time. Indeed, the zeal was so great in those days that people would not be taken for true connoisseurs who did not have the Juno with and without the crown, the Joseph with the light and dark face, and so forth.[59]

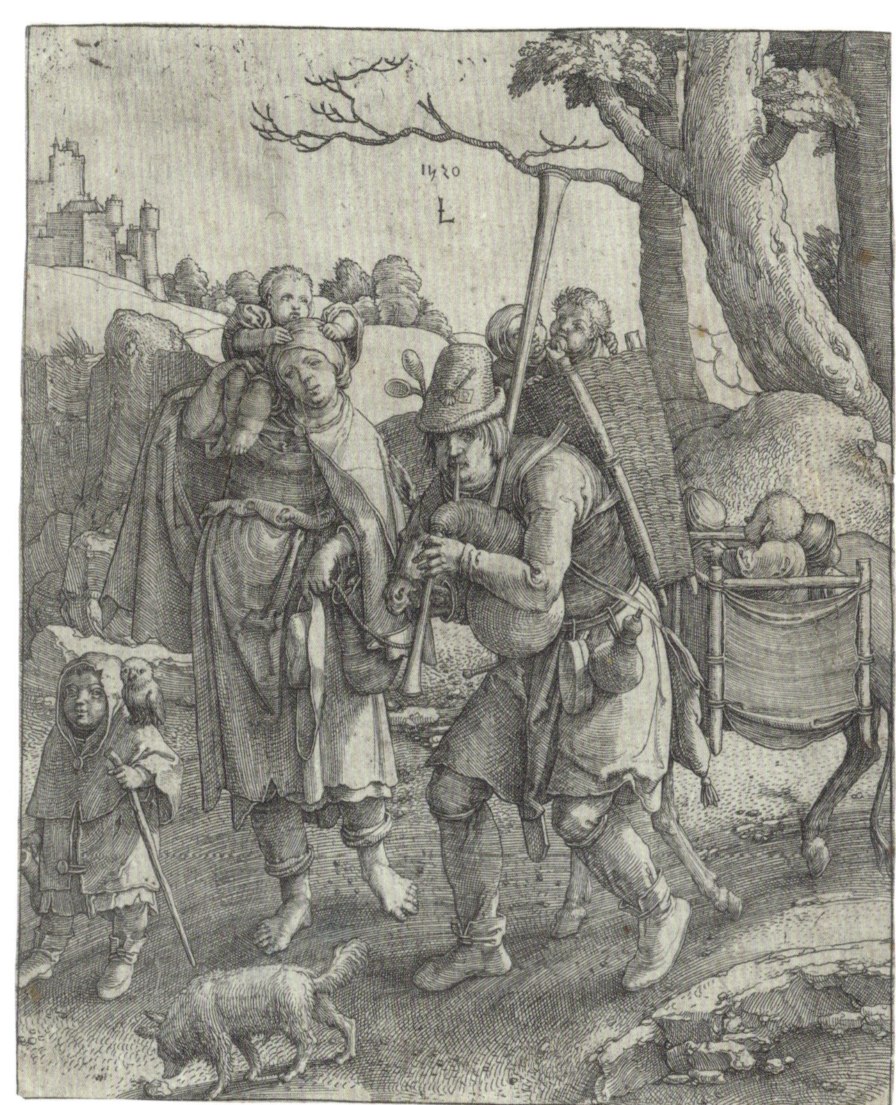

fig. 17.6 **Lucas van Leyden,** *Uylenspiegel* (*The Beggar's Family*)**, 1520, engraving on laid paper; 17.4 × 14.1 cm. Rijksmuseum, Amsterdam (RP-P-OB-1750)

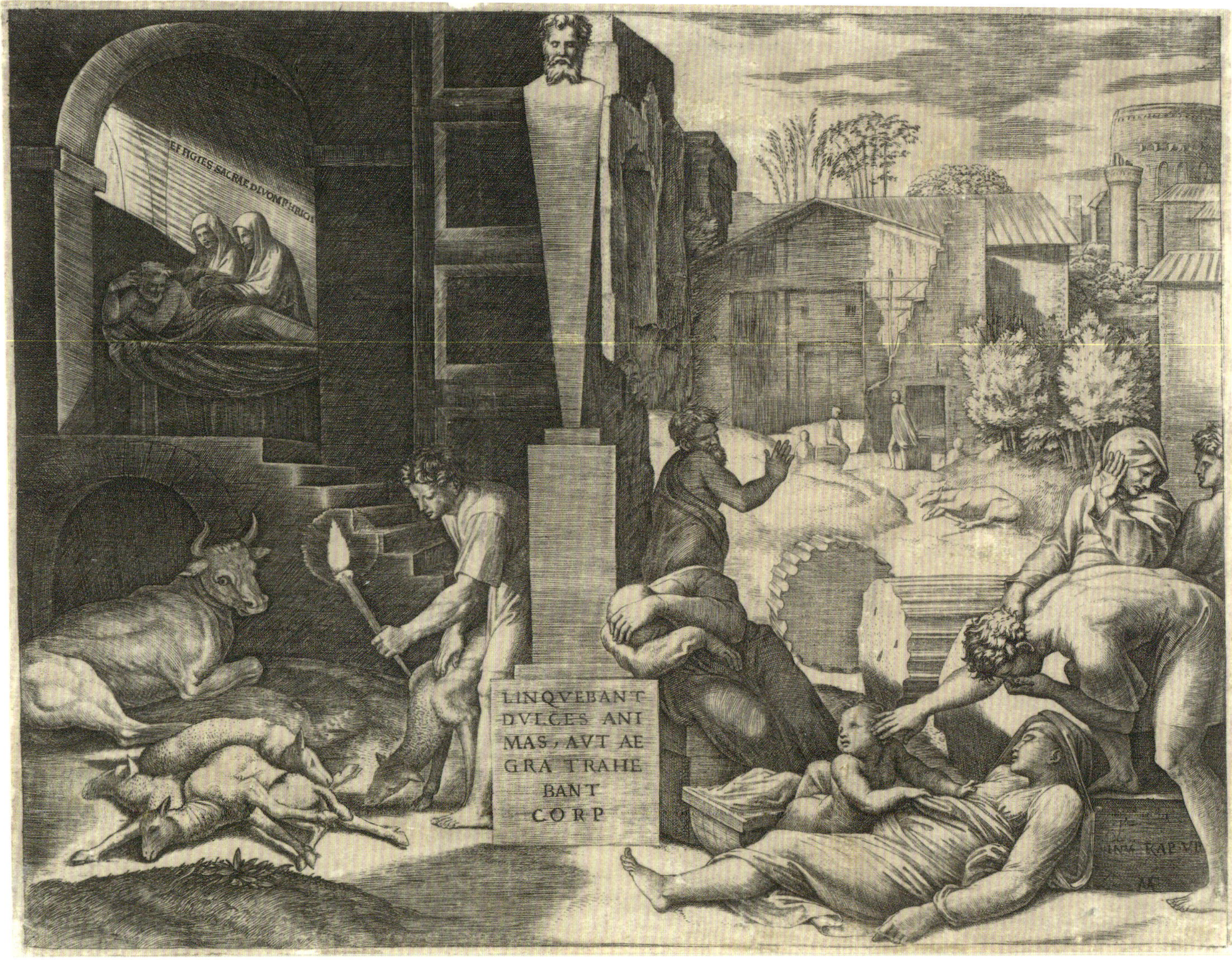

167 Marcantonio Raimondi (after Raphael), *Plague among the Trojans* (*Il Morbetto*), 1515–16. Rijksmuseum, Amsterdam

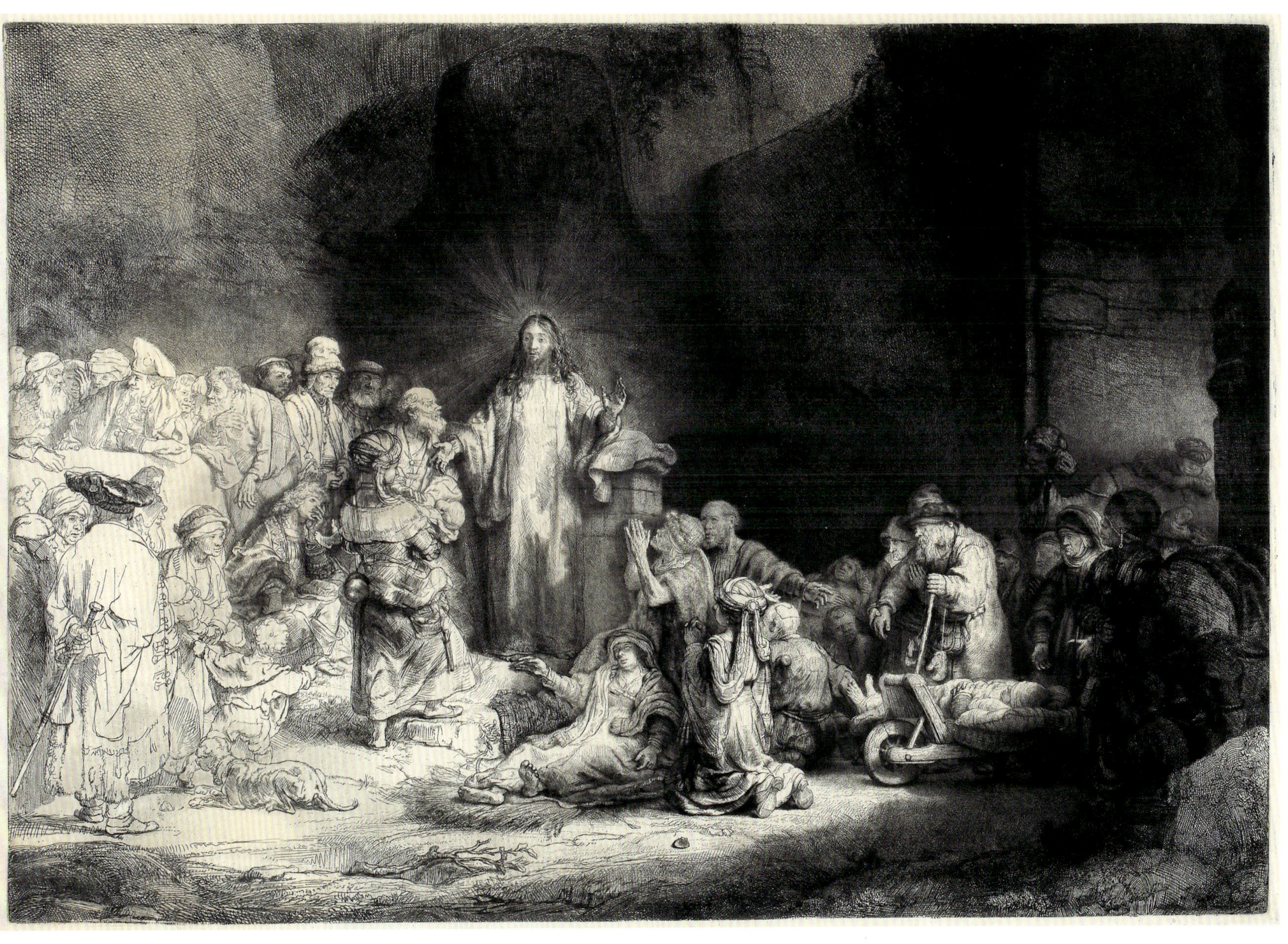

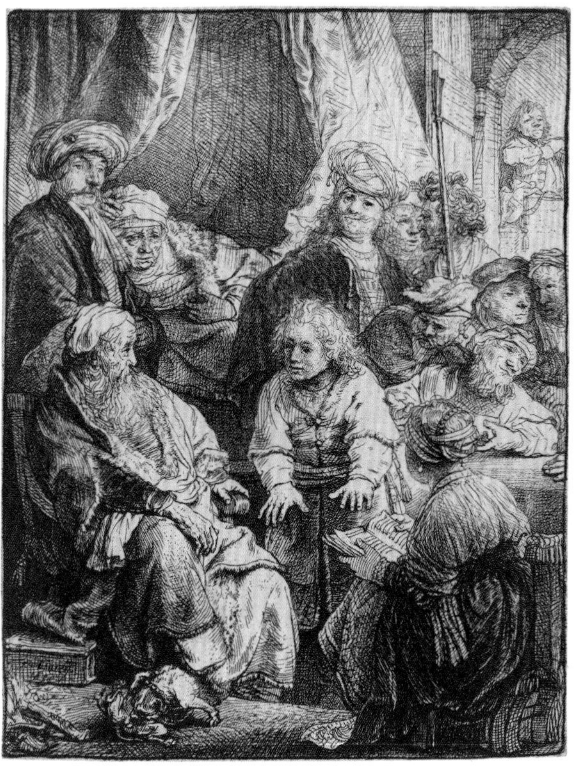

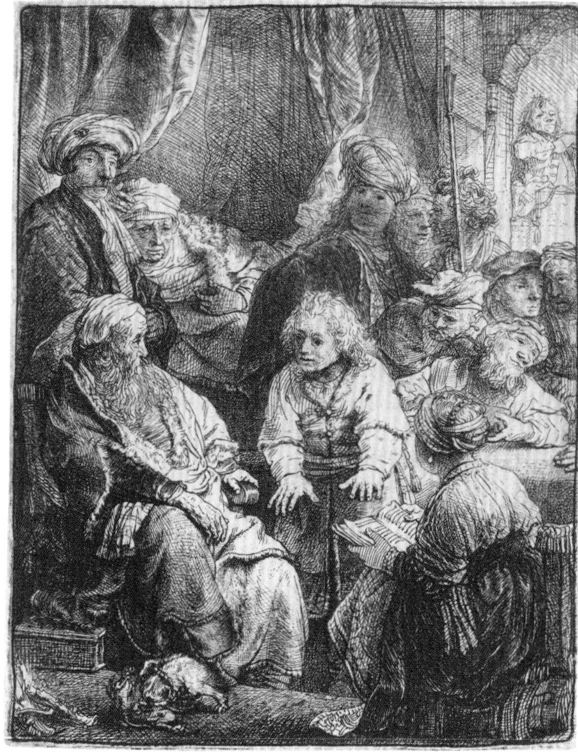

fig. 17.7 **Rembrandt van Rijn,**
Joseph Telling His Dreams, 1638,
etching on laid paper, second
state; 11 × 8.3 cm. Rijksmuseum,
Amsterdam (RP-P-OB-75)

fig. 17.8 **Rembrandt van Rijn,**
Joseph Telling His Dreams, 1638,
etching on laid paper, third state;
11.1 × 8.4 cm. Rijksmuseum,
Amsterdam (RP-P-OB-76)

In fact, Rembrandt's changes to some of his plates, such as *Christ Presented to the People,* were not so slight, but rather require us to rethink the artistic implications of the changing image.[60] Others, including some of the changes Houbraken specifically mentioned, such as for *Joseph Telling His Dreams* (figs. 17.7, 17.8), appear to be honest reworkings that Rembrandt carried out to strengthen the plate over the course of printing – in this case the addition of shading to the face of the central turbaned man and the drapery above him. Such corrections probably only fell under the eyes of collectors at a later point and were never intended to appeal to their interest in sequential states.[61]

The greatest challenge to Houbraken's statement, however, is that several of Rembrandt's most notable variations occur in his portrait prints. These are works that we generally assume were commissioned rather than made at Rembrandt's own instigation.[62] The fascinating changes found in the various states of *Portrait of Clement de Jonghe* (pls. 170, 171) and *Portrait of Abraham Francen* (pl. 24) must have been welcomed by these print connoisseurs.[63] An earlier state of *Portrait of Jan Lutma, Goldsmith* with the empty wall in the background (pl. 23) appears more proof-like in comparison with the later state with the window, yet both were printed in equally high numbers.[64] Rembrandt and his patrons may have

been inspired by Anthony van Dyck, who had extra proof impressions printed intentionally for his popular printed portrait series the *Iconography*.[65] As early as 1635, a publisher of prints by Jacques Callot in Paris was regularly printing extra proof impressions before the inscriptions were added.[66] In the case of Rembrandt's portrait prints, proof impressions would have appealed to collectors who valued them as works of art, rather than as mere documentary likenesses of the sitters.[67]

Since many of the states in Rembrandt's portrait prints survive today in nearly equal numbers of impressions, they should not be viewed as corrections, but rather as variations of a multiple finished product. This would have been a very modern concept at the time. Moreover, in certain cases watermark evidence shows that these different "editions" were all printed around the same time the plate was originally created, suggesting that they might even have been planned from the outset.[68] A recently discovered letter in the Staatsbibliothek, Munich, potentially sheds light on this. When the printmaker Jacob von Sandrart, nephew of the aforementioned Joachim von Sandrart, finished his portrait engraving of Frederick I of Saxe-Gotha-Altenburg, he sent the duke three separate bundles of impressions marked as best, medium, and least quality.[69]

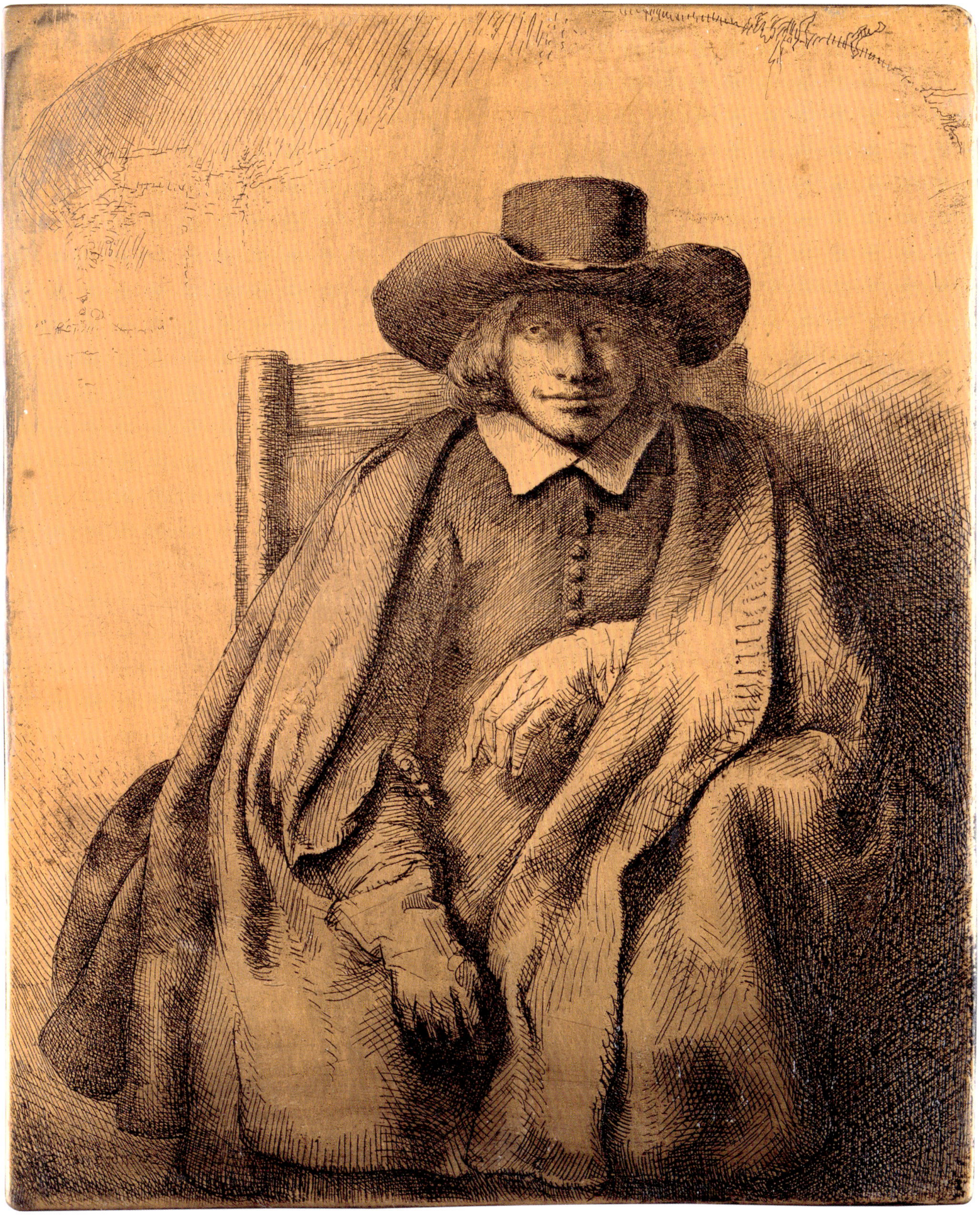

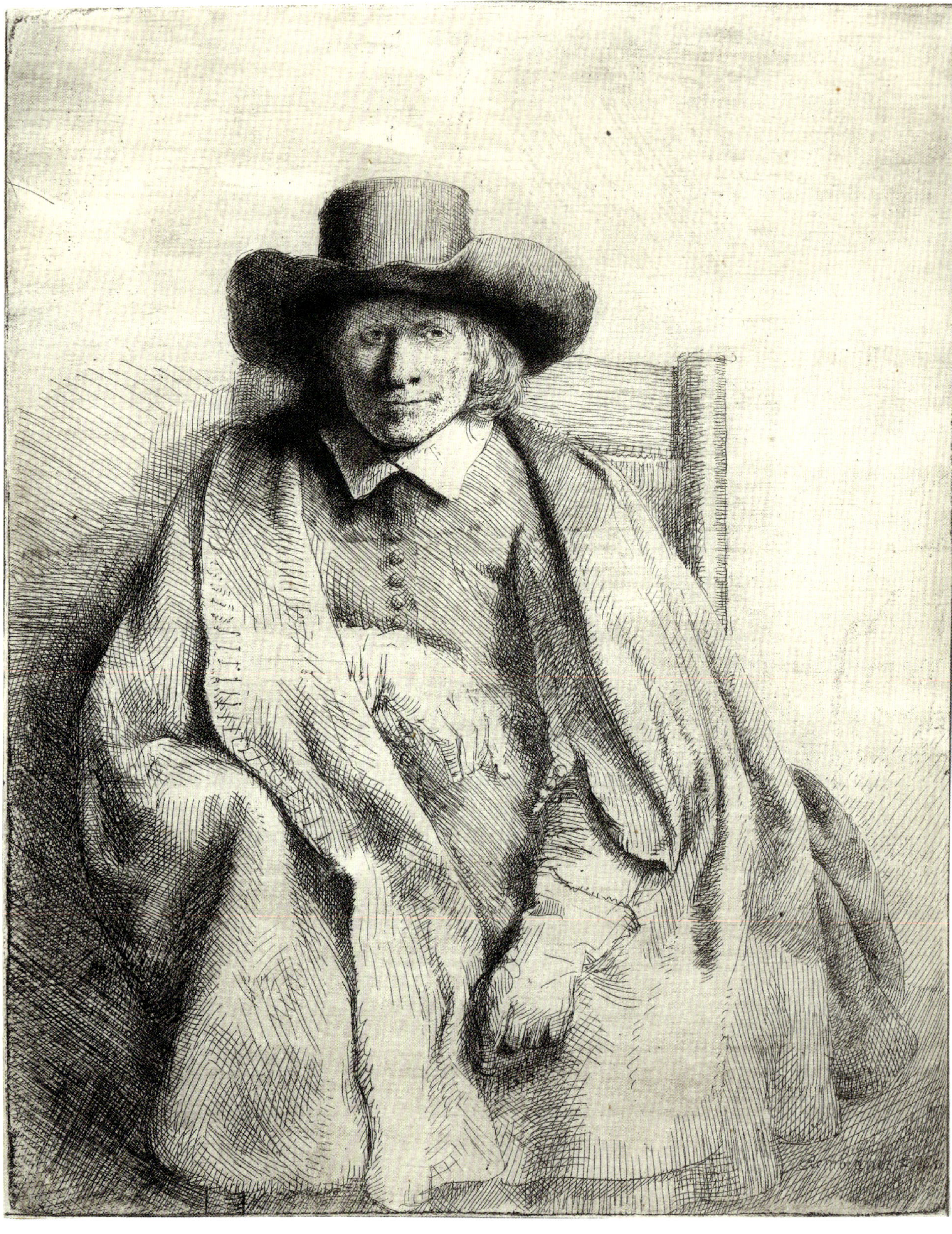

170 Rembrandt van Rijn, *Portrait of Clement de Jonghe*, 1651, first state. Städel Museum, Frankfurt am Main

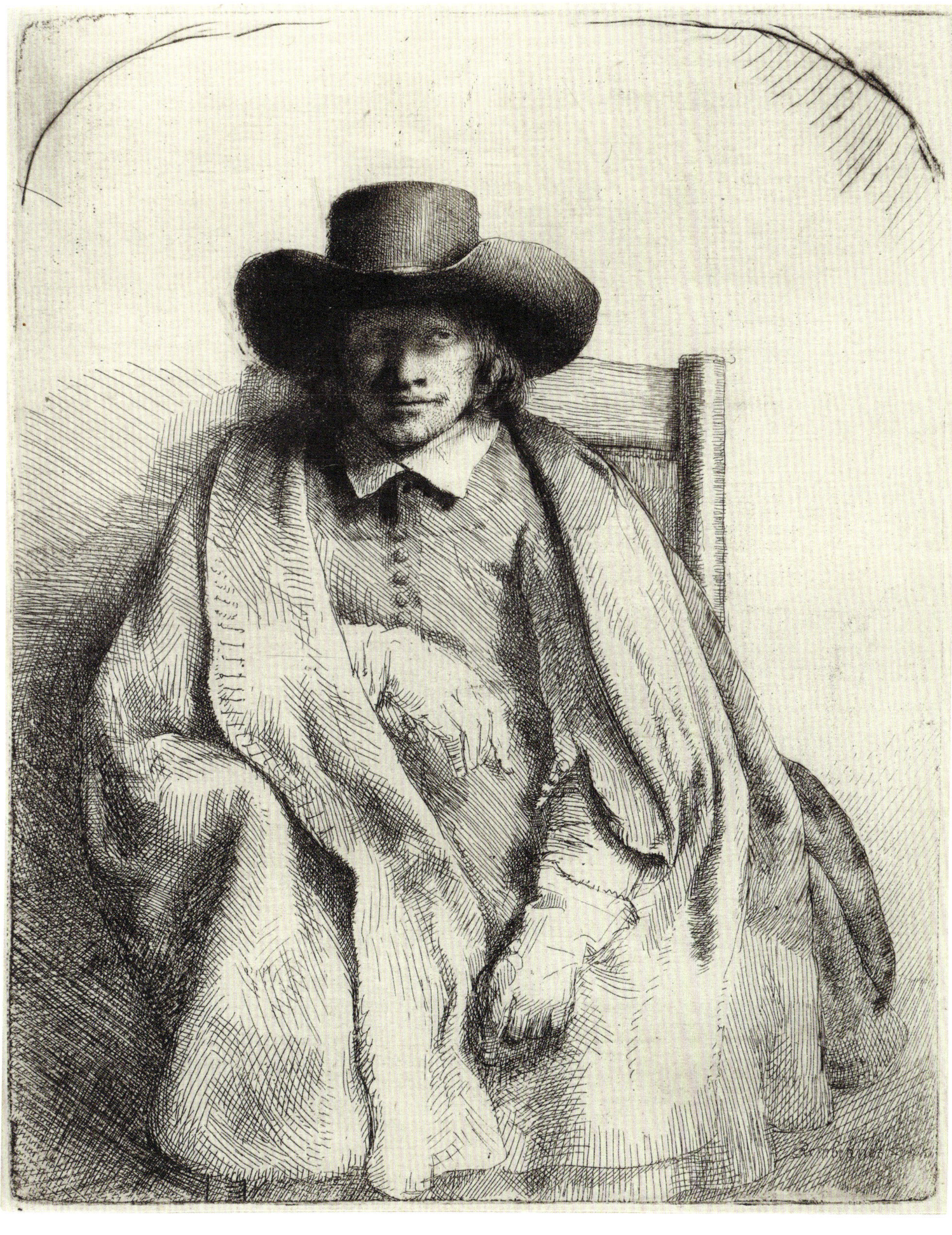

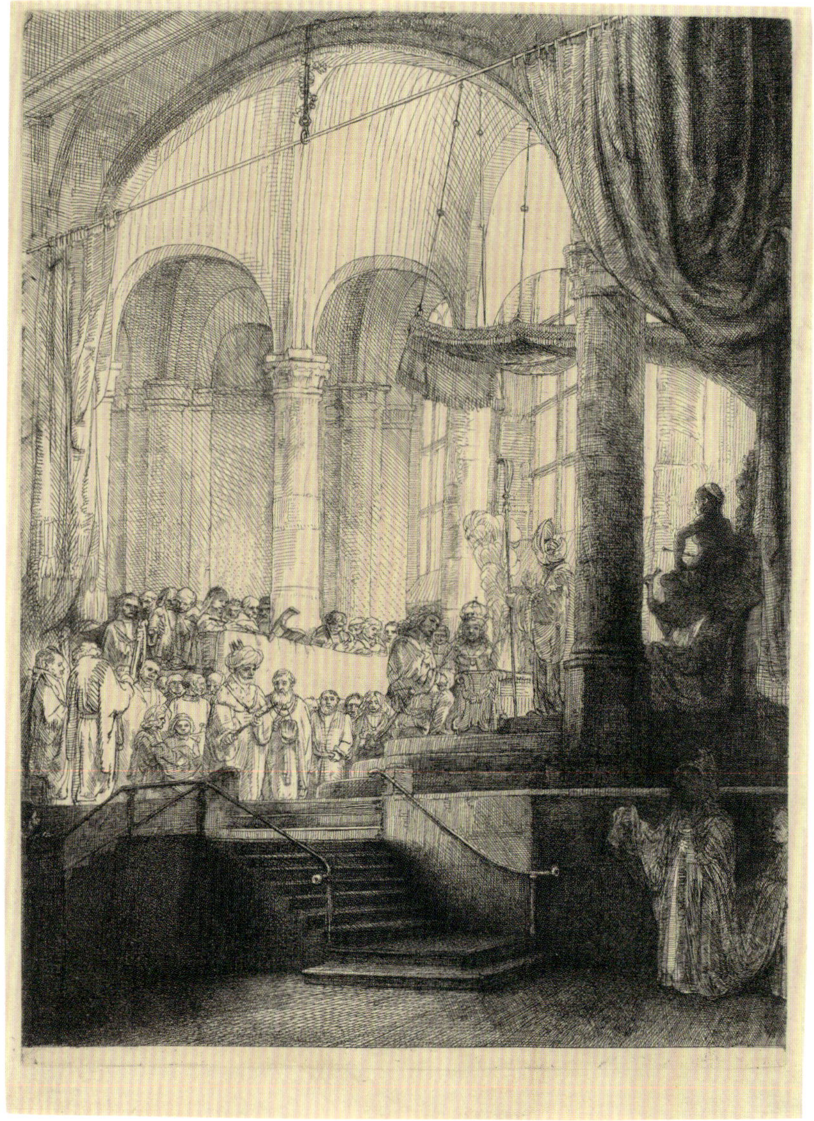

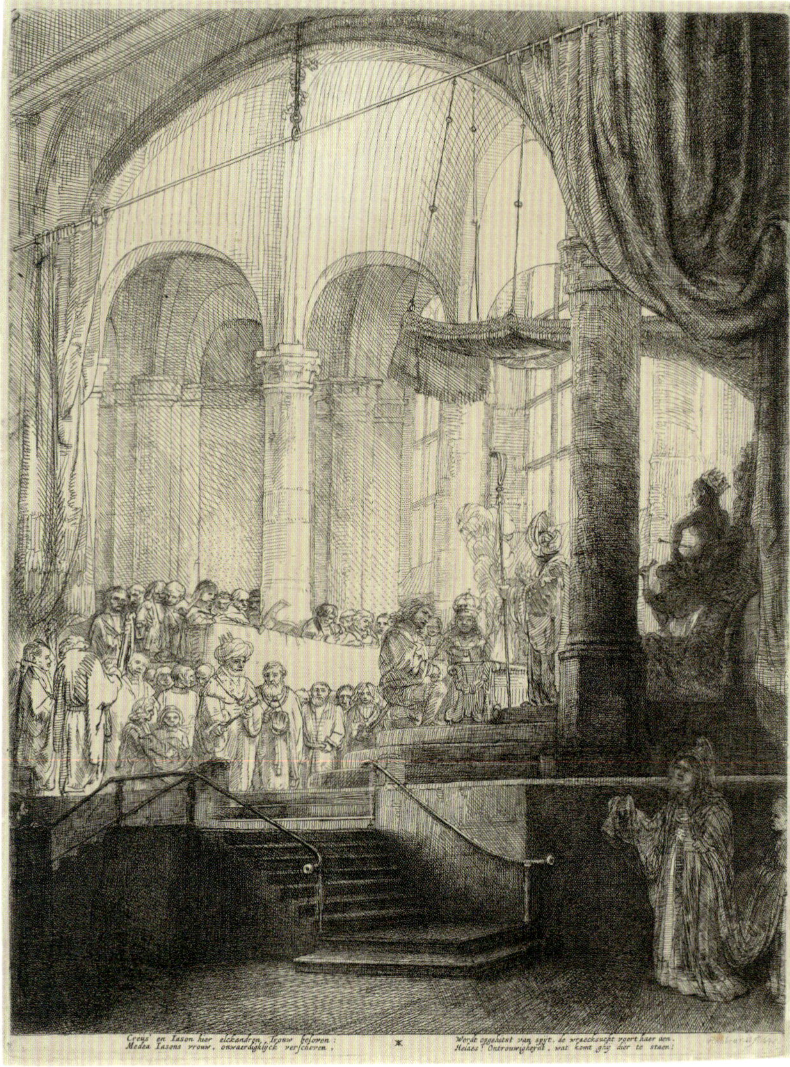

fig. 17.9 **Rembrandt van Rijn, *Medea, or the Marriage of Jason and Creusa*,** 1648, etching with touches of drypoint on Asian paper, first state; 24 × 17.6 cm. National Gallery of Art, Washington. Gift of W.G. Russell Allen (1955.6.8)

fig. 17.10 **Rembrandt van Rijn, *Medea, or the Marriage of Jason and Creusa*,** 1648, etching with touches of drypoint on laid paper, fourth state; 24 × 17.6 cm. National Gallery of Art, Washington. Rosenwald Collection (1943.3.7129)

Rembrandt and his patrons may have had something similar in mind when the artist made changes to his plates, not only to refresh them after a course of printing, but perhaps to create a visual shorthand for knowing which ones were printed before the others. It hardly seems coincidental that one finds the most dramatic variations in Rembrandt's portraits of artists, print collectors or a print dealer like De Jonghe, rather than sitters who were physicians or preachers.[70]

We have some idea that Rembrandt's portrait prints were highly valued commissions at the time since he was once offered 400 guilders to execute one "equal in quality to his portrait of Jan Six."[71] In the magnificent *Portrait of Jan Six* (pl. 13), Rembrandt radically enlivened the portrait print genre through an intensely wrought yet remarkably informal representation of the notable art collector and future burgomaster.[72] Further worth noting, two of Rembrandt's earliest securely dated uses of Asian papers were both commissions for Jan Six: one for his portrait dated 1647; the other for the frontispiece of his play *Medea*, published in 1648.[73] One cannot help wondering if Jan Six himself requested the use of these special papers. In the *Medea* frontispiece, as mentioned by Houbraken, the goddess Juno "with and without the crown" (seated on the throne at right) provides an easy to spot marker between earlier and later states (figs. 17.9, 17.10), and thus between impressions that were printed as part of

a special edition of loose single-sheet prints and those bound into the book with the text of the play.[74] Almost all of the "pre-press" edition "without the crown" is printed on Asian papers, while the bound edition "with the crown" is entirely on standard European papers.

We can conclude that Rembrandt's patrons and collectors were enthusiastic about – and perhaps even complicit in – the production of various effects that can be found throughout his printed oeuvre. Despite this, Houbraken's accusation is often dismissed as unfair and untrue.[75] There are good reasons to be hesitant about accepting his characterization of Rembrandt as mercenary and avaricious, but we can recast his comment more positively: Rembrandt indeed crafted some variants of his prints to cater to an increasingly avid collectors' market, and many collectors welcomed the production of such novel and intriguing variations.

Many of Rembrandt's changes, whether through inking, paper or revision of the design, arguably emerged in the first place from artistic concerns. While his novel methods may have helped to build his market, they also constitute an exploration of the potential of the print medium in its own right. In the end, Rembrandt did not just sell prints. He successfully marketed exciting new techniques and materials in a matchless and innovative style that elevated his viewers' appreciation, then as now, for the art of the print. ■

NOTES

1   Sandrart 1675–80, vol. 2, book 3, 326.

2   For an overview of Amsterdam print publishing in Rembrandt's time, see Amsterdam 2011.

3   Ibid., 64.

4   See NHD 264. For Clement de Jonghe, see Laurentius 2010; Hinterding 2006, vol. 1, 141–144; Dickey 2004, 138–141.

5   De Hoop Scheffer and Boon 1971. These form the core of the eighty-two surviving copperplates, on which see Hinterding 1993–94. An additional plate surfaced after Hinterding's study appeared for *Abraham Entertaining the Angels* from 1656 (NHD 295), now in the National Gallery of Art, Washington (inv. 1997.85.1).

6   William W. Robinson, "'This Passion for Prints': Collecting and Connoisseurship in Northern Europe during the Seventeenth Century," in Boston and St. Louis 1980–81, xxvii–xlviii; Rotterdam 2006b.

7   For engraving as a profession, see Stijnman 2012; Griffiths 2016; for the painter as etcher, see esp. Michael Cole and Larry Silver, "Fluid Boundaries: Formations of the Painter-Etcher," in Philadelphia 2006, 5–35.

8   Lievens produced around one hundred prints and Berchem around eighty, in comparison to Rembrandt's more than three hundred. For Lievens as a printmaker, see Stephanie S. Dickey, "Jan Lievens and Printmaking," in Washington, Milwaukee and Amsterdam 2008–09, 54–67; for Berchem, see Gerdien Wuestman, "Berchem as an Etcher: Effortless, Accomplished and Peerless," in Haarlem, Zürich and Schwerin 2006, 119–131.

9   Sandrart 1675–80, vol. 2, book 3, 326.

10 Lifetime impressions are identified on the basis of watermarks in the paper and other evidence. See Hinterding 1993–94 and listings in NHD.

11 Van Hoogstraten 1678, 195–196.

12 See recently Jaco Rutgers, "Rubens's Early Involvement in Printmaking," in Toronto 2019, 102–114.

13 See Amsterdam 1996.

14 See An van Camp, "Rembrandt's Early Works on Paper," in Leiden and Oxford 2019–20, 69, suggesting that there may have been no one else available in Leiden. Jaco Rutgers proposes that Van Vliet was not hired by Rembrandt, but worked on his own initiative; Jaco Rutgers, "Jan van Vliet and Rembrandt van Rijn: Their Collaboration Reassessed," in Dickey 2017b, 285–304, esp. 290. The evidence, while plausible, is not entirely convincing; see Fucci 2019, 358.

15 Hollstein, vol. 41, 146, no. 1. See also Amsterdam 1996, 40–41, no. 1a; An van Camp, in Leiden and Oxford 2019–20, 234–235, no. 111.

16 NHD 119.

17 Rutgers, "Jan van Vliet and Rembrandt van Rijn," in Dickey 2017b, 294–297, persuasively claims that arguments for Van Vliet's involvement are not entirely convincing; cf. Royalton-Kisch 1984a, Royalton-Kisch 1984b, Royalton-Kisch 1994; and Royalton-Kisch in Amsterdam 1996, 74–75, no. 18.

18 Hollstein, vol. 43, 36, no. 31. On Rembrandt and Vorsterman's engraving, see, among others, White 1999, 14–18; Royalton-Kisch in Amsterdam and London 2000–01, 132–134, no. 22.

19 For privileges on prints in the northern Netherlands, see esp. Nadine M. Orenstein, "Sleeping Caps, City Views, and State Funerals: Privileges for Prints in the Dutch Republic, 1593–1650," in Golahny, Mochizuki and Vergara 2006, 313–346. No document granting the privilege for this print has yet been found.

20 Around thirty impressions survive today from before the publisher's address of Uylenburgh was added (NHD 119, states 1 and 2). Hinterding 2006, vol. 1, 92–96, notes that watermark analysis proves inconclusive in clarifying this issue, but worth noting is that a Strasbourg Lily watermark dating to c. 1636–41 appears on impressions before Uylenburgh's name was added, as listed in NHD 119.

21 See Ernst van der Wetering, "Remarks on Oil-sketches for Etchings," in Amsterdam and London 2000–01, 52–56; *Corpus*, vol. 5, 176–185; *Corpus*, vol. 6, 176–179.

22 NHD 113; see recently Leiden and Oxford 2019–20, 152–155.

23 NHD 125.

24 Strauss and Van der Meulen 1979, doc. 1637/2. See also Hinterding 2006, vol. 1, 62.

25 Strauss and Van der Meulen 1979, doc. 1636/5.

26 Hinterding 2006, vol. 1, 35–42.

27 Erik Hinterding, "'The Incomparable Reinbrand': Rembrandt als onafhankelijk prentmaker in 17de-eeuws Amsterdam," in Amsterdam 2011, 191–192.

28 For printing-press prices, see Orenstein 1996, 124–128. For paper prices, see Hinterding 2006, vol. 1, 47. Rembrandt spent 4 guilders and 12 stuivers for three reams of blank paper at the Jan Bassé auction in 1637; Strauss and Van der Meulen 1979, doc. 1637/2. Prices for blank copperplates are more difficult to discern, but the publisher Broer Jansz paid 3 guilders and 2 stuivers for a blank copperplate of unspecified size; Orenstein 1996, 130. Rembrandt occasionally economized when it came to his copperplates, in one instance cutting up his large early plate of *St. Jerome* (NHD 3) to make smaller plates that he then reused; he etched a *Return of the Prodigal Son* (NHD 159) on a recycled plate used to illustrate a mathematics book from 1598; Hinterding 1993–94, 255–256. For a broader look at production costs across Europe, see Griffiths 2016, 63–66.

29 Hinterding, "The Incomparable Reinbrand," in Amsterdam 2011, 192. For commercial printing, see Orenstein 1996, 129–130; Landau and Parshall 1994, 28–29.

30 Griffiths 2016, 62–77.

31 NHD 214; Hinterding 2006, vol. 1, 51–53. Perhaps about one hundred impressions of *The Three Trees* survive today (extrapolating from the roughly seventy impressions listed in NHD), all of which appear to be lifetime or at least seventeenth-century impressions.

32 An average engraving might yield three hundred to six hundred impressions, but one of Rembrandt's etched plates might only produce "50 good and 200 reasonable impressions" before showing signs of wear; Hinterding 2006, vol. 1, 49–50. Griffiths 2016, 50–55, suggests higher numbers.

33 Hinterding 2006, vol. 1, 50; Griffiths 2016, 56–57.

34 NHD 290.

35 Houbraken 1718–21, vol. 1, 271.

36 Griffiths 2016, 246–247.

37 A document from 1665 shows Titus promoting his father's print-making ability when he secures a commission on his behalf for the *Portrait of Jan Antonides van der Linden* (NHD 314); Strauss and Van der Meulen 1979, doc. 1665/5, 1665/6. See Dickey 2004, 159–162.

38 Strauss and Van der Meulen 1979, doc. 1641/6.

39 Mariette frequently signed and dated his Rembrandt prints when he acquired them. An impression of *Student at a Table by Candlelight* (NHD 213) in the Morgan Library & Museum, New York, is signed *P. Mariette 1646*, making it the earliest thus far to come to light. My thanks to Erik Hinterding for sharing this information.

40 For the early distribution of Rembrandt's prints throughout Europe, see Hinterding, "The Incomparable Reinbrand," in Amsterdam 2011, 194.

41 Ricci 1918, 30; Münz 1952, vol. 2, 210. A document dated 8 December 1669 states "189 *stampe del Reimbrant Venutimi da Amsterdam*" (189 prints by Rembrandt arrived from Amsterdam). Allowing for travel time to Messina, one assumes Rembrandt sent the prints himself before his own death on 4 October.

42 De Roever 1884, 101–102; Münz 1952, vol. 2, 210. Magdalena van Loo died a few weeks after Rembrandt (Titus had died a year earlier); the prints appear in her inventory: "Three art books filled with all the most valuable prints that Rembrandt made during his life."

43 Hinterding 2006, vol. 1, 141–144, and vol. 2, 417–423, Appendix 4.

44 The plate appears in Danckerts' 1667 inventory, thus during Rembrandt's lifetime; see NHD 119.

45 Strauss and Van der Meulen 1979, doc. 1637/7.

46 For a documentary overview of prices paid for Rembrandt's prints, see Hinterding 2006, vol. 1, 59–65, and vol. 2, 424–425, Appendix 5.

47 NHD 239.

48 Amy Golahny, "Rembrandt's *One Guilder Print*: Value and Invention in 'the most beautiful [print] that ever came from the burin of this Master,'" in Dickey 2017b, 232–233; Hinterding 2006, vol. 1, 60–61; Antwerp and Amsterdam 1999, 368.

49 Houbraken 1718–21, vol. 2, 112.

50 Rembrandt's 1656 inventory contains three bound volumes containing prints after Raphael, the last called "very valuable"; Strauss and Van der Meulen 1979, doc. 1656/12, items 196, 205, 206.

51 Inscription on an impression in the Rijksmuseum, Amsterdam (inv. RP-P-OB-601); Golahny, "Rembrandt's *One Guilder Print*," in Dickey 2017b, 233; Amsterdam and London 2000–01, 253, no. 61, with transcription.

52 Noted in 1642 by the Burgomaster of Harderwijk; Strauss and Van der Meulen 1979, doc. 1642/10.

53 For Wtenbogaert's impression of *Uylenspiegel*, see New York 2015, 53 (with further references).

54 Strauss and Van der Meulen 1979, doc. 1656/12.

55 New York 2015, 15–40.

56 On Rembrandt's papers and supports, see Hinterding, "Incomparable Reinbrand," in Amsterdam 2011, 181–187; New York 2015, 19–20.

57 On Rembrandt's Asian papers (which were probably Japanese in origin), see Biörklund 1988, 170–173; Van Breda 1997; Akira Kofuku, "Papier de demi-teinte: Japanese Paper in Rembrandt's Oeuvre," in Tokyo 2011.

58 The two earliest known lists of individual impressions of Rembrandt's prints with their variations are the personal manuscript inventory of Valerius Röver (his *Memorie*) composed between 1731 and 1739, and the 1735 auction catalogue of the collection of Samuel van Huls. See Van Gelder and Van Gelder-Schrijver 1938; New York 2015, 34–35.

59 Houbraken 1718–21, vol. 1, 271. Houbraken here refers specifically to state changes in *Joseph Telling His Dreams* and *Medea, or the Marriage of Jason and Creusa* (figs. 17.7–17.10).

60 See, among others, Carroll 1981; Perlove and Silver 2009, 283–289; New York 2015, 108–112, no. 13.

61 New York 2015, 47–50, no. 2.

62 On Rembrandt's portrait prints, see esp. Dickey 2004. Plates were often in the possession of the sitters, sometimes even passed down through inheritance; for instance, the plate for *Portrait of Jan Six* is still in the family today.

63 NHD 264 and 301. For state changes, see also New York 2015, 89–94, no. 10. Francen was an avid print collector and likely Rembrandt's personal friend; Dickey 2004, 142–149.

64 NHD 293; New York 2015, 117–121, no. 15.

65 Antwerp and Amsterdam 1999, 92–100, no. 5; NHD Van Dyck, vol. 1, xxxii.

66 Griffiths and Chapman 2013.

67 See Dickey 2004, 104.

68 This is certainly the case with the first three states of *Portrait of Clement de Jonghe* (NHD 264) and the first two states of *Portrait of Jan Lutma, Goldsmith* (NHD 293), each of which have watermarks that carry over from state to state.

69 Griffiths 2016, 432, crediting Susanne Meurer for the reference.

70 New York 2015, 24.

71 Strauss and Van der Meulen 1979, doc. 1655/8.

72 NHD 238.

73 NHD 241. This has generally been overlooked, while the not precisely dated *Portrait of Jan Asselijn* (pl. 1, NHD 236) is invariably cited as his earliest use of Asian paper. While this portrait certainly dates to around 1647–48 on stylistic grounds, the last two digits of the inscribed date are illegible. A far more secure starting point for his uses of Asian papers, therefore, are the two plates commissioned by Jan Six, since the portrait is dated 1647 and the play *Medea* was published in 1648. Furthermore, the play premiered in 1647, and it is possible that the "pre-press" single-sheet states on Asian paper may have circulated before the bound version was released.

74 New York 2015, 25–27, 73–78, no. 7.

75 E.g., White 1999, 2–3; Griffiths 2016, 433. Hinterding 2006, vol. 1, 122, suggests only that Rembrandt would have been aware of the collectors' market for his early states; see also Hinterding 2011, 198n98. Alpers 1988, 100–101, on the other hand accepts Houbraken's statement at face value to argue for the effectiveness of Rembrandt's marketing operation.

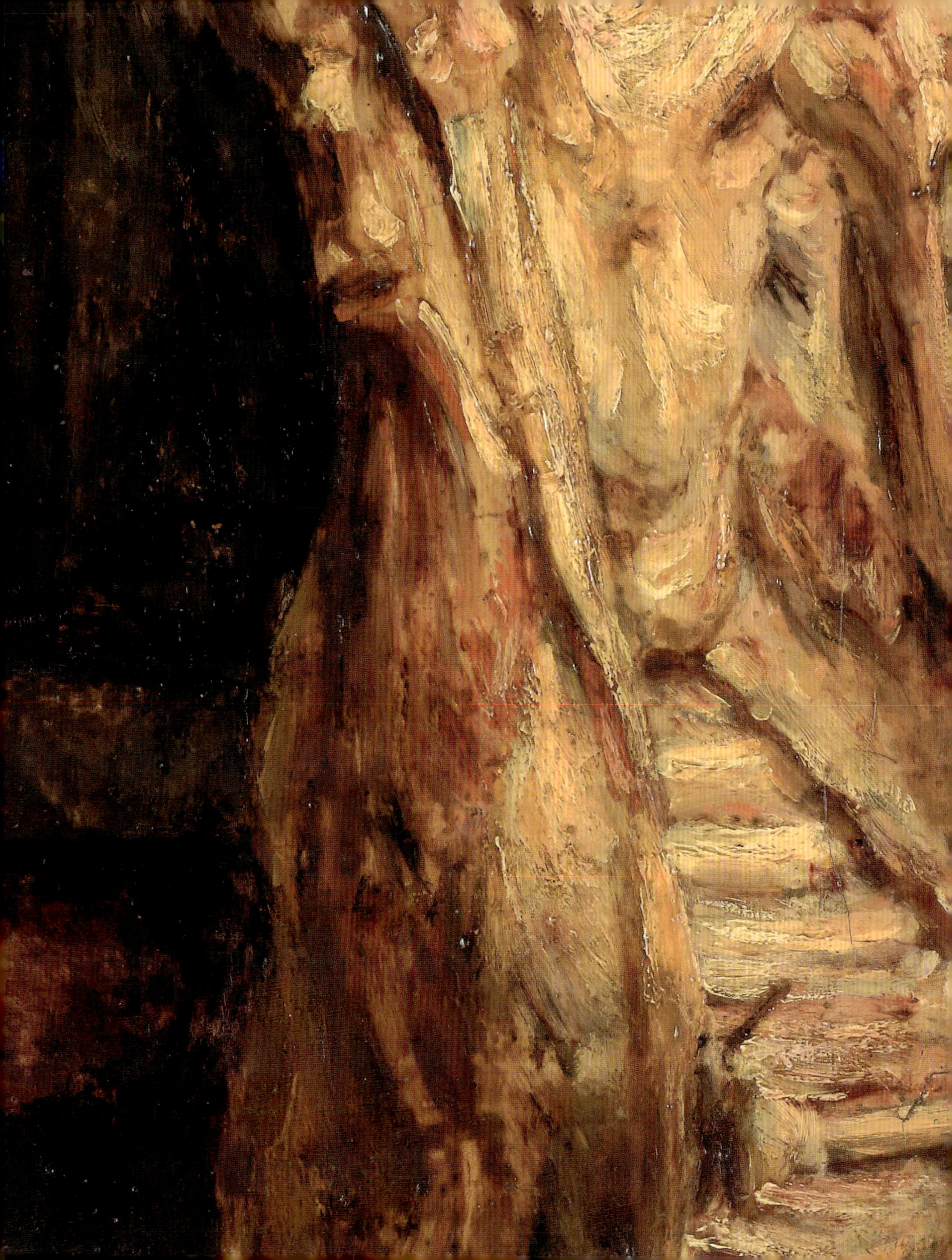

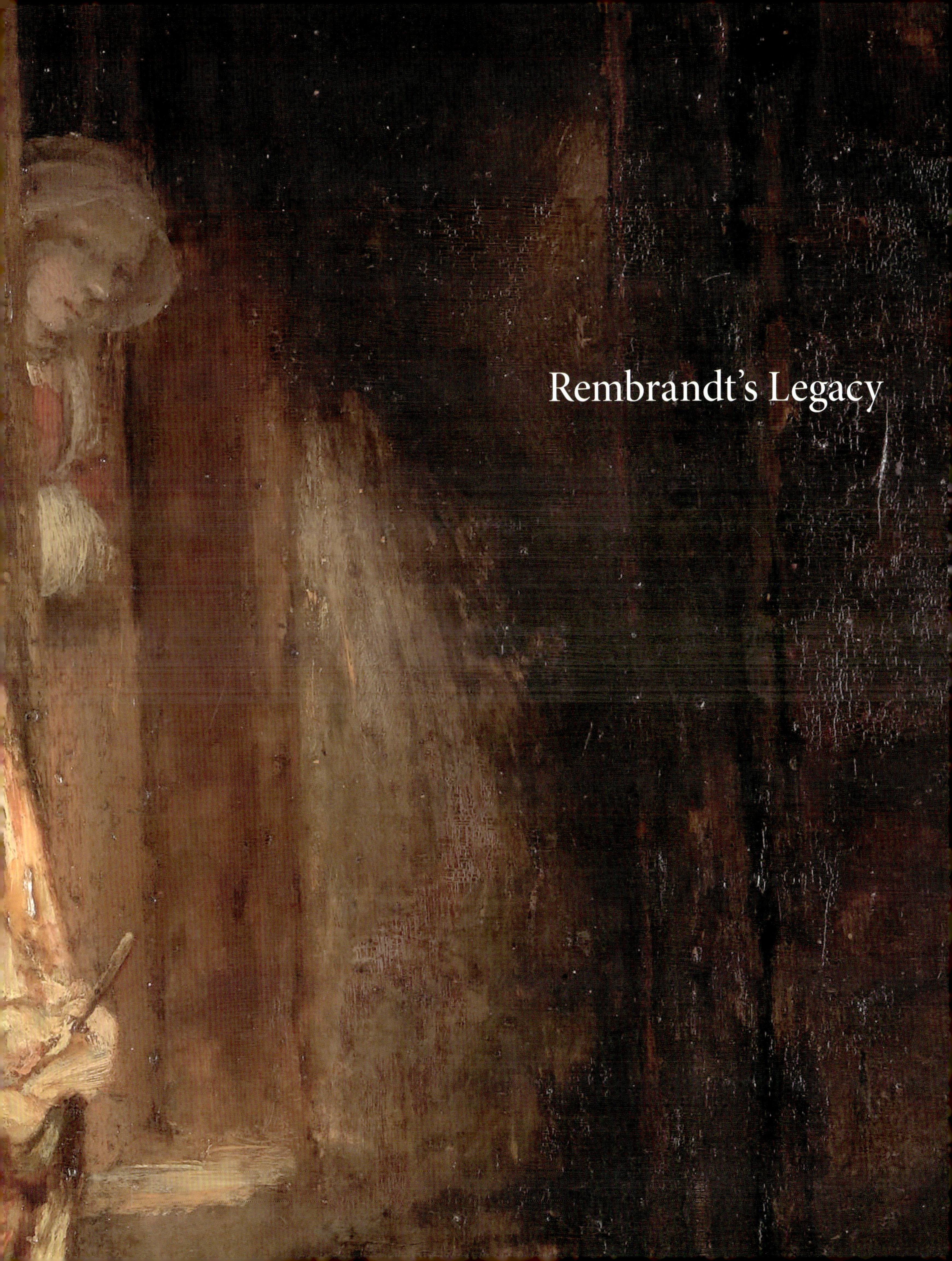

Rembrandt's Legacy

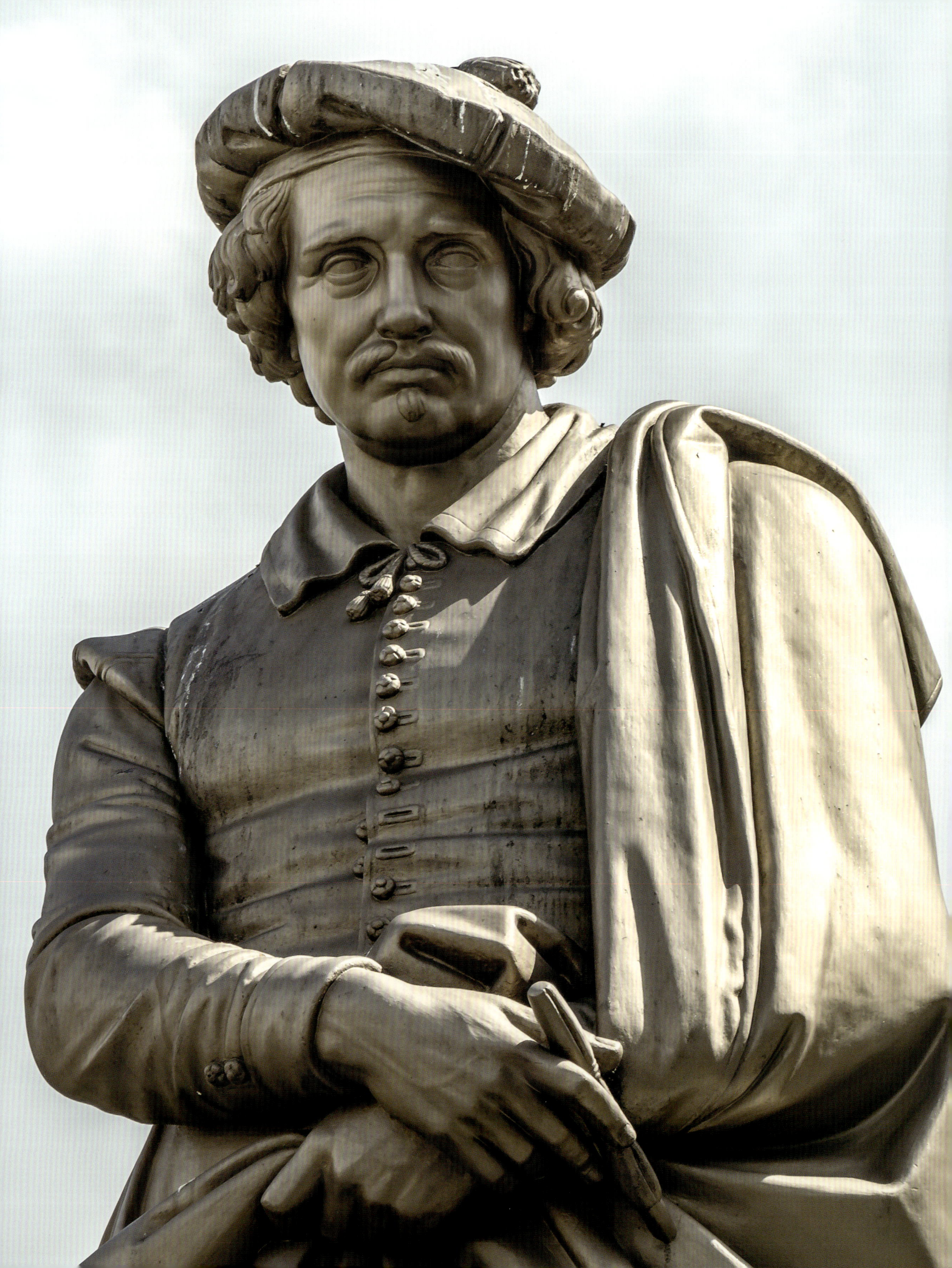

JAN BLANC

Why Rembrandt?

> For in the end, fame is no more than the sum of all the misunderstandings that gather around a new name.
>
> – Rainer Maria Rilke, *Auguste Rodin*, 1903[1]

There is something unfair about Rembrandt's fame. As he built his career, he was surrounded by brilliant colleagues, rivals and students – so why was his the only name to reverberate throughout Europe? And how did his name manage to survive the vicissitudes of time to become that of one of the world's most renowned artists?[2] To answer these questions it is not enough to simply cite the artist's "genius" or to evoke, like Rilke, the mysteries of a celebrity or a legacy that are ultimately inexplicable. Rembrandt's achievements, as demonstrated here, owe nothing to chance. The success of an oeuvre, both during its creator's lifetime and posthumously, is always a collective construction, and, as I hope to show, the reputation the master enjoyed from the very start of his career was to a large degree the result of strategies that he himself skilfully deployed to promote his name and works.

The Construction of an Image

Around February or March 1631, Constantijn Huygens noted in his journal his meeting with two young painters who were then sharing a studio in Leiden: Jan Lievens and Rembrandt van Rijn. Huygens compared the artists' abilities, judging Rembrandt's freedom of touch and talent for portraying emotions to be quite astounding, while declaring the originality of Lievens' subjects and ideas to be superior.

The two artists seemed to be working at the same level. Yet, it was Rembrandt, older by a year, who captured the attention of the poet and diplomat, and he did not hesitate to compare the young Dutchman to the greatest painters of antiquity: "I maintain that it did not occur to Protogenes, Apelles or Parrhasius, nor could it occur to them, were they to return to earth, that a youth, a Dutchman, a beardless miller, could put so much into one human figure and depict it all."[3] Half a century later, Joachim von Sandrart, who had almost certainly met Rembrandt and Lievens in person, expressed similar astonishment that a miller's son, a child of the Leiden countryside, could have succeeded in reaching the summit of European art.[4]

These accolades are not entirely to be trusted, for Huygens and Sandrart seem to have been unaware that Rembrandt's social and family background was actually quite prosperous, and that before embarking on his apprenticeship he had attended the Latin school in Leiden, and later Leiden University. The young painter appears to have mischievously suppressed these details, probably to give a pattern to his life that echoed that of the most celebrated Renaissance artists, often described in the legendary chronicles of Giorgio Vasari and Karel van Mander as coming from modest rural backgrounds, their natural talents emerging spontaneously, first in the solitude of early youth and later in their master's studio.[5]

The accounts that succeeded one another throughout the seventeenth century seemed to confirm the scenario concocted by Rembrandt himself. But the art theorist Filippo Baldinucci, who knew the painter only through his works, would be the first to speak of "Rembrandt's extravagance of manner," which, the writer explained, "was entirely commensurate with his mode of living, since he was a most temperamental man and despised everyone."[6] Later, the painter Jean-Baptiste Descamps would maintain that Rembrandt "associated only with the lower orders and people far beneath him."[7] How could these authors have imagined that Rembrandt, who at the height of his career was the most sought-after portraitist in Amsterdam, lived among beggars and paupers? It was possibly because the artist was fond of portraying such figures as extras in his paintings and of making them the subject of prints, even occasionally assuming their identity. He may have done this to set himself apart from rivals who were pursuing fame and riches, but also, with more than a touch of irony, to attract the attention of potential patrons.[8]

Rembrandt saw himself as a free man and was eager to broadcast the fact, both through his works and his declarations. Although the painter Arnold Houbraken and the playwright Andries Pels deplored the liberties Rembrandt took, seeing them as a form of libertinism, they were the first to recognize the master's unique place in the history of Dutch art, which he dominated by defending and illustrating his own freedom. "When I wish to rest my mind," Houbraken reported the artist as saying, "it is not honour that I seek, but freedom."[9] It was this freedom that distinguished Rembrandt from his peers, including Lievens, and from former pupils who sought initially to emulate him, such as Govert Flinck. But it was this same freedom that, as Sandrart noted with grudging admiration, enabled him to boldly flout the conventions of his art: "Accordingly, he would remain faithful to his habit of never hesitating to contravene the rules of art."[10]

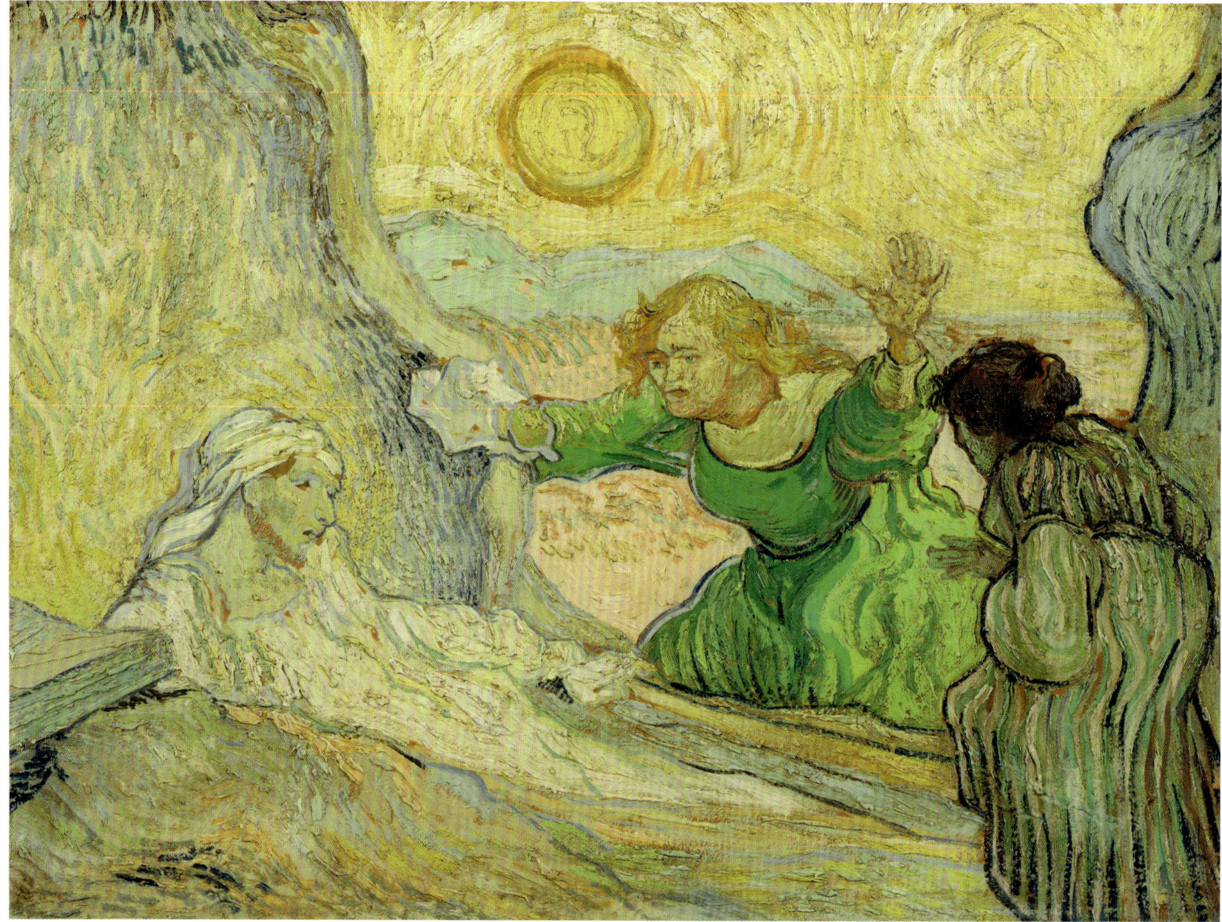

fig. 18.1 **Vincent van Gogh (after Rembrandt van Rijn)**, *The Raising of Lazarus*, 1890, oil on paper; 50 × 65.5 cm. Van Gogh Museum, Amsterdam. Vincent van Gogh Foundation (S0169V1962)

Artistic and Political Heroization

Early in the eighteenth century, a new myth was added to the image constructed by Rembrandt himself – that of the stubborn and visionary genius.[11] In the view of the French art theorist Roger de Piles, "every line etched by the needle, like every brushstroke of his painting, lends the parts of the face a quality of life and truth that prompts admiration of his *genius*."[12] Rembrandt's achievements began to be compared to those of Shakespeare.[13] If Rembrandt committed an error, explained the critic Pierre-Jean-Baptiste Chaussard, "he made it sublime," for he was a member of that elite of geniuses who knew how to "sin against art with art."[14] During the Romantic period, the myth escalated. In a play devoted to the Dutch artist published in 1800, he is portrayed – inaccurately, but in line with the growing mythologization of the modern genius, who must be damned before achieving recognition – as an artist who "during his life suffered every misfortune ... constantly exposed to the injustices of his contemporaries."[15] Along with Raphael and Rubens, Rembrandt was now one of the "true saints" (*wahre Heilige*) worshipped by Johann Wolfgang von Goethe.[16] He was a "Dutch sorcerer," a "painter of miracles," a "wizard" (*Zauberer*),[17] but also "the least classical and most romantic of all painters."[18]

During the 1830s, attitudes toward Rembrandt began to shift, and he became an icon of realism and anti-academicism. Théophile Thoré-Bürger contrasted him with Raphael, as he contrasted Eugène Delacroix with Jean-Auguste-Dominique Ingres.[19] A painter "of man for man," Rembrandt offered young realist artists some hope of posterity:

> For the past two centuries those who value nothing but the grand Italian style have always dealt harshly with Rembrandt, which has not prevented him from making his way into the museums and leading galleries of Europe. This should console the *realists* somewhat for current injustices, and give them a little hope for the future.[20]

Almost a year before he came up with a highly personal new interpretation of Rembrandt's *Raising of Lazarus* (figs. 18.1, 18.2), Vincent van Gogh also expressed a sense of a shared destiny with his Dutch compatriot, "alone or almost alone ... among painters" to have captured "that heartbroken tenderness, that glimpse of a superhuman infinite which appears

so natural."[21] The Old Master had become a new "painter of modern life."[22] When in the early 1950s the novelist Jean Genet saw the "two portraits of Madame Trip" (fig. 18.3) at London's National Gallery – "these two old women's heads that are decomposing, that are putrefying before our very eyes, that are painted with enormous love" – he in turn recognized Rembrandt as a kindred spirit for whom "decay is no longer considered outlandish but as worthy of love as anything else."[23] A few years later, in *Figure with Meat* (fig. 18.5),[24] Francis Bacon would express his admiration for the decomposing flesh of *The Slaughtered Ox* (fig. 18.4) and how the master's self-portraits captured the passage of time: "The way in which it's always Rembrandt that you see, in an image which changes each time, it's really astonishing, magnificent."[25]

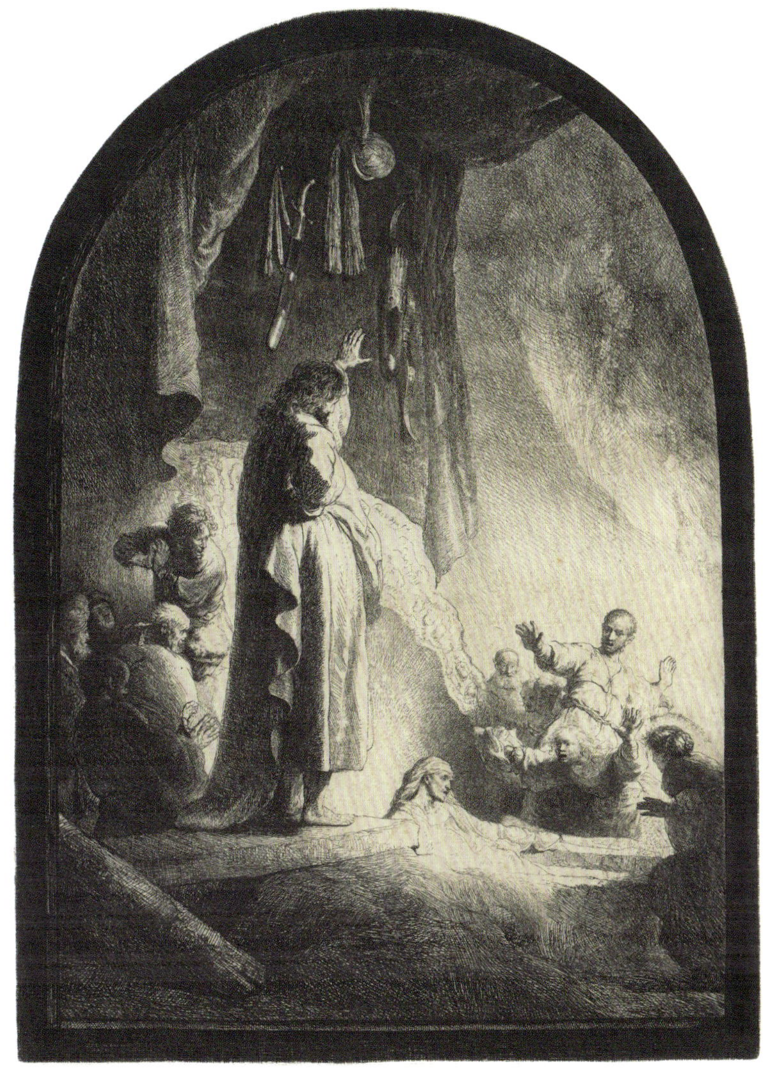

fig. 18.2 **Rembrandt van Rijn,** *The Raising of Lazarus*, 1630–34, etching on laid paper; 36.5 × 25.6 cm. Rijksmuseum, Amsterdam (RP-P-OB-596)

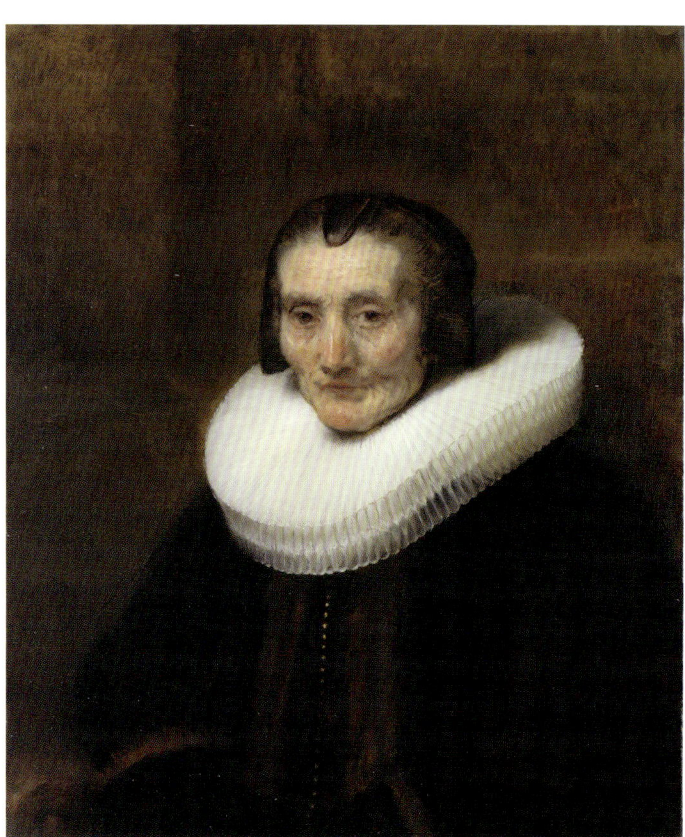

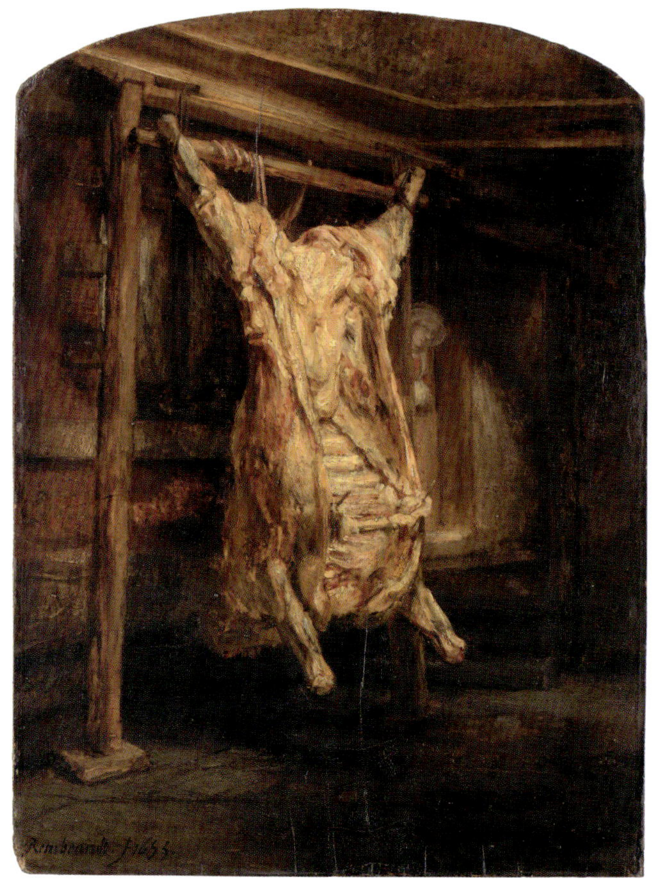

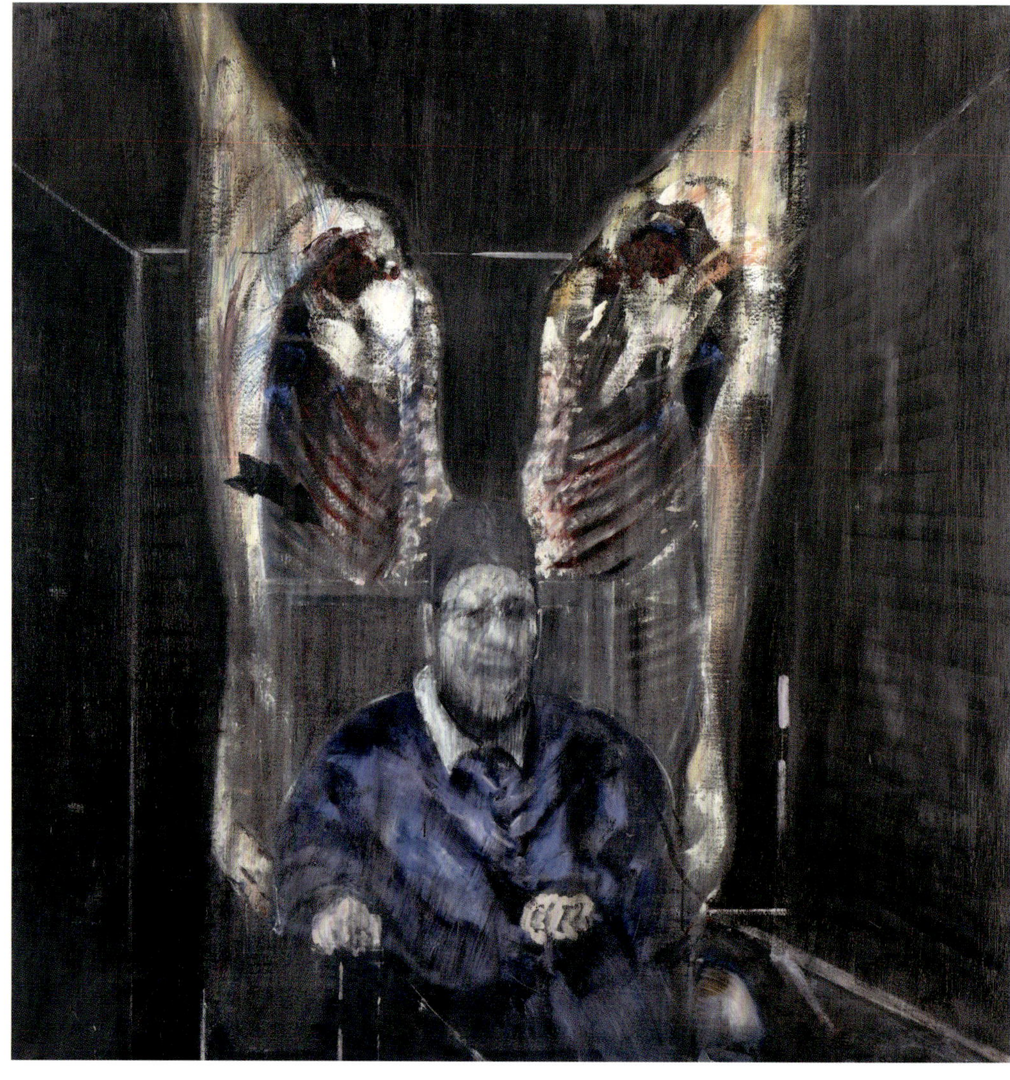

fig. 18.3 Rembrandt van Rijn,
*Portrait of Margaretha de Geer,
Wife of Jacob Trip*, 1661, oil on
canvas; 75.3 × 63.8 cm.
The National Gallery, London.
Presented by the Art Fund, 1941
(NG5282)

fig. 18.4 Rembrandt van Rijn,
The Slaughtered Ox, 1655,
oil on panel; 94 × 69 cm.
Musée du Louvre, Paris
(M.I.169)

fig. 18.5 Francis Bacon, *Figure
with Meat*, 1954, oil on canvas;
129.2 × 121.9 cm. The Art
Institute of Chicago. Harriet A.
Fox Fund (1956.1201)

The heroization of Rembrandt was political as well as artistic. After the creation of the United Kingdom of the Netherlands (1815) and the secession of its southern provinces following the Belgian Revolution (1830), Rembrandt became a veritable national hero whose love of freedom was identified with that of his "people," at last emancipated from the successive jurisdictions of revolutionary and imperial France. Twelve years after the statue of Peter Paul Rubens by Guillaume Geefs was erected on Antwerp's Groenplaats in August 1840, the Dutch performed a similar act of artistic patriotism with the unveiling on 27 May 1852 of the portrait of Rembrandt by Louis Royer (fig. 18.6), originally installed on the Kaasplein in Amsterdam. This early political appropriation of Rembrandt would lead to two other forms of distortion. The first was nationalist. According to the German art historian Carl Neumann, Rembrandt's life and work were symptoms of the "hypertrophic savagery," "burlesque humour," "devilish imagination" and "anti-academic barbarism" that characterize "all the medieval Northernness" that had "re-emerged for the umpteenth time" in his work.[26] Wilhelm von Bode, a leading expert on the artist, also maintained that Rembrandt was "the product of a purely Germanic background," a thesis that reappears in the writings of the racist and anti-Semitic ideologue Julius Langbehn.[27] The second distortion, older and more lasting, makes Rembrandt into a hero of Republicanism. He is portrayed as "the highest expression" of "Batavian genius," who developed independently "under the protection of a people's government" and the "republican model."[28] Rembrandt is seen as a true revolutionary, born of the "people," "among victors and free men," the "Luther of painting" who belonged "to the Third Estate, and barely to that, as they would have said in France in 1789."[29]

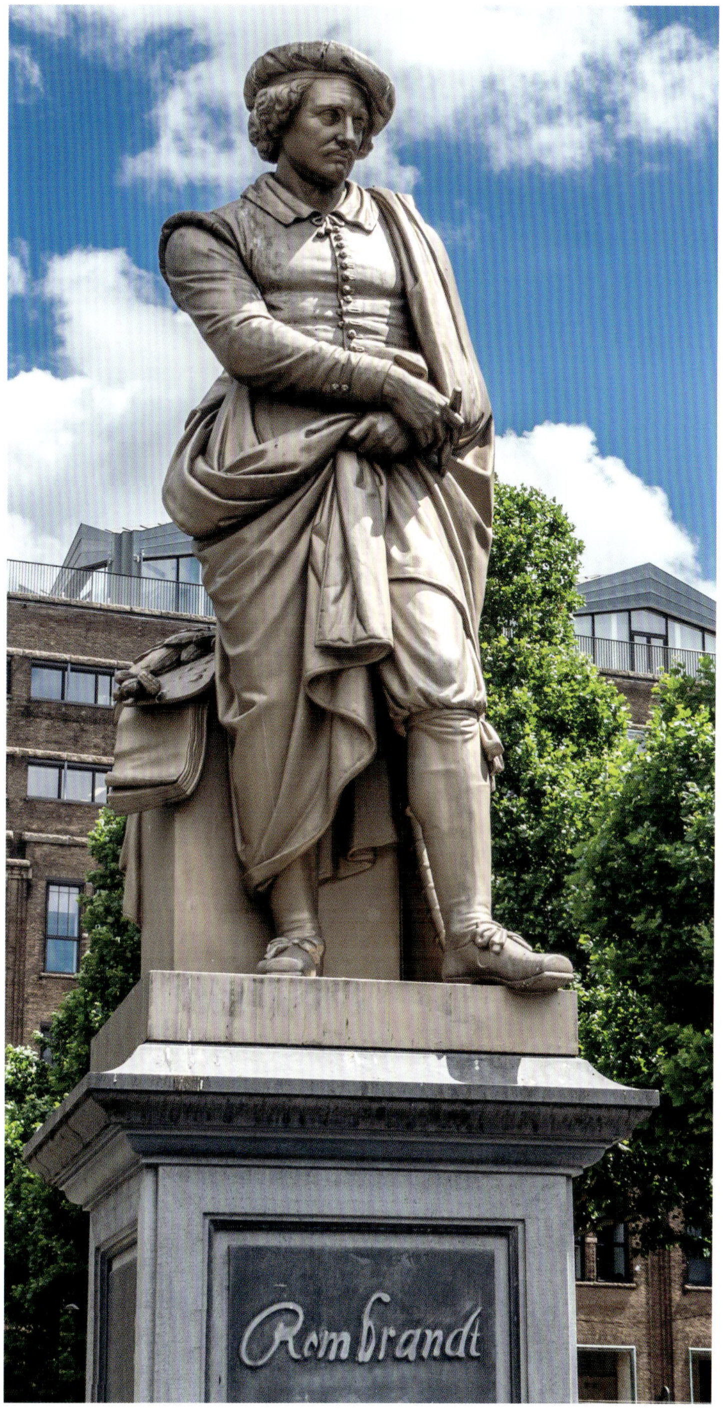

A Cultural Symbol

By the end of the nineteenth century, Rembrandt's art was being discussed not just for what it was but also for what it represented or embodied: it became a "cultural symbol."[30] When the first "catalogue raisonné" was published in 1751, based on notes that the *marchand-mercier* Edme-François Gersaint had put together on the subject of Rembrandt's etchings, the idea was to appeal to "lovers of the fine arts." The aim, according to the publishers, was "helping them

research the pieces of interest to them" – in other words, facilitating the assessments of dealers and collectors by enabling them to estimate the fair value of the master's prints.[31] Thus did Rembrandt become part of the history of connoisseurship and art dealing.[32] His illustrious name would henceforth frequently be the focus of controversies concerning attributions, disattributions and appraisals of his works. Newssheets were constantly reporting the

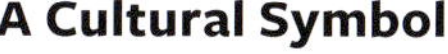

fig. 18.6 **Louis Royer,**
Rembrandt van Rijn, 1852,
cast iron; 816 cm (height).
Rembrandtsplein, Amsterdam

appearance on the market of some "new Rembrandt" or other. When the Flemish painter Pierre Joseph Lafontaine purchased *Christ and the Woman Taken in Adultery* (see fig. 9.2) in 1803, and subsequently exhibited it in Paris, there was much excited comment in the French press, not about the work itself but about the identity of its author: was the painting by Rembrandt or Rubens?[33] The same showcasing of the activities of art experts and historians dominated early catalogues devoted to Rembrandt's painted oeuvre. Those written by the first great Rembrandt specialists – Carel Vosmaer, Wilhelm von Bode, Wilhelm Valentiner, Cornelis Hofstede de Groot, Abraham Bredius and Horst Gerson – played a crucial

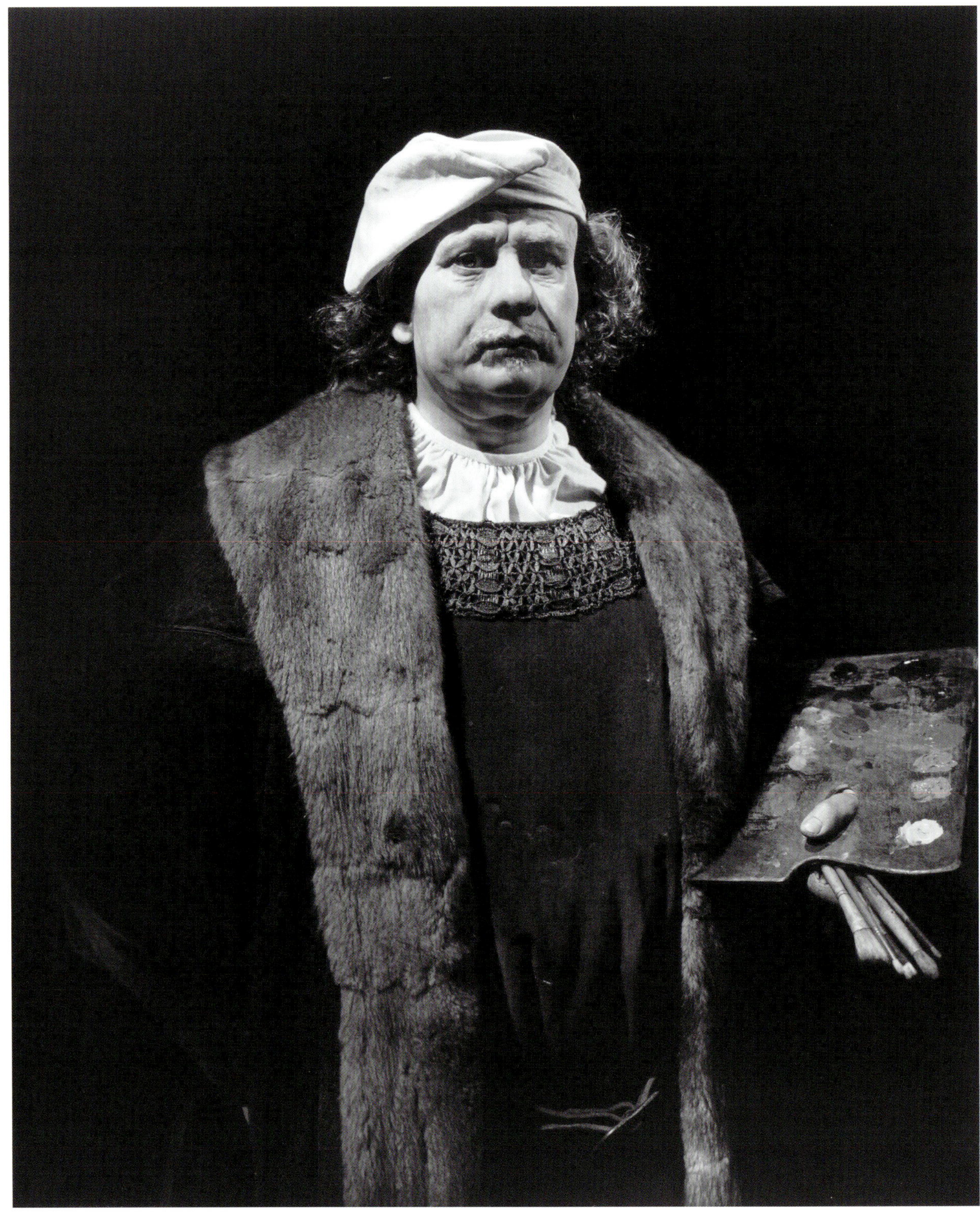

fig. 18.7 Hiroshi Sugimoto, *Rembrandt van Rijn*, 1999, gelatin silver print; 148.6 × 118.7 cm. Solomon R. Guggenheim Museum, New York. Commissioned by Deutsche Bank AG in consultation with the Solomon R. Guggenheim Foundation for the Deutsche Guggenheim, Berlin (2005.103)

role in how the artist's work and that of his emulators was received. But what lingers in the collective memory above all are the quarrels between different schools of thought and the methodological conflicts that accompanied them. This includes arguments provoked by a radical reduction in the mid-twentieth century of the corpus of autograph Rembrandt paintings and by early findings of the Rembrandt Research Project, between 1968 and 1989, which resulted in the sometimes controversial disattribution of a number of works previously considered iconic.[34]

These disputes have had two outcomes. For some, the successive mistakes and oversights of connoisseurs, likely to confuse Rembrandt's work with that of his pupils, have had the effect of desacralizing the Dutch painter by demonstrating that the artists he trained, or who drew inspiration from his works, were capable of rivalling him and thereby of confounding even the greatest experts.[35] This desanctification is evident in different forms of commercial exploitation of the artist's name or image, ranging from simple postcard reproductions of his works to Rembrandt® toothpaste – an example of what is known today as "artketing."[36] But it is also manifested more subtly, as with the recent project called *The Next Rembrandt* (2016), in which a machine with artificial intelligence was fed a vast amount of iconographical, formal and technical data characterizing the master's art, and

was tasked with creating and 3-D printing a new "Rembrandt" painting.[37]

There are those, however, who have come to renounce the marketing of Rembrandt, now virtually a brand. In 1956 and 1969 the two major Rembrandt retrospectives held to celebrate the 350th anniversary of his birth and the 300th anniversary of his death triggered public protests from numerous artists concerning the economic exploitation of the Dutch painter. In the name of the "freedom" that Rembrandt himself had defended throughout his life, they were calling for enhanced recognition of their profession, but also – like Hiroshi Sugimoto, who in photographing the wax figure of Rembrandt on view at Madame Tussauds purposefully reproduced a reproduction (fig. 18.7) – criticizing the cultural industry's appropriation of the artist's name and art, which they felt was contributing to the fossilization or (in Adornian terms) fetishization of his image.[38] For admirers of this type, the "cult of Rembrandt" (*Rembrandt-Kultus*), the "veneration" (*verering*) that originated in the nineteenth century must be protected at all costs,[39] even if it means fortifying it with a gloss of scholarly justification, by utilizing the notions of "quality" and "genius" to highlight the inimitable and unique character of his art,[40] or by employing the resources of literary or cinematic fiction to reinvent his life and work.[41]

fig. 18.8 **Andres Serrano,** *Black Rembrandt,* **1991, Cibachrome print mounted on aluminum, in three parts; 39.4 × 30.2 cm. Private collection**

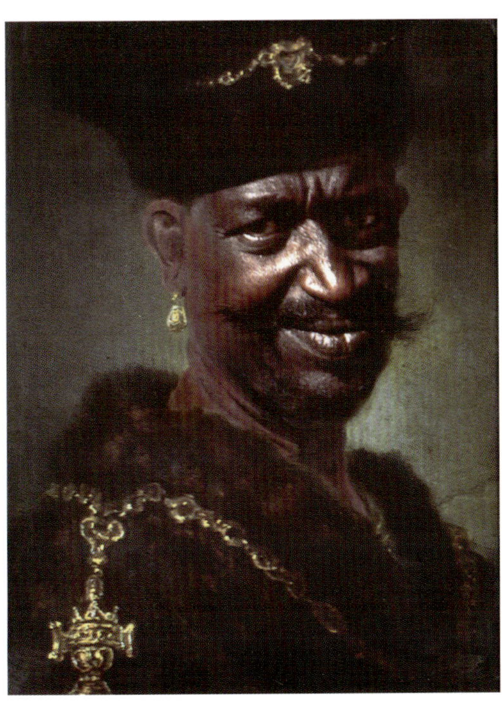
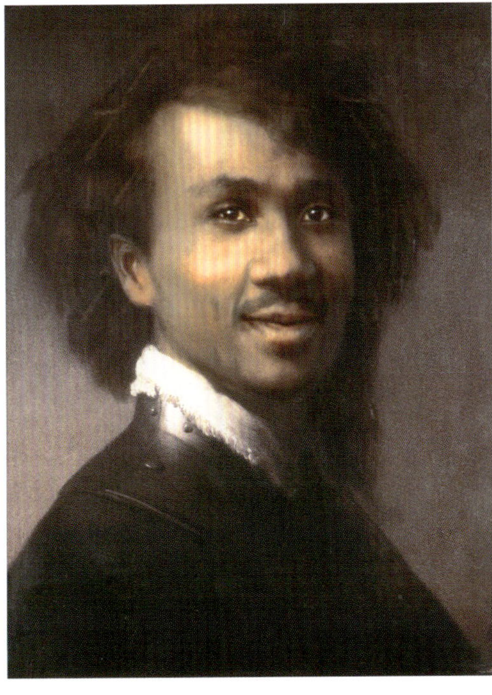
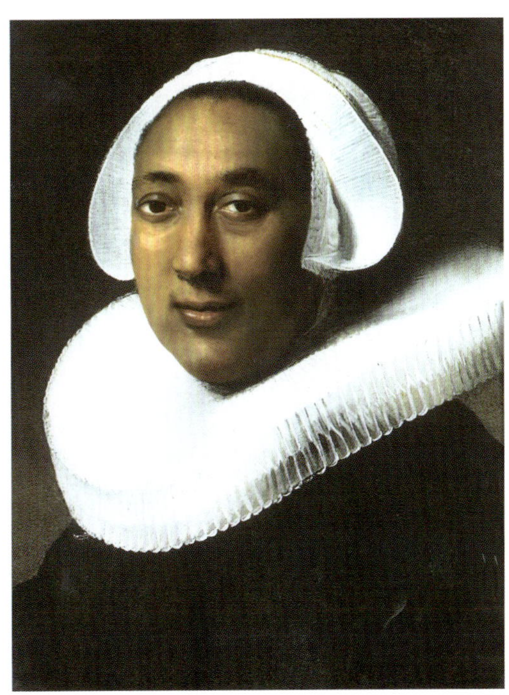

In his *Essays* (1580), Michel de Montaigne attempted to explain his friendship with Étienne de La Boétie, writing these famous words: "If you press me to tell you why I loved him, I feel that this cannot be expressed, except by answering: Because it was he, because it was I."[42] As we ponder the reasons for Rembrandt's enduring legacy, perhaps we also should respond: because it was he, because it was we.

Because it was he: for it is to Rembrandt himself and to the narratives surrounding his name and image that were developed during his lifetime that the painter owes his extraordinary fame, which far surpasses that of contemporaries less concerned about earning renown and admiration by making themselves the subjects of their art. Rembrandt's works thus offer access not to his private personality but rather to the ideal and tactical construction that he chose to present – what sociologists would call his social and artistic *ethos*.

Because it was we: for if Rembrandt has exerted such fascination since the early 1630s it is undoubtedly because his first admirers and spectators chose not only to believe the personal fictions he invented for them but also to recognize themselves in them, as in mirrors held up for the purpose. And this attitude to the Dutch master's work is still current today. When in 1991 the American photographer Andres Serrano, of Cuban and Honduran descent, reimagined three portraits by Rembrandt by making the models people of colour (fig. 18.8), it was clearly not to mock or ridicule them in an unseemly instance of blackface. The principal aim was to pay glowing tribute to a painter Serrano had admired since his childhood visits to the Metropolitan Museum of Art.[43] But he also wished to remind us of the world in which Rembrandt lived and of the cost of building the Dutch "Golden Age," which involved the marginalization of the poor, the incarceration of the mentally ill and the imprisonment of atheists, and which saw hundreds of thousands of slaves torn from their African homes. Unlike most of his contemporaries, the Dutch master sought to reflect these shameful and tragic realities in his art (see fig. 2.2), daring to bear witness to a complex world by portraying himself and forcing us – as Serrano does now – "to look squarely at what we tend today, increasingly, to avoid, to deny knowledge of, to refuse to contemplate."[44] ■

NOTES

1   Rainer Maria Rilke, "The Poet's Tribute to the Great Sculptor," in *Auguste Rodin*, trans. Victoria Charles (London: Parkstone Press International, 2011), 7.

2   Among the many publications to explore the critical reception of Rembrandt's work, see esp. Slive 1988; Scheller 1961, 81–118; Białostocki 1972, 131–157.

3   Huygens 1897, 79; trans. from Leiden 1991, 133.

4   Sandrart 1675–80, vol. 2, book 3, 326.

5   Kris and Kurz 2010.

6   Baldinucci 1686, 79; trans. from Ford 2007, 58.

7   Descamps 1753–64, vol. 2, 89.

8   Dickey 2013.

9   Houbraken 1718–21, vol. 1, 272–273. See also Pels 1978, 77.

10 Sandrart 1675–80, vol. 2, book 3, 326.

11 Evert van Uitert, "Rembrandts roem: hoe hij werd opgenomen in de kring van de grootste Geniën aller tijde," in Rijnders and Rutgers 2014, 135–169, 149–150.

12 De Piles 1699, 437.

13 Brom 1936, 169.

14 Pierre-Jean-Baptiste Chaussard, "Beaux-Arts. Exposition des ouvrages de peinture, sculpture, architecture, gravure dans les salles du Muséum," in *Décade* 1798, 468.

15 Étienne et al. 1800, 3.

16 Johann Wolfgang von Goethe, *Nach Falconet und über Falconet*, 1776, in Goethe 1975, 146.

17 Michelet 1876, vol. 14, 373–374; Verhaeren 1904, 8; Bode 1907, 15.

18 Hazlitt 1930–34, vol. 18, 123.

19 Thoré-Bürger 1870, vol. 2, 69 (Salon de 1864).

20 Thoré-Bürger 1870, vol. 1, 98 (Salon de 1861). The emphasis is Thoré-Bürger's.

21 Vincent van Gogh, letter to Theo van Gogh, 2 July 1889, *Vincent van Gogh: The Letters*, Van Gogh Museum, http://vangoghletters.org/vg/letters/let784/letter.html (accessed 9 Jan. 2020); Blanc 2017, 290. In analyzing the painting of Lazarus, Van Gogh made use of a heliogravure executed by Charles Amand-Durand after the fifth state of Rembrandt's original etching (1630), then part of the Dutuit Collection and published in the series *Eaux-fortes et gravures des maîtres anciens* (ibid., 343). On the relationship between Van Gogh and Rembrandt, see Hecht 2006.

22 On Rembrandt's place in modern and contemporary art, see Stückelberger 1996.

23 Genet 1979, 32. As well as the three-quarter portrait reproduced here, Genet saw another portrait of Margaretha de Geer, a frontal view painted around 1661 as a pendant to the one of her extremely wealthy husband, Jacob Trip (c. 1661, The National Gallery, London).

24 As well as paying tribute to *The Slaughtered Ox*, this work makes clear reference to the portrait of Pope Innocent X painted in 1650 by Diego Velázquez (Galleria Doria Pamphilj, Rome).

25 Bacon and Archimbaud 1993, 38.

26 Neumann 1902, 655.

27 Bode 1907, 5. See also Langbehn 1926, 48. This view was probably a response to the now-contested theories of Eduard Kolloff, one of the first art historians to claim that Rembrandt maintained close friendships with several leading members of Amsterdam's Jewish community; Zell 2000–01, 181–197.

28 Blanc 1883, vol. 1, 15–16, 20, 19.

29 Taine 1869, 165; Thoré-Bürger 1860, vol. 1, 321; Proudhon 1865, 85; Fromentin 1984, 776–777.

30 Robert W. Scheller, "Rembrandt als Kultursymbol," in Kelch and Von Simson 1973, 221–234.

31 Gersaint 1751, v–vi.

32 Alpers 1991, 14.

33 Van der Tuin 1948, 152. The painting was bought as a Rembrandt by John Julius Angerstein in 1807 and entered the collection of the National Gallery, London, in 1824.

34 On the turbulent history of the Rembrandt Research Project, which is currently under the direction of Ernst van de Wetering, see Bruin 1995, 100–105, and, for a broader view, Scallen 2004.

35 Gary Schwartz, "The Clones Make the Master: Rembrandt in 1650," in Albrecht and Imesch 2001, 53–64.

36 Christophe Rioux, "Le luxe et l'art : du marketing à l'*artketing*," in Assouly 2004, 331–352.

37 www.nextrembrandt.com. This "new work," created jointly by a team drawn from Microsoft, the Rembrandt House Museum in Amsterdam, the Mauritshuis in The Hague and the Technische Universiteit in Delft, was based on the digitization and interpolation of 346 paintings securely attributed to Rembrandt.

38 Chalard-Fillaudeau 2004, 219.

39 On the modern cult of Rembrandt, see McQueen 2003, 7–9.

40 Ernst van de Wetering, "On Quality: Comparative Remarks on the Functioning of Rembrandt's Pictorial Mind," in *Corpus*, vol. 5, 283–310.

41 Notable among the many novels and plays devoted to Rembrandt published during the twentieth century are *Crucial Instances* (1901) by Edith Wharton; *Rembrandt vor Gericht: eine romantische Komödie in vier Akten* (1933) by Hans Kyser; *Rembrandt van Rijn: The Life and Times of Rembrandt van Rijn* (1930) by Hendrik van Loon; *Rembrandt* (1961) by Gladys Schmitt; *Ferienreise mit Rembrandt* (1970) by Lothar Freund; *Rembrandt's Hat* (1973) by Bernard Malamud; *The Rembrandt Panel: A Novel* (1980) by Oliver T. Banks; and *Rembrandt till sin dotter* (1998) by Agne Erkelius. There have also been numerous films, including *Rembrandt* (1936, dir. Alexander Korda); *Rembrandt* (1940, dir. Gerard Rutten); *Rembrandt* (1942, dir. Hans Steinhoff); *Rembrandt fecit 1669* (1977, dir. Jos Stelling); *La Ronde de nuit* (1978, dir. Gabriel Axel); *Rembrandt* (1999, dir. Charles Matton); and *Nightwatching* (2007, dir. Peter Greenaway).

42 Michel de Montaigne, *Les Essais*, ed. Jean Céard (Paris: Le Livre de Poche, 2001 [1595]), vol. 1, chap. 28, 15; trans. from Donald M. Frame, *The Complete Essays of Montaigne* (Stanford, CA: Stanford University Press, 1958), 139.

43 Arasse 2006, 40.

44 Ibid., 33.

TIMELINE: REMBRANDT'S CREATIVE COMMUNITY IN AMSTERDAM

	1605	1610	1615	1620	1625	1630	1635	1640	1645

1600
Amsterdam has c. 50,000 inhabitants

1602
Founding of VOC (Dutch East India Company)

1609
VOC founds colony of Batavia on island of Java

1609–21
Twelve Years' Truce between the Netherlands and Spain

1621
Founding of WIC (Dutch West India Company)

1625
Frederik Hendrik of Orange becomes stadtholder

1626
Pieter Minuit buys island of Manhattan for Dutch colony of New Netherland (ceded to England in 1674)

1630
WIC establishes colony in Brazil (ceded to Portugal in 1654)

1637
Tulip speculation and market crash

1638
Visit of Marie de' Medici to Amsterdam

1642
VOC captain Abel Tasman Tasmania and New Zealand

Pieter Lastman (Amsterdam 1583–1633)

1617–19
Teacher of Jan Lievens

1624/25
Teacher of Rembrandt

Jan Lievens (Leiden 1607–1674 Amsterdam)

1617–19
Apprenticeship with Pieter Lastman

1625–31
Association with Rembrandt in Leiden

1632–34
Active in London

1635–44
Active in Antwerp; joins Guild of Saint Luke in 1635

1644–74
Travels to The H Berlin, Cleves ar

Jacob Backer (Harlingen 1608–1651 Amsterdam)

c. 1620–26
Possibly pupil of Jan Pynas

c. 1627–32
Apprenticeship with Lambert Jacobsz in Leeuwarden

Salomon Koninck (Amsterdam 1609–1656)

1621–30
Pupil of David Colijns, François Venant and Claes Moeyaert

1630
Member of Guild of Saint Luke

Jan Asselijn (Dieppe c. 1610–1652 Amsterdam)

1635–47
Travels in France and Italy

Thomas de Keyser (Amsterdam c. 1596–1667)

c. 1624
Possibly pupil of Cornelis van der Voort

REMBRANDT VAN RIJN (Leiden 1606–1669 Amsterdam)

1622–24
Pupil of Jacob van Swanenburg in Leiden

1624–25
Apprenticeship (six months) with Pieter Lastman

1632
Lodging with Hendrick Uylenburgh

1633
First self-portrait with signature "Rembrandt"

1634
Marriage to Saskia van Uylenburgh; joins Guild of Saint Luke

1635
Resides on Nieuwe Doelenstraat

1637
Resides on Binnen-Amstel

1639
Purchases house on St. Anthonisbreestraa

1642
Death of Saskia

Nicolaes Eliasz Pickenoy (Amsterdam 1588–1650/56)

1629
Member of Guild of Saint Luke

Dirck van Santvoort (Amsterdam 1609–1680)

c. 1630
Probably assistant in Hendrick Uylenburgh's workshop

Govert Flinck (Cleves 1615–1660 Amsterdam)

1630–34
Apprenticeship with Lambert Jacobsz in Leeuwarden

1634–35
Apprenticeship with Rembrandt in Hendrick Uylenburgh's workshop

1635–44
Workshop manager for Uylenburgh

Gerbrand van den Eeckhout (Amsterdam 1621–1674)

Bartholomeus van der Helst (Haarlem c. 1613–1670 Amsterdam)

1635–36
Possibly pupil of Nicolaes Eliasz Pickenoy

Ferdinand Bol (Dordrecht 1616–1680 Amsterdam)

1636–40
Assistant in Rembrandt's workshop

Joachim von Sandrart (Frankfurt am Main 1606–1688 Nuremberg)

1627
Pupil of Gerard van Honthorst in Utrecht

1628
Travels with Honthorst to London

1629–35
Active in Rome

1635–37
Active in Frankfurt

1645
Returns to Germany

Jan Victors (Amsterdam 1619–1676/77 Dutch East Indies)

Philips Koninck (Amsterdam 1619–1688)

1637–40
Pupil of his brother Jacob in Rotterdam

1641
Marries Cornelia Furnerius, sister Rembrandt's pupil Abraham Furn

Jacob van Loo (Sluis 1614–1670 Paris)

1635
Receives commission for ten paintings from Marten Kretzer in Amst

Carel Fabritius (Middenbeemster 1622–1654 Delft)

1642–43
Pupil of Rembrandt

Samuel van Hoogstraten (Dordrecht 1627–1678)

c. 1642–48
Pupil of Rembrandt

Barent Fabritius (Middenbeemster 1624–1673 Amsterdam)

Nicolaes Maes (Dordrecht 1634–1693 Amsterdam)

1646/
Pupil Remb

Willem Drost (Amsterdam 1633–1659 Venice)

Active in Amsterdam

1650 1655 1660 1665 1670 1675 1680 1685 1690

1650
Amsterdam has
c. 200,000 inhabitants

1655
Dedication of Amsterdam Town Hall

1663–64
Plague epidemic

1672–74
Third Anglo-Dutch War

1652
Old Amsterdam Town Hall destroyed by fire

1665–67
Second Anglo-Dutch War

1652–54
First Anglo-Dutch War

1653
First Saint Luke's Day Banquet honouring "Union of Apelles and Apollo"

[Peace of Münster, establishing independent Dutch Republic]

1652
Registers as citizen of Amsterdam

1656
Bankruptcy

1669
Death on 4 October; burial in Westerkerk on 8 October

1658
Sale of house and remainder of possessions;
moves to rented house on Rozengracht

1658
Headman of Guild of Saint Luke

1649
Independent
workshop on
Lauriergracht

1652
Registers as citizen of Amsterdam

1652
Registers as citizen of Amsterdam

1676
Departs for the East Indies

1652
Registers as citizen of Amsterdam

1650–54
Active in Delft

1657–61
Active in Leiden; joins Guild of Saint Luke in 1658

1653–73
Active in Dordrecht

1688
Joins Guild of
Saint Luke

1648–52
[Pupil] of Rembrandt

1655–59
Travels to Rome and Venice

References   Allgemeines Künstlerlexikon; Amsterdam 2017–18; Amsterdam 2019; Büttner 2014; Cologne and Prague 2019–20; ECARTICO; Grove Art Online; Frankfurt 2003a; Leiden and Oxford 2019–20; North 1999; RKD Database; Sluijter 2015. Compiled by Friederike Schütt. With thanks to Kambis Zahedi, Rebekka Hoummady, Samuel Fickinger and Leslie P. Zimmermann for their assistance.

LIST OF WORKS

Unless otherwise stated, all works are exhibited at the
National Gallery of Canada, Ottawa, and Städel Museum, Frankfurt am Main.

All dimensions are height × width.

Jan Asselijn
c. 1610–1652

The Tiber River with the Ponte Molle at Sunset c. 1650
oil on canvas
41.2 × 54 cm
National Gallery of Art, Washington
Florian Carr Fund, New Century Fund, and Nell
and Robert Weidenhammer Fund (2012.129.1)
plate 134

Jacob Backer
1608–1651

Portrait of a Man (Jan Pietersz van den Eeckhout?)
1632–33
oil on canvas
66.6 × 59.6 cm
Private collection
Frankfurt only
plate 51

The Drinker (Allegory of Taste) c. 1634
oil on panel
71.5 × 60 cm
Staatliche Museen zu Berlin, Gemäldegalerie
(935A)
Frankfurt only
plate 37

Portrait of a Woman with a White Cap c. 1634
oil on panel
45 × 35.5 cm
The Kremer Collection, Amsterdam
Frankfurt only
plate 52

Portrait of a Young Woman c. 1638
oil on canvas
127 × 102.2 cm
Los Angeles County Museum of Art
William Randolph Hearst Collection (50.28.1)
plate 69

Portrait of a Woman c. 1647
oil on canvas
95.3 × 74.9 cm
The J. Paul Getty Museum, Los Angeles (71.PA.18)
Ottawa only
plate 90

Gerrit Adriaensz Berckheyde
1638–1698

The Town Hall in Amsterdam c. 1674
oil on canvas
62.8 × 53.7 cm
Städel Museum, Frankfurt am Main (1051)
Frankfurt only
plate 30

Job Adriaensz Berckheyde
1630–1693

The Stock Exchange in Amsterdam c. 1675–80
oil on canvas
62.2 × 52.8 cm
Städel Museum, Frankfurt am Main (536)
Frankfurt only
plate 26

Joan Blaeu
1596–1673

Map of Amsterdam 1649–52
hand-coloured engraving on laid paper
42.1 × 54.5 cm
Amsterdam City Archives (10035/290)
Frankfurt only
plate 28

Ferdinand Bol
1616–1680

Portrait of a Man c. 1645
oil on canvas
87 × 72.5 cm
Bayerische Staatsgemäldesammlungen,
Alte Pinakothek, Munich (609)
plate 64

Woman at Her Dressing Table c. 1645
oil on canvas
128.9 × 91.8 cm
The Museum of Fine Arts, Houston
Museum purchase funded by Mrs. Harry C.
Hanszen (69.4)
Ottawa only
plate 92

Portrait of a Woman c. 1648
oil on canvas
87 × 72.5 cm
Bayerische Staatsgemäldesammlungen,
Alte Pinakothek, Munich (610)
plate 65

Self-portrait c. 1647
oil on canvas
97.5 × 77.5 cm
Michele and Donald D'Amour Museum of
Fine Arts, Springfield
The James Philip Gray Collection (42.02)
Frankfurt only
plate 40

Group Portrait of the Regents of the Leprozenhuis 1649
oil on canvas
224 × 310 cm
Amsterdam Museum (SA 7295)
Frankfurt only
plate 55

Pyrrhus and Fabricius (modello) c. 1655
oil on canvas
81 × 65 cm
Herzog Anton Ulrich-Museum, Kunstmuseum des
Landes Niedersachsen, Braunschweig (GG 248)
Frankfurt only
plate 94

Works on paper

The Holy Family in an Interior c. 1635–42
pen and ink with black, red and yellow ochre
chalks, with grey and brown wash, heightened with
white, outlines indented for transfer, on laid paper
18 × 20.7 cm
The British Museum, London (1836,0811.337)
Frankfurt only
plate 122

Abraham's Sacrifice of Isaac c. 1638–45
etching on laid paper
42.7 × 32.7 cm
Städel Museum, Frankfurt am Main (6098)
plate 115

Self-portrait 1642
etching on laid paper
13.7 × 11.2 cm
Städel Museum, Frankfurt am Main (6105)
Frankfurt only
plate 39

The Holy Family in an Interior 1643
etching on Asian paper
18.2 × 21.6 cm
Rijksmuseum, Amsterdam (RP-P-BI-1990)
Frankfurt only
plate 123

Woman with a Pear 1651
etching on laid paper
14.7 × 11.9 cm
Collection of Dr. Jonathan Meakins and
Dr. Jacqueline McClaran, Montreal
Ottawa only
plate 87

Bartholomeus Breenbergh
1598–1657

Landscape with the Rest on the Flight into Egypt 1634
oil on panel
54.8 × 78.4 cm
Bayerische Staatsgemäldesammlungen,
Alte Pinakothek, Munich (1647)
Frankfurt only
plate 121

Pieter Codde
1599–1678

Connoisseurs Visiting an Artist's Studio c. 1630
oil on panel
38.3 × 49.3 cm
Staatsgalerie Stuttgart
Acquired with lottery funds in 1976 (3249)
Frankfurt only
plate 11

Willem Drost, attributed to
1633–1659

The Liberation of Saint Peter from Prison c. 1650
pen and ink with wash, heightened with white,
on laid paper
19.7 × 29.9 cm
National Gallery of Canada, Ottawa
Gift of Frank and Marianne Seger, Toronto, 2013
(46101)
Ottawa only
plate 160

Portrait of Rembrandt in His Painter's Smock c. 1652
pen and ink on toned, laid paper
20.3 × 13.4 cm
Rembrandt House Museum, Amsterdam (246)
Ottawa only
plate 18

Anthony van Dyck
1599–1641

Samson and Delilah c. 1618–21
oil on canvas
152.3 × 232 cm
Dulwich Picture Gallery, London (DPG127)
Frankfurt only
plate 104

Gerbrand van den Eeckhout
1621–1674

Portrait of Isaac Commelin 1669
oil on canvas
70.7 × 55.6 cm
Städel Museum, Frankfurt am Main (705)
Frankfurt only
plate 27

Barent Fabritius
1624–1673

The Expulsion of Hagar and Ishmael c. 1650–60
oil on canvas
109.9 × 109.9 cm
Fine Arts Museums of San Francisco
Anonymous gift (50.34)
plate 111

Saint Matthew and the Angel 1656
oil on canvas
76.9 × 63.9 cm
Montreal Museum of Fine Arts
Gift of Mr. and Mrs. Michal Hornstein in honour
of Frederik J. Duparc (1990.13)
Not exhibited
plate 120

Carel Fabritius
1622–1654

Mercury, Argus and Io c. 1645–47
oil on canvas
73.5 × 104 cm
Los Angeles County Museum of Art
Gift of The Ahmanson Foundation (M.90.20)
Frankfurt only
plate 103

Govert Flinck
1615–1660

Portrait of a Woman in Profile c. 1636
oil on panel
78.1 × 68.6 cm
Wadsworth Atheneum Museum of Art, Hartford
Gift in memory of Mae Cadwell Rovensky (1961.191)
Frankfurt only
plate 49

Portrait of a Woman c. 1640
oil on panel
105 × 78 cm
Suermondt-Ludwig-Museum, Aachen (GK 154)
plate 70

The Sacrifice of Manoah 1640
oil on canvas
74.3 × 123.8 cm
Agnes Etherington Art Centre, Queen's University,
Kingston
Gift of Dr. and Mrs. Alfred Bader, 1975 (18-114)
plate 117

The Expulsion of Hagar and Ishmael c. 1642
oil on canvas
110.7 × 138.8 cm
Staatliche Museen zu Berlin, Gemäldegalerie (815)
Frankfurt only
plate 113

Portrait of a Man (Jan van Hellemont?) 1646
oil on canvas
124.8 × 94 cm
North Carolina Museum of Art, Raleigh
Purchased with funds from the State of North
Carolina (58.4.2)
plate 66

Portrait of a Woman (Margaretha van Raephorst?) 1646
oil on canvas
124.8 × 94 cm
North Carolina Museum of Art, Raleigh
Purchased with funds from the State of
North Carolina (58.4.3)
plate 67

Sketch for a Civic Guard Group Portrait 1648
oil on canvas
66.7 × 101.6 cm
Amsterdam Museum (SA 41181)
Frankfurt only
plate 54

Bartholomeus van der Helst
c. 1613–1670

Portrait of a Man (Joan Hulft?) 1644
oil on canvas
164.9 × 133.1 cm
Montreal Museum of Fine Arts
Gift of Louis-Joseph Forget Estate (1918.186)
Ottawa only
plate 74

Portrait of a Woman in Black Satin with a Fan 1644
oil on panel
104.6 × 76 cm
The National Gallery, London
Bought, 1904 (NG1937)
plate 71

Portrait of Jacob Trip 1655
oil on canvas
110 × 95 cm
Amsterdam Museum (SB 5783)
On loan from Rijksmuseum, Amsterdam
(SK-A-1255)
plate 77

François van den Hoeye
1590/91–1636

Panoramic View of Amsterdam c. 1620–25
etching and engraving on three sheets of laid paper
24.3 × 122.4 cm
Rijksmuseum, Amsterdam
Purchase June 1902 (RP-P-1902-A-22401)
Frankfurt only
plate 25

Cornelis Holsteyn
1618–1658

Venus and Cupid Lamenting the Dead Adonis c. 1655
oil on canvas
99 × 207 cm
Frans Hals Museum, Haarlem (Os I-224)
Frankfurt only
plate 101

Gerard van Honthorst
1592–1656

Portrait of Amalia von Solms 1632
oil on panel
75.5 × 62.5 cm
Centraal Museum, Utrecht (21659)
plate 48

Pieter de Hooch
1629–1679

Council Chamber of the Amsterdam Town Hall
c. 1663–65
oil on canvas
112.5 × 99 cm
Museo Nacional Thyssen-Bornemisza, Madrid
(196 / 1960.3)
Frankfurt only
plate 95

Samuel van Hoogstraten
1627–1678

Adoration of the Child 1647
oil on canvas
58.2 × 70.8 cm
Dordrechts Museum, Dordrecht
Purchased with support of the Rembrandt
Association, 1980 (DM/980/567)
plate 124

Works on paper

The Baptism of the Ethiopian Chamberlain c. 1660–65
pen and ink on laid paper
15.1 × 21.8 cm
National Gallery of Canada, Ottawa
Gift of Frank and Marianne Seger, Toronto, 2006
(42006)
Ottawa only
plate 162

Thomas de Keyser
c. 1596–1667

Portrait of a Man 1631
oil on panel
50.7 × 41.4 cm
National Gallery of Denmark, Copenhagen
(KMS8151)
Frankfurt only
plate 58

Portrait of a Young Woman 1631
oil on panel
50 × 41 cm
National Gallery of Denmark, Copenhagen
(KMS6703)
Frankfurt only
plate 59

Philips Koninck
1619–1688

Panoramic Landscape with a Village c. 1648–49
oil on wood
29.2 × 36.2 cm
Los Angeles County Museum of Art
Gift of Mr. and Mrs. Edward William Carter
(M.2009.106.9)
plate 132

Salomon Koninck
1609–1656

*Esther Reading the Decree of the Extermination of
the Jews* 1630s
oil on panel
74.7 × 57.3 cm
National Gallery of Denmark, Copenhagen
(KMSsp419)
Frankfurt only
plate 84

Pieter Lastman
1583–1633

The Expulsion of Hagar and Ishmael 1612
oil on panel
48.3 × 71.4 cm
Hamburger Kunsthalle, Hamburg (HK-191)
Frankfurt only
plate 107

The Triumph of Sesostris 1631
oil on panel
68.6 × 108.6 cm
Fine Arts Museums of San Francisco
Gift of Mr. and Mrs. Philip N. Lilienthal, Jr. (44.16)
plate 19

Jan Lievens
1607–1674

Job 1631
oil on canvas
171.5 × 148.6 cm
National Gallery of Canada, Ottawa
Gift of the National Art Collections Fund of
Great Britain, 1933 (4093)
Not exhibited
plate 22

Portrait of Adriaen Trip 1644
oil on canvas
107.5 × 83.5 cm
Rembrandt House Museum, Amsterdam
Long-term loan from private collection (BC0210)
plate 76

Works on paper

Saint Jerome Meditating in a Grotto c. 1630
etching on laid paper
24.7 × 21 cm
Städel Museum, Frankfurt am Main (6126)
Ottawa only
plate 21

Portrait of Joost van den Vondel c. 1644–50
etching and engraving on laid paper
32.6 × 24.7 cm
Städel Museum, Frankfurt am Main (10224)
Frankfurt only
plate 15

Wooded Landscape with Painter at His Easel c. 1655
pen and ink with wash on Asian paper
32.5 × 46 cm
Städel Museum, Frankfurt am Main (3289)
Frankfurt only
plate 141

Farm Buildings behind a Fence, and Cows c. 1655–65
pen and ink on Asian paper
22.6 × 37.6 cm
The Morgan Library & Museum, New York
Purchased by Pierpont Morgan (1837–1913) in 1909
(III, 186b)
Ottawa only
plate 164

Jacob van Loo
1614–1670

Diana and Her Nymphs 1654
oil on canvas
99.5 × 135.5 cm
National Gallery of Denmark, Copenhagen
(KMS1876)
Frankfurt only
plate 100

Nicolaes Maes
1634–1693

Abraham's Sacrifice of Isaac c. 1653–54
oil on canvas
113 × 91.5 cm
Agnes Etherington Art Centre, Queen's University,
Kingston
Purchase, Bader Acquisition Fund, 2014 (57-002)
plate 114

Theodor Matham
1605/06–1676
after Joachim von Sandrart (1606–1688)

Portrait of Joost van den Vondel c. 1643
engraving on laid paper
27.6 × 19.2 cm
Kunstsammlungen der Veste Coburg (VII, 159, 17)
Frankfurt only
plate 16

Jan Miense Molenaer
1609/10–1668

Tavern of the Crescent Moon c. 1637–40
oil on canvas
87.8 × 102 cm
Museum of Fine Arts, Budapest (288)
Frankfurt only
plate 142

Aert van der Neer
1603/04–1677

Nocturnal Canal Landscape with Fishing Boats
c. 1645–50
oil on panel
41.8 × 52.2 cm
Städel Museum, Frankfurt am Main (1092)
Frankfurt only
plate 133

Nicolaes Eliasz Pickenoy
1588–1650/56

Portrait of a Man 1628
oil on canvas
196 × 126 cm
Staatliche Kunsthalle Karlsruhe (2670)
Frankfurt only
plate 72

Portrait of a Man 1628
oil on panel
112 × 83 cm
Stedelijk Museum Alkmaar
Long-term loan from Stichting Van Foreest en
Van Egmond van de Nijenburg (027007)
plate 56

Portrait of a Woman 1628
oil on panel
112 × 83 cm
Stedelijk Museum Alkmaar
Long-term loan from Stichting Van Foreest en
Van Egmond van de Nijenburg (027008)
plate 57

Diana and Actaeon c. 1640
oil on panel
58.4 × 120.7 cm
Herbert F. Johnson Museum of Art, Cornell
University, Ithaca
Bequest of Roger P. Clark (55.045)
Frankfurt only
plate 98

Marcantonio Raimondi
c. 1470/80–1527
after Raphael (1483–1520)

Plague Among the Trojans (Il Morbetto) 1515–16
engraving on laid paper
19.8 × 25.5 cm
Rijksmuseum, Amsterdam (RP-P-OB-12.009)
plate 167

Rembrandt van Rijn
1606–1669

Bust of an Old Man in a Turban c. 1627–28
oil on panel
26.5 × 20 cm
The Kremer Collection, Amsterdam
Frankfurt only
plate 20

David Playing the Harp for Saul c. 1630–31
oil on panel
62 × 50.1 cm
Städel Museum, Frankfurt am Main (498)
plate 34

Portrait of Amalia von Solms 1632
oil on canvas
68.5 × 55 cm
Musée Jacquemart-André, Institut de France, Paris
(MJA-P839)
plate 47

Portrait of a Man 1632
oil on panel
64 × 47 cm
The Peter and Irene Ludwig Foundation, Aachen
Frankfurt only
plate 50

Portrait of a Young Woman 1632
oil on panel
89.2 × 73 cm
Allentown Art Museum
Samuel H. Kress Collection, 1961 (1961.035.000)
Ottawa only
plate 80

Self-portrait in a Wide-brimmed Hat 1632
oil on panel
21.8 × 16.3 cm
Private collection
plate 35

Young Girl in a Gold-trimmed Cloak 1632
oil on panel
59 × 44 cm
The Leiden Collection, New York (RR-104)
Ottawa only
plate 81

Heroine from the Old Testament 1632/33
oil on canvas
109.2 × 94.4 cm
National Gallery of Canada, Ottawa
Purchased 1953 (6089)
plate 85

Portrait of Maertgen van Bilderbeecq 1633
oil on panel
67.4 × 55.2 cm
Städel Museum, Frankfurt am Main (912)
Frankfurt only
plate 44

Portrait of a Young Woman with a Fan 1633
oil on canvas
125.7 × 101 cm
The Metropolitan Museum of Art, New York
Gift of Helen Swift Neilson, 1943 (43.125)
plate 68

*Diana and Her Nymphs Bathing, with the Stories
of Actaeon and Callisto* 1634
oil on canvas
73.5 × 93.5 cm
Sammlung der Fürsten zu Salm-Salm, Museum
Wasserburg Anholt, Isselburg
Frankfurt only
plate 99

Flora 1634
oil on canvas
125 × 101 cm
The State Hermitage Museum, St. Petersburg
(ГЭ-732)
Frankfurt only
plate 83

*Judith at the Banquet of Holofernes (formerly
Artemisia)* 1634
oil on canvas
143 × 154.7 cm
Museo Nacional del Prado, Madrid (P002132)
plate 82

Self-portrait in a Cap and a Fur-trimmed Cloak 1634
oil on panel
58.4 × 47.7 cm
Staatliche Museen zu Berlin, Gemäldegalerie (810)
Frankfurt only
plate 41

Saskia van Uylenburgh, the Wife of the Artist
c. 1634/35–1638/40
oil on panel
62.5 × 49 cm
National Gallery of Art, Washington
Widener Collection (1942.9.71)
plate 7

The Abduction of Ganymede 1635
oil on canvas
177 × 129 cm
Staatliche Kunstsammlungen Dresden,
Gemäldegalerie Alte Meister (1558)
Frankfurt only
plate 97

Portrait of Petronella Buys 1635
oil on panel
79.5 × 59.3 cm
The Leiden Collection, New York (RR-115)
Ottawa only
plate 61

Portrait of Philips Lucasz 1635
oil on panel
79.5 × 58.9 cm
The National Gallery, London
Bought, 1871 (NG850)
plate 60

Tronie of a Man with a Feathered Beret c. 1635–40
oil on panel
62.5 × 47 cm
Mauritshuis, The Hague (149)
Frankfurt only
plate 36

The Blinding of Samson 1636
oil on canvas
219.3 × 305 cm
Städel Museum, Frankfurt am Main (1383)
plate 106

Portrait of a Man Holding a Black Hat c. 1637
oil on panel
79.5 × 69.4 cm
Hammer Museum, UCLA, Los Angeles
The Armand Hammer Collection
Gift of the Armand Hammer Foundation
(AH.90.59)
plate 75

Landscape with a Stone Bridge c. 1638
oil on panel
29.5 × 42.5 cm
Rijksmuseum, Amsterdam
Purchased with the support of the Rembrandt
Association and A. Bredius, Amsterdam
(SK-A-1935)
plate 131

Portrait of a Standing Man (Andries de Graeff) 1639
oil on canvas
199 × 123.5 cm
Museumslandschaft Hessen Kassel,
Gemäldegalerie Alte Meister (GK 239)
plate 73

(Rembrandt van Rijn)

Still Life with Peacocks c. 1639
oil on canvas
145 cm × 135.5 cm
Rijksmuseum, Amsterdam (SK-A-3981)
plate 150

Self-portrait Wearing a Hat and Two Chains c. 1642–43
oil on panel
72 × 54.8 cm
Museo Nacional Thyssen-Bornemisza, Madrid
(331 / 1976.90)
plate 42

A Woman in Bed (*Sarah Awaiting Tobias*) 1647
oil on canvas
81.1 × 67.8 cm
National Galleries of Scotland, Edinburgh
Presented by William McEwan, 1892 (NG 827)
plate 89

Portrait of Hendrickje Stoffels c. 1654–56
oil on canvas
101.9 × 83.7 cm
The National Gallery, London
Bought with a contribution from the Art Fund,
1976 (NG6432)
Ottawa only
plate 91

Portrait of a Man with Arms Akimbo 1658
oil on canvas
107.4 × 87 cm
Agnes Etherington Art Centre, Queen's University,
Kingston
Gift of Alfred and Isabel Bader, 2015 (58-008)
Ottawa only
plate 78

Portrait of a Woman with a Lap Dog c. 1665
oil on canvas
81.3 × 64.1 cm
Art Gallery of Ontario, Toronto
Bequest of Frank P. Wood, 1955 (54/30)
Ottawa only
plate 79

Portrait of a Young Woman (Magdalena van Loo?)
c. 1668
oil on canvas
56.3 × 48 cm
Montreal Museum of Fine Arts
Mrs. R. MacD. Paterson Bequest (1949.1006)
Ottawa only
plate 93

Works on paper

The Drunken Lot c. 1630–33
black and white chalk, traces of red chalk, with wash,
on laid paper
25.3 × 18.9 cm
Städel Museum, Frankfurt am Main (857)
Ottawa only
plate 152

Self-portrait in a Soft Hat and a Patterned Cloak 1631
etching on laid paper
14.7 × 13.1 cm
Städel Museum, Frankfurt am Main (SG 4468)
plate 3

The Rat Catcher 1632
etching on laid paper
14 × 12.5 cm
Städel Museum, Frankfurt am Main (5870)
Frankfurt only
plate 146

The Descent from the Cross 1633
etching and engraving on laid paper
53 × 41 cm
Städel Museum, Frankfurt am Main (9001)
plate 166

The Ship of Fortune 1633
etching on laid paper
11.3 × 16.6 cm
Illustration from
Elias Herckmans (1596–1644)
Der zee-vaert lof
Amsterdam: Jacob Pieterss Wachter op den Dam, 1634
The Morgan Library & Museum, New York
Purchased 1920 (PML 21064)
Not exhibited
plate 8

Venus and Mars Caught in Vulcan's Net c. 1633–38
pen and ink on laid paper
30 × 42.5 cm
Amsterdam Museum (TA 10283)
Frankfurt only
plate 102

The Angel Appearing to the Shepherds 1634
etching, engraving and drypoint on laid paper
26 × 21.9 cm
National Gallery of Canada, Ottawa
Purchased 1953 (6245)
Ottawa only
plate 126

The Angel Appearing to the Shepherds 1634
etching, engraving and drypoint on laid paper
26.1 × 21.9 cm
Städel Museum, Frankfurt am Main (5784)
Frankfurt only

The Great Jewish Bride 1635
etching, engraving and drypoint on laid paper
22.4 × 16.7 cm
Städel Museum, Frankfurt am Main (6067)
plate 86

The Pancake Woman 1635
etching on laid paper
10.8 × 7.7 cm
Collection of Dr. Jonathan Meakins and
Dr. Jacqueline McClaran, Montreal
Ottawa only

The Pancake Woman 1635
etching on laid paper
10.9 × 7.7 cm
Städel Museum, Frankfurt am Main (5872)
Frankfurt only
plate 148

Two Studies of Saskia Asleep c. 1635–37
pen and ink with wash on laid paper
13 × 17.1 cm
The Morgan Library & Museum, New York
Purchased by Pierpont Morgan (1837–1913) in 1909
(I, 180)
Ottawa only
plate 156

Self-portrait with Saskia 1636
etching on laid paper
10.7 × 9.7 cm
National Gallery of Canada, Ottawa
Purchased 1913 (590)
Ottawa only

Self-portrait with Saskia 1636
etching on laid paper
10.4 × 9.5 cm
Städel Museum, Frankfurt am Main (5752)
Frankfurt only
plate 6

Studies of the Head of Saskia and Others 1636
etching on laid paper
15.1 × 12.6 cm
Städel Museum, Frankfurt am Main (6091)
Ottawa only
plate 5

Two Butchers at Work c. 1636–39
pen and ink on laid paper
14.9 × 19.9 cm
Städel Museum, Frankfurt am Main (3626)
plate 153

Samson and Delilah 1636–40
pen and ink on laid paper
14.7 × 20.2 cm
Staatliche Kunstsammlungen Dresden,
Kupferstich-Kabinett (C 1966-66)
Frankfurt only
plate 105

The Expulsion of Hagar and Ishmael 1637
etching and drypoint on laid paper
12.6 × 9.5 cm
Städel Museum, Frankfurt am Main (5764)
plate 112

The Expulsion of Hagar and Ishmael c. 1637
black chalk on laid paper
19.2 × 15 cm
Albertina, Vienna (8766)
plate 108

A Young Woman (the Artist's Wife, Saskia?) being Coiffed
c. 1637
pen and ink, brown and grey wash, on laid paper
(grey wash by a later hand)
23.4 × 18 cm
Albertina, Vienna (8825)
Ottawa only
plate 157

Two Studies of a Woman Reading c. 1638
pen and ink on laid paper
17.3 × 15 cm
The Metropolitan Museum of Art, New York
H.O. Havemeyer Collection, Bequest of
Mrs. H.O. Havemeyer, 1929 (29.100.932)
Frankfurt only
plate 143

Self-portrait Leaning on a Stone Sill 1639
etching on laid paper
20.6 × 16.3 cm
National Gallery of Canada, Ottawa
Purchased 1951 (5830)
Ottawa only
plate 45

Self-portrait Leaning on a Stone Still 1639
etching on laid paper
20.6 × 16.3 cm
Städel Museum, Frankfurt am Main (5754)
Frankfurt only

Cottages under a Stormy Sky c. 1640
pen and ink with wash and white bodycolour
on prepared laid paper
18.2 × 24.5 cm
Albertina, Vienna (8880)
Frankfurt only
plate 163

Saskia Asleep in Bed c. 1640–42
pen and ink with wash on laid paper
14.4 × 20.8 cm
Ashmolean Museum, University of Oxford
Purchased 1954 (WA1954.141)
Frankfurt only
plate 155

Landscape with Cottages and Haybarn 1641
etching and drypoint on laid paper
12.9 × 32.2 cm
Städel Museum, Frankfurt am Main (5961)
Frankfurt only
plate 138

*View of Amsterdam Seen from the Kadijk, from
the Northeast* c. 1641
etching on laid paper
11.1 × 15.3 cm
Städel Museum, Frankfurt am Main (5948)
plate 32

The Expulsion of Hagar and Ishmael c. 1642–46
pen and ink with wash on laid paper
18.8 × 23.7 cm
The British Museum, London (1860,0616.121)
Frankfurt only
plate 110

The Hog 1643
etching and drypoint on laid paper
14.5 × 18.4 cm
National Gallery of Canada, Ottawa
Purchased 1989 (30379)
Ottawa only

The Hog 1643
etching and drypoint on laid paper
14.4 × 18.4 cm
Städel Museum, Frankfurt am Main (5903)
Frankfurt only
plate 145

The Three Trees 1643
etching, engraving and drypoint on laid paper
21.3 × 28 cm
National Gallery of Canada, Ottawa
Purchased 1939 (4481)
Ottawa only
plate 140

The Three Trees 1643
etching, engraving and drypoint on laid paper
21.3 × 27.8 cm (trimmed)
Städel Museum, Frankfurt am Main (5950)
Frankfurt only

Satire on Art Criticism 1644
pen and ink, corrected with white, on laid paper
15.5 × 20.1 cm
The Metropolitan Museum of Art, New York
Robert Lehman Collection, 1975 (1975.1.799)
plate 12

View of the Montelbaans Tower in Amsterdam
c. 1644–45
pen and ink with wash on laid paper
14.5 × 14.4 cm
Rembrandt House Museum, Amsterdam (244)
Ottawa only
plate 2

*Landscape with Cottages and Farm Buildings and
a Man Sketching* c. 1645
etching on laid paper
13.1 × 20.7 cm
Städel Museum, Frankfurt am Main (5954)
Frankfurt only
plate 136

Three Women and a Child by a Door c. 1645
pen and ink on laid paper
23.3 × 17.8 cm
Rijksmuseum, Amsterdam
Purchased with the support of the Rembrandt
Association (RP-T-1889-A-2056)
Ottawa only
plate 144

Portrait of Jan Asselijn 1647
etching, engraving and drypoint on cartridge paper
21.8 × 17.1 cm
Städel Museum, Frankfurt am Main (55899)
plate 1

Portrait of Jan Six 1647
etching, engraving and drypoint on laid paper
24.4 × 19.3 cm
Städel Museum, Frankfurt am Main (6017)
plate 13

Beggars Receiving Alms at the Door of a House 1648
etching, engraving and drypoint on laid paper
16.6 × 13 cm
National Gallery of Canada, Ottawa
Purchased 1961 (9695)
Ottawa only

Beggars Receiving Alms at the Door of a House 1648
etching, engraving and drypoint on laid paper
16.5 × 12.8 cm
Städel Museum, Frankfurt am Main (5918)
Frankfurt only
plate 147

Christ Preaching (*The Hundred Guilder Print*)
c. 1648
etching, engraving and drypoint on India proof
paper, mounted on Asian paper
27.7 × 38.9 cm
National Gallery of Canada, Ottawa
Purchased 1957 (6879)
Ottawa only
plate 168

Christ Preaching (*The Hundred Guilder Print*) c. 1648
etching, engraving and drypoint on laid paper
27.8 × 38.8 cm
Städel Museum, Frankfurt am Main (8992)
Frankfurt only

Self-portrait Etching at a Window 1648
etching, engraving and drypoint on laid paper
15.6 × 12.9 cm
Städel Museum, Frankfurt am Main (61530)
plate 9

Farmhouses by the Diemerdijk c. 1648–50
pen and ink with wash on laid paper
11.3 × 24.8 cm
Ashmolean Museum, University of Oxford
Presented by Chambers Hall, 1855 (WA1855.22)
Ottawa only
plate 135

The Expulsion of Hagar and Ishmael c. 1650
pen and ink on laid paper
17.1 × 22.4 cm
Rijksmuseum, Amsterdam
Gift of C. Hofstede de Groot, The Hague
(RP-T-1930-2)
Ottawa only
plate 109

Three Gabled Cottages 1650
etching and drypoint on laid paper
16.2 × 20.3 cm
Städel Museum, Frankfurt am Main (5952)
Frankfurt only
plate 139

Portrait of Clement de Jonghe 1651
etching, engraving and drypoint on laid paper,
first state
20.7 × 16.1 cm
National Gallery of Canada, Ottawa
Gift in memory of Margaret Wade Labarge from
her collection, 2010 (43100)
Ottawa only

Portrait of Clement de Jonghe 1651
etching, engraving and drypoint on laid paper,
first state
20.7 × 16.1 cm
Städel Museum, Frankfurt am Main (5992)
Frankfurt only
plate 170

Portrait of Clement de Jonghe 1651
etching, engraving and drypoint on laid paper,
third state
20.7 × 16.1 cm
Städel Museum, Frankfurt am Main (5994)
Frankfurt only
plate 171

Portrait of Clement de Jonghe 1651
etching, engraving and drypoint on laid paper,
fourth state
20.7 × 16.1 cm
Städel Museum, Frankfurt am Main (5995)
Frankfurt only

The Baptism of the Ethiopian Chamberlain c. 1652
pen and ink, partially incised, on laid paper
18.2 × 21.1 cm
National Gallery of Canada, Ottawa
Purchased 1977 (18909)
Ottawa only
plate 161

(Rembrandt van Rijn)

Abraham's Sacrifice of Isaac c. 1652–54
pen and ink on laid paper
18 × 15.5 cm
Staatliche Kunstsammlungen Dresden,
Kupferstich-Kabinett (C 1373)
Frankfurt only
plate 154

The Flight into Egypt, altered from Hercules Segers
c. 1653
etching, engraving and drypoint on laid paper
21.2 × 28.4 cm
Collection of Dr. Jonathan Meakins and
Dr. Jacqueline McClaran, Montreal
Ottawa only
figure 1.8

The Three Crosses 1653–54
drypoint on laid paper, fourth state
38.4 × 44.7 cm
National Gallery of Canada, Ottawa
Purchased 1944 (4871)
Ottawa only

The Three Crosses 1653–54
drypoint on vellum, first state
37/34.1 × 42.9 cm
Städel Museum, Frankfurt am Main (8998)
Frankfurt only

The Three Crosses 1653–54
drypoint on laid paper, fourth state
38.5 × 45 cm
Städel Museum, Frankfurt am Main (8999)
Frankfurt only
plate 129

Abraham's Sacrifice of Isaac 1655
etching and drypoint on laid paper
15.6 × 13.2 cm
National Gallery of Canada, Ottawa
Purchased 1915 (1086)
Ottawa only
plate 116

Abraham's Sacrifice of Isaac 1655
etching and drypoint on laid paper
15.6 × 13.1 cm
Städel Museum, Frankfurt am Main (5767)
Frankfurt only

Christ Presented to the People: Oblong Plate 1655
drypoint on laid paper
35.6 × 45.2 cm
National Gallery of Canada, Ottawa
Purchased 1921 (1853)
Ottawa only
plate 128

Girl Asleep in a Window c. 1655
pen and ink with wash, corrected with white,
on laid paper
16.3 × 17.5 cm
Nationalmuseum, Stockholm (NMH 2084/1863)
Frankfurt only
plate 158

Portrait of Jan Lutma, Goldsmith 1656
etching and drypoint on vellum
18.6 × 14.5 cm
National Gallery of Canada, Ottawa
Purchased 1966 (14986)
Ottawa only
plate 23

Portrait of Abraham Francen c. 1657
etching, engraving and drypoint on Asian paper
15.8 × 20.8 cm
Städel Museum, Frankfurt am Main (5997)
Frankfurt only
plate 24

Other

Rembrandt's Funeral Medallion 1634
brass
2.8 cm (diameter)
Rembrandt House Museum, Amsterdam (2428)
plate 4

Letter from Rembrandt to Constantijn Huygens
12 January 1639
pen and ink on laid paper
30 × 21 cm
The Royal Collections of the Netherlands,
The Hague (G001-18)
plate 96

Copperplate for Etched Portrait of Clement de Jonghe
1651
copper
21 × 16.5 cm
Amsterdam Museum
Purchased with the support of the Rembrandt
Association (KA 19319)
plate 169

Rembrandt and Workshop

Portrait of Willem Burchgraeff 1633
oil on panel
67.5 × 52 cm
Staatliche Kunstsammlungen Dresden,
Gemäldegalerie Alte Meister (1557)
Frankfurt only
plate 43

Rembrandt Workshop

The Liberation of Saint Peter from Prison c. 1640–50
pen and ink with wash, corrected in white,
on laid paper
19.5 × 22.2 cm
Städel Museum, Frankfurt am Main (858)
Ottawa only
plate 159

**Rembrandt Workshop
here attributed to Ferdinand Bol
1616–1680**

The Angel Departing from the Family of Tobias
c. 1637–40
oil on panel
66 × 49.5 cm
Private collection
Frankfurt only
plate 119

**Rembrandt Workshop
attributed to Carel Fabritius
1622–1654**

A Girl with a Broom c. 1646/48–51
oil on canvas
107.3 × 91.4 cm
National Gallery of Art, Washington
Andrew W. Mellon Collection (1937.1.74)
plate 151

**Rembrandt Workshop
attributed to Constantijn Daniël van Renesse
1626–1680**

The Descent from the Cross 1650–52
oil on canvas
142 × 110.9 cm
National Gallery of Art, Washington
Widener Collection (1942.9.61)
plate 127

**Rembrandt Workshop
attributed to Pieter de With
c. 1635–1689**

Amsterdam Town Hall after the Fire of 7 July 1652
c. 1652
pen and ink on laid paper
13.8 × 17.7 cm
Herzog Anton Ulrich-Museum, Kunstmuseum des
Landes Niedersachsen, Braunschweig (Z 363r)
Frankfurt only
plate 14

**Peter Paul Rubens
1577–1640**

Hero and Leander c. 1604
oil on canvas
95.9 × 128 cm
Yale University Art Gallery, New Haven
Gift of Susan Morse Hilles (1962.25)
Frankfurt only
plate 46

**Jacob van Ruisdael
1628/29–1682**

*The Amstel River near Amsterdam, Seen from
the Southeast* c. 1656
oil on canvas
52.5 × 43.5 cm
Museum of Fine Arts, Budapest (4278)
Frankfurt only
plate 31

Works on paper

The Little Bridge c. 1650–55
etching on paper
19.3 × 28.1 cm
Rijksmuseum, Amsterdam (RP-P-OB-4858)
Frankfurt only
plate 137

Joachim von Sandrart
1606–1688

Portrait of Jacob Bicker 1639
oil on panel
93.5 × 71 cm
Amsterdam Museum (SA 2078)
Frankfurt only
plate 62

Portrait of Alida Bicker 1641
oil on panel
92 × 72 cm
Amsterdam Museum (SA 2077)
Frankfurt only
plate 63

Dirck van Santvoort
1609–1680

Group Portrait of the Regentesses of the Spinhuis 1638
oil on canvas
187.5 × 214 cm
Amsterdam Museum (SA 7402)
Frankfurt only
plate 53

Salomon Savery
1593/94–1683
after Jan Martszen de Jonge (1609/10–1647)

Mayors of Amsterdam Bidding Farewell to Marie de' Medici in Front of the Amsterdam Town Hall on Dam Square 1638
etching on laid paper
28 × 37.5 cm
Illustration from
Caspar Barlaeus (1584–1648)
Medicea Hospes, sive Descriptio publicae gratulationis...Mariam de Medicis...
Amsterdam: Joan and Cornelis Blaeu, 1638
Amsterdam City Archives
Atlas Dreesmann Collection
(10094/010094006324)
Frankfurt only
plate 10

Hercules Segers
1589/90–1633/40

River Valley c. 1620
oil on panel
22.5 × 53 cm
Mauritshuis, The Hague (1033)
plate 130

Wallerant Vaillant
1623–1677

Self-portrait with Helmet c. 1655
oil on canvas
63.7 × 57.7 cm
Niedersächsisches Landesmuseum, Hannover
(PAM 967)
Frankfurt only
plate 38

Jan Victors
1619–1676/77

Young Woman at a Window 1640
oil on canvas
93 × 78 cm
Musée du Louvre, Paris (1286)
plate 88

The Angel Departing from the Family of Tobias 1649
oil on canvas
104.1 × 131.8 cm
The J. Paul Getty Museum, Los Angeles (72.PA.17)
plate 118

Cornelis Visscher
1628/29–1658

The Pancake Woman c. 1650
engraving on laid paper
43.3 × 34.8 cm (trimmed)
Städel Museum, Frankfurt am Main (8989)
Frankfurt only
plate 149

Portrait of Joost van den Vondel c. 1657
etching and engraving on laid paper
26.1 × 21.5 cm
Städel Museum, Frankfurt am Main (7159)
Frankfurt only
plate 17

Jan van Vliet
c. 1600–1668

Lot and His Daughters 1631
etching on laid paper
26.7 × 22.4 cm
Städel Museum, Frankfurt am Main (6175)
Ottawa only
plate 165

Jan Baptist Weenix
1621–1659

The Rest on the Flight into Egypt c. 1647–50
oil on canvas
55.2 × 50.8 cm
Philadelphia Museum of Art
Purchased with the George W. Elkins Fund, 1984
(E1984-1-1)
plate 125

Zeeman (Reinier Nooms)
c. 1623/24–1664

A View of Amsterdam Harbour c. 1643–64
oil on canvas
61.9 × 77.2 cm
High Museum of Art, Atlanta
Gift of the Walter and Frances Bunzl Foundation
(1991.300)
Frankfurt only
plate 33

Philipp von Zesen
1619–1689

Map of Amsterdam 1664
engraving on laid paper
24.1 × 46.2 cm
Illustration from
Philipp von Zesen
Beschreibung der Stadt Amsterdam
Amsterdam: Noschen, 1664
Städel Museum, Frankfurt am Main (129/60 8°)
Frankfurt only
plate 29

BIBLIOGRAPHY

Abrahamse 2010
Jaap Evert Abrahamse. *De Grote Uitleg van Amsterdam. Stadsontwikkeling in de Zeventiende Eeuw*. Bussum: Thoth, 2010.

Adams 1998
Ann Jensen Adams, ed. *Rembrandt's "Bathsheba Reading King David's Letter."* Cambridge: Cambridge University Press, 1998.

Albrecht and Imesch 2001
Jürg Albrecht and Kornelia Imesch, eds. *Horizons. Essais sur l'art et sur son histoire*. Ostfildern-Ruit: Hatje Cantz, 2001.

Allgemeines Künstlerlexikon
Andreas Beyer, Bénédicte Savoy and Wolf Tegethoff, eds. *Allgemeines Künstlerlexikon – Internationale Künstlerdatenbank*. 2009. www.degruyter.com/view/db/akl?lang=en (accessed 6 May 2020).

Alpers 1988
Svetlana Alpers. *Rembrandt's Enterprise: The Studio and the Market*. Chicago: University of Chicago Press, 1988.

Alpers 1991
Svetlana Alpers. *L'atelier de Rembrandt. La liberté, la peinture et l'argent*. Paris: Gallimard, 1991.

Amsterdam 1992
Ellinoor Bergvelt and Renée Kistemaker, eds. *De wereld binnen handbereik. Nederlandse kunst- en rariteitenverzamelingen, 1585–1735*. Exh. cat. Amsterdams Historisch Museum, Amsterdam, 1992.

Amsterdam 1996
Christiaan Schuckman, Martin Royalton-Kisch and Erik Hinterding. *Rembrandt & Van Vliet: A Collaboration on Copper*. Exh. cat. Rembrandt House Museum, Amsterdam, 1996.

Amsterdam 1999–2000
Bob van den Bogaert, ed. *Rembrandt's Treasures*. Exh. cat. Rembrandt House Museum, Amsterdam, 1999–2000.

Amsterdam 2002–03
Norbert Middelkoop, J.B. Bedaux, et al. *Kopstukken. Amsterdammers geportretteerd 1600–1800*. Exh. cat. Amsterdams Historisch Museum, Amsterdam, 2002–03.

Amsterdam 2011
Elmer Kolfin and Jaap van der Veen, eds. *Gedrukt tot Amsterdam. Amsterdamse prentmakers en -uitgevers in de Gouden Eeuw*. Exh. cat. Rembrandt House Museum, Amsterdam, 2011.

Amsterdam 2015
David de Witt, Leonore van Sloten and Jaap van der Veen. *Rembrandt's Late Pupils: Studying under a Genius*. Exh. cat. Rembrandt House Museum, Amsterdam, 2015.

Amsterdam 2016
Judith Noorman and David de Witt, eds. *Rembrandt's Naked Truth: Drawing Nude Models in the Golden Age*. Exh. cat. Rembrandt House Museum, Amsterdam, 2016.

Amsterdam 2017
Menno Jonker, ed. *Rembrandt en Jan Six. De ets, de vriendschap*. Exh. cat. Rembrandt House Museum, Amsterdam, 2017.

Amsterdam 2017–18
Norbert Middelkoop, ed. *Ferdinand Bol and Govert Flinck: Rembrandt's Master Pupils*. Exh. cat. Rembrandt House Museum and Amsterdam Museum, Amsterdam, 2017–18.

Amsterdam 2019
Epco Runia et al. *Rembrandt's Social Network: Family, Friends and Acquaintances*. Exh. cat. Rembrandt House Museum, Amsterdam, 2019.

Amsterdam 2020
Elmer Kolfin and Epco Runia, eds. *Black in Rembrandt's Time*. Exh. cat. Rembrandt House Museum, Amsterdam, 2020.

Amsterdam and Aachen 2008–09
Peter van den Brink and Jaap van der Veen. *Jacob Backer (1608/9–1651)*. Exh. cat. Rembrandt House Museum, Amsterdam, and Suermondt-Ludwig-Museum, Aachen, 2008–09.

Amsterdam and Berlin 2006
Ernst van de Wetering et al. *Rembrandt: Quest of a Genius*. Exh. cat. Rembrandt House Museum, Amsterdam, and Gemäldegalerie, Berlin, 2006.

Amsterdam and Cleveland 1999–2000
Alan Chong and Wouter Kloek. *Still-life Paintings from the Netherlands, 1550–1720*. Exh. cat. Rijksmuseum, Amsterdam, and Cleveland Museum of Art, 1999–2000.

Amsterdam and Groningen 1983
Albert Blankert et al. *The Impact of a Genius: Rembrandt, His Pupils and Followers in the Seventeenth Century: Paintings from Museums and Private Collections*. Exh. cat. Waterman Gallery, Amsterdam, and Groninger Museum, Groningen, 1983.

Amsterdam and London 2000–01
Erik Hinterding, Ger Luijten and Martin Royalton-Kisch. *Rembrandt the Printmaker*. Exh. cat. Rijksmuseum, Amsterdam, and The British Museum, London, 2000–01.

Amsterdam and Paris 1998–99
Boudewijn Bakker et al. *Landscapes of Rembrandt: His Favourite Walks*. Exh. cat. Gemeentearchief Amsterdam and Institut Néerlandais, Paris, 1998–99.

Antwerp and Amsterdam 1999
Carl Depauw and Ger Luijten, eds. *Anthony van Dyck as a Printmaker*. Exh. cat. Plantin-Moretus Museum, Antwerp, and Rijksmuseum, Amsterdam, 1999.

Arasse 2006
Daniel Arasse. *Anachroniques*. Paris: Gallimard, 2006.

Assouly 2004
Olivier Assouly, ed. *Le luxe. Essais sur la fabrique de l'ostentation*. Paris: Éditions du Regard-Institut français de la mode, 2004.

Athens and Dordrecht 2000–01
Peter Schoon and Sander Paarlberg, eds. *Greek Gods and Heroes in the Age of Rubens and Rembrandt*. Exh. cat. National Gallery / Alexandros Soutzos Museum, Athens, Netherlands Institute, Athens, and Dordrechts Museum, Dordrecht, 2000–01.

Bacon and Archimbaud 1993
Francis Bacon and Michel Archimbaud. *Francis Bacon: In Conversation with Michel Archimbaud*. Edited by Michel Archimbaud. London: Phaidon, 1993.

Bakker 2012
Boudewijn Bakker. *Landscape and Religion: From Van Eyck to Rembrandt*. Translated by Diane Webb. Farnham and Burlington: Ashgate, 2012.

De Balbian Verster 1932
Jan François Leopold de Balbian Verster. *Burgemeesters van Amsterdam in de 17e en 18e eeuw*. Zutphen: W.J. Thieme, 1932.

Baldinucci 1686
Filippo Baldinucci. *Cominciamento e progresso dell'arte dell' intagliare in rame, colle vite di molti de' più eccellenti maestri della stessa professione*. Florence: Piero Matini, 1686.

Baldinucci 1974
Filippo Baldinucci. *Notizie del professori del disegno da Cimabue in qua*. 7 vols. Edited by Ferdinando Ranalli. Florence: Studio per Edizioni Scelte, 1974 [1681–1728].

Baraude 1933
Henri Baraude. *Lopez, agent financier et confident de Richelieu*. Paris: Éditions de la Revue mondiale, 1933.

Barlaeus 1638
Caspar Barlaeus. *Medicea hospes, sive Descriptio publicae gratulationis, qua ... Mariam de Medicis excepit Senatus Populusque Amstelodamensis*. Amsterdam: Joan and Cornelis Blaeu, 1638.

Barlaeus 2019
Caspar Barlaeus. *The Wise Merchant*. Edited by Anna-Luna Post. Translated by Corinna Vermeulen. Amsterdam: Amsterdam University Press, 2019.

Barnes et al. 2004
Susan J. Barnes et al. *Van Dyck: A Complete Catalogue of the Paintings*. New Haven and London: Yale University Press, 2004.

Benesch 1954–57
Otto Benesch. *The Drawings of Rembrandt: A Critical and Chronological Catalogue*. London: Phaidon, 1954–57.

Van Beresteyn 1940
Eltjo A. van Beresteyn. *Ikonografie der leden van het geslacht Van Beresteyn en van hunne aanverwanten, Bijlage I der Genealogie van het geslacht Van Beresteyn*. 's-Gravenhage: 1940.

Van den Berghe 1992
E.H. van den Berghe. "Italiaanse schilderijen in Amsterdam in de zeventiende eeuw." *Jaarboek Amstelodamum* 84 (1992): 21–40.

Bergvelt and Jonker 2020
Ellinoor Bergvelt and Michiel Jonker. *Catalogue of Dulwich Picture Gallery: Dutch, Flemish and German Schools, with addenda to the British School*. Edited by Emily Lane (forthcoming in 2020 as an online publication).

Van Berkel and De Goei 2010
Klaas van Berkel and Leonie de Goei, eds. *The International Relevance of Dutch History* (special issue of *Bijdragen en Mededelingen betreffende de Geschiedenis der Nederlanden*). The Hague: Royal Netherlands Historical Society, 2010.

Berlin, Amsterdam and London 1991–92a
Holm Bevers, Peter Schatborn and Barbara Welzel. *Rembrandt: The Master and His Workshop, Drawings and Etchings*. Exh. cat. Altes Museum, Berlin, Rijksmuseum, Amsterdam, and The National Gallery, London, 1991–92.

Berlin, Amsterdam and London 1991–92b
Christopher Brown, Jan Kelch and Pieter van Thiel. *Rembrandt: The Master and His Workshop, Paintings*. Exh. cat. Altes Museum, Berlin, Rijksmuseum, Amsterdam, and The National Gallery, London, 1991–92.

Białostocki 1972
Jan Białostocki. "Rembrandt and Posterity." *Netherlands Yearbook for History of Art / Nederlands Kunsthistorisch Jaarboek* 23 (1972): 131–157.

Bikker 2019
Jonathan Bikker. *Rembrandt: Biography of a Rebel*. Amsterdam: Rijksmuseum, 2019.

Biörklund 1988
George Biörklund, with O.H. Barnard. *Rembrandt's Etchings: True and False: A Summary Catalogue*. New York: Hacker Art Books, 1988 [1968].

Blanc 1883
Charles Blanc. *Histoire des peintres de toutes les écoles. École hollandaise*. 2 vols. Paris: Renouard, 1883 [1849].

Blanc 2006
Jan Blanc. *Dans l'atelier de Rembrandt. Le maître et ses élèves*. Paris: Éditions de la Martinière, 2006.

Blanc 2017
Jan Blanc. *Van Gogh. Ni Dieu ni maître*. Paris: Citadelles & Mazenod, 2017.

Blankert 1982
Albert Blankert. *Ferdinand Bol (1616–1680): Rembrandt's Pupil*. Doornspijk: Davaco, 1982.

Blocksom 2018
Megan C. Blocksom. "Procession, Pride and Politics in the *Medicea hospes* (1638): A Dutch Festival Book for a French Queen." *Dutch Crossing* 42, no. 1 (2018): 3–27.

Bloemendal and Korsten 2012
Jan Bloemendal and Frans-Willem Korsten, eds. *Joost van den Vondel (1587–1679): Dutch Playwright of the Golden Age*. Leiden and Boston: Brill, 2012.

Bode 1907
Wilhelm von Bode. *Rembrandt und seine Zeitgenossen*. Leipzig: E.A. Seemann, 1907.

Boers 2012
Marion Boers. *De Noord-Nederlandse kunsthandel in de eerste helft van de zeventiende eeuw*. Hilversum: Uitgeverij Verloren, 2012.

Bok 1994
Marten Jan Bok. *Vraag en aanbod op de Nederlandse kunstmarkt 1580–1700*. PhD diss., University of Utrecht, 1994.

Bok and Schwartz 1991
Marten Jan Bok and Gary Schwartz. "Schilderen in opdracht in Holland in de 17e eeuw." *Holland* 23 (1991): 183–195.

Bonebakker 1999
Odilia Bonebakker. *Denomination and Iconography: The Baptism of the Eunuch in Netherlandish Art from the Reformation to 1750*. MA thesis, Queen's University, Kingston, 1999.

Boschloo et al. 2011
Anton W.A. Boschloo et al., eds. *Aemulatio: Imitation, Emulation and Invention in Netherlandish Art from 1500 to 1800. Essays in Honor of Eric Jan Sluijter*. Zwolle: Waanders, 2011.

Bosman 2019
Machiel Bosman. *Rembrandts plan. De ware geschiedenis van zijn faillissement*. Amsterdam: Athenaeum-Polak & Van Gennep, 2019.

Boston 2000–01
Alan Chong, ed. *Rembrandt Creates Rembrandt: Art and Ambition in Leiden, 1629–1631*. Exh. cat. Isabella Stewart Gardner Museum, Boston, 2000–01.

Boston and Chicago 2003–04
Clifford S. Ackley et al. *Rembrandt's Journey: Painter, Draftsman, Etcher*. Museum of Fine Arts, Boston, and Art Institute of Chicago, 2003–04.

Boston and St. Louis 1980–81
Clifford S. Ackley. *Printmaking in the Age of Rembrandt*. Exh. cat. Museum of Fine Arts, Boston, and Saint Louis Art Museum, St. Louis, 1980–81.

Van Breda 1997
Jacobus van Breda. "Rembrandt Etchings on Oriental Papers: Papers in the Collection of the National Gallery in Victoria." *Art Bulletin of Victoria* 38 (1997): 25–38.

Bredius 1892
Abraham Bredius. "De Schilder Johannes van de Cappelle." *Oud Holland* 10 (1892): 26–40.

Bredius 1893
Abraham Bredius. "De portretten van Joris de Caullery." *Oud Holland* 11, no. 2 (1893): 127–128.

Bredius 1910
Abraham Bredius. "Bol's kunstschatten." *Oud Holland* 28 (1910): 233–238.

Bredius 1915–22
Abraham Bredius. *Künstler-Inventare*. 8 vols. The Hague: M. Nijhoff, 1915–22.

Bredius 1934
Abraham Bredius. "Een Schilderscontract." *Oud Holland* 51 (1934): 188–190.

Bredius and Gerson 1969
Abraham Bredius, revised by Horst Gerson. *Rembrandt: The Complete Edition of the Paintings*. London: Phaidon, 1969 [1935].

Brewer and Porter 1993
John Brewer and Roy Porter, eds. *Consumption and the World of Goods*. London and New York: Routledge, 1993.

Van den Brink 2016
Peter van den Brink. "Tussen Rubens en Rembrandt. Jacob Adriaensz. Backer als portret- en historieschilder in Amsterdam." *Kroniek van het Rembrandthuis* (2016): 4–39.

Brom 1936
Gerard Brom. *Rembrandt in de literatuur*. Groningen: J.B. Wolters, 1936.

Brook 2008
Timothy Brook. *Vermeer's Hat: The Seventeenth Century and the Dawn of the Global World*. London: Profile Books, 2008.

Broos 1975–76
B.P.J. Broos. "Rembrandt and Lastman's Coriolanus: The History Piece in 17th-century Theory and Practice." *Simiolus: Netherlands Quarterly for the History of Art* 8, no. 4 (1975–76): 199–228.

Broos 2012
Ben Broos. *Saskia. De vrouw van Rembrandt*. Zwolle: W Books 2012.

Brown 1995
Jonathan Brown. *Kings and Connoisseurs: Collecting Art in Seventeenth-century Europe*. New Haven and London: Yale University Press, 1995.

Bruin 1995
Kees Bruin. *De echte Rembrandt. Verering van een genie in de twintigste eeuw*. Amsterdam: Balans, 1995.

Brusati 2003
Celeste Brusati. "Hoogstraten [Hoostraeten], Samuel van." *Grove Art Online*. 2003. https://doi.org/10.1093/gao/9781884446054.article.T038856 (accessed 7 Mar. 2020).

Brussels 2005
Stefaan Hautekeete. *Les dessins de Rembrandt et ses élèves.* Exh. cat. Musées royaux des beaux-arts de Belgique, Brussels, 2005.

Busch 1989
Werner Busch. "Das keusche und das unkeusche Sehen. Rembrandts 'Diana, Aktaion und Callisto.'" *Zeitschrift für Kunstgeschichte* 52 (1989): 257–277.

Budapest 2014–15
Ildikó Ember, ed., with Nikoletta Koruhely, Júlia Tátrai and Axel Vécsey. *Rembrandt and the Dutch Golden Age.* Exh. cat. Museum of Fine Arts, Budapest, 2014–15.

Büttner 2014
Nils Büttner. *Rembrandt. Licht und Schatten. Eine Biographie.* Stuttgart: Reclam, 2014.

Van Campen and Eliëns 2014
Jan van Campen and Titus Eliëns, eds. *Chinese and Japanese Porcelain for the Dutch Golden Age.* Zwolle: Waanders, 2014.

Carroll 1981
Margaret Deutsch Carroll. "Rembrandt as Meditational Printmaker." *Art Bulletin* 63 (1981): 587–610.

Ten Cate 1988
Flip ten Cate. *Dit volckje seer verwoet. Een geschiedenis van de Sint Antoniesbreestraat.* Amsterdam: 1988.

Caves 2000
Richard E. Caves. *Creative Industries: Contracts between Art and Commerce.* Cambridge, MA: Harvard University Press, 2000.

Chalard-Fillaudeau 2004
Anne Chalard-Fillaudeau. *Rembrandt, l'artiste au fil des textes. Rembrandt dans la littérature et la philosophie européennes depuis 1669.* Paris: L'Harmattan, 2004.

Chapman 1990
H. Perry Chapman. *Rembrandt's Self-portraits: A Study in Seventeenth-century Identity.* Princeton: Princeton University Press, 1990.

Chicago 2019–20
Victoria Sancho Lobis, ed. *Rubens, Rembrandt, and Drawing in the Golden Age.* Exh. cat. The Art Institute of Chicago, 2019–20.

Chong and Zell 2002
Alan Chong and Michael Zell, eds. *Rethinking Rembrandt.* Zwolle: Waanders, 2002.

Cleves 2015–16
Tom van der Molen et al. *Govert Flinck: Reflecting History.* Exh. cat. Museum Kurhaus Kleve, Cleves, 2015–16.

Cologne and Dordrecht 1998–99
Udo Brüssow and Volker Manuth, eds. *Arent de Gelder, 1645–1727. Rembrandts Meisterschüler und Nachfolger.* Exh. cat. Wallraf-Richartz-Museum, Cologne, and Dordrechts Museum, Dordrecht, 1998–99.

Cologne and Prague 2019–20
Anja K. Sevčík, ed. *Inside Rembrandt, 1606–1669.* Exh. cat. Wallraf-Richartz-Museum & Fondation Corboud, Cologne, and National Gallery, Prague, 2019–20.

Corpus
Josua Bruyn, Bob Haak, Simon H. Levie, Pieter J.J. van Thiel and Ernst van de Wetering. *A Corpus of Rembrandt Paintings.* Stichting Foundation Rembrandt Research Project. 6 vols. Dordrecht, Boston and London: Martinus Nijhoff Publishers / Dordrecht: Springer, 1982–2015.

Courtright 1996
Nicola Courtright. "Origins and Meanings of Rembrandt's Late Drawing Style." *The Art Bulletin* 78, no. 3 (1996): 485–510.

Crenshaw 2006
Paul Crenshaw. *Rembrandt's Bankruptcy: The Artist, His Patrons, and the Art Market in Seventeenth-century Netherlands.* Cambridge: Cambridge University Press, 2006.

Crenshaw 2013
Paul Crenshaw. "The Catalyst for Rembrandt's *Satire on Art Criticism.*" *Journal of Historians of Netherlandish Art* 5, no. 2 (summer 2013). https://jhna.org/articles/catalyst-rembrandt-satire-on-art-criticism/ (accessed 12 Mar. 2020).

Cruz Yábar 2013
Juan Maria Cruz Yábar. "Judit o Ester? El Rembrandt del Museo del Prado." *Anales de historia del arte* 23 (2013): 99–112.

Davids 2008
Karel Davids. *The Rise and Decline of Dutch Technological Leadership: Technology, Economy and Culture in the Netherlands, 1350–1800.* 2 vols. Leiden and Boston: Brill, 2008.

Décade 1798
La Décade philosophique, littéraire et politique 35 (1798).

Dekiert 2006
Marcus Dekiert. *Alte Pinakothek. Holländische und deutsche Malerei des 17. Jahrhunderts.* Munich: Hatje Cantz, 2006.

Descamps 1753–64
Jean-Baptiste Descamps. *La vie des peintres flamands, allemands et hollandais.* 4 vols. Paris: Charles-Antoine Jombert, 1753–64.

Dickey 1986
Stephanie S. Dickey. "'Judicious Negligence': Rembrandt Transforms an Emblematic Convention." *Art Bulletin* 68, no. 2 (1986): 253–262.

Dickey 2004
Stephanie S. Dickey. *Rembrandt: Portraits in Print.* Amsterdam and Philadelphia: John Benjamins Publishing Company, 2004.

Dickey 2007
Stephanie S. Dickey. "Rethinking Rembrandt's Renaissance." *Canadian Journal of Netherlandic Studies* 21 (2007): 1–22.

Dickey 2008
Stephanie S. Dickey. "Jan Lievens in Rembrandt's House." *Kroniek van het Rembrandthuis* (2008): 36–53.

Dickey 2010
Stephanie S. Dickey. "Damsels in Distress: Gender and Emotion in Seventeenth-century Netherlandish Art." *Netherlands Yearbook for History of Art / Nederlands Kunsthistorisch Jaarboek* 60 (2010): 52–81.

Dickey 2013
Stephanie S. Dickey. "Begging for Attention: The Artful Context of Rembrandt's Etching Beggar Seated on a Bank." *Journal of Historians of Netherlandish Art* 5, no. 2 (summer 2013). www.jhna.org/articles/begging-for-attention-artful-context-rembrandts-etching-beggar-seated-on-a-bank (accessed 14 Nov. 2019).

Dickey 2017a
Stephanie S. Dickey, ed. *Ferdinand Bol and Govert Flinck: New Research.* Zwolle: W Books, 2017.

Dickey 2017b
Stephanie S. Dickey, ed. *Rembrandt and His Circle: Insights and Discoveries.* Amsterdam: Amsterdam University Press, 2017.

Van den Doel et al. 2005
Marieke van den Doel et al., eds. *The Learned Eye: Regarding Art, Theory, and the Artist's Reputation. Essays for Ernst van de Wetering.* Amsterdam: Amsterdam University Press, 2005.

Van Domselaer 1660
Tobias van Domselaer, ed. *Hollantsche Parnas, of verscheide gedichten…* Amsterdam: Jacob Lescaille, 1660.

Dresden 2006–07
Uta Neidhardt and Thomas Ketelsen, eds. *Rembrandt van Rijn. Die Entführung des Ganymed.* Exh. cat. Staatliche Kunstsammlungen Dresden, Gemäldegalerie Alte Meister, Kupferstich-Kabinett, 2006–07.

Dresden 2019
Stephanie Buck and Jürgen Müller, with Mailena Mallach, eds. *Rembrandt's Mark.* Exh. cat. Staatliche Kunstsammlungen Dresden, Kupferstich-Kabinett, 2019.

Dudok van Heel 1969
Sebastien A.C. Dudok van Heel. "Het maecenaat de Graeff en Rembrandt." *Maandblad Amstelodamum* 56 (1969): 150–155.

Dudok van Heel 1978
Sebastien A.C. Dudok van Heel. "Mr Joannes Wtenbogaert (1608–1680), een man uit een Remonstrants milieu en Rembrandt van Rijn," *Jaarboek Amstelodamum* 70 (1978): 146–169.

Dudok van Heel 2006
Sebastien A.C. Dudok van Heel. *De jonge Rembrandt onder tijdgenoten. Godsdienst en schilderkunst in Leiden en Amsterdam.* PhD diss., Radboud University, Nijmegen, 2006.

Dudok van Heel 2020
Sebastien A.C. Dudok van Heel. "Rembrandt als portretschilder bij Hendrick Uylenburgh, met opdrachten in Den Haag, Leiden en Rotterdam, 1631–1634." *Maandblad Amstelodamum* 107, no. 2 (2020): 56–91.

Dumas, Ekkart and Van de Puttelaar 2020
Charles Dumas, Rudi Ekkart and Carla van de Puttelaar, eds. *Connoisseurship: Essays in Honour of Fred G. Meijer.* Leiden: Primavera Pers, 2020.

Ebert 2009
Bernd Ebert. *Simon und Isaack Luttichuys. Monographie mit kritischem Werkverzeichnis.* Berlin: Deutscher Kunstverlag, 2009.

Ebert-Schifferer and Mazzetti di Pietralata 2009
Sybille Ebert-Schifferer and Cecilia Mazzetti di Pietralata, eds. *Joachim von Sandrart. Ein europäischer Künstler und Theoretiker zwischen Italien und Deutschland*. Munich: Hirmer Verlag, 2009.

ECARTICO
University of Amsterdam, Amsterdam Centre for the Study of the Golden Age. *ECARTICO*. www.vondel.humanities.uva.nl/ecartico/ (accessed 6 May 2020).

Edinburgh and London 2001
Julia Lloyd Williams. *Rembrandt's Women*. Exh. cat. National Gallery of Scotland, Edinburgh, and Royal Academy of Arts, London, 2001.

Van Eeghen 1977
I.H. van Eeghen. "Drie portretten van Rembrandt (Bruyningh, Cater, Moutmaker) Vondel en Blaeu." *Jaarboek Amstelodamum* 69 (1977): 55–72.

Emmens 1968
Jan Emmens. *Rembrandt en de regels van de kunst*. Utrecht: Dekker & Gumbert, 1968.

England 2018
Yaffa England. "The Expulsion of Hagar: Reading the Image, (Re)viewing the Story." *Religion and the Arts* 22 (2018): 261–293.

Étienne et al. 1800
Charles-Guillaume Étienne et al. *Rembrandt, ou la Vente après décès, vaudeville anecdotique en un acte*. Paris: Magasin de pièces de théâtre, 1800.

Fatah-Black and Van Rossum 2015
Karwan Fatah-Black and Matthias van Rossum. "Beyond Profitability: The Dutch Transatlantic Slave Trade and its Economic Impact." *Slavery and Abolition* 36, no. 1 (2015): 63–83.

Flynn, Giráldez and Von Glahn 2003
Dennis O. Flynn, Arturo Giráldez and Richard von Glahn, eds. *Global Connections and Monetary History, 1470–1800*. Farnham and Burlington: Ashgate, 2003.

Fontaine Verwey 1969
Herman de la Fontaine Verwey. "Michel le Blon: Graveur, kunsthandelaar, diplomaat." *Jaarboek Amstelodamum* 61 (1969): 103–128.

Ford 2007
Charles Ford, ed. *Lives of Rembrandt by Joachim von Sandrart, Filippo Baldinucci and Arnold Houbraken*. London: Pallas Athene, 2007.

Franits 2004
Wayne Franits. *Dutch Seventeenth-century Genre Painting: Its Stylistic and Thematic Evolution*. New Haven and London: Yale University Press, 2004.

Franits 2016
Wayne Franits, ed. *The Ashgate Research Companion to Dutch Art of the Golden Age*. London and New York: Routledge, 2016.

Frankfurt 2000
Annette Strech. *Nach dem Leben und aus der Phantasie. Niederländische Zeichnungen vom 15. bis 18. Jahrhundert aus dem Städelschen Kunstinstitut*. Exh. cat. Städel Museum, Frankfurt am Main, 2000.

Frankfurt 2003a
Jeroen Giltaij. *Rembrandt Rembrandt*. Exh. cat. Städel Museum, Frankfurt am Main, 2003.

Frankfurt 2003b
Martin Sonnabend. *Rembrandt. Die Radierungen im Städel*. Exh. cat. Städel Museum, Frankfurt am Main, 2003.

Frankfurt 2015–16
Max Hollein, ed. *Masterworks in Dialogue: Eminent Guests for the Anniversary*. Exh cat. Städel Museum, Frankfurt am Main, 2015–16.

Freedberg and De Vries 1991
David Freedberg and Jan de Vries, eds. *Art in History, History in Art: Studies in Seventeenth-century Dutch Culture*. Santa Monica: Getty Center for the History of Art and the Humanities, 1991.

Fremantle 1959
Katherine Fremantle. *The Baroque Town Hall of Amsterdam*. From the series *Orbus Artium*, vol. 4. Utrecht: Haentjens, Dekker et Gumbert, 1959.

Frijhoff and Prak 2004
Willem Frijhoff and Maarten Prak, eds. *Geschiedenis van Amsterdam*. Vol. 2–1: *Centrum van de Wereld, 1578–1650*. Amsterdam: SUN, 2004.

Fromentin 1984
Eugène Fromentin. *Œuvres complètes*. Edited by Guy Sagnes. Paris: Gallimard, 1984.

Fucci 2019
Robert Fucci. "Rembrandt in the Spotlight: Recent Studies and Exhibitions." *Print Quarterly* 36 (2019): 354–361.

Fusenig 2006
Thomas Fusenig. *Suermondt-Ludwig-Museum Aachen. Bestandskatalog der Gemäldegalerie, Niederlande von 1550 bis 1800*. Munich: Hirmer Verlag, 2006.

Van Gelder 1957
Hendrik E. van Gelder. *Ikonografie van Constantijn Huygens en de zijnen*. Dordrecht, Boston and London: Martinus Nijhoff Publishers, 1957.

Van Gelder and Van Gelder-Schrijver 1938
J.G. van Gelder and N.F. van Gelder-Schrijver. "De 'Memorie' van Rembrandt's prenten in het bezit van Valerius Röver." *Oud Holland* 55 (1938): 1–16.

Genet 1979
Jean Genet. *Le secret de Rembrandt* [1958], in *Œuvres complètes, V*. Paris: Gallimard, 1979.

Van Gent 2011
Judith van Gent. *Bartholomeus van der Helst (ca. 1613–1670). Een studie naar zijn leven en werk*. Zwolle: W Books, 2011.

Gersaint 1751
Edme-François Gersaint. *Catalogue raisonné de toutes les pièces qui forment l'œuvre de Rembrandt*. Edited by P.C.A. Helle and J.B. Glomy. Paris: Hochereau, 1751.

Gerson 1961
Horst Gerson, transcribed by Isabella H. van Eeghen. *Seven Letters by Rembrandt*. Translated by Yda D. Ovink. The Hague: L.J.C Boucher, 1961.

Gerson 1969
Horst Gerson. "Rembrandt's portret van Amalia van Solms." *Oud Holland* 84 (1969): 244–249.

Giltaij 1997
Jeroen Giltaij. *Ruffo en Rembrandt. Over een Siciliaanse verzamelaar in de zeventiende eeuw die drie schilderijen bij Rembrandt bestelde*. PhD diss., Vrije Universiteit Amsterdam, 1997.

Giltaij 2017
Jeroen Giltaij. "A Note on Rembrandt's *Aristotle, Alexander, and Homer*." *Journal of Historians of Netherlandish Art* 9, no. 1 (winter 2017). https://jhna.org/articles/note-rembrandt-aristotle-alexander-homer/ (accessed 7 Mar. 2020).

Glasgow 2012
Peter Black. *Rembrandt and the Passion*. Exh. cat. Hunterian Art Gallery, Glasgow, 2012.

Goethe 1975
Johann Wolfgang von Goethe. *Aus Goethes Brieftasche. Die schönsten Aufsätze über Natur, Kunst, Volk*. Edited by Margot Böttcher and Hans Jürgen Geerdts. Berlin: Verlag der Nation, 1975.

Golahny 1984
Amy Golahny. *Rembrandt's Paintings and the Venetian Tradition*. PhD diss., Columbia University, New York, 1984.

Golahny 1990
Amy Golahny. "Rubens' *Hero and Leander* and Its Poetic Progeny." *Yale University Art Gallery Bulletin* (1990): 21–37.

Golahny 2000
Amy Golahny. "Rembrandt's *Artemisia*: Arts Patron." *Oud Holland* 114, no. 2/4 (2000): 139–152.

Golahny 2003
Amy Golahny. *Rembrandt's Reading: The Artist's Bookshelf of Ancient Poetry and History*. Amsterdam: Amsterdam University Press, 2003.

Golahny 2007
Amy Golahny. "The Disappearing Angel: Heemskerck's 'Departing Raphael' in Rembrandt's Studio." *Canadian Journal of Netherlandic Studies* 28 (2007): 38–52.

Golahny 2013
Amy Golahny. "Italian Paintings in Amsterdam around 1635: Additions to the Familiar." *Journal of Historians of Netherlandish Art* 5, no. 2 (summer 2013). https://jhna.org/articles/italian-paintings-amsterdam-around-1635-additions-familiar/ (accessed 25 Oct. 2019).

Golahny, Mochizuki and Vergara 2006
Amy Golahny, Mia M. Mochizuki and Lisa Vergara, eds. *In His Milieu: Essays on Netherlandish Art in Memory of John Michael Montias*. Amsterdam: Amsterdam University Press, 2006.

Goossens 1996
Eymert-Jan Goossens. *Treasure Wrought by Chisel and Brush: The Town Hall of Amsterdam in the Golden Age*. Zwolle: Waanders, 1996.

Gottwald 2011
Franziska Gottwald. *Das Tronie. Muster, Studie und Meisterwerk. Die Genese einer Gattung der Malerei vom 15. Jahrhundert bis zu Rembrandt*. Berlin: Deutscher Kunstverlag, 2011.

Griffiths 2016
Antony Griffiths. *The Print before Photography: An Introduction to European Printmaking 1550–1820.* London: The British Museum Press, 2016.

Griffiths and Chapman 2013
Antony Griffiths and Hugo Chapman. "Israel Henriet, the Chatsworth Album and the Publication of the Works of Jacques Callot." *Print Quarterly* 30 (2013): 273–293.

Van de Grind 2016
Åse van de Grind. "Rembrandts ets *Het scheepje van Fortuin* voor *Der zee-vaert lof* van Elias Herckmans." *Kroniek van het Rembrandthuis* (2016): 37–46.

Grohé 1996
Stefan Grohé. *Rembrandts mythologische Historien.* Vienna: Böhlau Verlag, 1996.

Grove Art Online
Grove Art Online | Oxford Art Online. www.oxford-artonline.com/groveart (accessed 6 May 2020).

Haarlem and Paris 2001–02
Michiel C. Plomp. *Collectionner, passionnément.* Vol. 1: *Les collectionneurs hollandais de dessins au XVIIIe siècle.* Exh. cat. Teylers Museum, Haarlem, and Institut Néerlandais, Paris, 2001–02.

Haarlem, Zürich and Schwerin 2006
Pieter Biesboer et al. *Nicolaes Berchem: In the Light of Italy.* Exh. cat. Frans Hals Museum, Haarlem, Kunsthaus, Zürich, and Staatliches Museum Schwerin, 2006.

Hadjinicolaou 2016
Yannis Hadjinicolaou. *Denkende Körper. Formende Hände. Handeling in Kunst und Kunsttheorie der Rembrandtisten.* Berlin and Boston: De Gruyter, 2016.

The Hague 1997
Peter van der Ploeg and Carola Vermeeren, eds. *Vorstelijk Verzameld. De kunstcollectie van Frederik Hendrik en Amalia.* Exh. cat. Mauritshuis, The Hague, 1997.

The Hague and San Francisco 1990–91
Ben Broos et al. *Great Dutch Paintings from America.* Exh. cat. Mauritshuis, The Hague, and Fine Arts Museums of San Francisco, 1990–91.

Hamann 1936
Richard Hamann. "Hagars Abschied bei Rembrandt und im Rembrandt-Kreise." *Marburger Jahrbuch für Kunstwissenschaft* 8/9 (1936): 471–578.

Hamburg 2006
Martina Sitt, ed. *Pieter Lastman. In Rembrandts Schatten?* Exh. cat. Hamburger Kunsthalle, Hamburg, 2006.

Hamburg 2017–18
Franz Wilhelm Kaiser and Michael North, eds. *Die Geburt des Kunstmarktes. Rembrandt, Ruisdael, Van Goyen und die Künstler des Goldenen Zeitalters.* Exh. cat. Bucerius Kunst Forum, Hamburg, 2017–18.

't Hart 2014
Marjolein 't Hart. *The Dutch Wars of Independence: Warfare and Commerce in the Netherlands, 1570–1680.* London and New York: Routledge, 2014.

Haverkamp-Begemann 1982
Egbert Haverkamp-Begemann. *Rembrandt: The Nightwatch.* Princeton: Princeton University Press, 1982.

Hazlitt 1930–34
William Hazlitt. *The Complete Works.* 21 vols. Edited by Arnold Glover, P.P. Howe, James Thornton and Alfred Rayney Waller. London: J.M. Dent and Sons, 1930–34.

Hecht 2006
Peter Hecht. *Van Gogh en Rembrandt.* Amsterdam: Van Gogh Museum, 2006.

Heckscher 1958
William S. Heckscher. *Rembrandt's Anatomy of Dr. Nicolaas Tulp: An Iconological Study.* New York: New York University Press, 1958.

Heinen 2010
Ulrich Heinen. "Huygens, Rubens and Medusa: Reflecting the Passions in Paintings, with some Considerations of Neuroscience in Art History." *Netherlands Yearbook for the History of Art | Nederlands Kunsthistorisch Jaarboek* 60 (2010): 151–178.

Hillegers et al. 2014
Jasper Hillegers et al. *Salomon Lilian Old Masters 2014.* Amsterdam: Salomon Lilian, 2014.

Hillegers et al. 2019
Jasper Hillegers et al. *Salomon Lilian Old Masters 2019.* Amsterdam: Salomon Lilian, 2019.

Hinterding 1993–94
Erik Hinterding. "The History of Rembrandt's Copperplates, with a Catalogue of Those That Survive." *Simiolus: Netherlands Quarterly for the History of Art* 22, no. 4 (1993–94): 253–315.

Hinterding 2006
Erik Hinterding. *Rembrandt as an Etcher: The Practice of Production and Distribution.* 3 vols. Ouderkerk aan den IJssel: Sound & Vision Publishers, 2006.

Hinterding 2008
Erik Hinterding. *Rembrandt Etchings from the Frits Lugt Collection.* Bussum: Thoth Publishers / Paris: Fondation Custodia, 2008.

Hirschfelder 2008
Dagmar Hirschfelder. *Tronie und Porträt in der niederländischen Malerei des 17. Jahrhunderts.* Berlin: Gebrüder Mann Verlag, 2008.

Hoet 1752–70
Gerard Hoet. *Catalogus of naamlyst van schilderyen, met derzelver pryzen.* 3 vols. The Hague: 1752–70.

Hofstede de Groot 1908–27
Cornelis Hofstede de Groot. *A Catalogue Raisonné of the Works of the Most Eminent Dutch Painters of the Seventeenth Century, Based on the Work of John Smith.* 10 vols. London: MacMillan and Co., 1908–27.

Hollstein
Friedrich Wilhelm Hollstein, ed. *Dutch and Flemish Etchings, Engravings and Woodcuts, ca. 1450–1700.* 72 vols. Amsterdam: M. Hertzberger, 1949–.

Van Hoogstraten 1678
Samuel van Hoogstraten. *Inleyding tot de hooge schoole der schilderkonst. Anders de Zichtbare Werelt.* Rotterdam: François van Hoogstraten, 1678.

De Hoop Scheffer and Boon 1971
D. de Hoop Scheffer and K.G. Boon. "De inventaris-lijst van Clement de Jonghe en Rembrandts etsplaten." *Kroniek van het Rembrandthuis* 25 (1971): 1–17.

Houbraken 1718–21
Arnold Houbraken. *De groote schouburgh der Nederlantsche konstschilders en schilderessen.* 3 vols. Amsterdam: 1718–21.

Huygens 1897
Constantijn Huygens. *De vita propria sermonum inter liberos libri duo (Fragment eener autobiographie van Constantijn Huygens)* [c. 1681]. Published by J.A. Worp, in *Bijdragen en Mededeelingen van het Historisch Genootschap* 18 (1897): 1–121.

Huygens 1987
Constantijn Huygens. *Mijn jeugd.* Translated by C.L. Heesakkers. Amsterdam: Em. Querido's Uitgeverij, 1987.

Israel 1979
Jonathan I. Israel. "The Holland Towns and the Dutch-Spanish Conflict, 1621–1648." *Bijdragen en Mededelingen betreffende de Geschiedenis der Nederlanden* 94 (1979): 41–69.

Israel 1989
Jonathan I. Israel. *Dutch Primacy in World Trade, 1585–1740.* Oxford: Clarendon Press, 1989.

Jager 2015
Angela Jager. "'Everywhere illustrious histories that are a dime a dozen.' The Mass Market for History Painting in Seventeenth-century Amsterdam." *Journal of Historians of Netherlandish Art* 7, no. 1 (winter 2015). https://jhna.org/articles/everywhere-illustrious-histories-that-are-a-dime-a-dozen-mass-market-history-painting-seventeenth-century-amsterdam/ (accessed 19 Nov. 2019).

Jager 2016
Angela Jager. *"Galey-schilders" en "dosijnwerck." De productie, distributie en consumptie van goedkope historiestukken in zeventiende-eeuws Amsterdam.* PhD diss., University of Amsterdam, 2016.

Janssen 2017
Geert H. Janssen. "The Republic of the Refugees: Early Modern Migrations and the Dutch Experience." *The Historical Journal* 60, no. 1 (Mar. 2017): 233–252.

Judson 1969
J. Richard Judson. "Rembrandt in Canada." *The Burlington Magazine* 111, no. 800 (Nov. 1969): 703–704.

Judson and Ekkart 1999
J. Richard Judson and Rudolf E.O. Ekkart. *Gerrit van Honthorst, 1592–1656.* Doornspijk: Davaco Publishers, 1999.

Kaaring 2005
David Burmeister Kaaring. "Nicolaes Eliasz Pickenoy (1588–1650/56) and Portraiture in Amsterdam around 1620–45." *SMK Art Journal* (2005): 127–137.

Kahr 1966
Madlyn Kahr. "Rembrandt's Esther: A Painting and an Etching Newly Interpreted and Dated." *Oud Holland* 81 (1966): 228–244.

Kassel 2005–06
Gregor J.M. Weber. *Rembrandt im Kontrast.*
Die Blendung Simsons und der Segen Jakobs. Exh. cat.
Staatliche Museen Kassel, Gemäldegalerie Alte
Meister, 2005–06.

Kassel and Leiden 2006–07
Christiaan Vogelaar and Gregor J.M. Weber, eds.
Rembrandt's Landscapes. Exh. cat. Staatliche
Museen Kassel, Gemäldegalerie Alte Meister, and
Stedelijk Museum De Lakenhal, Leiden, 2006–07.

Keblusek and Noldus 2011
Marika Keblusek and Badeloch Vera Noldus, eds.
*Double Agents: Cultural and Political Brokerage in
Early Modern Europe.* Leiden and Boston: Brill, 2011.

Kelch and Von Simson 1973
Jan Kelch and Otto von Simson, eds. *Neue Beiträge
zur Rembrandt-Forschung.* Berlin: G. Mann, 1973.

Kingston, Edmonton, Regina and Hamilton 2019–21
Jacquelyn N. Coutré, ed. *Leiden circa 1630: Rembrandt
Emerges.* Exh. cat. Agnes Etherington Art Centre,
Kingston, Art Gallery of Alberta, Edmonton,
MacKenzie Art Gallery, Regina, and Art Gallery of
Hamilton, 2019–21.

Klemm 1986
Christian Klemm. *Joachim von Sandrart: Kunst-
Werke u. Lebens-Lauf.* Berlin: Deutscher Verlag für
Kunstwissenschaft, 1986.

Klep et al. 1987
P.M.M. Klep et al., eds. *Wonen in het Verleden,
17ᵉ-20ᵉ Eeuw. Economie, Politiek, Volkshuisvesting,
Cultuur en Bibliografie.* Amsterdam: NEHA, 1987.

Kofuku 2004
Akira Kofuku, ed. *Rembrandt and Dutch History
Painting in the 17th Century.* Tokyo: The National
Museum of Western Art, 2004.

Kok 2013
Erna Kok. *Culturele ondernemers in de Gouden Eeuw.
De artistieke en sociaal-economische strategieën van
Jacob Backer, Govert Flinck, Ferdinand Bol en Joachim
von Sandrart.* PhD diss., University of Amsterdam,
2013.

Kolfin 2013
Elmer Kolfin. "Rembrandt's *Reclining Nude*
Reconsidered." *Print Quarterly* 30, no. 1 (2013): 39–43.

Kooijmans 1997
Luuc Kooijmans. *Vriendschap en de kunst van het
overleven in de zeventiende en achttiende eeuw.*
Amsterdam: Bert Bakker, 1997.

Krempel 2000
Léon Krempel. *Studien zu den datierten Gemälden
des Nicolaes Maes (1634–1693).* Petersberg: Michael
Imhof Verlag, 2000.

Kris and Kurz 2010
Ernst Kris and Otto Kurz. *La légende de l'artiste.
Un essai historique.* Paris: Éditions Allia, 2010.

Kuijpers 2005
Erika Kuijpers. *Migrantenstad. Immigratie en Sociale
Verhoudingen in 17e-eeuws Amsterdam.* Hilversum:
Verloren, 2005.

Landau and Parshall 1994
David Landau and Peter Parshall. *The Renaissance
Print, 1470–1550.* New Haven and London: Yale
University Press, 1994.

Langbehn 1926
August Julius Langbehn. *Niederdeutsches. Ein Beitrag
zur Völkerpsychologie.* Edited by Benedikt Momme
Nissen. Buchenbach-Baden: Felsen-Verlag, 1926 [1887].

Laurentius 2010
Frans Laurentius. *Clement de Jonghe (ca. 1624–1677).
Kunstverkoper in de Gouden Eeuw.* Houten: Hes &
De Graaf, 2010.

Leerintveld 1989
A.M. Th. Leerintveld. "'T quam soo wel te pass.'
Huygens' portretbijschriften en de datering van
zijn portret geschildered door Jan Lievens." *Leids
Kunsthistorisch Jaarboek* 8 (1989): 159–183.

Leeuwarden and Kassel 2018–19
Marlies Stoter and Justus Lange, eds. *Rembrandt
and Saskia: Love and Marriage in the Dutch Golden
Age.* Exh. cat. Fries Museum, Leeuwarden, and
Museumslandschaft Hessen Kassel, 2018–19.

Leiden Collection Catalogue
Arthur K. Wheelock, Jr., ed. *The Leiden Collection
Catalogue.* www.theleidencollection.com/archive/
(accessed 10 Feb. 2020).

Leiden 1991
Christiaan Vogelaar, ed. *Rembrandt and Lievens in
Leiden.* Translated by Ruth Koening. Exh. cat.
Stedelijk Museum De Lakenhal, Leiden, 1991.

Leiden and Oxford 2019–20
Christopher Brown, An Van Camp and Christiaan
Vogelaar, eds. *Young Rembrandt.* Exh. cat. Museum
De Lakenhal, Leiden, and Ashmolean Museum,
Oxford, 2019–20.

Lesger 1986
Clé Lesger. *Huur en Conjunctuur. De Woningmarkt
in Amsterdam, 1550–1850.* Hilversum: Verloren, 1986.

Lesger 2006
Clé Lesger. *The Rise of the Amsterdam Market and
Information Exchange: Merchants, Commercial
Expansion and Change in the Spatial Economy of the
Low Countries, c. 1550–1630.* Farnham and Burlington:
Ashgate, 2006.

Li 2018
Weixuan Li. *Deciphering the Art and Market in the
Dutch Golden Age: Insights from Digital Methodologies.*
MA thesis, University of Amsterdam, 2018.

Li 2019
Weixuan Li. "Innovative Exuberance: Fluctuations
in the Painting Production in the 17th-century
Netherlands." *Arts* (2019). www.mdpi.com/2076-
0752/8/2/72 (accessed 29 May 2020).

Liedtke 2004
Walter Liedtke. "Rembrandt's 'Workshop' Revisited."
Oud Holland 117 (2004): 48–73.

Liedtke 2007
Walter Liedtke. *Dutch Paintings in the Metropolitan
Museum of Art.* 2 vols. New York: The Metropolitan
Museum of Art, 2007.

Logan 1979
Anne-Marie S. Logan. *The "Cabinet" of the Brothers
Gerard and Jan Reynst.* Amsterdam, Oxford and
New York: North-Holland Publishing Company, 1979.

London 1993
Christopher Brown et al. *Rembrandt van Rijn: Girl
at a Window.* Exh. cat. Dulwich Picture Gallery,
London, 1993.

London and Amsterdam 2006
Friso Lammertse and Jaap van der Veen. *Uylenburgh
and Son: Art and Commerce from Rembrandt to
De Lairesse, 1625–1675.* Exh. cat. Dulwich Picture
Gallery, London, and Rembrandt House Museum,
Amsterdam, 2006.

London and Amsterdam 2016
Jonathan Bikker et al. *Rembrandt: The Late Works.*
Exh. cat. The National Gallery, London, and
Rijksmuseum, Amsterdam, 2016.

London and The Hague 1999–2000
Christopher White and Quentin Buvelot, eds.
Rembrandt by Himself. Exh. cat. The National
Gallery, London, and Mauritshuis, The Hague,
1999–2000.

London and The Hague 2007–08
Rudi Ekkart and Quentin Buvelot. *Dutch Portraits:
The Age of Rembrandt and Frans Hals.* Exh. cat.
The National Gallery, London, and Mauritshuis,
The Hague, 2007–08.

London and The Hague 2019–20
Bart Cornelis, Ariane van Suchtelen and Nina
Cahill. *Nicolaes Maes: Dutch Master of the Golden
Age.* Exh. cat. The National Gallery, London, and
Mauritshuis, The Hague, 2019–20.

Lootsma 2007–08
Hilbert Lootsma. "Tracing a Pose: Govert Flinck and
the Emergence of the Van Dyckian Mode of Portraiture
in Amsterdam." *Simiolus: Netherlands Quarterly for
the History of Art* 33, no. 4 (2007–08): 221–236.

Los Angeles 2009–10
Holm Bevers et al. *Drawings by Rembrandt and His
Pupils: Telling the Difference.* Exh. cat. The J. Paul
Getty Museum, Los Angeles, 2009–10.

Los Angeles 2018
Stephanie Schrader, ed. *Rembrandt and the
Inspiration of India.* Exh. cat. The J. Paul Getty
Museum, Los Angeles, 2018.

Van Lottum 2007
Jelle van Lottum. *Across the North Sea: The Impact of
the Dutch Republic on International Labour Migration.*
Amsterdam: Aksant, 2007.

Lourens and Lucassen 1997
Piet Lourens and Jan Lucassen. *Inwoneraantallen
van Nederlandse steden, ca. 1300–1800.* Amsterdam:
NEHA, 1997.

Lugt 1915
Frits Lugt. *Wandelingen met Rembrandt in en om
Amsterdam.* Amsterdam: P.N. van Kampen, 1915.

Madrid 2008
Alejandro Vergara, ed., with Teresa Posada Kubissa and Mariët Westermann. *Rembrandt Pintor de Historias*. Exh. cat. Museo Nacional del Prado, Madrid, 2008.

Madrid 2020
Norbert Middelkoop and Rudi Ekkart, eds. *Rembrandt and Amsterdam Portraiture, 1590–1670*. Exh. cat. Thyssen-Bornemisza Museo Nacional, Madrid, 2020.

Magnani 2007
Lauro Magnani. "1666. Een onbekende opdracht uit Genua voor Rembrandt." *Kroniek van het Rembrandthuis* (2007): 3–18.

Magnusson 2018
Börje Magnusson. *Dutch Drawings in Swedish Public Collections*. Berlin: Hatje Cantz / Stockholm: Nationalmuseum, 2018.

Van Mander 1973
Karel van Mander. *Den grondt der edel vry schilder-const*. 2 vols. Edited by Hessel Miedema. Utrecht: Haentjens Dekker & Gumbert, 1973.

Mandrella 2011
David Mandrella. *Jacob van Loo, 1614–1670*. Paris: Arthena, 2011.

Manuth 1990
Volker Manuth. "Die Augen des Sünders. Überlegungen zu Rembrandts 'Blendung Simsons' von 1636 in Frankfurt." *Artibus et Historiae* 11, no. 21 (1990): 169–199.

Manuth 1993–94
Volker Manuth. "Denomination and Iconography: The Choice of Subject Matter in the Biblical Painting of the Rembrandt Circle." *Simiolus: Netherlands Quarterly for the History of Art* 22, no. 4 (1993–94): 235–252.

Manuth, De Winkel and Van Leeuwen 2019
Volker Manuth, Marieke de Winkel and Rudie van Leeuwen. *Rembrandt: The Complete Paintings*. Cologne: Taschen, 2019.

Manuth and Rüger 2004
Volker Manuth and Axel Rüger, eds. *Collected Opinions: Essays on Netherlandish Art in Honour of Alfred Bader*. London: Paul Holberton Publishing, 2004.

McCants 2008
Anne E.C. McCants. "Poor Consumers as Global Consumers: The Diffusion of Tea and Coffee Drinking in the Eighteenth Century." *Economic History Review* 61, no. S1 (Aug. 2008): 172–200.

McQueen 2003
Alison McQueen. *The Rise of the Cult of Rembrandt: Reinventing an Old Master in Nineteenth-century France*. Amsterdam: Amsterdam University Press, 2003.

Melbourne and Canberra 1997–98
Albert Blankert et al. *Rembrandt: A Genius and His Impact*. Exh. cat. National Gallery of Victoria, Melbourne, and National Gallery of Australia, Canberra, 1997–98.

Michelet 1876
Jules Michelet. *Histoire de France*. 19 vols. Paris: A. Lacroix, 1876.

Middelkoop 2019
Norbert Middelkoop. *Schutters, gildebroeders, regenten en regentessen. Het Amsterdamse corporatiestuk 1525–1850*. PhD diss., University of Amsterdam, 2019.

Von Moltke 1965
Joachim Wolfgang von Moltke. *Govaert Flinck, 1615–1660*. Amsterdam: Hertzberger & Co., 1965.

Von Moltke 1994
Joachim Wolfgang von Moltke. *Arent de Gelder. Dordrecht 1645–1727*. Doornspijk: Davaco, 1994.

Montias Database
John Michael Montias. *The Montias Database of 17th Century Dutch Art Inventories*. https://research.frick.org/montias/ (accessed 17 Dec. 2019).

Montias 1987
John Michael Montias. "Cost and Value in Seventeenth-century Dutch Art." *Art History* 10, no. 4 (Dec. 1987): 455–466.

Montias 1990
John Michael Montias. "Estimates of the Number of Dutch Master-painters, Their Earnings and Their Output in 1650." *Leidschrift* 6 (1990): 59–74.

Montias 1999
John Michael Montias. "Auction Sales of Works of Art in Amsterdam (1597–1638)." *Netherlands Yearbook for History of Art / Nederlands Kunsthistorisch Jaarboek* 50 (1999): 145–194.

Montias 2002
John Michael Montias. *Art at Auction in 17th Century Amsterdam*. Amsterdam: Amsterdam University Press, 2002.

Montias 2004–05
John Michael Montias. "Artists Named in Amsterdam, 1607–80." *Simiolus: Netherlands Quarterly for the History of Art* 31, no. 4 (2004–05): 322–347.

Montreal and Toronto 1969
Josua Bruyn et al. *Rembrandt and His Pupils: A Loan Exhibition of Paintings Commemorating the 300th Anniversary of Rembrandt*. Exh. cat. Montreal Museum of Fine Arts and Art Gallery of Ontario, Toronto, 1969.

Müller 2015
Jürgen Müller. *Der sokratische Künstler. Studien zu Rembrandts Nachtwache*. Leiden and Boston: Brill, 2015.

Münster, Amsterdam and Jerusalem 1994
Christian Tümpel, ed. *Im Lichte Rembrandts. Das Alte Testament im Goldenen Zeitalter der niederländischen Kunst*. Exh. cat. Westfälisches Landesmuseum, Münster, Joods Historisch Museum, Amsterdam, and Israel Museum, Jerusalem, 1994.

Münz 1952
Ludwig Münz. *Rembrandt's Etchings*. 2 vols. London: Phaidon, 1952.

Nadler 2011
Steven M. Nadler. *A Book Forged in Hell: Spinoza's Scandalous Treatise and the Birth of the Secular Age*. Princeton: Princeton University Press, 2011.

Neumann 1902
Carl Neumann. *Rembrandt*. Berlin: Spemann, 1902.

Neumeister 2005
Mirjam Neumeister. *Holländische Gemälde im Städel, 1550–1800*. Vol. 1. *Künstler geboren vor 1615*. Edited by Herbert Beck, Michael Maek-Gérard and Jochen Sander. Petersberg: Michael Imhof Verlag, 2005.

New York 1995
Walter Liedtke et al. *Rembrandt/Not Rembrandt in the Metropolitan Museum of Art: Aspects of Connoisseurship*. Vol. 2. Exh. cat. The Metropolitan Museum of Art, New York, 1995.

New York 2015
Robert Fucci. *Rembrandt's Changing Impressions*. Exh. cat. Miriam and Ira D. Wallach Art Gallery, Columbia University, New York, 2015.

New York 2017
Joanna Sheers Seidenstein. *Divine Encounter: Rembrandt's Abraham and the Angels*. Exh. cat. The Frick Collection, New York, 2017.

NHD
Erik Hinterding and Jaco Rutgers, comps. "Rembrandt." *The New Hollstein Dutch and Flemish Etchings, Engravings and Woodcuts, 1450–1700*. 7 vols. Edited by Ger Luijten. Ouderkerk aan den Ijssel: Sound & Vision Publishers, 2013.

NHD Heemskerck
Ilja M. Veldman, comp. "Marten van Heemskerck." *The New Hollstein Dutch and Flemish Etchings, Engravings and Woodcuts, 1450–1700*. 2 vols. Edited by Ger Luijten. Roosendaal: Koninklijke van Poll, 1993–94.

NHD Van Dyck
Simon Turner, comp. "Anthony van Dyck." *The New Hollstein Dutch and Flemish Etchings, Engravings and Woodcuts, 1450–1700*. 9 vols. Edited by Carl Depauw. Ouderkerk aan den IJssel: Sound & Vision Publishers, 2002.

North 1999
Michael North. *Art and Commerce in the Dutch Golden Age*. New Haven and London: Yale University Press, 1999.

North and Ormrod 1998
Michael North and David Ormrod, eds. *Art Markets in Europe, 1400–1800*. Farnham and Burlington: Ashgate 1998.

O'Brien et al. 2001
Patrick O'Brien et al., eds. *Urban Achievement in Early Modern Europe: Golden Ages in Antwerp, Amsterdam and London*. Cambridge: Cambridge University Press, 2001.

Onnekink and Rommelse 2019
David Onnekink and Gijs Rommelse. *The Dutch in the Early Modern World: A History of a Global Power*. Cambridge: Cambridge University Press, 2019.

Orenstein 1996
Nadine Orenstein. *Hendrick Hondius and the Business of Prints in Seventeenth-century Holland*. Ouderkerk aan den IJssel: Sound & Vision Publishers, 1996.

Orlers 1641
Jan Jansz Orlers. *Beschrijvinge der Stad Leyden*. Delft: Andries Jansz Cloeting / Leiden: Abraham Commelijn, 1641 [1614].

Ottawa 2004
Odilia Bonebakker, Joaneath Spicer and David Franklin. *Dutch and Flemish Drawings from the National Gallery of Canada*. Exh. cat. National Gallery of Canada, Ottawa, 2004.

Ottenheym 1989
Koen Ottenheym. *Philips Vingboons (1607–1678), Architect*. Zutphen: De Walburg Pers, 1989.

Paris 2016–17
Peter Schatborn, Emmanuel Starcky and Pierre Curie, eds. *Rembrandt Intime*. Exh. cat. Musée Jacquemart-André, Paris, 2016–17.

Paris, Dublin and Washington 2017–18
Adriaan E. Waiboer et al. *Vermeer and the Masters of Genre Painting: Inspiration and Rivalry*. Exh. cat. Musée du Louvre, Paris, National Gallery of Ireland, Dublin, and National Gallery of Art, Washington, 2017–18.

Paris, Philadelphia and Detroit 2011–12
Lloyd DeWitt, ed. *Rembrandt and the Face of Jesus*. Exh. cat. Musée du Louvre, Paris, Philadelphia Museum of Art, and Detroit Institute of Arts, 2011–12.

Parker 2010
Charles H. Parker. *Global Interactions in the Early Modern Age, 1400–1800*. Cambridge: Cambridge University Press, 2010.

Pels 1978
Andries Pels. *Gebruik én misbruik des tooneels*. Edited by Maria Adriana Schenkeveld-Van der Dussen. Culemborg: Tjeenk Willink/Noorduijn, 1978 [1681].

Perlove and Silver 2009
Shelley Perlove and Larry Silver. *Rembrandt's Faith: Church and Temple in the Dutch Golden Age*. University Park: Pennsylvania State University Press, 2009.

Peters 2010
Marion Peters. *De wijze koopman. Het wereldwijde onderzoek van Nicolaes Witsen (1641–1717), burgemeester en VOC-bewindhebber van Amsterdam*. Amsterdam: Bert Bakker, 2010.

Pettegree and Der Weduwen 2019
Andrew Pettegree and Arthur der Weduwen. *The Bookshop of the World: Making and Trading Books in the Dutch Golden Age*. New Haven and London: Yale University Press, 2019.

Philadelphia 2006
Michael Cole, ed. *The Early Modern Painter-Etcher*. Exh. cat. Arthur Ross Gallery, University of Pennsylvania, Philadelphia, 2006.

De Piles 1677
Roger de Piles. *Conversations sur la connaissance de la peinture et sur le jugement qu'on doit faire des tableaux*. Paris: Nicolas Langlois, 1677.

De Piles 1699
Roger de Piles. *Abrégé de la vie des peintres*. Paris: François Muguet, 1699.

De Piles 1706
Roger de Piles. *The Art of Painting, and the Lives of the Painters*. London: J. Nutt, 1706 [1699].

De Piles 1708
Roger de Piles. *Cours de peinture par principes*. Paris: Jacques Estienne, 1708.

Poelwijk 2003
Arjan Poelwijk. *"In dienste vant suyckerbacken:" De Amsterdamse suikernijverheid en haar ondernemers, 1580–1630*. Hilversum: Verloren, 2003.

Prak 2005
Maarten Prak. *The Dutch Republic in the Seventeenth Century*. Cambridge: Cambridge University Press, 2005.

Prater 2015
Andreas Prater. "Apotheose wider Willen und göttliche Torheit. Überlegungen zur Lektüre von Rembrandts 'Raub des Ganymed' als calvinistische Allegorese." *Marburger Jahrbuch für Kunstwissenschaft* 42 (2015): 153–181.

Price 1994
J.L. Price. *Holland and the Dutch Republic in the Seventeenth Century: The Politics of Particularism*. Oxford: Clarendon Press, 1994.

Proudhon 1865
Pierre-Joseph Proudhon. *Du principe de l'art et de sa destination sociale*. Paris: Garnier frères, 1865.

Raleigh, Cleveland and Minneapolis 2011–12
George S. Keyes, Tom Rassieur and Dennis P. Weller, in collaboration with Jon L. Seydl. *Rembrandt in America: Collecting and Connoisseurship*. Exh. cat. North Carolina Museum of Art, Raleigh, Cleveland Museum of Art and Minneapolis Institute of Art, 2011–12.

Rasterhoff 2017
Claartje Rasterhoff. *Painting and Publishing as Cultural Industries: The Fabric of Creativity in the Dutch Republic, 1580–1800*. Amsterdam: Amsterdam University Press, 2017.

Van Regteren Altena 1983
Ioan Q. van Regteren Altena. *Jacques de Gheyn. Three Generations*. 3 vols. Dordrecht, Boston and London: Martinus Nijhoff Publishers, 1983.

Remdoc
Radboud University Nijmegen. *Remdoc*. http://remdoc.huygens.knaw.nl/ (accessed 12 Dec. 2019).

Reznicek 1977
E.K.J. Reznicek. "Opmerkingen bij Rembrandt / Observations on Rembrandt." *Oud Holland* 91 (1977): 75–107.

Ricci 1918
Corrado Ricci. *Rembrandt in Italia*. Milan: Alfieri & Lacroix, 1918.

Ridolfi 1648
Carlo Ridolfi. *Le maraviglie [meraviglie] dell'arte*. Venice: Presso Gio. Battista Sgava, 1648.

Rijnders and Rutgers 2014
Mieke Rijnders and Jaco Rutgers, eds. *Rembrandt in perspectief. De veranderende visie op de meester en zijn werk*. Zwolle: Waanders, 2014.

RKD Database
RKD – Netherlands Institute for Art History. *Database: RKD Artists*. www.rkd.nl (accessed 8 May 2020).

De Roever 1884
N. De Roever. "Rembrandt: Bijdragen tot de geschiedenis van zijn laatste levensjaren." *Oud Holland* 2 (1884): 81–105.

Roscam Abbing 2006
Michiel Roscam Abbing, ed. *Rembrandt 2006: Essays and New Rembrandt Documents*. 2 vols. Leiden: Foleor Publishers, 2006.

Van Rossum 2015
Matthias van Rossum. "'Vervloekte goudzugt.' De VOC, slavenhandel en slavernij in Azië." *Tijdschrift voor Sociale en Economische Geschiedenis* 12, no. 4 (2015): 29–57.

Rotterdam 2006a
Peter van der Coelen. *Rembrandts passie. Het Nieuwe Testament in de Nederlandse prentkunst van de zestiende en zeventiende eeuw*. Exh. cat. Museum Boijmans Van Beuningen, Rotterdam, 2006.

Rotterdam 2006b
Jan van der Waals. *Prenten in de Gouden Eeuw. Van kunst tot kastpapier*. Exh. cat. Museum Boijmans Van Beuningen, Rotterdam, 2006.

Rotterdam and Frankfurt 1999–2000
Albert Blankert, Jeroen Giltaij and Friso Lammertse, eds. *Holländischer Klassizismus in der Malerei des 17. Jahrhunderts*. Exh. cat. Museum Boijmans Van Beuningen, Rotterdam, and Städel Museum, Frankfurt am Main, 1999–2000.

Royalton-Kisch 1984a
Martin Royalton-Kisch. "Over Rembrandt and Van Vliet." *Kroniek van het Rembrandthuis* 36 (1984): 2–23.

Royalton-Kisch 1984b
Martin Royalton-Kisch. "Rembrandt: Two Passion Prints Reconsidered." *Apollo* 119 (1984): 130–132.

Royalton-Kisch 1994
Martin Royalton-Kisch. "Some Further Thoughts on Rembrandt's *Christ before Pilate*." *Kroniek van het Rembrandthuis* (1994): 3–13.

Royalton-Kisch 2010
Martin Royalton-Kisch. *Catalogue of Drawings by Rembrandt and His School in The British Museum*. The British Museum, London, 2010. https://projects.britishmuseum.org/research/publications/online_research_catalogues/rembrandt_drawings/drawings_by_rembrandt/full_catalogue_list.aspx (accessed 5 Mar. 2020).

Royalton-Kisch 2011
Martin Royalton-Kisch. "Drawings by Rembrandt and His Pupils." *The Burlington Magazine* 153, no. 1295 (Feb. 2011): 97–102.

Royalton-Kisch 2012
Martin Royalton-Kisch. *The Drawings of Rembrandt: A Revision of Otto Benesch's Catalogue Raisonné.* 2012–, http://rembrandtcatalogue.net/home/4564920240 (accessed 28 Apr. 2020).

Royalton-Kisch and Schatborn 2011
Martin Royalton-Kisch and Peter Schatborn "The Core Group of Rembrandt Drawings, II: The List." *Master Drawings* 49, no. 3 (autumn 2011): 323–346.

Rutgers 2003
Jaco Rutgers. "'Sijn' kunst-faem over 't spits der Alpen heen gevlogen? Rembrandts naam en faam in Italië in de zeventiende eeuw." *Kroniek van het Rembrandthuis*, nos. 1–2 (2003): 3–19.

Salem and Amsterdam 2015–16
Karina H. Corrigan et al., eds. *Asia in Amsterdam: The Culture of Luxury in the Golden Age.* Exh. cat. Peabody Essex Museum, Salem, MA, and Rijksmuseum, Amsterdam, 2015–16.

Sandrart 1675–80
Joachim von Sandrart. *Teutsche Academie der edlen Bau-, Bild- und Mahlerey-Künste.* 3 vols. Nuremberg: Jacob von Sandrart / Frankfurt am Main: Matthäus Merian, 1675–80.

Scallen 2004
Catherine B. Scallen. *Rembrandt, Reputation, and the Practice of Connoisseurship.* Amsterdam: Amsterdam University Press, 2004.

Schaeps and Van Duin 2019
Jef Schaeps and Mart van Duijn. *Rembrandt en de universiteit Leiden.* Leiden: Leiden University Press, 2019.

Schatborn 2011
Peter Schatborn. "The Core Group of Rembrandt Drawings, I: Overview." *Master Drawings* 49, no. 3 (autumn 2011): 293–322.

Schatborn and Hinterding 2019
Peter Schatborn and Erik Hinterding. *Rembrandt: The Complete Drawings and Etchings.* Cologne: Taschen, 2019.

Scheller 1961
Robert W. Scheller. "Rembrandt's reputatie van Houbraken tot Scheltema." *Netherlands Yearbook for History of Art / Nederlands Kunsthistorisch Jaarboek* 12 (1961): 81–118.

Scheller 1969
Robert W. Scheller. "Rembrandt en de encyclopedische kunstkamer." *Oud Holland* 84 (1969): 81–147.

Schnackenburg 2016
Bernhard Schnackenburg. *Jan Lievens: Friend and Rival of the Young Rembrandt.* Petersberg: Michael Imhof Verlag, 2016.

Schnapper 1994
Antoine Schnapper. *Curieux du grand siècle. Collections et collectionneurs dans la France du XVIIe siècle.* Paris: Flammarion, 1994.

Schneider 1990
Cynthia P. Schneider. *Rembrandt's Landscapes.* New Haven and London: Yale University Press, 1990.

Schneider and Ekkart 1973
Hans Schneider, with a supplement by Rudi Ekkart. *Jan Lievens. Sein Leben und seine Werke.* Amsterdam: B.M. Israël, 1973.

Schwartz 1977
Gary Schwartz. *Rembrandt: All the Etchings Reproduced in True Size.* London: Oresko Books, Ltd., 1977.

Schwartz 1983
Gary Schwartz. "Jan van der Heyden and the Huydecopers of Maarseveen." *The J. Paul Getty Museum Journal* 11 (1983): 197–220.

Schwartz 1985
Gary Schwartz. *Rembrandt: His Life, His Paintings: A New Biography with all Accessible Paintings Illustrated in Colour.* New York: Viking, 1985.

Schwartz 2006
Gary Schwartz. *The Rembrandt Book.* Brussels: Mercatorfonds, 2006.

Schwartz 2020
Gary Schwartz. *A Rembrandt Invention: A New Baptism of the Eunuch.* Leiden: Primavera Pers, 2020.

Seidel 2000
Max Seidel, ed. *L'Europa e l'arte italiana.* Venice: Marsilio, 2000.

Seifert 2011
Christian Tico Seifert. *Pieter Lastman. Studien zu Leben und Werk. Mit einem kritischen Verzeichnis der Werke mit Themen aus der antiken Mythologie und Historie.* Petersberg: Michael Imhof Verlag, 2011.

Sellin 1998
Paul R. Sellin. "Michel Le Blon and England, 1632–1649, with observations on Van Dyck, Donne, and Vondel." *Dutch Crossing* 22, no. 1 (1998): 102–125.

Sellin 2006
Christine Petra Sellin. *Fractured Families and Rebel Maidservants: The Biblical Hagar in Seventeenth-century Dutch Art and Literature.* New York: T & T Clark International, 2006.

Sigal 1961
C. Sigal. "Bijbelbladen: Burchgraef, van Bilderbeeck, Tierens, de Ruyter, van Breda, Rijzendael, Hoogebaat, Scholten, Fockebergh." *De Nederlandsche Leeuw* 78 (1961): 340–342.

Slive 1988
Seymour Slive. *Rembrandt and His Critics, 1630–1730.* New York: Hacker Art Books, 1988 [1953].

Slive 2009a
Seymour Slive. *The Drawings of Rembrandt: A New Study.* London: Thames & Hudson, 2009.

Slive 2009b
Seymour Slive. *Rembrandt Drawings.* Los Angeles: Getty Publications, 2009.

Sluijter 2006
Eric Jan Sluijter. *Rembrandt and the Female Nude.* Amsterdam: Amsterdam University Press, 2006.

Sluijter 2009
Eric Jan Sluijter. "On Brabant Rubbish, Economic Competition, Artistic Rivalry, and the Growth of the Market for Paintings in the First Decades of the Seventeenth Century." *Journal of Historians of Netherlandish Art* 1, no. 2 (summer 2009). https://jhna.org/articles/brabant-rubbish-economic-competition-artistic-rivalry-growth-market-paintings-first-decades-seventeenth-century/ (accessed 12 Mar. 2020).

Sluijter 2010
Eric Jan Sluijter. "Rembrandt's Portrayal of the Passions and Vondel's 'Staetveranderinge.'" *Netherlands Yearbook for History of Art / Nederlands Kunsthistorisch Jaarboek* 60 (2010): 285–305.

Sluijter 2014
Eric Jan Sluijter. "How Rembrandt Surpassed the Ancients, Italians and Rubens as the Master of 'the Passions of the Soul.'" *BMGN – Low Countries Historical Review* 129, no. 2 (2014): 63–89.

Sluijter 2015
Eric Jan Sluijter. *Rembrandt's Rivals: History Painting in Amsterdam, 1630–1650.* Amsterdam and Philadelphia: John Benjamins Publishing Company, 2015.

Sluijter 2017
Eric Jan Sluijter. "Breenbergh and Rembrandt in Dialogue." *Journal of Historians of Netherlandish Art* 9, no. 1 (winter 2017). https://jhna.org/articles/breenbergh-rembrandt-dialogue/ (accessed 16 Mar. 2020).

Soltow and Van Zanden 1998
Lee Soltow and Jan Luiten van Zanden. *Income and Wealth Inequality in the Netherlands, 16th–20th Centuries.* Amsterdam: Het Spinhuis, 1998.

Stechow 1998
Wolfgang Stechow. "Rembrandt and the Old Testament." *Allen Memorial Art Museum Bulletin* 1, no. 2 (1998): 15–58.

Stijnman 2012
Ad Stijnman. *Engraving and Etching, 1400–2000: A History of the Development of Manual Intaglio Printmaking Processes.* Houten: Hes & De Graaf, 2012.

Stijnman 2015
Ad Stijnman. *Rembrandt's Etchings and Japanese Echizen Paper.* Exh. text. Rembrandt House Museum, Amsterdam, 2015. www.academia.edu/35913380/REMBRANDTS_ETCHINGS_AND_JAPANESE_ECHIZEN_PAPER (accessed 13 May 2020).

Straat 1928
H.L. Straat. "Lambert Jacobsz, Schilder." *Jaarboek De Vrije Fries* 28 (1928): 53–94.

Van Straten 2005
Roelof van Straten. *Young Rembrandt: The Leiden Years, 1606–1632.* Leiden: Foleor Publishers, 2005.

Strauss and Van der Meulen 1979
Walter L. Strauss and Marjon van der Meulen. *The Rembrandt Documents.* New York: Abaris, 1979.

Stückelberger 1996
Johannes Stückelberger. *Rembrandt und die Moderne. Der Dialog mit Rembrandt in der deutschen Kunst um 1900*. Munich: W. Fink Verlag, 1996.

Sumowski 1983–94
Werner Sumowski. *Gemälde der Rembrandt-Schüler*. 6 vols. Landau: PVA, 1983–94.

Taine 1869
Hippolyte-Adolphe Taine. *Philosophie de l'art dans les Pays-Bas. Leçons professées à l'École des Beaux-arts*. Paris: Baillière, 1869.

Tallemant des Réaux 1834
Gédéon Tallemant des Réaux. *Les historiettes de Tallemant des Réaux*. Vol. 2. Edited by René Charles Hippolyte de Châteaugiron, Louis Jean Nicolas de Monmerqué and Jules-Antoine Taschereau. Paris: Alphonse Levavasseur, 1834.

Thoré-Bürger 1860
Théophile Thoré-Bürger. *Musées de la Hollande*. 2 vols. Paris: Veuve Jules Renouard, 1860 [1858].

Thoré-Bürger 1870
Théophile Thoré-Bürger. *Salons de W. Bürger, 1861 à 1868*. 2 vols. Edited by Marius Chaumelin. Paris: Veuve Jules Renouard, 1870.

Van Tielhof 2002
Milja van Tielhof. *The "Mother of All Trades": The Baltic Grain Trade in Amsterdam from the Late 16th to the Early 19th Century*. Leiden and Boston: Brill, 2002.

Tilly and Blockmans 1994
Charles Tilly and Wim P. Blockmans, eds. *Cities and the Rise of States in Europe, A.D. 1000 to 1800*. Boulder: Westview Press, 1994.

Tokyo 2011
Akira Kofuku et al. *Rembrandt: The Quest for Chiaroscuro*. Exh. cat. National Museum of Western Art, Tokyo, 2011.

Tonkovich 2005
Jennifer Tonkovich. "'Rymsdyk's Museum': Jan van Rymsdyk as a Collector of Old Master Drawings." *Journal of the History of Collections* 17, no. 2 (Dec. 2005): 155–171.

Toronto 2019
Sasha Suda and Kirk Nickel, eds. *Early Rubens*. Exh. cat. Art Gallery of Ontario, Toronto, 2019.

Trentmann 2016
Frank Trentmann. *The Empire of Things: How We Became a World of Consumers, from the Fifteenth Century to the Twenty-first*. New York: Harper Collins, 2016.

Van der Tuin 1948
H. van der Tuin. *Les vieux peintres des Pays-Bas et la critique artistique en France de la première moitié du XIXe siècle*. Paris: Vrin, 1948.

Tummers and Jonckheere 2008
Anna Tummers and Koenraad Jonckheere, eds. *Art Market and Connoisseurship: A Closer Look at Paintings by Rembrandt, Rubens and Their Contemporaries*. Amsterdam: Amsterdam University Press, 2008.

Turner 2017
Jane Turner, ed. *Drawings by Rembrandt and His School in the Rijksmuseum*. Amsterdam, 2017. www.rijksmuseum.nl/en/collection/RP-T-1930-2/catalogue-entry (accessed 22 Mar. 2020).

Van der Veen 2003
Jaap van der Veen. "Onbekende opdrachtgevers van Rembrandt (3). Portretten van leden van de familie Sijen door Rembrandt, hoogstwaarschijnlijk Pieter Sijen (ca. 1592–1652) en Marretje Cornelisdr. van Grotewal (ca. 1593–1666)." *Kroniek van het Rembrandthuis*, nos. 1–2 (2003): 46–60.

Verhaeren 1904
Émile Verhaeren. *Rembrandt. Biographie critique*. Paris: Henri Laurens, 1904.

Vienna 2004
Klaus Albrecht Schröder and Marian Bisanz-Prakken, eds. *Rembrandt*. Exh. cat. Albertina, Vienna, 2004.

Vlieghe 2001
Hans Vlieghe, ed. *Van Dyck, 1599–1999: Conjectures and Refutations*. Turnhout: Brepols, 2001.

De Vries and Van der Woude 1997
Jan de Vries and Ad van der Woude. *The First Modern Economy: Success, Failure, and Perseverance of the Dutch Economy, 1500–1815*. Cambridge: Cambridge University Press, 1997.

Van Wagenberg-Ter Hoeven 2018
Anke A. van Wagenberg-Ter Hoeven. *Jan Baptist Weenix and Jan Weenix: The Paintings*. 2 vols. Zwolle: Waanders, 2018.

Washington 1990
Cynthia P. Schneider. *Rembrandt's Landscapes: Drawings and Prints*. Exh. cat. National Gallery of Art, Washington, 1990.

Washington and Paris 2016–17
Ger Luijten, Peter Schatborn and Arthur K. Wheelock, Jr. *Drawings for Paintings in the Age of Rembrandt*. National Gallery of Art, Washington, and Fondation Custodia – Collection Frits Lugt, Paris, 2016–17.

Washington, Detroit and Amsterdam 1980–81
Albert Blankert, ed. *Gods, Saints and Heroes: Dutch Painting in the Age of Rembrandt*. Exh. cat. National Gallery of Art, Washington, Detroit Institute of Arts, and Rijksmuseum, Amsterdam, 1980–81.

Washington, London and The Hague 2000–01
Ronni Baer, Arthur K. Wheelock, Jr., and Annetje Boersma. *Gerrit Dou, 1613–1675: Master Painter in the Age of Rembrandt*. Exh. cat. National Gallery of Art, Washington, Dulwich Picture Gallery, London, and Mauritshuis, The Hague, 2000–01.

Washington, Milwaukee and Amsterdam 2008–09
Arthur K. Wheelock, Jr., ed. *Jan Lievens: A Dutch Master Rediscovered*. Exh. cat. National Gallery of Art, Washington, Milwaukee Art Museum and Rembrandt House Museum, Amsterdam, 2008–09.

Weller 2009
Dennis P. Weller. *Seventeenth-century Dutch and Flemish Paintings: Systematic Catalogue of the Collection*. Raleigh: North Carolina Museum of Art, 2009.

Westermann 2000
Mariët Westermann. *Rembrandt*. London: Phaidon, 2000.

Weststeijn 2008
Thijs Weststeijn. *The Visible World: Samuel van Hoogstraten's Art Theory and the Legitimation of Painting in the Dutch Golden Age*. Amsterdam: Amsterdam University Press, 2008.

White 1999
Christopher White. *Rembrandt as an Etcher: A Study of the Artist at Work*. New Haven and London: Yale University Press, 1999 [1969].

De Winkel 2006
Marieke de Winkel. *Fashion and Fancy: Dress and Meaning in Rembrandt's Paintings*. Amsterdam: Amsterdam University Press, 2006.

De Witt 2008
David de Witt. *The Bader Collection: Dutch and Flemish Paintings*. Kingston: Agnes Etherington Art Centre, 2008.

De Witt 2014
David de Witt. *The Bader Collection: European Paintings*. Kingston: Agnes Etherington Art Centre, 2014.

Zandvliet 2002
Kees Zandvliet. *Mapping for Money: Maps, Plans, and Topographic Paintings and Their Role in Dutch Overseas Expansion during the 16th and 17th Centuries*. Amsterdam: Batavian Lion International, 2002 [1998].

Zandvliet 2018
Kees Zandvliet. *De 500 rijksten van de Republiek. Rijkdom, geloof, macht en cultuur*. Zutphen: De Walburg Pers, 2018.

Van 't Zelfde 2012
Reinier van 't Zelfde. "Rembrandts naam en faam." *RKD Bulletin* 2 (2012): 213–216.

Zell 2000–01
Michael Zell. "Eduard Kolloff and the Historiographic Romance of Rembrandt and the Jews." *Simiolus: Netherlands Quarterly for the History of Art* 28, no. 3 (2000–01): 181–197.

Zell 2003
Michael Zell. "A Leisurely and Virtuous Pursuit: Amateur Artists, Rembrandt, and Landscape Representation in Seventeenth-century Holland." *Netherlands Yearbook for History of Art / Nederlands Kunsthistorisch Jaarboek* 54 (2003): 337–373.

Zell 2011
Michael Zell. "Rembrandt's Gifts: A Case Study of Actor-Network-Theory." *Journal of Historians of Netherlandish Art* 3, no. 2 (summer 2011). https://jhna.org/articles/rembrandts-gifts-case-study-actor-network-theory/ (accessed 12 Mar. 2020).

De Zwart and Van Zanden 2018
Pim de Zwart and Jan Luiten van Zanden. *The Origins of Globalization: World Trade and the Making of the Global Economy, 1500–1800*. Cambridge: Cambridge University Press, 2018.

INDEX

Page numbers in italics denote illustrations.
Page numbers in bold italics denote illustrations and text.

National Gallery of Canada
380 Sussex Drive
Ottawa, ON, K1N 9N4
Canada
Tel. +1-613-990-1985
www.gallery.ca

Städel Museum
Städelsches Kunstinstitut and Städtische Galerie
Schaumainkai 63
60596 Frankfurt am Main
Germany
Tel. +49 69 60 50 98-0
Fax +49 69 60 50 98-111
www.staedelmuseum.de

Published in conjunction with the exhibition *Rembrandt in Amsterdam:*
Creativity and Competition, organized by the National Gallery of Canada, Ottawa,
and the Städel Museum, Frankfurt am Main.

Itinerary

National Gallery of Canada, Ottawa: 14 May – 6 September 2021
Städel Museum, Frankfurt am Main: 6 October 2021 – 30 January 2022

National Gallery of Canada

Chief, Publications and Copyright: Ivan Parisien
Editor: Caroline Wetherilt
Picture Editors: Anne Tessier and Andrea Fajrajsl
Production Manager: Anne Tessier

Translators: Martina Dervis, Kist & Kilian and Judith Terry
Designed and typeset in Freight Text Pro and Freight Sans Pro by Réjean Myette
Printed in Italy on GardaMatt by Conti Tipocolor

Also published in French under the title *Rembrandt à Amsterdam. Créativité et concurrence* and in
German under the title *Nennt mich Rembrandt. Kreativität und Wettbewerb in Amsterdam um 1630–1655.*

Cover: Rembrandt van Rijn, *Heroine from the Old Testament* (detail), 1632/33 (pl. 85)
Back cover: Rembrandt van Rijn, *View of Amsterdam Seen from the Kadijk, from the Northeast*, c. 1641 (pl. 32)
Frontispiece: Rembrandt van Rijn, *Self-portrait with Saskia* (detail), 1636 (pl. 6)
Front endpapers: François van den Hoeye, *Panoramic View of Amsterdam* (detail), c. 1620–25 (pl. 25)
Back endpapers: Philipp von Zesen, *Map of Amsterdam* (detail), 1664 (pl. 29)

Catalogue © National Gallery of Canada, Ottawa, 2021

ISBN 978-0-300-24993-4
Library of Congress Control Number: 2020943142

Distributed by
Yale University Press
302 Temple Street
P.O. Box 209040
New Haven, CT 06520-9040
www.yalebooks.com/art

Supported by the Government of Canada

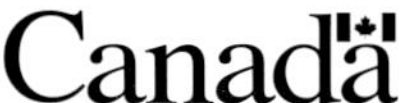

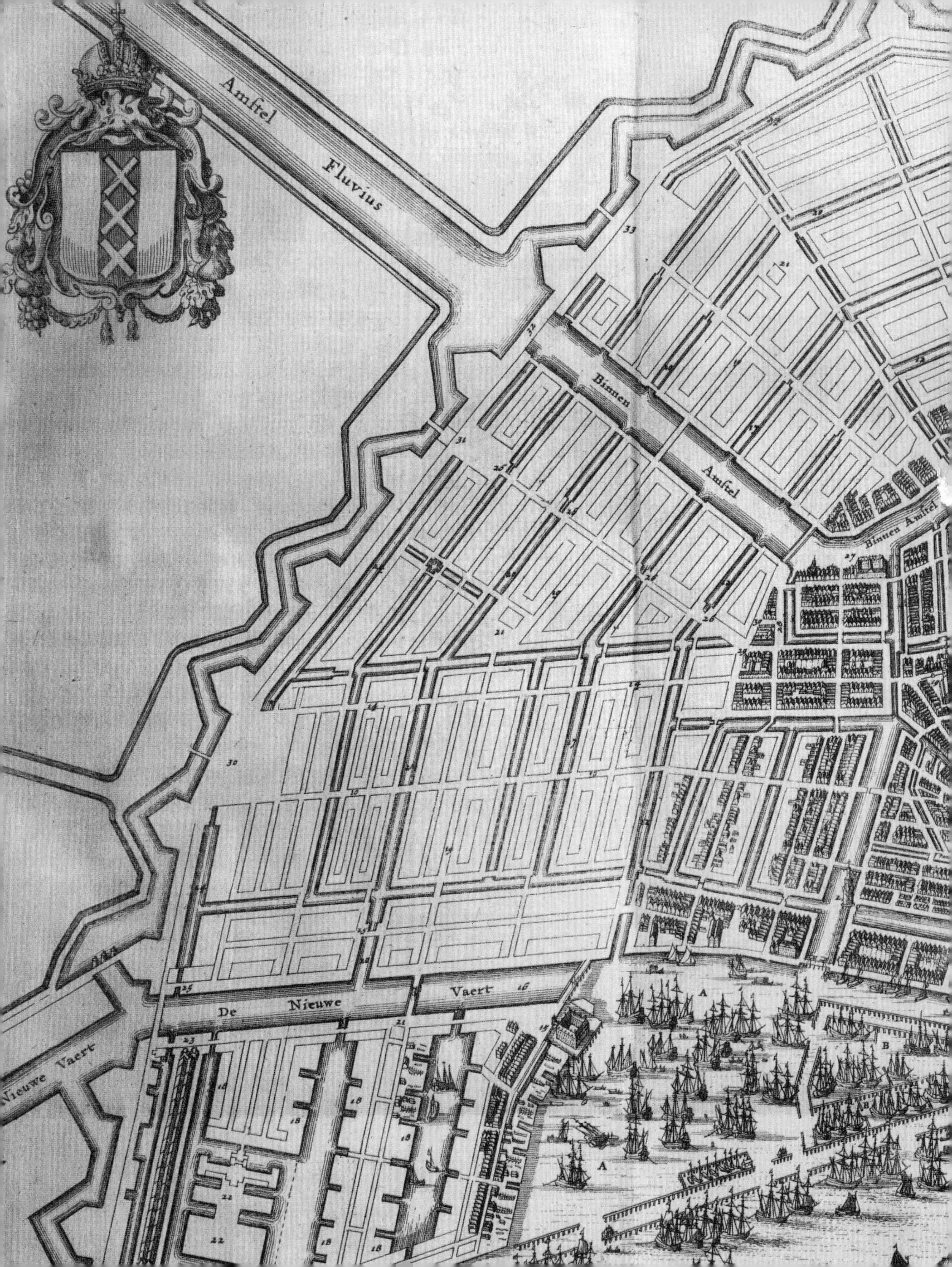

Amstel
Fluvius
Binnen
Amstel
Binnen Amstel
De Nieuwe Vaert
Nieuwe Vaert
A
B